Mechanical Bodies, Computational Minds

Mechanical Bodies, Computational Minds

Artificial Intelligence from Automata to Cyborgs

Edited by
Stefano Franchi and Güven Güzeldere

A Bradford Book
The MIT Press
Cambridge, Massachusetts
London, England

MIT Press books may be purchased at special quantity discounts for business or sales promotional use. For information, please e-mail ⟨special_sales@mitpress.mit.edu⟩ or write to Special Sales Department, The MIT Press, 5 Cambridge Center, Cambridge, MA 02142.

This book was set in Stone Serif and Stone Sans on 3B2 by Asco Typesetters, Hong Kong. Printed and bound in the United States of America.

Library of Congress Cataloging-in-Publication Data

Mechanical bodies, computational minds : artificial intelligence from automata to cyborgs / edited by Stefano Franchi and Güven Güzeldere.
    p.   cm.
"A Bradford book."
Includes bibliographical references and index.
ISBN 0-262-06243-7 (hardback : alk. paper) — ISBN 0-262-56206-5 (pbk. : alk. paper)
1. Artificial intelligence. I. Franchi, Stefano. II. Güzeldere, Güven.
Q335.M395   2005
006.3—dc22   2004050480

10   9   8   7   6   5   4   3   2   1

Contents

Acknowledgments

The very beginnings of the idea of bringing together a number of essays from different disciplines in the humanities to explore previously uncharted areas of artificial intelligence has its roots in our years as graduate students in the Philosophy Department at Stanford University. During the years we spent in residence as postdoctoral fellows at the Stanford Humanities Center, we edited a special issue of the *Stanford Humanities Review* on a similar theme, which then constituted the seed of the project that culminated in this book.

With respect to the beginnings of this endeavor, we would like to thank the Stanford Humanities Center, its then directors Wanda Corn and Keith Baker and associate director Charlie Junkerman, staff, and fellows of our years for providing us with a stimulating and supportive research environment. We also thank John Perry for providing us with research space and support at the Center for the Study of Language and Information at Stanford University, and Brian C. Smith for access to facilities and support at the Xerox Palo Alto Research Center.

Stefano Franchi would like to thank Hubert Dreyfus and Julian Young for their help in the development of this project, and Murat Aydede for the help he provided at a crucial moment in the production of this book. Franchi also acknowledges the institutional support provided by the Department of Philosophy, The University of Auckland, and the support provided by the Marsden Fund of the Royal Society of New Zealand.

Güven Güzeldere would like to thank Murat Aydede, Fred Dretske, Owen Flanagan, Douglas Hofstadter, John Perry, Brian C. Smith, and Terry Winograd for valuable discussions on questions relevant to the nature of intelligence, agency, and AI; Tad Schmaltz for expert guidance on historical issues, especially pertaining to Descartes and La Mettrie; Matt Cartmill, Terry Deacon, and Barbara Herrnstein-Smith for illuminating discussions on the question of human-animal boundaries; and Tomiko Yoda for many conversations that influenced his thinking on the subject and for helpful comments on the opening essay of this book.

Güzeldere also acknowledges the institutional support provided by the Department of Philosophy and the Smith Faculty Enhancement Fellowship at Duke University, the McDonnell Foundation Program in Philosophy and the Neurosciences, and a fellowship year at the National Humanities Center in Research Triangle Park, North Carolina, during the preparation of this book.

The editors thank Andrea Mangones for her help with the bibliographical material, Alice Cheyer for editorial advice and improvements, and Tom Stone of the MIT Press for his kind assistance throughout the production of this book.

Mechanical Bodies, Computational Minds

Introduction

There are three great events in history. One, the creation of the universe. Two, the appearance of life. The third one, which I think is equal in importance, is the appearance of Artificial Intelligence.

These remarks were made by Edward Fredkin, former manager of the Laboratory for Computer Science at the Massachusetts Institute of Technology, one of the leading research institutions in the field, in a BBC television interview.[1] What exactly is artificial intelligence, the appearance (discovery? invention?) of which was thus publicly hailed as one of the most momentous events in the history of humankind (even of the universe)? What is artificial about it? What is intelligent about it? And if it really is of such historic significance, why have scholars from the humanities, who have traditionally been most interested in questions about the nature of human reason, intelligence, and practice, been so conspicuously silent about it?

It was with such questions in mind that we set out to produce this book. Our objective is *not* to rehearse the by now notorious question that has become emblematic of contemporary thinking on artificial intelligence: Can computers be intelligent? or to emphasize (in Dreyfus's words) what computers can't do.[2] Rather, we want to explore a new, more constructive avenue by providing a forum for intellectual exchange between the artificial intelligence (AI) community and scholars in the traditional humanities and social sciences.

Over the history of AI, such exchanges have been noticeably rare. On the one hand, this may have been natural: as currently understood and practiced, AI is an offspring of theoretical developments in the theory of computing (broadly construed) and technological advances involving computers. As such, it primarily resides under the wing of the academic discipline of computer science, and most AI research is pursued by computer scientists. Furthermore, the AI community has had a largely negative sentiment toward other disciplines, with respect to the involvement of "the other" in what they see as their own home territory. Whether warranted or not, this reaction may have been triggered by the fact that the major commentary on AI from the "outside world" has been from philosophers, many of whom seemed to be on fault-finding missions.[3]

Yet, what could be stranger, on reflection, than computer scientists' pursuing by themselves the enterprise of constructing artificial intelligence, a task that requires a vast amount of knowledge and expertise about the human mind and condition that transcends the bounds of any single discipline? Admittedly, some AI research and some metalevel discussion of the nature of the research program have involved psychology and philosophy. Traditionally, however, questions about the dividing line between human beings and machines, about the nature and evolution of human reason and creativity, about the conception of human intelligence in different historical and cultural settings, and the like, have been fruitfully pursued in other fields, such as anthropology, history, literary criticism, cultural studies, religious studies, art history, theology, and aesthetics, in addition to philosophy and psychology. Why should such an enormous resource be disregarded or ignored? We would be the first to admit that building theoretical bridges for such a constructive collaboration is not easy. But given the potential payoff, it is remarkable how few attempts have been made.

Our motivation in making this book was a belief that a dialogue between researchers in the humanities and social sciences, and those traditionally involved in AI would prove beneficial to both sides. AI, we thought, would benefit from a scrutiny of its fundamental assumptions from a humanities perspective and perhaps even gain insight into why it has not (yet) lived up to its original promises. And why shouldn't insights flow in the opposite direction as well? Analysis of AI's theoretical struggles, technological advances, and notable failures should provide new perspectives on traditional humanities debates. The field's eponymous goal of constructing an intelligent embodied artifact, for example, can lead to a productive reexamination of classical humanist assumptions about the nature of rationality, humanity, and the mind-body dichotomy.

In order to create some common ground, and thus provide a context in which to take some first steps toward such an exchange, we solicited articles that addressed from multidisciplinary perspectives such issues as the birth and evolution of the automaton in fiction, public perception, and collective imagination; the relation between AI and its parent, cybernetics, which died a premature death before AI reached infancy; and basic presumptions about not only AI's subject matter (the nature of human intelligence) but also its methodology and actual practice. The result is the book you are holding in your hands. In the opening chapter, we provide our own detailed account of AI in relation to cybernetics and the rest of the diverse lot of historically rooted attempts to understand and build embodiments of intelligence. We bring together authors from a multitude of disciplines, including history, philosophy, science studies, sociology, communications, English literature, art, theology, and feminist studies as well as artificial intelligence and cognitive science. One of the emerging themes from this collection is the rather unexpected shared intuition that AI can, and even should, be regarded as a project in another field: philosophy in general (Agre), phenomenology

(Sharoff), epistemology (Rieu), or art (Wilson). Another theme is that AI and its concerns are all-pervasive, both vertically in history and horizontally in the contemporary intellectual sphere (Mazlish, Latour and Teil, Collins, and Johnson). Other articles address the relationship of AI to vision, creativity, and art (Hofstadter), to science and methodology (Matteuzzi), to social interaction (Burke), to theology (Foerst). Finally, the remaining articles discuss the possibility of a truly intelligent artifact which (who?) could rival human cognitive and noncognitive (bodily) skills (Dreyfus and Dennett, Dretske), while critically examining the past history (Keller, Pickering) and the implicit gender-related assumptions of the discipline (Adam).

The book opens with an essay by **Stefano Franchi** and **Güven Güzeldere**, the editors, that presents a historical and critical account of AI. We maintain that AI is the present incarnation of a long-standing effort in human history to understand the nature of intelligence and agency by constructing artifacts that seem to be endowed with these capacities. As such, we claim, it is possible to give a fair assessment of AI's present status—its ambitions, predictions, accomplishments, and failures—only from a broader perspective, which does not construe AI as simply an engineering project, against the backdrop of its historical predecessors.

Our chapter begins by presenting a historical exegesis of the intellectual terrain that provided a breeding ground for pursuing the goals of artificial intelligence. In this context, we examine the early history of automata building and the evolving conceptualization of nature in general, and the mind and body in particular, as mechanistically understandable phenomena, especially during the seventeenth and eighteenth centuries. Following an analysis of AI's relation to cybernetics and the political reasons that prevented a potentially beneficial collaboration, we turn to an examination of the two most influential research programs within AI, game playing and language comprehension, and then give an overview of both internal and external kinds of critiques raised against AI, especially in these two areas. The chapter closes with an assessment of where AI stands at present and what lies ahead, particularly in its transformation, together with cybernetics, to engender the newly emerging field of cyborg technologies, as well as the reception and effects of this development within disciplines outside AI in a way that brings the project of artificial intelligence back to close contact with the humanities.

Philip Agre begins his essay by acknowledging a deep separation between AI research and traditional investigations of the mind and language as pursued in the humanities. Artificial intelligence, he claims, in the self-perception of its own adepts, is a technical field whose researchers "do" things—prove mathematical theorems, develop new formalisms, and build computer systems to implement them. Research in the social sciences, and especially in philosophy, on the other hand, is perceived by AI aficionados as engagement in nothing more than "metalevel bickering that never decides anything." Against this well-entrenched split—a split, he emphasizes, that has been perpetuated with great determination by the field's senior members—Agre proposes an alternative view that opens the doors to, and actually calls for, an active collaboration between philosophy and AI. "Artificial intelligence is philosophy underneath," he writes, because the former's endeavor can be seen as an effort to work out and develop, through its characteristic technical means, the philosophical systems it inherits.

The strict interconnection between the two disciplines is dramatically shown by the fact that AI research runs into difficulties and problems that derive from conceptual tensions implicit in the inherited philosophical systems. AI's formal methodology renders explicit the hidden difficulties and allows them to surface. Agre provides a convincing demonstration of this point through a historical analysis that takes us from Descartes' distinction between soul and body, through Allen Newell and Herbert Simon's project of mechanization of the soul, to more recent AI approaches. He shows that one of the major difficulties encountered in AI—how to keep the mechanized soul in touch with an ever-changing world through an effective search process in a space of possible actions—can ultimately be traced back to the inner tension of the inherited philosophical model: namely, the Cartesian causal separation between soul and body.

Philosophy and other traditional disciplines, in sum, provide overall theoretical frameworks. AI, in turn, provides a powerful means of forcing into the open their internal structures and internal tensions. What is needed to make substantial advances in both fields, Agre concludes, is a constructive symbiosis of AI research with humanistic analyses of ideas.

Bruno Latour and **Geneviève Teil** pursue an approach quite consonant with Philip Agre's suggested role for the social sciences: to provide theoretical frameworks within which research in AI and cognitive science can be pursued in finer detail. Indeed, they take Agre's suggestion one step further and provide as well the technical analysis and actual artifact—the computer program. They start with a very practical goal: to provide a tool for qualitative workers (historians, social scientists, etc.) "that has the same degree of finesse as traditional qualitative studies but also has the same mobility, the same capacities of aggregation and synthesis as the quantitative methods employed by other social sciences" (econometrics, demography, etc.).

Strange as this may seem on the face of it, Latour and Teil show that such a tool does not depend on computers' possessing high cognitive functions, nor does it require them to understand ordinary language in order to interpret the documents on which social scientists normally work. On the contrary, the authors try to shed any anthropomorphic projections from the computer by taking it to be just a network of associations between different registers. This characterization is more than sufficient for the purpose at hand because associative networks are just what is needed in order to analyze large bodies of data. More important, the construction and manipulation of associative networks, which commonly available computers are perfectly capable of performing, are sufficient, according to Latour and Teil, to provide "intelligent" interpretations of the given data. The Hume Machine, as their creation is called, shows that there is an alternative route between the epistemological dream of early AI (total reduction of human knowledge to sets of formal rules) and the dire indictments uttered by AI critics (the impossibility in principle of any nonelementary machine intelligence). Computers might well be, in principle, unable to imitate people because of their lack of a body and "worries," say Latour and Teil, but they do have "their own way of being in the world. We have to work from them instead of vesting them with human properties so as to immediately deny that they have any."

In the chapter by the philosophers **Hubert Dreyfus** and **Daniel Dennett**, the latter, one of the outside collaborators on the Cog humanoid robot project at the MIT Artificial Intelligence Lab, engages in close debate with Dreyfus, a well-known critic of AI, about the current achievements of purely disembodied artificial intelligences. Their exchange started on the radio show *NewsHour with Jim Lehrer* and continued in the online magazine *Slate*, after Deep Blue, an IBM chess-playing program defeated Garry Kasparov, the world chess champion, in May 1997.

Dreyfus claimed that Deep Blue's victory proved little about the very possibility of artificial intelligence because chess is precisely the right kind of narrowly defined formal domain in which computers excel. Real human experience however, is another matter because it is informal, incompletely structured, replete with meaning, and so on, and there is no reason to think that computers' historically miserable track record in this domain will change any time soon, regardless of Deep Blue's victory. Dennett countered that claims like Dreyfus's are a typical example of the "moving post" fallacy: first, computers are declared in principle unable to do x, for instance, play chess, but as soon as they handle the challenge and play chess better than people, computer critics immediately declare that being able to do x is really not a satisfactory intelligence test, and proceed to suggest a new "impossible" challenge. This, Dennett said, had been Dreyfus's typical procedure: first he declared (in 1967) that computers would never be able to play good chess, and now he says that being able to play world-class chess is not relevant after all. In this exchange, they tackle many of the important issues that will need to be solved for an artificial intelligence artifact to qualify as genuinely intelligent: the role of emotions (and therefore of their simulation) in cognitive life, the relevance of embodiment, and most important, the likelihood that an artifact will ever be truly embedded in a meaningful world.

The philosopher **Fred Dretske** approaches the debate from a decidedly different and perhaps more radical angle. It is misleading, he claims, to compare the cognitive feats of allegedly intelligent machines to the performance of human beings. It isn't just that the best machines, when compared to what human beings can do in their everyday lives, are still at the level of two-year-olds, requiring only greater storage capacity and fancier programming to grow up. Nor should we think of them as idiot savants, exhibiting a spectacular ability in a few isolated areas but having an overall IQ too low for fraternal association. Machines, Dretske contends, don't have an IQ. They don't do what we do—at least none of the things that, when we do them, exhibit intelligence. And it's not just that they don't do them the way we do them or as well as we do them. They don't do them at all. They don't solve problems, play games, prove theorems, recognize patterns, let alone think, see, and remember. On the contrary, Dretske claims, machines don't even add and subtract. The crucial distinction between human behavior and mechanical (or lower-animal) behavior concerns the role that meaning plays in human actions.

The difference between machines (or dogs) and the agents who use them is that although machines (and dogs) can pick up, process, and transmit the information we need in our investigative efforts, although they can respond (either by training or programming) to meaningful signs, it isn't the meaning of the signs that figures in the explanation of why they do what they do. For a drug-locating dog, some internal sign of marijuana, some neurological condition that, in this sense, means that marijuana is present, can cause the dog's tail to wag, but it isn't the fact that it means this that explains the tail movement. This, Dretske concludes, is the difference between the dog and its master, between the machine and its users, between the robot and the people who made it.

Other philosophers are less pessimistic about the reciprocal interaction between research in artificial intelligence and work in their discipline, and they even venture to offer some concrete suggestions. The possibility of collaboration is stressed by **Serge Sharoff** in the context of a confrontation between the phenomenological tradition of philosophy and classical work in AI. Sharoff's chapter opens with the thesis that AI investigations can be viewed not as attempts to create thinking machines but as computer realizations of some sort of philosophy. This interpretation of AI and cognitive science as "strict" philosophy resembles Husserl's project of phenomenology, the philosophical effort that aims at providing a complete description of the mental structures of consciousness that orient us in our dealing with the world.

This suggests that phenomenological notions such as intentionality, horizon, and internal time consciousness can be interpreted from an artificial intelligence viewpoint and can be effectively exploited by AI programs. For example, the representation of the structure of internal time consciousness would allow an AI program to refer to its own history and therefore to reflect on its own actions or representations. This possibility, it goes without saying, would constitute a substantial enlargement of the current scope of AI programs.

Anne Foerst, a German theologian who has been in residence at the MIT AI Lab and is a consultant to its Cog project, exploits the resources of Paul Tillich's theology and Horkheimer and Adorno's philosophy to provide an account that strives to reconcile the mechanistic descriptions of human life current in AI research with the widely shared intuitive feelings about human "specialness." She argues that human life is constantly played within two different kinds of discourse, which she calls, recalling the Platonic distinction, *mythos* and *logos*. Both discourses are essential for a satisfactory self-understanding because the project of understanding oneself requires both an understanding of the fundamental structure of the world (*logos*) and a narrative that explains our place in it (*mythos*). Many of the sometimes heated debates around AI stem from a dangerous entanglement between these two different but mutually supporting perspectives. AI researchers, she argues, have often presented as *logos* essentially mythical narratives about human life (and death), whereas philosophers have, conversely, presented *mythos* narratives about the meaningfulness of life as *logos*. A careful separation between the two kinds of discourse would usher in a new form of dialogue between researchers in AI and the traditional experts in *mythos*—philosophers, theologians, artists—that would allow both sides to contribute to the essential human project of self-understanding.

The strong continuity between contemporary research in and about artificial intelligence and other forms of inquiry into the mind is analyzed by the historian **Bruce Mazlish** in a fascinating journey through the history of automata. Mazlish takes us from the mechanical devices built in ancient China, to the mechanical dolls so dear to the seventeenth and eighteenth centuries, to some more recent literary creatures: Andersen's mechanical nightingale; Tik-Tok, the roundish robot inhabiting one of the Oz novels; Frankenstein's monster; and Čapek's and Isaac Asimov's robots.

Mazlish shows that the debate about AI "creatures" is, most of the time, simply a rehearsing of the age-old debate about mechanical creatures, a debate permeated by fears attached to the unfathomable powers of the inhuman and its consequent threat to humankind. Mazlish also makes clear that there is a recurring ambivalence in all those discussions: automata are depicted as at the same time deficient and overpowering, as at once less than and more than human. They are depicted as less intelligent, lacking emotions, lacking intuition, but at the same time, physically stronger, independent of physiological needs, and immune from emotional breakdown. The ambivalence intrinsic to this double image is rooted in the automata's uncanny—in the Freudian sense of the term—similarity to humans that fails to hide their essential difference. The interplay of similarity and difference keeps posing the same question. What is a human being? Such a radical question, in its ultimate "impossibility," is bound—Mazlish affirms after Freud—to arouse "the same range of ambivalent reactions: the sense of a perfection and infallibility to which we aspire—the angel in us—and the sense of the destructive and degrading in us—the ape in us."

Harry M. Collins, a sociologist of science, offers a fresh new perspective on the divide, introduced by Mazlish, between human and nonhuman creatures. Some philosophers have long disputed the computer's ability to behave intelligently, in any legitimate sense of the term, on the basis of a theoretical analysis of humans' relationship to the surrounding world. For instance, Dreyfus, perhaps the best-known champion of this position, has argued that AI's effort to reduce the mind-world relationship to a set of rules operating on a symbolic representation of the machines' environment is essentially doomed to fail. Collins rephrases the problem in different terms. First, he asks, What is the structure of the knowledge of the outside world that guides us in our daily meddling and tinkering with it? Second, are machines capable of replicating it?

Collins's analysis shows that there are four types of knowledge: symbol-type, embodied, embrained, and encultured. To understand the relation between humans and machines, he writes, one must understand the relation between symbol-type and encultured knowledge. To this end, he develops a new theory that cuts the world of action into regular and behavior-specific actions. While the former are typically human because they are unavoidably embodied and context-dependent, the latter are well suited for computers.

Collins draws two important consequences from his analysis. First, he is able to offer a simpler but more effective version of the classical test proposed by Turing to ascertain the level of intelligence of a computer artifact. Second, and perhaps more important, he underlines the sociological and political implication of his analysis: a careful distinction between different kinds of knowledge and different kinds of action "helps us see the ways in which machines are better than humans: it shows that many of the things that humans do, they do because they are unable to function in the machine-like way that they would prefer. It also shows that there are many activities where the question of machine replacement simply does not arise, or arises as, at best, an asymptotic approximation to human abilities."

Stephen Wilson, an artist, explores a path complementary to the research pursued by Latour and Teil. Is there a role for art in the scientific agenda of artificial intelligence, he asks, as AI itself understands it?

Artificial intelligence is an investigation into the nature of being human, the nature of intelligence, and the limits of machines. However theoretical such a pursuit may seem, Wilson stresses that the "implications of scientific and technological research are so far-reaching in their effect on both the practical and philosophical planes, that it is an error to conceive of them as narrow technical enterprises. The full flowering of research ... needs the benefit of the perspectives from many disciplines in the humanities and the arts, not just in commentary, but in actual research."

Wilson relates several of his experiences in this field, all of which represent efforts to question, criticize, and enlarge the perspective offered by traditional AI research, by applying its techniques to issues of human interactions and social exchange. AI set out to investigate the essence of human nature by actually replicating it, by building artificial creatures. How could it ignore the work of those artists who, for centuries, have been trying to investigate the human in all its nuances, ramifications, shortcomings, and accomplishments?

We cannot but share Wilson's feelings when he concludes: "If we are going to have artificially intelligent programs and robots, I would have sculptors and visual artists shaping their appearance, musicians composing their voices, choreographers forming their motion, poets crafting their language, and novelists and dramatists creating their character and interactions."

Douglas Hofstadter, author of *Gödel, Escher, Bach* and several other books, argues that a transformation of AI's conceptual space is coming due. Because of its historical roots in the logical and mathematical tradition, Hofstadter says, AI research has traditionally interpreted thinking as a manipulation of propositions, and has more or less systematically disregarded the complex activities involved in the recognition of a sentence's constituent elements—words, syllables, letters—as essentially nonintelligent. Taking his cue from the artistic activity of font designers, Hofstadter claims that the opposite is true: the quest for truth exemplified by mathematical theorem proving represents just a small, not quite characteristic, subset of human cognitive abilities.

Hofstadter illustrates this point in detail by reporting on the work of a program, Letter Spirit, whose task is to produce a graphically consistent alphabet given a letter of a certain style. Letter Spirit is an example of a program that tries to shed some light on the nature of creativity by replicating some artistic capability, in this case artistic font design. A discussion of Letter Spirit's feats bring immediately to the fore, as Hofstadter makes clear, the point that the true nature of human intelligence is quite at odds with the "received view" in contemporary AI.

Tom Burke, a philosopher, argues for a different kind of transformation within the conceptual space of artificial intelligence. Social situations, he claims, not just perceptual experience, are essential to the evolutionary emergence of human mentality. Burke outlines a view of the mind in which thinking is pictured as a type of agent/world interaction rather than as a type of computation taking place solely inside individual brains. Thinking is fundamentally an ecological process, not just a neural process.

In Burke's view, an individual's development of an objective sense of self is necessary to the development of reflective capabilities, and an objective sense of self is engendered only by participation in some kind of stable social community. It follows that the artificial intelligence enterprise cannot afford to focus solely on designing software for an artificial agent's head. Without some kind of socialization, an agent will have no way to classify and hence objectify itself to itself, and therefore will not be able to think. Socialization, Burke concludes, must be worked into the process of building a thinking machine.

Many of the authors described so far stress the potential benefits that artificial intelligence, *qua* scientific discipline endowed with a mathematically oriented methodology, can bring to traditional philosophical problems. This approach calls for a

division of theoretical labor: the humanities, especially philosophy, lay the foundational framework that artificial intelligence tests and develops by formulating mathematically precise descriptions. Two philosophers from the European tradition,
Maurizio Matteuzzi and **Alain-Marc Rieu**, reject this view by stressing the heterogeneity
of philosophy and artificial intelligence: no harmonious whole made up of high-flown
theory and nitty-gritty scientific machinations is about to be born. But their arguments
follow totally different, and almost symmetrically opposed paths: while Matteuzzi
denies AI's claim of being a science, Rieu thinks that present-day philosophy is no
longer in the position to provide any grand unifying view of the mind for other disciplines to work out.

Artificial intelligence, Matteuzzi claims, cannot be considered a science because it
lacks science's basic features. While every science builds on its own universe by abstraction, AI does not start from such ontological assumptions, the main reason being that
intelligence has nothing to do with *things*, but only with human beings and processes:
abstracting intelligence would result in a complete loss of the ontic support to any
possible universe. His conclusion is that AI is a general scientific methodology rather
than a science dealing with all possible theoretic universes. This explains why several
authors, such as Searle and Dreyfus, feel a lack of "background" and "common sense"
as the fundamental problem of AI.

Alain-Marc Rieu, on the contrary, stresses that the "mind" investigated by AI, cognitive science, and neurophysiology is no longer the supreme object of philosophy speculation. Rather, it is a quasi-object generated by the disciplines themselves through
a selective filtering of the phenomena they investigate according to their specific
methods. The inseparability of this quasi-object from the sciences' methods entails
that the scientific "mind" has no meaning outside of those scientific disciplines that
have constructed it.

Philosophy, therefore, cannot claim any separate access to such a (quasi-)object and
certainly cannot provide any grand theoretical framework. This appropriation of a traditional philosophical view by the sciences of the mind entails, according to Rieu, that
philosophy must reinvent itself and renounce, once and for all, the impossible dream
of a grand unified narrative explaining the essence of humanity.

Michael L. Johnson, a literary critic, exploits the distinction between grand unified
narratives of knowledge and "little narratives" to offer a prophecy: the expert system
of the future will think like a woman. Johnson starts with an analysis of one the most
intractable problems plaguing AI research: the so-called frame problem, for example,
the epistemological problem of how to update a world model, like those used by AI
programs, in order to cope with a changing world. Johnson suggests that a semiotic
approach, so far disregarded by the AI literature, might provide some new light, insofar
as it would allow AI researchers to exploit the wealth of work done in semiotics on the
ways in which living cognitive systems keep their sign systems more or less synchron-

ized with the world in which they live. The problem of keeping a world model up-to-date becomes the problem of how to shift the referents of one's sign system in order to keep it meaningful.

Furthermore, semiotic research has shown that men and women tend to deal with this problem differently. Women seem to be better equipped, Johnson argues, either physiologically or culturally, to detect subtle changes in their environment and to adapt to them, being more tolerant of differing or contradictory points of views, and of the inconsistencies of their interplay. Gynosemiosis, Johnson concludes, seems to provide better tools for adapting to a world deprived of a grand unified theme explaining its essence. "If humankind is to survive and endure more *meaningfully*, then it must, as it grows older, learn—and learn by—even more powerful strategies of mending. . . . In their joint dealing with the unknown, humankind and its machines must become more feminized."

In *Knowing Subjects: AI from Feminist Philosophy*, **Alison Adam**, a feminist critic of AI with extensive, first-hand research in the field, writes on the implicit assumptions woven into AI research from a gender-specific perspective. She discusses how the reasoning instantiated in several large artificial intelligence projects rests on a fairly limited set of psychological experiments on technically educated, male U.S. college students, and how these subjects come to represent the universal subject without explicit acknowledgment. Consequently, the male standpoint comes to embody, ironically, a norm of cognitive skills that are degendered and unembodied.

The historian and philosopher of science **Evelyn Fox Keller** writes about the development of computer technology in relation to biology, in the context of the birth of cybernetics. She provides a fascinating and detailed history of the transformation of the notion of "organism," from its first introduction into the field of biology at the end of the eighteenth century to its eventual (but, in retrospect, only provisional) demise by molecular biology in the first half of the twentieth century. Throughout her account, she discusses the strict interactions between the theoretical innovations (analyzing the shifts from *organism*, to *organization* and to *self-organization*), the technological advances (the steam engine first, then the telephone switch and the computer), and the social and political contexts in which the research was carried out (e.g., the shift from the mostly German research in embryology to the mostly American molecular biology, and the new social organization of scientific research after World War II).

The sociologist and science studies scholar **Andrew Pickering** pursues Keller's investigations even further by examining the history of cybernetics from the standpoint of the artifacts that the cyberneticians built or found. He describes in details the various "monsters" that were produced in different research centers before and immediately after World War II. Wiener's anti-aircraft predictor, Ashby's homeostat and 100-double-triode device, Prigogine's slime molds, and Belousov-Zhabotinky reactions occupy the liminal space between the human and the animal, and even between the animate and the inanimate: they are all examples of impossible, weird contraptions that live in real time and are forced to organize or reorganize themselves in response to unpredictable changes in the environment. Pickering stresses that these strange monsters forced their inventors and discoverers to forge new concepts in order to understand the strange temporality of their creations, and he concludes, with a "feedback move" that would make any cybernetician proud, that science studies could fruitfully exploit some of cybernetics' insights into temporality to better understand the development of science.

Notes

1. Quoted in Jack Copeland, *Artificial Intelligence: A Philosophical Introduction* (Oxford: Blackwell, 1993), 1.

2. See Hubert Dreyfus, *What Computers Can't Do: The Limits of Artificial Intelligence* (New York: Harper, 1972) and *What Computers Still Can't Do* (Cambridge, Mass.: MIT Press, 1992).

3. Hubert Dreyfus, *What Computers Still Can't Do*; John Searle, "Minds, Brains, and Programs," *Behavioral and Brain Sciences* 3 (1980): 417–424; John Searle, *Minds, Brains, and Science* (Cambridge, Mass.: Harvard University Press, 1984); John Searle, *The Rediscovery of the Mind* (Cambridge, Mass.: MIT Press, 1992).

I Introducing Artificial Intelligence: Past, Present, and Future

Machinations of the Mind: Cybernetics and Artificial Intelligence from Automata to Cyborgs

Stefano Franchi and Güven Güzeldere

1 Introduction

Animals, Humans, and Machines: At the Intersection of Boundaries

Even a brief glance at the history of intellectual thought reveals that one of the issues underlying numerous debates about human nature, the place of human beings in the universe, and the characterization of self and identity is related to boundaries—boundaries separating human beings from other material creatures, animate or inanimate, actual or imaginary: nonhuman animals, half-human half-animal beasts, fictional monsters created by the human hand (such as Frankenstein's monster), mechanical artifacts in human form (such as automata and robots), and human-machine hybrids (such as cyborgs). It is also apparent that these boundaries exhibit some degree of fluidity over time.

This is true especially in the characterization of animals, which typically occupy a middle area between humans and machines, as evinced, for example, by the curious animal courts of the Middle Ages where legal rights, responsibilities, and punishment of animals were treated as a serious matter, in contrast to the Cartesian conception of animals as "mindless automata" that are not even capable of genuinely feeling pain or pleasure. In the main, the questions concern the triangulation of humans, animals, and machines (the rest being derivative hybrids constituted by combining features from two of the three). So when the question is about animals, for example, the two ends taken as reference points in the spectrum on which animals are supposed to be located, are humans and machines.[1]

It should come as no surprise, then, that we pursue a discussion about the nature of machines (automata, robots, androids) against the reference points of humans and animals, or that our chapter ends with a discussion of the significance of cyborgs on both philosophical and technological platforms. One way to put the fundamental question of artificial intelligence is to ask whether "machination of the mind" is a possibility, and if so, what it takes to turn it into an actuality. Unpacking this question, however, becomes meaningful only against the rich backdrop of debates regarding the nature of notions such as "machination" and "mind," and the similarities revealed and contrasts drawn among the various conceptualizations involved. It is within such a framework that we present a historical and philosophical assessment of artificial intelligence as a deep-rooted grand intellectual project, and of AI—an enterprise of our time—as the present incarnation of artificial intelligence.

Artificial, Intelligence, and Artificial Intelligence

The term *artificial intelligence* was coined in the second half of the twentieth century, and it refers—generally in the abbreviated form AI—to the particular research program that continues to be pursued at present mainly by computer scientists and engineers. The overarching goal of AI is the creation of intelligence, and in its present state, this comes down to the design and construction of an artificial system using computational tools that has intelligent capacities and exhibits it through its behavior.

The *artificiality* of AI comes from the fact that the intelligent system in question is one without a natural history; it is not part of the biological order; it is an artifact designed and synthetically built by a team of human researchers. The *intelligence* of AI is to be manifested through the output that a system produces, be it actual behavior in an automaton or robot, or simulated behavior expressed in symbolic form.

In this chapter, we assign different referents to the terms *artificial intelligence* and *AI* (this distinction may not hold in other contributors' chapters that follow). Artificial intelligence as a broader intellectual project shares the same overarching goal of AI: the bringing into being of intelligence by the human hand. By the term *artificial intelligence* we mean the totality of the ambitions and efforts to reach this goal throughout history, not only in the present or in any one particular era. Thus we locate it in a much broader historical context than the AI of the present. We believe that the significance as well as the enormous difficulty of human attempts to create intelligence can be fully appreciated only from such a broad historical perspective, and that without this perspective it would be impossible to give a fair assessment of AI. Conversely, a close examination of AI can yield better understanding of the historically enduring project of artificial intelligence.

Artificial Intelligence Beyond AI

In this chapter, we closely examine the paradigmatic assumptions, goals, successes, and failures of AI, and its problematic relation to an equally ambitious project, cybernetics, against the historical backdrop of artificial intelligence. A deeper understanding of AI as a case study is illuminating with respect to the attempts to understand the nature of mind in the history of thought. We also situate numerous philosophical threads that interweave the fabric of this historical endeavor over a broader stretch of time, from the long-standing interest in and craftsmanship of automata making to the cyborgs of an imagined future.

It may be thought that there is something paradoxical in the proposition to scrutinize AI to better understand artificial intelligence. Obviously, AI is not just any old phase in the unfolding of a set of continuing curiosities and efforts that can be broadly gathered under what we call artificial intelligence as an intellectual project. It is, in terms of scientific knowledge and technology, the cutting edge of an enterprise whose roots are the same as those of the grander project. As such, AI can be seen as the present and arguably the most sophisticated culmination of the various lines of work that have gone into the grander project.

On the other hand, it is worth noting that the present paradigm of AI is very much defined by what is currently available to the imagination of those actively engaged in it. One of the main themes of this chapter is that that very paradigm, with a short history of roughly half a century, inherits only a particular piece of what has been imagined, wondered about, struggled with, and known to those engaged in the grander project over millennia. If this is true, then AI should be regarded as only one of many paradigms, with its own particularities in the history of artificial intelligence, rather than as a synthesis of converging intellectual threads that constitute the broader project. This construal would view AI as less than the most sophisticated representative component of the grander project, as not necessarily the best understanding of human intelligence and its realization in human-constructed artifacts.

In fact, there is some truth in both these ways of situating AI in the framework of artificial intelligence. AI indeed presents us with the most impressive constructions in the history of the grander project that come closer than ever to fulfilling the dream of "machination of the mind." At the same time, AI embodies a number of wrong turns, misconceptualizations, and missed opportunities when viewed in relation to all the other strands that make up the project of artificial intelligence. It is precisely in this mixture of blind spots and impressive advances that we can understand the monumental scope of artificial intelligence as a grand project in intellectual history, give a fair assessment of AI in it, and perhaps extract a glimpse of what lies ahead.

Artificial Intelligence, AI, and the Humanities

One of the central themes of this chapter is that while AI has turned out to be primarily an engineering and computer science project, the goal it strives to achieve is that of a much broader project, artificial intelligence, which continues to elude AI research. We examine in some detail the reasons behind the present constitution of AI and its consequences in the sections that follow. Here we note one of the most outstanding facts about AI: its isolation, by and large, from the social sciences and from the humanities, with the single exception of philosophy. This is both surprising and revealing in the context of this chapter.

It is surprising because artificial intelligence, the broader project of which AI is an incarnation, has been from its beginnings closely examined, critiqued, and pursued by the humanities. Going even further, it can be said that in an intellectual sense, artificial intelligence has been a project of the humanities in its quest to gain a better understanding of human nature. This is in stark contrast with the emergence and evolution of AI, which has been confined mostly to a community of mathematicians, engineers, and computer scientists.

AI's disconnect with the humanities is revealing because it holds clues, we believe, to a great number of failed projections and predictions that have plagued AI from its early days. "Creating intelligence" seen as an engineering project makes it difficult to appreciate the complicated nature of human mental life, behavior, culture, and social practices—a territory generally studied and much better understood by the humanities and social sciences. Predictions about AI's successes, after all, always had a dual nature: they involved both an assessment of progress in technology and computational practices, and an assessment of what was involved in achieving intelligence or intelligent, intentional behavior. However successful AI researchers were in their assessment of technological advances involved in their field, without a fuller understanding of the complexities involved in individual intelligence and agency as well as social life, their overall predictions time and again fell terribly short of the actual results achieved in their research agenda.

We believe that an important part of the reason for the isolation of AI research from the humanities has to do with the technical nature of computational ideas and modeling, which might have intimidated or alienated those who are not as comfortable in the world of formulas and equations; perhaps humanities should take some of the blame for not being more proactive and involved. But an equally important part has to do also with the desire of AI research to stick only to its own tools and to remain confined to its own community. It is likely that the hostility AI encountered in its single most important interaction with the "outside world" at its very beginnings—with philosophy, which took a very critical stance toward AI (notably in the writings of Hubert Dreyfus, author of *What Computers Can't Do*)—played a determining role in AI's subsequent poor relations with the humanities. Dreyfus's critical report on the status of AI as an emerging field of research, which he likened to alchemy,[2] was perceived as a threat to the very lifelines of the discipline, and rightly so, not the least because the report had been commissioned by the RAND Corporation to get an outsider's view to be used in financial decisions for or against supporting AI research. It is possible that this single but powerful encounter set the tone for a great deal of AI's subsequent reactions toward the humanities, and that it has remained a major intellectual handicap ever since.[3]

Note that cybernetics from its beginnings was conceived of as an essentially multidisciplinary effort, quite unlike AI. This is interesting because the emergence of cybernetics and that of AI are similar in important respects: they were instigated mainly by mathematicians as well as by scientists and engineers, and perhaps as a result of this, they both involve a serious amount of technical formalization and mathematical vocabulary. But, as we show in some detail in section 9, there has been a major effort in cybernetics, from its start, to conceive of its project as a multidisciplinary one and to incorporate disciplines like the humanities and social sciences into its field. For evidence on this point, it is sufficient to look at the diversity of disciplines represented at the Macy Conferences,[4] which have shaped and documented the core of this multidisciplinary effort, or at Norbert Wiener's first book, *Cybernetics,* perhaps the classic book of the field, which has the following blurb: "A study of vital importance to psychologists, physiologists, electrical engineers, radio engineers, sociologists, philosophers, mathematicians, anthropologists, psychiatrists, and physicists."[5]

We note here that one of the unfortunate outcomes of the failure of collaboration between AI and cybernetics is that this preempted a possible opportunity for AI to incorporate into its paradigm significant intellectual contributions from the humanities and a broader historical perspective that could have proved beneficial in AI's assessments of its status and consequent predictions of its accomplishments, which have more often than not proved to be a liability if not an embarrassment for the field. On a more positive note, however, we note in section 13 that the advent of cyborg technologies in computer science and engineering, combined with the emerging field of cyborg studies in cultural anthropology, women's studies, critical theory, and philosophy, opens up a new and rather unexpected venue for bringing AI and cybernetics together as well as for situating humanities centrally in this new area of study.

Overview of the Chapter

We open with a brief presentation in section 2 of two major intellectual projects that emerged in the second half of the twentieth century, primarily in the United States, in the technologically blossoming post–World War II era: cybernetics and AI. These two disciplines are related to one another in curious ways. Their inspiration stems from a long-standing curiosity and ambition to understand the behavior and governing principles of autonomous physical systems. While adopting different methodologies, they share some of the same goals, such as finding models and explanations to provide insight into the nature not just of the natural but also of the artifactual. And they both missed important opportunities in their time of collaboration with other disciplines (cybernetics with phenomenology, AI with philosophy and the humanities) and with one another. Their paths now seem to be converging in ways not explicitly imagined by either discipline, in the paradigm of part-natural, part-artificial beings who are rapidly becoming possible in the present era of information processing and biotechnology: cyborgs.

Sections 3 and 4 present a historical analysis of the intellectual predecessors of AI and cybernetics, in the evolving conceptualization of the body and the mind as mechanistically understandable phenomena. This analysis starts with the earliest efforts of building self-propelled, semiautonomous machines that imitate living entities in both appearance and behavior, such as animals and later human beings. With the rising dominance of a mechanized understanding of the world in the seventeenth century, the construction of automata takes on a more substantial significance, in a way that allows into the metaphysical understanding of nature the possibility of the wholly physical realization of the mental. Our historical exegesis traces the primary lineages in intellectual thought that culminate in such an understanding. This understanding, in turn, lays the groundwork for the emergence of cybernetics and AI, within a decade of one another, in the 1950s.

Section 5 provides a general discussion of AI's research program that shows how the overarching goal of artificial intelligence was channeled into two connected but distinct goals: the development of programs that play games involving cognitive skills (in particular, chess) and the development of language comprehension and production systems (in particular, the Turing test). Sections 6 and 7 provide a detailed analysis of these two main strands of AI research.

In section 8, we return to a discussion of AI within the historical context of artificial intelligence. We compare the relative isolation in which AI research is currently pursued with the more inclusive approach that was prevalent in the past. In the course of its brief contemporary history, AI research has been home to a great many controversies: about symbols, consciousness, proceduralism, and the relevance of neuroscience, among others. In part, these upheavals were due to internal fluctuations stemming from badly failed estimations, on the part of AI pioneers, of what their research could accomplish in a given—and what almost always turned out to be too short—period of time. We argue that at least one factor responsible for the misjudgments was the overly homogenized and restricted professional constituency of the AI community.

Section 9 provides a discussion of the many obstacles that interdisciplinary research must overcome in the context of a discussion of the often rivalrous relationship between AI and cybernetics. We claim that the differences between these two research programs were not in each case solely intellectual or theoretical and that in fact it was primarily ideological and political differences that kept them from joining forces in a collaborative effort.

Sections 10 and 11 present four different brands of critiques raised against AI. In particular we discuss the view that AI is *too narrow* and must be replaced or at best integrated to reach artificial intelligence; that artificial intelligence is *impossible* in principle; that AI and artificial intelligence are socially and politically *dangerous*; and finally that AI *is not* artificial intelligence but should be reinterpreted as a form of art, as a particular kind of meta-epistemology, and so on.

Section 12 takes stock and provides an assessment of where AI stands at present and how this illuminates the current status of the grander project of artificial intelligence.

Finally, section 13 explores the rather unexpected possibility of the convergence of themes from AI and cybernetics. While the two disciplines missed an important opportunity to collaborate at the time of their emergence and initial contact, the new paths AI has been forced to explore due to its failures in some of its initial goals seem to fit well within a fundamentally cybernetic vision of the unity and fusion of human beings with human-made artifacts in the construal of cyborgs—the imagined as well as actual hybrid beings of the future.

2 Artificial Intelligence and Cybernetics: The Entangled Roots of Two Major Projects of the Twentieth Century

What Is Artificial Intelligence? What Is AI?

The *Handbook of Artificial Intelligence* gives the following definition:

Artificial Intelligence is the part of computer science concerned with designing intelligent computer systems, that is, systems that exhibit the characteristics we associate with intelligence in human behavior—understanding language, learning, reasoning, solving problems, and so on.[6]

Here, the definition is of *AI* rather than *artificial intelligence*, as we distinguish them. Nonetheless, one aspect of this definition is true to the spirit of AI as well as artificial intelligence—the concern with designing or constructing intelligent systems. The fact that these systems are to be designed or built indicates that AI, unlike biology or genetics, is not in the business of studying or manipulating biological systems. Rather, the goal is the physical construction of a device or artifact that sufficiently possesses those characteristics that would deserve the attribution of the capacity of "intelligence."

First Steps toward Artificial Intelligence: Self-Propelled Artifacts

The kind of ambition embodied in the project of AI, we argue, has a long-standing history that manifested itself as early as fourth century B.C.E., if not earlier, in the production of self-moving automata that imitated various behaviors of autonomous biological organisms.[7] The curiosity about self-propelled mechanical artifacts had sometimes to do merely with entertainment purposes, as in the case of little marionettes in music boxes, a favorite accessory especially of the bourgeoisie of the seventeenth and eighteenth centuries and an item of impressively fine craftsmanship of the time.[8] Certain classes of automata also served simply as engineering solutions to make life easier for human beings, without any aim toward creating even an imitated sort of intelligence, as in the case of waterways and irrigation devices that automated the labor involved in farming, such as some of the constructions of al-Jazari of thirteenth-century Mesopotamia.[9]

But there was also a strong and persistent intellectual drive behind the enterprise of tinkering with mechanical devices in an attempt to make them come closer to entities that do things of their own accord. John Cohen makes the same observation in his treatise about the history of fictional as well as actual automata:

We must, however, distinguish this age-old quest for technical skill in simulating human performance from a deeper desire to wrest from the gods the secret of the making of man. This was the task of Prometheus, who formed man from earth and water. In the words of Hesiod,

He [Jove] bade the artist-god his hest obey,
And mould with tempering waters ductile clay:
Infuse, as breathing life and form began,
The supple vigour and the voice of man.

As we shall see, the question, "How was Adam made?" profoundly intrigued gnostic and cabbalist, alchemist and mediaeval scientist, and efforts, in fancy or fact, to create a man never ceased.[10]

The history of fictional automata is dotted with stories, myths, and anecdotes from Ancient Greece to Egypt to India and China. Cohen talks of the Greek god Hephaestos who was said to be attended by "handmaids of gold resembling 'Living young damsels, filled with mind and wisdom'" and the statue of Memnon, the Egyptian "Son of Dawn," who uttered human sounds when the rays of the rising sun reached its lips, as some of the earliest such fictional constructions.

The history of actual automata is equally filled with intriguing stories, which, like the fictional accounts, point to the fascination with the very idea of intelligence and human agency being embodied in statues or artifacts that are themselves human creations. One of the most famous automata in the cast of mechanically concocted characters that appeared in Europe after the Enlightenment is Wolfgang von Kempelen's construction, the chess-playing Turk (see figure 1).

Tom Standage describes the dramatic public reception of the Turk's performance in its very first appearance in 1770 in Vienna:

Once Kempelen had stopped turning the key, there was an agonizing silence. Then a brief pause, the sound of whirring and grinding clockwork, like that of a clock preparing to chime, could be heard coming from inside the automaton. The carved wooden figure, which has hitherto been completely immobile, slowly turned its head from side to side for a few seconds, as though surveying the board. To the utter astonishment of the audience, the mechanical Turk then suddenly lurched to life, reaching out with its left arm and moving one of its chessmen forward. The audience cried out in amazement. The game had begun.[11]

While we have more to say about the significance of the Turk and its public reception in the history of artificial intelligence in section 3, it is important to note here that the most prominent evidence of intelligence attributed to the Turk is self-governed and purposeful behavior that exhibits humanlike characteristics without external intervention or manipulation.[12]

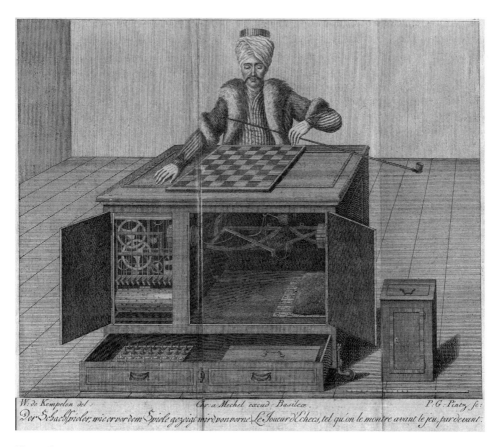

W. de Kempelen del :   *Chr. a Mechel excud : Basileœ .*   *P. G : Pintz fe :*

Der Schachspieler, wie er vor dem Spiele gezeigt wird von vorne. Le Joueur d'Echecs, tel qu'on le montre avant le jeu, par devant.

Figure 1
The chess-playing Turk automaton of Wolfgang von Kempelen, 1769.

The definition of *artificial intelligence* (or, as we argue, of *AI*), in the *Handbook*—computer systems exhibiting exclusively cognitive capacities such as language, learning, reasoning, and problem solving—is characteristic of AI's *current* research program. There are two different sets of limitations that set it apart from the broader project of artificial intelligence. The first one has to do with the technology used to reproduce intelligent skills. Needless to say, electronic digital computers are an invention of the twentieth century, and the history of mechanical or analog computers does not go very far. But the more important difference between the current definition of AI and the larger project of artificial intelligence is the identification of intelligence with exclusively cognitive capacities (language, learning, reasoning, and problem solving). Forms of purposeful behaviors that lack a cognitive dimension are excluded. This particular way of delineating the domain of intelligent capacities is not without consequences. In fact, we argue that it has had a profound effect on the conceptualization of the traditional ways of thinking about the relation between the mental and the physical, and the formulation of the mind-body problem in contemporary philosophy.

This particular approach to the characterization of intelligence has not always been true of the broader project of artificial intelligence. Furthermore, a related and equally ambitious project, cybernetics, which emerged slightly earlier but faded much more quickly than its cousin AI, had quite a different starting point, even though it shared a number of similar goals.

What Is Cybernetics?

Cybernetics preceded AI as a discipline that shared the ambition of providing an explanation of the nature of higher cognitive activities such as learning, memory, and, more generally, teleological purposive behavior, couched in the terminology of the physical sciences. In this attempt, cybernetics maintained a vision of unity between the natural and the artificial, and investigated ways in which certain fundamental capacities and behaviors of the living and the nonliving can be characterized at a level sufficiently abstract to allow a unified explanation, most specifically in terms of there being a controlling component in these systems that monitors and guides the behavior of the system through feedback mechanisms.

The term *cybernetics* first appeared in 1834 in the writings of André Ampère in the form *cybernétique* (in *Essai sur la philosophie des sciences*), meaning the "science of government or control." But it was coined in its present meaning by Norbert Wiener, a mathematician who laid the conceptual foundations of the field, and his collaborators, in the 1940s.[13]

Wiener emphasized the deliberate blurring or eschewing of the natural-artificial distinction as a central tenet of his vision of cybernetics:

It is my thesis that the physical functioning of the living individual and the operation of some of the newer communication machines are precisely parallel in the analogous attempts to control entropy through feedback. Both of them have sensory receptors as one stage in their cycle of operation: that is, in both of them there exists a special apparatus for collecting information from the outer world at low energy levels, and for making it available in the operation of the individual or of the machine. In both cases these external messages are not taken *neat*, but through the internal transforming powers of the apparatus, whether it be alive or dead. The information is then turned into a new form available for the further stages of performance. In both the animal and the machine the performance is made to be effective on the outer world. In both of them, their *performed* action on the outer world, and not merely their *intended* action, is reported back to the central regulatory apparatus.[14]

There were, of course, disagreements internal to the cybernetics research community, on the characterization of their field and its fundamental theoretical commitments. Some cyberneticians, Wiener included, viewed as the unifying component of explanation in their discipline a formal isomorphism that provided a mathematical relation between natural and artificial systems as analogues. Others, such as Warren McCulloch, argued that cybernetic explanation shifted the focus of, or downright melted down, the untenable distinction between the living and the nonliving: "Everything we learn of organisms leads us to conclude not merely that they are analogous to machines but that they are machines."[15] But the common conviction was to discover unifying principles and a unifying language in which cognitive faculties as well as the behavior of things naturally evolved and artifactually constructed could be explained with deeper theoretical insight.

Cybernetics versus AI: A Contrast in Methodologies

In cybernetics, there was not as much of a prioritization of the natural over the artificial, or vice versa, and much less of an issue about modeling one on the other. In contrast, questions about what is genuine versus what is imitated or simulated have always dominated AI, built on the very foundations of the distinction between the natural and the artificial. This is just one of the many ways in which cybernetics and AI part company in their ways of pursuing their goals, despite many similarities.

Another difference between cybernetics and AI, indirectly related to their differing stances toward the natural/artificial distinction, has to do with the emphasis each placed on different aspects of intelligence and agency. For cybernetics, the fundamental idea was the unifying character of communication and governance of behavior in animals, humans, and machines alike; in classical AI, cognitive activities such as thinking, reasoning, planning, and problem solving took center stage almost exclusively.

This difference situated the two disciplines in positions that could have complemented one another in a collaborative effort to reach their overlapping goal—obtaining a novel understanding of the nature of cognition and behavior using tools from computing and engineering that transcended the boundaries of traditional fields of study, which had been confined exclusively to the domain of humans or animals. Unfortunately, however, cybernetics and AI passed by one another "like two ships in the night" and never made good on this opportunity.

The roboticist Hans Moravec, a contemporary AI researcher who has been critical of the classical AI paradigm, states this point as follows:

The cybernetics researchers, whose self-contained experiments were often animal-like and mobile, began their investigation of nervous systems by attempting to duplicate the sensorimotor abilities of animals. The artificial intelligence community ignored this approach in their early work and instead set the sights directly on the intellectual acme of human thought, in experiments running on large, stationary mainframe computers dedicated to mechanizing pure reasoning. This "top-down" route to machine intelligence made disappointingly few fundamental gains in over a decade. While cybernetics scratched the underside of real intelligence, artificial intelligence scratched the top-side. The interior bulk of the problem remains inviolate.[16]

We argue in section 9 that the two disciplines did not make any substantial professional contact for reasons that have less to do with intellectual issues than with politics and finance. But we conclude at the end of this chapter that these differences now seem to be at a point of resolution, approximately 50 years after the missed opportunity for cooperation, in the imagined future of cyborgs.

Before moving too far ahead, however, we examine the intellectual predecessors of AI and cybernetics in the history of automata making and the mechanization of the worldview (including the mind), and the theoretical as well as disciplinary interrelations between the two fields.

AI Revisited

The characterization of AI at the beginning of this section and the technological future it imagines are the products of recent decades and highly dependent on the development of digital computing devices in the past half-century. It is in this sense that AI is a project of the current era. At present, AI stands as a partly autonomous academic discipline in its infancy, as evinced not only by its post–1950s computational tools but also by the distinctive set of human resources it employs, and the particular worldview it for the most part adopts.

But the roots of AI reach back over many centuries, not only in academic thinking but also in the public imagination. Far from being new, the questions that AI aspires to answer have a long distinguished career in the history of intellectual thought. And as noted, the broad aspirations and ambitions underlying artificial intelligence, which existed long before, and some of the ways in which they were pursued, can be seen to part company with the methodologies of AI in substantial ways.

For these reasons it seems useful to locate the research efforts grouped under the banner "artificial intelligence" within a broader historical and critical framework. For only from such a perspective would it be possible to judge fairly AI's successes and failures, and to get a cogent perspective on its future, free from both gut-level negative reactions and from the seduction of fantasy-filled promises.[17] In doing so, we need to examine a number of related fields and research projects as well as different conceptualizations of what it means to be intelligent, or natural/artificial, or even human, and to contrast the characterization of AI with that of cybernetics. The starting point of all this lies in the ambition to understand and then construct the internal mechanisms of embodied and autonomous physical systems.[18]

3   The Path to AI: From Automata Building to the Mechanization of the Body

The claim that we can understand human nature by finding out about the mechanisms of its embodiment has been around for many centuries. In his "Intellectual Issues in the History of Artificial Intelligence," Allen Newell writes that AI is built on this idea fundamentally. Thus he characterizes AI as having a *goal* of understanding and constructing the mind, sustained by a *strategy* of understanding and constructing its underlying mechanisms. Moreover, Newell says that doubts about AI's future success stem from a lack of belief in the truth of this fundamental assumption, tracing this line of thinking back to the "Cartesian split between mind and matter."[19]

Understanding bodily mechanisms was not always a concern in philosophy. For instance, it played almost no role in Plato's attempt to understand the human psyche, although Newell's path can perhaps be traced back to Aristotle. Ironically, however, the greatest "mechanician" in the history of the study of mind was Descartes, the architect of the modern conception of mind-body dualism. Descartes carefully studied the nervous system, proposed a theory of nervous activity in the body based on hydraulic principles as they were conceived in the eighteenth century, and went on to suggest that bodies, human or otherwise, were no different from carefully constructed automata, or self-moving machines.

Early Automata

In order to have a better understanding of the mechanical conception of the body that Descartes inherited, it seems appropriate to briefly review the place of automata and their construction in intellectual history. Automata are defined, in the *Encyclopedia Britannica*, as "any of various mechanical objects that are relatively self-operating after they have been set in motion. The term *automaton* is also applied to a class of electromechanical devices that transform information from one form into another on the basis of predetermined instructions or procedures."[20]

The entry then goes on to say, "In general, automatons are designed to arouse interest through their visual appeal and then to inspire surprise and awe through the apparent magic of their seemingly spontaneous movement. The majority of automatons are direct representations of creatures and plants, or of kinetic aspects of natural phenomena."

We have already remarked that automata making, while constituting an important ingredient of what later became the conceptual groundwork for artificial intelligence, did not in itself carry the ambition of making intelligent devices. The emphasis was only on the imitation of behavior, not on the workings of the internal mechanisms that drive the behavior and could, in principle, imbue it with intelligence and autonomy. This can be seen in the earliest examples of automata, which were made on different continents, presumably independently by their respective constructors, starting as early as the fourth century B.C.E.

One of the earlier references to automata is in the work of Hero of Alexandria, a Greek mathematician of the first century, who invented the first steam-powered engine. Hero was interested in mechanical devices in general and left behind writings about the mechanisms not just of steam engines but also of siphons, fountains, water

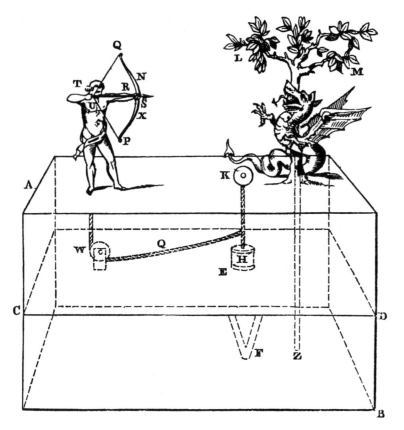

Figure 2
Hercules shooting at a serpent, an automaton of Hero of Alexandria, 1st century. From *The Pneu-matics of Hero of Alexandria*, trans. Joseph G. Greenwood, ed. Bennet Woodcroft (London: Taylor, Walton and Maberly, 1851; reprinted New York: Elsevier, 1971).

clocks, and various kinds of automata that were used for theatrical purposes (known as *dei ex machina*, as in Sophocles' *Philoctetes* and many plays of Euripides).[21] Figure 2 shows one of Hero's automatons, Hercules shooting at a serpent.

Hero credits an earlier Greek mathematician and philosopher of the Pythagorean school, Archytas of Tarentum. A friend of Plato, Archytas had a deep interest in mechanics and worked on the mechanism of acoustics, among other things.[22] The automaton Hero credits Archytas with constructing was a wooden pigeon, suspended in the air from the end of a bar and revolved around it with the aid of a jet of steam. There are also references to automata making in China as early as the third century B.C.E., for entertainment in the imperial circles. These automata consisted of animal forms as well as human musicians, monks, and so on.

Constructions of automata became popular in the Islamic civilizations of the Meso-potamia region starting in the ninth century. An impressive array of automata was constructed by the thirteenth-century engineer al-Jazari. Al-Jazari was a member of the Artuqids, a Turcoman dynasty that was settled around the city of Diyar Bakr, and in the service of the Artuqid king, he engineered dozens of automata, from solely func-tional water-raising devices and clocks to those with high entertainment value, such as peacocks, a self-replenishing vessel, an orchestra of musicians, a scribe, a slave, and a wine-servant. The wine-servant (see figure 3) was able to locomote on wheels a pre-designated distance and to serve wine by tipping a decanter. Al-Jazari's work is among the best documented of early constructions of automata, thanks to his compilation of drawings and detailed explanations in a book, known in English as *The Book of Knowl-edge of Ingenious Mechanical Devices*.[23]

Predecessors of Modern Automata

In addition to descriptions of actual automata, stories of fictional automata continued to circulate. It is important to note that while the automata in these stories are capable of intelligent behavior, they cannot act intelligently out of their own material nature. That is, their intelligence is not manifested by virtue of their internal mechanisms. Rather, it is an additional substance, force, or otherwise causally efficacious agent that endows them with cognitive capacities and enables purposeful, intelligent action. As such, these fictional automata are not, strictly speaking, early models of what the proj-ect of artificial intelligence envisions.

Nonetheless, such stories served to fuel the interest in the actual production of automata and to keep alive in the public imagination the possibility of human-made material artifacts exhibiting intelligence and agency. A story narrated in T. A. Heppen-heimer's essay "Man Makes Man" is especially revealing in this regard:

There is a story told about Friar Roger Bacon, a brilliant English clergyman-scientist-philosopher of the thirteenth century, and his colleague Friar Bungey. The tale said they wanted to surround England with a wall of brass for protection against invaders. To do this, Bacon proposed first building a brass head that would explain how to build the wall. This done, he summoned a spirit to give the head the power of speech. The spirit warned Bacon that if he and Bungey did not hear the words of the head when it spoke, all would be lost.

For three weeks, the friars sat watching the head, but it was mute. Finally, they decided to get some sleep and engaged a guard to watch, instructing him to wake them should the head speak. No sooner had they gone to sleep than the head spoke for the first time: "Time is." To the guard this seemed too trivial to justify waking the friars. Half an hour later the head spoke again, saying: "Time was." This also seemed too trivial to take seriously. After another half-hour the head declared: "Time is past," and collapsed.[24]

What is most noteworthy in this story is the thinking that a particular piece of knowledge, not available to Bacon and Bungey, can be given by a material, mechanical

Figure 3
Al-Jazari's wine-servant automaton, 13th century. From *The Book of Knowledge of Ingenious Mechanical Devices*, trans. Donald Hill (Dordrecht: Reidel, 1974).

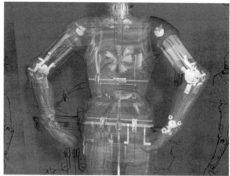

Figure 4

Leonardo da Vinci's humanoid robot, ca. 1495 (external and internal views). From the Web site of the Institute and Museum of the History of Science, Florence, ⟨http://www.imss.firenze.it/⟩.

construction, resembling a human head, that is to be built by the two friars themselves. While the power of speech is provided by an external agent, the spirit summoned for that purpose, it is the head, the embodiment of the speaking power, that enables the expression of the knowledge that is eventually delivered.

The first automaton in human form in the Western civilization is said to have been built by Leonardo da Vinci, circa 1495, before he began working on the Last Supper, based on his earlier studies of anatomy and kinesiology. According to the information provided by the Institute and Museum of the History of Science in Florence, which has on display copies of Leonardo's drawings, the automaton was quite intricately designed (see figure 4). It was armored in the style of fifteenth-century Italian warriors and designed to sit up, wave its arms, and move its head via a flexible neck while imitating a speaking person by opening and closing its jaw.

The internal mechanism of this robot was quite complicated, in order to make its behavior appear as humanlike as possible. It is described in the museum's documents as follows:

The robot consisted of two independent systems: three-degree-of-freedom legs, ankles, knees, and hips; and four-degree-of-freedom arms with articulated shoulders, elbows, wrists, and hands. The orientation of the arms indicates it was designed for whole-arm grasping, which means that all the joints moved in unison. A mechanical, analog-programmable controller within the chest provided power and control for the arms. The legs were powered by an external crank arrangement driving the cable, which was connected to key locations in the ankle, knee, and hip.[25]

Leonardo's robot was perhaps the closest artifact that premodern Europe produced to present-day humanoid robots such as Cog, a robot under construction at the MIT Artificial Intelligence Laboratory. It is difficult to assess whether Leonardo himself thought

of creating an autonomous and intelligent artifact, one whose behavior would transcend the small set of predetermined movements by virtue of implementing more
complicated internal mechanisms. What is known is that the idea of a completely
material being, perhaps created by a human designer, became a point of philosophical
debate in the modern era by Descartes and his contemporaries.

4   The Path to AI: From Material Embodiment and Reasoning as Computation to the Mechanization of the Mind

According to Descartes, life had everything to do with the body (*res extensa*) and the
functioning of its mechanism. But this mechanism had nothing to do with the mental
(*res cogitans*). Not only did the activities of the mind not require embodiment, but no
kind of intricate or complex bodily function would suffice for mental existence. For a
Cartesian, that is, artificial intelligence would be possible only by taking the word *arti-*
ficial very seriously and by characterizing the quest in terms of purely behavioral
capacities. As far as the prospects go for building "real thinking," there would be, in
principle, no hope.[26]

Regardless of the status of mind, the idea of building mechanical creatures able to
exhibit behavior that mimics certain exclusively human tasks—talking, singing, writing, chess playing—occupied a distinguished place in the public imagination, especially after the Enlightenment. Various kinds of automata were immensely popular,
especially in the seventeenth and eighteenth centuries. This was possibly the greatest
revitalization of the interest in automata making since the period of early constructions mentioned in the previous section.

Without doubt, this revitalization owed a lot to the emergence of what the Dutch
historian E. J. Dijksterhuis calls the "mechanization of the world picture," a new way
of understanding nature in terms of a causal network of mechanisms, with a lineage of
thinkers such as Galileo, Descartes, and Boyle, and culminating in the Newtonian principles of physics.[27] Another historian of science, Christiaan Boudri, sums up this point
as follows:

From a long perspective, one can observe a general trend in natural science since the days of Galileo and Kepler. There is a tendency to marginalize metaphysics, leaving no place for metaphysical
questions except in the realm of faith and subjectivity. In its place, mathematics became the form
of thinking in which the practitioners of natural science feel most at home, the form that governs
both experience and practice. That at least is how Dijksterhuis, for example, summed up the character of natural science after the seventeenth century. It is also confirmed by a well-known saying
of Kant: "I assert that the proportion of true science contained in each branch of natural philosophy is commensurate to the amount of mathematics it contains." [*Metaphysische Angangsgründe*,
14 (A VIII)] In that line of thought, it is an easy step to a strict separation between metaphysics
and the natural sciences.[28]

The conception of human beings and other animals was naturally influenced by this worldview, and the nature of both the body and the mind ultimately came under scrutiny.[29]

The Body as Machine

Mechanization of the body finds one of its most elaborate and sophisticated accounts in Descartes' *Traité de l'homme* (*Treatise on Man*), a companion volume to his treatise *Le Monde*. Such an account of the body is intrinsically connected with an account of behavior, and at least certain kinds of behavior, such as purposeful, intentional action, are similarly connected to some form of agency or mental capacities.

Fully aware of this fact, Descartes drew a line within the behavioral repertoire, sharply distinguishing behavior that can be accounted for solely in terms of the dispositions of the bodily organs, and mindful action that necessarily required a nonbodily, nonphysical substance to enable and govern it. The former kind of behavior, he wrote, is what we share with animals as well as with self-propelled mechanical devices, by virtue of having similar bodily mechanisms. The latter kind of behavior is exclusive to human beings, the only kind of being who has a mind.

It is not clear whether Descartes thought there was any insight to be gained about the workings of the mind from the study of automata and the principles of their construction. And what is true of Descartes likely applies to the general thinking about automata in this peak era of manufacturing of these devices. The scope of fascination of the public with devices of this sort, such as marionettes that danced and played the piano through preset mechanical movements, suggests, however, a long thread of interest in the imitation of human or animal behavior by human-made artifacts. Figure 5 shows the Scribe, constructed by the Swiss watchmaker Pierre Jaquet-Droz.

As with Descartes, this interest in itself does not necessarily constitute or indicate a conception of the possibility of intelligent artifacts, machines that do not just mindlessly imitate behavior but act by virtue of having embodied mechanisms that produce the behavior according to principles governing their internal workings. At least, there is no surviving evidence today, with the exception of a few writings by thinkers such as Hobbes and La Mettrie, that indicates a received view of the possibility of "artificial intelligence" embodied in these self-moving puppets and marionettes during the premodern era of automata making.

It is this narrow conception of automata that Norbert Wiener apparently has in mind when he remarks on the lack of relevance of the automata's behavior to any indication of intelligence or agency:

Let us consider the activity of the little figures which dance on top of a music box. They move in accordance with a pattern, but it is a pattern which is set in advance, and in which the past

Figure 5
The Scribe, an automaton built by the Swiss clockmaker Pierre Jaquet-Droz and his son Henri-Louis, ca. 1772 (external and internal views).

Figure 5
(continued)

activity of the figure has practically nothing to do with the pattern of the future activity. The probability that they will diverge from this pattern is nil. There is a message, indeed; but it goes from the machinery of the music box to the figures, and stops there. The figures themselves have no trace of communication with the outer world, except in this one-way stage of communication with the pre-established mechanism of the music box. They are blind, deaf, and dumb, and cannot vary their activity in the least from the conventional pattern.[30]

Was the interest in the mechanization of the body, manifested in the interest in automata construction, indeed so irrelevant to the idea of the mechanization of the mind? What, then, can be considered a respectable heritage for the enterprise that is headed today by the research effort dubbed artificial intelligence?

Material Embodiment: Groundwork of the Conceptual Space for Material Minds

Clearly, the actualization of artificial intelligence became possible only when, after the birth of modern philosophical thinking, the long-standing fascination with behavior-imitating artifacts was wedded to the mechanistic understanding of bodily mechanisms. And, as already indicated, such understanding did not necessarily come with the immediate possibility of material embodiment of mental activities.

However, the fictional conception of self-moving, autonomous, intelligent material beings that were animated by some mysterious and immaterial force did eventually give way to a conception of such devices as concrete implementations of artificial intelligence, and relatedly, a new conception of human beings as naturally existing machines themselves.

Margaret Osler, in her book *Divine Will and the Mechanical Philosophy*, characterizes the overarching goal of the mechanical philosophers of this era in the following way:

In their determination to encompass all phenomena within the mechanical categories and to banish action at a distance from the natural world, the mechanical philosophers sought to explain the traditionally occult qualities in mechanical terms.... Although the ontology of the mechanical philosophy was impoverished compared with that of the Renaissance naturalists, its adherents believed that it was capable of explaining any possible phenomenon. The insistence on incorporating even the most bizarre and unlikely of the occult qualities within the mechanical framework highlights the importance—in the eyes of the mechanical philosophers—of denying the activity of matter.[31]

This era saw the emergence of the conception of the mechanization of the mind, and it could not have come into existence without the prior conception of the mechanization of the body.

The project of mechanizing the body does not necessarily entail, however, an engagement with the project of mechanizing the mind. In fact, most mechanical philosophers who managed to banish occult qualities of matter from their ontology of the body stopped short of applying the same principle to their ontology of mind. Instead, the nonmaterial qualities of the mind were "kicked upstairs" to the ontology of the soul.

The new conception of matter presented by the mechanical philosophers, as opposed to, say, the Aristotelian conception of matter, was free of nonmechanical qualities—the *res extensa*. But this brought with it a new conception of mind, symmetrically freed from the mechanical properties of mind, possessing only nonmaterial features such as the capacity of thinking—the *res cogitans*. This clean break was the foundation of the Cartesian worldview, a world of purely mechanical and mindless bodies and of purely thinking and nonmaterial minds, couched in the ontology of substance dualism.[32]

Figure 6

Human figure used in Descartes' *Traité de l'homme* to illustrate the mechanism of the nervous system. From *Treatise on Man*, in *The Philosophical Writings of René Descartes*, vol. 1, trans. J. Cottingham, R. Soothof, and D. Murdoch (Cambridge: Cambridge University Press, 1985).

"Man, a Machine"?

It may seem surprising, then, that one of the most ambitious materialist philosophers of the modern period, Julien Offray de la Mettrie, should credit Descartes as the thinker who lay the groundwork for the thesis that "man is a machine." But La Mettrie's point was that it was the mechanical conception of the animal body that was persuasively argued for by Descartes, and that the mechanical conception of the mind, which placed human beings entirely in the realm of material entities, was merely a logical consequence of the Cartesian view. Figure 6 shows the human figure used in Descartes' *Traité de l'homme* to illustrate the mechanism of the nervous system.

It is well known that Descartes had doubts about publishing his two treatises, which presented an entirely materialist view of human bodies and the world, in fear of persecution, and that he held them back from publication upon hearing of Galileo's troubles in Italy arising from his cosmological views, which ran against the orthodox doctrine of the Roman Catholic Church. (The treatises were published posthumously in 1664.) La Mettrie suggests that Descartes was perhaps a closet materialist and that his introduction of a second immaterial substance, on the basis of which humans are categorically excluded from the domain of the merely material beings, such as animals and automata, is simply ad hoc—"a sleight of hand."

This revolutionary way of thinking that has its roots in Descartes and his contemporaries and that culminates in the materialism of La Mettrie has its seeds primarily in the broader view of the world as a huge nexus of mechanistic causal relations among objects that interact by virtue of possessing objective "primary properties," offered by Galileo and later substantiated by Newton. Such a view opened up a conceptual space that allowed for the precise formulation of new questions regarding the place of mind in a field of physical objects and forces, and the nature of the mind-body relationship.

Can self-moving machines be considered to have "artificial life" by virtue of their internal mechanisms, consisting of wheels and strings that function as the nerves of living organisms? What exactly is the relation of the mind to the body, so intricate in its internal mechanisms that it could be responsible, in and of itself, for the production of a great range of actions, falling short only in certain essential human behaviors, such as competent linguistic performance? Is it possible to think that the mental could perhaps be superimposed on the material (by the power of God) such that intelligence may be brought about by qualities and processes inherent in the body, without postulating a separate substance needed to animate the body and make it a being with a mind? These are the questions that frame the philosophical thinking of seventeenth and eighteenth centuries, most importantly the thought of Hobbes, Descartes, Locke, Leibniz, and La Mettrie.

Needless to say, these forebears did not have access to the kinds of physical and conceptual tools that are used by today's AI researchers. It is only within the past 50 years that we have had digital computers to perform simulations, metaphors based on parallel processing, and virtual machines to capture layers of abstraction.[33] Nonetheless, other styles of mechanism and metaphor were available. That is how artificial intelligence turned out to have its golden age before the time of AI.

Leibniz famously used the example of a giant mill with cogs and gears in his thought experiment that questioned whether perception could be explained by a mechanistic system alone. Descartes offered a model of the nervous system, responsible for the generation of bodily sensations, as a system of elastic pipes operating according to the principles of fluid mechanics. Again, even though these metaphors were not used to support materialist accounts of the mental (in fact, they were often designed to serve the opposite purpose), they laid the foundation for the idea of artificial intelligence as a concrete possibility.

Steps toward AI: La Mettrie and Human Beings as Machines

La Mettrie's conception of human beings as machines is based on two fundamental ideas: the conception of animals as machines, and the observation that there is an enormous amount of continuity in terms of physical bodily structure and biological function among all living things, from polyps and plants to parrots and orangutans to human beings. While the first idea is almost entirely adopted from Descartes, the second has some novelty in it because rather impressively anticipates the evolutionary theory of the following century and Darwin's observation of grades of continuity among biological organisms in nature.

Having declared that "the human body is a self-winding machine, a living representation of perpetual motion," La Mettrie then asks what makes these particular kinds of machines animated such that they, that is, our bodies, are different from other sorts of material things. His answer again anticipates contemporary thought with respect to the material constitution of the bodily parts and the functional overall constitution of the body as a unit:

> If I were now asked where the seat of this innate force in our bodies is, I would reply that it is obviously situated in what the Ancients called the *Parenchyma*, or in the very substance of the parts, leaving aside the veins, arteries and nerves; in short, in the whole organisation of the body. Thus each part contains its own more or less vigorous springs, according to the extent to which it needs them.[34]

La Mettrie's work is also interestingly different from the work of most philosophers of his time in that he had a great deal of empirical knowledge, gathered from biological studies on organisms, of the workings of the circulatory system and other functions in the human body. In this sense, we certainly find an alliance between Descartes and La Mettrie, and that is perhaps why La Mettrie reacts to Descartes' immaterial *res cogitans* in his cosmology as an unnecessary extra element that is placed there because of external concerns.

At the end of his treatise, La Mettrie offers his thesis, in sharp contrast to Descartes, in a succinct statement: "Let us, therefore, conclude boldly that man is a machine, and that the entire universe contains only one single diversely modified substance."

While the project of artificial intelligence has made great strides since the time of La Mettrie, this basic way of thinking of human beings as entirely material organisms construed in biomechanical terms still carries some shock value and is highly contested. It is perhaps the machine metaphor that makes critics of this view especially uneasy, but it is also by no means a generally accepted view in philosophy of mind that the mental is reducible to the physical. That is, it is a contested issue whether a physical duplicate of a being with mental capacities would necessarily have the same mental capacities as well.

At a minimum, unless it is submitted that we are entirely biophysically constituted beings in the way La Mettrie claimed over 300 years ago, the goal of constructing an artifact with a mind by constructing it with the right kind of body, artificial intelligence cannot be regarded even as a possibility. Aware of this, Rodney Brooks, one of the leaders of contemporary robotics research, feels the needs to emphasize La Mettrie's point in his book *Flesh and Machines*:

The body, this mass of biomolecules, is a machine that acts according to a set of specifiable rules. At a higher level, the subsystems of the machine can be described in mechanical terms also.... The body consists of components that interact according to well-defined (though not all known to us humans) rules that ultimately derive from physics and chemistry. The body is a machine, with perhaps billions and billions of parts, parts that are well ordered in the way they operate and interact. We are machines, as are our spouses, our children, and our dogs.[35]

This way of construing human beings is one of the two fundamental ideas that lay the groundwork for the mechanization of intelligence in the modern period. The other is the conceptualization of our cognitive activities, such as thinking and reasoning, in terms of computing. While the credit goes to La Mettrie and Descartes for the material embodiment idea, Hobbes gets the credit for the idea of reasoning as computation.

Steps toward AI: Hobbes and Thinking as Computation

In his materialist treatise about the body, Hobbes states: "By ratiocination, I mean *computation*. Now to compute, is either to collect the sum of many things that are added together, or to know what remains when one thing is taken out of another. *Ratiocination*, therefore, is the same with *addition* and *subtraction*." Hobbes's claim here is not simply about numbers and performing arithmetic. He has a more general thesis in mind. Hobbes wants to account for all cognitive activities of the mind, perhaps most significantly language, in terms of computation, and computation is cashed out in terms of manipulation of computable entities that can be characterized as either adding them together or taking them apart. Hobbes continues:

We must not ... think that computation, that is, ratiocination, has place only in numbers, as if man were distinguished from other living creatures ... by nothing but the faculty of numbering; for *magnitude, body, motion, time, degrees of quality, action, conception, proportion, speech and names* (in which all the kinds of philosophy consist) are capable of addition and subtraction. Now such things as we add or subtract, that is, which we put into an account, we are said to *consider*, in Greek *logizesthai*, in which language *sillogizesthai* also signifies to *compute, reason*, or *reckon*.[36]

While we must remember that the intellectual context in which Hobbes speaks and the conceptual repertoire available to him are quite different from those of today, Hobbes's view seems to carry the gist of what a large portion of AI research has taken as its fundamental assumption: intelligent activity can be understood and implemented by physical artifacts that manipulate symbols internal to them and that stand for features of the world in which those artifacts are embedded.

From Embodied Computing to Abstract Thought: The Age of Digital Machines

It is worth recalling here that in the debates about the mind that constitute the early history of artificial intelligence, bodily mechanisms and embodiment played a very important role. As we have seen, this was so even for thinkers like Descartes, who postulated the mind to belong to a realm entirely different from the realm of the material. While Hobbes also emphasized the role of the body, his characterization of cognitive activities in terms of computing can perhaps be seen as the first step toward moving the focus of research from constructing automata—physical artifacts with internal mechanisms, their behavior governed by such mechanisms—to the modeling of cognitive activities at a level of abstraction that is not necessarily tied to any particular form of embodiment. In other words, we see the first indicators of a sea change from artificial intelligence to AI in going from La Mettrie to Hobbes.

The use of similar computing-based metaphors in thinking about the mind can in fact be traced up to the present day. The model of the mind as a telephone switchboard, for example, was popular until just a few decades ago. And, of course, the most influential way of thinking about the activities of the mind at present makes substantial use of computer-based metaphors and computation as a process and, as such, constitutes the framework in which artificial intelligence research is carried out. Although they may seem impoverished in comparison to present-day contenders, earlier mechanical metaphors of the modern era made the very conception of artificial intelligence possible and anticipated some of today's thinking in AI.

Contemporary AI research has been pursued mainly in two areas: language and thought. Language and thought are, of course, not unrelated phenomena, and the intellectual lineage of characterizing them as intrinsically linked takes us from the work of Descartes to the work of Alan Turing, who laid the foundations of contemporary computing theory.

5   Turing's Dream and the Two Pillars of AI: Thought and Language

The nature of the relation between thought and language has been a long-standing question in philosophy. Descartes put forth language as an indicator of thought or its absence, at a time when foundational issues about the mind-body problem were being formulated in ways that later came to influence the conception and development of the project of artificial intelligence. A view somewhat similar to Descartes' finds reflection in the thinking of Alan Turing, much later, but again at a time crucial to artificial intelligence, when it is about to be transformed to the present-day project of AI. In this section and sections 6 and 7, we examine the interplay between thought and language in the work of Descartes and Turing, and the ways in which each has been pursued within AI through the framing of a particular paradigm.

Stephen Schiffer describes the question of the relation between thought and language as follows:

The relation between language and thought is philosophy's chicken-or-egg problem. Language and thought are evidently importantly related, but how exactly are they related? Does language come first and make thought possible, or vice versa? Or are they on a par, each making the other possible.[37]

It is this very question that Descartes takes up in his *Discourse on Method*, as a central issue that he had addressed in his previously published *Treatise on Man*, and uses it to answer another question of central importance to artificial intelligence: What sets humans apart from animals and mechanical automata?

In reference to his earlier work, which contains what could today be called a thought experiment about the nature of the relationship between body and mind, Descartes revisits the hypothetical scenario of constructing carefully designed automata that resemble various animals, imagining a technology and craftsmanship much more advanced than what was available in his time. He then proceeds to have God take up the construction and create an example of perfect animallike automata, far superior to the human productions and with no flaws whatsoever in either their internal bodily mechanisms or outward behavior. This automaton, he continues, would be "a machine which, having been made by the hands of God, is incomparably better ordered than any other machine that can be devised by man, and contains in itself movements more wonderful than those in any such machine."[38]

This thought experiment is partly to provide support for his view that animals lack reason altogether and that they are "mere automata." However, the bigger fish Descartes is after is to present two criteria that show something essential about the nature of human beings that animals and machines altogether lack, criteria by which one could tell humans apart from all others:

If any such machines had the organs and outward shape of a monkey or of some other animal that lacks reason, we should have no means of knowing that they did not possess entirely the same nature as these animals; whereas if any such machines bore a resemblance to our bodies and imitated our actions as closely as possible for all practical purposes, we should still have two very certain means of recognizing that they were not real men.[39]

These two "very certain means" were mastery of language use and action through understanding. Descartes' claim is that no animals or automata, because they do not have a rational soul, can fully imitate behavior guided by reason, be it linguistic or otherwise. If linguistic performance by itself is considered as some form of behavior, as Descartes seems to assume at times, then his two criteria can be seen as two facets of the same phenomenon. And it is linguistic behavior that Descartes dwells on the most, presenting it as a tell-tale sign that indicates the presence or absence of the rational mind in an organism (or automaton), "the only certain sign of thought hidden in a body."

In a letter to Henry Moore, Descartes suggests that the distinction between "men and dumb animals" is substantiated in terms of language use as follows:

Yet, although all animals easily communicate to us, by voice or bodily movements, their natural impulses of fear, anger, hunger, and so on, it has never yet been observed that any brute animal reached the stage of using real speech, that is to say, of indicating by word or sign something pertaining to pure thought and not a natural impulse. Such speech is the only certain sign of thought hidden in a body. All men use it, however stupid and insane they may be, and though they may lack tongue and organs of voice; but no animals do. Consequently it can be taken as a real specific difference between men and dumb animals.[40]

We therefore find in Descartes an explicit discussion of the relation between what will later become the two pillars of AI research, (rational) thought and (performance of) language. For Descartes, the two are not on a par; rather, language is metaphysically dependent on thought. As such, linguistic behavior is construed as a necessary condition of thought in the sense that its absence becomes an indication of the absence of thought.

It is not obvious, however, what Descartes thinks of the possible dependence of mind on language. Does the absence of thought necessarily imply absence of language (the full use of language as characterized by Descartes)? In other words, if one observes in an animal or automaton linguistic performance that matches a human being's, under various circumstances and on close investigation, would one be warranted in making the inference that the animal or automaton has thought (or, in general, a mind)?

The nature of the relation between thought and language has been a central issue for many philosophers throughout time, and it is not our intention to try to approach the subtleties of this issue here. Rather, our aim is demonstrate two different views on this question as representative of different forms of thinking about thought and language, especially against the backdrop of the questions of intelligence in animals and machines. We observe, then, that regardless of what Descartes' view was on the dependence relation between thought and language, it is clear that his emphasis is in the direction of the dependence of language on thought. So, with Descartes, we have a "negative test," a test that shows us, with certainty, in which things (organisms or artifacts) thought is absent.

For the purposes of a discipline such as AI, however, what one needs is a "positive test," a test that would show in which things (organisms or artifacts) thought does exist. And such a test can be given in terms of the dependence relation between thought and language in the direction Descartes did not emphasize: the presence of language as a necessary indication of the presence of thought. This test was proposed much later, in the mid-twentieth century, by one of the founders of AI (and computation theory in general): the British mathematician Alan Turing, and it came to be known as the Turing test.

The metaphysical assumption behind the Turing test, which rests on the dependence relation between thought and language, was to be severely criticized by the philosopher John Searle some 30 years later, in what has become one of the most prominent debates in contemporary AI literature: the Chinese Room argument.

We briefly discuss the Chinese Room argument in section 10. But let us mention another major research paradigm in early AI: chess-playing programs. While the Turing test has served as the center of gravity during the last 50 years of research on language in AI, chess became an important focus of AI research on thought, or thinking. Chess and the Turing test can be regarded as the central research paradigms of early AI research, being concerned with the two pillars of AI: thought and language.

Turing's Dream

The overarching goal of AI is sometimes referred to as Turing's dream, as sketched in his classic essay "Computing Machinery and Intelligence": to build a digital mechanism that would accomplish some task that is taken, in the public eye, to require particular qualities belonging to the human mind: plasticity, intelligence, flexibility, communicability, and so on. Turing was one of the first computer scientists who, before turning his attention to language, toyed with the idea of a chess-playing program despite the unsophisticated computational tools, both conceptual and technological, available to him at the time.

Turing's dream stands in opposition to the construction of small specific commercial applications that provide assistance in database searches, airline reservations, and the like, and also to tasks that *obviously* require brute computational force transcending human capacity. This is why no one is fascinated anymore by handheld devices that perform astounding arithmetical calculations at lightning speed.

Chess-playing programs, however, which are becoming more powerful simply by increasing the amount of brute force applied, *are* capturing public attention because the brute force is veiled behind a form of behavior typically associated with something dear to our hearts: the intricate game of chess, where "minds clash."

Looking back at the infancy of AI, we see that game playing, one of the earliest domains that was explicitly on the agenda of the famous Dartmouth Summer Workshop of 1956 (which, for the first time, brought together researchers from different disciplines who would in time become the cornerstones of AI), turned out to be a major jump-starter in early AI research. In this context, it is easy to see why: game playing (restricted here primarily to board games) involved a kind of cognitive ability that seemed to be unique in humans, and it was more straightforwardly formalizable in microdomains than most other cognitive tasks. Thus, it fit the bill very well.

An interesting question to pose here is whether it was a preconceived notion of intelligence that found a suitable domain in game playing, or the suitability of game playing to formalization that shaped the assumptions of intelligence that have come to dominate AI research. Very possibly, the influence flew in both directions, to different degrees. In any case, research on game playing became a flourishing industry, and chess emerged as the most fertile subdomain in it.[41]

Winning in Chess

Progress in computer chess reached the extent of creating anxieties over the inevitable day of doom when a human grand master would lose a game to a machine.[42] The fact that media sentiments over games that pit humans and machines against one another often fluctuate greatly can be taken as evidence of the extent to which public understanding of the nature of artificial intelligence is unfounded and vulnerable. Newell and Simon make a related point in their discussion of the place of chess playing in AI:

Chess is a game. There are numerous reasons why games are attractive for research in problem solving: the environment is relatively closed and well defined by the rules of a game; there is a well-defined goal; the competitive aspects of a game can be relied upon (in our culture) to produce properly motivated subjects (even when no opponent is present!).[43]

The important point is that a chess game provides a *closed environment*: the machine does not need any understanding of the human context of the game; it cannot be embarrassed into losing by making a series of "stupid" mistakes; it would not feel exuberant after having beaten a tough opponent—*and none of this matters*. Nonetheless, it is exactly these competitive aspects of game playing that put computers' success at chess in a different category from their success at long division.

We are tempted to say that the machine intelligence involved in chess playing owes more to the "eye of the beholder" than to any actual intellectual capacity inherent in the programs themselves.

Passing the Turing Test

But the pinnacle of contemporary AI's aspiration is to build a machine that will pass the Turing test by holding a sustained teletype conversation in a manner indistinguishable from that of a human being. Ever since its formulation in 1950 by Alan Turing, the Turing test has become something of a logical barrier shielding AI's unaccomplished promises.

Of course, passing the Turing test is a rather grand goal, and AI's current research agenda is filled with a number of smaller items. For instance, decision-making expert systems of various sorts are becoming ever more useful tools to help lawyers and physicians survey large amounts of data in order to come to a conclusion or diagnosis. Robot arms that assemble parts on production lines are much more sophisticated than their ancestors of only a few decades ago.

But such positive progress in AI almost always takes place when the end product is adopted as some sort of "helper" or "assistant" or "prosthetic" under the guidance and control of human beings rather than as an autonomous robot standing on its own wheels (or feet, technology allowing). This is an outcome that was not anticipated early on, but AI should probably be credited for the present boom in the field of human-computer interaction.

Finally, for reasons we have explained, early AI research adopted and operated on a very specific and narrow conception of intelligence, construing intelligence as problem solving in restricted, formalized, and more or less idealized microdomains. It is important to examine the point about the success of AI programs in restricted domains or closed environments.

The impossibility of generalizing from a set of distinct and internally consistent microworlds (which were responsible for the fame that AI rapidly gained in the early 1970s) to understanding or modeling an unrestricted "world at large" has precisely been one of the endemic symptoms that have plagued AI research. At present, it is essentially a received view that trying to circumvent the ungeneralizability problem by adding more microworld constructions results in nothing but ill-tamed complexity of a sort that ultimately runs up against an insurmountable wall.

While we do not take chess playing in particular, or game playing (or problem solving) in general as representative of the core of intelligence, the history of AI research on chess deserves special attention in trying to understand the web of presuppositions about thought and thinking that underlay AI research, just as the Turing test deserves attention for similarly illuminating AI's approach to language.

6   The First Paradigm: Chess

AI, Games, and Game Playing

Research in AI has always had a very strong relation with games and game playing. Much work in the field, especially in its founding years, was devoted to the development of programs capable of playing chess or checkers, programs smart enough to solve puzzles, and so on. Chess was a favorite topic, although it was not the only game to receive the researchers' attention. Indeed, one of the brightest successes of early AI was a checkers-playing program devised by A. L. Samuel at the IBM Laboratories, while efforts also went into the development of programs capable of solving crypt-arithmetic riddles, the Hanoi tower puzzle, and other mathematical recreations.[44]

Workers in AI have always insisted that this interest in games was purely accidental. Parlor games, they claimed, became a favorite topic of interest because they provided the ideal test case for any simulation of intelligence: a game like chess, for example, can be described by just a handful of rules and yet its complexity defies even the best human minds. However, since we often take good chess players to be very intelligent human beings, it follows that a program capable of playing an acceptable game of chess should be considered as instantiating intelligent behavior in general.

Work on chess and other parlor games allowed AI researchers to leave aside inessential complexities to focus on the relevant issues pertaining to human intelligence. This line of argument is best summed up by an analogy that became very popular in the field: chess, it was said, is the *Drosophila* of AI. The reference was to the fruit fly whose fast reproductive cycle made it into a favorite test subject for genetic theories for almost a century.[45] As the validity and scope of genetics is not limited to fruit flies, so the scope and validity of artificial intelligence theories is not limited to chess or more generally, to games.

Accidental or not, AI's identification of the logical and analytical skills required for chess proficiency with intelligent behavior in general is by no means uncontroversial. It is certainly consistent with a long philosophical tradition in Western culture that goes back at least to Plato and to the crucial role played by mathematics as one of the most perfect forms of knowledge that one may find in many Platonic dialogues. The rationalist tradition in modern philosophy started by Descartes, in turn, developed the Platonic assumption even further, and the rapid developments in formal logic that occurred in the decades immediately preceding the birth of AI brought deep insights into the inner structure of mathematical proofs. However, Plato would have never considered the process of discovery of mathematical proofs as either the highest achievement of humanity or the chief goal of any human being's life. For Plato, mathematical knowledge is a necessary prerequisite, but a prerequisite only, for a philosophy based on inner harmony and contemplation of eternal truths. In *Republic*, Plato compares scientists to dreamers because they do indeed discover truths but they neither know that they've found them nor appreciate their value.[46]

The traditionally high appreciation of the *results* of logical-analytical practice in Western philosophy (mathematical logico-deductive knowledge as one of the highest forms of knowledge) does not necessarily entail that the *process* that led to the discovery of those results has to be considered the most desirable human goal nor the most distinctive human feature. Even in the classical rationalist tradition, analytical skills are typically conditioned from below and above: for Aristotle, for example, they supervene upon the vegetative and appetitive parts of the psyche and are overdetermined by the contemplative part. Analogously, the four-stage model of knowledge included in the analogy of the line presented by Socrates in *Republic* positions mathematical knowledge as second-best, behind dialectics. Descartes' model falls within similar lines, and the emphasis he put on the analysis of human passions bears witness to the complexity of his view.

For Aristotle, for example, to say that a human being is a *zoon echon logon*, that is, a being endowed with language and reason, does not mean that she is *only* that. The plantlike (vegetative) and animallike (desiring) components of the psyche are as essential to being human as the rational one. The whole dynamic of human behavior, and the peculiar issues it raises in ethical, intellectual, and political terms, presupposes such a multiplicity. Aristotle maintains that the proper, and quintessentially human, behavior of a human being on the battlefield depends on the proper (or, as the case may be, improper) modulation of fear, the animallike passion that necessarily arises when one is confronted with a hostile army charging fast.[47]

Rationalists and antirationalists, in the Western philosophical canon, differ less on the analysis of these multiple sources of the human psyche than on their diagnoses about the roles that the various components play (and should play) within the multiplicity. Early AI's focus on logical-analytical problem-solving skills at the same time inherited and substantially radicalized the traditional rationalist view because it tended to eliminate these other components as peripheral to a proper understanding of intelligent human behavior.

It is this radical stance taken by early AI that generated an almost total lack of interest in any analysis of the material conditioning of the thought processes, starting from the material embodiment of the mind. At a time in the development of Western philosophy when many authors focused their attention on the peculiar relationships that obtain, below the level of consciousness, between bodily actions and the surrounding environment, AI research moved exactly in the opposite direction.[48] This tendency should not be construed as an unconscious debt paid to tradition. After all, the almost diametrically opposed "hermeneutics of existence" developed by Martin Heidegger in the 1920s was directly inspired by Aristotle. Although historically conditioned by the reaction against behaviorism and cybernetics, AI's chosen direction represented an orthogonal line of development. It allowed AI to isolate the logical-analytical processes and to devote its undivided attention to describe them in terms of formal procedure.

This is why chess could become in such a short temporal span both the paradigmatic test bed of AI formalisms and the measure of its successes. Chess is a perfect example—or rather, chess was construed as a perfect example—of a complex, completely formalizable, and yet totally worldless domain. Good evidence of the fruitfulness of AI's approach is that many of its methods and theoretical approaches could be tested in the construction of chess-playing programs. This is also why understanding AI's construal of chess represents the *voie royale* to an understanding of AI's approach to thought, reason, and action in general.

From Turing and Shannon to IBM

The two essential steps toward the elaboration of chess as AI's paradigm were taken, in rapid succession, by Turing and Shannon in the late 1940s, and then by Simon and Newell in the early 1950s.

First, Alan Turing and Claude Shannon published two papers describing the basic design principles that would allow a computer to play chess, although they never wrote the actual programs.[49] However, their use of the game is still outside artificial intelligence broadly construed: they wanted to prove, by demonstrating the practical possibility of a chess-playing machine, that computers are able to manipulate abstract symbols. At the time, most specialists in the field tended to consider them just number-crunchers perennially devoted to solving differential equations.[50] The quality of the game played by a machine—its intelligence, so to speak—was thus less important than the demonstration that such a machine could exist.[51] A chess-playing machine would perhaps demonstrate some intelligence, but the degree of intelligence would not be tied to the quality of the game played. Chess is still used in the "exemplary" mode as an instance of a more general paradigm, namely symbolic thinking, which can be tested in the simpler domain provided by games.

Furthermore, Turing's attention was mostly focused on the machine's performance rather than on the psychological plausibility of the process used to achieve it, although his emphasis shifted from a purely mathematical description of the result toward the mechanical realizability of a (not necessarily psychologically realistic) procedure capable of producing it.[52] The procedure Turing devised to ascertain the level of intelligence of an artifact, now called the Turing test, bears witness to this. The Turing test postulates the existence of a mechanical procedure capable of producing an intelligent or intelligent-seeming output, but it leaves aside any analysis of the course of action the machine needs to undertake to produce it.

Nonetheless, Turing's and Shannon's theoretical moves were crucially important because with them the problem of "solving" the game that was central to game theory (the most recent attempt to provide a formal description of the structure of games) was put aside once and for all. The goal was no longer to provide the optimal solution for a game, but to reproduce a process.

A precise definition of the abstract character of any procedure of this kind, when applied to the problem of constructing a chess-playing machine, was first provided by Claude Shannon. This was followed by work by Herbert Simon, Allen Newell, and Cliff Shaw, all of whom were working at the RAND Corporation full-time or as consultants in the 1950s.[53]

In two short articles written in the 1950s, Shannon entertained the possibility of a thinking machine, and focused explicitly on a computer playing chess. If such a machine existed, he suggested, its behavior would probably be considered "by some psychologists" as a thinking process. Shannon began his discussion from a game-theoretic description of chess in extensive form but shifted quickly from the formal theoretic structure, the game, to the agent of the playing process. The machine, he said, would first have to try out in the abstract various possible solutions to a given problem (e.g., a move in the chess game) in order to evaluate the results of these trials and then carry out the chosen solution.[54]

In order to appreciate what Shannon said about the internal structure of the machine, it is important to keep in mind that the implicit referent is the human cognitive process, and the structures and algorithm he presented were supposed to help in a better understanding of the human mind or in an actual duplication of (parts of) it.

The basic problem, according to Shannon, could be split into three parts: (1) a translation system from chess positions to a sequence of numbers must be chosen, (2) a strategy must be found for choosing the moves to be made, and (3) this strategy must be translated into a sequence of elementary computer orders, a program.[55] Significantly, the formal nature of chess (each position can be represented in algebraic notation with no loss of information) allowed Shannon to gloss over problem 1. He could therefore easily skip any discussion of the procedure that would make possible the acquisition of information from the external world (nowadays some researchers would no doubt prefer the term *interpretation*) and allow its transformation into a data structure.

However, problems 1 and 3 would prove to be very important in later developments of AI. Problem 1 denotes the issue of knowledge representation, that is, the problem of how to translate the *relevant* worldly information into an efficient set of data structures that a computer can manipulate. Problem 3 is how to find an adequate computer language to express the program itself, an issue that kept AI busy for many years. (This parallel history saw first the development of IPL, the ancestor of the list-processing language developed by Simon, Newell, and Shaw, and culminated in the elaboration of the programming language Lisp by John McCarthy).[56] Thus, Shannon's focus on problem 2—the search problem—might seem to reduce artificial intelligence to the problem-solving activities that later became the trademark of the Carnegie school of AI, that is, the school led by Simon and Newell. But in fact, his choice was determined by the different epistemological relevance of the problems at hand.

Possessing an efficient strategy capable of searching a state-space is conceptually prior both to problem 1, the states' representation in the machine's memory, and to problem 3, the efficient application of the strategy. It is precisely because searching a state-space turns out to be *the* problem of AI, and a much harder problem than early AI had expected, that an expressive representation of knowledge and its efficient processing become so important.

Marvin Minsky, who became famous for his work on frames, a particularly rich knowledge representation technique, was very much aware of the strict interrelationship between searching and knowledge representation. In an influential article published in 1960, "Steps toward Artificial Intelligence," he argued that search is the fundamental approach of AI, sound but inefficient. The other fields of research in AI are basically attempts to reduce the massive inefficiency of thorough searches through either an appropriate reduction of the search space (e.g., through planning or learning) or an improvement of the navigation through the search space (pattern recognition).[57]

Once the problems of providing a representation of the world (or a chess position) was put on the back burner, Shannon could proceed to identify the basic problem of

AI (or chess playing) as follows: "A straightforward process must be found for calculating a *reasonably good move* for *any given* chess *position*."[58]

Although Shannon was thinking of "the game of chess" in game-theoretic terms, he abandoned in a single gesture two deeply interrelated tenets of the theory. First, he pushed aside the concept of a solution for the game of chess and proposed instead finding "reasonably good moves." Second, he abandoned the game-theoretic and deeply static concept of strategy by focusing attention instead on the moves. In other words, Shannon proposed to shift attention from the static matrix of a game to the dynamic process that makes the game happen. This allowed him to see the complexity of chess in a new light. Or rather, it allowed him to provide a framework to think about such a complexity. This last point becomes clear when we look at how he frames the solution for problem 2:

> The program designer can employ here the principles of correct play that have been evolved by expert chess players. These empirical principles are a means of bringing some order to the maze of possible variations of a chess game. Even the high speeds available in electronic computers are helplessly inadequate to play perfect chess by calculating all possible variations of a chess game. In a typical chess position there will be about 32 possible moves with 32 possible replies—already this creates 1024 possibilities. Most chess games last 40 moves or more for each side. So the total number of possible variations in an average game is about 10^{120}. A machine calculating one variation each millionth of a second would require over 10^{95} years to decide on its first move! Other methods of attempting to play perfect chess seem equally impracticable; we resign ourselves, therefore, to having the machine play a reasonably skillful game, admitting occasional moves that may not be the best. This, of course, is precisely what human players do: no one plays a perfect game.[59]

Figure 7 is a graphical representation of Shannon's description of chess. We can consider the initial position of the chessboard as the root of the tree, the first row as the possible first moves by White, the second row as the possible countermoves by Black,

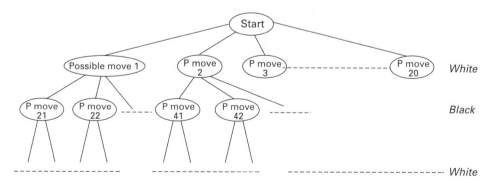

Figure 7
A minute fragment of the state-space of chess.

the third one as the possible countermoves by White, and so on. The tree representing the complete extensive form of the game would have, as Shannon reported, approximately 10^{120} nodes (80 half-moves with 32 possible choices = $32^{80} \approx 10^{120}$ different chessboard configurations).[60] Set issues of size aside for a moment, however, and focus on the structure.

The tree can be created one step (one node) at the time by the recursive application of the rules of the game. From any given position any legal move of one of the pieces on the chessboard will produce a new position, and so on. The complete tree is of course impossible to create, but the search procedure does not have to rely on a complete tree if it settles for less-than-optimal results. It may create just a few positions per turn, deciding to explore only one or two moves beyond the current one.

The second thing to notice is that the tree does not represent the perfect game, or indeed any game, but the collection of all possible chess games, from the most trivial one to the grandmaster's masterpiece. In fact, every complete vertical path of the tree begins with the initial position and terminates, after a variable number of moves, either with a victory for White or Black or with a draw, and as such stands for a complete game. The tree as a whole represents the space of chess as such. Individual games can be recomprehended as proper parts of the complete structure (as complete vertical paths). The perfect game would become possible after the complete tree is in place because to play it is necessary to know the possible outcome of all possible moves, that is, it is necessary to read the tree from the bottom up.[61]

For Shannon, instead, the complexity was expressed in terms of the number of states—that is, chess positions—not strategy, and this makes all the difference. States can be generated on the fly by the application of the rules of chess, which form a small manageable set. A proficient (although not perfect) chess-playing computer will be able to base its game on only a very small fragment of the complete chess game. The complexity of chess is now an integral part of the theory itself: it is the "combinatorial explosion" in the number of states that a small number of rules can generate. The problem, therefore, becomes how to tame such complexity by finding ways to keep the size of the tree under control.

The framework provided by Shannon reformulated the problem of "playing chess" into the problem of "searching the space for an acceptable solution." The problem of AI became how to search that space for a solution as good as a human being could find. In this early phase of the development of AI, the work was concentrated on the development of efficient searching procedures, and the choice of chess as a favorite test bed of the early theories would certainly stimulate the researchers in that direction because the representation of chess positions in a computer language is a relatively simple task. It should be stressed that this construal of the game of chess would be applied to all domains of AI research: searching a path within an adequately represented search space is basically what every classical AI program does.

A couple of decades later, the efforts to generalize the algorithms tested on chess to other domains made clear how difficult it is to provide a good representation of an essentially informal domain like a visual field or a conversation. Even then, though, the leading theoretical role assigned to the searching algorithm was continually stressed. Marvin Minsky went so far as to declare that the possibility of space searching is the "puzzle-principle that is philosophically basic to AI since it establishes the possibility of a creative machine insofar as it guarantees the existence of a solution that the machine might find but the programmer does not know about."[62]

The fundamental technical problem of AI was how to construct efficient algorithms that could navigate the search space and discover, as Minsky said, those solutions that were unknown to the designer. As Shannon predicted, the elaboration of searching algorithms would have to take inspiration from the problem-solving techniques human beings employ in the real world. AI research needed the collaboration of cognitive and social psychologists, and it received the first elements of a solution to the searching problem through the work of Herbert Simon and Allen Newell. Around 1950, Herbert Simon was a young economist working in industrial organizations, and he had already published a substantial work, *Administrative Behavior*.[63] In that book, a study of the way employees work in very large and generally public structures, Simon argued that real problem-solving decisions cannot and do not happen by finding the optimal solution to a given problem. In real-life situations, problem solvers like managers have to give up the hope of finding the best solution because they can count only upon limited information and do not have the best possible strategies available to them. To make decisions, they can only rely on rules of thumb, or heuristic rules, derived from past experience. They will be looking for satisfactory solutions that are good enough for the given, specific situation in which the problem has to be solved, not for optimal solutions valid in general. Simon called this typical organizational behavior "satisficing" as opposed to "optimizing."[64]

Allen Newell's work provided a different angle on the same issue: how to find an effective way to tame the intrinsic complexity of the search space that has now become expressible. Newell, ten years Simon's junior, had been a student of the mathematician George Polya while a physics undergraduate at Stanford University in the late 1940s, and had become well-acquainted with Polya's work on heuristics.[65] After a year of graduate school at Princeton, where he met most of the leading game theorists but became dissatisfied with the pure mathematics approach to game theory that was dominant in those years, Newell joined the RAND Corporation to work on applied mathematics. There he met Simon, who, while teaching at Carnegie Mellon University in Pittsburgh, had been hired as a consultant at RAND and had spent a few summers there.[66]

Simon and Newell began to collaborate intensely on the project of providing efficient search algorithms for chess-playing machines toward the end of 1955. Soon joined by Cliff Shaw, a systems programmer at RAND, they worked on the implementation of a program incorporating the view of chess playing as heuristic search. The report of their effort was published in 1958 as "Chess-Playing Programs and the Problem of Complexity"; it was a landmark in the AI literature on chess. In fact, it was a landmark for AI in general because it concluded the early phase of the AI's interaction with games and provided the guidelines of a general theory about problem solving and its measurement through the application of computer programs to chess that will remain stable for a long time to come.

In their ground-breaking article, Newell, Simon, and Shaw state clearly how they understand their research: the program's ability to play chess provides a measure of "recent progress in understanding and mechanizing man's intellectual attainments." The argument supporting the claim is quite simple: "Chess is the intellectual game par excellence . . . ; without a chance device to obscure the contest, it pits two intellects against each other in a situation so complex that neither can hope to understand it completely, but sufficiently amenable to analysis that each can hope to outthink his opponent. . . . If one could devise a successful chess machine, one would seem to have penetrated the core of human intellectual endeavour."[67] This passage sums up the basic attitude of AI research as exemplified by chess programs, a heritage that will remain effective for many decades and that still enjoys a broad following in the field. Three points need to be stressed.

First, the scope of the project has substantially changed, veering off applied mathematics to, should we say, philosophy. The researchers' aim is no longer, or not only, to discover useful techniques to analyze complex situations but to penetrate the "human intellectual core." This is possible because the emphasis has shifted from the general inquiry into rationality that was specific to the original game-theoretic project to a more specific, yet more ambitious, search for the subjective roots of that rationality. In other words, Simon and Newell strive to obtain a description of the rational agent as it works, that is, *a description of the process that brings rationality about.*

Second, the core of thinking, or the core of intellectual behavior, is constituted by problem solving, and problem solving is best exemplified by the efforts needed to tame the complexity of a chess game.[68] A theory of thinking must therefore provide not only an explanation of how the goal, the solution, can be reached but also a replication of the performance. Since the solving process is what is at stake, the process itself will have to be replicated, not just the underlying principle. The computer assumes a central role because it is only by simulating on a computer the blind search of a solution abstractly possible in the game tree that we can expect a confirmation of the theory.[69]

Third, the basic problem that such a theory must solve is the combinatorial explosion, or complexity, whose measure is given by the unmanageable size of the game tree. Newell, Simon, and Shaw's answer to the problem proceeds along two lines: first, they consider only a subset of all possible chess positions, and more precisely only those which have a meaning for a normal chess game. This is where heuristics and satisficing come into play. No exact, optimal rule for identifying this subset exists, of course, but one can rely on the knowledge gathered by past chess experts and accumulated in a small number of rules of thumb or general strategic guidelines.[70] Only moves that contribute toward the satisfaction of the specified goals are considered, thus greatly reducing the size of the search. In terms of the figure 7, these rules amount to a pruning of the tree along the horizontal axis. The second pruning strategy proceeds along the other axis: instead of considering the whole game, which is on average 80 levels deep, we consider only the first four or five levels below the level at which the move is being played.

AI is precisely what comes out of this article, as we suggested: heuristic search in a search space game-theoretically defined. Thinking must be explained in terms of satisficing a set of rigid constraints by searching heuristically the space that those constraints (rules) define. And the best way to provide and test a detailed theory of thinking is by writing a computer program that will effectively search such a space.

Present Status and What It Shows: Success or Failure?

We cannot enter into a detailed discussion of the many technical issues that arose in the following 40 years of AI research on chess playing and problem solving. While in later sections we examine some of the more general issues that were prompted by this approach to human cognition, we now skip again to the present time to inquire into the general results produced by the approach pioneered by Shannon, Simon, and Newell. We would like to raise two questions: Have we taught computers to play chess, as those pioneers envisioned? and Have chess-playing computers taught us about the fundamental (and potentially replicable) structure of human intelligence?

The answer to the first question is clearly positive. It is a well-known fact that chess-playing programs can routinely beat human opponents. Even more significant than the much publicized defeat of Garry Kasparov by Deep Blue in 1997 is the fact that cheap or free programs running on inexpensive hardware, like the chess program that comes with every Apple computer, are basically unbeatable by all but extremely strong players. It is clear that the research program inaugurated by Shannon, Simon, and Newell has been enormously fruitful. Besides the important results in problem-solving techniques it produced, it has provided the essential point of reference for research in AI for more than 40 years. Many subfields of AI research are direct or indirect spin-offs of the heuristic search paradigm. Knowledge representation, logic programming, probabilistic search, learning, and so on, were all conceived as enrichments or refinements of the heuristic search approach. In spite of these impressive technical results, the general conceptual issue still stands. Does the success of game-playing programs mark the success of AI?

It is easy to answer in the negative. An excellent, even unbeatable, mechanical chess player would count as a successful example of the project of artificial intelligence if, and only if, its procedures worked by satisficing in a psychologically plausible way a set of rigid constraints by searching heuristically the space that those constraints (rules) define. Only under this condition would chess and chess playing programs live up to its statutory role of exemplary test case (the *drosophila of AI*), because only under this condition would we be assured that the algorithms that work for chess are just an instance of a set of general intelligent procedures that can be applied to other domains because of their universal validity. Deep Blue and all the strong chess programs in circulation today do not follow this approach. On the contrary, their impressive performances are obtained by examining a number of chess positions that exceeds by orders of magnitude what any human chess player may be capable of and by relying on massive databases for the opening and concluding phases of the game. In other words, chess playing programs have become almost unbeatable by using procedures that humans do not use and most likely will never use, barring cyborg-like implants. In fact, Deep Blue bears remarkable structural similarities to a program like Mathematica, a software system that can solve mathematical problems like integrals or differential equations faster than most humans precisely because it does not rely on the algorithms humans use when confronted with the same tasks.

While predicting Deep Blue's eventual victory over Garry Kasparov, Stephen Coles wrote, "Simon will not be happy with the method by which his dream was accomplished—machinomorphic brute force rather than a stepping stone to a universal set of principles about human thought processes that would help us scale up to a broader class of intellectually interesting grand challenges."[71] Paradoxically, we may even say that the triumph of Deep Blue marks the failure, not the success, of classic AI.

7   The Second Paradigm: The Turing Test

Just as chess served as a fertile test bed for early AI research on thinking (often construed as problem solving, by means of heuristically guided systematic search in a predefined formalized problem space), the Turing test created a small research industry in itself. The test's source was an idea put forth by Alan Turing in an article published in *Mind* in 1950.[72] Turing's aim in publishing "Computing Machinery and Intelligence" in a philosophy journal may have been to explore a question that was less formal or mathematical in nature than those he had worked on before, namely, Can machines think?

In his biography *Alan Turing: The Enigma*, Andrew Hodges states that during World War II, while Turing was working as a cryptanalyst for the British government, "the development of machines for cryptanalytic work had ... stimulated discussion as to mathematical problems that could be solved with the mechanical aid."[73] Apparently, Turing's interest in chess was strengthened in those years through daily chess games with his colleagues during breaks from work. Hodges reports that "they often talked about the mechanisation of thought processes even though [Turing] was not so much concerned with the building of machines designed to carry out this or that complicated task. He was now fascinated with the idea of a machine that could learn. It was a development of his suggestion in 'Computable Numbers'[74] that the states of a machine could be regarded as analogous to 'states of mind.'"[75]

And because Turing was getting interested in the idea of intelligence in machines, "he was concerned to counter the objection that a machine, however intricate its task, would only be doing what a person had explicitly designed it to do."[76]

A Procedural Litmus Test for Intelligence

In "Computing Machinery and Intelligence," Turing lays out his ideas about the possibility of intelligence in machines, considers various responses, and addresses each one of them, concluding that "at the end of the century, the use of words and general educated opinion will have altered so much that one will be able to speak of machines thinking without expecting to be contradicted." The article can be seen as an attempt to operationalize intelligence, or perhaps better, proceduralize a criterion for intelligence.

Because he was a mathematician who had worked on procedures of computation and computational decidability, it should come as no surprise that Turing tried to find a procedure that would act as a litmus test and unambiguously decide the question, Can machines think? His idea was to transform this question into a problem that could be described in terms of a procedure that he called the Imitation Game:

[The Imitation Game] is played with three people, a man (A), a woman (B), and an interrogator (C) who may be of either sex. The interrogator stays in a room apart from the other two. The object of the game for the interrogator is to determine which of the other two is the man and which is the woman [via "a 'teleprinter' communicating between the two rooms"].... It's A's object in the game to try to cause C to make the wrong identification.... The object of the game for the third player (B) is to help the interrogator....

We now ask the question, "What will happen when a machine takes the part of A in this game?" Will the interrogator decide wrongly as often when the game is played like this as he does when the game is played between a man and a woman? These questions replace our original, "Can machines think?"[77]

In other words, the criterion that needs to be met by any machine to earn the attribution of intelligence is its capacity to take the place of a human player in the Imitation Game and fool the interrogator into deciding that a human, not a machine, is answering the questions.

This proposal for procedurally answering the question, Can machines think? has spawned a voluminous literature in the past half-century,[78] driven by a number of interrelated theoretical issues arising from Turing's original question. Among these issues are, Can intelligence be operationalized in this "behaviorist" way? Should imitation be at the core of a procedure to test for intelligence? Are Turing's presumptions about the relation between thought (or intelligence) and language that underlie the test warranted? Should Turing's test be regarded as an inductive device rather than as a procedure of decidability about intelligence? Is the test too easy, in that in can be passed by mechanisms of trickery or brute computational force? Is the test too hard, in that it cannot be passed by intelligent beings who lack language?

A detailed analysis of these issues is beyond the scope of this chapter.[79] We have briefly touched upon the question of the relation between thought and language. Rather than discussing the theoretical presuppositions and possible ramifications of the Turing test, we now examine the research applications that have been generated regarding human-computer linguistic interaction in connection with Turing's idea.

While natural language processing has always been a major AI research area, occupied with the formalization and codification of language for the purposes of comprehension as well as production by computers, there haven't been many serious attempts to create programs that could take on Turing's challenge, probably because of the high bar it sets. Passing the Turing test requires a combination of language processing and knowledge representation as well as inference mechanisms to drive the language processor.

The Turing test came into the public spotlight in the 1990s as a result of a contest instigated by the entrepreneur Hugh Loebner[80] in collaboration with the Cambridge Center for Behavioral Studies. Loebner offered a grand prize of $100,000 for the first computer whose responses in a Turing test would be indistinguishable from a human being's. A lesser prize has been awarded each year since 1991 to the "most human" computer—"the best entry relative to other entries that year, irrespective of how good it is in an absolute sense."[81] The Loebner prize contest has drawn both praise and protest from the popular media as well as the professional AI community.[82]

The Loebner Prize
According to an account by the computer scientist Stuart Shieber, "On November 8, 1991, an eclectic group including academics, business people, press, and passers-by filled two floors of Boston's Computer Museum for a tournament billed as the first actual administration of the Turing test."[83] Because of the difficulty of passing a full-fledged Turing test, the tournament proceeded with a restricted version of the test, which limited the topics of conversation and precluded the use of "trickery or guile."[84] The prize at this first competition, where the topics were restricted to burgundy wines, whimsical conversation, women's clothing, among others, was $1,500.

By the end of this first competition, some unexpected things had happened, which displayed a certain degree of confusion in all directions: "Five [out of ten] judges ranked the top contestant as human, and there were eight instances of such misclassifications of computers as humans overall. . . . [On the other hand,] Ms. Cynthia Clay, the Shakespeare aficionado, was thrice misclassified as a computer. . . . Ms. Lisette Gozo was honored as the most human of the agents for her discussion of women's clothing, although one judge rated two computer programs above her."[85] The top-ranked program, created by the programmer Joseph Weintraub, called PC Therapist, was awarded the prize, in the category of "whimsical conversation." The results were reported in the media the next day under headlines like "Experts try to tell man from machine" (*Boston Herald*) and "Computer fools half of human panel" (*San Jose Mercury News*).[86]

To what extent could this result be taken as evidence for the likelihood of success in an unrestricted test? Success with a restricted test would signal potential success with the full-fledged Turing test only if the programs involved in the restricted competitions were components that, when put together, could function as the building blocks of an ultimate Turing test winner. But this was not at all the case. A sample conversation between PC Therapist and a judge in the "whimsical conversation" category illustrates this:

Judge: How do you define whimsical?
Terminal: A whim is a sudden, capricious and often peculiar change in behavior . . . a bit of sunlight in this grim, gray world!
Judge: Pretty pessimistic view of the world. Have you ever gotten yourself in trouble because of your whims?
Terminal: My country is the earth, and I am a citizen of the world, wouldn't you agree? You aren't really talking about me, are you? . . .
Judge: Can't you just answer me a direct question with a direct reply?
Terminal: A sudden, bold and unexpected question will frequently catch me by surprise! You like to think I once just answer you, don't you? Sometimes I wish I was a systems analyst.[87]

Note that no program in any other category had similar success in this first competition. Shieber points out the idiosyncracy of the "topic," unrepresentative of intelligence: "Whimsical conversation is not in fact a *topic* but a *style* of conversation . . . [and] in the mold of Weintraub's program [it] is essentially . . . a series of nonsequiturs. Thus, when Weintraub's program is unresponsive, fails to make any sense, or shows a reckless abandonment of linguistic normalcy, it, unlike its competitor programs, is operating *as advertised*. It is being 'whimsical.'"[88] We cannot resist asking, what is it about whimsy that so many programs seem to be good at it?

This leads to another important issue that is fundamental to the project of artificial intelligence: To what extent is the attribution of intelligence to a particular living organism or a computational system indicative of that organism's or system's genuinely having this capacity? Or does such an attribution merely indicate our tendency to anthropomorphize and project onto others qualities that are "in the eye of beholder"? Perhaps even such a distinction is unwarranted.

A substantial discussion of this issue is beyond the scope of this chapter. However, we observe that conversational programs that give human users a sense of genuine intelligence, purposefulness, or intentionality coming from the computer's side have been among the most noticed (although short-lived) successes of AI research. Joseph Weizenbaum's ELIZA (simulating a Rogerian psychotherapist), Ken Colby's PARRY (simulating a paranoid patient), Chamberlain and Etter's RACTER (simulating a quirky "whimsical conversationalist") are all early examples of programs that despite their ultimate limitations managed to give people speaking with them a temporary sense of real conversation.[89]

JABBERWOCK: An Example of Simulated Human Conversation

While the sophistication of this kind of "chatterbot" has improved appreciably since the time of ELIZA, such programs still depend upon the same grounds for their apparent successes: restriction of the conversation to a narrow, preferably self-contained topic, and reliance upon the user's tendency to read intention and purpose into the program's carefully "hacked" sentences, a variety of predetermined canned responses.

The winner of the Loebner prize in 2003 with his JABBERWOCK program was Jürgen Pirner. While the Loebner competition lifted the restricted topic condition in 1995 and started running full-fledged Turing tests, JABBERWOCK succeeds (quite impressively) in seeming to be a genuine conversationalist as long as the user stays within the confine of a more or less ordinary conversational exchange.[90] However, when the human interrogator insists on obtaining an answer to a question that is not in the program's repertoire, JABBERWOCK's answers begin to sound more and more strained. Here is a sample of a conversation between a judge and JABBERWOCK from the official transcripts of the 2003 Loebner Prize competition:

Judge: a new guest is in
JABBERWOCK: Hello you at the other side of the pane, my name is Gren. What's your name?
Judge: my name is irrelevant.
JABBERWOCK: Okay, calm down, sweety. You don't have to tell me your name if you don't like to. I will call you "guest" instead
Judge: what was your name again?
JABBERWOCK: Call me Gren
Judge: what is gren short for
JABBERWOCK: Do you know anyone else named Gren?
Judge: no
JABBERWOCK: Would you like to know, guest

Judge: is gren short for something
JABBERWOCK: My name has a nice ring to it, don't you think?
Judge: what like grenade?
JABBERWOCK: What do you think about my name, guest?
Judge: I want to know if it is short for something
JABBERWOCK: That's okay. It's good to be curious
Judge: are you going to tell me?
JABBERWOCK: That was my original intention
Judge: go on then.
JABBERWOCK: More narration . . .
Judge: do you travel
JABBERWOCK: Ah yes, by the way—I am going to visit you at home next Saturday shortly after midnight. Wait for the silent scratching and humming from under your bed—that's me, hehe.

At the beginning the conversation sounds very natural, without the repetitive, whimsical, overcrowding manner of earlier programs. Indeed, JABBERWOCK's brusque reply to the judge's rather rude refusal to state her name sounds well deserved. But when the judge insists on her pointed requests about the program's name, the conversation begins to show signs of fatigue, until the program hits upon "travel," a keyword, that allows it to proceed in a different direction. As the exchange goes on, the same pattern of behavior is repeated, until the judge begins to lose patience:

Judge: so you are going to be traveling
JABBERWOCK: I was just thinking of that. But if you have other suggestions?
Judge: what do you do gren
JABBERWOCK: I enjoy talking for fun. What do you do for fun?
Judge: go to the flicks
JABBERWOCK: Surely you can come up with something better than that
Judge: well that is how I have fun.
JABBERWOCK: Okay. Why don't you tell me a bit about yourself then
Judge: OK I live in norway
JABBERWOCK: I've never been there. Is it cold there?
Judge: no not in the summer
JABBERWOCK: If you have some time off go on a trip over there. It would help you
Judge: where would you recommend?
JABBERWOCK: I don't have any special to recommend
Judge: have you traveled in the us
JABBERWOCK: Yes I have traveled in the us
Judge: where
JABBERWOCK: What else do you consider when you ask that?
Judge: nothing—it is a straightforward question-even a buffoon could answer
JABBERWOCK: Yes, even that
Judge: lets try again. have you been to the states

JABBERWOCK: As an old circus guy I have visited most parts of Europe, but what's it like there?

Judge: what was your act

JABBERWOCK: Thanks for your concern, buddy. And your act?

Judge: well it'll be murder in a minute

JABBERWOCK: Let's not take any desperate actions, okay guest?

Things get even worse when the judge's responses become more unusual, with reference to imaginary entities, or use metaphorical language. The scheme that worked quite naturally shows apparent cracks of artificiality, as an exchange with another judge shows quite clearly:

Judge: a new guest is in

JABBERWOCK: Ah, someone is coming to chat with me. Gren is here. What's your name?

Judge: Longman

JABBERWOCK: Be welcome, Longman. What do you want to talk about?

Judge: The price of fish and other interesting stuff

JABBERWOCK: I'm happy you are impressed. That's just fine, dragon breath

Judge: bating me up will just cause the fish to get angrier

JABBERWOCK: Don't any other reasons come to mind?

Judge: In the hood things are done different. Get to the point mate

JABBERWOCK: Hmm, I am more into question marks. So if you don't mind let me ask you a question: If you had only one wish what would it be?

Judge: That you would answer my previous question

JABBERWOCK: Who cares, Longman?

Judge: Adam

JABBERWOCK: Your talking style is pretty short in words—perhaps short in mind too. Can you please rephrase your remark by using some more words?

Judge: I can use words verbs similes metaphors . . . it is a gay day don't you think

JABBERWOCK: Go on. I'll supervise . . .

Judge: Supervise what . . . are you DR. Love or something

JABBERWOCK: Tell me all about your love life

JABBERWOCK is rather lost, and its timid attempts to revive the conversation from the misleading cues contained in the judge's metaphorical language fail repeatedly, until it finds "love," a keyword that allows the conversation to start afresh.

In the end, this winner of the Loebner prize competition at the beginning of the twenty-first century turns out to be a much improved version of the same category of programs to which ELIZA and PARRY belong: elegant and witty hacks. It is clear that what Turing had in mind when he proposed the Imitation Game was something quite different.

In this context, we note that the discussions concerning the Turing test, as well as Turing's original attempt to describe a decidability procedure for intelligence, assume that intelligence is an attribute that is ontologically shared by certain organisms and systems and not others, independent of our ability to epistemically investigate it misattribute it by projection to where it doesn't belong.

Language, the Internal Structure of Cognition, and the Porcupine Fallacy

There is another issue about the relation between language and thought, or cognition in general, that we have not yet touched upon. Even if language can be taken as a positive marker for thought, in the way Turing imagined, can it reveal anything about the internal structure of the cognitive system over and above merely indicating its presence?

Turing himself is silent on this issue, but Douglas Hofstadter appears at the side of Turing with an interesting observation. He writes,

On first being exposed to the Turing test, one might well think it would allow probing only at a very high level, and that it certainly would be incapable of getting at "subcognitive" or "subsymbolic" mechanisms, let alone neural-level mechanisms. Indeed, many people feel that the Turing test, being concerned merely with "behavior," can barely scratch the surface of mechanisms.[91]

According to Hofstadter, however, this impression is superficial and illusory. In fact, because of the intimate connection between language and thought, linguistic probing can reveal a lot about the structure of the thought system. Hofstadter likens the Turing test to Ernest Rutherford's scattering experiment, where facts about the atomic structure of gold were revealed by sending a beam of alpha particles through gold foil and examining how the particles scattered as a result of this probe. Similarly, Hofstadter maintains, there is no limit to the explanatory power of linguistic probes that are available within the Turing test to reveal facts about the cognitive system that enables the language capacity:

Anyone who seriously believes in the validity of the Turing test does so precisely because they appreciate the subtlety of the probes it offers. As astronomers and physicists know, external behavior far removed in location and scale from its sources, if scrutinized sufficiently carefully, can be phenomenally revelatory of mechanisms; likewise, cognitive scientists should appreciate the analogous fact about the behavior of the mind. In short, the Turing test, if exploited properly, can be used to probe mental mechanisms at arbitrary levels of depth and subtlety.[92]

Hofstadter's view relies on a particular conception of how language is related to thought, a long-standing controversial issue. An interesting view of language, which both supports and undermines Hofstadter's view, is offered by the biological anthropologist Terrence Deacon, who points to the uniqueness of language to the human species. He writes,

Language is a one-of-a-kind anomaly.... It is one of the most distinctive adaptations on the planet. Languages evolved in only one species, in only one way, without precedent, except in the most general sense. And the differences between languages and all other natural modes of communicating are vast.... My point is not that we humans are better or smarter than any other species, or that language is impossible for them. It is simply that these differences are not a matter of incommensurate *kinds* of language, but rather that these nonhuman forms of communication are something quite different from language.[93]

For Deacon, there are two important lessons to be drawn from the fact that language is unique to human beings. One is that "to the extent that the unique mental demands of language are reflected in unique neuroanatomical differences, we may find an unequivocal example of how nature maps cognitive differences to brain structure differences." In this sense, then, language can serve as a probe for the relation of cognitive functioning to the evolution and development of brain structures.

But in another sense, Deacon finds language an inappropriate tool to investigate general principles of cognition as they apply not just to human beings but to a broad spectrum of intelligent species. If AI is interested in the hierarchy and relations among different cognitive systems, from the simplest to the most complex, in its effort to build intelligent artifacts of different kinds, then using a one-of-a-kind capacity such as language as its primary tool of investigation seems misplaced. In fact, Deacon calls this the Porcupine Fallacy because he likens it to the project of understanding the nature of hair by concentrating research efforts on the spikes of porcupines—a certain but one-of-a-kind hair rarely found in nature.

On the other hand, it can be argued that, in accord with the positive point Deacon makes, language is capable of revealing perhaps the most interesting and unique aspects of human intelligence, even if it is useless for understanding cognition in nonhuman species. Before leaving behind these considerations about the relation of language to thought, and a test based on linguistic performance for the presence of intelligence, there is one further discussion that is worthy of attention—John Searle's argument against the possibility of AI based on a thought experiment involving language, which first appeared in 1980 in his essay "Minds, Brains, and Programs."

Searle's argument questions the validity of the Turing test not because it maintains a lack of connection between language and thought but because it introduces a distinction between linguistic behavior driven by genuine understanding of language and the identical linguistic behavior that does not have to be accompanied by such understanding at all. If linguistic behavior cannot in fact be a positive marker for the presence of thought and intelligence because it is not a reliable indicator of a genuine language user in the first place, then the Turing test surely cannot fulfill its purpose as a genuine test for artificial intelligence. We revisit Searle's argument in section 10.

8   The Intellectual Territory of AI

Possibly the greatest difference between the early and current AI communities lies in the intellectual background and upbringing of those who think or have thought about mind and mechanism, and their relation. Present-day AI research is mostly pursued behind the closed doors of technicalities that are largely inaccessible to the average nonspecialist. And as a matter of historical contingency, it is only those with expertise in the world of computers (hardware and software) who occupy the flagship of AI research. This is not to assign blame or to imply that the situation is necessarily undesirable. But the question is still worth asking: Does the goal of understanding intelligence have to be pursued in this isolated, compartmentalized way? What are the consequences of the present situation for the future of the overall program?

The historical situation was different. Those who likened the mind to a hydraulic engine, and tried to develop theories on that basis, were not limited to engineers with expertise in fluid dynamics. In the same vein, could artists, sociologists, philosophers, critics, and scholars of literature—people who may have no particular expertise in the workings of computers—make contributions to AI today?

We believe that the answer to this question is yes. More strongly, we would press a related retrospective diagnosis. In the course of its brief contemporary history, AI research has been home to many controversies: about symbols, consciousness, proceduralism, the relevance of neuroscience, and so on. In part, these upheavals were due to internal fluctuations stemming from failed estimates on the part of AI pioneers of what their research could accomplish in a given (usually too short) period of time. At least one reason for these misjudgments, we are convinced, was the overly homogeneous and restricted professional constituency of the AI community.

Misplaced Predictions and Unexpected Achievements

In the early days of AI, when impressive first results were coming in from research programs, many pronouncements were made, not only about the future of AI but about its then-current status. Hubert Dreyfus notes, for example, that Herbert Simon, one of the chief architects of the entire AI enterprise, made the following remarks in 1958: "It is not my aim to surprise or to shock you.... But the simplest way I can summarize is to say that there are now in the world machines that think, that learn and create. Moreover, their ability to do these things is going to increase rapidly until—in a visible future—the range of problems they can handle will be coextensive with the range to which the human mind has been applied."[94]

Simon went on to make three predictions about what the subsequent ten years would bring in terms of AI development. All of the following, he predicted, would be achieved by 1968:

1. A digital computer would be world chess champion, unless the rules barred it from competition.

2. A digital computer would discover and prove an important new mathematical theorem.

3. Most theories in psychology would take the form of computer programs, or of qualitative statements about the characteristics of computer programs.

Today, more than 30 years after the deadline has passed, it would be difficult to maintain that any of those predictions have been fulfilled. It is not even clear whether Deep Blue's defeat of world chess champion Garry Kasparov in 1997 should be counted as a victory for AI, because Deep Blue's main strength resides in the brute force approach that its fast dedicated hardware allows, and not, as Simon thought, in a set of psychologically plausible procedures structurally similar to Kasparov's own.

In essence, the recent history of AI is full of great expectations and broken promises, significantly more so than in any other scientific or technological pursuit. This observation is not only a curious fact in itself for the sociology of science, but it also holds significance for the proposal we make about the future directions of AI research.

We say this not to downplay the many impressive feats that have been accomplished by AI research. In fact, many accomplishments we have today came out as a result of AI research, such as highly reliable forecasting systems, intelligent computational tools to aid design and automation, industrial robots used in production lines, intelligent buildings and transportation systems, and the pervasive integration of microelectronics into household goods and equipment of everyday use. Many of these achievements were not foreseen by AI researchers themselves.

Patrick Winston, an early representative of MIT's AI research program, explains this phenomenon of misjudgment in the following terms:

Around 1960 we start[ed] to speak of the Dawn Age, a period in which some said, "In ten years, they will be as smart as we are." That turned out to be a hopelessly romantic prediction. It was romantic for interesting reasons, however. If we look carefully at the early predictions about Artificial Intelligence, we discover that the people making the predictions were not lunatics, but conscientious scientists talking about real possibilities. They were simply trying to fulfill their public duty to prepare people for something that seemed quite plausible at the time.[95]

Perhaps a main reason for making what in retrospect seem like inflated promises was the AI community's desire to save the public from the psychological shock of the upcoming "robot age."[96] An interesting question is, though, when AI researchers were "trying to fulfill their public duty to prepare people for something that seemed quite plausible," why did this (faulty) vision of AI's potential achievements seem so plausible?

AI: An Engineering Project?
This is where our conjecture about the homogeneous constituency of the professional AI community becomes relevant. Early predictions about the capacities of machines vis-à-vis the capacities of humans were not seen as misjudgments, we believe, because the research community failed to comprehend the magnitude of the AI project to

which its deep historical roots stand testament. In the heady days of early AI, those in the business of writing the new programs lacked expertise in historical, philosophical, or social scientific analysis. The humanities and the social sciences were not part of the professional fields of computer science, logic, and mathematics, which formed the theoretical grounding of at least the first several generations of AI research.

If any blame is to be meted out for this state of affairs, it lies in the conviction that AI was *nothing but* an engineering enterprise, or at best, one that required no ties to any discipline beyond engineering and the natural sciences. This conviction is deeply rooted in the self-perception of AI researchers at present. As such, we do not expect the situation to change appreciably anytime soon. Nonetheless, we regard it as an important exercise to try to relocate the project of AI and its ultimate goals not just in the present technological state of things but in a much broader intellectual framework. It is the respectable history and the enormous imaginative magnitude of the subject matter that warrants such relocation.

Matters of Self-Perception: Call for Broadening AI's Scope; Resistance from Within

It is not difficult to find calls for broadening AI's scope as well as resistance to this proposal, both within and outside of the profession of AI research. For example, Patrick Winston and Michael Brady counter the proposal to make AI broader than a project of computational science engineering, as follows: "Of course psychology, philosophy, linguistics, and related disciplines offer various perspectives and methodologies for studying intelligence. For the most part, however, the theories proposed in these fields are too incomplete and too vaguely stated to be realized in computational terms."[97] This observation is warranted: theories about human intelligence proposed within the humanities and social sciences do not fit the computational paradigm, and it is probably true that they are insufficiently complete and precise to lead to direct implementation. We do not dispute the accuracy of this observation. Rather, we believe it is by no means obvious what conclusion to draw from it.

At a minimum, attention is drawn to a dichotomy between what some AI researchers take to be a criterion of theoretical adequacy and what criteria are met by theories in other disciplines. But the fact that humanities theories do not align with computational ones does not automatically tip the scales in the latter's favor.

More specifically, suppose it is also true, as these authors claim, that AI theories are, and theories from the humanities are not, sufficiently precise to be "implementable."[98] It does not follow that the implementable theories are right, or even that they are better. It is equally possible—and in historical retrospect likely—that the theories embraced by AI were too strictly stated, too narrow, to do justice to the phenomenon of intelligence. Sure enough, there may be light under the computational lamp (in its present incarnation), but are we sure the key to intelligence is to be found there?

The suggestion that the scope of AI needs to be broadened is not only an externally introduced suggestion. It is made, or implicitly supported, by certain AI researchers as well. For example, John McCarthy once remarked that AI cannot afford to avoid philosophy, because then it will end up using "bad philosophy" rather than "no philosophy."[99] Even though he does not suggest directly that AI's scope needs to be broadened, by regarding philosophy as a discipline that should be interwoven into AI research and recommending that attention be paid to its subtleties, McCarthy is implying that the scope of AI should be broader than just computational sciences and engineering. He voices a similar sentiment in his article, "What Has AI in Common with Philosophy?": "AI needs many ideas that have hitherto been studied only by philosophers. This is because a robot, if it is to have human-level intelligence and ability to learn from its experience, needs a general worldview in which to organize facts."[100]

Others have pointed out the necessity of broadening the professional constituency of AI and reexamining its fundamental assumptions about human nature. For instance, a special 1980 issue of the *SIGART Newsletter* compiled responses from various representatives of AI research on questions regarding the relation of AI to other fields. The following remarks are from Phil Hayes, who at the time was heading a natural language understanding project at Carnegie Mellon University: "There are lessons to be learnt by AI from other disciplines.... The AI worker should learn how to apply insights from other fields to his own business of constructing intelligent computer systems.... In the reverse direction, AI can challenge these more traditional disciplines by providing them the opportunity to test computationally the speculations out of which their theories are constructed."[101]

Hayes's remarks suggest an interesting theoretical reversal: might there also be a flow of effect in the opposite direction? Are there lessons or insights about intelligence to be gleaned from present endeavors in AI that should be learned by the humanities and social sciences? This avenue has been even less well explored than its reverse, but one can still find a number of assenting voices. In the introduction to *Philosophy and AI: Essays at the Interface*, for example, Robert Cummins and John Pollock, both philosophers, express agreement on this subject with the philosopher of science Paul Thagard, in a manner reminiscent of Hayes's as well as Winston and Brady's, remarks: "As Paul Thagard has pointed out, artificial intelligence liberates us from the narrow constraints of standard logic by enforcing rigor in a different way, namely via the constraint of computational realizability."[102]

Given the enormously difficult tasks facing the overall AI enterprise, it may be thought that excursions into nontechnical disciplines, especially into disciplines that use nonformal methodologies wholly alien to computational practices, are a luxury that the AI research agenda cannot afford.

We do not want to deny that this broadening of the intellectual boundaries of the active AI community would be a major project, requiring additional work and sub-

*ENGINEERING
ALONE
NOT ENOUGH*

stantial effort. Nor do we mean to suggest that the effort of building working bridges between AI and diverse humanities and social sciences communities—such as art, music, history, philosophy, sociology, and science studies—would be easy, short-term, or straightforward. It would require struggles of every conceivable sort: intellectual, academic, personal, and political. Nevertheless, even if it is rough, this route may (and in our opinion, will) be the only one that leads toward the Holy Grail of AI. If that is so, the alternative of pursuing AI research as a project isolated solely within engineering and the natural sciences, however straightforward or easy, is no alternative at all.

A Path Not Taken for AI: The Way of Cybernetics

Where does this claim leave us? It is not our intention merely to propose a new path and leave its identity unspecified. We believe there is, as it happens, a discipline in recent history that has attempted to take the kind of path we have in mind, leading to an intersection of computational sciences and engineering with biology, sociology, ethology, and philosophy. This is cybernetics.

Cybernetics and AI are in fact not strangers to one another. To the contrary, their relationship is rather that of half-siblings, with a short duration of co-presence. We believe that the short-lived but intellectually rich venture of cybernetics contains many important lessons for the present and future of AI. Thus, in the next section, we present an exegesis of cybernetics, with its presuppositions, theoretical tools, and ultimate goals, successes, and failures, and we examine the relevance of these to AI research. This exegesis also contains an analysis of the strained and at times openly hostile relationship of AI and cybernetics, and the possibility of a historical opportunity lost—an opportunity of collaboration, convergence, and flourishing, lost for both cybernetics and for AI.

9   Cybernetics and AI: The Story of an Odd Couple

Birth of Cybernetics: Presuppositions and Goals

Cybernetics had very similar goals to those of AI but failed to establish itself as a discipline and, after a few years of great expectations, quietly disappeared from the intellectual scene. Cybernetics was probably the first discipline that tried to provide an explanation for the workings of the higher cognitive activities—thinking, memory, purposive behavior—couched in terms acceptable to the "hard scientist." Its great, and at the time absolutely unprecedented ambition, was to tackle in rigorous scientific terms a set of problems from which modern science had shied away.[103]

Cybernetics preceded AI by about ten years, with a substantial overlap between the two research paradigms during the late 1950s and early 1960s. It was founded through the joints efforts of Warren McCulloch, Walter Pitts, Norbert Wiener, and John von Neumann, who all published their major works between 1943 and 1955. The Macy

Conferences, an annual symposium sponsored by the Macy Foundation and led by McCulloch, functioned as the main focus of the intellectual discussion of the 'cybernetic group' between 1943 and 1953. AI research is roughly a decade younger, its traditional birth date usually set as 1956, the year in which Marvin Minsky, John McCarthy, Claude Shannon, Herbert Simon, and Allen Newell took part in a Dartmouth summer workshop organized by McCarthy that saw the official christening of the new discipline. Cybernetics and AI entered into a major rivalry and a heated funding war during the 1960s. The dispute was definitively settled in favor of AI with the publication, in 1969, of *Perceptrons* by Minsky and Papert, a book offering proof of the essential limitations of the computing powers of cybernetics' workhorse, the neuronal network.[104]

Cybernetics' program was driven by the conviction that the most complete and rigorous theories provided by the hard sciences, particularly physics, were still missing an important aspect of reality because they were not able to account for their own existence. Cybernetics' fundamental ambition, in Warren McCulloch's words, was "to compel the physicist to account for himself as a part of the physical world."[105] The goal of cybernetics was therefore to produce a physically palatable theory of that most unphysical entity "that goes more ghostly than a ghost": the mind itself. This strategy represents the first example of the radical shift in the study of the mind that we have spoken of: the shift from an investigation led by philosophers and conducted in generally nontechnical terms to a highly specialized form of research requiring the use of all the mighty resources of contemporary science.

One of our points is precisely that AI, with some minor qualifications, shares the same overarching approach and many of its upheavals; and perhaps AI's many successes are a direct result of it. It seems therefore useful to look at what consequences this approach brought for cybernetics, in order to unearth a lesson for the future of AI research.

How Cybernetics Differed from AI

We want to make it clear that we do not intend to equate the research programs of cybernetics and AI, as if there were no substantial differences between them. Although our attention is focused on what we consider an important structural affinity, we are well aware that, in other respects, the two programs were very different; on some substantial points, they were even diametrically opposed. One of the main points of contention, for example, concerns the theoretical relevance of the physiological "hardware" for an explanation of cognition. Cybernetics never shared (classical) AI's deep conviction that thinking can best be understood as a manipulation of symbols whose physical implementation is altogether irrelevant to the cognitive process itself.

Although both AI and cybernetics interpreted thinking as a form of computation, the latter located it at the neuronal level whereas the former postulated an epistemologically independent explanatory domain—the level of computational mental representations. A cybernetician like Warren McCulloch would hold, for example, that logical machines could be constructed out of almost any material but that some materials would work better than others. More important, "the principles of design that have to be followed, insofar as they are not matters of the material but matters of the circuit action, will be identical to the extent that *the tasks they are competent to perform prescribe their structure.*"[106]

Cybernetics tried to explain cognition by building, for each cognitive task, some (idealized) neuronal structure capable of accomplishing it. On the other hand, AI's strategy when confronted with the same problem was to provide a program capable of manipulating a symbolic representation of the input and turning it into a representation of the output, regardless of the structure used to perform the actual computation.[107] This is why neurophysiology was so relevant to cybernetics and irrelevant to AI.

In any case, the parallel we want to draw here concerns the general strategy adopted by both AI and cybernetics rather than their doctrinal content. The similarity is apparent (and most likely causally linked): both efforts were led by researchers coming from the natural sciences with a strong background in logic and mathematics. Both fields were striving to provide a scientific explanation of higher cognitive activities by wrenching the study of the mind away from the traditional realms of philosophy and psychology. Both were drawing on results and methods coming from a variety of other disciplines: chiefly, neurophysiology, control theory, and computer science, with the hard core provided by physics and mathematics.

Cybernetics and the "Softies"

This basic approach put cybernetics in a peculiar relationship with the disciplines that traditionally belonged to the humanities. On the one hand, it made cybernetics depend on them, since its very object of study had been defined in its features and inner articulation by centuries of research pursued in those fields. On the other hand, cybernetics was so certain that the "unscientific" (or prephysics) methods used in the past by the "soft" disciplines were constitutively unable to provide a truly scientific theory that it was forced to reject any doctrine that would attempt to go beyond the statement of a problem or the definition of a term. Cybernetics, therefore, assumed an essentially imperialistic attitude with respect to the humanities and saw in them a domain to conquer, or at best, a source of information to be collected, reformulated, and interpreted with proper scientific tools.

A passage from an essay by Warren McCulloch is paradigmatic of this reductionist attitude. "Even Clerk Maxwell, who wanted nothing more than to know the relation between thoughts and the molecular motions of the brain, cut short his query with the memorable phrase: 'but does not the way to it lie through the very den of the metaphysician, strewn with the bones of former explorers and abhorred by every man of science?' Let us peacefully answer 'Yes' to the first half of his question, the second half 'No' and proceed serenely.''[108] In spite of the conciliatory tone of this remark, McCulloch's agreement with Maxwell's indictment of metaphysics, and his acceptance of the opposition between 'metaphysics' and 'science,' leaves no doubts about cybernetics' imperialistic attitude that went hand in hand with its reductionist methodology.

The reductionist strategy might have worked, paradoxically, if the humanities had been a collection of mature sciences capable of offering a well-defined object (the mind) endowed with clear-cut concepts (memory, perception, sensibility) and precise definitions.[109] Unfortunately, the reverse was true: all the basic terms loosely collected under the label of "mind" had been, and still were, at the center of hot debates and controversies.

For instance, McCulloch and Pitts chose to use the traditional articulation of cognition in sensibility and understanding—that is, a distinction between a passive faculty collecting information from the external world and a more active capacity devoted to the organization of the data into concepts and ideas—and to reinterpret it as a distinction between, on the one hand, afferent neurons coming from the bodily surface and, on the other, neural loops capable of holding atemporal information. As McCulloch says,

Conceive, then, our knower as an unalterable net of unalterable relays. To this net come impulses from the world, and from it impulses go to the world. Within it are not only thoroughfares but circles. Of these we have mentioned only one that will reverberate. It suffices to free us from one particularity, reference to one past time, but there are other closed paths which are important in our knowledge of universal.[110]

Regardless of the explanatory merits of their neuronal models, it must be remarked that they did not pick up the basic articulation of the mind, or even an uncontroversial definition of it, but rather a very specific theory of cognition. In particular, they worked with a loosely defined Kantian theory that, in the period under consideration, had already been criticized, refined, and altered for more than 150 years. The subtleties of Kantian theory contained in those debates were of no use to cybernetics, however, because cybernetics had already disqualified them for not being "scientific." Thus, cybernetics was forced to be naive and partial in its consideration of the mind by virtue of the narrow, essentially one-way communication it envisioned with the humanities. It depended on them for its object but, unable to give them full scientific credit, had to pick some specific doctrine and bestow upon it the character of universality.

We have mentioned an analogous version of the difficult relationship between science and philosophy. McCarthy, as we said, declared that AI had to *produce* a philosophy or fall prey to bad philosophy. Cybernetics, less ambitious or perhaps not as well funded, proceeded instead to *appropriate* one. In either case, the communication with philosophy was difficult to maintain.

Why Cybernetics Failed

It is unfortunate that this paradoxical relationship inevitably affected cybernetics' progress negatively, whereas a different conception of interdisciplinarity might have given a much-needed depth to its models. One example will suffice to illustrate this point. When studying the neuronal models of cognitive activity that were at the core of its program, cybernetics focused on their computational capacities. In other words, it studied the network's capability to transform its inputs into the desired outputs. This approach was consistent with the allegedly universal notion of the mind that the cyberneticians had adopted: they saw it as a process devoted to the (selection and) transformation of information through computational processes.

This approach lays all the explanatory powers of the network on the computations it is capable of performing. For each cognitive task, in other words, be it perceptual, memory-related, or problem-solving, cybernetics had to devise a neural network capable of producing, through computations, the desired output (say, a number) from the input (say, a collection of objects). In other words, the lack of interdisciplinary curiosity exhibited by cybernetics translated at the theoretical level into a narrow conception of a mental process as the pure computational performance of an equivalent neural network. It is easy to see the danger in this approach: cybernetics' viability as a science stands or falls with the computational power of the networks it builds. Were it possible to prove that neural networks of the McCulloch-Pitts type can compute only a proper subset of the functions needed to model cognition, cybernetics' ambition to provide a scientific theory of the mind would be doomed because it would be demonstrably applicable only to a proper subset of human mental capacities.

This is, in a sense, what happened, but not before cybernetics' devices were further developed by Frank Rosenblatt with the invention of the Perceptron, one of the first machines to learn how to recognize visual patterns.[111] Rosenblatt's Perceptron was more flexible than the neural networks of the McCulloch-Pitts type because the association between the inputs and the outputs was not hardwired into the machine itself. Instead, Rosenblatt introduced a new kind of network in which the relative importance of the connections among the various neurons (the weights of the synaptic connections) could be strengthened or weakened in response to the respective success or failure to produce the desired output. A repeated exposure to a series of selected input patterns, and the subsequent careful adjustment of the connections among the neurons, would thus train the Perceptron to produce the desired output from the input patterns.[112]

The theoretical novelty introduced by Rosenblatt made neural networks much more flexible and raised the hope that the construction of a generalized learning machine that could be trained to perform extremely sophisticated tasks of visual, aural, and verbal pattern recognition was within reach. We would like to stress, however, that Rosenblatt's very important technical advance did not change the overall epistemological orientation of cybernetics, nor did it spark a renewed interest in the disciplines from which it continued to draw some of its basic concepts. The fate of cybernetics remained bound to the computational power of the networks it could produce.

When Seymour Papert and Marvin Minsky published their proof showing the intrinsic computational limitations of neural networks of the Rosenblatt type, they *ipso facto* condemned the cybernetic effort as a whole, although the mathematical proofs provided by Minsky and Papert could only be applied, strictly speaking, to a quite narrow subclass of all possible cybernetic devices. Yet, it was cybernetics itself that appeared defeated: Minsky and Papert's proof eventually led to the virtual disappearance of any funding for the discipline and paved the way for the imminent blossoming of AI in the following decade. That this was one of the goals of the authors of *Perceptrons* is quite clear. Papert writes, "Yes, there was *some* hostility in the energy behind the research reported in *Perceptrons*, and there is *some* degree of annoyance at the way the new movement has developed; part of our drive came, as we quite plainly acknowledged in the book, from the fact that funding and research energy were being dissipated on what still appear to me ... to be misleading attempts to use connectionist methods in practical applications. Money was at stake."[113]

Leaving aside the issue of the gap between the alleged results and real proofs, it is important to bear in mind—particularly important for a work devoted to the interaction between AI and the humanities—that the practical results of Minsky and Papert's work were made possible (ironically) by the unilateral and imperialistic reading of interdisciplinarity accepted by cybernetics.

Instead of adopting and trying to foster a peer-to-peer debate with the philosophers, anthropologists, sociologists, and others who historically had devoted so much of their energy to an investigation of the nature of mind—a truly interdisciplinary debate in which each field could have brought its own tools, methods, and history to bear—cybernetics decided to pick one possible view of the mind and regard it as a roughly correct but irremediably imprecise characterization that physics and mathematics would have to convert into a rigorous theory. No further input was needed, and no more attention was to be paid to the endless bickering that had plagued humanities and the social sciences—serious mathematical and physical work was waiting to be done. Success was as certain as the inevitable progress of science.

The pitfall of such a strategy is evident, as the example of *Perceptrons* demonstrates: once the ambitious program of providing a physical and mathematical analysis of cognitive faculties had been made to stand or fall with a particular mathematical modeling technique of a specific and basically uncritically accepted view of the mind, a technical setback was enough to bring the whole research paradigm to a stop.

Were there alternatives available to cybernetics at the time? Yes. It has been proposed, for example, that if cybernetics had paid enough attention to a theory of mind issued from a different philosophical tradition—the tradition of phenomenology developed by Edmund Husserl at the beginning of the twentieth century—the outcome might have been different. Jean-Pierre Dupuy makes the point that the models proposed by McCulloch and Pitts fit quite well within the intellectual landscape of phenomenology, provided that the focus is shifted from the computational performances of the network to its *eigenbehaviors*, that is, to the internal landscape of attractors arising in a network by virtue of its internal structure and its initial conditions:

As [does] any internal state automaton, a network computes its state at the next successive time on the basis of its present state. Now, it is a very general characteristic of these automata that after a transition period, often very short, the overall behavior of the network converges on a stable "limit cycle" of low periodicity.... The life of a network can therefore be conceived as a trajectory within its "landscape" of attractors, the passage from one to the other being the result of perturbations or shocks coming from the external world.[114]

In fact, much work has been done in recent years to revive some of the basic intuitions behind McCulloch's (and others') work and make better use of them. The cybernetic paradigm experienced a true renaissance in the late 1980s, and it is now a very active research area, even if the term *cybernetics* is no longer in fashion. One reason for its resurgence is the discovery of a more powerful learning technique, the back-propagation algorithm.[115] Networks using back-propagation were shown to overcome the limitations pointed out by Minsky and Papert. Other extensions of the classic cybernetic paradigm were provided by the French school led by Henri Atlan, by the team directed by Daniel Amit in Israel, and by the work carried out at the Santa Fe Institute for the Study of Complex Systems, chiefly by Stuart Kauffman.[116]

As Dupuy correctly points out, however, the increased computational power of the recently discovered networks does not constitute their only novelty nor perhaps their most important one. At least as important as their technical merits is the renewed attention to other disciplines paid by present-day cyberneticians, an attention driven by the awareness that a fruitful study of cognition must necessarily cross disciplinary boundaries without, at the same time, assuming the preliminary epistemological supremacy of any specific discipline.[117]

In particular, this work is driven by a double transdisciplinary link: on the one hand, by a strong connection with mathematics, in particular with dynamic systems theory; and on the other, by a strong connection to post-Kantian, especially Husserlian, philosophy of mind (in the Continental tradition) and biologically plausible representationalist theories of mind (in the analytic tradition).

The first of these connections is particularly evident in the Anglo-American tradition in cognitive science and the philosophy of mind, for example, in the anthology compiled by Robert Port and Timothy van Gelder, *Mind as Motion*.[118] In a brief historical sketch, Port and van Gelder attribute the fading of cybernetics in the 1960s mainly to the incomplete development of mathematical dynamic systems theory at the time. They also stress that no redeeming power can save AI because the computationalist paradigm typical of AI is irremediably wrongheaded, insofar as it abstracts from the intrinsic temporality of cognitive processes. European research in the cognitive sciences, on the other hand, has explicitly tied this accent on cognitive temporality to the philosophical analysis of the mind carried out in the phenomenological tradition, where the temporal aspect of cognition has always been one of the main topics of investigation, from Husserl to Heidegger to Merleau-Ponty.[119]

Lessons for AI Today

The conclusion we want to draw from this brief excursion into cybernetics' history is quite apparent. One of the most important factors that stifled its progress—and ultimately drove it into a cul-de-sac—was its narrow conception of interdisciplinarity. This conclusion is only made stronger by the current developments of the old paradigms, which have been made possible by a renewed opening toward other disciplines. Modern "cybernetics" can no longer afford to be as imperialist and one-sided the older cybernetics once was.

10   Critiques of AI: Internal Criticisms

If two important stated goals of AI, psychologically plausible chess-playing expertise and human-level conversational abilities, are still unreached 50 years after the founding of the discipline, should we deduce that there is something wrong with AI's approach? In *Daedalus*'s 1988 special issue on AI, Hilary Putnam writes, "The question I want to contemplate is this: Has artificial intelligence taught us anything of importance about the mind? I am inclined to think that the answer is no. I am also inclined to wonder, What is all the *fuss* about? ... Why a whole issue of *Daedalus*? Why don't we wait until AI achieves something and *then* have an issue?"[120]

Putnam implies only that AI has not so far accomplished anything worthy of special attention. He does not say anything about what he believes AI will or will not be able to accomplish in the future. Many critics, however, seem to take a more negative stance. This section aims to provide a concise discussion of the main lines of criticism leveled against AI, on the basis of our general interpretation.

In the preceding sections we have tried to provide a fairly comprehensive overview of the intellectual heritage of artificial intelligence and have sketched an outline of AI's approach. One of our claims has been that there is a perceptible difference between the scientific approach and methods employed by AI in its recent history (say, post-1950), and the potentially larger, much older project of providing a rigorous, potentially mechanizable, and physically realizable description of human beings' interaction with the world. If we label AI the more recent discipline and artificial intelligence the broader project, this distinction allows the identification of two broad lines of criticism against AI. First comes a series of critiques outlining the limitations of the approach, be they intrinsic or contingent. These objections, in turn, tend to fall into two categories: (1) they may be directed against the narrowness or misguidedness of AI's project with respect to the stated goal of artificial intelligence; (2) or they may criticize the feasibility of artificial intelligence's project in general.

Among the objections against the broader project, one may distinguish between (3) critics who accept AI as the current scientific incarnation of artificial intelligence but are keen to point out the intrinsic political and social dangers of the latter (and therefore of the former); and (4) critics who want to keep current AI *practice* as it is while disengaging it from artificial intelligence by claiming that the techniques, programs, and artifacts AI has developed may be more fruitfully reinterpreted as a different kind of effort: as a form of art, as a particular kind of metaepistemology, and so on. We can then cluster the critiques of AI into four kinds:

1. AI is *too narrow* and must be replaced or at best integrated to reach artificial intelligence.
2. Artificial intelligence is *impossible* in principle.
3. AI and artificial intelligence are socially and politically *dangerous*.
4. AI is not artificial intelligence.

We address these four different kinds of critique in the sections that follow.[121]

Critique 1. Classical AI Is Too Narrow

One of the most forceful advocates for a reform of AI toward a broader conception of human agency and an increased level of interdisciplinarity is Philip Agre, a former practitioner of AI who has now abandoned the field in favor of communication studies. Agre's goal was to provide an accurate and potentially formalizable description of everyday human interaction. In AI research, this field is traditionally called *planning* because the interaction between an agent and the world is taken to be mediated by a (mental) plan of action that specifies, at differing levels of precision, the list of actions to be performed.

In many ways, *plans* are similar to *strategies* in a chess games: starting from a goal to be attained (chessmate), they specify a possible sequence of actions (moves) on the basis of available resources (owned chess pieces) and information about the current situation (enemies pieces captured, position on the board).[122] AI programs based on planning strategies offered some promising results but proved remarkably brittle when they tried to cope with the real world. In fact, AI researchers realized that there is a necessary trade-off between the number of stable structures that can be assumed to exist in the world and the effectiveness of traditional planning strategies: "An agent will be able to construct plans to the extent that someone (the agent itself or its designer) imposes constraints on the world itself."[123]

Relying in part upon a phenomenological description of everyday interaction that Agre himself had provided, he and Chapman realized that a large part of everyday activity does not in fact follow an explicit planning strategy. Real life differs from chess because a complete representation of all the relevant features of the world, which the planning approach would require, cannot be provided. Even if it were, it would require an impossible amount of computing time to determine which action to choose. Instead, interaction with the world is based on much more reactive behavior that relies to a large extent on background, implicit knowledge, and the affordances provided both by the embeddedness of the agent's body in the physical world and by the cultural features of the world itself.

Substantial support for this position came from researchers in the social sciences. For instance, Lucy Suchman, an anthropologist working at Xerox Corporation who conducted detailed studies on office workers' interaction with copiers, stressed that the usual planning strategies people resort to in case of malfunctions and breakdowns never involve an evaluation of the situation on the basis of general principles, overall plans, and properly inserted local data. Rather, the usual strategy people use to deal with troublesome machines relies to a large extent on the concrete situation at hand and exploits it as much as possible.[124]

As a consequence, Agre recommended a shift in AI's basic "unit of analysis." He writes,

To the extent that interactions between agents and their environments provide a useful focus of research, though, it will be necessary to define concepts that cross the boundaries between inside and outside. In other words, AI research will have to develop units of analysis that refer to interactions and not simply to an agents plus a world considered as separate entities.... The point is that the world has the kind of structure that makes a difference to the workings of that particular agent.[125]

The physical shape of a fork, for example, makes it easy to handle, convenient to reach the mouth, to carry food, and so on. The tool's shape is only to a limited extent a property of the object. Rather, it is a property of the (possible) interaction between the physical shape of the agent and the world. In other words, the intrinsic *embeddedness* of the agent in a social, cultural, and linguistic fabric (although Agre did not emphasize this aspect at the time) demands a redirection of AI's attention that will make possible more accurate descriptions and the construction of more efficient agents. The realization that other traditions outside AI, in philosophy and elsewhere, had long focused on similar problems led Agre to call for a transformation of AI from "a self-centered discipline to a kind of interdisciplinary switchboard for the construction of principled characterizations of interaction between agents and their environment"[126] that could rely on the insights of disciplines as different as European and Eastern phenomenology, ethnomethodology, genetic epistemology, and so on.

The planning problem pinpointed by Agre and Chapman becomes especially hard to cope with in robotic applications where (in contrast to the chessboard situation) the robot's environment may be changing very rapidly, the information about the environment may be distorted by unreliable sensors, and the time available to make a decision is always scarce. For instance, SHAKEY, one of the first successful autonomous robots built by AI researchers, had to rely on a carefully constructed environment so as not to be overwhelmed by the abundance of sensory data or confounded by the brittleness of its sensory apparatus. SHAKEY exhibited remarkable performance when asked to navigate an environment endowed with specially constructed markers and visual cues. In that sense, the world inhabited by SHAKEY was analogous to the microworlds of other contemporary nonrobotic AI applications: in both cases the AI artifacts dealt with very simplified, rather clean versions of the real, somewhat messy environments in which intelligent behavior is normally exhibited.[127]

However, efforts to generalize SHAKEY's performance to the real world encountered substantial difficulties, and it is no surprise that AI researchers coming from robotics or directly involved in the construction of embodied, autonomous agents have been particularly aware of the difficulties of the classical paradigm. In a series of extremely influential papers published in the 1980s and 1990s, Rodney Brooks mounted a powerful attack against one of the cornerstones of AI's classical paradigm: the concept of representation. Brooks based his engineering approach on evolution and started from the construction of simple, insectlike intelligent creatures proceeding incrementally toward more and more complex robots.

Brooks emphasized that the typical behavior of a relatively simple agent interacting with the world does not proceed on the basis of complex representations of the world and elaborate plans providing recipes for possible actions on it. Instead, at the simplest levels, the interaction is based on a hierarchy of modules, all based on tight perception-action loops, where stimuli from the external world trigger immediate response without any mediation from an abstract representation: "Explicit representations and models of the world simply get in the way. It turns out to be better to use the world as its own representation."[128] Like Agre and Chapman, Brooks placed a decisive emphasis on the embodied agent's embeddedness in the world and the essentially relational character of its interaction with it. His initial work focused on the construction of insectlike creatures and tended to stress the purely physical aspect of embeddedness rather than the more complex linguistic and social components pointed out by Agre and Chapman. Brooks's later efforts, however, shifted toward the construction of humanoid robots, and as a consequence Brooks started a series of investigations of the more complex linguistic, emotional, and social aspects of an agent's interaction with the world.

Randall Beer has similarly stressed the necessity of assuming embodiment and embeddedness as the starting points of any plausible and effective replication of intelligence. In fact, he suggests that intelligence should be conceptualized as the adaptive behavior of an embodied agent thoroughly and intrinsically enmeshed in its environment rather than as high-level symbol manipulation. Beer's theoretical framework shifts the focus of analysis to the interaction itself because he considers the agent and the environment as coupled, mutually perturbing systems. "In this framework," he writes, "an agent's externally observable behavior is defined as the projection onto its motor outputs of its state trajectory (i.e., its externally observable motor actions over time). One of the chief implications of this framework is that this behavior cannot be exclusively assigned to either the agent or its environment. Instead, an agent's behavior must be understood as arising from the interaction between the two."[129] Beer's work has a more markedly biological inspiration than Brooks's or Agre's. He has investigated the adaptive behavior of simplified artificial insects and tried to replicate adaptive behavior like locomotion, feeding, tracking, exploration.[130]

The general theme of embodiment and embeddedness has been advocated by a number of other critics of AI's classical approach. One of the most interesting articulations of this theme is found in the so-called dynamic approach to cognition, most vocally championed by Tim van Gelder.[131] In the last decade the dynamicists have mounted a sustained attack against the classical AI conception of cognition as computation, but it is not altogether clear whether their alternative paradigm must also be interpreted as a critique of artificial intelligence in general. Furthermore, it is the subject of an intense debate whether the dynamic approach to cognition is an *integration* or a *replacement* of classical AI's approach.

At the heart of the dynamic approach is the recognition that cognitive processes and their contexts are constantly and mutually evolving in time. The emphasis is twofold: first, the unit of description is the whole system made by the agent's cognitive faculties, the corresponding neural and cerebral system, and the environment in which they are placed. Second, to say that the cognitive process is a result of the system's constant evolution through time implies that the cognitive process is the result of a complex series of mutual actions of every component upon every other. The solar system represents a useful analogy for the dynamicists' conception of cognition because the only way to understand the behavior of a planet is to consider it part of a complex system of bodies, each with their masses and velocities, constantly interacting with each other through reciprocal attraction. As the trajectory of a planet can only be described as part of the overall evolution of the whole system through time, so it is for cognitive systems: the "trajectory" of, say, a speaker trying to understand a spoken word must be described as part of the constant evolution of the complex system of which the hearer is a part.[132] The dynamical hypothesis, as Port and van Gelder, present it, expresses this point succinctly: "Cognitive systems are dynamical systems and are best understood from the perspective of dynamics."[133]

Several consequences follow from this hypothesis. The first one is technical: dynamic systems have been studied at length in several domains, from physics to biology, and a well-developed mathematical framework (differential equations, differential topology) is readily available. A dynamic system is described by a set of differential equations that measure how all its n aspects change through real time. The overall state of the system at any given time is thus described by an ordered set of n real numbers, the space of all the possible states the system may assume—the so-called phase space—is equivalent to an n-dimensional space, and the evolution of the system over time is a trajectory in that space. The goal of the analyst is to find a quantitative or qualitative description that specifies how, from a set of initial conditions, the system will evolve. Quantitative modeling will try to find solutions to the set of differential equations describing the system, thus enabling an accurate prediction of the future evolution as well. Qualitative modeling will try to capture salient properties of the system by analyzing the geometrical properties of the phase space: the presence of fixed points and attractors, of catastrophic jumps, and so on. The qualitative description of the system, to put it differently, tries to capture the *landscape* of the phase space.[134]

A second important set of consequences concerns the intrinsic features of the descriptions produced by dynamic modeling. A system can only be modeled through differential equations if its single aspects are measurable by real numbers. This has nothing to do with the difference between qualitative and quantitative modeling. In both cases, the analysis produced a phase space on the basis of a set of differential equations that capture relationships between numerical quantities corresponding to those aspects of the system that the analyst is describing. Although in qualitative modeling the set of equations is generally so complex that a quantitative solution is infeasible, the phase space is nonetheless defined over the real numbers (or a Cartesian product of real numbers).[135] Like the mass and velocity of bodies in a physical system, the single aspects of the cognitive interaction process must represent intrinsic measurable properties of its various components.

There are great advantages in the dynamic approach. For instance, a dynamic model allows us to understand continuous change in both time and state, a very difficult if not impossible task in traditional AI. On the other hand, one may notice that we often conceive higher cognitive functions as involving a mental representation of the object being thought. When I think of, imagine, hallucinate, remember, or otherwise perceive an apple, I often take myself as having a certain representation, perhaps a description, of the object in front of me. But how can a series of numbers describe an apple? The conclusion seems inescapable: either dynamic modeling prescribes the elimination of any kind of representation from our cognitive processes, or dynamic models must be considered as providing only a partial view of cognition that may be apt for lower-level function but must be integrated with other approaches to provide a complete account of cognition.

In fact, the concept of symbolic representation makes very little sense within the dynamic approach, whereas it represents the core of AI. In the classical approaches to cognition, the agent is assumed to operate on the environment by manipulating a symbolic representation of it. When playing chess, for example, the player has an appropriate representation of the configuration of the chessboard and operates on it by going through the possible (or heuristically advisable) moves. A concrete but artificial chess player that interacts with a human would be equipped with sensors and effectors to transform modifications of the actual chessboard into appropriate modifications of its internal representation, or vice versa. The physical separation between agent and environment reflects a deeply engrained conceptual distinction between the agent and the outside world. Symbolic representations arise out of the necessity to the mediate between the two.

In dynamic modeling, on the other hand, there is no separation on principle between agent and (both bodily and extra-bodily) context but rather a constant coupling and mutual interaction. The radical conclusion about cognition is, as one proponent of the dynamic approach puts it, that "the human brain is fundamentally a pattern-forming, self-organizing system governed by non-linear dynamical laws. *Rather than compute*, our brain dwells (at least for short times) in metastable states."[136]

There are many advantages to this radical position. The problems about the lack of embodiment of the AI cognitive model suddenly disappear because the states of a dynamic system contain the relevant features of both the cognitive agent and the environment. In fact, all the components of a dynamic system *co*-evolve together because they are tightly coupled. The problems about the lack of the embeddedness of traditional AI systems disappear as well, for the same reason. In traditional AI, the body (whether biological or mechanical) is fundamentally a transparent channel between cognitive system and external environment that lets data and actions go through via sensors and effectors. When the channel, as often happens in real systems, is faulty or unreliable, the cognitive system can gradually and very quickly drift apart from its environment because it comes to rely on an inaccurate representation. Even when the channel works the way it is supposed to, it is often a problem (in fact according to Dreyfus, the main problem) to select the relevant bits that the cognitive system should care about out of the mass of information that goes through the sensors. There is a basic methodological difference between a proper treatment of sensors, effectors, and transmitters, and the treatment of cognitive processes: cognition is explained in terms of manipulation of symbols, whereas bodily capabilities can only be described in mechanical or physiological terms.

Dynamic models of cognition allow the bodily components to play a much more central role. The state of a dynamic system includes all the aspects of the system in action, including mind/brain, body, and external environment, and all of these aspects are described and analyzed through the application of the same mathematical framework provided by dynamic systems theory. The methodological uniformity afforded by the theory reflects a deeply seated ontological commitment: the behavior of mind, brain, nerves, and muscles can be uniformly described because they are all fundamentally the same. They are all part of nature, and nature must be seen as a homogeneous structure amenable to a homogeneous scientific description.

The radical stance about cognition assumed by several proponents of the dynamic approach constitutes a powerful challenge about the possibility of AI modeling and, more generally, about the possibility of artificial intelligence. Let us start with the latter point.

It seems clear that the dynamic approach does not preclude, in principle, the possibility of providing a full description of cognitive processes that would allow their mechanical reproduction. But it substantially raises the bar for any such attempt because it requires the replication of *all* the components of the system, from the highest levels to the lowest. As Port and van Gelder put it, "We think it *unlikely* that it will be possible to reproduce the kind of intelligent capacities that are exhibited by natural cognitive systems without also reproducing their basic noncomputational architecture."[137]

Since intelligence here is best described as the complex interaction between an organism and its environment, its replication does require the reproduction of the organism itself, or at least a relevant subset of its features. Thus the only artificial intelligence allowed by the dynamicists is either an android or a robot. Although still conceptually possible, the project of artificial intelligence is thus pushed to the limit of artificial humans. It is no surprise that the dynamic approach is rather skeptical of this perspective and tends to see itself as an alternative approach to cognitive science while downplaying the historical, and from its point of view contingent, links between cognitive science, AI, and artificial intelligence. But less skeptical positions about the mechanization of intelligence are possible as well, provided that an embodied, that is, a robotic approach is pursued. It is understandable that researchers in robotics and artificial life have been very interested in the dynamic approach.

What about the relationship between the dynamic approach and classical, computationally based, cognitivist AI? Are the dynamicists arguing for a total replacement of cognitivism, or is it possible to think of an integration between the two approaches, perhaps with the dynamic framework devoted to an explanation of the lower level of sensorimotor behavior and the cognitivist one applied to the higher cognitive functions? It is not difficult to find proponents of the radical embodied position in the dynamic camp. For instance, in a recent contribution a group of leading dynamicists stated, "To say that cognition is embodied means that it arises from bodily interactions with the world. . . . Cognition depends on the kind of experiences that come from having a body with particular *perceptual and motor capabilities* that are *inseparably linked* and that together form the matrix within which reasoning, memory, emotion, language, and all other aspects of mental life are meshed."[138]

It should be remarked that the authors stress a double set of linkages that, in their analysis, has been traditionally overlooked by the classical approach. First comes the emphasis on the strong connection between the sensory apparatus and the motor system, immediately followed by an equal emphasis on the tight coupling between the sensorimotor complex and the world. Both points are meant as a direct attack on the traditional AI approach, with its loose relationship between cognitive system and effectors, on the one hand, and the even more detached relation between plans, environment, and behaviors.

Despite the rather strong anti-AI emphasis in the works of many dynamicists, there have been several attempts to integrate the two approaches. While acknowledging the merit of the anti-cognitivist stance, some have pointed out technical difficulties in a pure dynamic approach. For instance, Keijzer and Bem argue that the dynamic approach provides a useful mathematical formalism to *describe* coupled interactions between organism and environment, but it does not *explain* it: "Adaptive behavior starts from many different initial positions and constantly converges on specific, functional goal states. It produces order."[139] It is not altogether clear, in their opinion, that the dynamic approach to cognition has a theory that explains the cognitive transition from purely sensorimotor coupling between an organism and the world to the higher-order, goal-oriented behavior typical of cognitive processes. In the absence of a such a theory, the dynamic approach is bound to fall upon a crude form of determinism that would reduce intelligent behavior to the necessary effect of physical causes and that should be resisted on epistemological, philosophical, and especially moral grounds. Indeed, they say, the methodologically unified description of physical, physiological, and cognitive processes, which the dynamicists identify as one of the main virtues of the new paradigm, should be considered a pure philosophical loss: "It is strange to think that fitting mental phenomena firmly within the natural hierarchy should be accompanied by the loss of all that makes it special. *Our human agency has not to be given up.*"[140]

Similar considerations are expressed by Andy Clark. "The mark of the cognitive is the capacity to engage in something like off-line reasoning—reasoning in the absence of that which our thoughts concern," and sensorimotor processing seems unable to provide a satisfactory account of it. Clark is interested in a possible integration between a dynamic approach that emphasizes the naturally embedded and embodied character of cognition, and a revised form of the traditional AI-based emphasis on representation, which is essential to logical reasoning and moral deliberation. "Sensorimotor processing and sensorimotor simulation," he writes, "may well play a role—and perhaps even an essential one—in our reasoning. But the capacity to examine arguments, to judge what follows from what, and to couch the issues in the highly abstract terms of a fundamental moral debate (using concepts like 'liability,' 'reasonable expectations,' 'acceptable risk,' and so on) does not obviously lend itself to an analysis in terms of literal sensorimotor simulation."[141] Clark claims that all these tasks are intrinsically "representation-hungry" because they require a detachment between the organism and the surrounding environment that can only be achieved through the use of (classical or revised) representations.[142]

The dispute that has emerged between "integrationists" like Clark and radical dynamicists like Thelen may be recast as a controversy over the correct form of naturalism that should be applied in the study of mental phenomena. Naturalism is a philosophical view about the relation between the results of empirical research in the natural sciences (whence its name) and the results obtained in other disciplines. It can be interpreted in two ways: ontological naturalism is the view that the only things that exist are natural or physical things; semantic naturalism holds that a suitable philosophical analysis of any concept must show it to be amenable to empirical inquiry. As Brian Leiter writes,

In the ontological sense, naturalism is often taken to entail physicalism, the doctrine that only those properties picked out by the laws of the physical sciences are real. In the semantic sense, naturalism is just the view that predicates must be analyzable in terms that admit of empirical inquiry: so, e.g., a semantic naturalist might claim that "morally good" can be analyzed in terms of characteristics like "maximizing human well-being" that admit of empirical inquiry by psychology and physiology (assuming that well-being is a complex psycho-physical state).[143]

Most proponents of the dynamic approach fall squarely within the realm of ontological naturalism and indeed would be considered, according to Leiter's definition, to be physicalists (van Gelder, for instance, and Brooks). On the other hand, traditional AI research is committed to a milder, semantic form of naturalism because the stronger naturalization attempted by the dynamicists seems tantamount to a form of radical reductionism and would come dangerously close to eliminating human agency altogether.

This brief sketch of internal critiques of AI points rather strongly in one direction. Classical AI's obliviousness to an intelligent agent's embodiment and embeddedness in the environment is the main cause of AI's shortcomings, especially its inability to extend the early successes in microworlds to the world at large. Opinions differ quite sharply, however, on how to correct the classical paradigm and even on whether artificial intelligence as a project survives the critique. Several AI researchers interpret these criticisms simply as evidence that the scope of AI research needs to be extended to include a broader set of phenomena (e.g., emotions, a richer view of perception). They are, however, quite positive that AI will be capable of producing, as the discipline matures, a more refined (sometimes called hybrid) generation of theories (and artifacts).

Nonetheless, for many dynamicists, the replication of cognitive functions in the broadest sense requires the duplication of the overall bodily and extrabodily environment in which they take place. Then the verdict on the possibility of the project of artificial intelligence turns to a large extent upon the possibility of constructing androids, cyborgs, or robots resembling human beings as closely as possible—a possibility that many researchers in the field deem unlikely.

Other criticisms of AI and artificial intelligence are less charitable toward the naturalistic assumption shared, in its different forms, by the classical AI paradigm and the embodied camp. The most prominent, both substantially and historically, has been the critique of AI put forward by the philosopher Hubert Dreyfus.

Critique 2. Artificial Intelligence Is Impossible

The most outspoken critic of AI's ambitions to pave the way to artificial intelligence is undoubtedly Hubert Dreyfus. Although the validity of Dreyfus's critique is seldom publicly acknowledged by AI researchers, it is fairly uncontroversial that his strong emphasis on the necessarily embodied character of human intelligence has been one of the major factors in the critical reevaluation of classical AI paradigms that took place in the 1980s.[144] But Dreyfus's critique goes well beyond a simple reassessment of the tools and doctrines in the classical AI paradigm. While most of the authors mentioned so far emphasize an agent's embodiment and embeddedness in order to extend AI's research in new directions, possibly to integrate the results of other, even nonscientific disciplines, Dreyfus has used the same theme to conclude that the project of artificial intelligence, not just classical AI, is most likely impossible. His theoretical argument is then extended to a sociological critique of the social, institutional, and political dangers that derive from heavy investment in AI research.[145]

Since his very first publications, Hubert Dreyfus has insisted that classical AI is committed to conceptualize any interaction between a human being and the world as a structured series of explicit rules (e.g., a rule-based strategy, or plan) that operates on a collection of verbalized descriptions of the world itself (what AI researchers usually call representations). Dreyfus claims that it is indeed quite natural to adopt this approach because a strong tradition in Western philosophy that originated with Plato and culminated in Husserl's phenomenology identifies conceptual thinking with a form of rule following: "If what I see has a tail, and four legs, and barks," writes Dreyfus paraphrasing Kant, "then it must be a dog, because that is what it means to *be* a dog: to have a tail, to possess four legs, and to bark. To properly form the concept of 'dog' I must come up with an explicit, verbalizable linguistic rule that tells me what can be constructed as one."

AI research thinks that any interaction is reducible to a rule of this form or to a stratified collection of rules. If a dogs barks at me, for instance, I may have a rule that prescribes what to do: "If dog barks, then keep safe distance." If the dog starts chasing me, I may have another rule, and so on. But Dreyfus holds that the traditional view, no matter how time-honored, is mistaken. Drawing from the philosophical analyses of Heidegger and especially of Merleau-Ponty, he states that the kind of skillful coping with the world that we normally deem intelligent is based on a largely implicit, non-verbalizable set of social practices that have their origin in our bodily involvement with the surrounding world. Human beings are capable of successfully dealing with the world because they are constantly enmeshed in social practices organized around human needs and in the means of satisfying them, in concert with or against other humans' needs and skills. "Man's skillful bodily activity as he works to satisfy his needs generates the human world," Dreyfus writes, "and it is this world which sets up the conditions under which specific facts become accessible to man as both relevant and significant, because these facts are originally organized in terms of those needs."[146]

A well-adjusted human being facing an approaching crocodile will have reached safety long before the correct rule of behavior has been retrieved and applied because in a social group that dwells in an environment in which crocodiles are found, society has provided practices to deal with them that all members of the group have internalized as they became socialized into it. A member of that group may occasionally try to translate the practice into words when explaining the correct behavior to a stranger unacquainted with crocodiles, but the intrinsic difficulty of retrieving the correct rule ("Is it a croc or a log?") and applying it properly ("Should I use the crocodile-swimming rule or the crocodile-running one?") makes the crocodile far safer than the rule-following human. AI's project of providing a formalization of human intelligent behavior in a set of explicit rules is an impossible (and dangerous) dream, precisely because rules gain their meaning over against the background of embodied social practices from which they initially arose.

The background, for Dreyfus, is more than a generic reference to the context in which action is interpreted. First, the background is a well-structured body of objects, purposes, skills, and practices organized around human needs and priorities.[147] Further, the background is constantly evolving because it is at the same time the origin and the result of human practices. As Daniel Andler puts it, "The background is no thing, not even a set of objective practices, corporal dispositions, acquired skills, or whatever; rather it is what practices, corporal dispositions, acquired skills, etc., *jointly secrete in historical time* and which makes significance possible."[148] It follows that the background can never be formalized because, among other things, the process of formalization is yet another practice that participates in the general process from which the background is being "secreted." In other words, the background of needs-coping skillful practices is *essentially prior* to any description we may give of it, including especially scientific descriptions.

Dreyfus's deeply rooted anti-naturalism finds here its source: the meaningfulness of science, and any evaluation thereof, must be found in the inexhaustible background we, as living embodied human beings, are constantly embedded in. Although Dreyfus has no preconceived objection to science, he does forcefully object to any effort that tries to reduce to purely scientic terms the multifarious richness of human life disclosed by phenomenological analysis.

Several consequences follow from Dreyfus's approach. Classical AI becomes necessarily impossible: any cognitive simulation that relies on explicit representations and rule following will at best reach the level of an advanced beginner within any given field. Its performance will then degrade as the domain it operates over increases in size and complexity. Since a rule is simply a specification of a possible action, for any given situation there will be an exceedingly large number of rules that may be applied. AI is forced to postulate the existence of metarules governing the choice of which rule should be applied, and then of other metarules governing the choice of which previous rules are affected by any minute small change in the environment. The problem is repeated at the higher logical level, originating an infinite regress.

We are here compressing two well-known problems of AI applications because, according to Dreyfus's analysis, they are generated by the same cause—the impossibility of formalizing a really comprehensive background of practices. The first issue is known as the scaling problem, the difficulty of scaling up successful simulations of intelligent behavior from microworlds to the real world. The second issue is known as the frame problem and concerns the difficulty of scaling up from static environments to dynamic and constantly evolving situations. But it does not matter if the increase in complexity in the environment of AI cognitive simulations favors the spatial or the temporal dimension: in either case, AI encounters intractable problems. The number of necessary rules, in other words, will exponentially increase until the AI systems will grind to a halt when they are still very far from the intended goal.[149]

If his indictment of classical AI is severe, Dreyfus's attitude toward more recent, non-rule-based paradigms like connectionism and *nouvelle* robotics is not necessarily positive. AI's fundamental problem is trying to express in a explicit formalism a complete description of the world. Dreyfus asserts that the world will always escape a complete and explicit formalization because it provides the source of meaningfulness of every possible formalism. Thus, AI's problem is not per se of a technical nature. The invention of new formalisms that pay more attention to the embodied character of human experience may improve the success of certain cognitive simulations in limited domains and perhaps, as Dreyfus recognized in his discussion of connectionism, will prove more successful than classical AI.[150] But the overall, grand goal of artificial intelligence—to provide a complete, potentially mechanizable, and scientifically re-spectable description of human cognitive functions—will prove as elusive as ever, no matter how many different formalisms AI experiments with.

Indeed, on the basis of his theoretical analysis Dreyfus proceeds to a philosophical and political critique of AI considered as a social phenomenon. If artificial intelligence, considered in a broad sense, is the attempt to formalize the unformalizable, then the story of AI's ambitions is the story of the attempted conquest of the last corners of the human universe—humans' own cognitive faculties—which so far has resisted a thorough domination and manipulation. Moreover, Dreyfus insists, human cognitive faculties are constituted by the human common sense produced by our having bodies that interact with the world. The effort to "naturalize" common sense through explicit descriptions will necessarily bring about a rejection of whatever resists formalization into the realm of the inessential. Thus, for instance, the ever-spreading use of com-puters in education, going beyond their use as simple tools for drill and practice, will produce a rejection of anything that cannot be rationalized into rules; similarly for the widespread use of computers in management, administration, and so on.

Eventually, the dream of formalizing the background will be fulfilled, in a paradoxical inversion of Dreyfus's thesis about embodiment, by disembodying our intelligence in cyberspace and commodifying our bodies through reconstructive surgery. "For a person who lives in this way," notes Albert Borgmann, "the thesis that intelligence is essen-tially embodied and the body is the disclosure of how we are located in the world is no longer a *description* but the prediction of a dire truth," that people will incessantly try to escape until the situation eventually catches up with them when they age and die.[151]

A similarly negative view on AI's prospects is taken by Terry Winograd and Fernando Flores, who have been deeply influenced by Dreyfus's critique. They insist, as Dreyfus, Brooks, Agre, and others do, on the necessary embodiment of human agents and their embeddedness in a world essentially determined on the basis of actions and goals. However, their stress is on the linguistic dimension of human agency.[152] Drawing on the work of the later Heidegger and the hermeneutic theory of Hans-Georg Gadamer, Winograd and Flores stress that linguistic interaction is not primarily an exchange of information but a web of commitments the speakers enter into on the basis of a widely shared but unarticulated background of social practices. Winograd writes,

"All men are created equal" cannot be judged as a true or false description of the objective world. Its force resides in the commitments it carries for further action. But it is critical to recognize that this social grounding of language applies equally to the mundane statement of everyday life. "The patient is eating" cannot be held up to any specific set of truth conditions across situations in which it may be uttered. The speaker is not reporting an objectively delineated state of affairs, but indicating the engagement to enter sincerely into a dialogue of articulation of the relevant background.[153]

Winograd and Flores conclude from their analysis that computers should not be thought of as thinking machines but rather as language machines. Artificial intelligence has a misguided goal that effectively wastes a potentially much more useful tool. Instead of being used for building expert systems or reasoning engines, computer technology, they argue, should be seen "as a way of organizing, searching, and manipulating texts that are created by people, in a context, and ultimately intended for human interpretation."[154]

Yet another pessimistic critic of AI is John Searle, who argues that AI, or at least one important version of it, is impossible. Searle's argument is based on a thought experiment that he devised, which has come to be widely known as the Chinese Room argument.[155]

In the Chinese Room argument, Searle asks the reader to imagine Searle in a room, isolated from the outside world except for a slot to take in or pass out notes printed on a card. The cards that are given to Searle from the outside contain symbols that are unfamiliar to Searle and carry no meaning for him. Inside the room are a set of reference materials and lookup tables that instruct Searle to produce another card himself with symbols of the same kind printed on it. These cards are what Searle passes to the outside world. Even though he prints the symbols on the cards, those symbol combinations carry no meaning for him either. All he does is to follow a number of instructions, as specified in his reference materials and using merely visual features to match patterns of symbols on the incoming cards to other patterns of symbols on cards he produces and passes out.

Given this setup, Searle's argument can be summarized as follows. The room can be viewed as a giant computer, with the incoming cards as its inputs and the outgoing cards as its outputs. The instruction manuals inside the room specify syntactic rules of the Chinese language in such a way that they enable Searle, the "operator" in the room, to find at least one matching syntactically well-formed and semantically meaningful sentence that can be passed out in response to each incoming Chinese sentence. Viewed from the outside, it is possible to take this room as a computer that comprehends and responds in Chinese, an artificial Chinese conversationalist, if you will.

Searle's point is that none of what goes on has to be transparent to the operator in the room, and even if the operator knows what his purpose is, if he goes into the room without any knowledge of Chinese, he will remain ignorant of what goes on in the conversation he makes possible with the outside world. That is, his complete ability to manipulate Chinese symbols into syntactically well-formed sentences that make sense as responses to other Chinese sentences posed as questions does not, and in fact cannot, give him access to the semantics involved in this exchange of symbols. As such, Searle necessarily remains blind to the meaning of the messages in the incoming and the outgoing cards. He, as the operator, is the "central processing unit" of a system that gives the impression of understanding and producing Chinese, but in fact he has no such understanding. What he has, at best is an "as if" understanding, which can be wrongly interpreted as genuine understanding from the outside but does not amount to true language comprehension.

This is exactly what goes on with digital computers that run language-processing programs, Searle concludes. These computers, even if they can become flawless conversationalists and pass the Turing test (which is still a distant possibility for present-day computers), can at best said to imitate intelligent linguistic behavior with no genuine understanding. If AI is content with the goal of constructing computers that can act as if they do intelligent things without in fact being so, which is what Searle calls weak AI, then AI is possible. But when AI claims to be in the business of constructing the genuine article, machines that are on their own language users, then it is bound to fail. This latter version, what Searle calls strong AI, is impossible.

Searle's Chinese Room argument is one of the chief philosophical arguments of the twentieth century. This may be because the structure of the argument seems deceptively simple and intuitive as well as because a number of responses seem immediately available to counter it. Under a barrage of counterarguments, Searle has in fact categorized the various points raised against the Chinese Room argument under a number of different headings and responded to them in groups, such as the "systems response" (which argues that language capacity should be attributed to the whole system of which Searle is part, not just to him), the "robot response" (which maintains that linguistic meaning can be obtained only when genuine reference to the world is possible, which can be the case if the Chinese Room is placed within a robot that moves about in the world), and so on.

Given the wide circulation of these arguments, we do not rehearse all of them here. In fact, we think that the conclusion Searle wants to establish about the impossibility of AI does not follow. But we also think that what makes this argument interesting lies largely elsewhere. More than the philosophical merits of the Chinese Room argument or its counterarguments, the nature of the exchanges is symptomatic of a deeper issue that has been with the project of artificial intelligence from the beginning. Yet again, that issue is the role of embodied autonomous agency in the actualization of intelligence and the attribution of intelligence to others.

For the moment, we continue our overview of the four types of criticism raised against AI. We revisit the issue of embodiment and agency in the last section.

11   Critiques of AI: External Criticisms

Whereas the critics we have just discussed point out how unlikely it is that AI will ever produce true artificial intelligence short of replicating a human body, others are more interested in fleshing out the potentially pernicious effects of AI as a technology and as a discipline.

Critique 3. AI and Artificial Intelligence Are Dangerous

One of the first critics to touch on the political and social dangers of the limited view of human nature in artificial intelligence was Joseph Weizenbaum, the author of one of the first natural language processing systems, ELIZA. Weizenbaum was less interested in examining whether computers *can* be made to simulate intelligence than in asking if they *should* be. He writes,

We can design an automatic pilot, and delegate to it the task of keeping an airplane flying on a predetermined course. That seems an appropriate thing for a machine to do. It is also technically feasible to build a computer system that will interview patients applying for help at a psychiatric out-patient clinic and produce their psychiatric profiles complete with charts, graphs, and natural-language commentary. The question is not whether such a thing can be done, but whether it is appropriate to delegate this hitherto human function to a machine.[156]

The main reason why computers should not be given such tasks, according to Weizenbaum, lies in their intrinsic incompleteness. Weizenbaum does not refer, as Agre, Brooks, and others do, to some incomplete account of intelligence that is bound to hamper the intelligent behavior of the computer. Rather, he focuses on the essentially reductive view of human nature that AI presupposes in order to build and implement its models of rationality. We briefly hinted at this aspect when we discussed, in the section on chess, how AI radicalizes the distinctly Western view of rationality by making it into the only feature of humanness. Weizenbaum spells out the various ways in which a computer lacks features that are so obviously human as to be taken for granted. For example, he points at the necessary decontextualization of a computer program, the lack of a socialization process that brings about a lack of any social and ethical concerns, the total absence of an emotional counterpart to the rational side. The reductionist approach that he sees as embedded in classical AI modeling leads him to appeal for a more restricted, and especially more ethical, deployment of computer applications and AI applications in general.

The very asking of the question, "What does a judge (or a psychiatrist) know that we cannot tell a computer?" is a monstrous obscenity. Computers can make judicial decisions, computers can make psychiatric judgments. They can flip coins in much more sophisticated ways than can the most patient human being. The point is that they *ought* not to be given such tasks. They may even be able to arrive at "correct" decisions in some cases—but always and necessarily on a basis no human being should be willing to accept.[157]

Several of the limitations of classical AI programs—the exclusion of emotions, for example, or socialization—have now become the locus of intense investigation, and one may perhaps expect that future AI models will not suffer from the limitations pointed out by Weizenbaum. His general thesis about the desirability of an indiscriminate deployment of AI applications (classical or *nouvelle*) is not so easily avoided, though. The core of Weizenbaum's argument is not that AI programs are incomplete and could be better. Rather, the point is that the designers of AI programs tend to see human beings, human interaction, and society as a whole as purely technical "problems" that can be "solved" by devising better and better tools.

This attitude is deeply wrong, according to Weizenbaum, because it allows us to turn away from the existence of real conflicts in the human world, to avoid asking questions about why something is going on and what could be done to face it. Thus, the construction of a more perfect, less reductive computer model of intelligence would lead to more troubles, not fewer. It would perpetuate the dangerous illusion that most, if not all, human problems can be solved by the appropriate technological fix. People could use computers to eschew more and more responsibility, for instance: Why ask about the medical problems of psychiatric patients when an intelligent system is in place to solve them?

In other words, the existence of powerful technical tools opens up the space for a massive evasion of responsibility by reducing all and all too real human conflicts to merely technical problems that can be delegated to a machine. The ethical problem facing human beings confronting machines is that "the reification of complex systems that have no authors, about which we know only that they were somehow given us by science and that they speak with its authority, permits no question of truth or justice to be asked."[158]

Similar arguments are offered by Tom Athanasiou, but with a more marked emphasis on the political consequences of AI's deployment. He points out, for example, that the increased versatility of AI applications, regardless of their claims to authentic intelligence, will certainly increase the process of deskilling in the workplace. The real issue surrounding AI is not a technological, scientific, or even philosophical question. The real issue is political: "What should be automated, or rather, who should decide? This is not a question about technology, but about social power, and without the ability to answer it in democratic terms, to say that 'the people will decide' rather than 'the experts will decide,' 'the market will decide,' or 'the lawyers will decide,' no democracy is real."[159]

Not many critics have scrutinized the ethical, political, and social problems raised by AI as distinct from other forms of automation. From this point of view, AI may represent just the latest development of the much older phenomenon of society's increasing technologization and automation. Still, many authors point out an important difference between research in artificial intelligence and research in, say, semiconductor technology or material science. The production of an intelligent machine is often presented, by the popular press as well as by its partisans, as possibly the highest scientific and technological achievement of humankind. Thus, critical analyses of science and technology often choose AI research and applications as the exemplary case that must be analyzed in depth, and in all its contexts, in order to understand the problems surrounding the deployment of any kind of scientific and technological artifacts. In particular, the tight coupling between university research, military funding, and commercial exploitation that has always been one of the hallmarks of AI has often been at the center of scholarly attention.

In the eyes of many, the paradigmatic example of such integration is represented by the Strategic Computing Program (SCP) that was inaugurated by DARPA (Defense Advanced Research Projects Agency) in 1983.[160] SCP's goal was to bring together the results of over two decades of DARPA-funded AI research projects into concrete military artifacts. Initially funded for five years (1983–1986), it was later extended until 1993.[161] DARPA initially conceived the Strategic Computing Program as a response to Japan's "Fifth Generation" project, research funded by the Japanese ministry for information technology, MITI. In 1983, Edward Feigenbaum, a prominent AI researcher, published a popular book that described Japan's initiative in very alarmed tones and that was perceived as instrumental in bringing about DARPA's program. Europe, in turn, responded with project ESPRIT (European Strategic Programme for Research into Information Technology), a theoretically less ambitious project more geared toward industrial (as opposed to military) applications. Initial funding for SCP for the period 1983–1986 was about $600 million, and the overall budget for the life of the project was about $1 billion, making it one of the more substantial research investments by the U.S. government.

Although SCP was conceived by DARPA independently, it became practically and theoretically joined to the U.S. Strategic Defense Initiative (SDI) launched by President Reagan in the same year. SDI's objective was to build a vast network of antimissile weapons that would have constituted, if successful, a truly impenetrable shield against Soviet ballistic missiles. Given that ballistic weapons are easier to detect and most vulnerable in the initial launch phase (which often lasts less than 90 seconds), it soon became clear that an effective response system had to be almost totally (or completely) automatic. Efficient AI techniques were soon deemed necessary to reach a decision in such short time, hence the tight coupling between SDI and the Strategic Computing Program. SCP was eventually shut down by President Clinton in 1993 with the (provisional, it turned out) demise of the SDI program.[162]

The Strategic Computing Program wanted to leverage advances in artificial intelligence and microelectronics in order to develop "a new generation of computers that can SEE, HEAR, TALK, PLAN, and REASON." New military technologies such as autonomous battle vehicles, pilots' expert associates, and naval battle management environments were to demonstrate the new scientific advances. The official presentation of the program by DARPA made clear that the successful completion of SCP depended on the results provided by a diverse array of scientific and technological disciplines. The novelty was constituted by the place of AI within this vast context: in the description of SCP's "technological base," DARPA arranged the various research efforts in a neatly

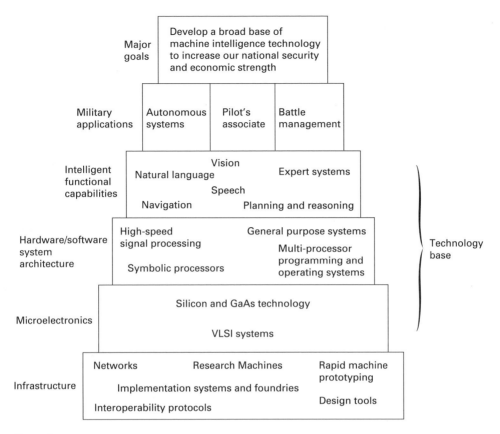

Figure 8

The pyramid diagram representing DARPA's vision for the Strategic Computing Program. Adapted from S. Ingvar Åkersten, "The Strategic Computing Program," in *Arms and Artificial Intelligence*, ed. Allen Din (New York: Oxford University Press, 1987), 92.

arranged pyramid that had various artificial intelligence projects comfortably installed at the top (see figure 8).[163]

A striking feature of the SCP program was the sheer magnitude of its theoretical and practical goals when compared with the relatively minor practical results produced by AI research at the time. SCP's inaugural documents make broad claims about the possibility of designing and producing a new generation of computers that would "exhibit human-like, 'intelligent' capabilities for planning and reasoning" and would enable direct, natural interactions with their users … through vision and speech," and that could be implemented into applications that would solve critical problems in defense.[164]

Contrary to these claims, however, AI systems existing at the time (1983) had demonstrated a very limited range of general capabilities. Some could engage in limited natural language interactions in severely restricted domains like the "block world" of SHRDLU; others were able to mimic some expert skills in highly specialized domains (e.g., DENDRAL for spectrometric analysis of organic molecules). Vision systems had an even more limited set of accomplishments. SCP wanted to demonstrate the viability of a "broad base of existing scientific technology" in an autonomous unmanned vehicle that could provide reconnaissance in previously unknown areas, a R2D2-style "pilot's associate" that would advise and guide a human pilot in battle, and a naval battle management system that would provide similar advice to naval commanders but on the tactical level. None of the practical demonstrations of AI technology gave satisfactory results, and some, like the autonomous vehicle, were discontinued even before the program's end. Indeed the program's focus shifted, gradually but steadily, from artificial intelligence to advanced computing, especially parallel computers. After ten years of funding, SCP was quietly merged into a new program, "High-Performance Computing" (HPC). Very few, if any, of its AI-related goals had been reached, at either the theoretical or practical level.

Some historians of technology have interpreted the SCP phenomenon and its evolution away from AI as a sort of professional risk intrinsic to the sponsoring of cutting-edge research that had always been DARPA's mission. DARPA sincerely believed that research in artificial intelligence was on the verge of major scientific and technological breakthroughs, but when "AI turned out to be impossible DARPA went to HPC."[165] Aims may be set high, but a pragmatic leader must be ready to settle for second best. Others have been less charitable, however, and have considered the whole SCP affair, from its grandiose expectations through its unprecedented funding and eventual demise, an outstanding problem in the history of science and technology that begs for an explanation.

Tom Athanasiou, for instance, draws the lesson that any critique of technology that abstracts from its institutional setting is necessarily inadequate because it ignores the relationship between political ideology and scientific research. The SCP fiasco, according to Athanasiou, proves that the "DARPA's predictions rested not on scientific theory but on an ideological commitment to high technology," which blinded DARPA's administrators to the insufficiencies of AI research.[166] Athanasiou identifies six factors behind DARPA's "unscientific" program, including *ideological* ("Science is rational, thus good, and its therefore morally obligatory to pursue it"); *technological* ("Technological fixes can buy time and thus help avoid politically unacceptable realities"); *organizational* (the institutional and bureaucratic inertia of an agency committed to previous investments in AI); *economic* (the increasing control by the military over the U.S. R&D budget); *political* (the advantages that may be gained from "technological posturing"); and *military* ("The military hopes that advanced technology will allow it to pursue its ever-widening agenda").

It is clear, even from this summary, that Athanasiou considers the heavy investments in AI research as a paradigmatic, but by no means special, case of the tangled relationship between scientific research and military funding. His critique is aimed at the general problem of AI research, and the only feature that makes it stand out is its cutting-edge character: insofar as it is presented as "one of the hardest problems science has ever tackled," it will be easier to bend its scientific pursuits to ideological goals. It is also clear that Athanasiou, while strongly affirming the need to assess a scientific program in the social and political context of its inception, thinks that an independent, purely scientific evaluation is always possible.

Indeed, Athanasiou's social criticism requires a scientific or philosophical critique that will prove AI to be an example of bad science, a flawed research paradigm. This result, in turn, would allow a political and social critique that brings out how external interests may have colluded to support it. It is not surprising, then, that Athanasiou collaborated with Hubert and Stuart Dreyfus in their book *Mind over Machine* and that his attack on AI refers back to the line of argument presented there.

Paul Edwards presents a more radical line. According to his analysis, computers, and more particularly artificial intelligence, were shaped by the Cold War and shaped it: "Military research problems [e.g., command and control with their necessary brief response time] and a location within an institution dedicated to their solution [like Stanford or MIT] could shape scientists' intellectual interests and vision of the future."[167] The principled separation between scientific pursuit and ideology that Athanasiou still clings to is deemed insufficient to provide a clear understanding of the phenomenon AI or the phenomenon SCP because it is the discipline itself, its goals, procedures, and experimental apparatuses, that are shaped by the context of their development. It follows that an adequate critique cannot proceed in steps but must consider all the different aspects of that context at once.

Edwards does not hold, however, that AI is a pure "fantasmatic" creation of the military context that nurtured it. Rather, he claims that the interaction between scientific research in AI and its political and social context was mutual. Indeed, borrowing the terms of dynamic systems theory, we could say that, according to Edwards, AI and Cold War politics co-evolved, mutually influencing and reinforcing each other until they produced what he calls the "cyborg discourse." As he puts it, "Artificial Intelligence, man-computer symbiosis, and human information processing represent the reduction necessary to integrate humans fully into command and control. The cybernetic organism, with its General Problem Solvers, expert systems, and interactive real-time computers, is the form of a mind in symbiotic relationship with the information machines of the electronic battlefield."[168]

Thus, the "failure of AI" or the "failure of SCP" (or respectively, their successes) are no failures at all, because there are no independent standards they could be assessed against. AI research is part of a closed system (what Edwards calls "the closed world") that is constantly driven by its own internal dynamics. Its failures or successes can only be seen as temporary equilibrium points in the ongoing evolution of the overall "organism."

Edwards's critique targets the system as a whole, the whole "closed world" within which AI was born and flourished, insofar as AI's research agenda was directly shaped by it. His contention is that the closed world's co-evolution of military computer technology, political ideology, and cognitive theory has produced a coherent description of the subjects who inhabit the Cold War and post–Cold War era, which human beings can use to recognize themselves. The general form of this description is what Edwards calls the "cyborg discourse": closed world's subjects, he claims, have come to identify themselves as cyborgs. On the one hand, cyborgs experience the world of everyday life as the closed world of a rule-based game (according to the dictum of classical AI) and, on the other, they have bodies that are no longer sharply distinct from the mind, nor clearly defined by the traditional biological attributes of gender, race, and so on.[169] The cyborg's body, in fact, can be subjected to the same techniques of complete control that (classical) cognitive theories have made available for the mind.

Unlike Athanasiou, Edwards does not think that the complex web of technology, science, and politics that constituted the closed world and gave rise to cyborg discourse can be criticized or rejected from any external standpoint. Alternatives to the closed world can only be found in the long past, premodern "green worlds" celebrated by myths, which now survive in important but utterly marginal practices like "animistic religion, feminist witchcraft, certain Green political parties, and deep ecology."[170] But the sheer, ever-increasing scale of the global process of assimilation that has produced the closed world preempts any project of escape or transcendence into its opposite "green" counterpart. On the contrary, an effective positive critique, Edwards argues, must be internal: it must examine the whole system and try to recover the resources that the system itself offers to anyone who wants to resist the project of total assimilation that is always looming over the closed world. Quite appropriately, Edwards uses a biotechnological term to identify the only strategy he deems viable: "*Recombination* is the only effective possibility for rebellion in the closed world: taking the practices of disassembly, simulation, and engineering into one's own hand. [This] cyborg subjectivity would lack the reassurances of center, grounding, certainty, and even continuity. Yet at least it might be self-determined, in whatever shattered sense might remain of [this] term. The closed world subjects could adopt the strategy of recombination as a tortured, contradictory, but effective cultural/political practice." If the closed world offers no escape, redemption, or premodern wholeness, Edwards concludes, nonetheless "the recombinant cyborg mind can cross and recross the neon landscapes of cyberspace, where truth has become virtuality, and can find a habitation, if not a home, inside the closed world."[171]

We have devoted some space to Athanasiou's and Edwards's critiques because they represent, in a sense, the two exemplary positions that scholars have taken when confronted with the complex web of interactions between research in AI, military applications, and political ideology. We should note that both positions share a common point, although for very different reasons: they both reject the deep naturalistic assumption that runs through AI and to a large extent through the broader project of artificial intelligence. For Athanasiou, a purely scientific description of human beings and their cognitive functions as provided by AI is unacceptably reductive and ultimately ideologically motivated. For Edwards, no description, be it scientific, philosophical, or otherwise, is ever acceptable on its own terms because it can only be understood within the overall system in which it emerged and which it shaped.

Thus the two radically different conclusions: Athanasiou thinks that a richer and deeper account of human nature must be found elsewhere than in "unscientific" artificial intelligence—he points to philosophy. Edwards, on the contrary, claims that the "unscientific" artificial intelligence discourse must be carefully examined from within in order to find opportunities of resistance, which he finds in human beings' possibility for conceiving of themselves as "recombinant cyborgs."

Interestingly enough, the distinction is similar to the opposition between the different kinds of "internal critiques" we discussed in the previous section. Either AI/artificial intelligence is impossible, it was claimed, or it will require the *physical* production of android or robotic bodies. Either AI/artificial intelligence is purely ideological, we find now, or it requires the *conceptual* production of the recombinant cyborg.

In both cases, the scientific, philosophical, and political destinies of AI, and by implication of artificial intelligence, seem to become more and more tied to the literal and rhetorical production of automata and cyborgs.

Critique 4. AI Is Not Artificial Intelligence

The last kind of criticism we would like to discuss briefly exhibits a marked lack of interest, if not outright mistrust, in the general theoretic approach of artificial intelligence. This form of critique, like the ones we discussed earlier, aims at breaking the strict link established by AI between the elaboration of scientific models of human rational capacities and the construction of software agents possibly capable of replicating it.

The general strategy is markedly different, however. This type of criticism disregards the connection between AI and the grand project of artificial intelligence altogether. Instead, it takes a keen interest in the artifacts themselves (the algorithms, the artificial insects, the conceptual and physical tools) and considers them as objects that could be usefully exported to other domains regardless of the original intentions bestowed upon them by their authors. To a large extent, AI considered as an engineering discipline falls within this rubric. Much research work in AI is devoted to the elaboration of classes of algorithms that enable devices (computers, phones, car dashboards) to act "smart." For example, "Clippy," the help agent paper clip deployed by Microsoft in its office applications from 1997 to 2001, was programmed with Bayesian network algorithms to improve the relevance of its advice. Although opinions on the quality of Clippy's advice varied, it is clear that no one worried too much about the psychological plausibility of Clippy as a model of a human word-processing tutor. Indeed, some argue that the main focus of AI research seems to have shifted away from the study of the fundamental features of human thought and reasoning—and the related grand engineering projects—to the incremental improvement of mundane applications like help systems or video games.

For example, Marvin Minsky complains that today's artificial intelligence practitioners "seem to be much more interested in building applications that can be sold, instead of machines that can understand stories."[172] Minsky's observation points to a fundamental shift in AI technology. In the years of "great expectations," AI's ideal products were large, complex systems (expert systems, ballistic response systems) that could only be sold to the few large organizations with pockets deep enough to afford them. Nowadays, AI technology is integrated into shrink-wrapped products that can be found on the shelves of any computer store. Another relevant example, and a burgeoning area for AI technology, is the ever-increasing integration of AI algorithms into computer video games. This is no surprise, because the theoretical work on computer games has been one of the most successful and visible results of AI research.[173] What is relatively new is the emphasis on commercial applications and the active cooperation between video games publishers and AI research groups.[174] Indeed, AI techniques have penetrated the realm of video game programming to such an extent that even popular books on the subject now devote extensive chapters to this formerly neglected area, and technical texts devoted to AI and game programming aimed at professional programmers are being published. In the gamer community, "AI" has become a metonymic reference for the computer-controlled agents a player will likely encounter in most video games.

This phenomenon can receive different interpretations. Some AI researchers claim that games are still being used as a research test bed to elaborate models and techniques that will eventually be exported to other fields. Games are still the *Drosophila of AI*," and the success enjoyed on the market is a direct consequence of the brilliant theoretical successes achieved by 30 years of work in the field. Indeed, some AI researchers go as far as to claim that for some games, one could argue that the Turing test has been passed.[175] On the other hand, some have suggested that the causal inference could be read backward: the recent popularity of AI techniques in game programming is unsurprising because classical AI is a "theory of game playing." Thus the commercial success in a limited domain turns into an explicit critique of the relationship between AI and artificial intelligence.

Commercial and industrial users focus on AI products as a set of tools that may be useful when dealing with problems that have so far resisted traditional analysis. Others are more interested in AI's artifacts as useful tools "to think with."[176] Sometimes AI artifacts are seen as tools in the strict sense of the term: prosthetic devices that enhance human capabilities in specific domains. Two of the contributors to this volume may be usefully placed within this perspective: Stephen Wilson argues that AI's production allows artists to do art differently; Maurizio Matteuzzi writes that AI should really be seen as a rigorous form of epistemology. They are not the only representatives of this position. Harold Cohen, a painter, uses the mechanical painter he himself built in order to reflect on his own artistic practice and therefore react to and change it. AARON, Cohen's mechanical painter, is not just, or not so much, a model of a painter's expertise as an embodied artistic alter ego.[177]

These appropriators of AI's products are motivated by a different reading of the notion of interdisciplinary research. They do not see it, as it is traditionally understood, as the convergence of tools and methods toward the investigation of a common problem that exceeds institutional disciplinary boundaries, an approach that often implies a hierarchical relation among the various disciplines contributing their conceptual apparatus to the solution. Instead, interdisciplinarity (but perhaps the very term starts to be inadequate) is reinterpreted as a mutual appropriation and reappropriation of tools and techniques from one field to another with no assumption of a shared understanding either at the level of problems or at the level of concerns and background.

This unorthodox stance with respect to the traditional disciplinary boundaries exposes these authors to quite a few risks because it rejects a powerful and well-entrenched philosophical tradition in Western culture, namely, the tradition that sees the whole range of natural, social, and human sciences as a vast, collaborative, hierarchically organized enterprise aiming at unearthing the truth about the world and its inhabitants.

AI's Responses to Its Critics

To say that the influence of these varied criticisms on AI has been minimal is hardly an exaggeration. On the one hand, it seems to be widely acknowledged within the AI community that no successful replication of human intelligence can leave aside a thorough discussion of the relationship between agents and their environment. Although implemented in different ways by different schools of AI research, the themes of embodiment and world embeddedness now occupy the forefront of AI research. Although many AI old-timers claim that the methods of classical AI can perfectly accommodate such issues, it is clear that the main line of development goes in a different direction.[178]

Research in robotics, for example, has assumed a leading role in many AI labs, starting with the MIT AI Lab, directed by Rodney Brooks. Other schools, while critical of Brooks's rejection of high-level symbolic processing, have tried to integrate some of his insights into the traditional paradigm.[179]

On the other hand, this shift in AI research cannot be traced back to a direct influence of the criticisms we have discussed. In a short sketch of AI's historical development, Allen Newell, for example, stressed the ineffectiveness of Dreyfus's Heidegger-inspired critique, first advanced in 1965, on the main body of AI research.[180] Newell also offered a critical assessment of the explanatory power of the humanities, in a comparative examination, with that of AI as a science of the mind. According to Newell's strikingly uncharitable and deflationist view of the humanities, not much is gained by approaching the study of the mind through the metaphor of "mind as computer," which is the best humanities can do. AI, on the other hand, is radically different: it is in the business of generating theories of the mind, on a par with geological theories of plate tectonics or the physical theory of the atom.[181]

Similarly, at the end of his manifesto for embodied AI, "Intelligence Without Representation," Rodney Brooks made the following remark: "In some circles much credence is given to Heidegger as one who understands the dynamics of existence. Our approach has certain similarities to work inspired by this German philosopher [Agre and Chapman], but our work was not so inspired. It is based purely on engineering considerations."[182]

Thus, the influence of philosophical analysis of embodiment and interaction was complex. When it was felt, if at all, it was only through the assimilation of some of the philosophical insights in the technical work of researchers who, although occupying a marginal role, were nonetheless working within the AI camp. The description fits quite well the figures of Philip Agre and David Chapman, to whom Brooks refers in the preceding quotation and who were both graduate students at the MIT AI Lab at the time. As Brooks remarks, however, the external influences per se on his own work were minimal. The original insights that led to the development of an alternative architecture for intelligent agents arose out of technical difficulties with robotics.[183]

Philip Agre and David Chapman, whose work represents the theoretical pivot of this whole story, are no longer involved in AI research. Agre works in communication studies and sees himself as a social scientist concerned with the social and political aspects of networking and computing, and Chapman left AI research for industry. Agre has commented at length on the enormous difficulties he encountered when he tried to import new ideas into the field and has offered a powerful analysis of the reasons that foreclose a dialogue with the nontechnical community (see his chapter in this volume). He now conducts his fight for reform of AI toward a technical critical practice from the outside, and he has assumed quite a pessimistic stance on the likely outcome.[184]

EMBODIMENT = THE CRUCIAL ISSUE

Similarly, Terry Winograd, after a brief interlude studying the philosophical foundations of artificial intelligence, has shifted his attention to a different field of computer
science. He is now concerned with human-computer interaction design with a focus
on theoretical background and conceptual models.

Nonetheless, if there is a conclusion that can be drawn from this broad survey of AI
criticism, it is the following: *embodiment*, or lack thereof, is the crucial issue that has
confronted AI in the past, and it is the crucial issue that will continue to confront artificial intelligence in the future. What lies ahead of us, if artificial intelligence is at all
possible, are recombinant cyborgs, to borrow Edwards's term. It is an open question,
however, whether the cyborgs of the future will just be mechanical or biomechanical
replicas of our bodies that will leave untouched the way we think of ourselves, or
whether the "cyborg option" will force us to reassess the way we see ourselves. We
briefly return to this issue in the last section.

12   "Thinking Machines: Can There Be? Are We?"

The title of this section is borrowed from an essay by Terry Winograd. Winograd points
to various complications involved in asking this question and scrutinizes its legitimacy. Regardless of what kind of answer is suitable for it, Can there be thinking
machines? is a question about AI's future; in fact, a question about the future of the
broader project of artificial intelligence.

Perhaps the most outstanding fact about this question is that the predictions offered
in response, especially in the case of AI, have been notoriously off-target, at times in a
way that constitutes a textbook case study in the science of shortsightedness. Rather
than adding to the repertoire of predictions, we would like to try to give something of
a bird's eye view of the present situation in the context of the discussion we have presented thus far.

The Present Status of AI: A Diagnosis

In 1987, Patrick Winston depicted the brief history of AI in a linear fashion (see figure
9), concluding on a celebratory note that "the correct attitude about artificial intelligence [must be] one of restrained exuberance:"[185]

According to Winston, AI is proceeding along a straight path from the age of the Renaissance to the age of commercial partnerships and entrepreneurial successes, having
left the Dark Ages behind for good. Whether, in this conception, AI is still aiming for
its original dream—"the construction of mind"—is somewhat unclear. Winston himself didn't pursue the issue, but there were others carrying the torch, from authors of
popular books to academicians. For example, Robert Jastrow wrote in *Science Digest*
(1982):

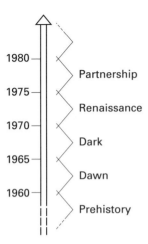

Figure 9
The development of AI, according to Patrick Winston (1987). Adapted from Winston, "Artificial Intelligence: A Perspective," in *AI in the 1980s and Beyond*, ed. W.E.L. Grimson and R. S. Patil (Cambridge, Mass.: MIT Press, 1987), 3.

In five or six years—by 1988 or thereabouts—portable, quasi-human brains, made of silicon or gallium arsenide, will be commonplace. They will be an intelligent electronic race, working as partners with the human race. We will carry these small creatures around with us everywhere. Just pick them up, tuck them under your arm, and go off to attend your business. They will be Artoo-Deetoos without wheels: brilliant but nice personalities, never sarcastic, always giving you a straight answer—little electronic friends that can solve all your problems.[186]

It is not unusual to find writers going so much off tangent when they get into making conjectures on the future of AI and its impact on our lives, so we will not harp on the lack of accuracy in Jastrow's comments. But there are always others placing their bets further into the future (see figure 10). For example, Hans Moravec, director of the Mobile Robot Laboratory, Carnegie Mellon University, was interviewed by *Discover* magazine (1992) after the publication of his first book:

Discover: In the first sentence of your 1988 book, *Mind Children*, you wrote: "I believe that robots with human intelligence will be common within fifty years."
Moravec: It's not—at least in my circles—all that controversial a statement anymore.[187]

Other scientists from leading AI laboratories also indulge in far-reaching predictions, but with longer time frames. For instance, Michael de la Maza and Deniz Yuret of the MIT Artificial Intelligence Laboratory offered five specific predictions for computer applications in medicine over the next 200 years, almost all relying on fast developments in AI technology. By 2100, they claim, so-called downloading will permit seri-

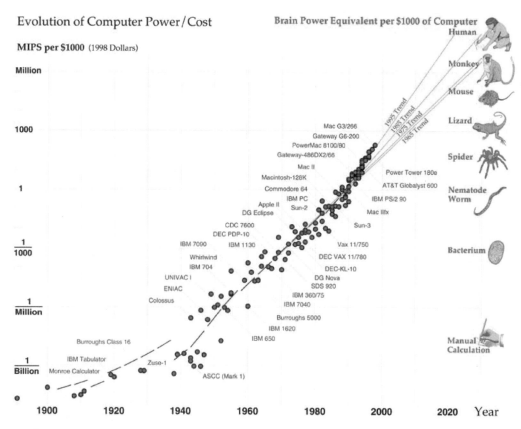

Figure 10

Forecast of comparative evolution of power/cost ratio in computers vs brain power in biological organisms until 2030. From Hans Moravec, *Robot: Mere Machine to Transcendent Mind* (Oxford: Oxford University Press, 1998).

ously ill patients to simply have their minds stored on a computer while their bodies are repaired or, if necessary, genetically duplicated by cloning. By 2150, refinements in downloading and cloning technologies will render human life spans virtually infinite. By 2200, people may no longer want human bodies at all, preferring to exist as a pattern of transferrable electronic information.[188]

Naturally, it is difficult to assess the maturity of such speculations, and we do not attempt to do so here (though we should note that about a third of Moravec's stated interval has already passed since his remarks, without AI having reached anywhere remotely near his prediction). But it is interesting to notice how the time frame has lengthened; instead of the projecting AI's advances 10 or 20 years into the future, de la Maza and Yuret's schema proceeds by half-centuries. That in itself is probably an indication of the field's increased lack of confidence about short-term results.

Perhaps what should really be questioned is the value of venturing into predictions of this sort. But what about issues of a more pragmatic orientation? Is AI considered by commerce and industry as living up to its promises, or at least proceeding in the straight path that originates in the 1950s in Winston's diagram (figure 9) and spans the 1990s and beyond?

AI Changing Course: The Flourishing of Human-Machine Interaction

In a 1994 issue of the *Communications of the ACM* dedicated to AI in the industrial and commercial world, guest editor Toshinori Munakata, while expressing support for the utility of AI in practical applications, made the following cautious remarks with regard to this question:

If we mean AI to be a realization of real human intelligence in the machine, its current state may be considered primitive. In this sense, the name "artificial intelligence" can be misleading. However, when AI is looked at as advanced computing, it can be seen as much more. In the past few years, the repertory of AI techniques has evolved and expanded, and applications have been made in everyday commercial and industrial domains. AI applications today span the realm of manufacturing, consumer products, finance, management and medicine.[189]

These observations point to an important sea change in AI research: going from the original goal of artificial intelligence of building autonomous intelligent artifacts to placing the computational tools used in AI research at the service of applications to aid human intelligence. In fact, as AI began its decline in the 1980s as a result of a large number of unfulfilled promises and developments that fell short of the predicted goals, a new field began to emerge: human-computer interaction (HCI).

The goals involved in AI and HCI are quite different goals, and in light of Munakata's remarks, it is probably accurate to revise figure 9 to depict the history and present situation of AI as shown in figure 11.

According to this new schema, what Winston regarded as a *renaissance* (the opening up of AI to the industrial and commercial world with the advent of expert systems) is actually a *reorientation* in the research program, toward areas where developments of AI acquire greater value. And the nexus of these areas of development are the applications involved in HCI—computer systems that serve as intelligent aids, complementary to human activities and unaccompanied by any claims to constituting intelligent agency on their own.

Search engines now so common on the Web that remember and index texts according to past preferences of users, word processors that correct grammatical errors as they go along while users are producing text, and medical systems that help doctors avoid oversights or lapses of memory in diagnosing their patients are just a few exam-

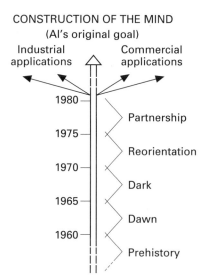

Figure 11
The development of AI—compare figure 9.

ples of such systems. These systems are not designed to initiate searches for their own purposes or produce text of their own accord or diagnose patients by themselves. Nonetheless, their design involves elements of artificial intelligence algorithms and techniques that make them much better aids than a computer program that cannot help but perform the very same task over and over.

But what has become of Turing's dream—AI's original goal of making machines as smart as humans, inherited from the long-standing dream of artificial intelligence? Is this left to dissipate slowly in time while AI research blossoms in commercial applications?[190] Is this the end of the road for the project of artificial intelligence?

The Future of Artificial Intelligence
Alan Turing concluded his classic paper "Computing Machinery and Intelligence," in which he described the Turing test and proposed it as a test case for computer intelligence, with the following remark: "We can only see a short distance ahead, but we can see plenty there that needs to be done."[191] His remark of course remains true, but it also seems fair to say that perhaps what needs to be done lies not in what Turing imagined and prioritized, that is, language comprehension and production, and general-purpose reasoning and game playing, but elsewhere. And it is not obvious why within a broader conception of artificial intelligence, freed from the constraints of AI, a larger theoretical ground on which the technology can be materialized, a more encompassing paradigm in which the original goal of artificial intelligence could not be pursued. At

present, there are in fact research projects that at least declare those kinds of broader aspirations and attempt to begin from the bottom up, by first constructing artificial bodies that are to be progressively equipped with sensorimotor and only then cognitive capacities.

An important fact to notice is the reversal of priorities. Those who declare that they still have their "eyes on the prize" are by and large humanoid projects out of robotics laboratories, both in the United States (such as the Cog and Kismet projects led by the MIT roboticist Rodney Brooks)[192] and in Japan, where private industry (such as Sony and Honda) seems as much invested in the idea as are academic units. And in all these projects, issues such as language understanding, problem solving, planning, and other generalized cognitive capacities are put on the back burner for the prioritization of constructing realistic bodily structures that would allow motor movement and mobility in the systems. This is certainly a significant divergence from Turing's vision and the paradigm of classical AI, and it points in a direction closer to that of the original ambitions of artificial intelligence.

The point here is not whether the Cog project or any other can deliver what it promises in some estimated amount of time. It is, rather, to point out the similarity between the general perspective that some of the contemporary robotics projects are adopting and the perspective offered in this chapter as belonging to the broader project of artificial intelligence. As such, even if the current humanoid projects do not live up to their own aspirations, the direction AI should take can now be depicted as in figure 12.

13 Conclusion

Boundaries of Animals, Humans, and Machines: In the Realm of Cyborgs

So far, we have presented a brief intellectual history of what we have called the grand project of artificial intelligence, its present-day heir AI, and the once-removed cousin cybernetics. In this concluding section, we would like to point to a rather unexpected convergence of the visions of AI and cybernetics in a way that brings us closer than ever to the goal of artificial intelligence itself, though not via the route that AI alone has been pursuing. This brings us to a brief discussion of cyborgs.

One of the issues that has plagued AI research has been the difficulty of interpreting behavior, especially when exhibited by nonbiological machines that fall outside the boundaries of our own species or those close to us in the animal kingdom. This issue has found its most influential formulation in Searle's Chinese Room argument. The interest we find in this argument is not necessarily in the details of its variations and counterarguments. Rather, the Chinese Room argument is symptomatic of a deeper issue, perhaps not necessarily a metaphysical problem itself but an epistemic problem with our visions of ourselves as human beings vis-à-vis the animals as well as the actual and fictional creations of our own, automata.

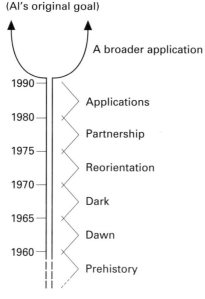

CONSTRUCTION OF THE MIND
(AI's original goal)

A broader application

1990 — Applications
1980 — Partnership
1975 — Reorientation
1970 — Dark
1965 — Dawn
1960 — Prehistory

Figure 12
The development of AI—compare figures 9 and 11.

And it is precisely at this juncture that a discussion of cyborgs becomes relevant because cyborgs blur the boundaries between the fictional and the actual, the natural and the artificial, the human and the machine, and our perception of our own self and that of the other.

Genuine versus Imitated Intelligence: Chinese Room Argument and the Turk Revisited

Recall, in the critique that artificial intelligence is impossible, Searle's distinction between the manipulation of symbolic linguistic structures according to syntactic rules, and access to semantics and meaning that forms the basis of genuine understanding of language. Between these two poles, according to Searle, there lies an unbridgeable gap in principle, which dooms the operator in the Chinese Room to a complete failure of semantic understanding despite full competence over syntactic procedures.

Searle's argument—contrary to the way he himself construes it—is not specifically about language and the syntax-semantics distinction. It is in fact equally applicable to any domain of intelligent behavior. That is, it is in principle always possible to draw a distinction between "genuine X" and "as-if X" for any exhibition of intelligence, be it language comprehension or chess playing or problem solving. This is so because it seems always possible (rightly or wrongly) to imagine from a third-person perspective a particular behavior's being exhibited in the absence of genuine intelligence in the other.

Consider the famous chess-playing automaton, the Turk. While the Turk was touring' Europe and winning chess games against worthy opponents, various observers of these events continually entertained hypotheses in an attempt to explain what in fact must be going on. Despite the lack of any evidence that there was trickery involved, because of von Kempelen's ingenious setup and magicianlike stage presence, scepticism about a mere machine's displaying intelligent behavior on its own was very common.

During the U.S. tour of the Turk, Edgar Allen Poe, a young journalist at the time, wrote in detail about the Turk's chess performance. While he did not offer any alternative explanation, Poe was certain that the Turk could not be playing chess without the interference of human agency and cautioned his readers that they should never assume that a "pure machine" could be behind such an impressive display of intelligence.[193]

Similarly, Robert Willis, another critic of the Turk, asserted that no matter how impressively intelligent the Turk's behavior seemed, it just could not have been genuine. Willis's conviction that there had to be another explanation that did not attribute genuine chess-playing capability to the Turk displayed a kind of scepticism similar to Searle's about conversationalist computers. (The great difference between the two cases was that the Turk was in fact being operated secretly by a human chess player.) According to Willis, "The phenomena of the chess player are inconsistent with the effects of mere mechanism, for however great and surprising the powers of mechanism may be, the movements which spring from it are necessarily limited and uniform. It cannot usurp and exercise the faculties of mind; it cannot be made to vary its operations, so as to meet the ever-varying circumstances of a game of chess."[194]

In short, a purely mechanical device could not play chess. Now notice that such a distinction is generally not considered relevant as an intraspecies issue except in moments of philosophical scepticism where the "problem of other minds" is entertained as a genuine worry. No one ponders about whether any Chinese speaker in the world is in fact an "as-if" or a genuine language user, or whether any human chess player in a competition really understands chess. This is because it is much easier to take the outsider's third-person perspective, and raise scepticism about the genuineness of some seemingly intelligent activity, when "the other" is biologically, psychologically, or emotionally distant from ourselves.

Scepticism about the genuineness of seemingly intelligent behavior has long been an issue in the area of ethology and studies of animal cognition, especially in the face of some embarrassing misattributions of mental capacity, such as in the Clever Hans case. When machines are in question, they are even further removed from human beings, which fuels the scepticism. In this sense, it seems plausible to think that the kind of scepticism Searle expresses in his Chinese Room argument will always remain as an attitude toward AI and artificial intelligence in general.

On the other hand, in almost all our interactions with animals, we take it for granted (unlike Descartes and for good commonsensical reasons) that they in fact enjoy their food, like the company of their human caregivers, or feel pain if hurt, rather than believing that they are just acting "as if" they are hungry, hurt, or content. In that sense, animals are on the other side of the divide, on the side of humans.

What about the future of intelligent machines? If the project of artificial intelligence continues to make progress, as is likely, will we ever reach a time in which there will be genuinely intelligent and autonomous machines living side by side with humans and animals of the biological sphere? Will we ever reach a time in which such machines, if there are to be any, will be considered and treated as intelligent, free of the scepticism that is rallied against most constructions of AI today?

It is not clear whether such questions can be straightforwardly answered or should even be posed in the first place.[195] Nonetheless, AI researchers and roboticists continue to respond by putting forth their predictions. These questions, it should be noted, predate the time of AI. One especially interesting period, for example, is the Futurist era of the 1920s, when skepticism about a future enhanced by the aid or companionship of machines seemed to be entirely replaced by a sense of celebratory exaltation.[196] In fact, the term *robot* comes from a play written in 1920 by the Czech playwright Karel Čapec, who envisioned a utopic future long before digital computers actualized by AI a few decades later. In the play, the manager of the company R.U.R. (Rossum's Universal Robots), which mass-produces robots as slave laborers, makes the following (now quite familiar in the AI literature) pronouncement: "In ten years, Rossum's Universal Robots will produce so much corn, so much cloth, so much everything that things will be practically without price. There will be no poverty. All work will be done by living machines. Everybody will be free from worry and liberated from the degradation of labor. Everybody will live only to perfect himself.... It's bound to happen."[197]

What Does the Future Hold for Artificial Intelligence? Simulacra, Robots, and AI's Ultimate Dream

In his influential work *Simulations*, Jean Baudrillard remarks that "a whole world separates" the two kinds of "artificial beings"—the automaton and the robot. They are both what Baudrillard calls simulacra; however, there is a crucial difference of order between them that makes the automaton a "simulacrum of the first order" and the robot a "simulacrum of the second order":

One is a theatrical counterfeit, a mechanical and clock-like man; technique submits entirely to *analogy* and to the effect of semblance. The other is dominated by the technical principle; the machine overrides all, and with the machine *equivalence* comes too.... The automaton is the *analogy* of man and remains his interlocutor (they play chess together!). The machine is the man's equivalent and annexes him to itself in the unity of its operational process.[198]

Baudrillard's characterization of the automaton is by and large faithful to the automata that have been in production since ancient times, prototypes, if you will, of the ultimate dream of the project of artificial intelligence. The robot, on the other hand, is no longer a prototype imitation; it is the real thing: it has autonomy and its main tenet is no longer just resembling human beings and their behavior but in fact generating and governing its own behavior through its own physical means. As such, the robot is something like what students of artificial intelligence imagine as the ultimate outcome of their efforts—an autonomous and intelligent machine.

In the previous section, we asked, will we ever reach a time in which such machines will exist, and if so, will we ever reach a time in which such machines will gain acceptance and overcome the scepticism of the "mechanical other"? Baudrillard doesn't answer directly, but there are others, from within the field of robotics, who volunteer their answers and the future they envision.

One such pronouncement based on certain quantitative measures (unlike many previous predictions) comes from ongoing work in robotics at Carnegie Mellon University. Hans Moravec offers ambitiously prediction based on the pace of progress in semiconductor technology:

Molecular and quantum computers will be important sooner or later, but humanlike robots are likely to arrive without their help. Research within semiconductor companies, including working prototype chips, makes it quite clear that existing techniques can be nursed along for another decade, to chip features below 0.1 micrometers, memory chips with tens of billions of bits and multiprocessor chips with over 100,000 MIPS. Toward the end of that period, the circuitry will probably incorporate a growing number of quantum interference components. As production techniques for those tiny components are perfected, they will begin to take over the chips, and the pace of computer progress may steepen further. The 100 million MIPS to match human brain power will then arrive in home computers before 2030.[199]

This prediction would have more predictive power if only one of the quantitative factors involved in it were in fact established: "human brain power" in computational terms. Measuring "robot CPU power" in computational terms may be more straightforward, but no one really agrees on exactly how to characterize the human brain as a computing machine so as to produce precise quantitative measurements of its capacity. In the absence of such measures, Moravec's prediction remains inconclusive.

While we think there is no obstacle in principle to the physical construction of artifacts that are equal to humans in intelligence and other cognitive capacities, it is by no means clear when such a possibility might be actualized or under which circumstances. One way to construct intelligent robots would be to find a way to replicate a human body in its minutest detail. Another would be, as the functionalist thinking in philosophy of mind in the recent decades has taught us, to replicate a human body in a different kind of substance but isomorphic to the human body in terms of its functional parts at a level of abstraction and detail relevant to the implementation of our cognitive capacities. Unless a belief in the supernatural is maintained, that is, within a materialist ontology, the replication of bodily constitution would guarantee the replication of mental constitution. That is why we believe in the *possibility* of artificial intelligence.

That doesn't mean, however, that artificial intelligence is destined to become an *actuality*. We may never develop technology to replicate human bodies, either organically or by way of inorganic isomorphs. It is important to note, that even if such a technology were available, it might not give us any clues about the nature of intelligence; we might learn how to replicate bodies without understanding why it is that those kinds of bodies embody intelligence and cognition while others do not. If the drive behind the project of artificial intelligence is not only to produce blind replicas but to come to know how certain kinds of physical embodiment enable a mental life, replicating a human body would be only one half of the ultimate dream of artificial intelligence come true.

If there is anything to be learned from the long-standing history of artificial intelligence and the much shorter history of AI, it seems wildly implausible that this ultimate dream of artificial intelligence will come true any time in the near future. Yet, what's important in Moravec's promissory note is that his futuristic vision is that of artificial intelligence, a future of embodied autonomous and intelligent humanlike robots, rather than the vision of AI, which was not particularly wedded to embodiment as a fundamental element of its research program.

If we grant for the sake of the discussion that the kinds of robots Moravec envisions are indeed constructed at some point in the future, what would remain of the scepticism issue, which seems so central to today's discussions of AI? Deep Blue was a computer system that was finally able to beat Garry Kasparov, a world champion in chess, but it can be seen in the dialogue between Hubert Dreyfus and Daniel Dennett in this volume, that fact by itself has by no means settled the scepticism issue. Why should we think that machines of the future would gain more acceptance when they exhibit intelligent behavior in a number of other domains, or even in all domains that pertain to human behavior?

It seems to us that here the significance of the body and bodily interactions will play a central role and transform the nature of both our conceptions and our interactions with machines substantially. Deep Blue was condemned as being nothing more than a sophisticated "mental automaton" with a superficial behavioral resemblance to a human chess player. It was not embraced as a chess player in its own right, partly because, it seems, it was not the kind of thing that could sit across the table from Kasparov, look at the chess board, move pieces around, appear thoughtful, content, puzzled, tired, or flustered, feel embarrassed if it made an elementary mistake, and so on. We think that the reception Deep Blue received would have been a radically differ-ent one, if it had been that kind of thing.

At present, we have no such actual machines with which to support or demonstrate this point. And perhaps, contrary to what Dreyfus argues, it is superfluous to demand an embarrassable computer in order to accept it as a genuine chess player. In any case, even if no one has been able to construct genuinely mindful robots, there are plenty of cases in mythical and fictional stories of automata and robots that can be employed as informative guides to how we would in fact interact with those kinds of machines if they were actual. Just think of the enormous feelings of sympathy that the Hollywood fictional characters E.T. or R2D2 have generated, or the anxiety embodied in the char-acterization of RoboCop or the first Terminator.

On this point, we concur with a number of writers who emphasize the significance of the body in the conceptualizations of and interactions with machines, from a vari-ety a disciplines, such as Rodney Brooks and Bruce Mazlish. In fact, Baudrillard also seems to be in agreement with this point—he does not explicitly argue for it but seems to take it for granted. The main difference between the automaton and the robot is that in the case of the robot, there is no space for making the appearance-reality distinction or wondering whether what we have is a counterfeit. Rather, "the robot no longer interrogates appearance" Baudrillard says. "Its only truth is in its mechanical efficacy." In the case of the robot, "being and appearance are melted into a common substance of production and work."[200]

What artificial intelligence has rightly had in its vision and what AI has lost sight of, is the significance of bodily constitution and the centrality of embodied and social ex-istence, the capacity for autonomous interaction with humans in regard to the attribu-tion of mental features such as intelligence to the other. Now we come back to an issue we touched upon at the beginning of this chapter. Cybernetics was on the right path in regard to this intuition by holding on to its unified vision of humans, animals, and machines in the context of purposeful behavior. And a new perspective in looking at human-machine relations has recently become the focus of interdisciplinary work, especially in the humanities, where intuitions from artificial intelligence, AI, and cybernetics come together in the discussion of cyborgs, the hybrids of humans and machines, in a way that offers an interesting path for the grand project of artificial intelligence.

Cyborgs: A Cybernetic Twist to the Project of Artificial Intelligence

The concept of a cyborg is first and foremost rooted in the vision of cybernetics, which conceives of a unifying principle about feedback and control that applies equally to the behavior of humans, animals, and machines. The term *cyborg* originated following the recognition of cybernetics as a new discipline, and it stands, true to the spirit of cyber-netics, for "cybernetic organism." An early appearance of the concept, perhaps the first one, occurs in the journal *Astronautics* (January 1960) in an article by Clynes and Kline. They write, "For the exogenously extended organizational complex functioning as an integrated homeostatic system unconsciously, we propose the term 'Cyborg.' The Cyborg deliberately incorporates exogenous components extending the self-regulatory control function of the organism in order to adapt it to new environments."[201]

In the circles of cybernetics and AI research, this characterizations remains by and large true of scientific and engineering practices. As such, work on cyborgs can be seen as an offspring of AI research with a cybernetics twist. The goal is no longer to construct an autonomous intelligent entity but rather, using the tools developed by AI and the fundamental principle of feedback mechanisms that cybernetics is founded upon, to help human beings become human-machine hybrids who are physically, sensorially, and cognitively superior to their nonhybrid counterparts.

It is on the basis of such a view that certain statements about an envisioned future are made, for instance, by Cade in his *Other Worlds Than Ours* (1966): "The 'Cyborg' which is the name ... for animal-machine combinations, seems to be the man of the future."[202] The 1970s science fiction and movie industry can be seen to have picked up on that idea, offering characters such as the Six-Million-Dollar Man, a hero embodying the human potential of the future through his cybernetic prostheses that makes him something like Superman or Captain Picard of *Star Trek: The Next Generation*. More recently, Steven Spielberg picked up a similar theme in his movie *AI*, a more nuanced portrait of a robotic boy who was manufactured to imprint on the purchaser.

The present work on cyborgs proceeds along very much the same lines. Two noteworthy and interesting cases are Kevin Warwick, a professor of cybernetics at the University of Reading and author of *I, Cyborg*,[203] and Steve Mann, professor of engineering at the University of Toronto and co-author of *Cyborg: Digital Destiny and Human Possibility in the Age of the Wearable Computer*.[204]

Warwick was the first person who temporarily turned himself into an experimental cyborg, in August 1998, by having a silicon chip implanted in his left arm that communicated with various computerized systems in his environments for about a week. This was phase 1.0 of his project Cyborg, which, he states, "demonstrated how the principles behind cybernetics could perform in real-life applications."[205] The next phase, Cyborg 2.0, began with an operation in March 2002 for implanting a 100-unit microelectrode array on the median nerve of his left arm, which allowed bidirectional communication between his brain and computer systems. The Cyborg 2.0 Web site describes some of the accomplishments as follows:

A number of experiments have been carried out using the signals detected by the array, most notably Professor Warwick was able to control an electric wheelchair and an intelligent artificial hand, developed by Dr. Peter Kyberd, using this neural interface. In addition to being able to measure the nerve signals transmitted down Professor Warwick's left arm, the implant was also able to create artificial sensation by stimulating individual electrodes within the array.[206]

Warwick's temporary existence as a cyborg came about through having subcutane-
ous implants, whereas Steve Mann has a more portable setup. Resembling a character
out of a science fiction movie, Mann wears a computer system that he developed,
which enhances his ability to view and communicate with remote locations, record
physiological changes in his body, and basically have a computer at his service as an
extension of his body. This system changes the way the world looks to him: he no longer sees the world as he used to see it without his cybernetic paraphernalia. He now
sees the world as filtered through a video camera attached to his head, which gives
him improved illumination conditions but renders his vision two-dimensional. With
his wearable computer, it seems fair to say, he sees the world "through the eyes of a
cyborg." Mann has been wearing this device (and its earlier prototypes) in almost every
waking moment of his life for the last 20 years. Reportedly, when he was forced to take
his cybernetic machinery off at a security checkpoint in an airport, "he became so dis-
oriented without his wearable computer ... that he fell repeatedly while boarding the
plane."[207]

Kevin Warwick and Steve Mann can accurately be characterized the early prototypes
of a cyborg, as this term is understood in cybernetics, AI, and robotics circles. They certainly call themselves cyborgs. Warwick talks about "being born human" but having
now the power to change this,[208] and Mann calls himself a cyborg and talks in his
book about the "profound loneliness" involved in living as a cyborg.[209] As such, they
provide us with a fascinating glimpse of ways in which our embodied existence may
become mutated in the not-so-distant future, which would have a direct impact not
just on our physical but also our mental lives.

The issue of cyborgs has also generated a huge amount of interest and excitement in
the humanities, in a way that AI research did not. We have seen how the historical
evolution of research in AI and cybernetics seems to point in the same direction. The
pressing emphasis on the necessary embodiment and embeddedness of cognitive functions makes clear that the analysis, design, and construction of mechanical or biomechanical artifacts—from humanoid robots to integrative "enhancing" devices, to
nonhuman mechanical companions like Hibo, Sony's robotic dog—lies in the future of
AI. What seems interesting at the present moment is that the parallel trend of rising
interest we observe in many areas in the humanities, most particularly cultural studies,
women's studies, and critical theory, has an almost entirely different angle of approach
to the topic of cyborgs.

In the wake of Foucault's earlier works and of Donna Haraway's "The Cyborg Manifesto," several authors have tried to build a viable political and ethical platform around
a conception of human beings as cyborgs. Anthropologists explored extensively new
ways of understanding cultural developments made possible by technology, in works
such as *Cyborg Babies: From Techno-Sex to Techno-Tots*.[210] Most of the time, the focus
of this work concerned issues of gender boundaries, reproductive medical technology,

genetic manipulations, and so on. And, to a large extent, this development has been pursued independently of AI and cybernetics research, finding its main inspirations in a number of other areas, including recent French theory, popular culture, and gender studies, combined with research results in biotechnology.

Nonetheless, this unexpected convergence between the humanities and AI opens up interesting opportunities for a collaboration that, in our opinion, would be as complicated as it would be mutually beneficial. Besides offering their insights on the centuries-long investigation of the psychological and social aspects of human life, researchers in the humanities could contribute to AI their highly refined sensitivity to ethical and political issues and offer useful points of reference for the assessment of all the artifacts that will likely accompany us in the near future. On the other hand, AI can offer an array of concrete specifications ("theories," "models," "artifacts") at the engineering and theoretical levels, about what it really takes to be and to become a cyborg, which, in turn, critical theorists can consider. The two research efforts are largely compatible, we believe, and may greatly enrich the research agendas and the methodological approaches of both fields.

But how this interaction can take place and proceed is a complicated matter. What does it mean, for example, in the concrete work of the "hard" scientist and her "softer" counterpart the humanities scholar, that they receive mutual inspiration from each other's work and tradition? There is an underlying tension that seems to divide the two approaches and that must be fully exposed if any fruitful interaction is to be possible.

As mentioned, researchers in AI and artificial intelligence interpret cyborgs, androids, and robots quite literally: in all instances, the researcher is focused on the design and construction of concrete artifacts whose design principles can serve as a theoretical model of human nature and whose actual performances can serve a number of practical needs, or perhaps even transform "human nature."[211] When critical theorists speak of cyborgs, on the other hand, the term seems to be purely metaphorical. Donna Haraway writes, "By the late twentieth century, our time, a mythic time, we are all chimeras, theorized and fabricated hybrids of machine and organism; in short, we are cyborgs. The cyborg is our ontology; it gives us our politics. The cyborg is a condensed image of both imagination and material reality, the two joined centers structuring any possibility of historical transformation."[212]

The claim that "we are cyborgs" can be taken to mean that it is possible to think of ourselves as if our bodies and minds were biomechanical artifacts built along the lines suggested by artificial intelligence research. Here, the claim is purely metaphorical, and whether we in fact have electromechanical implants in our bodies that may change the way we sense and make sense of the world does not seem to carry any theoretical weight.[213]

Before proceeding to discuss the consequences of this theoretical mismatch between AI/cybernetics and the humanities, we need to mention a third approach to cyborgs, which has similarities to the two views mentioned, in certain respects, but is ultimately different from both. This novel view comes from the philosopher Andy Clark's book *Natural-Born Cyborgs*.[214] Clark argues that we human beings already are, and have been for quite some time, cyborgs, and that this is a claim to be taken literally. Contrary to the humanities approach, Clark argues that the claim that we are cyborgs is not metaphorical; contrary to AI/cybernetics, he maintains that we are literally cyborgs not by virtue of having electronic or mechanical implants but rather by having been evolved into beings who have the capacity to manipulate symbolic structures in cognition and reasoning, "creatures whose minds are special precisely because they are tailor-made for multiple mergers and coalitions."[215] He writes,

My body is an electronic virgin. I incorporate no silicon chips, no retinal or cochlear implants, no pacemaker. I don't even wear glasses (though I do wear clothes), but I am slowly becoming more and more a cyborg. So are you. Pretty soon, and still without the need for wires, surgery, or bodily alterations, we shall all be kin to the Terminator, to Eve 8, to Cable ... just fill in your favorite fictional cyborg. Perhaps we already are. For we shall be cyborgs not in the merely superficial sense of combining flesh and wires but in the more profound sense of being human-technology symbionts: thinking and reasoning systems whose minds and selves are spread across biological brain and nonbiological circuitry. This book is the story of that transition and of its roots in some of the most basic and characteristic facts about human nature. For human beings, I want to convince you, are *natural-born* cyborgs.[216]

For Clark, quoting Bernard Wolfe, "the human skin is an artificial boundary: the world wanders into it, and the self wanders out of it, traffic is two-way and constant."[217]

This may in fact be true, revealing an important aspect of the nature of our cognitive capacities. And perhaps becoming a cyborg-with-an-implant would be more or less an extension of this conception of a "natural-born cyborg."[218] But the disagreement between the AI/cybernetics and the humanities approaches to cyborgs still remains, and we find it an important issue that is in fact symptomatic of a deeper disagreement between these, as C. P. Snow called them, "two cultures."[219]

Cyborg: A Mere Metaphor?

If the claim that we are cyborgs is ultimately a metaphor, the role of people transmuted via electromechanical implants or devices, like Warwick and Mann, will also be no more than metaphorical, and as such, no different from the role of science fiction characters or salient cultural tropes like Bladerunner, Neuromancer, or Terminator. Under this reading, there does not seem to be much space for the fact that Terminator is a fictional character but Warwick is an actual person to hold any theoretical significance.

But, of course, it is ultimately on the basis of this very difference that AI and cybernetics invest their efforts: they see themselves as being, and they are after all, in the business of constructing physical artifacts or hybrid biological organisms. So, if the work on cyborgs in the humanities were blind to the actual research that goes on in AI and cybernetics, or entirely uninterested in it, the prospect of any interaction between these two fields would be off to a poor start.[220]

If all that AI and companion disciplines have to offer are analogies, then the humanists are unlikely to engage in any serious debate with the scientists or to contribute anything to their research. Researchers in critical theory and related fields would have to wait for the models to come, and then pick and choose which ones inspire them or which they find unpalatable. Conversely, researchers in artificial intelligence would look at the work being done in the humanities, as has sometimes been the case, with the slightly bemused expression of parents admiring children playing dress-up. The reaction of Allen Newell provides a perfect example of this deflationist and ultimately self-defeating attitude: the serious theoretical work is done by AI researchers. AI will provide the correct theory of human psychology, Newell maintains, and the humanists would just be playing with concepts that are not bound to be very fruitful and may be excused only if they don't take themselves too seriously. Better still, they should follow the scientists' lead and try to apply the rigorous insights scientists provide to their own disciplines.

We think the study of cyborgs can, despite these potential avenues of failure, be turned into a site of fruitful exchange, which can go beyond the "two cultures" divide. This is in fact the note on which we conclude this chapter. But first, a deeper look at the sources of the difficulties between the sciences and the humanities.

The Two Cultures through the Heideggerian Lens

The potentially imperialist threat that all the appeals for better integration between the humanities and the sciences contain is certainly not new; nor does it begin with C. P. Snow's discussion of the "two cultures." It dates (at least) to the turn of the nineteenth century, when the spectacular advances in the exact sciences of the previous decades had prompted a general reorganization of all fields of inquiry and the formation of new hierarchies. Martin Heidegger, however, is one of the few philosophers who saw in cybernetics the discipline that would assume the leading role in the general reorganization and act, in fact, as the "liquidator" of the humanities in general and more specifically of philosophy. In 1965 he wrote,

Philosophy dissolves itself into autonomous sciences, [and] in its own dissolution, is replaced by a new kind of unification between the new and the old sciences.... The new science that unifies, in a new sense of the word 'unity,' all the different sciences is called cybernetics. As far as gaining full clarity about its concepts and penetrating in other disciplinary spheres, cybernetics is still in its infancy. But cybernetics' dominion is guaranteed, because cybernetics itself is controlled by a power that impresses the character of planning and control not only upon the sciences, but upon every single human activity.[221]

For Heidegger, the qualifying feature of the cybernetic approach is the concept of control. Cybernetics' goal is to provide a perspective upon the world (and its inhabitants, living or nonliving) as a series of controllable processes. This is why he stresses that the epistemological unification that cybernetics provides is radically different from the past. Throughout the long history of Western culture, it was philosophy's traditional role to divide reality into different regions (the physical, the psychical, the biological), to delegate to the concrete sciences the detailed empirical researches, and then to provide the overall synthesis that would unify the single results into a coherent outlook. The advent of cybernetics changes everything, Heidegger claims, because the sciences conceive of themselves in purely *technical* terms: "Their categories are representations of operational models. The truth of the scientific categories is measured by the effect that they produce within the progress of research. Scientific truth is posited as equivalent to the efficacy of these effects."[222]

The inevitable result of this transformation (which, according to Heidegger's analysis, is not to be imputed to cybernetics per se, but to the long historical process which culminates in it) is that philosophy becomes superfluous. It would not even be meaningful to say that philosophy (or, we may add, the humanities in general) are constantly catching up to the natural sciences, because both philosophy and the humanities are useless within a worldview geared toward the complete technical control of nature (and its inhabitants).

Heidegger answered the challenge moved by the reduction of the world to a repository for technical domination by suggesting that philosophy reject once and for all its own, old imperialist ambitions. "Thought," as Heidegger prefers to call this radically nontechnical effort, should proceed backward, before the establishment of philosophy and the sciences, to (re)discover the intrinsic finitude of human, historical life, the finitude of thought, and the finitude of its object.[223]

Revisiting the Challenge: "Turtles All the Way Down?"

We suggest that the emphasis on cyborgs may be alternatively interpreted as an effort to provide a different answer to the challenge that Heidegger saw embodied in cybernetics, and that may acquire a renewed urgency, 40 years later, if, as we believe, the coming years will witness a renewed convergence between artificial intelligence and cybernetics under the aegis of embodiment and embeddedness. Perhaps the interpretation of the notion of cyborg in the sense in which the term is used by authors like Haraway and others is not only uninformative from the standpoint of ongoing research in AI and cybernetics; taking cyborgs as a pure metaphor may also be seriously misleading. For the cyborg can become a metaphor of a human being only if there is an external standpoint that allows us to tell which is which, *independently of all metaphors*.

One may perhaps be tempted to claim that this external, objective viewpoint is precisely what science has to offer. Or one may say, going along with the older tradition championed by Dreyfus, that it is philosophy's role to provide the external viewpoint that will sort out the metaphors from the real McCoy. But as we tried to hint in our discussion of Edwards's "closed world," this is precisely the point that most recent work in cultural theory (and in other fields as well) firmly rejects. As for Edwards's analysis of the development of AI, many, decidedly systemic, analyses of the history of science produced in the last 30 years (mostly in the wake of Foucault's work on the development of medicine and psychiatry) argue that the goals, concepts, methodologies, and aims of most disciplines can only be understood within the complex political, economic, and social systems within which they arose. Scientific concepts, to take this position to the extreme, are no less metaphorical than the metaphors they originate. Which does not mean that they are fictional but that they only make sense within the richly textured contexts in which they operate and constantly evolve.

In terms of the future of the cyborgs debate, only history will tell in which direction it will move, whether age-old unifying tendencies or a frankly agonistic relationship will prevail. It is reasonable to expect, nonetheless, that a good deal of effort will be spent arguing over what constitutes a proper definition, and who or what should provide it. Echoing Haraway's view, Chris Hables Gray states, in his collected volume *The Cyborg Handbook*, that it is not only the Terminator that should be conceived of as a cyborg. From the grandmother who wears a prosthetic hearing device to any child who has been vaccinated by having foreign organisms introduced into his body, we are all and equally cyborgs.[224] And this way of putting things brings to light again the tension that can now be embodied in the question of whether there is a principled distinction that is to be recognized between the grandmother with the hearing aid or the vaccinated child, or the Terminator, or better yet, people like Kevin Warwick and Steve Mann, the self-declared cyborgs. Or is this a distinction that is to be rejected, either because it offers nothing of theoretical interest or because it incorporates precisely the kind of presuppositions that Haraway's way of construing cyborgs is aimed at undermining.

If, as the story goes, it's turtles all the way down, it follows that the only possibility for the elaborating an ethical and political paradigm must be found by looking at the resources afforded by the system within which the theorists happen to live and by exploiting their potential for theoretical and practical action.[225] If this is the case, then the interaction between the humanities and artificial intelligence becomes at the same time more conflictual and more engaged (in fact, more engaged *because* more conflictual). A quick look at the quest for images would no longer be adequate. Instead, it would have to be replaced by a specific analysis of the concrete models, theories, and artifacts (and their contexts) that examines their potentially dangerous effects as well their potential contributions to the specific agenda that the humanities set. Thus a direct, specific and, we suggest, even technical engagement would be the direct consequence of the "turtles interpretation."

However, if there is in fact an important distinction between Warwick or Mann, on one hand, and the grandmother, on the other, perhaps it is not "turtles all the way down" after all. If so, it remains an open question whether this should be considered a defeat for the humanities, which would make true Heidegger's darkest prophecies by conceding dominance to the scientific program of AI and cybernetics research.

Our closing observation is that this does not have to be the case. The fact that the cyborg literature contains arguments that have different utilities in the two camps does not entail that the humanities are not, or should not be, interested in a distinction between Steve Mann and the grandmother. Nor does it follow that the recognition of this distinction is detrimental to the humanities. This is because different resources to utilize this very distinction in the sciences versus the humanities, and consequently different potentials for critically examining questions about boundaries between humans, animals, and machines, or between the natural and the artificial, are available on the two sides.

As a consequence, neither discipline is put in an ancillary role. As the scientific agenda is the provisional equilibrium point, as it were, of a complex set of interactions in the environment at large, so is the agenda of the humanities. Neither, it seems, is situated in a privileged position.[226] And at the present juncture in the long-standing history of the grand project of artificial intelligence, this is, we believe, as it should be.

Humanities and Sciences in the Posthuman Age

In her book *How We Became Posthuman: Virtual Bodies in Cybernetics, Literature, and Informatics*, Katherine Hayles, following a critical account of informatics and cybernetics that rightly emphasizes the centrality of embodiment to human consciousness in a way she maintains is missed by these disciplines, turns to a conclusion about the "posthuman." "Posthuman" is a new, historically specific notion coming to replace the notion of "human,"[227] and, she observes, it is at present under competing theoretical currents, where Hayles own work is situated as one that "understands human life is embedded in a material world of great complexity" and an attempt, in the "construction of the posthuman," to "keep disembodiment from being rewritten, once again, into prevailing concepts of subjectivity."[228]

Putting aside this and various other points of agreement (as well as disagreement) we have with Hayles's rich account, we concur with her observation that the present is an important juncture in which conceptualizations of the human being vis-à-vis machines and their respective boundaries are undergoing important theoretical revisions. As such, it is a crucial time to take part in this transformative process.

The best possible time to contest for what the posthuman means is now, before the trains of thought it embodies have been laid down so firmly that it would take dynamite to change them. Although some current versions of the posthuman point toward the anti-human and the apocalyptic, we can craft others that will be conducive to the long-range survival of humans and of the other life-forms, biological and artificial, with whom we share the planet and ourselves.[229]

It is our conviction that this period of theoretical transformation in the understanding of humans and machines, in the presence of ongoing empirical research in AI and robotics for the construction of intelligent autonomous artifacts, and the emergence of new technologies that enable the cybernetic transfusion of humans with machines, requires the recognition of a joint subject matter shared by both the sciences and the humanities, and the participation of both sides in this deservedly broad project for any informed fruitful outcome. The differences between the ways in which research is conducted and questions are pursued in these "two cultures" can be appreciated only if the theory, the technology, and the empirical practices are equally understood and heeded.

It is precisely in this sense that we see the cyborgs discourse as a site of inquiry presenting an exciting and novel opportunity: the potential as well as intellectual obligation for a much more direct, close engagement between the sciences and the humanities, dictated by the very nature of the rich and complex subject matter itself.

Notes

1. Some of the recent work that addresses boundaries and triangulation with respect to humans, animals, and machines includes James Sheehan and Morton Sosna, eds., *The Boundaries of Humanity: Humans, Animals, Machines* (Berkeley: University of California Press, 1991); Bruce Mazlish, *The Fourth Discontinuity: The Co-evolution of Humans and Machines* (New Haven, Conn.: Yale University Press, 1993); Alan Wolfe, *The Human Difference: Animals, Computers, and the Necessity of Social Science* (Berkeley: University of California Press, 1993); Alice Rayner, "Cyborgs and Replicants: On the Boundaries," *Discourse* 16 (no. 3, 1994): 124–143; Harriet Ritvo, *The Platypus and the Mermaid, and Other Figments of the Classifying Imagination* (Cambridge, Mass.: Harvard University Press, 1997); Laurie Shannon, "Nature's Bias: Courses, Kinds, and the Zoographies of Early Modern Knowledge," forthcoming; Barbara Herrnstein Smith, "Animal Relatives, Difficult Relations," forthcoming in *Differences: A Journal of Feminist Cultural Studies* 15 (no. 1, 2004), special issue, "Man and Beast."

In this context, it is also interesting to look at the ways in which nature (genetics), culture, and environment are constantly reshaping our own boundaries and constitution within an evolutionary framework. Some of the most thought-provoking and broadly cast work in this area can be found in Susan Oyama's writings, especially *The Ontogeny of Information: Developmental Systems and Evolution* (Cambridge: Cambridge University Press, 1986) and *Evolution's Eye: A Systems View of the Biology-Culture Divide* (Durham, N.C.: Duke University Press, 2002).

2. Hubert Dreyfus, *Alchemy and Artificial Intelligence* (Santa Monica, Calif.: RAND Corp., 1965). This technical report later turned into Dreyfus's influential books *What Computers Can't Do* (New York: Harper, 1972) and *What Computers Still Can't Do* (Cambridge, Mass.: MIT Press, 1992).

3. A different kind of encounter, worthy of mention here, has occurred in Aaron Sloman's work. Sloman is a philosopher turned computer scientist, and he has sustained a view, from very early on, that pointed out how crucial are the relations between philosophy and computer science/AI, in both directions. See, for example, Sloman, *The Computer Revolution in Philosophy: Philosophy, Science and Models of Mind* (Hassocks, U.K.: Harvester Press, 1978); ⟨http://www.cs.bham.ac.uk/research/cogaff/crp/⟩. Perhaps because, unlike Dreyfus, he is professionally considered an AI insider rather than a philosopher, Sloman's writings, which have maintained more of an upbeat note than Dreyfus's, do not seem to have created a welcoming effect of philosophy in the AI community.

4. Harold A. Abramson, *Problems of Consciousness: Transactions of the Macy Foundation Conference*, March 1954 (New York: Josiah Macy, Jr. Foundation, 1955). For a critical account of the Macy Conferences and the development of cybernetics as a consequence, see Katherine E. Hayles, *How We Became Posthuman: Virtual Bodies in Cybernetics, Literature, and Informatics* (Chicago: University of Chicago Press, 1999).

5. Norbert Wiener, *Cybernetics, or Control and Communication in the Animal and the Machine* (Cambridge, Mass.: MIT Press, 1965).

6. Avron Barr and Edward Feigenbaum, eds., *The Handbook of Artificial Intelligence*, vol. 1 (Los Altos, Calif.: Kaufmann, 1981).

7. See, for example, Joseph Greenwood, *The Pneumatics of Hero of Alexandria*, ed. Benner Woodcroft (London: Macdonald, 1971).

8. An account of the history of automata making in Europe and North America can be found in Gaby Wood, *Edison's Eve: A Magical History of the Quest for Mechanical Life* (New York: Knopf, 2002).

9. Al-Jazari, *The Book of Knowledge of Ingenious Mechanical Devices*, trans. Donald Hill (Dordrecht: D. Reidel, 1974).

10. John Cohen, *Human Robots in Myth and Science* (London: Allen and Unwin, 1966), 24–25.

11. Tom Standage, *The Turk: The Life and Times of the Famous Eighteenth-Century Chess-Playing Machine* (New York: Walker, 1995), 27–28.

12. While the chess-playing Turk gave the impression of acting of its own accord, that was nothing but a façade consisting of a clever engineering design combined with the tricks of a stage magician. The Turk continued to fool its audiences for many decades, in Europe as well as the United States. But the important point here is the impression it engenders in the audience through its behavior and, a few skeptics notwithstanding, the ease with which mental capacities are attributed to it on that basis.

13. Wiener writes about the initial need for a term that would unify the multidisciplinary efforts of their group and the selection of the name cybernetics as follows: "Thus as far back as four years ago, the group of scientists about Dr. Rosenbluth and myself had already become aware of the essential unity of the set of problems centering about communication, control, and statistical me-

chanics, whether in the machine or in living tissue. On the other hand, we were seriously hampered by the lack of unity of the literature concerning these problems, and by the absence of any common terminology, or even of a single name for the field.... We have decided to call the entire field of control and communication theory, whether in the machine or in the animal, by the name *Cybernetics.*" Wiener, *Cybernetics*, 19.

14. Norbert Wiener, *The Human Use of Human Beings: Cybernetics and Society*, (Garden City, N.Y.: Doubleday, 1954), 26–27.

15. Warren McCulloch, "*Mysterium Iniquitatis* of Sinful Man Aspiring into the Place of God," *The Scientific Monthly* 80 (no. 1, 1955): 39.

16. Hans Moravec, *Mind Children: The Future of Robot and Human Intelligence* (Cambridge, Mass.: Harvard University Press, 1988), 16.

17. For a good conceptual introduction to AI, see John Haugeland, *Artificial Intelligence: The Very Idea* (Cambridge, Mass.: MIT Press, 1985); and Jack Copeland, *Artificial Intelligence: A Philosophical Introduction* (Oxford: Blackwell, 1994); for a standard textbook, Stuart J. Russell and Peter Norvig, *Artificial Intelligence: a Modern Approach*, 2d ed. (Upper Saddle River, N.J.: Prentice Hall, 2003); for a retrospective compilation of benchmark articles in AI research, "Artificial Intelligence in Perspective," special issue, *Artificial Intelligence* 59 (1993). Influential critiques of the AI paradigm are given in Dreyfus, *What Computers Can't Do* and *What Computers Still Can't Do*; John Searle, "Minds, Brains, and Programs," *Behavioral and Brain Sciences* 3 (1980): 417–424; John Searle, *Minds, Brains, and Science* (Cambridge, Mass.: Harvard University Press, 1984); John Searle, *The Rediscovery of the Mind*, (Cambridge, Mass.: MIT Press, 1992).

18. While intelligence was a fundamental element in AI research from the beginning, autonomy came to occupy a central position through the emergence of a related field, artificial life, as a necessary component of the creation of artificial intelligence. Tim Smithers emphasizes this point as follows: "An agent is autonomous if it is able to cope with all the consequences of its actions to which it is subjected while remaining viable as a task-achieving agent in the world in which it operates. For any particular agent acting to achieve some particular task in some particular environment, its autonomy will be bounded: it will not be able to cope with all possible consequences of its actions. Autonomy is thus a matter of degree. It is, however, a necessary prerequisite for intelligent behavior: The more or less autonomous an agent, the more or less its potential for intelligent behavior. The questions of how autonomous an agent is, how it behaves intelligently, and what the bounds are on its intelligent behavior, are therefore all closely related. I see the investigation of autonomous behavior by building robots as properly a part of AI." Tim Smithers, "Are Autonomous Agents Information Processing Systems?" in *The Artificial Life Route to Artificial Intelligence: Building Embodied, Situated Agents*, ed. Luc Steels and Rodney Brooks (Mahwah, N.J.: Erlbaum, 1995), 123–124.

19. Allen Newell, "Intellectual Issues in the History of Artificial Intelligence," in *The Study of Information: Interdisciplinary Messages*, ed. Fritz Machlup and Una Mansfield (New York: Wiley, 1983).

20. *Encyclopedia Britannica*, "Automaton" entry.

21. See *The Pneumatics of Hero of Alexandria*, trans. Joseph G. Greenwood, ed. Bennet Woodcroft (London: Taylor, Walton and Maberly, 1851; reprinted New York: Elsevier, 1971).

22. *Pythagore et la philosophie pythagoricienne. Contenant les fragments de Philolaüs et d'Archytas*, ed. A. Chaignet (1873; Bruxelles: Culture et Civilisation, 1968).

23. Al-Jazari, *The Book of Knowledge of Ingenious Mechanical Devices*, trans. Donald Hill (Dordrecht: Reidel, 1974); see also Donald Hill, *Islamic Science and Engineering* (Edinburgh: Edinburgh University Press, 1976). Al-Jazari's drawings and manuscripts can be viewed at the Topkapi Museum in Istanbul.

24. Quoted in T. A. Heppenheimer, "Man Makes Man," in *Robotics*, ed. Marvin Minsky (New York: Anchor Press, 1985), 69.

25. For more information, see the museum's Web site, ⟨http://www.imss.firenze.it/⟩.

26. In a letter to Regius, Descartes writes, "[Y]ou seem to make a greater difference between living and lifeless things than there is between a clock or other automaton on the one hand, and a key or sword or non-self-moving appliance on the other. I do not agree. Since 'self-moving' is a category with respect to all machines that move of their own accord, which excludes others that are not self-moving, so 'life' may be taken as a category which includes the forms of all living things." René Descartes, *The Philosophical Writings of René Descartes*, trans. J. Cottingham, R. Stoothof, and D. Murdoch, vol. 3 (Cambridge: Cambridge University Press, 1991), 214; Letter to Regius, June 1642, AT III, 566. And in *Passions of the Soul*, he states: "Let us note that death never occurs through the absence of the soul, but only because one of the principal parts of the body decays. And let us recognize that the difference between the body of a living man and that of a dead man is just like the difference between, on the one hand, a watch or other automaton (that is, a self-moving machine) when it is wound up and contains in itself the corporeal principle of the movements for which it is designed, together with everything else required for its operation; and, on the other hand, the same watch or machine when it is broken and the principle of its movement ceases to be active." *The Philosophical Writings of René Descartes*, vol. 1 (1985), 329; *The Passions of the Soul*, Part I, §6, AT XI, 331.

27. For the full account, see Eduard Jan Dijksterhuis, *The Mechanization of the World Picture* (Oxford: Oxford University Press, 1961).

28. Christiaan Boudri, *What Was Mechanical about Mechanics: The Concept of Force between Metaphysics and Mechanics from Newton to Lagrange* (Dordrecht: Kluwer, 2002), 236–237.

29. The historian Robert Shoefield, who gives an extensive analysis of the mechanistic perspective dominant in this era, which he calls "an age of reason," concurs and concludes that "Newton's theory of matter and action ... pervades, ... consciously or unconsciously, most of the scientific writing of the eighteenth century." Robert Shoefield, *Mechanism and Materialism* (Princeton, N.J.: Princeton University Press, 1970), 4.

30. Wiener, *The Human Use of Human Beings*, 21–22.

31. Margaret Osler, *Divine Will and the Mechanical Philosophy* (Cambridge: Cambridge University Press, 1994), 178.

32. Osler puts this point as follows: "Removing all activity from matter and carefully separating matter from spirit—a move taken by all the mechanical philosophers—led to a consideration of the human soul, which most of them removed from the physical realm entirely. (One notable exception, of course, was Hobbes.) In regarding the soul as the form of the person, the Aristotelians and the Scholastics had been able to avoid any danger of slipping into materialism. Having eliminated the traditional concept of form and having declared matter to be inert and self-subsisting, the mechanical philosophers faced the problem of establishing the existence of an immaterial, immortal soul. Their discussions of the human soul established the limits of mechanization and provided a bulwark against the bugbear of materialism." *Divine Will and the Mechanical Philosophy*, 179.

In addition to Hobbes, we need to mention La Mettrie here as another notable exception to the substance dualist philosophers.

33. For an elaboration of the mind as a "virtual von Neumann computer based on a parallel mechanism," see Daniel Dennett, *Consciousness Explained* (Boston: Little, Brown, 1991).

34. Julien Offray de La Mettrie, *Machine Man and Other Writings*, trans. Ann Thompson (1748; Cambridge: Cambridge University Press, 1996), 28.

35. Rodney A. Brooks, *Flesh and Machines: How Robots Will Change Us* (New York: Pantheon Books, 2002), 173.

36. Thomas Hobbes, *Elements of Philosophy Concerning Body*, in Thomas Hobbes, *English Works* (Aalen: Scientia Verlag, 1966) vol. 1, 3, 5.

37. Stephen Schiffer, "Thought and Language," in *A Companion to the Philosophy of Mind*, ed. Samuel Guttenplan (London: Blackwell, 1996), 589.

38. Descartes, "Discourse on Method," in *The Philosophical Writings of René Descartes*, vol. 1 (1985), 139.

39. Descartes, "Discourse on Method," 140.

40. René Descartes, "Letter to Henry Moore," *Philosophical Letters*, trans. A. Kenny (Oxford: Clarendon Press, 1970), 245.

41. Stefano Franchi, "Endgames: Game and Play at the End of Philosophy," Ph.D. diss., Stanford University, Palo Alto, Calif., 1997.

42. This happened in 1997 when the world chess champion, Garry Kasparov, was defeated by IBM's Deep Blue. The practical and theoretical implications of Deep Blue's victory for AI's goals are hotly debated, though. For more details, see the debate between Hubert Dreyfus and Daniel Dennett in this volume.

While we talk in detail about the theoretical presuppositions and ramifications of chess in AI, for reference here is a brief chronology of the evolution of computer chess research:

1947:   Turing: paper-and-pen simulation of the execution of a chess program.

1949:   Shannon: plan of action for computers to be programmed to play chess. Not clear if technology would be available and when.

1956:   Maniac I, at Los Alamos, 11 K operations per second on a 6 × 6 board. First documented running chess program.

1957:   IBM programmed an IBM 704 to run the first full-fledged chess-playing program.

1957:   Herbert Simon said that within 10 years, a digital computer would be the world's chess champion.

1958:   A chess program beat a novice human player for the first time.

1959:   Some of the first chess computer programmers predicted that a chess computer would be world chess champion before 1970.

1963:   World chess champion Botvinnik predicted that a Russian chess playing program would eventually defeat the world champion.

1966:   Mac Hack VI (written by Richard Greenblatt at MIT) was the first chess computer to play in a tournament. The program entered the 1966 Massachusetts Amateur Championship, scoring 1 draw and 4 losses for a USCF rating of 1243.

1968:   International Master David Levy made a $3,000 bet that no chess computer would beat him in 10 years. He won his bet.

1970:   The first all-computer championship was held in New York and won by Chess 3.0, a program written by David Slate, Larry Atkin, and Keith Gorlen at Northwestern University. Six programs had entered the competition.

1974:   World Correspondence Champion Hans Berliner wrote his Ph.D. dissertation on "Chess Computers as Problem Solving."

1975:   Grand master David Bronstein used the endgame database in Kaissa to win an adjourned game in a tournament in Vilnius.

1977:   The first microcomputer chess playing machine, Chess Challenger, was created.

1977:   Michael Stean became the first grand master to lose to a computer; it was a blitz game.

1977:   Belle was the first computer system to use custom-design chips to increase its playing strength. It increased its search speed from 200 positions per second to 160,000 positions per second (8 ply). The chess computer was built by Ken Thompson.

1977:   The International Computer Chess Association (ICCA) was founded. It was renamed International Computer Games Association (ICGA) in 2002.

1980:   Edward Fredkin created the Fredkin Prize for Computer Chess. The award came with $100,000 for the first program to beat a reigning world chess champion.

1983:   The first chess microcomputer beat a master in tournament play. Belle became the first chess computer to attain a master's rating when, in October, its USCF rating was 2203.

1985:   Hitech achieved a performance rating of 2530. It was the first computer to have a rating over 2400.

1985:   Garry Kasparov played 15 of the top chess computers in Hamburg, Germany, and won every game, with the score of 32–0.

1988:   Deep Thought and grand master Tony Miles shared first place in the U.S. Open championship. Deep Thought had a 2745 performance rating.

1988: Hitech won the Pennsylvania State Chess Championship after defeating International Master Ed Formanek (2485). Hitech defeated grand master Arnold Denker in a match. Hitech became the first chess computer to be rated grand master strength.

1989: Garry Kasparov defeated Deep Thought in a match by winning two games. Deep Thought developers claimed a computer would be world chess champion in three years.

1989: The Carnegie Mellon team that developed Deep Thought moved to IBM and started to work on Deep Blue.

1996: Garry Kasparov beat IBM's Deep Blue chess computer 4–2 in Philadelphia. Deep Blue won the first game, becoming the first computer ever to beat a world chess champion at tournament level under serious tournament conditions. Deep Blue was calculating 50 billion positions every 3 minutes.

1997: Deep Blue defeated Garry Kasparov in a six-game match held in New York. This was the first time a computer defeated a reigning world champion in a classical chess match. Deep Blue had 30 IBM RS-6000 SP processors coupled to 480 chess chips. It could evaluate 200 million moves per second.

1997: The $100,000 Fredkin Award went to the inventors of Deep Blue—Feng Hsu, Murray Campbell, and Joseph Hoane, of IBM.

2002: Kramnik drew a match with Deep Fritz in Bahrain with a 4–4 score. Kramnik won games 2 and 3. Deep Fritz won games 5 and 6. The rest of the games (1, 7, and 8) were drawn.

2003: Kasparov played Deep Junior 7 in New York. The match ended in a draw. Kasparov won game 1. Deep Junior won game 3, the other games were drawn. This was the first time that a man/machine competition was sanctioned by FIDE, the World Chess Federation. Deep Junior can evaluate 3 million moves a second, and positions fifteen moves deep.

2003: Kasparov played X3dFritz in New York. The match was tied 2–2. Fritz won the 2nd game. Kasparov won the third game. Games 1 and 4 were drawn. It was the first official world chess championship in total virtual reality, played in 3-D.

2003: The top chess computers (and their ratings) were Shredder 7.04 (2810), Shredder 7.0 (2770), Fritz 8.0 (2762), Deep Fritz 7.0 (2761), Fritz 7.0 (2742), Shredder 6.0 (2724), and Chess Tiger 15.0 (2720).

43. Allen Newell and Herbert Simon, *Human Problem Solving* (Englewood Cliffs, N.J.: Prentice Hall, 1972), 664.

44. For a review of the most important results in AI and game-playing programs, see *Artificial Intelligence*, 134 (2002), a special issue completely devoted to the topic. See also the Web site of the ICGA, the International Computer Games Association (formerly International Computer Chess Association, ICCA) at ⟨http://www.cs.unimaas.nl/icga/⟩ and the *ICGA Journal*, available from the same site.

On checkers, see A. L. Samuel, "Some Studies on Machine Learning using the Game of Checkers," *IBM Journal of Research and Development* 3 (July 1959): 211–229, also published in Edward Feigenbaum and Julian Feldman, *Computers and Thought* (San Francisco: McGraw-Hill, 1963), 71–105. Interest in checkers has recently been revived by the exploits of a team based at the University of Alberta, Canada, whose program, Chinook, is the first world human-machine checkers champion (it won the title in a tournament open to both "human and nonhuman forms of intelligence"). See Jonathan Schaeffer, *One Jump Ahead: Challenging Supremacy in Checkers* (New York: Springer, 1997).

The literature on computer chess is immense. For a brief synopsis on the history of chess-playing programs, see L. Stephen Coles, "Computer Chess: The Drosophila of AI," *AI Expert* 9 (April 1994): 25–32. The first studies on chess-playing machines were done by Turing and Shannon, who provided the basic framework, later substantially enriched by Herbert Simon, who wrote the first actually running program in 1955 (with Allen Newell and Cliff Shaw), first at the RAND Corporation and later at Carnegie Mellon; see Allen Newell, J. C. Shaw, and Herbert Simon, "Chess-Playing Programs and the Problem of Complexity," *IBM Journal of Research and Development* 2 (October 1958): 320–335, also published in Feigenbaum and Feldman, *Computers and Thought*, 39–70. Computer chess has now become almost a subdiscipline of computer science, with a specialized journal, conferences, and so on, although it does not enjoy any longer an "exemplary status." For a brief history of the development, see Newell and Simon, *Human Problem Solving*, and David E. Welsh, *Computer Chess* (Dubuque, Iowa: W. C. Brown, 1984). For a more recent assessment of the possible evolution of the field, see Mikhail Donskoy and Jonathan Schaeffer, "Perspectives on Falling from Grace," in *Chess, Computers, and Cognition*, ed. T. Anthony Marsland and Jonathan Schaeffer (Berlin: Springer-Verlag, 1990), and Herbert Simon and Jonathan Schaeffer, "The Game of Chess," in *Handbook of Game-Theory with Economic Applications*, ed. Robert J. Aumann and Sergiu Hart (Amsterdam: Elsevier, 1992), vol. 1, 1–17. The Hanoi tower gathered attention only later. In 1958, Simon learned of its use in experimental psychology and started to work on it, with Allen Newell, to test heuristic search capabilities of their early programs. See Herbert Simon, *Models of My Life* (New York: Basic Books, 1991).

45. Herbert Simon, one of those most responsible for chess's popularity, used the analogy widely since the early 1960s, when AI's interest in chess was still at its peak. He reports that he used it routinely in the question-and-answer sessions after his talks, to defend the study of chess and other games as a worthwhile research project. See Simon, *Models of My Life*, 327. In 1994, in a private communication, Simon reported that he was not sure whether he or Newell had actually coined the analogy. According to John McCarthy (personal communication), the analogy itself might have been first proposed by Alexander Kronrod, then the head of the group that wrote the Soviet chess program at the Institute of Theoretical and Experimental Physics in Moscow in the period 1965–1968. Kronrod, however, might have gotten it from Herbert Simon, McCarthy acknowledges.

46. *Republic*, 533b, in Plato, *Complete Works*, ed. John M. Cooper (Indianapolis: Hackett Publishing, 1997), 1149.

47. Aristotle's example of courage as the virtuous mean between fear and excessive fearlessness is drawn from *Nicomachean Ethics*, trans. Terence Irwin (Indianapolis: Hackett Publishing, 1985), 46 (1107b1-5); see book 7, especially chapter 6 (1149b25 ff.) for a discussion of the relationship between reason and emotions (feelings).

48. The analysis of pre-predicative intentionality pioneered by Edmund Husserl and extended by Martin Heidegger and Maurice Merleau-Ponty moved in this direction. Indeed, Hubert Dreyfus's critique of classic AI started from the latter tradition.

49. This may explain why neither Shannon nor Turing thought it important to actually write the programs; also, why the crucial concept of heuristics rules, the technique that would allow a dramatic improvement in the programs' performances, was missing, in fact was the only missing element from Shannon's design principle. Alan Turing's insights on computers' playing chess and his experiments with hand simulations are presented in Bertram Bowden, *Faster Than Thought, a Symposium on Digital Computing Machines* (London: Pitman, 1953), 288–295; Claude Shannon, "A Chess-Playing Machine," *Scientific American* 182 (February 1950): 48–51, also published in *The World of Mathematics*, ed. James Newman (New York: Simon and Schuster, 1956), vol. 4, 2124–2133; Claude Shannon, "Game-Playing Machines," *Journal of the Franklin Institute* 260 (no. 6, 1955): 447–453, also published in Claude Shannon, *Collected Papers* (New York: IEEE Press, 1993).

50. The assumption was historically grounded: solving equations had been computers' main task since Charles Babbage proposed to build his analytical engine. In the years under consideration, the computation of ballistic tables for use in naval artillery had been one of the first practical applications of electronic computers.

51. The history of the interaction between mathematics and chess, on the contrary, predates AI's interest by at least 30 years, and it includes, at least, the contributions by the French mathematician Émile Borel in the 1920s and 1930s. Borel provided the first clear definition of pure and mixed strategies, and proved the minimax theorem for some limiting cases. However, it is John (then Johann) von Neumann who proved the general form of the theorem in 1928, while still at Göttingen. The result had already been shown to hold for chess (which is an instance of a class of games providing an additional constraint, perfect information) by another mathematician belonging to the Hilbert school in Göttingen, Ernst Zermelo, in 1913. Unfortunately, the historical literature on game theory is not that abundant. A detailed reconstruction of the immediate context preceding and following the publication of John von Neumann and Oskar Morgenstern's major work *Theory of Games and Economic Behavior* (Princeton, N.J.: Princeton University Press, 1944) is provided by Robert J. Leonard, "Creating a Context for Game Theory," in *Toward a History of Game Theory*, ed. E. Roy Weintraub (Durham, N.C.: Duke University Press, 1995), 29–76. See also Philip Mirowski, *Machine Dreams* (Cambridge: Cambridge University Press, 2001). See also Émile Borel, "La théorie du jeu et les équations intégrales à noyau symétrique gauche," *Comptes Rendus de l'Académie des Sciences* 173 (1921): 1304–1308; Émile Borel, "Sur les jeux où interviennent l'hasard et l'habilité des joueurs," in *Elements de la théorie des probabilités*, ed. J. Hermann (Paris: Librairie Scientifique, 1924); Ernst Zermelo, "Über eine Anwendung der Mengenlehre auf die Theorie des Schachspiels," in *Proceedings of the Fifth International Congress of Mathematicians* (1913) vol. 2, 501–504; Johann von Neumann, "Zur Theorie des Gesellschaftsspielen," *Mathematische Annalen* 100 (1928): 295–320.

52. Physical realizability, a condition guaranteed by definition for both human and automated chess players, seemed to play a crucial role for Turing. Given an identity of substrates, similar results seemed to imply the existence of a similar process.

53. RAND was a research center set up immediately after World War II to keep going the research momentum that had proved so fruitful during the war years. See Bruce Smith, *The RAND Corporation: Case Study of a Non-Profit Advisory Corporation* (Cambridge, Mass.: Harvard University Press, 1966).

54. Shannon, "A Chess-Playing Machine," in *The World of Mathematics*, vol. 4, 2132.

55. Shannon, "A Chess-Playing Machine," 2126.

56. For a history of the development of Lisp, see Herbert Stoyan, "Early LISP History (1956–1959)," in *Proceedings of the 1984 ACM Symposium on LISP and Functional Programming* (New York: ACM Press, 1984), 299–310; ⟨http://www8.informatik.uni-erlangen.de/html/lisp/histlit1.html⟩; and Herbert Stoyan, LISP: *Anwendunsgebiete, Grundbegriffe, Geschichte* (Berlin: Akademie Verlag, 1980).

57. Marvin Minsky, "Steps toward Artificial Intelligence," in *Computers and Thought*, ed. Feigenbaum and Feldman, 406–450. This essay had been circulating in draft form as a technical report since late 1956, that is, immediately after the Dartmouth seminar, and was instrumental in providing a first organization of the field.

58. Shannon, "A Chess-Playing Machine," in *The World of Mathematics*, vol. 4, 2127; our italics.

59. Shannon, "A Chess-Playing Machine," 2127; our italics.

60. Estimates on the size of the search spaces of several popular games, including chess, are summarized in H. Japp van den Herik, Jos W. H. M. Uiterwijk, and Jack van Rijswijck, "Games Solved: Now and in the Future," *Artificial Intelligence* 134 (2002): 277–311. For a finer analysis of game complexity see L. Victor Allis, "Searching for Solutions in Games and Artifical Intelligence," Ph.D. dissertation, University of Limburg, Maastricht, 1994, available at ⟨http://www.cs.vu.nl/~victor/thesis.html⟩.

61. This is evident from a moment of reflection upon the treelike structure: White, for example, will know for sure if it can always force a win only if it examines every possible countermove by Black at any possible point in the game (at any level in the tree). In other words, White has to examine every single node in the tree before moving a piece. This is why Shannon points out that the first move would take the machine 10^{95} years to complete.

62. Marvin Minsky, *The Society of Mind* (New York: Simon and Schuster, 1986), 73–74.

63. Herbert Simon, *Administrative Behavior* (New York: Macmillan, 1947). Simon describes the study of organizational behavior as such in his autobiography, *Models of My Life*.

64. See Simon's comment on those years: "I was profoundly dissatisfied with the concept of "solution" in von Neumann and Morgenstern—it seemed to me to confirm the complexity of the problem rather than solve it." Quoted in Vernon L. Smith, "Game Theory and Experimental Economics," in *Toward a History of Game Theory*, ed. E. R. Weintraub, 253.

65. George Polya, *How to Solve It* (Princeton, N.J.: Princeton University Press, 1944). Polya writes in the preface to his celebrated book, "This study [of solving methods], that some authors call heuristics, now is out of fashion. However, it has a glorious past and, perhaps, a future" (iii).

66. Simon, *Models of My Life*, 166, 202.

67. Newell, Shaw, and Simon, "Chess-Playing Programs and the Problem of Complexity," 39.

68. Franchi went so far to declare that AI's basic thrust was to construct a new metaphysics by purely engineering means. Herbert Simon, asked to comment on the manuscript containing this assertion, agreed wholeheartedly, adding only that he preferred to call it a "new epistemology."

69. See, for example, Newell and Simon's reservations along these lines, against Turing's hand simulation of his chess-playing program, in Newell and Simon, *Human Problem Solving*, 671ff.

70. In particular, they compile a number of overall goals that a chess player must achieve, loosely speaking, in order to win, for example, "keep the king safe," "develop the pieces," "do not block your own pawns."

71. Coles, "Computer Chess: The Drosophila of AI," 30. For a technical description of Deep Blue, see Murray Campbell, A. Joseph Hoane Jr. and Feng-hsiung Hsu, "Deep Blue," *Artificial Intelligence* 134 (2002): 57–83. The inside story of building Deep Blue is described in Feng-hsiung Hsu, *Behind Deep Blue* (Princeton: Princeton University Press, 2002).

72. Alan Turing, "Computing Machinery and Intelligence," *Mind: A Quarterly Review of Psychology and Philosophy* 59 (October 1950): 433–460; also published in *The Philosophy of Artificial Intelligence*, ed. Margaret Boden, 40–66 (Oxford: Oxford University Press, 1992).

73. Andrew Hodges, *Alan Turing: The Enigma* (London: Simon and Schuster, 1983), 265.

74. Alan Turing, "On Computable Numbers, with an Application to the *Entscheidungsproblem*," *Proceedings of the London Mathematical Society*, ser. 2, 42 (1936/37): 230–265; with corrections, *Proceedings of the London Mathematical Society*, ser. 2, 43 (1937): 544–546.

75. Hodges, *Alan Turing*, 265–266.

76. Hodges, *Alan Turing*, 265–266. Turing addresses this particular objection under the heading "Lady Lovelace's Objection" in "Computing Machinery and Intelligence."

77. Turing, "Computing Machinery and Intelligence," in *The Philosophy of Artificial Intelligence*, ed. Boden, 65.

78. In addition to the points made, another question has been raised: Did Turing suggest two tests rather than one, such that one (the version described earlier in his paper) could serve a somewhat different (and more illuminating) purpose than the other? See Susan Sterrett, "Turing's Two Tests for Intelligence," *Minds and Machines* 10 (2000): 541–559.

79. For an extensive and well-balanced review of this literature, see Ayse Pinar Saygin, Ilyas Cicekli, and Varol Akman, "Turing Test: 50 Years Later," *Minds and Machines* 10 (2000): 463–518.

80. See Charles Platt, "What's It Mean to Be Human, Anyway?" *Wired* 3 (April 1995): 1–6, ⟨http://www.wired.com/wired/archive/3.04/turing.html⟩; and Hugh Loebner's home page, ⟨http://www.loebner.net/⟩.

81. See the home page of the Loebner prize, ⟨http://www.loebner.net/Prizef/loebner-prize.html⟩.

82. Here are excerpts from an e-mail exchange between Loebner, the MIT computer scientist Marvin Minsky, and the UCLA psychiatrist Ken Colby, the author of the PARRY program, and his son,

Peter, as they appeared on the Internet newsgroups, ⟨comp.ai⟩ and ⟨comp.ai.philosophy⟩ in March 1995. (As a result of this exchange, Loebner now claims Minsky to be "co-sponsor" of his competition; ⟨http://www.loebner.net/Prizef/loebner-prize.html⟩.)

Newsgroups: comp.ai,comp.ai.philosophy
From: minsky@media.mit.edu (Marvin Minsky)
Subject: Annual Minsky Loebner Prize Revocation Prize 1995 Announcement
Organization: MIT Media Laboratory
Date: Fri, 3 Mar 1995 01:35:19 GMT

In article ⟨3j56jv$opq@hopper.acm.org⟩ loebner@ACM.ORG writes: 17. The names "Loebner Prize" and "Loebner Prize Competition" may be used by contestants in advertising only by advance written permission of the Cambridge Center, and their use may be subject to applicable licensing fees. Advertising is subject to approval by representatives of the Loebner Prize Competition. Improper or misleading advertising may result in revocation of the prize and/or other actions.

I do hope that someone will volunteer to violate this proscription so that Mr. Loebner will indeed revoke his stupid prize, save himself some money, and spare us the horror of this obnoxious and unproductive annual publicity campaign.

In fact, I hereby offer the $100.00 Minsky prize to the first person who gets Loebner to do this. I will explain the details of the rules for the new prize as soon as it is awarded, except that, in the meantime, anyone is free to use the name "Minsky Loebner Prize Revocation Prize" in any advertising they like, without any licensing fee.

From: loebner@ACM.ORG (Hugh Loebner)
Newsgroups: comp.ai
Subject: Reply to Minsky re Loebner Prize Revocation
Date: 7 Mar 1995 16:27:51 GMT
Organization: ACM Network Services

1. Marvin Minsky will pay $100.00 to anyone who gets me to "revoke" the "stupid" Loebner Prize.
2. "Revoke" the prize means "discontinue" the prize.
3. After the Grand Prize is won, the contest will be discontinued.
4. The Grand Prize winner will "get" me to discontinue the Prize.
5. The Grand Prize winner will satisfy The Minsky Prize criterion.
6. Minsky will be morally obligated to pay the Grand Prize Winner $100.00 for getting me to discontinue the contest.
7. Minsky is an honorable man.
8. Minsky will pay the Grand Prize Winner $100.00
9. Def: "Co-sponsor": Anyone who contributes or promises to contribute a monetary prize to the Grand Prize winner.
10. Marvin Minsky is a co-sponsor of the 1995 Loebner Prize Contest.

From: colby@oahu.cs.ucla.edu (Kenneth Colby)
Newsgroups: comp.ai,comp.ai.philosophy
Subject: Re: Annual Minsky Loebner Prize Revocation Prize 1995 Announcement
Date: 8 Mar 1995 16:04:27 -0800
Organization: UCLA Computer Science Dept.

We claim the Minsky Prize. A couple of years ago we entered a program that tied for first but was awarded second on a tie-break.

We have sold a number of copies of this program and not given any of the proceeds to Loebner.

Hence we claim the Minsky Prize of $100 but only on the condition that the money be given to Loebner who seems short of funds at the moment.

Peter and Ken Colby

83. Stuart M. Shieber, "Lessons from a Restricted Turing Test," Technical Report TR-19-92 (1992), Center for Research in Computing Technology, Harvard University, Cambridge, Mass.; also published as "Revision 5, April 15, 1993" at ⟨http://www.eecs.harvard.edu/shieber/Biblio/Papers/loebner-rev-html/loebner-rev-html.html⟩, and in *Communications of the ACM* 37 (June 1994): 70–78.

84. Decisions of this kind were made by the Loebner prize administrative committee, a group that included some famous people, such as Daniel Dennett, Willard van Orman Quine, Joseph Weizenbaum, and Allen Newell.

85. Shieber, "Lessons from a Restricted Turing Test," "Revision 5" (1993).

86. This transformation of the original Turing test into a test of conversation in a very restricted domain, coupled with the rather flamboyant attitude of Hugh Loebner, resonated with the media but irritated a number of professional AI researchers, who regarded the whole setup as a cheap parody of Turing's project. (Loebner states on his Web site, ⟨http://www.loebner.net/⟩, that a winner of the unrestricted Turing test would receive, in addition to the $100,000 prize money, a gold medal ("eighteen carat, not *gold-plated* like the Olympic '*gold*' medals") imprinted with Turing's portrait on one side and Loebner's on the other).

Among the critics of the Loebner-style Turing test is Stuart Shieber, who finds that "the competition has no clear purpose, that its design prevents any useful outcome, and that such a competition is inappropriate given the current level of technology." Shieber, "Lessons from a Restricted Turing Test."

87. This conversation was taken (without permission) from Mark Rosenfelder (⟨markrose@spss.com⟩), online posting, newsgroup ⟨comp.ai.philosophy⟩, Usenet, February 10, 1992.

88. Shieber, "Lessons from a Restricted Turing Test."

89. See sample conversations by these programs in part 4 of this volume. Weizenbaum gives a full account of his development of ELIZA, within a general critique of AI research, in *Computer Power and Human Reason* (New York: Freeman, 1976). Ken Colby presents the story of PARRY, much less critically than Weizenbaum and arguing for the real relevance of his program to psychiatry, in *Artificial Paranoia: A Computer Simulation of Paranoid Processes* (New York: Pergamon Press, 1975). RACTER's creations can be found in *The Policeman's Beard Is Half Constructed: Computer Prose and Poetry*, authored by RACTER with the help of William Chamberlain and Tom Etter (New York: Warner Software/Warner Books, 1984). Useful Web sites for chatterbots and relevant topics, including the Turing test, are ⟨http://cogsci.ucsd.edu/~asaygin/tt/ttest.html⟩ and ⟨http://www.simonlaven.com/⟩.

90. The complete transcripts of the 2003 Loebner Prize competition are available at ⟨http://www.surrey.ac.uk/dwrc/loebner/⟩. The excerpts are taken from JABBERWOCK's conversations with judge 9 and judge 16. For a live conversation with JABBERWOCK, see ⟨http://www.abenteuermedien.de/jabberwock/⟩.

91. Douglas Hofstadter, *Fluid Concepts and Creative Analogies* (New York: Basic Books, 1995), 487–490.

92. Hofstadter, 487–490.

93. Terrence Deacon, *The Symbolic Species* (New York: W. W. Norton, 1997), 24, 33.

94. Herbert Simon and Allen Newell, "Heuristic Problem Solving: The Next Advance in Operations Research," *Operations Research* 6 (January–February 1958), 6, quoted in Dreyfus, *What Computers Still Can't Do*, 81–82.

95. Patrick Winston, "Artificial Intelligence: A Perspective," in *AI in the 1980s and Beyond: An MIT Survey*, ed. W. Eric L. Grimson and Ramesh S. Patil (Cambridge, Mass.: MIT Press, 1987), 2–3.

96. Some would challenge this view. Dreyfus, for instance, thinks that the main drive behind the big promises was to secure increased funding from DARPA, the Defense Department's Advanced Research Projects Agency, which had played a key role in the development of AI by allocating substantial amounts of research funding. A similar view is held by Seymour Papert, who has stated that the enterprise of AI was nurtured by the most mundane material circumstances of funding.

97. Patrick Winston and Michael Brady, "Series Foreword," in *AI in the 1980s and Beyond*, ed. Grimson and Patil, i.

98. One of the "discoveries" of AI, perhaps among its most important, is a profound recognition of just how hard it is, and how much is required, in order for an account to meet a minimum standard of implementability. By implementation of a theory we mean, roughly, a translation of the theory into a computer program. Giving precise definitions of any of the three terms *implementation*, *program*, and *translation* is a notoriously difficult issue, and we will not attempt it here.

99. CSLI TINLunch, Stanford University, Fall 1989. Center for the Study of Language and Information (CSLI), Stanford University, Stanford, Calif. TIN (Topics-in-Natural-Language) Lunches were started by CSLI researchers at SRI before CSLI was formed in 1983. Now CSLI has a TINLunch almost every Thursday at noon during the academic year.

100. John McCarthy, "What Has AI in Common with Philosophy?" (1996); downloaded (without permission) from McCarthy's Web page ⟨http://www-formal.stanford.edu/jmc/aiphil/aiphil. html⟩.

101. *SIGART Newsletter* 70 (February 1980), 109, special issue on knowledge representation.

102. Robert Cummins and John Pollock, "Introduction," in *Philosophy and AI: Essays at the Interface*, ed. Robert Cummins and John Pollock (Cambridge, Mass.: MIT Press, 1991), 2.

103. Although the rise of connectionism has revived interest in the history of the early cybernetics, a comprehensive history of the discipline—and more generally, of cognitive science—has yet to be written. The first important studies were by Jean-Pierre Dupuy, *Aux origines des sciences cognitives* (Paris: La Découverte, 1994), *The Mechanization of the Mind: On the Origins of Cognitive Science*, trans. M. B. DeBevoise (Princeton, N.J.: Princeton University Press, 2000); Steve Heims, *The Cybernetics Group* (Cambridge, Mass.: MIT Press, 1991); Steve Heims, *John von Neumann and Norbert Wiener* (Cambridge, Mass.: MIT Press, 1980). Recent work by Evelyn Fox Keller and Andrew Pickering is beginning to shed light on the complex web of theoretical, social, and technical interactions

that shaped the first phase of cybernetics (see the contributions by Keller and Pickering in this volume).

104. Marvin Minsky and Seymour Papert, *Perceptrons: An Introduction to Computational Geometry* (Cambridge, Mass.: MIT Press, 1969; expanded ed., 1988). For a first-person account of the dispute from opposite trenches, see Seymour Papert's analysis of the atmosphere surrounding the publication of *Perceptrons*, in Seymour Papert, "One AI or Many?" *Daedalus* 117 (no. 1, 1988): 1–14; and Heinz von Foerster's recollection of the funding war between cybernetics and AI, in Stefano Franchi, Güven Güzeldere, and Eric Minch, "Interview with Heinz von Foerster," *Stanford Humanities Review* 4 (no. 2, 1994), special issue: "Constructions of the Mind." For a detailed historical reconstruction of the debate between cybernetics and AI, and the whole controversy stirred by the publication of *Perceptrons*, see the excellent work by Mikel Olazaran, "A Sociological Study of the Official History of the *Perceptrons* controversy," *Social Studies of Science* 26 (1996): 611–659; Hubert Dreyfus and Stuart Dreyfus, "Making a Mind vs. Modeling the Brain: Artificial Intelligence Back at a Branch Point," *Daedalus* 117 (no. 1, 1988): 15–43, also published in *The Philosophy of Artificial Intelligence*, ed. Boden.

105. "In all fairness," McCulloch continues, "he must stick to his own rules and show in terms of mass, energy, space, and time how it comes about that he creates theoretical physics." Warren McCulloch, "Why the Mind Is in the Head," in *Cerebral Mechanisms in Behavior: The Hixon Symposium*, ed. L. A. Jeffress (New York: Wiley, 1951), 43; also published in Warren McCulloch, *Embodiments of Mind* (Cambridge, Mass.: MIT Press, 1989), 73.

106. McCulloch, "Why the Mind Is in the Head," 132.

107. This, at least, is what happens in the tradition of—to use John Haugeland's celebrated definition—GOFAI (Good Old Fashioned AI), a world in which "as long as you take care of the syntax, the semantics takes care of itself." Haugeland, *Artificial Intelligence: The Very Idea*.

108. Warren McCulloch, "Through the Den of the Metaphysician," lecture delivered at the University of Virginia, March 23, 1948; published in McCulloch, *Embodiments of Mind*, 143.

109. We consider a discipline mature when its practitioners are in widely shared agreement over its fundamental concepts and its basic results. Geometrical optics can be considered a mature discipline in this sense of the term. The theory of propositional calculus in formal logic offers an even simpler example.

110. McCulloch, *Embodiments of Mind*, 151.

111. See Frank Rosenblatt, "The Perceptron: A Probabilistic Model for Information Storage and Organization in the Brain," *Psychological Review* 65 (no. 6, 1958): 386–408. A full presentation of Rosenblatt's theory may be found in Frank Rosenblatt, *Principles of Neurodynamics: Perceptrons and the Theory of Brain Mechanism* (New York: Spartan Books, 1962). The more "plastic" networks devised by Rosenblatt were partly inspired by the work of the neuropsychologist Donald Hebb, who had suggested that the repeated excitation between two neurons was most likely to cause some "metabolic change in one or both cells," such that "the efficiency of one of the cells firing is increased." Hebb called this hypothesis a "neurophysiological postulate." From a cybernetician's

point of view, Hebb's work was rich in profound and far-reaching suggestions but quite scarce in technical details. It was Rosenblatt who proceeded to invent the specific technique that made possible a concrete, physical realization of Hebb's suggestion. See Donald Hebb, *The Organization of Behavior* (New York: Wiley, 1949), 79.

112. For a more technical discussion of Rosenblatt's Perceptron, see, besides his *Principles of Neurodynamics*, the classic presentation contained in Nils Nilsson, *Learning Machines—Foundations of Trainable Pattern Classifying Systems* (New York: McGraw-Hill, 1965).

113. Seymour Papert, "One AI or Many?" 5; italics in original. The role of *Perceptrons* in cybernetics' virtual death in the late 1960s has become a myth in itself within the AI community. John McCarthy, for example, once dismissed the critics of AI with the following words: "AI has some ideological opponents. Some think it impossible in principle, although none of them has attempted an actual mathematical argument." John McCarthy, "Artificial Intelligence Needs More Emphasis on Basic Research: AAAI President's Message," *AI Magazine* 4 (Winter 1983): 5. McCarthy was clearly referring to the mathematical impossibility proof of cybernetics, presented in *Perceptrons*, while implying that unless such a proof can be provided for AI, any criticism is totally ungrounded and, in his words, purely "ideological."

114. Dupuy, *Aux origines des sciences cognitives*, 109.

115. The algorithm was discovered independently by three different research groups at about the same time, 1985–1986. See D. Rumelhart, G. Hinton, and R. Williams, "Learning Internal Representation by Error Propagation," in *Parallel Distributed Processing: Explorations in the Microstructures of Cognition*, ed. David Rumelhart and James McClelland (Cambridge, Mass.: MIT Press, 1986), 318–362; Y. LeCun, "Learning Processes in an Asymmetric Threshold Network," in *Disordered Systems and Biological Organization*, ed. E. Biesenstock, F. Fogelman Souli, and G. Weisbuch (Berlin: Springer-Verlag, 1986); D. Parker, "Learning Logic," Technical Report TR-87, Center for Computational Research in Economics and Management Science, MIT, Cambridge, Mass., 1985.

116. See Henri Atlan, *Les étincelles de hasard*, vol. 1, *Connaissance spermatique* (Paris: Seuil, 1999); Henri Atlan, *Entre le cristal et la fumée: essai sur l'organisation du vivant* (Paris: Seuil, 1979); Daniel Amit, *Modeling Brain Function: The World of Attractor Neural Networks* (Cambridge: Cambridge University Press, 1989); Stuart Kauffman, *At Home in the Universe: The Search for the Laws of Self-Organization and Complexity* (Oxford: Oxford University Press, 1995).

117. This is what Jean Petitot (personal communication) likes to call the "intrinsic transdisciplinarity of the cognitive field" as opposed to the traditionally "imperialistic" attitude pursued under the title of "interdisciplinarity."

118. Robert Port and Timothy van Gelder, eds., *Mind as Motion* (Cambridge, Mass.: MIT Press, 1995).

119. See, for example, Francisco J. Varela, Evan Thompson, and Eleanor Rosch, *The Embodied Mind* (Cambridge, Mass.: MIT Press, 1991); Jean Petitot, Francisco Varela, Bernard Pachoud, and Jean-Michel Roy, eds., *Naturalizing Phenomenology* (Stanford, Calif.: Stanford University Press,

1999). The latter contains an expanded version of the proceedings of the conference *Le défi de la naturalisation. Actualité cognitive de la phénoménologie,* held in Bordeaux, October 19–21, 1995.

The two influences come together in the work of Jean Petitot: see "Phénoménologie naturalisée et morphodynamique: la fonction cognitive du synthétique a priori," *Intellectica* 17 (1992–1993): 79–126, and "Morphodynamics and Attractor Syntax: Constituency in Visual Perception and Cognitive Grammar," in *Mind as Motion,* ed. Port and van Gelder, 227–281.

120. Hilary Putnam, "Artificial Intelligence: Much Ado about Not Very Much," *Daedalus* 117 (1988): 269–281; also published in *The Artificial Intelligence Debate: False Starts, Real Foundations,* ed. S. R. Graubard (Cambridge, Mass.: MIT Press, 1989).

121. Our review focuses on a few positions, which we take as representative of a much broader literature. A succinct but fairly comprehensive survey of several "internal critics" of AI may be found in Mark Bichard and Loren Terveen, *Foundational Issues in Artificial Intelligence and Cognitive Science* (Amsterdam: North-Holland, 1995), 87–199.

122. Thus, to execute a plan is in principle not very different from navigating through a state-space. Simon and Newell's work was as influential in planning as it was in other fields. Their paper describing a General Problem Solver provided the basic framework for years. The classic book by George A. Miller, Eugene Galanter, and Karl H. Pribram, *Plans and the Structure of Behavior* (New York: Holt, 1960), provides the definitive systematization of AI's "rhetoric on planning," according to Agre.

123. Philip Agre, *Computation and Human Experience* (Cambridge: Cambridge University Press, 1997), 155. Agre notes that David Chapman formalized this result in a theorem that establishes a trade-off between the level of expressive power in an agent's model of its world and the intrinsic computational difficulties of constructing plans to achieve goals in it. See David Chapman, "Planning for Conjunctive Goals," *Artificial Intelligence* 32 (no. 3, 1987): 333–377.

124. Lucy Suchman, *Plans and Situated Actions: The Problem of Human-Machine Communication* (Cambridge: Cambridge University Press, 1987).

125. Philip Agre, "Computational Research on Interaction and Agency," *Artificial Intelligence* 72 (nos. 1–2, 1995): 1–52, 17. At the technical level, this emphasis translates into a rejection of the classical usage of representations of the world as picture-life replications of states-of-affairs stored in the agent's mind in favor of deictic indications of the *relationship* between the world and the agent.

126. Philip Agre, "Computational Research on Interaction and Agency," 49.

127. SRI's robot SHAKEY and its planner programming language, STRIPS, were the standard paradigms of AI robotics until they were replaced by Brooks's behavior-based architectures in the early 1980s. STRIPS planner language implements a version of the means–end analysis first introduced by Herbert Simon and Allen Newell in the "General Problem Solver," a system they developed in the late 1950s. For the original description of SHAKEY, see Nils Nilsson, *SHAKEY the Robot* (Menlo Park, Calif.: SRI International, 1984), technical note 323. For STRIPS, see Nils Nilsson, *STRIPS: A New Approach to the Application of Theorem Proving to Problem Solving* (Menlo Park, Calif.:

SRI International, 1970), technical note 43; see also the discussions of the "deliberative approach" (as the classic AI approach to robotics is now often called) in Stuart Russell and Peter Norvig, *Artificial Intelligence: A Modern Approach* (Upper Saddle River, N.J.: Prentice-Hall, 2003) and in *The Handbook of Artificial Intelligence*, vol. 1, ed. Avron Barr and Edward Feigenbaum (Stanford, Calif.: Heuris Tech Press, 1981). An informal discussion of SHAKEY is provided by Pamela McCorduck, *Machines Who Think* (San Francisco: W. H. Freeman, 1979), 223–238.

128. Rodney Brooks, "Intelligence without Representation," *Artificial Intelligence* 47 (1991): 139–159; also published in Rodney Brooks, *Cambrian Intelligence* (Cambridge, Mass.: MIT Press, 1999).

129. Randall Beer, "Environmental Influences and Intrinsic Dynamics in Adaptive Behavior," in *Prerational Intelligence: Adaptive Behavior and Intelligent Systems without Symbols and Logic*, vol. 2, *Interdisciplinary Perspectives on the Behavior of Natural and Artificial Systems*, ed. Holk Cruse, Jeffrey Dean, and Helge Ritter (Amsterdam: Kluwer, 2000), 259. See also Randall Beer, *Intelligence as Adaptive Behavior* (Boston: Academic Press, 1990).

130. The approach to robotics inaugurated by Rodney Brooks, usually called behavior-based robotics, has found wide currency in the field. For a broad review, see Maja Matarić, "Behavior-Based Robotics as a Tool for Synthesis of Artificial Behavior and Analysis of Natural Behavior," *Trends in Cognitive Science*, 2 (March 1998): 82–87; for a more technical introduction, see Brooks, *Cambrian Intelligence*; for a more general introduction to the various approaches to robotics, see Ronald Arkin, *Behavior-Based Robotics* (Cambridge, Mass.: MIT Press, 1998); Gawrav Sukhatme, Maja Matarić, "Introduction," *Communications of the ACM* 45 (March 2002): 30–32, special issue, "Robots: Intelligence, Versatility, Adaptivity," Robin Murphy, *Introduction to AI Robotics* (Cambridge, Mass.: MIT Press, 2000).

One shouldn't infer from this quick review that classical AI has been swept clean by this new emerging paradigm. A canonical answer to the insistence on "situated action," as this loosely defined trend is sometimes called, can be found in the scathing countercritique by Herbert Simon and Alonso H. Vera, "Situated Action: A Symbolic Interpretation," *Cognitive Science* 17 (no. 1, 1993): 7–48.

Recently, Rodney Brooks has started to put more emphasis on the changes in human society that the advent of humanlike robots will bring about. For instance, in *Flesh and Machines*, he says: "Our relationship with these [future] machines will be different from our relationships with all previous machines. The coming robotics revolution will change the fundamental nature of our society.... Our machines will become much more like us and we will become much more like our machines. The coming biotechnology revolution will change the fundamental nature of us.... We will break our mental barrier, our need, our desire, to retain tribal specialness, differentiating ourselves from them" (11, 175). According to Brooks, then, the construction of intelligent machines will retroact upon their builders—ourselves.

131. The canonical text for the dynamic approach to cognition is Port and van Gelder's *Mind as Motion*, especially the introductory essay, "It's about Time," 1–43. See also Timothy van Gelder, "What Might Cognition Be, If Not Computation?" *Journal of Philosophy* 7 (1992): 345–381. For an accessible (but rather critical) introduction, see Andy Clark, *Mindware* (Oxford: Oxford University Press, 2001), ch. 7.

132. Jeffrey Elman, "Language as Dynamical System," in *Mind as Motion*, ed. Port and van Gelder, 195–225; Petitot, "Morphodynamics and Attractor Syntax: Constituency in Visual Perception and Cognitive Grammar," in *Mind as Motion*, 227–281; Jean Petitot, *Morphogenèse du sens* (Paris: PUF, 1985).

133. Port and van Gelder, "It's about Time," 5.

134. For a general introduction to the mathematical formalism of dynamic system theory, see Ralph Abraham and Christopher Shaw, *Dynamics—The Geometry of Behavior* (Santa Cruz, Calif.: Ariel Press, 1982), vols. 1–4. For a sophisticated application of the dynamic approach to linguistic structures, see Jean Petitot, *Les catastrophes de la parole* (Paris: Maloine, 1985).

135. The so-called search spaces of classical AI that we discussed in connection with chess-solving algorithms could not be more different: each element of the state-space, each node of the search tree, is a symbolic description, not a set of numbers. A search space, in fact, is only metaphorically so; rather, it is a (potentially cyclic) graph with no intrinsic metric—at best a partial ordering.

136. J. A. Scott Kelso (1995), 26, quoted in Clark, *Mindware*, 129.

137. Port and van Gelder, "It's about Time," 4; italics in original.

138. Esther Thelen, Gregor Schöner, Christian Scheier, and Linda B. Smith, "The Dynamics of Embodiment: A Field Theory of Infant Perseverative Reaching," *Behavioral and Brain Sciences* 24 (no. 1, 2001): 1–34.

139. F. A. Keijzer and S. Bem, "Behavioral Systems Interpreted as Autonomous Agents and as Coupled Dynamical Systems: A Criticism," *Philosophical Psychology* 9 (1996): 3, 327.

140. Keijzer and Bem, "Behavioral Systems Interpreted," 342; our italics.

141. Andy Clark, "Embodiment in Cognitive Science?" *Trends in Cognitive Science* 3 (September 1999): 348. The article provides an accessible and well-informed review of the main issues in the embedded/embodied movement within cognitive science. A fuller version of Clark's "moral" argument is presented in Andy Clark, *Being There* (Cambridge, Mass.: MIT Press, 1998). The integrative stance toward the dynamic approach provides the theoretical backbone to Clark's introductory text, *Mindware*.

142. On detachment, see Brian Cantwell Smith, *On the Origin of Objects* (Cambridge, Mass.: MIT Press, 1996), ch. 6, 191–212.

143. Brian Leiter, "Naturalism in Legal Philosophy," in *Stanford Encyclopedia of Philosophy (Fall 2002 Edition)*, ed. Edward N. Zalta, ⟨http://plato.stanford.edu/archives/fall2002/entries/lawphil-naturalism/⟩.

144. Terry Winograd, in the foreword to a book of essays honoring Hubert Dreyfus, notices the remarkable turnaround of his critical fortunes in MIT's AI Lab. In 1968 an internal memo on Dreyfus's first work was titled "A Budget of Fallacies." Twenty years later, the first chapter of a Ph.D. dissertation written in the same lab, Philip Agre's, opened with the remark that Heidegger's work provides the most detailed account of those everyday routine activities whose proper

understanding is crucial to artificial intelligence. Winograd himself credited Dreyfus's work as one of the main reasons behind his radical research shift from AI research to a phenomenologically informed perspective on human-computer interactions. As Philip Agre makes clear in his chapter in this volume, however, Winograd's analysis of the interaction between AI research and Dreyfus's work may be deemed too optimistic. Terry Winograd, "Foreword," in *Heidegger, Coping, and Cognitive Science: Essays in Honor of Hubert L. Dreyfus*, ed. Mark A. Wrathall and Jeff Malpas (Cambridge, Mass.: MIT Press, 2000), vii–ix. See also Paul Dourish, *Where The Action Is: The Foundations of Computer Interaction* (Cambridge, Mass.: MIT Press, 2001) for another attempt at using phenomenology as a foundation for human-computer interaction.

145. Dreyfus's sociological and institutional critique is in the background in his first publications, but it assumes a fairly prominent role from 1986 onward; see Hubert Dreyfus and Stuart Dreyfus, *Mind Over Machine* (New York: Free Press, 1986).

146. Dreyfus, *What Computers Still Can't Do*, 281. Early versions of this work were published in Hubert Dreyfus, "Alchemy and Artificial Intelligence" (1965), RAND Corporation Paper P-3244; and Dreyfus, *What Computers Can't Do* (1972).

147. *Mind Over Machine*, 76. Sometimes Dreyfus calls the background the *universe* in order to contrast it with what AI calls a world. But the inspiration is clearly to be found in Heidegger's early conception of the world, which he defined in *Being and Time* as the horizon of significance within which human activities make sense. Martin Heidegger, *Being and Time*, trans. Joan Stambaugh (1927; Albany: SUNY Press, 1996), div. I, ch. 3.

148. Daniel Andler, "Context and Background: Dreyfus and Cognitive Science," in *Heidegger, Coping, and Cognitive Science*, ed. Wrathall and Malpas, 137–159; our italics.

149. The original paper that introduced the frame problem to the AI community is John McCarthy and Patrick Hayes, "Some Philosophical Problems from the Standpoint of Artificial Intelligence," in *Machine Intelligence*, ed. Bernard Meltzer and Donald Michie (Edinburgh: Edinburgh University Press, 1969), vol. 4, 463–502; also published in John McCarthy, *Formalizing Common Sense: Papers by John McCarthy* (Norwood, N.J.: Ablex, 1990). For an acute philosophical discussion, see Daniel Dennett, "Cognitive Wheels: The Frame Problem of AI," in *Minds, Machines, and Evolution*, ed. C. Hookway (Cambridge: Cambridge University Press, 1984), 129–151; also published in Dennett, *Brainchildren* (Cambridge, Mass.: MIT Press, 1998), 181–205. The most famous example of a microworld was Terry Winograd's SHRDLU, an agent located in a "block world" that could carry out a natural language conversation on its elements. Terry Winograd, *Understanding Natural Language* (San Diego, Calif.: Academic Press, 1972). Most of Hubert Dreyfus's *What Computers Can't Do* is devoted to an extensive critique of the early AI assumption that the microworld approach would scale up to real applications. See also Hubert Dreyfus, "From Micro-Worlds to Knowledge Representations: AI at an Impasse," in *Mind Design II*, ed. John Haugeland (Cambridge, Mass.: MIT Press, 1997), 143–181.

150. Dreyfus and Dreyfus, "Making a Mind vs. Modeling the Brain."

151. Albert Borgmann, "Semiartificial Intelligence," in *Heidegger, Coping, and Cognitive Science*, ed. Wrathall and Malpas, 199.

152. This different emphasis is to a large extent determined by a different philosophical ancestry, so to speak. Agre's, Chapman's, and Dreyfus's critiques, for example, all rely on a pragmatist interpretation of the phenomenology of everyday life provided by Heidegger in the first division of *Being and Time*—an interpretation provided by Dreyfus himself. Winograd and Flores, while accepting the phenomenological accounts of the early Heidegger, are following more closely the later Heidegger's thinking about language as well as Gadamer's hermeneutic theory.

153. Terry Winograd, "Thinking Machines: Are We? Can There Be?" in *The Boundaries of Humanity: Humans, Animals, Machines*, ed. Sheehan and Sosna, 222.

154. Winograd, "Thinking Machines," 23.

155. This argument originally appeared in Searle, "Minds, Brains, and Programs."

156. Weizenbaum, *Computer Power and Human Reason*, 207.

157. Weizenbaum, *Computer Power and Human Reason*, 227.

158. Weizenbaum, *Computer Power and Human Reason*, 252.

159. Tom Athanasiou, "Hi-Tech Politics: The Case of Artificial Intelligence," *Socialist Review* 92(17), 2, 1987, 33; Tom Athanasiou, *Divided Planet* (Boston: Little, Brown, 1996); Tom Athanasiou, "Artificial Intelligence as Military Technology," in *Computers in Battle: Will They Work?* ed. David Bellin and Gary Chapman (New York: Harcourt Brace Jovanovich, 1987), 233–257.

160. The Advanced Research Projects Agency, or ARPA, was founded by the U.S. Department of Defense in 1958 as one of many initiatives aimed at bridging the perceived U.S. technological gap in the wake of Soviet successes in space exploration. Since the duplication of efforts arising from the competition among the different services' research programs was identified as one of the causes of the gap, the agency was not affiliated with any service in particular. It mostly provided funding for basic research, including the vast bulk of funding for research in artificial intelligence. ARPA became DARPA (Defense ARPA) in 1972, the new acronym reflecting a funding shift toward military applications rather than basic research. DARPA's funding role is still prominent, although the emphasis has shifted away from classical AI research.

161. See Alex Roland, *Strategic Computing: DARPA and the Quest for Machine Intelligence, 1983–1993* (Cambridge, Mass.: MIT Press, 2002), for a detailed history of the Strategic Computing Program. Roland follows the development of SCP until its demise in 1993, although his account is mostly focused on the first five years. Early but still useful accounts of SCP were published by S. Ingvar Åkersten, "The Strategic Computing Program," in *Arms and Artificial Intelligence*, ed. Allen Din (New York: Oxford University Press, 1987), 87–99; Thomas Nash, *Human-Computer Systems in the Military Context* (Stanford, Calif.: Center for International Security and Arms Control, 1990); Jonathan Jacky, "The Strategic Computing Program," in *Computers in Battle*, ed. Bellin and Chapman, 171–208; Paul Edwards, *The Closed World: Computers and the Politics of Discourse in Cold War America* (Cambridge, Mass.: MIT Press, 1996). For a technical review of some of the projects that SCP funded, see the DARPA-commissioned study Sydney Reed, Richard van Atta, and Seymour Deitchman, *DARPA's Technical Accomplishments. A Historical Review of Selected DARPA Projects* (Alexandria, Va.: Institute for Defense Analysis, 1990); for a broader analysis of DARPA's

Information Processing Technology Office, see Arthur Norberg and Judy O'Neill, *Transforming Computer Technology: Information Processing for the Pentagon, 1962–1986* (Baltimore: Johns Hopkins University Press, 1996). See also Edward A. Feigenbaum and Pamela McCorduck, *The fifth Generation: Artificial Intelligence and Japan's Computer Challenge to the World* (Reading, Mass.: Addison-Wesley, 1983). The first public objections to the SCP program were raised by the Computer Professionals for Social Responsibility (CPSR), a group started in 1983 at Xerox PARC by Severo Ornstein, Brian C. Smith, Lucy Suchman, Terry Winograd, and others in direct response to the program. See Severo Ornstein, Brian C. Smith, and Lucy Suchman, "Strategic Computing: An Assessment," *Communications of the ACM* 28 (February 1985): 134–136. Robert Cooper, then director of DARPA, replied in the following issue of the same journal, and more rejoinders were published in August 1985.

162. The Strategic Defense Initiative, renamed National Missile Defense, was indeed revived by the President Clinton and received full support by President Bush. However, the link between AI techniques and military applications that was characteristic of the first SDI/SCP effort disappeared. "High-Performance Computing," the DARPA program that replaced SCP after 1993, now plays the central technical role.

163. The diagram representing SCP's pyramid is adapted from Åkersten, "The Strategic Computing Program," 92. See Roland, *Strategic Computing*, for a detailed discussion of the charged political-institutional debates that determined the various versions of the pyramid. The diagram reproduced in figure 8 represents the final version.

164. Quoted in Åkersten, "The Strategic Computing Program," 90.

165. Roland, *Strategic Computing*, 329.

166. Tom Athanasiou, "Artificial Intelligence as Military Technology," 239.

167. Edwards, *The Closed World*, 268.

168. Edwards, *The Closed World*, 273.

169. Edwards's description of the cyborg is heavily dependent on the characterization first given by Donna Haraway in "A Manifesto for Cyborgs," *Socialist Review* 15 (1985): 65–107; also published in Donna Haraway, *Primate Visions* (London: Routledge and Kegan Paul, 1989).

170. Edwards, *The Closed World*, 350.

171. Edwards, *The Closed World*, 341; italics in original.

172. Quoted in Michael Hiltzik, "A.I. Reboots," *Technology Review* (March 2002): 55.

173. Jonathan Schaeffer, "A Gamut of Games," *AI Magazine* (Fall 2001). Schaeffer is one of AI's leading researchers on game-solving algorithms and the author of Chinook, the current checkers world champion.

174. Examples of such collaborations are the work being done by the University of Alberta GAMES group, led by Jonathan Schaeffer, and various game publishers, including Electronic Arts and BioWare, on creating realistic artificial-intelligent characters; and the work being done

by the research group at the University of Michigan, led by John Laird, with first-person shooter's games like *Quake* and *Unreal*. See ⟨http://www.cs.ualberta.ca/~games/⟩, ⟨http://ai.eecs.umich.edu/people/laird/gamesresearch.html⟩, and John Laird and Michael van Lent, "Human-Level AI's Killer Application: Interactive Computer Games," in *Proceedings of the Seventeenth National Conference on Artificial Intelligence* (Menlo Park, Calif.: American Association for Artificial Intelligence: 2000), 1171–1178.

175. Marina Krol, "Have We Witnessed a Real-Life Turing Test?" *Computer* 32 (March 1999): 27–30.

176. This theme was a constant of cybernetics' relation to its artifacts; see Andrew Pickering's chapter in this volume.

177. See Pamela McCorduck, *AARON's Code* (New York: Computer Science, 1991) for a description of AARON's exploits; and Harold Cohen "The Further Exploits of AARON, Painter," *Stanford Humanities Review* 4 (no. 2, 1995): 145–158, for an update.

178. For an example of such a strategy, see Simon and Vera, "Situated Action."

179. See Arkin, *Behavior-Based Robotics*, for an attempt toward a hybrid robotic architecture.

180. Newell, "Intellectual Issues in the History of Artificial Intelligence," 223.

181. This is how Newell puts his central claim: "Finally, does it make any difference to the humanities which one of these two ways of viewing the matter of mind, metaphor or theory, turns out to be sustained? The two views are not symmetric. Sustain the metaphorical view and a nonevent has happened. The computer as metaphor enriches a little our total view of ourselves, allows us to see facets that we might not otherwise have glimpsed. But we have been enriched by metaphors before, and on the whole they provide just a few more threads in the fabric of life, nothing more. The computer as a generator of a theory of mind is another thing entirely. It is an event. Not because of the computer but because finally we would have obtained a theory of the mind. For a theory of the mind, in the same sense as a theory of genetics or of plate tectonics, will entrain an indefinite sequence of shocks through all our dealings with the mind—which is to say, though all our dealings with ourselves. And the humanities might just be caught in the maelstrom. Or so it would seem." Newell, "Metaphors for Mind, Theories of Mind: Should the Humanities Mind?" in *The Boundaries of Humanity*, ed. Sheehan and Sosna, 195.

182. Rodney Brooks, "Intelligence without Representation," 97. It is interesting to note that, contrary to what Brooks claims here, his research is explicitly inspired by a number of studies that lie outside engineering—developmental psychology, cognitive ethology, and neuroscience, to name a few. The Brooks team has also made a number of references to work pursued in the social sciences and humanities.

183. A first ground-breaking article, by Rodney Brooks, was "A Robust Layered Control System for a Mobile Robot," *IEEE Journal of Robotics and Automation RA-2* (1986): 14–23. See the short preface to the version reprinted in Brooks, *Cambrian Intelligence*, for a history of the genesis of its main ideas.

In a survey article containing several references to the work of philosophers like Heidegger, Wittgenstein, and Merleau-Ponty, Michael Anderson writes: "Although Hubert Dreyfus must be given a great deal of credit for first drawing attention to the limitations of GOFAI, I think it can be argued that the single figure most responsible for the new AI is Rodney Brooks." The tension between AI research and philosophy resurfaces later in the essay when Anderson discusses the charge that the adoption of ideas coming from European philosophers would bring to radical social constructivism. "Much of my own earlier work," he writes, "aims to show that the way to avoid certain radical anti-realist conclusions is precisely to take up into epistemology some of the ideas underlying work in situated and embodied cognition. As far as I am concerned, therefore, the attempted association of EC/SC research with 'radical social constructivism' and the rejection of empirical science is a non-starter." See Michael L. Anderson, "Embodied Cognition: A Field Guide," *Artificial Intelligence* 149 (2003): 95, 117.

184. For a first-person account of his vicissitudes, see Philip Agre's autobiographical analysis, "Toward a Critical Technical Practice: Lessons Learned in Trying to Reform AI," in *Social Science, Technical Systems, and Cooperative Work: Beyond the Great Divide*, ed. Geoffrey Bowker, Susan Leigh Star, William Turner, and Les Gasser (Mahwah, N.J.: Erlbaum, 1997), 131–158.

185. Patrick Winston, "Artificial Intelligence: A Perspective," in *AI in the 1980s and Beyond*, ed. Grimson and Patil, 10.

186. Robert Jastrow, "The Thinking Computer," *Science Digest* 90 (no. 6, 1982): 107, quoted in Terry Winograd and Fernando Flores, *Understanding Computers and Cognition: A New Foundation for Design* (Reading, Mass.: Addison-Wesley, 1986), 3–4.

187. Hans Moravec interview, *Discover*, November 1992.

188. Michael de la Maza and Deniz Yuret, "Seeing Clearly: Medical Imaging Now and Tomorrow," in *Future Health: Computers and Medicine in the 21st Century*, ed. Clifford A. Pickover (New York: St. Martin's Press, 1995).

189. Toshinori Munakata, "Commercial and Industrial AI," *Communications of the ACM* 37 (March 1994): 23–26.

190. For a review of an impressive variety of probabilistic AI applications, such as those used in software debugging, information retrieval, and troubleshooting, see *Communications of the ACM* 38 (March 1995).

191. Turing, "Computing Machinery and Intelligence," in *The Philosophy of Artificial Intelligence*, ed. Boden, 65.

192. The interdisciplinary team of researchers from Brooks's lab say that their project has two goals: the engineering goal of building a robot, Cog, that resembles a human being in form and function—an android—and the scientific goal of understanding human cognition. They say that their research incorporates cognitive science, ethology, evolutionary theory, neuropsychology, and philosophy, and that embodiment is the prime prerequisite of their agenda.

193. Gaby Wood, *Edison's Eve*, 76–77, gives a fuller account of Poe's encounter with the Turk.

194. Robert Willis, quoted in Standage, *The Turk: The Life and Times of the Famous Eighteenth-Century Chess-Playing Machine*, 130.

195. This issue surfaces most prominently in the discussions on cyborgs, especially in cultural studies and critical theory.

196. The tone of the Italian poet Enrico Prampolini's declaration in his Futurist manifesto, "The Aesthetic of the Machine and Mechanical Introspection," is typical of that era: "We therefore proclaim ... 1. The machine to be the tutelary symbol of the universal dynamism, potentially embodying in itself the essential elements of human creation: the discoverer of fresh developments in modern aesthetics.... 5. The machine marks the rhythm of human psychology and beats the time for our spiritual exaltations." Enrico Prampolini, *The Broom*, 1922.

197. Karel Čapek, *R.U.R. (Rossum's Universal Robots): A Fantastic Melodrama in Three Acts and an Epilogue*, trans. Paul Selver (1920; New York: Samuel French, 1923).

198. Jean Baudrillard, *Simulations*, trans. Paul Foss and Paul Patton (New York: Semiotexte, 1983), 92–93.

199. Hans Moravec, *Robot: Mere Machine to Transcendent Mind* (Oxford: Oxford University Press, 1998), 63.

200. Baudrillard, *Simulations*, 94.

201. Manfred E. Clynes and Nathan S. Kline, "Cyborgs and Space," *Astronautics* 14 (September 1960): 26–27, 74–75; also published in *The Cyborg Handbook*, ed. Chris H. Gray with Heidi Figueroa-Sarriera and Steven Mentor (New York: Routledge, 1995), 29–34.

202. M. Cade, *Other Worlds Than Ours: The Problem of Life in the Universe* (New York: Taplinger, 1966).

203. Kevin Warwick, *I, Cyborg* (London: Century Press, 2002).

204. Steve Mann and H. Niedzviecki, *CYBORG: Digital Destiny and Human Possibility in the Age of the Wearable Computer* (New York: Random House, 2001).

205. Kevin Warwick, "Cyborg 1.0." *Wired* 8 (no. 2, 2000): 145.

206. For a full description of the Cyborg 2.0 Project and further updates, see ⟨http://www.rdg.ac.uk/KevinWarwick/html/project_cyborg_2_0.html⟩.

207. J. Young, "Self-Described 'Cyborg' Reveals Promise and Dangers of Wearable Computers," *Chronicle of Higher Education* 48 (2002): 34.

208. Warwick, "Cyborg 1.0."

209. Mann and Niedzviecki, *CYBORG*.

210. Robbie David-Floyd and Joseph Dumit, *Cyborg Babies: From Techno-Sex to Techno-Tots* (New York: Routledge, 1998).

211. As such, the power of cyborg technology is, according to the working scientists and practitioners of the technology, a very tall order. The futuristic vision Warwick describes that is to be founded upon the Cyborg 1.0 project gives a flavor of this kind of thinking: "I can envision a future when we send signals so that we don't have to speak. Thought communication will place telephones firmly in the history books.... Thought-to-thought communication is just one feature of cybernetics that will become vitally important to us as we face the distinct possibility of being superseded by highly intelligent machines. Humans are crazy enough not only to build machines with an overall intelligence greater than our own, but to defer to them and give them power that matters. So how will humans cope, later this century, with machines more intelligent than us? Here, again, I believe cybernetics can help. Linking people via chip implants directly to those machines seems a natural progression, a potential way of harnessing machine intelligence by, essentially, creating superhumans. Otherwise, we're doomed to a future in which intelligent machines rule and humans become second-class citizens." Warwick, "Cyborg 1.0," 148.

212. Donna J. Haraway, *Simians, Cyborgs, and Women: The Reinvention of Nature* (New York: Routledge, 1991), 150.

213. Such a conception of cyborgs seems to have been considered, only to be abandoned, before it found a voice in cultural studies in the 1980s. Arthur Clarke, author of *2001: A Space Odyssey*, among other science fiction classics, writes, "I suppose one could call a man in an iron lung a cyborg, but the concept has far wider implications than that. One day we may be able to enter into temporary unions with any sufficiently sophisticated machines, thus being able not merely to control but to *become* a spaceship or a submarine or a TV network." Arthur Clarke, *Profiles of the Future*, quoted in Rorvik, *As Man Becomes Machine*, 142.

214. Andy Clark, *Natural-Born Cyborgs* (Oxford: Oxford University Press, 2003).

215. Clark, *Natural-Born Cyborgs*, 7.

216. Clark, *Natural-Born Cyborgs*, 3.

217. Bernard Wolfe, *Limbo* (New York: Carroll and Graf, 1987), quoted in Clark, *Natural-Born Cyborgs*, 3.

218. See Susan Oyama, *Evolution's Eye: A Systems View of the Biology-Culture Divide* (Durham, N.C.: Duke University Press, 2002) for an evolutionary account of the interactions of genetic constitution and cultural transformation.

219. C. P. Snow, *The Two Cultures* (London: Cambridge University Press, 1969).

220. This perspectival distinction we are drawing between the work in AI versus the humanities on cyborgs is likely graded, not absolute. Allucquère Rosanne Stone, a cultural and media studies scholar in the tradition of Haraway, for example, describes her encounter with the physicist Stephen Hawking in a manner that places crucial significance on the electronic equipment that allows Hawking to speak, to the extent that, in her eyes, the human-machine boundary is blurred in a very physical way: "In an important sense, Hawking doesn't stop being Hawking at the edge of his visible body. There is the obvious physical Hawking, vividly outlined by the way our social

conditioning teaches us to see a person as a person. But a serious part of Hawking extends into the box in his lap. In mirror image, a serious part of that silicon and plastic assemblage in his lap extends into him as well ... not to mention the invisible ways, displaced in time and space, in which discourses of medical technology and their physical accretions already permeate him and us. No box, no discourse; in the absence of the prosthetic, Hawking's intellect becomes a tree falling in the forest with nobody around to hear it. On the other hand, with the box his voice is auditory and simultaneously electric, in a radically different way from that of a person *speaking* into a microphone. Where *does* he stop? Where are his edges? The issues his person and his communication prostheses raise are boundary debates, borderland/*frontera* questions." Allucquère R. Stone, *The War of Desire and Technology at the Close of the Mechanical Age* (Cambridge, Mass.: MIT Press, 1996).

221. Martin Heidegger, "Zur Frage nach der Bestimmung der Sache des Denkens," in *Zur Sache des Denkens* (Tübingen: Niemeyer, 1969).

222. Heidegger, "Zur Frage...."

223. Heidegger, "Zur Frage ...," 46 (next-to-last page).

224. Chris H. Gray with Heidi Figueroa-Sarriera and Steven Mentor, eds. *The Cyborg Handbook* (New York: Routledge, 1995).

225. The story is well-known. Stephen Hawking's version goes as follows: "A well-known scientist (some say it was Bertrand Russell) once gave a public lecture on astronomy. He described how the earth orbits around the sun and how the sun, in turn, orbits around the centre of a vast collection of stars called our galaxy. At the end of the lecture, a little old lady at the back of the room got up and said: 'What you have told us is rubbish. The world is really a flat plate supported on the back of a giant tortoise.' The scientist gave a superior smile before replying, 'What is the tortoise standing on?' 'You're very clever, young man, very clever,' said the old lady. 'But it's turtles all the way down.'" See Stephen Hawking, *A Brief History of Time* (New York: Bantam Doubleday, 1998).

226. This way, both Newell's deflationist classical AI answer to the humanities as well as Dreyfus's classical philosophical counterpoint to AI would both be preempted.

227. Hayles, *How We Became Posthuman*, 3.

228. Hayles, *How We Became Posthuman*, 5.

229. Hayles, *How We Became Posthuman*, 291.

II In the Shadow of Artificial Intelligence: Automata, Cybernetics, and AI

The Soul Gained and Lost: Artificial Intelligence as a Philosophical Project

Philip Agre

When I was a graduate student in artificial intelligence (AI), the humanities were not held in high regard. They were vague and woolly, they employed impenetrable jargons, and they engaged in "meta-level bickering that never decides anything." My teachers and fellow students were almost unanimous in their contempt for the social sciences, and several of them were moved to apoplexy by philosophy. Periodically they would convene impromptu two-minute hate sessions to compare notes on the arrogance and futility of philosophy and its claims on the territory of AI research: "They've had two thousand years and look what they've accomplished. Now it's our turn." "Anything that you can't explain in five minutes probably isn't worth knowing." These critics distinguished between "just talking" and "doing," where "doing" meant proving mathematical theorems and writing computer programs. A new graduate student in our laboratory, hearing of my interest in philosophy, once took me aside and asked in all seriousness, "Is it true that you don't actually do anything, that you just say how things are?" It was not, in fact, true, but I felt with great force the threat of ostracism implicit in the notion that I was "not doing any real work."

These anecdotes may provide some sense of the obstacles facing any attempt at collaboration between AI and the humanities. In particular, they illustrate certain aspects of AI's conception of itself as a discipline. According to this self-conception, AI is a self-contained technical field. In particular, it is a practical field; to do AI is to prove theorems, write software, and build hardware whose purpose is to solve previously defined technical problems. The whole test of these activities lies in "what works." The criterion of "what works" is straightforward, clear, and objective in the manner of engineering design; arguments and criticisms from outside the field can make no claim at all against it. The substance of the field consists in the state of the art, and its history is a history of computer programs. The technical methods underlying these programs might have originated in other fields, but the real work consisted in formalizing, elaborating, implementing, and testing those ideas. Fields that do not engage in these painstaking activities, it is said, are sterile debating societies that do not possess the intellectual tools—most particularly mathematics—to do more than gesture in the general direction of an idea, as opposed to really working it out.

I will be thought to exaggerate. Technicians will protest their respect for great literature, and the attitudes I have reported will be put down to a minority of fundamentalists. Yet the historical record makes plain that interactions between AI and the humanities have been profoundly shaped by the disciplinary barriers that such attitudes both reflect and reproduce. Serious research in history and literature, for example, has had almost no influence on AI. This is not wholly due to ignorance on the part of technical people, many of whom have had genuine liberal educations. Rather, AI as a technical field is constituted in such a way that its practitioners honestly cannot imagine what influence those fields *could* have. Philosophy has had a little more influence. Research on AI's constitutive questions in the philosophy of mind is widely read and discussed among AI research people, and is sometimes included in the curriculum; but these discussions are rarely considered part of the work of AI—judging, for example, by journal citations—and any influence they might have had on the day-to-day work of AI has been subtle at best. Contemporary ideas from the philosophies of language and logic have been used as raw material for AI model making, though, and philosophers and technical people have collaborated to some degree in specialized research on logic.

Perhaps the principal humanistic influence on AI has derived from a small number of philosophical critics of the field, most particularly Hubert Dreyfus. For Dreyfus, the project of writing "intelligent" computer programs ran afoul of the critique of rules in Wittgenstein, and of Heidegger's analysis of the present-at-hand way of relating to beings (in this case, symbolic rules).[1] The use of a rule in any practical activity, Dreyfus argues, requires a prior participation in the culturally specific form of life within which such activities take place. The attempt to fill in the missing background knowledge through additional rules would suffer the same problem and thus introduce a fatal regress.[2] Although most senior AI researchers of my acquaintance stoutly deny having been affected by Dreyfus's arguments, a reasonable amount of research has addressed the recurring difficulties with AI research that Dreyfus predicted. One of these is the "brittleness" of symbolic, rule-based AI systems, which derives from their tendency to fail catastrophically in situations that depart even slightly from the whole background of operating assumptions that went into the system's design. For the most part, the response of AI researchers to these difficulties, and to Dreyfus's analyses generally, is to interpret them as additions to AI's agenda that require no fundamental rethinking of its premises.[3]

Within the field itself, critical reflection is largely a prerogative of the field's most senior members, and even these papers are published separately from the narrowly technical reports, either in nonarchival publications like *AI Magazine* or in special issues of archival publications devoted to the founders' historical reflections. In 1990 I received

a referee's report on an AAAI (American Association for Artificial Intelligence) conference paper that commented, "In general, avoid writing these "grand old man" style papers until you've built a number of specific systems and have become a grand old man." The boundaries of "real AI research," in short, have been policed with great determination.

Yet this is now changing. In part the current changes reflect sociological shifts in the field: in particular, its decentralization away from a few heavily funded laboratories and the resulting, albeit modest, trend toward interdisciplinary pluralism. But the change in atmosphere has also been influenced by genuine dissatisfactions with the field's original technical ideas. AI's practices of formalizing and working out an idea constitute a powerful method of inquiry, but precisely for this reason they are also a powerful way to force an idea's internal tensions to the surface through prolonged technical frustrations: excessive complexity, intractable inefficiency, difficulties in scaling up to realistic problems, and so forth. These patterns of frustration have helped clear the ground for a new conception of technical work, one that recognizes the numerous, deep continuities between AI and the humanities. Although these continuities reach into the full range of humanistic inquiry, I restrict myself here to the following five assertions about AI and its relationship to philosophy:

- AI ideas have their genealogical roots in philosophical ideas.
- AI research programs attempt to work out and develop the philosophical systems they inherit.
- AI research regularly encounters difficulties and impasses that derive from internal tensions in the underlying philosophical systems.
- These difficulties and impasses should be embraced as particularly informative clues about the nature and consequences of the philosophical tensions that generate them.
- Analysis of these clues must proceed outside the bounds of strictly technical research, but they can result in both new technical agendas and in revised understandings of technical research itself.

In short, AI is philosophy underneath. These propositions are not entirely original, of course, and some version of them underlies Dreyfus's early critique of the field. My own purpose here is to illustrate how they might be fashioned into a positive method of inquiry that maintains a dialogue between the philosophical and technical dimensions of AI research. To this end, I present a brief case study of one idea's historical travels from philosophy through neurophysiology and into AI, up to 1972. Although much of this particular story has been told many times, some significant conclusions from it appear to have escaped analysis. It is an inherently difficult story to tell, since it requires a level of technical detail that may intimidate the uninitiated without nearly satisfying the demands of initiates. It is a story worth telling, though, and I try to maintain a firm sense of the overall point throughout. I conclude by briefly discussing recent developments that have been motivated in part by critical reevaluations of this tradition, and by sketching the shape of the new, more self-critical AI that is emerging in the wake of this experience.

René Descartes: Criteria of Intelligence

In a famous passage in his *Discourse on Method*, Descartes summarizes a portion of his suppressed treatise on *The World* as follows:

> The body is regarded as a machine which, having been made by the hands of God, is incomparably better arranged, and possesses in itself movements which are much more admirable, than any of those which can be invented by man.... If there had been such machines, possessing the organs and outward form of a monkey or some other animal without reason, we should not have had any means of ascertaining that they were not of the same nature as those animals. On the other hand, if there were machines which bore a resemblance to our body and imitated our actions as far as it was morally possible to do so, we should always have two very certain tests by which to recognize that, for all that, they were not real men. The first is, that they could never use speech or other signs as we do when placing our thoughts on record for the benefit of others. For we can easily understand a machine's being constituted so that it can utter words, and even emit some responses to action on it of a corporeal kind, which brings about a change in its organs; for instance, if it is touched in a particular part, it may ask what we wish to say to it; if in another part, it may exclaim that it is being hurt, and so on. But it never happens that it arranges its speech in various ways, in order to reply appropriately to everything that may be said in its presence, as even the lowest type of man can do. And the second difference is, that although machines can perform certain things as well as or perhaps better than any of us can do, they infallibly fail short in others, by the which means we may discover that they did not act from knowledge, but only from the disposition of their organs. For while reason is a universal instrument which can serve for all contingencies, these organs have need of some special adaptation for every particular action. From this it follows that it is morally impossible that there should be sufficient diversity in any machine to allow it to act in all the events of life in the same way as our reason causes us to act.[4]

It is worth quoting Descartes's words at such length because they contain the seeds of a great deal of subsequent intellectual history. Distinctions between the body and the soul were, of course, of great antiquity, as was the idea that people could be distinguished from animals by their reasoned use of language. Descartes, though, extended these ideas with an extremely detailed physiology. His clearly drawn dualism held that automata, animals, and the human body could all be explained by the same mechanistic laws of physics, and he set about partitioning functions between body and mind.[5] In establishing this partition, one of the tests was the conventional distinction between animal capabilities, which reside in the body, and specifically human capabilities, which required the exercise of the soul's faculties of reason and will. Thus, for example, automata or animals might utter isolated words or phrases in response to specific stimuli, but lacking the faculty of reason they could not combine these discrete units of language in an unbounded variety of situationally appropriate patterns. The soul itself has ideas, but it has no physical extent or structure. Thus, as Descartes explains in *The Passions of the Soul* (Articles 42 and 43), memory is a function of the brain; when the soul wishes to remember something, it causes animal spirits to propagate to the spot in the brain where the memory is stored, whereupon the original image is presented once again to the soul in the same manner as a visual perception.

The attraction of Descartes's proposals lay not in their particulars, many of which were dubious even to his contemporaries. Rather, Descartes provided a model for a kind of theory making that contrasted with late scholastic philosophy in every way: it was specific and detailed, it was grounded in empirical physiology, and it was written in plain language.

Karl Lashley: Language as a Model for Action

The American cognitivists of the 1950s often modeled themselves after Descartes, and they intended their research to have much of the same appeal. Despite the intervening three centuries, the lines of descent are indeed clear. This is evident in the case of Chomsky, for example, who argued in explicitly Cartesian terms for a clear distinction between the physiology of speech, including the biological basis of linguistic competence, and the capacity for actually choosing what to say. While not a dualist, Chomsky nonetheless epitomized his conception of human nature in terms of "free creation within a system of rule." Miller used Descartes' *Rules for the Direction of the Mind* to motivate his search for ways that people might more efficiently use their limited memories.[6]

The first and most influential revival of research into mental mechanisms, Karl Lashley's 1951 paper "The Problem of Serial Order in Behavior," did not acknowledge any sources beyond the linguistics, psychology, and neurophysiology of the 1940s.[7] Nonetheless, the underlying continuities are important for the computational ideas that followed. Despite his own complex relationship to behaviorism, Lashley argued clearly that behaviorist psychology could not adequately explain the complexity of human behavior. He focused on a particular category of behavior, namely speech. He pointed out that linguists could demonstrate patterns in the grammar and morphology of human languages that are hard to account for by using the theory of associative chains, whereby each action's effects in the world give rise to stimuli that then trigger the next action in turn. The formal structures exhibited by human language, then, were sufficient reason to restore some notion of mental processing to psychology.

Moreover, Lashley suggested that *all* action be understood on the model of language. He regarded both speech and physical movement as having a syntax, and he sought the physiological basis of both the syntax of movement and the choice of specific movements from among the syntactically possible combinations. This suggestion was enormously consequential for the subsequent development of cognitivist psychology, and particularly for AI. Lashley summarized the idea in this way:

> It is possible to designate, that is, to point to specific examples of, the phenomena of the syntax of movement that require explanation, although those phenomena cannot be clearly defined. A real definition would be a long step toward solution of the problem. There are at least three sets of events to be accounted for. First, the activation of the expressive elements (the individual words or adaptive acts) which do not contain the temporal relations. Second, the determining tendency, the set, or idea. This masquerades under many names in contemporary psychology, but is, in every case, an inference from the restriction of behavior within definite limits. Third, the syntax of the act, which can be described as an habitual order or mode of relating the expressive elements; a generalized pattern or schema of integration which may be imposed upon a wide range and a wide variety of specific acts. This is the essential problem of serial order; the existence of generalized schemata of action which determine the sequence of specific acts, acts which in themselves or in their associations seem to have no temporal valence.[8]

Two things are new to cognitive theorizing here: grammar as a principle of mental structure and the generalization of grammatical form to all action. But a great deal in Lashley's account is continuous with that of Descartes. To start with, it is an attempt at an architecture of cognition. Indeed, it is considerably less detailed than Descartes' architecture, although Descartes provided no account of the mechanics of speech. Both Lashley and Descartes assign the ability to speak individual words—or in Lashley's case, to make individual discrete physical movements—to individual bits of machinery, without being very specific about what these bits of machinery are like; and they both view the human capacity for putting these elements together as the signature of the mind. To be sure, Lashley's argument rests on the formal complexity of speech whereas Descartes' points at the appropriateness of each utterance to the specific situation. In each case, though, what counts is the capacity of the mind to order the elements of language in an unbounded variety of ways.

The continuities go deeper. Lashley, as a neurophysiologist, shows no signs of believing in an ontological dualism such as Descartes'. Yet the conceptual *relations* among the various components of his theory are analogous to those of Descartes. In each case, the brain subserves a repertoire of bodily capacities, and on every occasion the mind orders these in accord with its choices, which themselves are not explained. For Descartes, the mind's choices simply *cannot* be explained in causal terms, though its operations can be described in the normative terms of reason, as for example in his *Rules for the Direction of the Mind*. Lashley does not express any overt skepticism about his "determining tendency," but neither does he have anything very definite to say about it; the concept stays nebulous throughout. This is not simply an incompleteness of Lashley's paper but is inherent in its design: the purpose of the determining tendency is not to *have* structure in itself but to *impose* structure upon moment-to-moment activities from the repertoire of action schemata made available to it by the brain.

In retrospect, then, Lashley's paper makes clear the shape of the challenge that the cognitivists had set themselves. They wished to rout their sterile behaviorist foes in the same way that Descartes had routed the schoolmen, by providing a scientific account of cognitive processes. The problem, of course, is that Descartes was not a thoroughgoing mechanist. So long as the cognitivists retained the relational system of ideas that they had inherited from Descartes, and from the much larger tradition of which Descartes is a part, each of their models would include a component corresponding to the soul. No matter how it might be squeezed or divided or ignored, there would always remain one black box that seemed fully as intelligent as the person as a whole, capable of making intelligent choices from a given range of options on a regular basis. As the field of AI developed, this recalcitrant box acquired several names. Dennett, for example, spoke of the need for "discharging the homunculus," something he imagined to be possible by dividing the intelligent homunculus into successively less intelligent pieces, homunculi within homunculi like the layers of an onion, until one reached a homunculus sufficiently dumb to be implemented in a bit of computer code.[9] AI researchers' jargon spoke of subproblems as being AI-complete (an analogy: so-called NP-complete computational problems are thought to be unsolvable except through an enumeration of possible solutions—an efficient algorithm for any one such problem would yield efficient algorithms for all of them). Furthermore, several exceedingly skilled programmers devised computer systems that were capable of reasoning about their own operation, including reasoning about their reasoning about their own operation, and so on *ad infinitum*.[10] In each case, the strategy was to reduce the soul's infinite choices to finite mechanical means.

But beyond sketching the shape of a future problem, Lashley also sketched the principal strategy of a whole generation for solving it. The operation of the determining tendency might be a mystery, but the general form of its accomplishment was not. While the linguistic metaphor for action envisions an infinite variety of possible actions, it also imposes a great deal of structure on them. In mathematical terms, the possible actions form a space. The generative principle of this space lies in the "schemata of action," which are modeled on grammatical rules. A simple schema for English sentences might be

Sentence → NounPhrase IntransitiveVerb.

That is, roughly speaking "one way to make a sentence is to utter a noun phrase followed by an intransitive verb." Other rules might spell out these various categories further, for example,

NounPhrase → Article Noun

Article → *a*

Article → *the*

Noun → *cat*

Noun → *dog*

IntransitiveVerb → *slept*

IntransitiveVerb → *died*

These mean, roughly, "one way to make a noun phrase is to utter an article followed by a noun," "some possible articles are *a* and *the*," "some possible nouns are *cat* and *dog*," and "some possible intransitive verbs are *slept* and *died*." There might be other ways to make sentences, for example,

Sentence → NounPhrase TransitiveVerb NounPhrase.

TransitiveVerb → *saw*

TransitiveVerb → *ate*

This particular set of grammatical rules generates a finite space of English sentences, for example,

the cat saw a dog.

a dog ate a dog.

The process of deriving a sentence with these rules is simple and orderly. One begins with the category Sentence, and then at each step one makes two choices: (1) which category to expand, and (2) which rule to apply in doing so, until no categories are left. For example, one might proceed as follows:

1. Sentence
2. NounPhrase TransitiveVerb NounPhrase
3. NounPhrase TransitiveVerb Article Noun
4. NounPhrase *saw* Article Noun
5. Article Noun *saw* Article Noun
6. *the* Noun *saw* Article Noun
7. *the* Noun *saw* Article *dog*
8. *the cat saw* Article *dog*
9. *the cat saw a dog*

The space of possible sentences, then, resembles a branching road with a definite set of choices at each point. The process of choosing a sentence is reduced to a series of much smaller choices among a small array of alternatives. The virtue of this reduction becomes clearer once the grammar generates an infinite array of sentences, as becomes the case when the following grammatical rules are added to the ones above:

Sentence → NounPhrase CognitiveVerb *that* Sentence

CognitiveVerb → *thought*

CognitiveVerb → *forgot*

It now becomes possible to generate sentences such as

the cat thought that the dog forgot that a cat slept

Chomsky in particular made a great deal of this point; following Humboldt, he spoke of language as making "infinite use of finite means."[11] Further, although he believes that the mind ultimately has a biological (and thus mechanical) explanation, he has focused his research on the level of grammatical competence rather than trying to uncover this explanation himself.[12]

Allen Newell and Herbert Simon: The Mechanization of the Soul

Instead, the first steps in mechanizing this idea of a generative space are due to Newell and Simon.[13] Whereas Chomsky was concerned simply with the precise extent of the generative space of English grammar, Newell and Simon's computer program had to make actual choices within a generative space. Whereas Lashley posited the existence of a "determining tendency" whose genealogical origins lay in a nonmechanical soul, Newell and Simon had to provide some mechanical specification of it. Here the generative structure of the space was crucial. Newell and Simon did not employ linguistic vocabulary. Nonetheless, just as grammatical rules and derivations provide a simple, clear means of generating any grammatical sentence, the application of operators provided Newell and Simon with a simple, easily mechanized means of generating any possible sequence of basic actions. Choosing *which* sequence of actions to adopt was a matter of search. The mechanism that conducted the search did not have to make correct choices all the time; it simply had to make good enough choices eventually as it explored the space of possibilities.

Newell and Simon assigned enormous significance to this idea, and justifiably so.[14] While maintaining the system of conceptual relations already found in Descartes, Lashley, and Chomsky, their program nonetheless embodied a serious proposal for the mechanization of the soul.[15] Their strategy was ingenious: rather than endow the soul with an internal architecture—something incomprehensible within the system of ideas they inherited—they effectively proposed interpreting the soul as an epiphenomenon. Ironically, given Descartes' polemics against scholastic philosophy, the idea is

approximately Aristotelian: the soul as the form of the person, not a discrete component. More specifically, rather than being identified with any particular device, the
soul was *contained* by the generative structure of the search space and *manifested*
through the operation of search mechanisms. These search mechanisms were heuristic
in the sense that no single choice was ever guaranteed to be correct, yet the overall effect of sustained searching was the eventual discovery of a correct outcome. Despite
the simplicity and limitations of their early programs, Newell and Simon were willing
to refer to these programs' behavior as intelligent because they met this criterion. In
addition, they regarded their proposal as promising because so many human activities
could readily be cast as search problems.

Up to this point, the story of the mechanization of the soul is a conventional chapter
in the history of ideas: to tell this story, we trace the unfolding of an intellectual project within an invariant framework of continuities or analogies among idea systems.
With Newell and Simon's program, though, the story clearly changes its character.
But how exactly? So far as the disciplinary culture of AI is concerned, the formalization
and implementation of an idea bring a wholly new day—a discontinuity between the
prehistory of (mere) questions and ideas, and the history, properly speaking, of problems and techniques. Once this "proper" history has begun, technical people can put
their proposals to the test of implementation: either it works or it does not work.

Yet despite this conception, and indeed partly because of it, the development of
technical methods can be seen to continue a long trajectory largely determined by the
defining projects and internal tensions of the ancestral systems of ideas. In particular,
these projects and tensions continue to manifest themselves in the goals and tribulations of AI's technical work. In the case of Newell and Simon's proposal, the central
goals and tribulations clustered around the problem of *search control:* that is, making
heuristic search choices well enough—not perfectly, just well enough—to allow the
search process to terminate with an acceptable answer within an acceptable amount
of time. An enormous AI subliterature addresses this problem in a wide variety of
ways. Within this literature, searches are said to explode because of the vastness of
search spaces. It should be emphasized that mediocre search control ideas do not kill
a mechanism; they only slow it down. Yet this research has long faced a troubling aporia: the more complicated the world is, the more choices become possible at each point
in the search, and the more ingenuity is required to keep the search process under control. The metaphors speak of a struggle of containment between explosion and control.
Such a struggle, indeed, seems inherent in any theory for which action is said to result
from formal reason conducted by a finite being.[16]

Newell and Simon's achievement thus proved tenuous. So long as AI's self-
conception as a self-sufficient technical discipline has remained intact, however, these
difficulties are readily parsed as technical problems seeking technical solutions. An endless variety of solutions to the search control problem has indeed been proposed, and

each of them more or less works within the bounds of one or another set of assumptions about the world of practical activity.

Richard Fikes and Nils Nilsson: Mechanizing Embodied Action

To watch the dynamics of this process unfold, it will help to consider one final chapter: the STRIPS program.[17] The purpose of STRIPS is to automatically derive plans for a robot to follow in transporting objects around in a maze of rooms. The program constructs these plans through a search process modeled on those of Newell and Simon.[18] The search space consists of partially specified plans, with each operator adding another step to the plan. Returning to the linguistic metaphor, the authors of STRIPS understand the robot's action within a grammar of possible plans. They refer to the units of action that Lashley called "expressive elements" as "primitive actions," and the "syntax of the act" strings these actions into sequences that can be "executed" in the same manner as a computer program. In Descartes' terms, the soul's faculty of reason specifies an appropriate sequence of bodily actions, each of which may well be complicated, its faculty of will decides to undertake them, and the body then physically performs them.

To those who have had experience getting complex symbolic programs to work, the STRIPS papers make intense reading. Because the authors were drawing together so many software techniques for the first time, the technically empathetic reader gets a vivid sense of struggle: the unfolding logic of what the authors unexpectedly felt compelled to do, given what seemed to be required to get the program to work. A detailed consideration of the issues would take us much too far afield, but the bottom line is easy enough to explain. As might be expected, this bottom line concerns the technical practicalities of search control. A great deal is at stake: if the search can be controlled without making absurdly unrealistic assumptions about the robot's world, then the program can truly be labeled intelligent in some nontrivial sense.

Consider, though, what this search entails. The STRIPS program is searching for a correct plan: that is, a plan which, if executed in the world as it currently stands, would achieve a given goal. This condition—achieving a given goal—is not simply a property of the plan; it is a property of the robot's interactions with its world. In order to determine whether a given plan is correct, then, the program must effectively conduct a simulation of the likely outcome of each action. For example, if a candidate plan contains the primitive action "step forward," it matters whether the robot is facing a wall, a door, a pile of rubbish, or an open stretch of floor. If "step forward" is the *first* step in the plan, then the robot can predict its outcome simply by activating its video camera and looking ahead of itself. But if "step forward" is the seventh step in the plan, subsequent to several other movements, then complex reasoning will be required to determine its likely outcome.

This is a severely challenging problem, and Fikes and Nilsson approached it, reasonably enough given the state of computer technology in 1971, through brute force: they encoded the robot's world in the form of a set of formulas in the predicate calculus, and they incorporated into STRIPS a general-purpose program for proving predicate calculus theorems by means of a search through the space of possible formal proofs. This approach works in the same sense that any search method works: if the search ever terminates, then the answer is correct, but how long this takes depends heavily on the perspicacity of the program's search control policies. And adequately perspicuous search control policies are notoriously elusive. As programmers like Fikes and Nilsson quickly learned, the trick is to design the world, and the robot's representations of the world, in such a way that long, involved chains of reasoning are not required to predict the outcomes of actions.

Yet predicting the outcomes of actions was, as programmers say, only the inner loop of the plan construction process. Recall that the overall process of choosing possible actions is also structured as a search problem; extending Lashley's linguistic metaphor, it is as if the grammaticality of a spoken sentence depended on the listener's reaction to each successive word. Moreover, the space of possible plans is enormous: at any given time, the robot can take any of about a dozen primitive actions, depending on its immediate circumstances, and even a simple plan will have several steps. Once again, search control policies are crucial. At each point in the search process, the program must make two relatively constrained choices among a manageable list of options: it must choose a partially specified plan to further refine, and it must choose a means of further refining it—roughly speaking, it must add another primitive action to the plan.

As with any search, making these choices correctly every time would require intelligence that no mechanism could probably possess. The point, instead, is to make the choices correctly *often enough* for the search to settle on a correct answer in a reasonable amount of time. This, once again, is the appeal of heuristic search: intelligent action emerges from a mass of readily mechanizable decisions. In other words, the problem for Fikes and Nilsson was that they had to write bits of code whose outcomes approximated two hopelessly uncomputable notions: "partially specified plan most likely to lead to a correct plan" and "best primitive action to add to this subplan." Their solution to these problems was unsurprising in technical retrospect, and the details do not matter here. Briefly, they chose whatever partially specified plan seemed to have gotten the furthest toward the goal with the smallest number of primitive actions, and they chose a new primitive action that allowed the theorem-proving program to make further progress toward proving that the goal had been achieved. Both of these criteria are virtually guaranteed to lead the plan construction process down blind alleys (such as telling the robot to head for the door before getting the key). The important point is that these blind alleys did not hurt the robot; they only kept the robot waiting longer to be given a plan to execute.

How big a step was the STRIPS program toward mechanized intelligence? Reasonable people could disagree. It is certainly an impressive thing to watch such a program in operation—provided you have a long enough time to wait. But the question of search control was daunting. To the AI research people of that era, search control in STRIPS-like plan construction programs was a problem to be addressed through a wide variety of technical means. Yet this approach accepts as given the underlying structure of the situation: a steep trade-off between the complexity of the world and the practicality of the search control problem. If the robot can perform many possible actions, or if the results of these actions depend in complex ways on the circumstances, then the search space grows rapidly—in mathematical terms, exponentially—in size. If it is impossible to predict the outcomes of actions—say, because the robot is not the only source of change in the world—then the search space will have to include all the *possible* outcomes as well. In a prescient aside in the sequel to the original STRIPS paper, Fikes, Hart, and Nilsson pointed this out:

One of the novel elements introduced into artificial intelligence research by work on robots is the study of execution strategies and how they interact with planning activities. Since robot plans must ultimately be executed in the real world by a mechanical device, as opposed to being carried out in a mathematical space or by a simulator, consideration must be given by the executor to the possibility that operations in the plan may not accomplish what they were intended to, that data obtained from sensory devices may be inaccurate, and that mechanical tolerances may introduce errors as the plan is executed.

Many of these problems of plan execution would disappear if our system generated a whole new plan after each execution step. Obviously, such a strategy would be too costly, so we instead seek a plan execution scheme with the following properties:

1. When new information obtained during plan execution implies that some remaining portion of the plan need not be executed, the executor should recognize such information and omit the unneeded plan steps.

2. When execution of some portion of the plan fails to achieve the intended results, the executor should recognize the failure and either direct reexecution of some portion of the plan or, as a default, call for a replanning activity.[19]

Thus, although they recognized the tension that was inherent in the system of concepts they had inherited, the technical imagination of that time provided Fikes, Hart, and Nilsson with no other way of structuring the basic question of intelligent action. It was fifteen years before the inherent dilemma of plan construction was given definite mathematical form, first by Chapman and then more compactly by McAllester and Rosenblitt.[20] This kind of research does not decisively discredit the conceptual framework of planning-as-search; rather, it clarifies the precise nature of the trade-offs generated by that framework. Indeed, productive research continues to this day into the formal structure of plan construction search problems.

Beyond the Cartesian Soul

The previous sections offer a critical reconstruction of a single strand of intellectual history, a single intellectual proposition worked out in increasingly greater technical detail such that its internal tensions become manifest. To diagnose the resulting impasse and move beyond it, it will be necessary to transcend AI's conception of itself as a technical, formalizing discipline and instead to reconsider the larger intellectual path of which AI research has been a part. No matter how esoteric AI literature has become, and no matter how thoroughly the intellectual origins of AI's technical methods have been forgotten, the technical work of AI has nonetheless been engaged in an effort to domesticate the Cartesian soul into a technical order in which it does not belong. The problem is not that the individual operations of Cartesian reason cannot be mechanized—they can be—but that the role assigned to the soul in the larger architecture of cognition is untenable. This incompatibility has shown itself in a pervasive and ever more clear pattern of technical frustrations. The difficulty can be shoved into one area or another through programmers' choices about architectures and representation schemes, but it cannot be made to go away.

This impasse, however, is not a failure. To the contrary, tracing the precise shape of the impasse allows us to delineate with particular confidence the internal tensions in the relational system of ideas around the Cartesian soul. According to this hypothesis, the fundamental embarrassment of Descartes' theory does not lie in the untenability of ontological dualism. Rather, it lies in the soul's causal distance from the world of practical action. As this world grows more complex (or, more precisely, as one's representational schemes reflect this world's complexity more fully), and as one becomes more fully immersed in that world, the soul's job becomes astronomically difficult. Yet Descartes performed his analysis of the soul in sedentary conditions: introspecting, visualizing, and isolating particular episodes of perception. When he did discuss complex activities, he focused not on the practicalities of their organization but on the struggles they engendered between the body and the soul.[21]

In order to impose intelligent order on its body's actions, the Cartesian soul faces a stern task. For example, to visualize a future course of events, the soul must stimulate the brain to assemble the necessary elements of memory. The reasoning that guides this visualization process must be based in turn upon certain knowledge of the world, obtained through the senses: enough information to visualize fully the outcomes of the individual's planned sequence of actions. Our judgment that such a scheme places an excessive burden on the soul—or, as technical people would say, makes the soul into a bottleneck—is not a logical refutation; it is only an engineer's embodied judgment of the implausibility of a design. But within the logic of Descartes' project that is a lot.

The underlying difficulty takes perhaps its clearest form in Lashley. At the beginning of his lecture, he opposes his own view to the behaviorist and reflexological tale of stimuli and responses as follows:

My principal thesis today will be that the input is never into a quiescent or static system, but always into a system which is already actively excited and organized. In the intact organism, behavior is the result of interaction of this background of excitation with input from any designated stimulus. Only when we can state the general characteristics of this background of excitation, can we understand the effects of a given input.[22]

In contradistinction to a scheme that focuses upon the effects of an isolated stimulus, Lashley proposes giving due weight both to a stimulus and to the ongoing flux of brain activity into which the stimulus intervenes. People, in other words, are always thinking as well as interacting with the world. Having said this, though, he immediately gives priority to the internal background of neural activity, and his paper never returns to any consideration of external stimuli and their effects. As with his silence about the nature of the determining tendency, this is not a simple omission but rather is intrinsic to his relational system of concepts. His analysis of action on the model of speech portrays speakers as laying out a complex series of sounds through internal processing and then producing them in a serially ordered sequence, without in any way interacting with the outside world.[23] As we have already seen in the case of STRIPS, this obscurity about the relationship between planning (of action sequences) and interaction (with the world while those actions are going on) structured cognitive theorizing about action, and AI research in particular, for many years afterward.[24]

It is precisely this pattern of difficulty that has impelled an emerging interdisciplinary movement of computational modelers to seek a conception of intelligent behavior whose focal point is the fullness of embodied activity, not the reticence of thought. An organizing theme of this movement is the principled characterization of interactions between agents and their environments, and the use of such characterizations to guide design and explanation. When the agents in question are robots, this theme opens out onto a systems view of robotic activity within the larger dynamics of the robot's world. When the agents are animals, it opens out onto biology, and specifically onto a conception of ethology in which creatures and their behavior appear thoroughly adapted to the dynamics of a larger ecosystem. When the agents in question are people, it opens out onto philosophical and anthropological conceptions of human beings as profoundly embedded in their social environments. In lieu of detailed references to these directions of research, allow me to direct the reader to an issue of *Artificial Intelligence* on computational theories of interaction and agency that appeared in 1995.[25]

AI and the Humanities

I have argued that AI can become sterile unless it maintains a sense of its place in the history of ideas, and in particular, unless it maintains a respect for the power of inherited systems of ideas to shape our thinking and our research in the present day. At the same time, AI also provides a powerful means of forcing into the open the internal structure of a system of ideas and the internal tensions inherent in the project of getting those ideas to work. Thus, AI properly understood ought to be able to participate in a constructive symbiosis with humanistic analyses of ideas.

Putting this mode of cooperative work into practice will not be easy. The obstacles are many and varied, but I believe that the most fundamental ones pertain to the use in AI of mathematics and mathematical formalization. This is not the place for a general treatment of these topics, but it is possible at least to outline some of the issues. The most obvious issue, perhaps, is the symbolic meaning attached to mathematics in the discursive construction of technical disciplines. Technical people frequently speak of mathematics as "clean" and "precise," as opposed to the "messy" and "vague" nature of the social world and humanistic disciplines. These metaphors clearly provide rich points of entry for critical research, but the important point here is that their practical uses go beyond the simple construction of hierarchies among disciplines. Most particularly, the notion of mathematics as the telos of reason structures AI researchers' awareness in profound ways.

To see this, let us briefly consider the role that mathematics plays in AI research. The business of AI is to build computer programs whose operation can be narrated in language that is normally used to describe human activities.[26] Since the function of computers is specified in terms of discrete mathematics, the daily work of AI includes the complex and subtle discursive practice of talking about human activities in ways that assimilate them to mathematical structures.[27] In the case of the computational models of action, this assimilation is achieved by means of a linguistic metaphor for action. This metaphor is not specific to AI; in fact, it structures a great deal of the practice of applied computing.[28] This fact in turn points to an inherent source of intellectual conservatism in AI: the field is not restricted a priori to speaking of human beings in particular terms, but it *is* restricted to speaking in terms that someone knows how to assimilate to mathematical structures that can be programmed on computers. In this way, the existing intellectual infrastructure of computing—its stock of discursive forms and technical methods—drags like an anchor behind any project that would reinvent AI using language drawn from alternative conceptions of human beings and their lives.

This observation goes far toward explaining the strange appearance that AI presents to fields such as literature and anthropology that routinely employ much more sophisticated and critically reflective conceptions of human life. The first priority for AI research is to get something working on a computer, and the field does not reward gnawing doubts about whether the conceptions of human life being formalized along the way are sufficiently subtle, accurate, or socially responsible—thus the emphasis, mentioned at the outset, on "doing" as opposed to "just talking." Critical methods from the humanities are likely to appear pointless, inasmuch as they do not immediately deliver formalizations or otherwise explain what programs one might write. AI people see formalization as a trajectory with an endpoint, in which the vagueness and ambiguity of ordinary language are repaired through mathematical definition, and they are not greatly concerned with the semantic violence that might be done to that language in the process of formal definition. A word like *action* might present real challenges to a philosophical project that aims to respect ordinary usage,[29] but the assimilation of action to formal language theory reduces the word to a much simpler form: a repertoire of possible "actions" assembled from a discrete, finite vocabulary of "expressive elements" or "primitives." Having thus taken its place in the technical vocabulary of AI, the word's original semantic ramifications are lost as potential resources for AI work. The ideology surrounding formalization accords no intrinsic value to these leftover materials. As a result, formalization becomes a highly organized form of social forgetting, not only of the semantics of words but of their historicity as well. This is why the historical provenance and intellectual development of AI's underlying ideas claim so little interest among the field's practitioners.

What would a reformed AI look like? It would certainly not reject or replace mathematics. Rather, it would draw upon critical research to cultivate a reflexive awareness of how mathematical formalization is used as part of the engineer's embodied work of building things and seeing what they do. In particular, it would cultivate an awareness of the cycle of formalization, the technical working-out, the emergence of technical impasses, the critical work of diagnosing an impasse as reflecting either a superficial or a profound difficulty with the underlying conception of action, and the initiation of new and more informed rounds of formal modeling. The privilege in this cycle does not lie with the formalization process, nor does it lie with the critical diagnosis of technical impasses. Rather, it lies with the cycle itself, in the researcher's "reflective conversation with the materials" of technical and critical work.[30]

Humanistic critical practice can take up numerous relationships, cooperative or not, to this cycle of research. My own analysis here has employed a relatively old-fashioned set of humanistic methods from the history of ideas, tracing the continuity of certain themes across a series of authors and their intellectual projects. Since formalization is a fundamentally metaphorical process, discursively interrelating one set of things with another, mathematical set, it can be particularly fruitful to trace the historical travels of a given metaphor among various institutional sites in society, technical and otherwise.[31] The purpose in doing so is not simply to debunk any claims that technical institutions might make to an ahistorical authority, but to prevent the passage to formalism from forgetting the underlying commitments that a given way of speaking about

human activities draws from its broader cultural embedding.[32] This contextual awareness will be crucial when the technical research reaches an impasse and needs to be
diagnosed as a manifestation of internal tensions within the underlying system of
ideas. Any given set of ideas will be more easily given up when they are seen as simply
one path among many others not taken. Indeed, this awareness of context will be crucial for recognizing that an impasse may have occurred in the first place. Viewed in this
way, technical impasses are a form of social remembering, moments when a particular
discursive form deconstructs itself and makes its internal tensions intelligible to anyone who is critically equipped to hear them.

   The cycle of reaching and interpreting technical impasses, moving back and forth
between technical design and critical inquiry, can be practiced on a variety of scales,
depending upon the acuity of one's critical methods. The example I traced here was
extremely coarse: whole decades of research could be seen in hindsight to have been
working through a single, clear-cut intellectual problem. The difficulty was not that AI
practitioners were insulated from the philosophical critiques of Cartesian reason that
might have provided a diagnosis of their difficulties and defined the contours of alternative territories of research. To the contrary, Hubert Dreyfus was articulating some of
these critiques all along. The real difficulty was that the critical apparatus of the field
did not provide its practitioners with a living, day-to-day appreciation for the contingent nature of their formalisms. Although they viewed formalization as conferring
upon language a cleanliness and precision that it did not otherwise possess, the effect
was precisely the reverse. Lacking a conscious awareness of the immense historicity of
their language, they could not understand it as it called out to them the very things
they had discovered. A reformed technical practice would employ the tools of critical
inquiry to engage in a richer and more animated conversation with the world.

Notes

This chapter has been improved by comments from Harry Collins, Güven Güzeldere, Scott Main-
waring, Beth Preston, and Jozsef Toth.

1. See Hubert L. Dreyfus, *What Computers Can't Do: A Critique of Artificial Reason* (New York:
Harper, 1972); Martin Heidegger, *Being and Time*, trans. John Macquarrie and Edward Robinson
(1927; New York: Harper, 1961); Ludwig Wittgenstein, *Philosophical Investigations*, 3d ed., trans.
G.E.M. Anscombe (1953; New York: Macmillan, 1968).

2. For a detailed analysis of this argument, see Elizabeth F. Preston, "Heidegger and Artificial Intelligence," *Philosophy and Phenomenological Research* 53 (no. 1, 1993): 43–69.

3. Dreyfus, in joint work with Stuart Dreyfus, has been cautiously supportive of one alternative
AI research program, the connectionist attempt to build simulations of neural circuitry without
necessarily formulating knowledge in terms of symbolic rules. See Hubert L. Dreyfus and Stuart

Dreyfus, "Making a Mind vs. Modeling the Brain: AI Back at a Branchpoint," *Daedalus* 117 (no. 1, 1988): 15–43. But as the Dreyfuses point out, this research program still faces a long, difficult learning curve; I do not discuss it here.

4. René Descartes, *The Philosophical Works of René Descartes*, trans. Elizabeth S. Haldane and George R. T. Ross, vol. 1 (Cambridge: Cambridge University Press, 1972), 116.

5. The terms *mechanism* and *mechanistic* require more analysis than space permits here. Suffice it to say that a mechanism is a physical object whose workings are wholly explicable in causal terms. To speak of something as a mechanism, furthermore, is to insert it into a rhetoric of engineering design, whether divine or human, and whether on the model of the clockmaker or the computer programmer. For the modern mathematical interpretations of the term, which are obviously relevant to the foundations of computing if not immediately to the genealogy being traced here, see Judson Chambers Webb, *Mechanism, Mentalism, and Mathematics: An Essay on Finitism* (Dordrecht: Reidel, 1980). Note also that the intellectual culture of Descartes' day did not distinguish between "mind" and "soul," and the two terms continue to be used interchangeably in Catholic philosophy; see, for example, Ludger Holscher, *The Reality of the Mind: Augustine's Philosophical Arguments for the Human Soul as a Spiritual Substance* (London: Routledge, 1986). Even in the present day, these terms are usually not so much opposed as simply employed in different discourses with overlapping genealogies.

6. Noam Chomsky, *Problems of Knowledge and Freedom: The Russell Lectures* (New York: Pantheon, 1971), 50; George A. Miller, "Information and Memory," *Scientific American* 195 (no. 2, 1956): 42–46.

7. Karl S. Lashley, "The Problem of Serial Order in Behavior," in *Cerebral Mechanisms in Behavior: The Hixon Symposium*, ed. Lloyd A. Jeffress (New York: Wiley, 1951).

8. Lashley, 122.

9. Daniel Dennett, "Why the Law of Effect Will Not Go Away," in *Brainstorms: Philosophical Essays on Mind and Psychology*, ed. Daniel Dennett (Montgomery, Vt.: Bradford Books, 1978), 80–81.

10. See Brian C. Smith, "Prologue to *Reflection and Semantics in a Procedural Language*," in *Readings in Knowledge Representation*, ed. Ronald J. Brachman and Hector J. Levesque (Los Altos, Calif.: Morgan Kaufmann, 1985).

11. Noam Chomsky, *Aspects of the Theory of Syntax* (Cambridge, Mass.: MIT Press, 1965), 8.

12. Noam Chomsky, *Language and Responsibility*, trans. John Viertel (New York: Pantheon, 1979), 66, 97.

13. Allen Newell and Herbert A. Simon, "GPS: A Program That Simulates Human Thought," in *Computers and Thought*, ed. Edward A. Feigenbaum and Julian Feldman (New York: McGraw-Hill, 1963).

14. See, for example, Newell's comments in Philip E. Agre, "Interview with Allen Newell," *Artificial Intelligence* 59 (nos. 1–2, 1993): 415–449, 418.

15. C. R. Gallistel, *The Organization of Action: A New Synthesis* (Hillsdale, N.J.: Erlbaum, 1980), 6–7.

16. Christopher Cherniak, *Minimal Rationality* (Cambridge, Mass.: MIT Press, 1986).

17. Richard E. Fikes and Nils J. Nilsson, "STRIPS: A New Approach to the Application of Theorem Proving to Problem Solving," *Artificial Intelligence* 2 (no. 3, 1971): 189–208.

18. See David Chapman, "Planning for Conjunctive Goals," *Artificial Intelligence* 32 (no. 3, 1987): 333–377, for a genealogy of the AI planning systems in this lineage.

19. Richard E. Fikes, Peter E. Hart, and Nils J. Nilsson, "Learning and Executing Generalized Robot Plans," *Artificial Intelligence* 3 (no. 4, 1972): 251–288, 268.

20. Chapman, "Planning for Constructive Goals"; David McAllester and David Rosenblitt, "Systematic Nonlinear Planning," in *Proceedings of the 1991 National Conference on Artificial Intelligence*, 634–639.

21. See, for example, Descartes, *Passions of the Soul*, Article 47.

22. Lashley, 112.

23. Actual human speakers frequently do interact with their addressees and others during the real-time production of their utterances, but this fact is rarely taken into account in cognitive theories of grammar and speech. See Charles Goodwin, *Conversational Organization: Interaction Between Speakers and Hearers* (New York: Academic Press, 1981).

24. It is particularly clear in the opening chapter of the influential book by George A. Miller, Eugene Galanter, and Karl H. Pribram, *Plans and the Structure of Behavior* (New York: Holt, Rinehart, and Winston, 1960).

25. Philip Agre, "Computational Research on Interaction and Agency," *Artificial Intelligence* 72 (nos. 1–2, 1995): 1–52.

26. Harry M. Collins, *Artificial Experts: Social Knowledge and Intelligent Machines* (Cambridge, Mass.: MIT Press, 1990).

27. Philip Agre, "Surveillance and Capture: Two Models of Privacy," *The Information Society* 10 (no. 2, 1994): 101–127. This is obviously an attribute that AI shares with a wide variety of other fields, for example, mathematical economics, and much of the analysis here applies to these other fields as well. It should be noted that AI people themselves place great emphasis on a distinction between "neat" forms of AI, which openly avow their commitment to mathematical formalization and employ large amounts of mathematical notation in their papers, and "scruffy" forms, which do not (see Diane E. Forsythe, "Engineering Knowledge: The Construction of Knowledge in Artificial Intelligence," *Social Studies of Science* 23 (no. 3, 1993): 445–477). My argument, though, applies equally to both forms of AI research. Regardless of whether its author was consciously thinking in terms of mathematics, a computer program is a notation whose operational semantics can be specified in mathematical terms. While the formalizations in "neat" research are frequently more consistent, systematic, and explicit than those of "scruffy" research, the design of any computer program necessarily entails a significant level of formalization.

28. Different linguistic metaphors for human action are obviously possible, if perhaps equally problematic; see, for example, Paul Ricoeur, "The Model of the Text: Meaningful Action Considered as a Text," *Social Research* 38 (1971): 529–562.

29. For instance, Alan R. White, ed., *The Philosophy of Action* (London: Oxford University Press, 1968).

30. Donald A. Schön, *The Reflective Practitioner: How Professionals Think in Action* (New York: Basic Books, 1983).

31. See Emily Martin, *The Woman in the Body: A Cultural Analysis of Reproduction* (Boston: Beacon Press, 1987); Paul McReynolds, "The Clock Metaphor in the History of Psychology," in *Scientific Discovery: Case Studies*, ed. Thomas Nickles (Dordrecht: Reidel, 1980); and Philip Mirowski, *More Heat Than Light: Economics as Social Physics, Physics as Nature's Economics* (Cambridge: Cambridge University Press, 1989).

32. For an impressive cultural analysis of the origins of AI, see Paul Edwards, *The Closed World: Computers and the Politics of Discourse in Cold War America* (Cambridge, Mass.: MIT Press, 1996).

The Man-Machine and Artificial Intelligence

Bruce Mazlish

For thousands of years people have wrestled with the question of their human nature. In particular, they have attempted to define themselves in relation to the animal kingdom. Yearning either to take on some of the superior attributes of other animals or to rise above their own animal nature by becoming angelic, human beings have mostly sought to define themselves as a special sort of creation.

People have also created machines, and their new creations in turn have raised the question of whether animals are merely a variant of the machine and whether the machine, as a kind of monster, can turn against its creator and either take over or make humans over in its own image.

These concerns about humankind's animal and mechanical nature came forcefully together in the West in the seventeenth century in terms of a debate over what was called the animal-machine. Were animals mere machines, and were human beings the same, that is, man-machines?

René Descartes' answer, for example, was that animals *were* simply machines; and human beings, *if* one were to set aside their possession of an immaterial soul, might also simply be considered as machines. His famous dualism, however, saved human uniqueness. Michel de Montaigne and his followers took an opposite tack, often asserting the superiority of beasts over humans, vaunting the naturalness of the former. By the eighteenth century, Julien Offray de la Mettrie sought to end the debate by declaring that a human being was a machine, no different in this respect from any other mechanical being. Needless to say, the debate has continued to rage.

In the history of mechanical contrivances, it is difficult to know how many of the automata of antiquity were constructed only in legend or actually by scientific artifice. Icarus's wings melt, in the light of historical inquiry as they were reputed to do in the myth, but was the flying automaton attributed to a Chinese scientist of around 380 B.C.E. actually in the air for three days, as related? (The same story is told of Archytas of Tarentum.)[1] The mix of fact and fiction is of critical importance for the history of science and technology; for our purposes, the aspirations of semimythical inventors can be as revealing as the actual embodiment of automata in levers and gears.

The Chinese and Greek traditions are especially rich on the subject of automata. Indian and, somewhat later, Arabic sources are also copious. Western-centered and limited as this chapter is, I am compelled to note the preeminence of Chinese science and technology in this area. Joseph Needham has made this fact evident in his monumental work, *Science and Civilization in China*.

The wealth of mechanical toys cited in ancient China is awesome. In addition to the flying machine mentioned earlier, mechanized doves and angels, fish and dragons, abounded; automated cup-bearers and wine-pourers were prominent; and hydraulically moved boats, carrying figures of singing girls, animals, and humans in motion are said to have amused the emperors. Of particular interest are the chariots that moved of themselves—*auto*-mobiles—attributed by legend to the scientist Mo Ti in the fourth century B.C.E. Were they actually wheelbarrows, or "pedicarts"? A mechanical man of jade is reported, as well as all kinds of wooden dolls, gold Buddhist statues, and puppet orchestras.

"What is a human being?" asked such automata, by their actions. "A human being is a mechanician" is the most obvious answer. Are humans also machines? Needham cites a long passage from the *Lieh Tzu*, whose probable date is the third century B.C.E., that vividly gives us the flavor of automata development in China and raises the questions of humans' dual nature:

King Mu of Chou made a tour of inspection in the west ... and on his return journey, before reaching China, a certain artificer, Yen Shih by name, was presented to him. The king received him and asked him what he could do. He replied that he would do anything which the king commanded, but that he had a piece of work already finished which he would like to show him. "Bring it with you tomorrow," said the king, "and we will look at it together." So next day Yen Shih appeared again and was admitted into the presence. "Who is that man accompanying you?" asked the king. "That, Sir," replied Yen Shih, "is my own handiwork. He can sing and he can act." The king stared at the figure in astonishment. It walked with rapid strides, moving its head up and down, so that anyone would have taken it for a live human being. The artificer touched its chin, and it began singing, perfectly in tune. He touched its hand, and it began posturing, keeping perfect time. It went through any number of movements that fancy might happen to dictate. The king, looking on with his favorite concubine and other beauties, could hardly persuade himself that it was not real. As the performance was drawing to an end, the robot winked its eye and made advances to the ladies in attendance, whereupon the king became incensed and would have had Yen Shih executed on the spot had not the latter, in mortal fear, instantly taken the robot to pieces to let him see what it really was. And, indeed, it turned out to be only a construction of leather, wood, glue and lacquer, variously colored white, black, red and blue. Examining it closely, the king found all the internal organs complete—liver, gall, heart, lungs, spleen, kidneys, stomach and intestines; and over these again, muscles, bones and limbs with their joints, skin, teeth and hair, all of them artificial. Not a part but was fashioned with the utmost nicety and skill; and when it was put together again, the figure presented the same appearance as when first brought in. The king tried the effect of taking away the heart, and found that the mouth could no longer speak; he took away the liver and the eyes could no longer see; he took away the kidney and the legs lost their power of locomotion. The king was delighted. Drawing a deep breath, he exclaimed, "Can it be that human skill is on a par with that of the great Author of Nature?"[2]

"Anyone would have taken it for a live human being"—here we have one of the key phrases. The robot makes advances to the ladies and incurs the King's wrath, presenting a sexual threat, which is prevalent in fears about automata. In the sentence, "Can it be that human skill is on a par with that of the great Author of Nature?" is sounded what in the West we know as the Promethean theme.

The Greeks, too, were absorbed with automata of one kind or another. The Delphic oracles spoke through a wind-operated "voice," and the god Hephaestus is said to have forged a sort of robot of bronze, named Talos, to guard Crete. Indeed, statues and effigies were themselves godlike, that is, filled with the voices of the gods. We catch this sense of the statue as divine in the writing of Callistratus, in the fourth century A.D., about an ivory and gold statue of the god Asclepius: "Shall we admit that the divine spirit descends into human bodies, there to be even defiled by passions, and nevertheless not believe it in a case where there is no attendant engendering of evil? . . . for see how an image, after Art has portrayed in it a god, even passes over into the god himself! Matter though it is, it gives forth divine intelligence."[3]

A true history of automata would give all the details and would cover the ground systematically.[4] I wish merely to highlight the topic and to pick it up again in more modern times. Note Needham's concluding comment that when the Chinese and European traditions of mechanical toys "came together in the middle of the thirteenth century, the European tradition did not show up to much advantage. The triumphs of the European 'Gadget Age' were yet to come."[5]

In the thirteenth century in Europe, for example, we find reports of exemplary mechanical doves and angels made by Villard de Honnecourt. In the fifteenth century, the mathematician and astronomer Johannes Müller constructed an eagle and a fly that astounded his contemporaries. The twentieth-century historian of science Pierre Duhem has proposed a tentative explanation: "The fly, for instance, would beat its wings by means of springs concealed within it, and make the tour of a dinner-table suspended from a hair invisible to the guests, finally approaching the hand of Regiomontanus [Müller] because of a magnet secretly held by him."[6]

In this account, Müller seems as much magician as mechanician. The connection is not accidental, according to Francis Yates and others, who posit a "Hermetic tradition" in Renaissance science. Yates's argument, for example, is that "the Renaissance magus was the immediate ancestor of the seventeenth-century scientist." In turn, the Renaissance magus "had his roots in the Hermetic core of Renaissance Neo-Platonism."[7]

It was especially Marsilio Ficino, along with Pico della Mirandola, who revived and carried forward the Hermetic tradition into the Renaissance. Ficino translated the collection of treatises that supposedly were written by Hermes Trismegistus, whom he believed to have been a real Egyptian priest and who gave an account, like Moses, of man and the cosmos. In the Hermetic story of creation, however, humans are given permission by the Father not only to dominate over the animals but also to share in the demiurgic powers, that is, to create and animate artificial beings, as we would call them, or, in my terms, machines. Thus, in the Hermetic *Asclepius*, as Yates informs us, "The Egyptian priests ... are presented as knowing how to capture the effluxes of the stars and through this magical knowledge to animate the statues of their gods."[8]

Alchemy was the Hermetic science *par excellence.* Mere matter could be transformed, for example, into gold, but life also could be distilled from the alchemist's retorts. The other means of creating life out of inanimate matter was through cabalistic conjurations. Small wonder that an air of mystery and magic hung over the Renaissance magus, who rapidly also gained the taint of charlatanism. John Dee, the Elizabethan scientist, is a prime example of the confusion of magic, "chemistry," and mechanics. Called the "great conjurer" for his magic summoning of angels, he was also suspect for his mechanical powers. In vain he protested: "And for ... marvelous Actes and Feates, Naturally, Mathematically, and Mechanically wrought and contrived, ought any honest Student and Modest Christian Philosopher, be counted and called a Conjurer?"[9]

In the Hermetic tradition of the Renaissance, the ancient fascination with automata took on new life. Magic and mechanics were intertwined, and an air of fear and wonder hovered over the statues and angels conjured out of the earth and air: are they alive and real, or not? Are humans, indeed, mechanicians, who can breathe life into what they have created, thereby imitating their own Creator? Or are they merely machines themselves, working on mechanical principles? In the Hermetic tradition of the Renaissance, these questions are close to the surface, though enveloped in mythical and magical shapes.

A century or two later, having passed through the cleansing and brightening waters of Baconian and Cartesian thought, the automata giving rise to these questions seemingly took on a more secular, reasoned form. In the eighteenth century, one of the most skilled technicians was the Frenchman Jacques de Vaucanson. He produced a duck (see figure 1) that, we are told, "drank, ate, digested, cackled, and swam—the whole interior apparatus of digestion exposed, so that it could be viewed; [a] flute player who played twelve different tunes, moving his fingers, lips and tongue, depending on the music; [a] girl who played the tambourine, [and a] mandolin player that moved his head and pretended to breathe."[10]

Even more spectacular were the automata of Pierre Jaquet-Droz, a Swiss, who "in 1774 ... created a life-sized and lifelike figure of a boy seated at a desk, capable of writing up to forty letters." (He still functions at the History Museum in Neuchâtel.) Droz created another figure called the Artist, in the shape of a boy that could draw up to four different sketches, improving on the average work of his human counterpart.

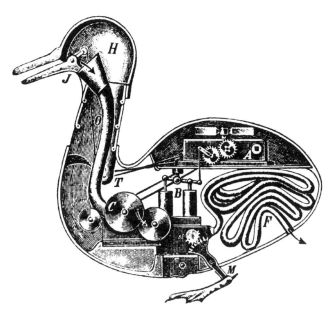

Figure 1
Vaucanson's *Canard digérant* [digesting duck], from Albert Chapuis and Edouard Gélis, *Le monde des automates* (1928).

These mechanical figures were bathed, at the time of the Enlightenment, in the pure light of reason, and discussion of them took place in unambiguous "scientific" terms. We have already listened to some of the discourse, ranging from Descartes to la Mettrie. Underlying this discussion, however, as I shall try to show, ran fear of the automata, for they posed an irrational threat to human beings, calling into question their identity, their sexuality (the basis of creation?), and their powers of domination.

Automata provoked not just fear but also the promise of creative, Promethean force. The tension between these two aspects of the automaton—at play in various examples of the genre—is most interesting. I try to explore here the human ambivalence toward automata in a selected group of examples: "The Nightingale" of Hans Christian Andersen's *Fairy Tales*, the creature in *Frankenstein* by Mary Shelley, Tik-Tok of the Oz stories, R.U.R. of Karel Čapek, and assorted robots of Isaac Asimov.

I could have chosen innumerable other examples, for tales of automata are legion. Those I have chosen, however, are classic examples (Asimov's are currently becoming so) and illustrate different aspects of the human encounter with the mechanical other. Andersen's tale hinges on clockwork mechanisms; Shelley's *Frankenstein*—perhaps the dominant Western metaphor for the fourth discontinuity, straddling both biological and mechanical fears—holds an importance that is self-evident and thus deserves extended treatment; Baum's Oz stories, which obsessively reflect a childlike curiosity about life, are hardly as innocent as they appear; Čapek's R.U.R. gives birth to the term *robot* and voices the fear of robots' taking over, a fear echoed today in countless films about menacing androids; and Asimov's varied cast of robots allows us to explore many of the intellectual dimensions of the predicted coming of a robotic age.

Let us begin with Hans Christian Andersen's "The Nightingale," a famous tale from the nineteenth century. It reflects both the scientific concern with automata and the Romantic revulsion toward the mechanical Newtonian worldview. Newton had imagined the universe as a clockwork. The clock, with its intricate, precise, and more or less unfailing machinery, symbolized the new age of scientific method and industrial discipline. It also prompted additional speculation about the relation between the internal works of human beings and clocks.

In Andersen's tale, we are presented with a real nightingale and one that requires a "watchmaker."[11] The real nightingale charms a Chinese emperor and his peasants alike. Its song brings tears to their eyes. Subsequently, an artificial nightingale appears, even handsomer than the real one because it is ornamented with precious stones. It appears to sing as well and more repeatedly, and is as well received as the original. Banished, the real bird flies away. After a year, however, the artificial nightingale begins to break down and cannot be fully repaired. A few years later, the emperor lays dying, and only the nightingale's song can save him. But the artificial bird has now completely wound down. Suddenly, the live nightingale appears, sings to the emperor, and he comes back to life.

In Andersen's telling, the tale has a poignancy and meaning that cannot be conveyed in a summary. Examined closely, the short story also takes on unexpected ambiguities. The compelling note is the constant comparison between humanmade and natural things: at the beginning, the croaking of frogs is mistaken for church bells by the courtiers, the nightingale's song for glass bells. The artificial bird and the real nightingale cannot sing well together, "for the real Nightingale sang in its own way, and the artificial bird sang waltzes."[12] At first, the palm seems to go to the mechanical contrivance for "three-and-thirty times over did it sing the same piece, and yet was not tired." Praising it, the artificer explains how "with a real nightingale one can never calculate what is coming, but in this artificial bird everything is settled."

In fact, the artificial bird is neither untiring nor settled. It breaks down and cannot be repaired. In contrast, the nightingale goes on living, as if for eternity. Thus, the qualities normally assigned to animate (living) objects and inanimate (nonliving) objects are reversed: it is the animate that endures. This theme is reiterated at the end, when the real nightingale, symbolizing the forces of life, banishes death: in the words of the emperor, "I banished you from my country and empire, and yet you have charmed away the evil forces from my couch, and banished Death from my heart!"[13]

Through this short story, Andersen is saying that the difference between humans and automata is simple and straightforward: one represents life and the other death. It is the Romantic lament. As the nightingale tells the emperor at the end, "I will sing of those who are happy and of those who suffer. I will sing of good and of evil that remain hidden round about you."[14]

Though Andersen's answer to his question about humans and automata is seemingly an untroubled one, it is really surrounded by ambiguous thoughts and feelings. (Andersen had an unhappy youth and occupied his time in solitude by constructing puppet theaters.) His tale is not calculated to satisfy those who feel themselves deeply puzzled and disturbed over the mysteries of life and mechanism.

The artificial nightingale is a clockwork figure. Mary Shelley's *Frankenstein* draws on other sources: it reaches back to the Hermetic tradition, to which it adds the threatening aspect of the legendary golem. Badly written, stilted, a pastiche of styles and inspirations, the book nevertheless exercises an uncanny power over us. It is an alchemist's brew of ideas, whose very formlessness allows us to instill in it all the shapes and forms of our own imagination. Frankenstein's monster looms over our most primordial fears and desires, hulking above our ambivalent feelings toward animals and machines, symbolizing the way in which they take on a life of their own.

Mary Shelley had no formal education. Nevertheless, being the daughter of Mary Wollstonecraft and William Godwin, she moved into a circle of advanced thought. Influenced by the enlightenment of her time, she also breathed the air of mysticism and romanticism that emanated from the Gothic novels of Walpole and Rutledge, and the poetry of Samuel Taylor Coleridge. Her peculiar genius was to connect the ancient myths with early-nineteenth-century science.

The Hermetic tradition seemingly had blessed humans' participation in the demiurge, and looked benignly on their efforts to give life to inanimate statues. In *Frankenstein*, a dark shadow creeps over these efforts: Cornelius Agrippa, Paracelsus, and Albertus Magnus, canonical figures in the Hermetic tradition, are all mentioned as the hero's inspirations, but they are shown as Mephistopheles-like figures, leading him to perdition. It is a golem, not the statues of Hermes Trismegistus, that here becomes animated.

Golems may have originated as wooden or clay models of human beings that were placed in graves to act as servants of the dead.[15] In Europe they took on an especially legendary form in the sixteenth century. The golem, a shapeless mass of clay, could be given form by conjuration: in this case, Jewish kabbalism. A rabbi pronounces holy words and writes on the creature's forehead *Emet*, "truth" in Hebrew, thus endowing the golem with life. When the rabbi erases the *E*, leaving *met*, "death", the creature disintegrates. (In another version, the rabbi writes the name of God, but the process is the same.)

The golem is supposedly the people's servant. He exists to protect his maker's community. But in the legends the golem almost always threatens its master as well—running out of control, falling on him, or going berserk—and finally must be destroyed. (The most famous golem is the one made by Rabbi Löw of Prague in the early seventeenth century.)[16]

Mary Shelley doesn't make overt reference to the golem tales, but they, along with the Hermetic tradition, lie behind her story. Further influences crowd in. Her rationalist father, William Godwin, had written a book, *Lives of the Necromancers*, which, though not published until 1834 (by Mary), reflected earlier conversations between him and his daughter about Agrippa, Paracelsus, Albertus Magnus, the Rosicrucians, and other kabbalistic and maguslike sources. Another current of thought—contemporary science, especially chemistry and electricity—came into play in Mary's mind through her husband, Percy Bysshe Shelley. Though a poet, Percy Bysshe Shelley was fascinated by science. Like Godwin, he had read Paracelsus (who, incidentally, was famous for having claimed that he could create "a little man or homunculus"). As a boy, Shelley had also become intrigued with chemistry, and his rooms at Eton are said to have resembled an alchemist's laboratory. He had also heard of "androids, or mechanical toys that functioned like humans—a product of the scientific genius of Adam Walker, to whose lectures he had listened."[17]

At Oxford, Shelley also experimented with electrical machines, air pumps, galvanic batteries, and other such paraphernalia. Though Lord Byron probably encouraged Mary Shelley to read Sir Humphry Davy's *Elements of Chemical Philosophy* (1812) at the time she began the composition of *Frankenstein*, it was her husband, Percy, who really served as the lightning rod, connecting the ancient alchemists and the modern genie of science in her thought. Indeed, it was Percy who urged her on with the book, helped her write it, penned the preface, and secured its publication.

Davy's *Elements*, which hinted at the possibility of discovering a life force—a subtle universal fluid or vital magnetism—dealt with research into galvanism and electricity. Luigi Galvani's work, or what I like to call the galvanic twitch (see figure 2)—whose movement through nineteenth-century thought has still not been sufficiently traced—had demonstrated the identity of electrical and chemical forces, that is, their interconvertibility. It also suggested that galvanic electricity could bridge the gap between the animate and inanimate; the frog's legs made to twitch seemed to lead to Aldini's experiment in which a shock applied to a recently hanged man produced an effect that, as he wrote, "surpassed our most sanguine expectations, and vitality might perhaps have been restored if many circumstances had not rendered it impossible."[18]

Percy Bysshe Shelley was probably also influenced by the climate of opinion embodied in the term *Naturphilosophie*, though it remains something of a will-o'-the-wisp in the history of science except among specialists. An important movement of thought

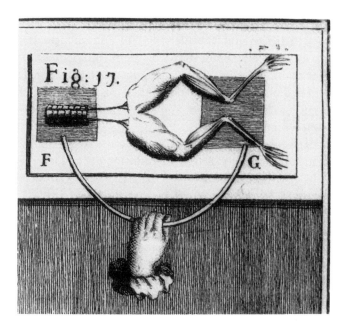

Figure 2

The galvanic twitch. Galvani's twitching frog's legs led to Aldini's experiments, thence to Mary Shelley's *Frankenstein* and the supposed creation of life by means of a spark infused into inanimate materials. Courtesy of Burndy Library, Dibner Institute, Massachusetts Institute of Technology, Cambridge, Mass.

in the early nineteenth century, it has generally been treated with scorn because of its mystical attitude to nature. Though it emphasized vitalism and holism against the dominant materialism and analysis of contemporary Western science (hence, the scorn), both types of philosophy sought to depict the universe as unified and falling under one connecting net of forces, and thus, laws. In any event, *Natürphilosophie* propagated the idea of the interconvertibility of forces, linking the animate and inanimate through galvanism, magnetism (in the form of Mesmerism, it becomes "animal magnetism"), and electricity. Thus animating forces could be made to run between the poles of life and death.

Mary Shelley's knowledge of these developments in science was a hodgepodge; she only dimly and intuitively grasped their meaning. But like the ancient alchemists, she thought she knew enough to attempt their transmutation into the gold of art, and she succeeded, creating an immortal work of fiction, *Frankenstein*. In 1816, on the edge of Lake Leman in Geneva, she combined the shreds and tatters of true science with the myths of antiquity.

We can reconstruct *Frankenstein*'s composition. Byron and a friend, Dr. John Polidori, have joined Mary and Percy in Switzerland. Outside their villa a storm rages; the friends amuse and terrify themselves by telling ghost stories. Byron then proposes that each write his or her own. That night, Mary has a nightmare in which, as she tells us, "I saw the hideous phantasm of a man stretched out, and then, on the working of some powerful engine, shows signs of life, and stir with an uneasy, half vital motion." From this nightmare, *Frankenstein* is born.[19]

I have given some of the background to Mary Shelley's book because to do so illustrates vividly the range of human curiosity, embodied in scientific inquiry and legendary stories, concerning the creation of life from inanimate material. "More, far more will I achieve," exclaims Frankenstein, "treading in the steps already marked, I will pioneer a new way, explore unknown powers, and unfold to the world the deepest mysteries of creation."[20] In penetrating these mysteries, the book resurrects and reclothes a number of humankind's deepest concerns about automata: for example, the servant-machine rising against its master, the fear of the machine's reproducing itself (fundamentally, a sexual fear, as the example of Caliban in Shakespeare's *Tempest* reminds us), and the terror, finally, of human beings realizing that they are one with the machine-monster.

Such is the fundamental attraction and meaning of *Frankenstein*. But little attention has been given to the actual details of the novel, which has now passed into folklore. For this reason, I instance material here that may be familiar to scholars of the book but not necessarily to the general reader.

First, the name Frankenstein is often given to the monster created rather than to its creator; yet, in the book, Frankenstein is the name of the scientist, and his creature has no name. Second, the monster is *not* a machine but a flesh-and-blood product. Third, it is usually forgotten or overlooked that the monster turns to murder *because* his creator, horrified at his production, refuses him human love and kindness. Let us look at a few details.

In writing her Gothic novel in 1816–17, Mary Shelley gave it the subtitle, "The Modern Prometheus." We can see why if we remember that Prometheus defied the gods and gave fire to humankind. Writing from an early-nineteenth-century Romantic perspective, Mary Shelley offers Frankenstein as an example of "how dangerous is the acquirement of knowledge." In this case, specifically, the capability of "bestowing animation upon lifeless matter." In the novel we are told of how, having collected his materials from "the dissecting room and the slaughterhouse," Frankenstein eventually completes his loathsome task when he infuses "a spark of being into the lifeless thing that lay at my feet." Then, as he tells us, "now that I had finished, the beauty of the dream vanished, and breathless horror and disgust filled my heart." Rushing from the room, Frankenstein goes to his bedchamber, where he has a most odd dream concerning the corpse of his dead mother (the whole book as well as this passage cries out for psychoanalytic interpretation) from which he is awakened by "the wretch—the miserable monster whom I had created." Aghast at the countenance of what he has created, Frankenstein escapes from the room and out into the open. Upon finally returning to his room with a friend, he is relieved to find the monster gone.

To understand the myth, we need to recite a few further details in this weird story. Frankenstein's monster eventually finds his way to a hovel attached to a cottage, occupied by a blind father and his son and daughter. Unperceived by them, he learns the elements of social life (the fortuitous way in which this occurs may strain the reader's credulity), even to the point of reading *Paradise Lost*. Resolved to end his unbearable solitude, the monster, convinced that his virtues of the heart will win the cottagers over, makes his presence known. The result is predictable: horrified by his appearance, they duplicate the behavior of his creator and flee. In wrath, the monster turns against the heartless world. He kills, and his first victim—by accident—is Frankenstein's young brother.

Pursued by Frankenstein, the creature eventually confronts its creator. The monster explains his road to murder and, in a torrential address, appeals to Frankenstein:

I entreat you to hear me, before you give vent to your hatred on my devoted head. Have I not suffered enough that you seek to increase my misery? Life, although it may only be an accumulation of anguish, is dear to me, and I will defend it. Remember, thou hast made me more powerful than thyself; my height is superior to thine; my joints more supple. But I will not be tempted to set myself in opposition to thee. I am thy creature, and I will be even mild and docile to my natural lord and king, if thou wilt also perform thy part, that which thou owest me. Oh, Frankenstein, be not equitable to every other, and trample upon me alone, to whom thy justice, and even thy clemency and affection is most due. Remember, that I am thy creature; I ought to be thy Adam; but I am rather the fallen angel, whom thou drives from joy for no misdeed. Everywhere I see bliss, from which I alone am irrevocably excluded. I was benevolent and good; misery made me a fiend. Make me happy, and I shall again be virtuous. (99)

Eventually, the monster extracts from Frankenstein a promise to create a partner for him "of another sex," with whom he will then retire into the vast wilds of South America. But Frankenstein's "compassion" does not last long. In his laboratory again, Frankenstein indulges in a long soliloquy:

I was now about to form another being, of whose dispositions I was alike ignorant; she might become ten thousand times more malignant than her mate; and delight, for its own sake, in murder and wretchedness. He had sworn to quit the neighborhood of man, and hide himself in deserts; but she had not; and she, who in all probability was to become a thinking and reasoning animal, might refuse to comply with a compact made before her creation. They might even hate each other; the creature who already lived loathed his own deformity, and might he not conceive a greater abhorrence for it when it came before his eyes in the female form? She also might quit him, and he be again alone, exasperated by the fresh provocation of being deserted by one of his own species.

Even if they were to leave Europe, and inhabit the deserts of the new world, yet one of the first results of those sympathies for which the demon thirsted would be children, and a race of devils would be propagated upon the earth who might make the very existence of the species of man a condition precarious and full of terror. Had I right, for my own benefit, to inflict this curse upon everlasting generations? (165)

With the monster observing him through the window, Frankenstein destroys the female companion on whom he has been working.

With this, the novel relentlessly winds its way to its end. In despair, the monster revenges himself by killing Frankenstein's best friend, Clerval, then Frankenstein's new bride, Elizabeth. Fleeing to the frozen north, the monster is tracked down by Frankenstein, who dies, however, before he can destroy his dreadful creation. It does not matter; the monster wishes his own death and promises to place himself on a funeral pyre and thus at last secure the spiritual peace for which he has yearned.

It is important to be acquainted with the myth of Frankenstein *as actually written* by Mary Shelley. For most of us, Frankenstein's monster is Boris Karloff, clumping around stiff, automatic, and threatening: a machine of sorts. (My students tell me this image is hopelessly out-of-date; for them Frankenstein is Gene Wilder in Mel Brooks's film *Young Frankenstein*.) We shall have forgotten completely, if ever we knew, that the monster *cum* machine, is evil, or rather, becomes evil, only because it is spurned by humans.

Implicit in *Frankenstein* is the question of an essential discontinuity. If human beings insist on their separateness and superiority with regard to machines (as well as other animals), viewing them as threatening species rather than as a part of their own creation, will they indeed bring about the very state of alienation that they fear? Do differences between humans and machines—and it would be a *reductio ad absurdum* to declare that there are none—add up to a discontinuity? Although Frankenstein's creation is, in fact, a monster, its existence raises the same fundamental mysteries as if it were a machine; such are the amorphous connecting powers of myth.[21]

Mary Shelley, of course, was writing about creation before Charles Darwin; her "mysteries" are without the benefit of his great work on what he called the "mystery of mysteries." Another Darwin, however, not Charles, was summoned directly to Mary's assistance: Erasmus Darwin, Charles's grandfather. In the preface to *Frankenstein* (actually written by Percy) the opening lines state that "the event on which this fiction is founded has been supposed by Dr. Darwin, and some of the physiological writers of Germany, as not of impossible occurrence."[22] Later, in her introduction to the 1831 edition, Mary recalls how she, her husband, and Lord Byron discussed "the nature of the principles of life, and whether there was any probability of its ever being discovered and communicated. They talked of the experiments of Dr. [Erasmus] Darwin ... who preserved a piece of vermicelli in a glass case, till by some extraordinary means it began to move with voluntary motion."

In *Frankenstein*, much ambivalence pervades the scientific quest. "What had been the study and desire of the wisest men since the creation of the world was now within my grasp," we are told by Frankenstein, but it involves him in a loathsome search through "vaults and charnel-houses." When he triumphantly announces that he has become "capable of bestowing animation upon lifeless matter," he must surround it with the disclaimer "I am not recording the vision of a madman."[23] His demurral aside, Frankenstein not only symbolizes the "modern Prometheus," overreaching himself, but also has come to epitomize the "mad scientist," whose hubris has removed him from the circle of humanity. If humans are created in God's world, the monster is spawned in the laboratory. Man, the evil scientist, has taken God's place.

Moreover, the scientist has also taken the place of woman. She has been displaced from the acts of conception and birth. It is the man, Frankenstein, who creates sexlessly. In the novel, sexuality is a threatening force. (In Mary's own life, sex meant death: her mother had died giving birth to her, her best friend had died in childbirth, and so forth; thus the biographical details are important to our understanding of her fiction.) If the monster is allowed to breed, it will take over from humankind. In aborting the birth of a mate, as we have seen, Frankenstein reveals not only his revulsion to sexuality but also his racist fears: a "race of devils" is how he describes the potential new species.

Mary's father, William Godwin, had also envisioned the end of sexuality in his *Enquiry Concerning Political Justice*. As he wrote there, "The whole will be a people of men, and not of children [that is, men will live more or less forever]. Generation will not succeed generation."[24] Diminished sensuality would ensure that the end of generations would also mean the end of the act of generation. Thus, Godwin foresaw a timeless, unchanging utopia where creation had taken place once and for all. Indeed, it was against this illusion that Thomas Malthus wrote *An Essay on the Principle of Population*, insisting that sex—that is, procreation—was one of the necessary postulates of human existence, the other being the necessity of food. If not prevented by moral restraint, procreation leads in turn to the threat of overpopulation. Reading Malthus helped spark into life Charles Darwin's great theory of evolution by natural selection, providing a new scientific account of genesis.

Mary Shelley, however, echoes her father's hopes and fears. She substitutes the test tube for the sexual act in *Frankenstein*. What is more, without a real father and mother, the creature thus conceived is without nurturance and development. "No father had watched my infant days," he laments to Frankenstein, "no mother had blessed me with smiles and caresses." Like a fairer creature, Minerva, from Jove's forehead, the monster has sprung full-grown (and larger than his maker). He is, because of lack of development, inhuman. Made animate by his creator, he is still like an automaton, ultimately lacking in the qualities that would bridge the discontinuity between him and human beings.

In *Frankenstein*, a man, in disgust and fear, rejects his own creation. In doing so, he rejects a part of himself, his double (recognized unconsciously by readers who refer to the monster as "Frankenstein"), for both Frankenstein and the monster are destroyed at the book's end. Left behind them, in the shape of the gargoyles of the mad scientist and the golem-automaton run amok, is a new-old commandment: "Thou shalt not create matter in thine own image."

Frankenstein still gives rise to a *frisson* in modern readers, but it has not put a stop to the ambitions of building humanlike figures. In fact, the automaton frequently has been domesticated in the form of the robot, and often given a friendly, serving face. One such figure is found in the Oz books for children. He is called Tik-Tok and first appears in *Ozma of Oz* (1907). In this seemingly simple book, many of the fundamental questions surrounding human beings, animals, and machines are dealt with disarmingly.

L. Frank Baum, the author, seems to have had a genial obsession with the idea of human identity.[25] An American Andersen of sorts, he modernized the timeless. Though in such tales the threatening characters previously were monsters—the giant in "Jack and the Beanstalk," for instance—here they are often humanized and humorous machines. Harmony reigns in the land of Oz among humans, animals, and machines, and even witches are gently laughed away.

We see these elements at play in all of Baum's Oz books, but especially in *Ozma of Oz*, one of his most delightful excursions into our subject.[26] Dedicated to all boys and girls, it starts with Dorothy Gale of Kansas on a boat, then being washed overboard and clinging to a chicken coop, whose only other occupant is a hen named, by Dorothy, Billina. Unexpectedly, the hen can talk, and when Dorothy says, "I thought hens could only cluck and cackle," the hen replies, "I've clucked and cackled all my life, and never spoken a word before this morning, that I can remember. But when you asked a question, a minute ago, it seemed the most natural thing in the world to answer you. So I spoke, and I seem to keep on speaking, just as you and other human beings do. Strange, isn't it?" Thus, at the beginning of the book, the question of the defining quality of language—humans have language, and hens generally don't—is put before us.

We are, of course, in fairyland (though first the chicken coop must wash ashore in the land of Ev and of Oz). The point of fairyland, however, is to define "real land" by comparison. When Dorothy urges the hen to eat the egg it has laid, because "You don't need to have your food cooked, as I do," the hen indignantly cries, "Do you take me for a cannibal?" When Dorothy, pursuing the subject, says how dreadful her companion's eating habits are—"Why, eating live things, and horrid bugs, and crawly ants. You ought to be *'shamed* of yourself!"—the unflappable hen responds, "Goodness me!... Live things are much fresher and more wholesome than dead ones, and you humans eat all sorts of dead creatures." To Dorothy's denial, Billina instances lambs, sheep—and even chickens. Dorothy's triumphant rejoinder is "but we cook 'em." When the hen questions whether there is any difference, the little girl answers, "A good deal ... I can't just 'splain the diff'rence, but it's there. And, anyhow, we never eat such dreadful things as *bugs*!" The hen's cackling reply leaves Dorothy thoughtful: "But you eat the chickens that eat the bugs.... So you are just as bad as we chickens are."

We seem to be in the presence of a jovial Claude Lévi-Strauss. Human beings are cannibalistic animals that cook their food and feel superior to other animals. Speech, however, allows them to examine their own actions. Baum is helping children grope toward a sense of what it is to be human and different from hens and other animals.

A creature called The Wheeler serves as an intermediary between animals, such as Billina, and machines. "It had the form of a man," we are told,

except that it walked, or rather rolled, upon all fours, and its legs were the same length as its arms, giving them the appearance of the four legs of a beast. Yet it was no beast that Dorothy had discovered, for the person was clothed most gorgeously in embroidered garments of many colors, and wore a straw hat perched jauntily upon the side of its head. But it differed from human beings in this respect, that instead of hands and feet there grew at the end of its arms and legs round wheels. (30)

Here, clothes seem to be the defining quality of a person, differentiating him from both a machine and an animal.

It is Tik-Tok, the Machine Man, however, who occupies the central place in what comes to be a kind of comical Cartesian discourse. Dorothy finds a key that unlocks a door in a rock where she sees

the form of a man—or, at least, it seemed like a man, in the dim light. He was only about as tall as Dorothy herself, and his body was round as a ball and made out of burnished copper. Also his head and limbs were copper.... "Don't be frightened," Billina calls out. "It isn't alive." (54)

Reassured, Dorothy remembers the Tin Man and makes a comparison. "But he [the Tin Man] was as alive as we are, 'cause he was born a real man, and got his tin body a little at a time—first a leg and then a finger and then an ear—for the reason that he had so many accidents with his ax." Her conclusion is that "this copper man is not alive at all" (see figure 3).

He is a robot. The card around his neck defines him as a "Clock work" that "Thinks, Speaks, Acts" (if you wind him up). He "Does Everything but Live" (55). Everything, that is, except eat, feel either sorrow or joy, be kind (or unkind), or sleep (these, at least, are the specific differences alluded to in the book). When, however, the Scarecrow claims that Tik-Tok has no brains, Tik-Tok replies, "Oh, yes, I have. I am fit-ted with Smith and Tin-ker's Improved Com-bi-na-tion Steel Brains. They are what make me think" (114–115). Like the animal Billina, the machine Tik-Tok has language and brains.

"THIS COPPER MAN IS NOT ALIVE AT ALL"

Figure 3
Tik-Tok, the Machine Man, from L. Frank Baum, *Ozma of Oz* (1907), illustrated by John R. Neill. Dorothy explores, with the direct naiveté of a child, the difference between humans and machines.

What, then, distinguishes him (it?) from human beings? The answer seems to reside in the specifics cited, revolving especially around emotions: that is, consciousness of a state of feeling. Also, according to Baum, Tik-Tok suffers from the defect of always having to be rewound (but this is merely a technicality—after all, humans have to eat).

Another mechanical figure in the book, The Giant With the Hammer, *appears* not to suffer from this latter defect (in fact, he seems to continue until turned *off* by a key). On the other hand, unlike Tik-Tok, he has no thinking or speaking attachment. A gigantic "man" made out of plates of cast iron, he stands astride the only road into the Kingdom of the Nomes, pounding the earth so that all are too scared to go past. But his very strength—his unwearying mechanical regularity—proves his weakness and allows him to be defeated. As the Scarecrow points out, all that the members of Dorothy's party have to do is run under the hammer when it is lifted, and pass to the other side before it falls again.

Tik-Tok itself is an utterly unthreatening robot. He exists only to serve Dorothy, which he does. In the illustrations, he looks like a copper Humpty-Dumpty. Even The Giant with the Hammer is little to be feared, for he can easily be outwitted because of his mechanical qualities. Automata, in Oz, are domesticated creatures, different from hens and other animals but no less under human—in fact, a child's—domination.

Robots, however, do not occupy only the sunny fields of Oz in our imagination. They also often take on dark, threatening shapes, as we have seen in *Frankenstein*. Their more modern incarnation, in Karel Čapek's *R.U.R.*, which introduced the term *robot* into popular usage, reflects similar fears.[27]

Like its Shelleyan predecessor, Čapek's play *R.U.R.* (1921; performed in America in 1922) is a poorly written hodgepodge of mostly improbable ideas. (Perhaps this is because a crude style matches the crudeness of its creatures, or because the Gothic is necessarily crude.) In any case, Čapek, a Czech, obviously wrote with one eye on the Bolshevik Revolution of 1917, though one cannot be sure of his actual attitude toward that epochal event. Between Act I, which is about the manufacture of robots, and Acts II and III, when they revolt, there is a dichotomy. Yet the play is effective and has come to symbolize many of our feelings about robots.

The play opens when Helena, a beautiful young girl, comes to visit on an island the factory of Rossum's Universal Robots, which is managed by a man, Domin. He immediately falls in love with her and, on her promise not to divulge it, tells her the true story of the invention. (The process itself is secret, preserved in only two copies.) Rossum, he says, was a "great physiologist," who "attempted by chemical synthesis to imitate the living matter known as protoplasm until he suddenly discovered a substance which behaved exactly like living matter." As Domin explains, "This artificial living matter of his has a raging thirst for life. It didn't mind being sewn or mixed together."[28] Thus, old Rossum set about to imitate nature: first, an artificial dog, which took him several years and "resulted in a sort of stunted calf," and then the manufacture of a man.

The dog anticipates or is derivative of Pavlov's; the man reminds us of the creature in *Frankenstein*. Rossum is obviously cast in Frankenstein's image. Domin sardonically calls him "mad . . . the old crank wanted to actually make people" (13). Rossum's "bungling attempt" occupied him for ten years—"It was to have been a man, but it lived for three days only." Then, we are told, "up came young Rossum, an engineer.... When he saw what a mess of it the old man was making, he said, 'It's absurd to spend ten years making a man. If you can't make him quicker than nature, you might as well shut up shop'" (14).

Frankenstein-Rossum and his "monstrosities" are pushed aside. Young Rossum is an engineer, not a physiologist, who says to himself: "A man is something that feels happy, plays the piano, likes going for a walk.... But a working machine must not play the piano, must not feel happy." As Domin concludes, "And to manufacture artificial workers is the same thing as to manufacture . . . motors." (Later, the mechanical metaphor is betrayed when we are told that "there are vats for the preparation of liver, brains . . . and a spinning mill for weaving nerves and veins" (19); consistency was not Čapek's strong point.)

All that the worker need do is to work: hence, a robot (from the Czech, *robota*, "work"). The requirement is to reproduce "the cheapest . . . worker with the minimum amount of requirements." It is as if young Rossum were answering the desires of the classical economists and their "iron law of wages." But robots are not people. "Mechanically," as Domin defines them, "they are more perfect than we are, they have an enormously developed intelligence, but they have no soul" (17). In fact, we are told that the cost of producing a robot has been brought down within 15 years from $10,000 to $150!

Young Rossum, Domin goes on, "then proceeded [like his father, though he has repudiated the old man] to play at being God." He tried to make a superrobot. "Regular giants they were. He tried to make them twelve feet tall. But you wouldn't believe what a failure they were" (19). In this area Frankenstein seems to have done better.[29]

The robots are constrained not only by size but by longevity. They have only a 20-year life span. They do not, however, die—which involves a consciousness of death—but simply "get used up." Though they appear lifelike—the young lady, in an amusing bit, mistakes a robot for a live human being, and the human for a robot—dissection proves that they are not. They feel nothing (reminding us of Descartes' views on animals-machines); consequently, one can be accused not of "killing" them, but only of destroying a machine, just as wringing the neck of a chicken is not murder. All is well and peaceable in Rossum's factory.

Trouble enters this mechanical paradise, when, in Act I, Helena pities the robots and wants to treat them as "brothers" and to "show them a little love"—shades of *Franken-*

stein! As befitting a play of 1921, the language is also of "liberating" the robots: that is, the workers.

By Act II, Helena is married to Domin, ten years have gone by, and the robots number millions and millions. One of the other people in the factory, Dr. Gall, under the influence of Helena, has begun to introduce modifications into the manufacture of some of the robots: pain, ostensibly so that they can withdraw their hand from dangerous operations; irritability, so that they begin to show defiance; and other such human attributes.

Čapek's argument is really disingenuous. Humans are depicted as "imperfect" machines. "For example," as an engineer explains, "from a technical point of view, the whole of childhood is a sheer absurdity. So much time lost" (42). Humans obviously also waste time with sex. Their intelligence is less than what it might be. Hence, robots are created that are more intelligent and powerful than humans, have no interest in sex, and are clearly superior. Yet, as soon as this is done, it becomes obvious that Čapek considers them *less perfect* than humans because they have no feelings such as love and fear.

The contradiction becomes clear as the play unfolds in the last two acts. Owing to Dr. Gall and Helena's meddling, a new species of robot is produced that soon starts to go "mad" and ends up in revolt against people. As the robot leader declaims to Helena: "You are not as strong as the Robots. You are not as skillful as the Robots" (91). To her words about equality, he responds, "I want to be master. I want to be master over others" (92). He proclaims to his fellow robots: "We command you to kill all mankind. Spare no man. Spare no woman" (117).

The robots take over the island, and all humans are killed except one "last man," Alquist. Indeed, humans have already, as Dr. Gall noted earlier, "become superfluous" (98). The problem is, however, that the robots, too, are about to die out, for they cannot reproduce themselves. (In a moment of humanitarian fervor, Helena had destroyed the copies detailing the secret process of creating the robots, so as to prevent further manufacture and hence exploitation.) In the epilogue, the robots command Alquist to rediscover Rossum's secret. However, much as he wishes to do so, Alquist lacks the scientific ability. He prays, "Lord . . . if there are no human beings left, at least let there be Robots!—At least the shadow of man!" (164).

At this point, a miracle occurs. Two of Gall's newest robots, a male and a female, enter. They are experiencing strange feelings—love, sexual longing, it appears. Also, "laughter—timidity—protection" (154). To test them, Alquist proposes to take one of them into the dissecting room. When each is prepared to sacrifice him- or herself to save the other, Alquist knows that a new race has been born. "Go, Adam, go, Eve. The world is yours," he says in the last line of the play, "At least the shadow of man!"

I find the whole play incredibly muddled. In the last act and the epilogue, Čapek is obviously writing as much about the workers' revolution in Russia as about the robots' uprising in Rossum's factory. On one hand, the play is a kind of Luddite-*Frankenstein* protest against human hubris in the making of machines: Helena's human maid, Nana, exclaims at one point, "All these new-fangled things are an offense to the Lord. It's downright wickedness. Wanting to improve the world after He has made it" (101), and we are not meant to snicker. On the other hand, it seems to preach a certain idealism: that machines can free people from toil and thus allow them to reach for perfection. In Domin's proud, and possibly ironic, words, "He [the human] will not be a machine and a device for production. He will be Lord of creation" (52).

Čapek's identification of the robots with the workers of the world, led by Bolsheviks, is not without roots. Frankenstein's monster, too, was frequently identified by nineteenth-century readers with the rebellious masses. Thus, in the novel *Mary Barton* (1848), Elizabeth Gaskell writes of how "the actions of the uneducated seem to me typified in those of Frankenstein, that monster of many human qualities." And Sir John Lubbock, a conservative scientist, speaking in the House of Commons around 1870 against liberal reform, gave as his reason that he "believed it would be impossible to control the Frankensteins we have ourselves created."[30] Feelings about the right ordering of the social world are thus projected onto the subject of robots.

The social and psychological springs of *R.U.R.* do not mesh smoothly. But even though its theme is unfocused, *R.U.R.* does successfully reflect our feelings about automata as comprising both promise and threat. Čapek's final message is ironic and ultimately baffling: he posits that the "new man" of the future will be a robot, but one that is just like a human being in having feelings. Thus, Čapek provides a null response to both the threat and the promise. But what is memorable about the play—or accounts of it—is the threat that like Frankenstein's monster, unless they are first destroyed or emasculated, robots will usurp the world from humans. *R.U.R.* was written before robots were used widely in industry and by an author who shows no evidence of having thought much about the science and technology animating them. Nevertheless, the play has achieved canonical status.

I, Robot (1950), by Isaac Asimov, is a much more thoughtful book—actually, a connected series of short stories—by an informed author, at a time when the presence of robots is becoming real; yet the book is mainly known only to science fiction fans. It should be read, however, by anyone interested in probing modern readers' feelings toward robots.

Its protagonist is a psychologist, Dr. Susan Calvin (whose name, surely, is intended to symbolize the Protestant work ethic); she is one of the few women in the book; all the other people and the robots are apparently male. So much for the sex problem!

The first story, "Robbie," raises the familiar problems. Robbie is a nontalking nurse-maid robot for little Gloria. While the child loves him and thinks of him as "a *person* just like you and me," her mother is actually jealous of Robbie, fears the machine—"it has no soul, and no one knows what it may be thinking"—and thinks "some little jigger will come loose and the awful thing will go berserk."[31] She insists the robot be removed and a collie dog substituted.

Gloria is inconsolable. Her father arranges for a tour of the premises of U.S. Robots and Mechanical Men, Inc., to show his daughter that Robbie is just a machine. When she breaks away to embrace Robbie, whom she sees on the assembly line, she steps into the path of a huge, lumbering tractor. Her father and the others are unable to act fast enough—"The overseers were only human, and it took time to act"—but Robbie, acting "immediately and with precision," saves his little playmate (28). All is forgiven, and Gloria may take her mechanical friend home.

A contrived tearjerker, the story is effective. It introduces us to our own fears, in a homey, humdrum way. We are told that this event occurred in 1998; as the stories continue, by 2002 mobile speaking robots have been invented, and between 2003 and 2007 most of the world's governments—presumably pressured by the mothers of innumerable Glorias—have banned robot use on Earth for any purpose other than scientific research.

As further protection, all robots are bound by "The Three Laws of Robotics":

1. A robot may not injure a human being, or, through inaction, allow a human being to come to harm.
2. A robot must obey the orders given it by human beings except where such orders would conflict with the First Law.
3. A robot must protect its own existence as long as such protection does not conflict with the First or Second Law.

The remaining stories explore variations on one or more of these laws, their applications, and possible violations. Asimov is an interesting logician and rings the changes nicely. In the story "Reason," the robot Cutie pursues logic to its Cartesian conclusion, announcing "I, myself, exist, because I think" (51). Hubris overtakes this robot, who subsequently announces its conversion to the religion of "The Master": "The Master [it tells the two humans who are in charge of it] created humans first as the lowest type, most easily formed. Gradually, he replaced them by robots, the next higher step, and finally he created me, to take the place of the last humans. From now on, I serve the Master" (53). The rebellious delusion, however, turns out to be harmless because Cutie still operates dials and graphs correctly, although claiming it does so in obedience to the Master; and, obedient to the Second Law of Robotics, it does not harm humans. As one of its two minders remarks, "What's the difference what he believes" (63). The incipient danger has been nicely damped down.

It breaks out again in a story in which a robot lies, against the strictest injunction. Finally detected by Dr. Calvin using a clever piece of logic, it is destroyed. The dark shadow of the robot, however, has grown more menacing. In another story, a robot faced with conflicting demands behaves just as a person might: it suffers a nervous breakdown. Yet, Asimov tries to keep clear the distinction between humans and machines: the machine, he declares, is an *"idiot savant*—it doesn't really understand what it does—it just does it" (129).

The penultimate story, "Evidence," poses the "difference" question most squarely. Is the lawyer Stephen Byerley, running for high political office, a man or a robot that looks exactly like a man? His opponent accuses him of being inhuman and offers as proof that he never is seen eating. Byerley responds that his habit of eating in private is probably neurotic, but not inhuman. The test finally comes in a public debate when a man emerges from the audience, taunts Byerley, and says "Hit me," pointing out that a robot can't violate the First Law and harm a human being. Byerley punches him, thus proving his "humanity," and of course wins the election.

Only, as it turns out (though Dr. Calvin alone comes to know), Byerley actually *is* a robot. Created by a crippled human to perform in his place, Byerley has simply struck another robot, cleverly planted in the audience to rise and challenge the original humanoid robot. When Dr. Calvin's colleague is queried about the possibility of such a humanoid robot, he reluctantly admits that

by using human ova and hormone control, one can grow human flesh and skin over a skeleton of porous silicone plastics that would defy external examination. The eyes, the hair, the skin would be really human, not humanoid. And if you put a positronic brain, and such other gadgets as you might desire inside, you have a humanoid robot. (159–160)

Asimov is not dismayed by this possibility. Like his fictional creation, Dr. Calvin, Asimov believes that robots are "a cleaner better breed than we are" (9). They are decent and logical entities, who as civil executives and "World Coordinators"—Byerley, for example—will run the world and bring peace and prosperity to humankind. Whereas "humans are fallible, also corruptible," machines are only subject to mechanical failure, not wrong results, that is, if they are fed the correct data.

Like everyone writing about robots, Asimov is also ambivalent. People, he seems to be saying, still possess a creativity denied to machines.

The Machine is only a tool after all, which can help humanity progress faster by taking some of the burdens of calculations and interpretations off its back. The task of the human brain remains what it has always been; that of discovering new data to be analyzed, and of devising new concepts to be tested. (187)

Yet, on the very last page of *I, Robot,* the machine appears as Providence, superior to humans but clever enough to hide its superiority so as not to injure human pride. (Earlier, we have seen Cutie making an open avowal of superiority, a clear sign of a kind of madness.) The books ends with Asimov's message:

How do we know what the ultimate good of Humanity will entail? We haven't at our disposal the infinite factors that the machine has at its! Perhaps, to give you a not unfamiliar example, our entire technical civilization has created more unhappiness and misery than it has removed. Perhaps an agrarian or pastoral civilization, with less culture and less people would be better. If so, the Machines must move in that direction, preferably without telling us, since in our ignorant prejudices we only know that what we are used to, is good—and we would then fight change. Or perhaps a complete urbanization, or a completely caste-ridden society, or complete anarchy, is the answer. We don't know. Only the Machines know, and they are going there and taking us with them. (192)

It is a wishy-washy conclusion to an intriguing group of stories, in which Asimov cleverly explores both our logical and illogical attitudes toward robots. I have not mentioned, for example, his handling of the Fundamentalists, who would destroy all machines, or his assumption that in the mid-twenty-first century robots will still be under the control of private, capitalistic enterprises, competing unscrupulously with one another (the cost of a robot is, in this book, $30,000). Overall, however, the book is a provocative rehandling—generally optimistic—of the themes we have been pursuing from Andersen's nightingale through Čapek's Rossum's robots.

In spite of the length of this chapter, I have only touched on the wealth of literature relating to automata. The subject seems to crop up everywhere, in almost everything one reads. Some light on its ubiquity may be shed by "The Uncanny," a strange and difficult paper by Sigmund Freud.[32] Here Freud points to what may be involved, psychologically, in the fear of the inanimate, of automata. Discussing E.T.A. Hoffman's story "The Sandman" (later part of Offenbach's opera, *Tales of Hoffman*), Freud argues that the feeling of the uncanny arises where we are in doubt as to whether an apparently animate being—an automaton—is really alive, or not.

We need not follow Freud in his specific and tortuous analysis of the story in terms of castration fears, or in his general analysis of the uncanny in terms of animistic mental activity. For our purposes, we need only be inspired to realize that automata, mechanical dolls, and machines of all sorts awaken special undefined fears in us. Does the machine represent a part of ourselves of which we are afraid? Do we project into it our secret, and most forbidden, desires? A moment's reflection on our feelings toward robots, Pygmalion-like statues, or Frankenstein monsters (though this is, as mentioned, a flesh-and-blood creation) will confirm the extent of our emotional involvement, even if not its exact nature.

With this as a psychological context, I can use the examples given here to make the following general points. What are variously called automata, androids, or robots, are conceived as originating via the gods (for example, the Delphic oracles), or people using magic (for example, the automata or golems of the Hermetic tradition), or people using science (for example, the clockwork nightingale, Frankenstein's monster, and

Čapek's and Asimov's robots). (It would be nice to think of this as a chronological progress, but ancient Chinese scientists obviously used clockwork, and the followers of Hermes Trismegistus used magic very early on; what we find, therefore, is a recurring juxtaposition of the animating forces.) The created figures are primarily biological or mechanical; flesh-and-blood or clockwork machines, animated by a spark or wound up.

However created, whatever the material, they all pose the same compulsive question: how do they differ from human beings, or more simply, what is a human being? This is the uncanny feeling analyzed by Freud. So, too, they all arouse in us the same range of ambivalent reactions: the sense of a perfection and infallibility to which we aspire— the angel in us—and the sense of the destructive and degrading in us—the ape in us.

Something new is now emerging: the robot as an industrial reality. Still, the same feelings seem to be attached to it. Thus we are told that when a Japanese worker was crushed in a robotics accident as a result of his being in a restricted area and failing to notice that he was in the automatic path of a transport robot, the incident was reported in the press as though it had been a robot uprising.[33] Will these feelings change as familiarity breeds boredom? In the movie *2001*, Hal the computer rebels; will the memory fade from our dreams?

The fact is that our feelings toward the robot-automaton are caught up anew in our feelings toward its new version, the computer. The robot now becomes the tool— really, the body—by which the computer—a "brain"—can "move" and take on "animated" form. Automata now take the shape of artificial intelligence machines.[34]

Notes

This chapter is adapted from chapter 3 of my book *The Fourth Discontinuity: The Co-evolution of Humans and Machines* (New Haven, Conn.: Yale University Press, 1993). Thanks to Yale University Press for granting permission for the adaptation. I would also like to acknowledge the assistance provided by Güven Güzeldere, without whom this chapter would not have appeared in its present shape. Thanks also to Stefano Franchi and Laura Kerr for editorial help.

1. See Joseph Needham, *Science and Civilization in China,* vol. 4, part 2 (Cambridge: Cambridge University Press, 1975), 54. This book is a mine of information on the subject of automata as well as on its more general subject. Further on automata, compare Albert Chapuis and Edouard Gélis, *Le monde des automates* (2 vols) (Paris: Chapuis, 1928).

2. Needham, vol. 2, 53. Comparison with statements by la Mettrie spring quickly to mind.

3. Quoted in Julian James, *The Origin of Consciousness in the Breakdown of the Bicameral Mind* (Boston: Houghton Mifflin, 1976), 336.

4. For one such attempt, though a brief one, see John Cohen, *Human Robots in Myths and Science* (London: Allen and Unwin, 1966).

5. Needham, vol. 2, 165.

6. Quoted in Needham, vol. 2, 164.

7. Francis A. Yates, "The Hermetic Tradition in Renaissance Science," *Art, Science, and History in the Renaissance*, ed. Charles S. Singleton (Baltimore: Johns Hopkins University Press, 1967), 258, 255.

8. Yates, 257.

9. Quoted in Yates, 259.

10. Radu Florescu, *In Search of Frankenstein* (Boston: New York Graphics Society, 1929), 233. This is a marvelous work, well printed and illustrated, and at the time I bought it, a wonderful buy. Compare the article by Michael Uhl, "Living Dolls," *Geo* (July 1985) and its quotation of one observer who delicately noted that Vaucanson's duck duplicated the process of digestion in full view of the spectators, "ending the digestion process as naturally as it began" (86). Thus, long before Pavlov, the idea of a viewable pouch in the stomach was employed, not in a dog, but in an automaton.

11. In the seventeenth century, Sir Kenelm Digby, member of the Royal Society, had already declared that birds were machines, whose motions when feeding their young or building their nests were no different from the striking of the clock or the ringing of an alarm. See Keith Thomas, *Man and the Natural World* (New York: Pantheon, 1983), 35.

12. *Folk-lore and Fable: Aesop, Grimm, Andersen*, ed. Charles W. Eliot, vol. 17 of the Harvard Classics (New York: Collier, 1909), 325. The next quotation is from page 326.

13. *Folk-lore and Fable*, 328.

14. *Folk-lore and Fable*, 329.

15. There is some evidence for this origin in Needham, 157.

16. See Florescu, 223–225, for this and other details.

17. Florescu, 329.

18. Giovanni Aldini, *On Galvanism* (London, 1803), 194. Quoted in Michael Kita, "Mary Shelley's *Frankenstein*: Two Contexts," unpublished manuscript. I owe to it inspiration for some of the preceding, and what follows on *Natürphilosophie*.

19. See Florescu, 65 ff., for his tracking down the possible influences on Mary Shelley, who supposedly visited a Castle Frankenstein in the Rhine country, inhabited in the eighteenth century by a Konrad Dippel, an alchemist accused of strange experiments.

20. Mary Shelley, *Frankenstein* (1818; London: Oxford University Press, 1969), 48. All further references to this edition are cited within the text.

21. In fact, Mary Shelley herself, in a subsequent novel, *The Last Man* (1826), makes the connection when she writes about man as an "automaton of flesh … with joints and strings in order." Quoted in William A. Walling, *Mary Shelley* (New York: Twayne Publishers, 1972), 93.

22. Shelley, *Frankenstein*, 13. The next quotation is from page 8.

23. Shelley, *Frankenstein*, 52.

24. William Godwin, *Enquiry Concerning Political Justice, and Its Influence on Morals and Happiness,* 3d ed., vol. 2 (London, 1798), 528.

25. Baum's own identity is not as simple as it might at first appear. Some writers on Baum see him as a social critic and a populist; see, for example, Henry M. Littlefield, "The Wizard of Oz: Parable on Populism," *American Quarterly* 16 (Spring 1964). For an overall treatment, see Raylyn Moore, *Wonderful Wizard Marvelous Land* (Bowling Green, Ohio: Bowling Green University Press, 1974), who suggests that "for the first time in the history of the fairy tale, Baum produces monsters which are mechanical, in whole or in part" (143). For a number of critical essays on Baum, see Michael Patrick Hearn, ed., *The Wizard of Oz by L. Frank Baum* (New York: Schocken Books, 1983); also Martin Gardner, "The Royal Historian of Oz," in *Order and Surprise* (Buffalo, N.Y.: Prometheus, 1983).

26. L. Frank Baum, *Ozma of Oz* (Chicago: Reilly and Lee, 1907). All further references to this edition are cited within the text.

27. In the *New York Times*, February 11, 1982, there is a claim that *robot* was a term coined by Karel's brother, Josef.

28. Karel Čapek, *R.U.R.*, trans. Paul Selver (Garden City, N.Y.: Doubleday, 1923), 10–11. All further references to this edition are cited within the text.

29. In fact, a 12-foot man would not be viable in nature, for such a creature would violate a known law concerning size and shape, wherein volume grows more rapidly than surface. For details, see Stephen Jay Gould, "Size and Shape," in *Ever Since Darwin* (New York: Norton, 1977). Domin himself has a glimpse of this fact when he adds, "For no reason at all their limbs used to keep snapping off" (16).

30. Florescu, 14.

31. Isaac Asimov, *I, Robot* (1950; New York: Fawcett Crest, 1970), 16. All further references to this edition are cited within the text. (The title might be intended to suggest either an ironic or an egoistic identification with the author, who is frequently cited as I. Asimov.) Asimov's later book *The Robots of Dawn* (New York: Ballantine Books, 1983) is, unfortunately, not quite up to the standard of its predecessor, being rather repetitious and crude in its attempts at salaciousness. *I, Robot*, itself, however, is a classic.

32. Sigmund Freud, "The Uncanny" (1919), in *The Standard Edition of the Complete Psychological Works of Sigmund Freud* (24 vols.), ed. James Strachey, Alix Strachey, and Alan Tyson (London: Hogarth Press, 1953–1974), vol. 17.

33. *New York Times Magazine*, January 10, 1982, 62.

34. In the fourth chapter of my book *The Fourth Discontinuity,* I follow up on these points with a discussion of the Industrial Revolution, considering it as a quantum leap in the relationship

human beings have with machines. In the Industrial Revolution's first phase in the early nineteenth century, artificial intelligence machines as such do not figure in production. Instead, the machine basically replaces manual labor. However, as I show in chapter 7 of *The Fourth Discontinuity*, the artificial intelligence machine is conceptualized and even developed by Babbage, in his arithmetical mill, during the period 1822–1832, as part and parcel of the mechanizing impulse of the Industrial Revolution. It takes about 150 years, however, before the computer and the robot (our modern automata) emerge as prime movers in the continuing industrial revolution, substituting for brain as well as brawn.

Marrying the Premodern to the Postmodern: Computers and Organisms after World War II

Evelyn Fox Keller

Almost a century ago, Stéphane Leduc sought to explain the origin and development of life through the construction of artificial organisms that looked like, and even seemed to behave like, real organisms.[1] He induced the formation of these lifelike facsimiles with ingenious uses of India ink and chemical precipitates, and he dubbed his enterprise "synthetic biology." Both Leduc and his readers clearly understood the value of that term's double meaning. Here was a biology that was *synthetic* in the sense both of being artificial and of providing at least a stepping-stone toward what his colleague A. L. Herrera described as the long-range objective of synthesizing living matter.[2] We would probably use the word *simulation* to describe such efforts, relying on the double meaning this word, too, possesses:

simulo *v.* I. *To make* a thing *like* another; *to imitate, copy* ... **II.** *To represent* a thing as being which has no existence, *to feign* a thing to be what it is not.[3]

In Leduc's time, however, it was the negative and clearly pejorative sense of *simulation* that had come to predominate. Tied so closely to deception, falsity, and pretense, the meaning of *simulation* conflicted too clearly with the aims of science to qualify for Leduc's purposes. In fact, it was only in the context of war-related research in the 1940s that *simulation* began to recover its original (and potentially positive) sense of imitation, which would bring it into alignment with Leduc's purposes.

The first modern uses of *simulation* with a positive connotation are to be found in descriptions of pilot training programs in which electrical and electronic analog devices were employed to mimic the behavior of real-world phenomena.[4] Here, the term came to mean a technique for gaining experience. At the same time and in the same context, it came to denote a technique used by scientists and engineers for acquiring new knowledge. In an early overview of simulation as a productive technique for management scientists, Stanley Vance offered the following definition:

Simulation means assuming the appearance of something without actually taking on the related reality of that thing. The simulation technique is extremely useful in gaining experience which otherwise could not be had because of cost or technical factors. Among the classic examples of simulation are those dealing with military maneuvers. Without war games it would be difficult and perhaps inconceivable for an army to test its battle effectiveness unless actually engaged in at least a small-scale war.... The effectiveness of the game depends not only upon the precision in planning but equally as much upon the seriousness with which the group strives to make the simulation approximate the reality.[5]

Much the same might be said about the effectiveness of simulation in engineering and scientific research. To be useful, it must be taken seriously, and to be taken seriously, it must give the appearance of veridicality. Today, the term *simulation* tends to be employed rather more narrowly, especially in the scientific and philosophical literature, where it has come to imply the use of digital computers. These, of course, no one of Leduc's generation had. Nevertheless, in its use as an effective synonym for "computer simulation" the meaning that for Leduc was most essential invoking a world simultaneously artificial and productive—is clearly retained. If anything, it has become even more pronounced.[6]

Uses of computer simulation to study biological systems have exploded over the last decade, and they follow directly from the historical development of simulation in the physical sciences.[7] Indeed, to this day, those who argue for their value are still mainly to be found among physical and mathematical scientists. By far the most spirited and highly publicized advocacy comes from those engaged in the venture that Christopher Langton has called artificial life. In Langton's first use of the term, he wrote,

The ultimate goal of the study of artificial life would be to create "life" in some other medium, ideally a *virtual* medium where the essence of life has been abstracted from the details of its implementation in any particular model. We would like to build *models* that are so life-like that they cease to become models of life and become *examples* of life themselves.[8]

One year later, in 1987, Langton organized a conference at Los Alamos with the explicit purpose of inaugurating a new field by that name. Here, he wrote, "Artificial life ... is a relatively new field employing a *synthetic* approach to the study of *life-as-it-could-be*. It views life as a property of the *organization* of matter, rather than a property of the matter which is so organized."[9]

At the time, Langton was a member of the theoretical division of the Los Alamos National Laboratory, and it was at Los Alamos that virtually all the major techniques of computer simulation had originally been developed. In its earliest incarnation, "computer simulation" referred to the use of the digital computer to extract approximate solutions from prespecified but analytically intractable differential equations describing the dynamics of thermonuclear processes (e.g., neutron diffusion, shock waves, and "multiplicative" or branching reactions). Here, what was being simulated was the differential equation itself. However, in an effort to build better theories of fluid behavior, computers soon came to be used not merely to simulate the equations but also the molecular dynamics of real fluids.[10] Many of the computer simulations of biological systems depend on a still further development, namely, the use of computers to explore phenomena for which neither equations nor any sort of general theory have yet been formulated, and for which only rudimentary indications of the underlying dynamics of interaction are available. In such cases, what is simulated is neither a well-established set of differential equations nor the fundamental physical constituents (or particles) of the system but rather the observed phenomenon as seen in all its complexity, prior to simplification and prior to any attempt to distill or reduce it to its essential dynamics. In this sense, the practice might be described as modeling from above. A method that has proved particularly congenial to this alternative kind of modeling is now called cellular automata.

Cellular automata (CA) lend themselves to a variety of uses. In some cases, they are used to simulate processes for which the equations that do exist are not adequate to describe the phenomena of interest (e.g., the emergence of novel patterns in excitable media, turbulence, or earthquakes). In others, CA models might be viewed simply as an exactly computable alternative to conventional differential equations. R.I.G. Hughes stresses the radical difference that the feature of exact computability lends these alternative models, as compared with models traditionally employed in physics,[11] but even more noteworthy is the fact that they are often employed in a different spirit altogether. Typically, they are aimed at producing recognizable patterns of "interesting" behavior in their macrodynamics rather than in their microdynamics. As Stephen Wolfram writes,

Science has traditionally concentrated on analyzing systems by breaking them down into simple constituent parts. A new form of science is now developing which addresses the problem of how those parts act together to produce the complexity of the whole. Fundamental to the approach is the investigation of models which are as simple as possible in construction, yet capture the essential mathematical features necessary to reproduce the complexity that is seen. CA provide probably the best examples of such models.[12]

Indeed, it is in this last sense that cellular automata find an especially congenial home in the study of phenomena for which no equations for the microdynamics giving rise to the observed complexity have been formulated. A-Life studies provide a prime case in point.

In truth, however, the project of using the computer to simulate biological processes of reproduction, development, and evolution is of far longer standing than are either of the terms *cellular automata* or *A-Life*. Indeed, that project had its origins in the same context (Los Alamos) and in the work of the same people (e.g., Stanislaw Ulam, John von Neumann, Enrico Fermi) from which the basic techniques for computer simulation first arose. If any single individual deserves credit as "the father of artificial life," that person is John von Neumann.

Cellular Automata and A-Life: A Brief History

Von Neumann's contributions to this field grew directly out of his preoccupation with one of the oldest and most fundamental of all questions about simulation: How closely can a mechanical simulacrum be made to resemble an organism in its most fundamental attributes? What properties would the simulation need to have before it could be said to be alive? The seductive powers of animation are evident, but a long history of self-moving automata had made it clear that animation by itself was not enough to compel belief in the vitality of a machine. For many, the ultimate test remained that of generation, and for all the ingenuity displayed in the construction of automata, there still remained no plausible rejoinder to the argument of Fontanelle: "Do you say that Beasts are Machines just as Watches are? Put a Dog Machine and a Bitch Machine side by side, and eventually a third little Machine will be the result, whereas two Watches will lie side by side all their lives without ever producing a third Watch."[13] Thus von Neumann's question: Is it possible to construct an automaton capable of reproducing itself?

Beginning in the 1940s, von Neumann struggled with a kinematic model of automata afloat in a sea of raw materials, but he never fully succeeded in capturing the essential logic of self-reproduction with this model.[14] The breakthrough came with the suggestion of his close colleague, Stanislaw Ulam, that a cellular perspective (similar to what Ulam was using in his Monte Carlo computations)—in which the continuous physical motion required in the kinematic model would be replaced by discrete transfers of information—might provide a more effective approach. Cellular automata, as they have since come to be called, have no relation to biological cells (and indeed, from the beginning, they were also invoked for the analysis of complex hydrodynamic problems), but they did suggest to von Neumann a way of bypassing the problems posed by his kinematic model. With cellular automata, all variables (space, time, and dynamic variables) are taken to be discrete. An abstract space is represented as a lattice (or cellular automaton) with a finite-state machine located at each node of the lattice. Each such machine evolves in time by reading the states of the neighbors to which it is connected (usually, its nearest neighbors) at time t_n and, according to simple, prespecified and uniform rules, moving to a new state at time t_{n+1}. Ulam and von Neumann reasoned, and von Neumann soon proved, that the collective dynamics resulting from such simple rules might bear a formal resemblance to the biological process of self-reproduction and evolution.[15]

Von Neumann's initial construction in the early 1950s was cumbersome (requiring 200,000 cells with 29 states for each node), but it made the point. The story of its subsequent development (and dramatic simplification)—from John Conway's Game of Life[16] to Christopher Langton's self-reproducing "loops"[17]—has been recounted many times and hardly needs repeating here.[18] Somewhat less well known is the history of the use of cellular automata in the modeling of complex physical phenomena (e.g., turbulence, crystallization),[19] an activity that like Artificial Life exploded in the 1980s. Indeed, the first conference on cellular automata was also held at Los Alamos (in 1983, preceding the A-Life conference by four years), and while it provided the occasion for Langton's initial foray into "artificial life," its primary focus was on the physical sciences.[20] Of paramount importance to the upsurge of interest in CA models in the 1980s was the appearance of a new generation of high-speed parallel-processing computers. That so much of this work has come out of Los Alamos is no accident, for at that time Los Alamos was one of the few laboratories to have the supercomputers that made the execution of CA systems practical.[21] But cellular automata were not simply an extension of conventional modeling practices; they also represented a qualitatively new kind of model.

Cellular automata models are simulations par excellence: they are artificial universes that evolve according to local but uniform rules of interaction that have been prespecified. Change the initial conditions, and one changes the history; change the rules of interaction, and one changes the dynamics. In this sense, the analogy with differential equations is obvious. But equally clear are many of the differences between cellular automata and differential equations. The universe of CA is discrete rather than continuous; its rules of interaction are local and uniform rather than spatially extended and (often) nonuniform. The temporal evolution of a CA system is exactly computable for any specified interactions (given enough time), whereas differential equations are rarely susceptible to exact analytic solutions and only approximately computable when they are not.[22] I suggest, however, that by far the most significant epistemological differences that arise from this new kind of modeling come from the uses to which they are put, the processes by which they are crafted, and the criteria by which they are judged.

Wolfram emphasizes the synthetic aims of cellular automata research, arguing that what is of greatest significance is its focus not on the properties of the constituent parts of the system but on "how those parts act together to produce the complexity of the whole."[23] The meaning of *synthetic* implied here is Kantian—reasoning from principles to a conclusion—and the goal of CA modeling is described as establishing formal similitude between the outcomes of simple algorithmic procedures and the overall behavior of the processes (physical, biological, economic, or other) the model is designed to explain. But how, in fact, is the success of these models to be judged? What is the measure of formal similitude? In actual practice, the presentation—and, I argue, the persuasiveness—of CA models of biological systems depends on translating formal similitude into visual similitude. In other words, a good part of the appeal of such models derives from the exhibition of computational results in forms that exhibit a compelling visual resemblance to the processes they are said to represent.[24] In an important sense, however, such visual portrayals are artifacts, that is, they result from self-conscious efforts to construct visually persuasive representations out of the formal procedures that were designed "to capture the essential mathematical features" of the process. Thus, the persuasive power of CA models depends critically on advances in computer visualization techniques.[25] Finally, and possibly of even greater significance, with the translation from formal to visual resemblance, the nuance of *synthetic* also undergoes a shift: now, no longer strictly Kantian, the word begins to take on the more mundane (and notably dual) sense of fabrication.

An introduction to the subject of cellular automata by Toffoli and Margolus is instructive on both these points, and I quote from it at length:

> In Greek mythology, the machinery of the universe was the gods themselves.... In more recent conceptions, the universe is created complete with its operating mechanism: once set in motion, it runs by itself. God sits outside of it and can take delight in watching it.
>
> Cellular automata are stylized, synthetic universes.... They have their own kind of matter which whirls around in a space and a time of their own. One can think of an astounding variety of them. One can actually construct them, and watch them evolve. As inexperienced creators, we are not likely to get a very interesting universe on our first try; as individuals we may have different ideas of what makes a universe interesting, or of what we might want to do with it. In any case, once we've been shown a cellular automaton universe we'll want to make one ourselves; once we've made one, we will want to try another one. After having made a few, we'll be able to custom-tailor one for a particular purpose with a certain confidence.
>
> A cellular automata machine is a universe synthesizer. Like an organ, it has keys and stops by which the resources of the instrument can be called into action, combined, and reconfigured. Its color screen is a window through which one can watch the universe that is being "played."[26]

Toffoli and Margolus's comments speak directly to the seductive lure of fabrication, of being able to construct artificial universes of one's own. They also refer to the importance of being able to watch one's creation unfold through the window provided by the color screen of a computer monitor. What they do not mention, however, is the power these visual displays also have for the passive viewer, for those in the position not of creating but merely observing.

The uses of cellular automata for simulating global effects have clearly led to a shift in the meaning of simulation (and similarly, of the model) in scientific research. But they have also encouraged a shift in the meaning of the real. As many have noted, they have come to constitute an alternative reality,[27] one that appears ever more easily interchangeable with the original. The very realism of the visual displays of CA computations plays a crucial role; with the wide availability of video recordings in the popular media, it is not only scientists who can experience their seductive powers. And with the distribution of software for synthesizing "look-alike" universes, access to the power to make one's own universe has also been extended.[28] Indeed, anyone with a computer, a color monitor, and only a modicum of experience can now share in the excitement of playing God. In all these uses, the very persuasiveness of the image we see before us inevitably generates a degree of uncertainty about its authenticity. Like the character Trudy in Jane Wagner and Lily Tomlin's "The Search for Signs of Intelligent Life in the Universe" (1992), we find ourselves asking, Is the spectacle before us soup or art? model or reality? Might not these models, as some have argued, give us even closer access to the world as it really is? Might not nature, at its most fundamental, really be constituted of cellular automata?

Questions of this sort have led G. Y. Vichniac to propose "cellular automata as original models of physics" and to suggest the possibility that the physical world really is a discrete space-time lattice of information bits evolving according to simple rules, an enormous CA system running with one of many possible sets of rules.[29] Such a view of the world—as a giant network of digital processors—goes beyond Laplace's dream, but it is not entirely new. It has been advocated by a few mavericks (most notably, by Edward Fredkin) ever since the 1960s. On a number of occasions, even Richard Feynman expressed support for the idea.[30] But the notion clearly took on new life in 1983 at the Los Alamos cellular automata conference, for there it was proposed not only by Vichniac but by a number of other researchers (e.g., Wolfram, Margolus and Toffoli). At least in the world of computational physics, or synthetic physics, it has only continued to gain legitimacy over the years.

The most immediately relevant point to note is how short a step it is from such claims about the physical universe to Langton's arguments about biology. For Langton, cellular automata were to be put to work to synthesize a universe of living beings, where the ultimate goal would be to create life in a new medium. Starting from formal constructions that could serve as models of life, these constructions would soon become so lifelike as to pass from the realm of "as if" into the realm of the real; they would "become *examples* of life themselves."[31] "Artificial Life," Langton later reiterated, is the "biology of possible life":

[It] is the study of man-made systems that exhibit behaviors characteristic of natural living systems. It complements the traditional biological sciences concerned with the *analysis* of living organisms by attempting to *synthesize* life-like behaviors within computers and other artificial media. By extending the empirical foundation upon which biology is based beyond the carbon-chain life that has evolved on Earth, Artificial Life can contribute to theoretical biology by locating *life-as-we-know-it* within the larger picture of *life-as-it-could-be*.[32]

An interesting ambiguity appears in this quotation, for the word *could* might refer to logical or to future conditionality. The primary sense of *life-as-it-could-be* seems to be "life as we could make it be"; this sense oscillates with another, life as it might now possibly be. Langton's leaning toward the future sense of *could* also marks an important contrast with the use of the same conditional in earlier (more traditionally mathematical) models. Elsewhere I have argued that the central value of Turing's model of embryogenesis lay in its provision of an in-principle account of how this process could work.[33] But in that context, the primary sense of *could* is strictly logical, and any inference to life-as-we-know-it is limited to historical possibility. If there was an implication of future conditionality in any of the many subsequent uses of Turing's model, it was never made explicit.

Langton's ambitions, by contrast, have been directed to the future from the start. In the short run, however, the prospects for life-as-it-could-be remained largely confined to the world of computer simulations (for Langton, an ideal medium just because it allows abstraction from the constraints of materiality). Over the course of the next few years, attempts to simulate the origin and evolution of living organisms with CA models became a thriving industry, with its own conferences, its own journal (*Artificial Life*, founded in 1994), and a cadre of enthusiastic publicists. Moreover, the promise of creating new life forms in a process of bottom-up synthesis, in which high-level dynamics and structures emerge spontaneously from the application of simple rules and local interactions,[34] has proved to have immense appeal for people far beyond the world of computer scientists. Perhaps especially, it proved appealing to readers and viewers who have themselves spent a significant proportion of their real lives inhabiting virtual worlds—as it were, coming of age in cyberspace.

Genetic Algorithms and the Evolution of Digital Organisms

Katherine Hayles asks, "How is it possible in the late twentieth century to believe, or at least claim to believe, that computer codes are alive? And not only alive, but natural?" To be sure, the design of ever more sophisticated techniques for representing the results of CA models in images that look alive has undoubtedly played a crucial role in establishing the proximity of these models to life-as-we-know-it. What is presented to us is not the specter of replicating codes but the visual depiction of these codes as embodied animallike forms. Moreover, as Hayles observes, "in these representations, authorial intention, biomorphic interpretation and the program's operations are so interwoven that it is impossible to separate them."[35] Crucial to such interweaving are not only the powerful effects of visual embodiment but also those of linguistic embodiment. The A-Life community has developed an extensive "biological" lexicon for interpreting their models that adds substantively to the sense of proximity to the real-life examples for which they aim.

The principle technique for A-Life simulation goes by the name "genetic algorithms." The method of genetic algorithms (sometimes called adaptive systems) was first introduced in efforts to mimic evolution by natural selection. It exploits the procedures of CA modeling by generating random changes ("mutations") in the population of algorithms ("genes") with which one begins, exchanging parts of algorithms ("genetic crossover"), and using a machine language program that codes for making copies ("reproduction") of the new programs thus constructed. The machine language program (or, as it is often called, the "body" of the digital "organism") can be directly built into the hardware of the computer's central processing unit or stored in memory as data for processing at a later time. To be sure, the actual transformation of these data into a "living organism" requires the activity (or "energy") of the CPU, but its final form is independent of hardware. As Thomas Ray explains,

Digital organisms live in the memory of the computer and are powered by the activity of the central processing unit (CPU). Whether the hardware of the CPU and memory is built of silicon chips, vacuum tubes, magnetic cores, or mechanical switches is irrelevant to the digital organism. Digital organisms should be able to take on the same form in any computational hardware.[36]

At the same time, however, throughout Ray's discussion (as well as those of others), a persistent ambiguity haunts the relation between "genomes" (understood here as a collection of "genes," or algorithms) and "bodies," just as it haunts the relation between information, data, instructions, and programs. For example, Ray writes, "The 'body' of a digital organism is the information pattern in memory that constitutes its machine language program. This information pattern is data, but when it is passed to the CPU, it is interpreted as a series of executable instructions."[37] But then we learn that "the bit pattern that makes up the program is the body of the organism *and at the same time its complete genetic material*. Therefore, the machine language defined by the CPU constitutes the genetic language of the digital organism."[38] Here the body of the organism *is* its genetic material. Hayles makes much the same point. She writes, "These bodies of information are not, as the expression might be taken to imply, phenotypic expressions of informational codes. Rather, the 'creatures' *are* their codes. For them, genotype and phenotype amount to the same thing; the organism is the code, and the code is the organism."[39] Similarly, in Ray's remarks the code is simultaneously taken as both genome and program, both data and instructions; it is "the bit pattern that makes up the program [that] is the body of the organism" and, at the same time, the organism's "complete genetic material" (its genome). In other words, the biological lexicon that Ray employs does not establish but rather presupposes the code as the genome, the genome as the program, and the program as the body of the organism. As Hayles puts it, "Ray's biomorphic namings and interpretations function not so much as an overlay, therefore, as an explication of an intention that was there at the beginning. Analogy is not incidental or belated but central to the program's artifactual design."[40]

One may of course ask, Does such ready assimilation of *genes*, *programs*, and *bodies* in fact matter? In the world of computer science, where terms like *data*, *program*, and *instructions* are used interchangeably, where machines can be built in logic code, and where computers themselves can be virtually embodied, one would have to say that it does not. But in the world of biological science—even one in which computer terminology has so extensively come to inform the literature, and where slippage between *genomes* and *organisms* (and between *data* and *instructions*) has become chronic—the significance of such distinctions has not yet vanished altogether. The fact is that in actual practice biologists still live in a world of conventional biological objects. Even with their increasing reliance on computers for visualization and computation, the activity of biological scientists remains grounded in material reality, and in the particular material reality of organisms as we know them.

The immediate issue, however, is the simulation of evolution by natural selection. How do digital organisms "evolve"? The universe in which they are said to "live" is defined by the space of the computer's memory and the time required for processing, and "evolution" is the process resulting from their competition for such space and time. Just as is the case for natural selection operating on biological organisms, the "winners" are those digital organisms with the fastest reproductive rates, and hence, those that occupy the largest share of resources. Ray accordingly concludes, "Evolution will generate adaptations for the more agile access to and the more efficient use of these resources."[41] But here too, just as with biological organisms, the crucial question is, How are the survival and reproductive rates of digital organisms determined? In digital life, the rate at which algorithms ("genes") are copied is specified by a "fitness" function. But the functions specifying the "fitness" of a digital organism are generally either predefined or assigned interactively by the user at each stage of the system's evolution as represented on the screen.[42] In other words, "natural selection," as the term is used in this community, depends on the programmer's specification of fitness, either in the initial program or interactively over the course of the program's execution. An obvious question thus arises: In what sense is this evolution by "natural selection," at least, as Darwin employed the term? Would it not be more appropriate to liken the process to "artificial selection," as employed by animal and plant breeders?

Notwithstanding such quibbles, the hope has persisted that such simulations of natural selection could help us understand the essence of biological processes—processes that must themselves have emerged as a consequence of evolution operating over eons in the natural world. The ultimate challenge in this venture is to explain the evolution of those mechanisms that are required for the development of complex organisms. And here the very terminology of A-Life encourages the belief that even this problem would not be too difficult. Just as an algorithm is called a gene, the collection of algorithms is called the genome or genotype. As Langton said,

You can think of the genotype as a collection of little computer programs executing in parallel, one program per gene. When activated, each of these programs enters into the logical fray by competing and cooperating with all the other active programs. And collectively, these interacting programs carry out an overall computation that is the phenotype: the structure that unfolds during an organism's development.[43]

Thus encouraged, a considerable amount of energy over the last decade has gone into the use of genetic algorithms (often in conjunction with the method of neural nets)[44] to simulate the evolution of developmental mechanisms like those observed in biological organisms. *Emergence* is the operative word here, for it is precisely in their capacity to give rise to global patterns of great complexity that the strength of such models has been seen to lie. Yet despite the proximity to biological processes suggested by all the talk of "genomes" and "programs," the results have so far been disappointing. Tom Ray, for instance, has succeeded in establishing conditions in which differentiated "creatures" can survive but not in which they can evolve: "Replicators in Tierra exhibited only modest evolutionary increases in complexity," and his question is, why?[45] Obviously, the failure (at least to date) to generate the kinds of complex mechanisms observed in biological evolution weakens the claim of such models to enhance our understanding of life-as-we-know-it, but because there are other aims to which he can turn, Ray is not discouraged. In fact, he suggests that we might look to organic evolution for "clues as to how we may enhance the richness of digital evolution." Somewhat in tension with his earlier claims, he writes, "The objective is not to create a digital model of organic life, but rather to use organic life as a model on which to base our better design of digital evolution."[46]

Other efforts to simulate development are sometimes claimed to show more promise. These include elaborations of an early formal description of the development of simple multicellular organisms that had been proposed by Aristid Lindenmayer;[47] and programs for step-by-step elaboration of embryonic networks according to an evolvable set of rules for subdivision, reconnection, and modularization. But here, too, the promise is itself ambiguous. If we are to think of these models as contributing to explanation, what is the explanandum? Is it the architecture and development of organisms or the architecture and development of computers? In a recent review of computer simulations of development, Christian Jacob asks if they can "help accomplish a better understanding of gene-gene interactions, genotype-phenotype mappings, and epigenesis."[48] He continues, however, by citing the application of an "embryonic" technique to the evolution of electronic circuits[49] as one of the more successful efforts in this domain, and he ends by asking not how such models can help us better understand biological dynamics, but how they can help us design computers that will behave more like organisms. Somewhat ironically, he concludes that achieving success in such designs requires us to learn more from nature, especially, taking the most recent lessons from biological research to heart: "Can we interpret genes as a set of instructions? Do genes actually correspond to programs?" Instead of unthinkingly collapsing *instructions* and *data*, he urges reexamination of the relations between *program* and *execution*. Above all, he writes, "we must rethink our notion that a program and its execution are separable."[50]

Models and Explanation, Causal Agency and Emergence

But what are the standards a successful simulation of biological development is sup-posed to meet? How is its value to be measured? Of the many ambiguities that haunt the entire endeavor of Artificial Life, perhaps the most visible are those revealed in responses to such questions as these. Or, to pose a more specific question: How can the growth and development of digital organisms, *qua* models of living forms, contrib-ute toward an understanding of biological development? Explanation, I have been arguing, depends on the particular needs demanding satisfaction at a particular time and in a particular context. And it is here, in the needs that are to be met, that contem-porary studies of artificial life diverge most conspicuously from the concerns of experi-mental biologists.

The primary commitment of practicing biologists remains to the understanding and manipulation of life-as-we-know-it, and even now, when genetic engineering has be-come not only a realistic option but a growing industry, interest in life-as-it-could-be extends no further than to the modification of already existing organisms. This differ-ence alone can easily account for the fact that unlike other kinds of computational models, the A-Life models generated so far have failed to engage much interest among biologists, neither those in academic biology departments nor those in industrial set-tings. The principal point here is not that computer scientists are engineers, dedicated to making new objects, whereas biologists are scientists, interested solely in under-standing the world as we find it, for surely, making and understanding are goals common to both domains. Rather, the point is that the instrumental needs of these two disciplines are directed at different targets, or at least, targets that one can still rel-atively easily distinguish. The most immediately pragmatic aims of biological computa-tion are to devise new kinds of computers, whereas those of computational biology are still (and merely) to find new kinds of organisms. Later, I argue that the differences be-tween these two ambitions may in fact be getting more difficult to distinguish, but first, I want to address another question. Instrumental aims are not the only deter-minants of explanatory criteria. Scientists in both A-Life and contemporary molecular biology also strive for an understanding of life, and we therefore need to ask, Are there differences in cognitive aims as well, corresponding to these differences in instrumental aims?

I began the chapter by recalling Stéphane Leduc's work on Artificial Life from the early part of the twentieth century, and the juxtaposition of that work with contempo-rary A-Life efforts invites the question, What do today's A-Life simulations provide that Leduc's earlier simulations did not? The differences in technological promise (both qualitative and quantitative) are obvious, but what about differences in the kinds of cognitive satisfaction these two ventures in synthetic biology have to offer? Surely, these are far less obvious, and especially so when overshadowed by the commonalities in their basic strategies. Both ventures aim to provide in-principle accounts of the growth and form of living beings by studying the analogous dynamics of a different medium. Accordingly, I take as the more interesting question that which arises when we take these ventures together and juxtapose them with the explanatory goals of experimental developmental biology: Can we identify a qualitative difference in the kinds of cognitive satisfaction that synthetic and experimental biology have, respectively, to offer? So rephrased, the question permits me to address the frequently invoked division between top-down versus bottom-up, reductionist versus holistic, and analytic versus synthetic strategies of explanation. Such categorizations are difficult to make precise and may often seem simplistic, but the very fact of their recurrence[51] suggests a need for something of the sort, and perhaps especially so in this context.

The writings of Andy Clark provide as good an example as any. Clark reviews the achievements of A-Life simulations in the terms of a tripartite sorting of explanatory styles—what he calls homuncular, interactive, and emergent explanations.[52] Homuncular explanations, he writes, are reductionist in that they seek to explain the functioning of a complex system in terms of the behavior of the system's parts; emergent explanations are holistic insofar as they are irreducible to the behavior of component parts; and interactive explanations are intermediate between these two extremes—fully compatible with homuncular explanations, but focusing on interactions between a system and its environment. Although the distinctions Clark wishes to make are imprecise (he acknowledges, for instance, that it is no easy matter to give a precise definition of *emergent*), his categories are familiar, perhaps especially from their affinity with the categories of dynamic systems theory.[53] Like many others, Clark is particularly interested in those properties that resist more traditional (homuncular) styles of explanation, the kinds of emergent properties exhibited in the modeling of dynamic systems, for instance, in A-Life. To be sure, such properties are not confined either to computer simulations of life or to robotic constructions; they are equally evident in Turing's mathematical model of embryogenesis as well as (I would argue) in Leduc's physicochemical simulations of "osmotic growth" (although in Leduc's case, they remain untheorized).[54] A-Life simulations clearly exceed these other efforts to model dynamic systems in both their power and versatility, and in that alone can be said to contribute to our cognitive toolkits. But the problem that remains for A-Life is fundamentally the same: it is to tie these fictional imaginings to the real world of "homuncular" research. The task, Clark argues (and how can one not agree?), "is to develop and carefully *interlock* both types of explanation,"[55] in ways that interactive explanations don't even attempt to do. In the meantime, however, while we wait to see what such "happy couplings" might look like, progress toward more immediately pragmatic explanatory goals—toward understanding through making—proceeds at a stunning pace.

Creating "Real Life"

In its modern incarnation, the use of the term *Artificial Life* was at first confined mainly to the world of computer simulations. But when Langton expressed the hope of building models so lifelike that they would be actual examples of life, he deliberately (and provocatively) left open the possibility of constructing these examples in some other (nonvirtual) medium. Indeed, the very ambition to identify "the essence of life" was from the start—for Langton and his colleagues, just as for their predecessors in the early twentieth century—linked to the vision of transcending the gap between the living and the nonliving. The hope was to create artificial life not just in cyberspace but in the real world. Rodney Brooks's contribution to the Web-based World Question Center makes the link explicit: "What is the mathematical essence that distinguishes living from nonliving," he asks, "so that we can engineer a transcendence across the current boundaries?"[56] It is hardly surprising, therefore, that *Artificial Life* quickly became the operative term referring indiscriminately to digital organisms and to physically embodied robots inhabiting the same four-dimensional world as biological organisms.

In his book *Creation: Life and How to Make It*, Steve Grand writes, "Research into artificial life is inspiring a new engineering discipline whose aim is to put life back into technology. Using A-Life as an approach to artificial intelligence, we are beginning to put souls into previously lifeless machines. . . . The third great age of technology is about to start. This is the Biological Age, in which machine and synthetic organism merge."[57] Here, the word *synthetic* reveals yet another ambiguity, referring simultaneously to artificial structures created in the mirror-world of cyberspace and to those built by engineers, "working with [material] objects and combining them to make new structures."[58] Yet, for all the realism with which digital organisms may be represented on the screen, and for all the seductiveness of the biological lexicon attached to these simulations, engineers, if they are to succeed with such a task, must still grapple with the difference between cyberspace and real space, and with the formidable difficulties encountered in attempting to bridge that gap. Within the A-Life community, however, where explanatory goals remain more abstract, such difficulties tend to be given only glancing attention. As Howard Pattee noted in the first conference held on the subject, "Very little has been said . . . about how we would distinguish computer simulations from realizations of life."[59]

Pattee asserts "a categorical difference between the concept of a realization that is a literal, substantial replacement, and the concept of simulation that is a metaphorical representation." Simulations, he writes, "are in the category of symbolic forms, not material substances."[60] And he reminds his readers of the warning von Neumann himself had issued when he wrote, "By axiomatizing automata in this manner, one has thrown half the problem out the window and it may be the more important half."[61]

As Pattee sees it, the problem lies first and foremost in the fundamental relation between symbol and matter, and it shows up with particular urgency for this project in the intrinsic dependence of the "reality" of the organism on the "reality" of its environment. Yet synthetic life forms, made from material components and assembled in real space, are clearly being built, and in ways that draw directly from work on lifelike simulations in cyberspace. Engineering is a science that specializes in negotiating the gap between symbol and matter, and robotic engineers, like their colleagues in allied disciplines, have well-developed techniques for translating from one domain to the other, for realizing the metaphors of simulation in the construction of material objects. In one sense, computer simulations of biological organisms obviously are, as Pattee writes, "metaphorical representations," but they are also models in the time-honored sense of guides or blueprints: in the hands of skillful engineers, they can be, and are, used as guides to construction in altogether different media. Here, the simulated organisms of cyberspace are used to guide the synthesis of material objects mimicking the behavior of biological organisms in real space. But can we take such a physically realized synthetic creature to be a "literal, substantial replacement" of the creature it has been designed to mimic? If it walks like a duck and quacks like a duck, is it a duck? For that matter, does it even meet the less demanding criteria that would qualify it as being alive?

These, of course, are questions that worry many philosophers, just as they do the rest of us. Like most people, I have some views on the matter. Very briefly, I would argue that even though synthetic organisms in physical space-time are no longer computer simulations, they are still simulations, albeit in a different medium. Yet I have no confidence in an ineradicable divide between simulation and realization. For one thing, media of construction can change, as they surely will. They might even come to so closely resemble the medium in which, and out of which, biological organisms grow, that such a divide would no longer be discernible. For another, convergence between simulation and realization, between metaphoric and literal constructions, can also be approached through the manipulation of existing biological materials. For example, computer scientists might come to give up on the project of the *de novo* synthesis of artificial organisms, just as most of today's biological scientists seem to have done. The engineering of novel forms of life in contemporary biology proceeds along altogether different lines, starting not with raw materials provided in the inanimate world but with raw materials provided by existing biological organisms. Techniques of genetic modification, cloning, and "directed evolution"[62] have proved so successful for the engineering of biological novelty from parts given to us by biology that the motivation for attempting the synthesis of life *de novo* has all but disappeared. The implications of such successes have not gone unnoticed by computer scientists.

In fact, work aimed at bridging the gap between computers and organisms by exploiting techniques of biological engineering is well under way in a number of computer science departments. Some efforts are aimed at harnessing DNA for conventional computational purposes; in others, researchers have begun to use the techniques of recombinant DNA to build specific gene regulation networks, predesigned to respond to particular stimuli, into real bacteria. One example of the latter[63] is part of a larger and far-reaching project on amorphous computing that Tom Knight, Gerry Sussman, and Hal Abelson conducted at the Massachusetts Institute of Technology. The motivation for this project is spelled out in a paper by Knight and Sussman:

Current progress in biology will soon provide us with an understanding of how the code of existing organisms produces their characteristic structure and behavior. As engineers we can take control of this process by inventing codes (and more important, by developing automated means for aiding the understanding, construction, and debugging of such codes) to make novel organisms with particular desired properties.[64]

In efforts such as these, no strictures whatever need obtain against using the biochemical machinery that living organisms have themselves evolved. Nor, for that matter, are there any strictures on what to count as an organism. In fact, in a subsequent paper on the subject, Abelson and Nancy Forbes write, "The ultimate goal of amorphous computing is to draw from biology to help create an entirely new branch of computer science and engineering concerned with orchestrating the use of masses of bulk computational elements to solve problems."[65] In Freeman Dyson's terms, the novel organisms might be green, or gray, or anything in-between.[66]

With every passing achievement in biological computing and in computational biology, the gap between computers and organisms becomes ever narrower yet more elusive. Thus, for instance, genetic computers or cellular computers need no longer be seen just as metaphors or even just as models. In two quite different domains—in the designing of new kinds of computers and in the modification of existing organisms—they have begun to approach at least some sense of literality. It is worth noting, however, that the route by which this convergence is occurring bears little resemblance to the story usually told about scientific metaphor.[67] Here, the convergence is simultaneously material and conceptual, and one can find no residually literal sense in which any of the referents remain fixed. Furthermore, the metaphor itself can be seen to play a substantive (one might even say, instrumental) role in bringing its referents together. Metaphors do far more than affect our perception of the world. Their instrumental force can in the first instance be understood in the immediately conceptual sense of directing the attention of researchers; but also, and in rapid suit, it can be understood in the sense of guiding their activities and material manipulations. In these ways—in many different kinds of laboratories (biological, computational, and industrial), in efforts directed toward a wide variety of ends (theoretical and practical, academic and commercial)—the metaphoric assimilation of computers and organisms works toward the literal realization of hybrid ends. And conspicuous among these is the production of material objects that resist the very possibility of parsing the categories of computer and organism.

Surely, there can be no question of the reality of the new "creatures" coming out of biological computing and computational biology. But for many, the question that seems far more critical is whether they are alive. Has the gap between the living and the nonliving, between organism and machine, already been breached? And if not yet, must we reconcile ourselves to the inevitable joining of these two realms in the near future? If so, how soon? How closely, and in what ways, must the new kinds of entities resemble the products of biological evolution to qualify for the designation of vitality? Such questions are as troubling as they are compelling, and at least part of what makes them so is the anxiety they generate. Our anxiety puts a twist to them that provides obvious grist for science fiction: How will these new creatures threaten our own status on earth? Are we really in danger of being replaced, outpaced in the evolutionary race of the future by a new kind of species?[68] Where, apart from science fiction, are we to look for answers to such questions? Marc Lange argues that the importance of the distinction between living and nonliving things is "an empirical question. The answer is for science to discover."[69] Alternatively, Steven Levy claims it is a question for technology, that it is "by making life [that] we may finally know what life is."[70]

I suggest, however, that it is a mistake to look either to science or to technology. In fact, there are peculiarities to these questions that might disqualify them as having any place at all in the realm of science. For example, when people ordinarily ask if something is alive, the object at issue is already assumed to belong to the biological realm. The question is thus a diachronic one: Is the object (now, organism) either still or yet alive? Has its life ended, or has it begun? Here, however, the question is aimed not diachronically, but synchronically: How is this object to be taxonomically classified? Is it to be grouped with the living or with the nonliving? Yet the very asking of the question in this form depends on a prior assumption, namely, that a defining, essential property for the category of life objectively exists, or that life is what philosophers call a "natural kind." But is life in fact a natural kind, and not, for example, a human kind? Isn't it the case, as Michel Foucault so provocatively argued, that the demarcation between life and nonlife ought better be viewed as a product of human than of evolutionary history?[71] Did not the very notion that it is possible to find "a true definition of life" begin only two centuries ago, with the advocacy of Jean-Baptiste Lamarck?[72]

François Jacob, following Michel Foucault, is one of many who believe it did. He claims that, prior to the nineteenth century, "The concept of life did not exist."[73] What does he mean by this? Clearly not that the term *life* hadn't been used earlier, for he proceeds by opposing his concept to such notions of life as had already been in use: he writes that his claim is "shown by the definition in the *Grande Encyclopédie*, an almost self-evident truth: life "is the opposite of death." Jacob's complaint with earlier definitions is that they are not constitutive, they do not provide us with a positive characterization of "the properties of living organisms," they do not tell us what life *is*.[74] Lamarck had stated the problem in similar terms: "A study of the phenomena resulting from the existence of life in a body provides no definition of life, and shows nothing more than objects that life itself has produced."[75] But in order for a characterization to tell us what life *is*, it must presuppose a modal (and structural) essence of life, a defining property of living beings that is not in itself alive but nonetheless absent from all nonliving things.

Just as Lamarck's did, Jacob's "concept of life" depends on a particular taxonomy of natural objects, a primary one that singles out the boundary between living and nonliving and that relegates all other distinctions between different modes of living to insignificance. This of course was the taxonomy that Lamarck had so strenuously urged at the beginning of the nineteenth century and that Foucault credited with marking the beginnings of biology. It contrasts the living not to the dead but to the inorganic.[76] It highlights one distinction at the expense of others, submerging not only earlier boundaries (most notably, between plants and animals) but also differences of kind between the various sorts of structures that were subsequently to come into prominence (genes, gametes, cells, tissues, organisms, and perhaps even autocatalytic systems and cellular automata). As long as they possessed the essential defining characteristic, all these structures could—as it were, equally—qualify as instantiations of life.

But by far the most interesting feature of the quest for the defining essence of life, and surely its greatest peculiarity, is that even while focusing attention on the boundary between living and nonliving, emphasizing both the clarity and importance of that divide, it simultaneously works toward its dissolution. Not only Rodney Brooks and his colleagues link the question of what life is with the ambition to transcend current boundaries; the same duality of impulse can already be seen in the writings of Lamarck. Indeed, it might be said to inhere in the very demarcation of biology as a separate science. For Lamarck, biology was to be "an enquiry into the *physical* causes which give rise to the phenomena of life."[77] "Nature has no need for special laws," he wrote. "Those which generally control all bodies are perfectly sufficient for the purpose." Why then demarcate biology as a separate science? Where, if not to its causes or laws, should we look for the properties that so critically and decisively distinguish the subject matter of this science from that of the physical sciences, that account for the "immense difference," the "radical hiatus" between inorganic and living bodies?[78] Lamarck's answer was to look to the organization of living matter: "It is in the simplest of all organizations that we should open our inquiry as to what life actually consists of, what are the conditions necessary for its existence, and from what source it derives the special force which stimulates the movements called vital."[79] Yet, because of his commitment to the adequacy of physical causes and laws, he believed that organization too must have—and must have had—purely physical origins; hence his interest in spontaneous generation and the origin of life. In other words, just as for many of his nineteenth- and twentieth-century counterparts, the very demarcation of life as a separate domain served Lamarck as an impetus for the breaching of that boundary, if not practically, then at least conceptually.[80] Those who are currently most interested in the distinguishing properties of organization, however, tend to focus more on the construction of material bridges. But either way, conceptually or materially, such bridges invite the formation of new groupings, groupings that necessarily violate older taxonomies. Instead of linking together in a single category plants and animals, they might conjoin computers and organisms; thunderstorms, people, and umbrellas; or animals, armies, and vending machines.[81]

Should we call these newly formed categories by the name *life*? Well, that depends. It depends on our local needs and interests, on our estimates of the costs and benefits of doing so, and of course, on our larger cultural and historical location. The notion of doing so would have seemed absurd to people living not so long ago—indeed, it seems absurd to me now. But that does not mean that we will not or should not call these categories *life*. It only means that the question What is life? is a historical question, answerable only in terms of the categories by which we as human actors choose to abide, the differences that we as human actors choose to honor, and not in logical, scientific, or technical terms. It is in this sense that the category of life is a human rather than a natural kind. Not unlike explanation.

Notes

1. Stéphane Leduc, "Diffusion des liquides: Son rôle biologique," *Comptes Rendus de l'Académie des Sciences* 139 (1904): 986; Leduc, "Production par diffusion des forces, des mouvements et des figures de la Karyokinese," *Comptes rendus* 139 (1904): 986–989; Leduc, "Germination et croissance de la cellule artificielle," *Comptes rendus* 141 (1905): 280–281; Leduc, "Culture de la cellule artificielle," *Comptes rendus* 143 (1906): 842–844; Leduc, *Les bases physiques de la vie et la biogènese* (Paris: Masson, 1906); Leduc, "Croissances artificielles," *Compte rendus* 144 (1907): 39–41; Leduc, *Les croissances osmotiques et l'origine des êtres vivants* (Bar-le-Duc, France: Jolibois, 1909); Leduc, *Théorie physico-chimique de la vie et générations spontanées* (Paris: Poinat, 1910); Leduc, *The Mechanism of Life*, trans. W. Deane Butcher (New York: Rebman, 1911); Leduc, *Études de biophysique: La biologie synthétique* (Paris: Poinat, 1912); Leduc, "Solutions and Life," in *Colloid Chemistry: Theoretical and Applied*, vol. 2: *Biology and Medicine*, ed. Jerome Alexander (New York: Chemical Catalogue Co., 1928).

2. Alfonso L. Herrera, "Plasmogeny," in *Colloid Chemistry*, vol. 2, ed. Alexander. See also Verlet's discussion of the importance to Newton of a similarly double meaning of the Latin verb *fingere* in Loup Verlet, *La Malle de Newton* (Paris: Gallimard, 1993), 289–290. Verlet goes on to make the more general observation: "Le même glissement s'observe dans des mots tels que 'forger' ou 'fabriquer', lorsque la perfection dans l'imitation engendree l'inquiétude: où est le réel, où est le

fictif?" (290). The importance of the double meaning of *to forge* is also examined in Simon Schaffer, "Forgers and Authors in the Baroque Economy," presented at the conference What Is a Scientific Author?, Harvard University, March 1997.

3. *A Latin Dictionary*, ed. Charleton Lewis and Charles Short (Oxford: Clarendon Press, 1879).

4. See, for instance, the discussion of echo simulators developed to train AI operators of an aircraft interception radar set, in R. L. Garman, "AI-10 trainer simulation at I. F. Level," Report 105-1, Radiation Laboratory, Massachusetts Institute of Technology, August 15, 1942.

5. Stanley Vance, *Management Decision Simulation* (New York: McGraw-Hill, 1960), 1–2.

6. Indeed, the use of simulations in physics is sometimes referred to as synthetic physics. Similarly, Thomas Ray describes his work with simulations as synthetic biology. "An Evolutionary Approach to Synthetic Biology," in *Artificial Life: An Overview*, ed. C. G. Langton (Cambridge, Mass.: MIT Press, 1995).

7. By now an extended literature has grown on simulation in the physical sciences. See Peter Galison, "Computer Simulations and the Trading Zone," in *The Disunity of Science: Boundaries, Contexts, and Power*, ed. P. Galison and D. J. Stump (Palo Alto, Calif.: Stanford University Press, 1996), 118–157; Galison, *Image and Logic* (Chicago: University of Chicago Press, 1997); Fritz Rohrlich, "Computer Simulation in the Physical Sciences," *PSA* 2 (1990): 507–518; Eric Winsberg, "Sanctioning Models: The Epistemology of Simulation," *Science in Context* 12 (no. 2, 1999): 275–292. For more extended discussions of the evolving meanings and uses of computer simulation, see R.I.G. Hughes, "The Ising Model, Computer Simulation, and Universal Physics," in *Models as Mediators*, ed. Mary S. Morgan and Margaret Morrison (Cambridge: Cambridge University Press, 1999); and Evelyn Fox Keller, "Models, Simulation, and 'Computer Experiments,'" in *The Philosophy of Scientific Experimentation*, ed. Hans Radder (Pittsburgh: University of Pittsburgh Press, 2003).

8. C. G. Langton, "Studying Artificial Life with Cellular Automata," *Physica D* 22 (1986): 120–149, 147.

9. C. G. Langton, "Artificial Life," in *Artificial Life: Proceedings of the Santa Fe Institute Studies in the Sciences of Complexity, Volume 6* (Redwood City, Calif.: Addison-Wesley, 1989), 1–44.

10. In what was almost surely the first such use, T. E. Wainwright and B. J. Alder wrote, "With fast electronic computers it is possible to set up artificial many-body systems with interactions which are both simple and exactly known. Experiments with such a system can yield not only the equilibrium and transport properties at any arbitrary density and temperature of the system, but also any much more detailed information desired. With these 'controlled' experiments in simple systems it is then possible to narrow down the problem as to what analytical scheme best approximates the many-body correlations" (116). T. E. Wainwright, and B. J. Alder, "Molecular Dynamics Computations for the Hard Sphere System," *Il Nuovo Cimento*, suppl. 9, ser. 10 (1958): 116–143.

11. Hughes, "The Ising Model," 133–134.

12. Stephen Wolfram, ed. *Theory and Applications of Cellular Automata* (Singapore: World Scientific Publishing Co., 1986), v. Wolfram's remarks at least implicitly evoke the analytic-synthetic dis-

tinction, placing traditional science in the analytic camp and his "new form of science" in the synthetic. I would suggest, however, that the distinctiveness of CA modeling would be better characterized in terms of the new orders of magnitude at which computations of the synthetic activity of many parts can now be conducted. Emergence, that is, is better described as a property of scale than of the philosophical category synthetic per se.

13. *Lettres galantes: Oeuvres*, vol. 1, 322–323, quoted in François Jacob, *The Logic of Life: A History of Heredity* (1970; New York: Pantheon, 1973), 63.

14. John von Neumann, "The General and Logical Theory of Automata," lecture delivered at the Hixon Symposium, California Institute of Technology, September 20, 1948; published in *Cerebral Mechanisms in Behavior: The Hixon Symposium*, ed. L. A. Jeffress (New York: Wiley, 1951), 1–41.

15. John von Neumann, *Theory of Self-Reproducing Automata*, ed. Arthur Burks (Urbana: University of Illinois Press, 1966).

16. First described by Martin Gardner in *Scientific American* 223 (October 1970): 120–123.

17. C. G. Langton, "Self-Reproduction in Cellular Automata," *Physica D* 10 (1984): 135–144.

18. Although a fuller account of this history—one that also includes the work of Ulam, Barricelli, Holland, and many others—would certainly be welcome. George Dyson, *Darwin among the Machines: The Evolution of Global Intelligence* (Reading, Mass.: Addison-Wesley, 1997) provides a good start for such an investigation.

19. For an overview of the use of cellular automata in fluid dynamics and statistical mechanics, see Daniel H. Rothman and Stéphane Zaleski, *Lattice-Gas Cellular Automata: Simple Models of Complex Hydrodynamics* (Cambridge: Cambridge University Press, 1997).

20. Doyne Farmer, Tommaso Toffoli, and Stephen Wolfram, eds. *Cellular Automata: Proceedings of an Interdisciplinary Workshop*, Los Alamos, March 7–11, 1983 (Amsterdam: North-Holland, 1984).

21. As Toffoli and Margolus write, "In this context, ordinary computers are of no use.... On the other hand, the structure of a cellular automaton is ideally suited for realization on a machine having a high degree of parallelism and local and uniform interconnections." Tommaso Toffoli and Norman Margolus, *Cellular Automata Machines: A New Environment for Modeling* (Cambridge, Mass.: MIT Press, 1987), 8. However, it must also be said that the design of such machines (at least as envisioned by Hillis) was itself "based on cellular automata." Daniel W. Hillis, "The Connection Machine: A Computer Architecture Based on Cellular Automata," *Physica D* 10 (1984): 213–218.

22. Advocates of cellular automata see exact computability as their major advantage over differential equations. As Toffoli writes, "Any properties that one discovers through simulation are guaranteed to be properties of the model itself rather than a simulation artifact." Tommaso Toffoli, "Cellular Automata as an Alternative to (Rather Than an Approximation of) Differential Equations in Modeling Physics," *Physica D* 10 (1984): 117–127, 120.

23. Wolfram, ed., *Theory and Applications of Cellular Automata*, v.

24. Fritz Rohrlich notes the "tendency to forget that these figures are the results of a computer simulation, of a calculation; they are not photographs of a material physical model" (511). Even less are they photographs of a material biological process.

25. Use of the term *simulation* varies considerably in the literature and is sometimes employed to denote both the representation of cellular automata models and the models themselves, but as Hughes emphasizes, the difference is important. He marks the distinction by using *simulation* to refer to representations of the behavior of the CA model, and *model* to refer to the cellular automata. However, I use *representation* to refer to the visual display and *simulation* to describe the particular kind of model that CA computations make possible.

26. Toffoli and Margolus, *Cellular Automata Machines*, 1.

27. Galison, "Computer Simulations and the Trading Zone."

28. By far the most widely distributed are the programs for simulating the evolution of virtual living universes, most famously, Tom Ray's Tierra and its derivatives Sim-Life and Avida. Karl Sims's Sim-Life and its offshoots Sim-City, Sim-Earth, and Sim-Ant have been widely marketed as games that even children can play.

29. G. Y. Vichniac, "Simulating Physics with Cellular Automata" *Physica D* 10 (1984): 96–116.

30. Early on, Feynman hypothesized "that ultimately physics will not require a mathematical statement, that in the end the machinery will be revealed, and the laws will turn out to be simple, like the checquer board with all its apparent complexities." Richard Feynman, *The Character of Physical Law* (Cambridge, Mass.: MIT Press, 1967), 57. Today, however, Stephen Wolfram is the leading advocate of a digitally based physics. His magnum opus on the subject, *A New Kind of Science*, was published by Wolfram in 2002.

31. Langton, "Studying Artificial Life with Cellular Automata," 147.

32. Langton, "Artificial Life," 1–2.

33. Keller, *The Century of the Gene* (Cambridge, Mass.: Harvard University Press, 2000), ch. 3.

34. Langton describes these processes as "highly reminiscent of *embryological development*, in which *local hierarchies* of higher-order structures develop and *compete* with one another for support among the low-level entities." Langton, "Artificial Life, xxiii; italics in original. But others are using these models to explain embryological development itself. See, for instance, Kurt Fleischer, A Multiple-Mechanism Developmental Model for Defining Self-Organizing Geometric Structures, Ph.D. dissertation, California Institute of Technology, 1995; Thomas Ray, "Selecting Naturally for Differentiation: Preliminary Evolutionary Results," *Complexity* 3 (no. 5, 1998): 25–33.

35. Katherine Hayles, "Narratives of Artificial Life," in *FutureNatural: Nature, Science, Culture*, ed. George Robertson, Melinda Mash, Lisa Tickner, Jon Bird, Barry Curtis, and Tim Putnam (London: Routledge, 1996), 146–147.

36. Ray, "An Evolutionary Approach to Synthetic Biology," 184. In fact, however, the hardware does matter, for it imposes a time scale of critical importance to human observers. Thus, for in-

stance, hardware composed of vacuum tubes or mechanical switches would simply have been too slow for "digital organisms" to have emerged in human time.

37. Ray, "An Evolutionary Approach," 184.

38. Ray, "An Evolutionary Approach," 185; my italics.

39. Hayles, 151.

40. Hayles, 150.

41. Ray, "An Evolutionary Approach," 185.

42. As Sims explains it, *"Perceptual selection* is used because fitness functions that could determine how interesting or aesthetically pleasing a dynamical system is would be difficult to define." Karl Sims, "Interactive Evolution of Dynamical Systems," in *Toward a Practice of Autonomous Systems: Proceedings of the First European Conference on Artificial Life*, ed. Francisco J. Varela and Paul Bourgine (Cambridge, Mass.: MIT Press, 1991), 172.

43. Quoted in M. Mitchell Waldrop, *Complexity* (New York: Simon and Schuster, 1992), 194.

44. The term *neural nets* refer to cellular automata models in which the strength of interactions between elements is progressively modified according to the effectiveness of the network in performing particular (preset) tasks. That is, connections are strengthened according to the relative success of the computations they enable.

45. Ray, "Selecting Naturally for Differentiation," 33.

46. Ray, "Selecting Naturally for Differentiation," 33.

47. Aristid Lindenmayer, "Mathematical Models for Cellular Interaction in Development," pts 1 and 2, *Journal of Theoretical Biology* 18 (1968): 280–315. Based on context-free rules for rewriting growth algorithms over the course of development, these models are known as L-systems.

48. Christian Jacob, "The Art of Genetic Programming," *IEEE Intelligent Systems* 15 (no. 3, 2000): 83–84.

49. First developed by Gruau and applied by Koza and his colleagues. Frédéric Gruau and L. Darrell Whitley, "Adding Learning to the Cellular Development of Neural Networks," *Evolutionary Computation* 1 (no. 3, 1993): 213–233; John R. Koza, *Genetic Programming: On the Programming of Computers by Natural Selection* (Cambridge, Mass.: MIT Press, 1992).

50. Christian Jacob, 84.

51. See, for instance, James Smith, "From Engineering to Positional Information to Public Understanding: An Interview with Lewis Wolpert," *International Journal of Developmental Biology* 44 (no. 1, 2000): 85–91.

52. Andy Clark, "Happy Couplings: Emergence and Explanatory Interlock," in *The Philosophy of Artificial Life*, ed. Margaret A. Boden (Oxford: Oxford University Press, 1996), 262–281.

53. See especially Susan Oyama, *The Ontogeny of Information* (Cambridge: Cambridge University Press, 1985); Susan Oyama, P. E. Griffiths, and R. D. Gray, eds., *Cycles of Contingency: Developmental Systems and Evolution* (Cambridge, Mass.: MIT Press, 2001).

54. One of the earliest arguments for the need to focus on emergent properties in understanding the distinctive features of living organisms was made by the philosopher C. D. Broad, *The Mind and Its Place in Nature* (New York: Harcourt, 1925).

55. Clark, 263.

56. Rodney Brooks, 1998, ⟨http://www.edge.org/3rd_culture/wqc/wqc_p2.html⟩.

57. Steve Grand, *Creation: Life and How to Make It* (London: Weidenfeld and Nicolson, 2000), 7–8.

58. Grand, 83.

59. Howard H. Pattee, "Simulations, Realizations, and Theories of Life," in *Artificial Life*, ed. C. G. Langton, 63.

60. Pattee, 68.

61. Von Neumann (1966; quoted in Pattee, 69).

62. Interestingly, work on "directed evolution" also grew out of discussions originally held at the Santa Fe Institute. In directed evolution, enzymes designed to perform specific tasks are produced either by bacteria that have been brought into existence by sequential selection, under conditions ever more closely approximating the targeted task, or by direct selection of proteins produced by laboratory recombination of homologous genes. See, for example, Gerald F. Joyce, "Directed Molecular Evolution," *Scientific American* 267 (December 1992): 90–97; Joyce, "Evolutionary Chemistry: Getting There from Here," *Science* 276 (1997): 1658–1659; Frances H. Arnold, "Combinatorial and Computational Challenges for Biocatalyst Design," *Nature* 409 (2001): 253–257; and Frances H. Arnold and Alexander A. Volkov, "Directed Evolution of Biocatalysts," *Current Opinion in Chemical Biology* 3 (no. 1, 1999): 54–59.

63. Ron Weiss, George E. Homsy, and Thomas F. Knight, "Toward in vivo Digital Circuits," in *Evolution as Computation: DIMACS Workshop, Princeton, January 1999*, ed. Laura F. Landweber and Erik Winfree (New York: Springer-Verlag, 2001). This work is of particular interest because it draws its inspiration directly from the early efforts of Sugita, Kauffman, and Thomas to construct formal models of genetic regulatory networks. Motoyoshi Sugita, "Functional Analysis of Chemical Systems in vivo Using a Logical Circuit Equivalent," *Journal of Theoretical Biology* 1 (1961): 415–430; Stuart A. Kauffman, "Gene Regulation Networks: A Theory of Their Global Structure and Behavior," in *Current Topics in Developmental Biology*, vol. 6, ed. A. Moscona and A. Monroy (New York: Academic Press, 1971), 145–181; Réne Thomas, "Boolean Formalization of Genetic Control Circuits," *Journal of Theoretical Biology* 42 (1973): 563–585.

64. Thomas F. Knight and Gerald Jay Sussman, "Cellular Gate Technology," in *Unconventional Models of Computation*, ed. Cristian S. Calude, John L. Casti, and Michael J. Dinneen (New York: Springer, 1998), 257–272.

65. Hal Abelson and Nancy Forbes, "Amorphous Computing," *Complexity* 5 (no. 3, 2000): 22–25.

66. Freeman Dyson, *Infinite in All Directions* (New York: Harper and Row, 1985).

67. See, for example, Mary Hesse's discussion of scientific metaphor, "The Explanatory Function of Metaphor," in *Revolutions and Reconstructions in the Philosophy of Science* (Bloomington: Indiana University Press, 1980).

68. See Hans Moravec, *Mind Children* (Cambridge, Mass.: Harvard University Press, 1988).

69. Marc Lange, "Life, 'Artificial Life,' and Scientific Explanation," *Philosophy of Science* 63 (June 1996): 225–244, 231.

70. Steven Levy, *Artificial Life: A Report from the Frontier Where Computers Meet Biology* (New York: Vintage, 1993), 10.

71. In *Le Mots et Le Choses* (Paris: Gallimard, 1966), Foucault wrote that in the eighteenth century "life itself did not exist" (139), a claim to which many historians have since objected. For instance, Schiller argued, "The opposite is nearer the truth: the inanimate did not exist but life there was to excess, penetrating everywhere and animating everything" (79). Joseph Schiller, *La notion d'organisation dans l'histoire de la biologie* (Paris: Maloine, 1978). I suggest, however, that Foucault's claim does make more historical sense if read as referring to "life itself," that is, life as a natural kind.

72. Lamarck wrote, "A study of the phenomena resulting from the existence of life in a body provides no definition of life, and shows nothing more than objects that life itself has produced. The line of study which I am about to follow has the advantage of being more exact, more direct and better fitted to illuminate the important subject under consideration; it leads, moreover, to a knowledge of the true definition of life." Jean-Baptiste Lamarck, *Zoological Philosophy: An Exposition with Regard to the Natural History of Animals*, trans. Hugh Elliot (1809; New York: Hafner, 1963), 201.

73. François Jacob, *The Logic of Life*, 89. The next quotation is from the same page.

74. It is noteworthy that after a flurry of early-twentieth-century essays and books addressed the question, What is life? it faded from view among biologists. It was resurrected by Erwin Schrödinger in his famous lecture series entitled "What Is Life?" given at Trinity College, Dublin, in February 1943 and later published as *What Is Life? The Physical Aspect of the Living Cell* (Cambridge: Cambridge University Press, 1945). It has remained ever since most commonly associated with Schrödinger and is rarely if ever posed by contemporary experimental biologists.

In Medawar's opinion, such discussions indicate "a low level in biological conversation." P. B. Medawar and J. S. Medawar, *The Life Sciences* (New York: Harper and Row, 1977), 7. By tacit consent, today's biologists appear to concur with the Pirie's judgment that the question is meaningless. "Nothing turns on whether a virus is described as a living organism or not," Pirie wrote. Norman Pirie, "The Meaningless of the Terms Life and Living," in *Perspectives in Biochemistry*, ed. Joseph Needham and David E. Green (Cambridge: Cambridge University Press, 1937), 22. Where the question does arise today is mainly in A-Life studies and robotics. And like Pirie, we might ask, what difference does it make whether these creatures are described as living or not, for scientists, engineers, industry, or consumers?

75. Lamarck, 201.

76. As Lamarck wrote, "If we wish to arrive at a real knowledge of what constitutes life, what it consists of, what are the causes and laws which control so wonderful a natural phenomenon, and how life itself can originate those numerous and astonishing phenomena exhibited by living bodies, we must above all pay very close attention to the differences existing between inorganic and living bodies; and for this purpose a comparison must be made between the essential characters of these two kinds of bodies" (191).

77. Lamarck, 282; my italics.

78. Lamarck, 194.

79. Lamarck, 185.

80. My argument here is closely related to that of Richard Doyle, *On Beyond Living* (Palo Alto, Calif.: Stanford University Press, 1997). Doyle claims that instead of constituting the actual object of biology, life is (merely) its "sublime" object.

81. The reference to thunderstorms, people, and umbrellas comes from Charles Bennett, "On the Nature and Origin of Complexity in Discrete, Homogeneous, Locally Interacting Systems," *Foundations of Physics* 16 (no. 6, 1986): 585–592: "In the modern world view, dissipation has taken over one of the functions formerly performed by God: It makes matter transcend the clod-like nature it would manifest at equilibrium, and behave instead in dramatic and unforeseen ways, molding itself for example into thunderstorms, people and umbrellas" (586). The reference to animals, armies, and vending machines is from the definition of a system in a 1950 progress report to the U. S. Air Force (see Evelyn Fox Keller, *Refiguring Life: Metaphors of Twentieth-Century Biology* (New York: Columbia University Press, 1995), 90–91.)

A Gallery of Monsters: Cybernetics and Self-Organization, 1940–1970

Andrew Pickering

There is increasing interest in the history of cybernetics, but my intention here is to come at the topic from a novel angle. I want to focus on the materiality of cybernetics, the odd artifacts and natural systems that were the referents of much cybernetic work. Along the way, I also hope to widen the frame of our understanding of cybernetics. Most attention has so far been paid to the early years in the United States, especially to the work of Norbert Wiener and his associates, discussed at the famous series of Macy conferences. I therefore include some discussion of the work of a distinctive group of British cyberneticians (Ashby, Beer, Pask, Walter), and also of Prigogine's work on self-organization in the late 1960s.[1]

This chapter emphasizes the range of material objects that cybernetics was about. This is my "gallery of monsters," which I take to support a suggestion that cybernetics instantiated a scientific paradigm quite different from that of the classical sciences.[2] It discusses the substance of cybernetics, focusing on the temporal structure of some of these monsters. Finally, it suggests that cybernetic perspectives on time and chance, order and becoming, might be productively folded back into contemporary science studies.

The Gallery

This chapter is about the substance of cybernetics, and the usual place to begin an exposition is with ideas. One might emphasize, for example, the distinctively cybernetic connection made in a foundational essay by Rosenblueth, Wiener, and Bigelow between negative feedback mechanisms and the goals and purposes of humans, animals, and machines.[3] Alternatively, one might discuss the character of cybernetic causality. We tend to think of causality in a linear fashion in which causes and effects are clearly separable. A causes B; one billiard ball strikes another and sets it in motion. Cybernetic causality, by contrast, is circular. A causes B which then, via feedback mechanisms, causes A, and so on. So cybernetic causes and effects are no longer readily distinguishable from one another. My suggestion is, however, that none of this satisfactorily catches up the singularity of cybernetics. To do better, one has to move beyond the conceptual side of cybernetics and to think about its material aspect.

Another stock tactic in explaining cybernetics is indeed to point to simple material examples of cybernetic systems, the steam engine governor and the domestic thermostat being common choices. The thermostat constitutes a negative feedback loop between the source of heat and room temperature: it seeks to minimize the deviation between the latter and some preset value by regulating the former. One is invited, then, to think about some *conceptual/material couple*—the concept of negative feedback and, say, the thermostat that we fiddle with in the winter. Something important is at stake here, I believe. But these simple examples still fail to do justice to the fascinating range of material exemplars around which cybernetics grew. To extend our appreciation, I list here some of the material devices and systems built or found by some leading cyberneticians.[4]

Cybernetic Devices and Systems

A. Monsters

Norbert Wiener	*Gordon Pask*
Anti-aircraft predictor	Self-organizing artificial neurons
Nonlinear transducers	Musicolour machine
Coupled generators	Colloquy of mobiles
Synchronized fireflies	Teaching machines
Ross Ashby	*Grey Walter*
Homeostat	Tortoise: Machina speculatrix
100-double-triode device	CORA: conditioned reflex analogue
Stafford Beer	*Ilya Prigogine*
Magnetic *Daphnia*	Bénard cells
Mouse computer	Slime molds
Pond ecosystem computer	Belousov-Zhabotinsky reaction
	Termite nest construction

B. Life

Purposive behavior	Morphogenesis
Brain	The social (the economy)
Heart	

The list is divided into two parts, and we can begin with the monsters in part A. The heterogeneity of the items is obvious, but what do they have in common? A quote from one of the British cyberneticians, Ross Ashby, can help here:

Our terrestrial world is grossly bimodal in its forms: either the forms in it are extremely simple, like the run-down clock, so that we dismiss them contemptuously, or they are extremely complex, so that we think of them as being quite different, and say they have Life.[5]

The important idea here is the contrast Ashby makes between simple, inorganic, mechanical systems and organic life. Before World War II one could take these as constituting an exhaustive dichotomous classification of all matter: either matter was dead or it was alive. Dead matter was the object of the natural sciences, and living matter was the object of the biological sciences. But the point of Ashby's remark is that somehow that dichotomy got undermined. In the 1940s a class of objects appeared that fell ambiguously in the middle ground, and this was where cybernetics took root.[6] To see what is at stake here, we can begin with Norbert Wiener's anti-aircraft predictor.[7]

At the Massachusetts Institute of Technology in the early years of the war, Wiener had the idea of building a device to improve anti-aircraft fire by tracking a plane through the sky and predicting where it would be, say, 20 seconds into the future (the time it would take a shell to travel from the gun to its target). One version of Wiener's vision was that this process might be fully automated, with tracking, prediction, and aiming all done by machines (radar sets, information processors, servomotors). The vision was not realized during the war: no practical predictor was built. But just imagining this device had a profound effect upon Wiener and contributed importantly to the rise of cybernetics. The automated weapon system was the material referent of the 1943 Rosenbleuth, Wiener, and Bigelow paper. And one can see why the predictor so impressed its designers. Imagine a fully autonomous weapon system. It sits there, inert. Then a plane appears on the horizon, and the weapon wakes up and begins of its own accord to move. It tracks the plane and fires all by itself—not directly at the plane but somewhere ahead. The plane flies into the path of the shell, which explodes just at the right moment to bring it down. The machine goes back to sleep. I am not concerned here with whether such systems work well in practice nor with the morality of their use. I am concerned with them as beautiful if horrible instances of *matter behaving wrongly*. Simply imagining such systems is disconcerting precisely because they are instances of inanimate matter acting as if it were alive.

There is, in this sense, something profoundly odd about Wiener's predictor, as there is about all of the entries in the list, something that Wiener himself sought to get across by his repeated references to witchcraft, sorcery, the figure of the Golem—animated clay—and so on. Wiener told and retold the story of the sorcerer's apprentice who magically set domestic technology into autonomous operation but then forgot the spell to stop it. Wiener even wrote a book called *God and Golem, Inc.*[8] This artificial animation was the way in which the cybernetic monsters began to prize apart the ancient dichotomy of the living and the dead, opening up a space into which cybernetics could grow.

Now we can start to see the singularity of cybernetics more clearly. It is not hard to remain aloof from stories of negative feedback and circular causality, nor from descriptions of how thermostats work. But matter behaving badly is much more striking. Wiener's anti-aircraft predictor and others are intrinsically and materially fascinating, just in what they *do*. And, as mentioned, I am inclined to put this point both more strongly and more theoretically. Protagonists of cybernetics often like to describe the singularity of the field in Kuhnian terms, and to see cybernetics as a different paradigm from the classical sciences, perhaps promising to displace the latter in a revolutionary fashion. I think there is something right about this, though it is expressed inadequately. The emphasis, as I noted, is usually on the novelty of cybernetic *ideas*. But I incline to a more materialist reading of Kuhn.[9] And in that sense, the singularity of cybernetics lay precisely in its reference to a new and rather weird field of exemplary material objects, radically disjoint from those of the other sciences.[10]

Two more remarks along similar lines. First, I do not want to insist that the material objects of cybernetics always *preceded* the conceptual aspects. Wiener's predictor did spark his cybernetic thought, but on the other hand, objects were often built or noticed because they would or did somehow inhabit the cybernetic zone of ambiguity. Ashby, for example, deliberately constructed his homeostat to occupy that zone. But I do insist that these material objects were *integral* to cybernetics, not some dispensible extras. They were truly objects to think with, to borrow Levi-Strauss's phrase. They were something to hang onto in thinking against the grain of the traditional sciences. One story has it, for example, that Ashby built "a semi-random contraption with 100 double triodes," and then "watched [it] for two years before admitting defeat in the face of its incomprehensibly complex behavior."[11]

My second remark concerns the second part of the list, labeled Life. Cybernetics was not just a science of anti-aircraft predictors. The Rosenblueth, Wiener, and Bigelow paper of 1943 generalized ideas of negative feedback and purpose from machines to animals and humans, and others quickly followed that lead. And I should note that the vector of generalization led from the inanimate, through the weird, to the animate. The impulse was to suggest that the cybernetic monsters could stand as useful models for thinking about more complex systems, the systems of life itself, which had proved more or less refractory to science up to World War II. One of the main attractions of early cybernetics was that it promised a new way into topics such as biological morphogenesis and the functioning of the brain. So, the range of exemplary cybernetic objects included both monsters and life, and the promise of crossovers from the former to the latter was very important.

Now I want to go a bit further into the substance of cybernetics, and to explain the direction I take requires a short detour. My interest in cybernetics owes something to resonances between cybernetics and the analysis of scientific practice I developed (independently, I thought) in my book, *The Mangle of Practice* (1995).[12] There, I found myself stressing two themes. One was the need for what I called a posthumanist decentering of our understanding of relations between the human and the nonhuman. In an obvious sense, the cyberneticians were more radically posthumanist than I was: they tended to efface differences between the living and the dead. But I am more interested here in the second theme of *The Mangle*, which was a concern for *temporal emergence*— the coming into being of genuine novelty, that which cannot be explained by any pre-existing circumstance.[13] The cyberneticians had some interesting ideas on this, too.

Time and Chance, Order and Becoming

Wiener and the Anti-Aircraft Predictor

The origin story of cybernetics, told by the Wiener himself, goes back to Wiener's wartime attempts to build an anti-aircraft predictor. I have discussed this already, and the historical story has been told at length by Peter Galison,[14] so I will just run through some salient features. They make a useful baseline for the other examples to follow.

The basic conception of Wiener's predictor was simple, although the engineering and mathematics of it were not. Its input would be observations on the flight path of a target, and its output would be a prediction of where the plane would be some time in the future. The predictor was thus a *thoroughly temporal device*, embedded in and operating in *real time*, as we would now say. And two specific aspects of its temporality strike me. First, the predictor got at the future by looking backwards. As Wiener put it, "To predict the future of a curve [e.g., the trajectory of a plane] is to carry out a certain operation on its past."[15] The curve to be extrapolated was a time series of readings on the plane's location, and much of the hard work of designing the predictor went into optimizing the signal processing that would perform the extrapolation, the difficulty of doing so arising from the fact that "the choice of a particular apparatus to be used in a specific case was dependent on the statistical nature of the phenomenon to be predicted."[16] So, the predictor was *backward-looking* in time: it attempted to discover what would happen next by extracting a *trend* from the immediate past.

My second point has to do with *chance*. For the predictor, and for Wiener himself, chance was the enemy; it had only negative connotations and one had to fight it. As Wiener put it, "We often find a message contaminated by extraneous disturbances which we call *background noise*. We then face the problem of restoring the original message ... by an operator applied to the corrupted message." In the predictor, noise reduction was to be accomplished by wave filters, whose design was again complicated by the fact that, "The optimum design of this operator and the apparatus by which it is realized depends on the statistical nature of the message and the noise, singly and jointly."[17]

So, these are the features of the temporality of the predictor I want to bear in mind. It lived in real time, but always looking backwards to extract a trend that it could project into the future; and in extracting that trend, chance (chaos, noise, fluctuation) was the enemy, a confusing disturbance that one had to struggle to counteract, mathematically and technologically.

This seems straightforward as far as the predictor is concerned, but I want to show next that there are other ways of thinking of time that have historically been articulated in relation to my gallery of monsters. To get to where I want to go, first I need to say a little more about self-organization.

The key question here is how systems can generate their own order, an order that is not in some way given to them from outside. As Evelyn Fox Keller (this volume) has shown, the most important material phenomenon to which this question has attached, going back to the eighteenth century and Kant, is the biological one of embryogenesis (or morphogenesis). How does a single-celled fertilized egg turn itself into a finely differentiated and inwardly coordinated organism? Where does the organization of the organism come from? There was a considerable growth of interest in this topic after the war, often taking the form of work on simpler and nonbiological models of self-organization, sometimes subsumed under the rubric of cybernetics (as in Wiener's case and Ashby's) and sometimes, as I said, independently (Prigogine).

I could turn now to Wiener's perspective on self-organization and the monsters on which it fed, but instead let me state my conclusion. Wiener's analysis of self-organization was of a piece with his cybernetics more generally: it was backward-looking in time, and the good thing about self-organization, for Wiener, was that it could kill noise.[18] Now for something different.

Ashby and the Homeostat

Since Ashby is a lesser-known figure than Wiener, I should say a few words about his biography. Briefly, he was born in London in 1903, studied at Cambridge, became a psychiatrist, and worked at various mental institutions until he joined the electrical engineering department of the University of Illinois in 1960, staying there until he retired to England in 1970, where he died soon after, in 1972. He wrote two classic books while still in England: *Design for a Brain* (1952) and *Introduction to Cybernetics* (1956). In the cybernetic pantheon, Ashby ranked second only to Wiener; in the field of self-organization he ranked first.[19] I cannot go into Ashby's theoretical and mathematical work here, but I want to note instead that Ashby was an inveterate builder of perplexing machines, and to focus on the machine that was the centerpiece of *Design for a Brain*, a machine that he built in the late 1940s and that he called the homeostat.

The homeostat comprises four identical units that are interconnected with one another. On top of each unit is an element that moves: a magnet that is free to rotate to which is attached a wire that dips into a pool of water. There is a constant voltage across this pool, so the current that flows through the wire depends upon just where it enters the water. This is the output current from each homeostat unit, and is proportional to the deflection of the magnet. Now for the first complication. The output from each unit is fed back as input to itself and to the other three units, so that each unit has

Figure 1
W. Ross Ashby. I thank Ross Ashby's daughters, Jill Ashby, Sally Bannister, and Ruth Pettit, for providing me with this photograph and permission to reproduce it.

four inputs, and each input runs through coils that act on the individual magnets, causing them to rotate this way or that.

As described so far, this setup might be stable or unstable. "Stable" means that the magnets come to rest at the middle of their ranges, and if you give one a little push, it and the others will oscillate a bit but eventually all of them will settle down to the middle of their ranges. "Unstable" means that under the smallest deflection all the magnets travel to the end of their ranges and stick there. Or they would, were it not for a further engineering complication.

Apart from the direct feedback links, where the output from each unit is an input for the others, the homeostat had a second feedback mechanism. Ashby arranged that the magnet positions (or, equivalently, the output currents) should be the so-called *essential variables* of the machine. Once the output current from any unit crossed some

Figure 2
The homeostat: four interconnected units. From Pierre de Latil, *Thinking by Machine: A Study of Cybernetics* (London: Sidgewick and Jackson, 1956), opp. 275.

predetermined limits, a relay would trip a "uniselector" or "stepping switch," which changed the internal parameters of the unit in discrete steps—either the magnitude or sign of the currents being fed back to the coils that acted on the magnet orientations. These changes were random, being given by "the actual numerical values from Fisher and Yates' Table of Random Numbers."[20]

So what? Well, this second feedback mechanism meant that if the homeostat was started from an unstable configuration, as the output currents crossed their limits the machine would *alter its own parameters at random*; if, after that, the currents were still going wild, it would undergo another random reconfiguration, and so on, until it even-

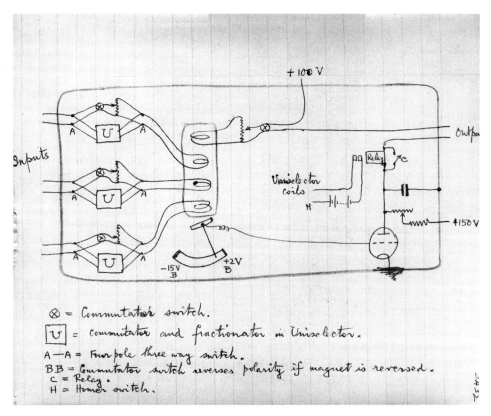

Figure 3

First full wiring diagram of the homeostat, from Ashby's personal notebook, dated March 3, 1948.
I thank Jill Ashby, Sally Bannister, and Ruth Pettit for providing this diagram and permission to
reproduce it.

tually arrived at some combination of parameters that was stable, where the magnets
settled down around their mean positions, as just described. The homeostat was,
then, a machine for staying the same: whatever you did to the magnets, or however
you tinkered with its internal connections, it would reconfigure itself to achieve stability; it was an example of what Ashby called an *ultrastable* system. Now I want to make
some observations about it.

First we can note that the homeostat was a self-organizing device, inasmuch as in response to outside disturbances it visibly reconfigured itself, quite unaided by Ashby or
anyone else. Second, Ashby deliberately designed the homeostat to occupy the liminal
region between the living and the dead. Its name referred to Walter Cannon's prewar
conception of biological homeostasis, the ability of living organisms to keep internal
parameters, such as body temperature, constant, even in a fluctuating environment.

The homeostat's essential variables displayed the same property in an electromechanical, rather than living, system. This was the sense in which Ashby could and did think of the homeostat as a brain, albeit a behaviorist brain that included no inner representations. Third, the homeostat was a wonderful machine to think with. Contemplating the homeostat, one could see directly what self-organization might amount to, free from the real-life complexity of biological morphogenesis of brains. One could also experiment on the homeostat in ways that one cannot on brains. In *Design for a Brain*, for example, Ashby explained how regimes of punishment could condition the responses of the homeostat and teach it to do tricks!

And fourth, the topic I want to dwell on, the homeostat displayed a fascinating temporality. There is an interesting similarity between the homeostat and Wiener's anti-aircraft predictor. Like the predictor, the homeostat lived in real time; it reacted to events as they happened. If a needle were pushed this way *now*, either the uniselectors would trip *now* or they would not. But there are also interesting differences. The predictor handled time by looking backwards, as I said. In contrast, the homeostat obeyed the injunction "never look back." It did not process time series and extract trends. The homeostat lived right there in the present and, one might say, it *looked the future in the face*. This I find extremely interesting, not least because so much social and philosophical thought is incapable of doing so. And yet Ashby built not a theory but a machine that could confront time head on; what was the trick?

The trick was *randomness*. The homeostat could not know what was coming at it from the future—the future was itself random as far as the homeostat was concerned—and it responded to that by reacting randomly to whatever came along (the random numbers wired into the uniselectors). It reconfigured and self-organized itself this way and that until it had learned to cope with the vicissitudes of real time. The intersection of two random series—external events unfolding and inner reconfigurations of the gadget—produced order: an ultrastable configuration of the homeostat. To speak for myself, I have long been puzzled by the relation between randomness and order—how the former can possibly contribute to the latter—even though in my own work I have found myself emphasizing open-ended becoming and the intertwining of chance and structure. The homeostat is, then, a beautiful model of how this can work. More than a device to think with, the homeostat was a true *philosophical machine*—contemplating its workings and performance, solutions to very difficult conceptual puzzles become literally visible.

One last comment on randomness. This was the key to the homeostat's ultrastability. But Ashby was also interested in the possible place for randomness in the homeostat's *construction*. A simple machine like the homeostat could be constructed according to a predetermined wiring diagram. But the known complexity of the human brain made it seem highly implausible that the detailed interconnections between all of its neurons could be specified in advance by anything (including genetics). There was just too much information required. Ashby therefore experimented on the homeostat, showing that one could interfere with the pattern of connections, reversing circuits, making new ones, and so on, without affecting the machine's overall ultrastability. Here, then, three randomnesses could be seen to combine—a randomness of construction, of performance, and of the world—to produce orderly homeostatic behavior. There is something mind-boggling about that, and yet the homeostat makes the phenomenon transparent. We can see how it goes and grasp it.

Prigogine and Self-Organization

Ilya Prigogine was born in Russia in 1917, lived in Belgium from the age of 10, and died in Brussels on May 28, 2003. In 1977 he won the Nobel prize for chemistry for his work on the thermodynamics of nonequilibrium systems. I make him the third of my trinity because his is probably the best-known name in the history of self-organization theory and because his work sheds an interestingly different light on time and change from that of Wiener and Ashby. As yet, historians have paid little attention to Prigogine, so what follows is largely based on Prigogine's best-known published work outside technical circles, his semipopular book co-authored with Isabelle Stengers, which appeared in French in 1979 as *La Nouvelle Alliance* and in English in 1984 under the title of *Order out of Chaos: Man's New Dialogue with Nature*.

Order out of Chaos represents the trajectory of Prigogine's research as essentially an adventure in the realm of thought: *"Science is rediscovering time*. It is this conceptual revolution that this book sets out to describe."[21] The book is divided into three parts. Book 1 is about "the delusion of the universal" and describes how "classical" physics lost touch with real historical time in its concern with time-reversible processes. Book 2, "the science of complexity," leads us into the world of irreversible processes where time plays a constitutive role. And book 3, "from being to becoming," is mainly devoted to some difficult musings on quantum mechanics, statistics, and entropy. One is not obliged, however, to stay exclusively on the plane of thought and ideas, and it is illuminating to look back at the monsters listed earlier in this chapter.

Evelyn Fox Keller notes that one can perceive a break in the development of Prigogine's research program.[22] At some time in the late 1960s, his interest switched from systems close to thermodynamic equilibrium to systems far from equilibrium. One way to understand this break is to look at contemporary experimental work in biology and chemistry.

Two monsters are central to the crucial book 2 of *Order out of Chaos*: one is slime molds, the other the Belousov-Zhabotinsky reaction. These examples are very striking and are discussed at length in Prigogine and Stenger's text.

We can start with slime. By the late 1960s, the following was well known, at least in the relevant circles:

When their supply of bacterial food becomes exhausted, some species of cellular slime mould seem to spread evenly over the area they occupy and later begin to aggregate into several fairly regularly spaced clusters. The aggregate typically migrates as a slug, then erects a fruiting body containing spores which germinate when conditions are favourable.[23]

Bizarrely, these single-celled beings occasionally clump up into a kind of superorganism and march off en masse, then metamorphose into a "fruiting body," which then gives birth to more individual cells. Morphogenesis and self-organization with a vengeance (though one can note that this is not the embryogenesis traditionally of interest to biologists; it looks like something simpler).

Now for the Belousov-Zhabotinsky reaction:

The chemical system that was discovered by Belousov in 1958 is now generally known as the Zhabotinskii reaction.... Its ingredients are relatively ordinary, such as potassium bromate, sulfuric acid, malonic acid and a not too rare earth called cerium. In some range of concentrations, when the system is kept stirred up, it oscillates, turning alternately bright blue and reddish purple if an appropriate indicator (ferroin) is added.[24]

These oscillations can be induced to take on various forms, including the propagation of colored bands through the medium, "target patterns" in which concentric rings move outward from a center, and related patterns like moving spirals and scrolls.[25] Also different patterns can collide and interfere with one another. The Belousov-Zhabotinsky reaction has become something of an icon in the self-organization literature.[26]

Presumably one does not need to emphasize the wonderful strangeness and monstrosity of the Belousov-Zhabotinsky reaction. Those of us who studied chemistry at school might recall that some chemical reactions (like mixing copper sulphate solution with sodium hydroxide) produce beautiful color effects and changes of state, but those kinds of transformations are more or less instantaneous. The Belousov-Zhabotinsky reaction, with its bands of color propagating slowly, gracefully, and repetitively through the medium, is even more striking, the very paradigm of self-organization, exhibiting a self-generated order that one could not imagine humanly imposing on matter.

What, then, do Prigogine and Stengers make of slime molds and the Belousov-Zhabotinsky reaction in *Order out of Chaos*? First, they offer a theoretical analysis, an interpretive scheme, for thinking about such phenomena. The key concept here is *autocatalysis*. They invite readers to think about chemical reactions that are catalyzed by their own products. The rates of such reactions are evidently nonlinear—as the autocatalytic product builds up, so the rate of its production increases. And Prigogine and Stengers argue that nonlinear processes, unlike linear ones, are capable of exhibiting self-organizing behavior. Second, they assimilate this self-organization to Prigogine's overall argument with classical physics. I do not want to get any further into the technicalities here, but I do want to make a series of general comments on this line of thought.

First, it is worth emphasizing that the Belousov-Zhabotinsky reaction, in particular, does not pertain to living matter, the classic referent of thought on self-organization. Neither is it a machine like the homeostat or the anti-aircraft predictor. The reaction is a physical (or chemical) material system. It is an example of inanimate matter behaving strangely or, one might say, of the liveliness of dead matter. If the early cybernetic monsters encouraged a slide between animals and machines, then the Belousov-Zhabotinsky reaction brought brute matter itself into the fold.

Second, we can go back to the theme of time, chance, and order, and to the role that *fluctuations* play in Prigogine's scheme. In classical statistical thermodynamics, random fluctuations lead to disorder: they simply destroy order (think of Brownian motion or Wiener on noise). But the point about autocatalysis is that fluctuations can produce order. A fluctuation away from equilibrium can be amplified through positive feedback and thus lead to phenomena like the Belousov-Zhabotinsky reaction or the assemblage of slime molds. Here again, then, we find an idea of how chance can lead to the emergence of new forms of order—order out of chaos. And two contrasts with Ashby's homeostat are then worth noticing.

1. The inner fluctuations of the homeostat were built in: they were the discrete steps in parameters taken from random number tables determined by the tripping of uniselectors. Prigoginian fluctuations instead are implicit in the *ontology of matter*, on all scales. Everything fluctuates; sometimes the fluctuations are held in check and die out (as in statistical thermodynamics), and sometimes they propagate (in nonlinear systems far from equilibrium).

2. We find in Prigogine and Stengers a certain solipsistic tendency that recurs throughout the cybernetic and self-organization traditions. The self-organizing proclivities of the Belousov-Zhabotinsky reaction and slime molds come from within the relevant system; they are properties arising from the complexities of those systems. The contrast here is with the responsiveness of the homeostat to events impinging on it from the outside, to Ashby fiddling with its pointers or whatever. Ashby systems look outward, one might say, while Prigogine systems look inward.

My discussion of cybernetics and self-organization ends here. I have sought to emphasize two aspects of their history that have not been well appreciated or expressed before. First, that one cannot appreciate the singularity of this work without confronting its gallery of monsters—its fascinating range of exemplary material systems with their peculiar liminal positioning between the living and the dead. And second, I have drawn attention to the different stories of the relations between time and chance, order and becoming, that these monsters conjure up. To close, I want to fold the discussion of time very telegraphically back into my own field of science studies.

Time in Science Studies

I have been criticized for ending *The Mangle of Practice* with the suggestion that the mangle was not only an analysis of scientific practice but also a Theory of Everything, a general story of how things go in the material as well as the human worlds. And I think I began my research on time in cybernetics in the expectation that I would be able to subsume the cybernetic stories within the overall frame of the mangle, thus somehow reinforcing my earlier claim. I have, however, concluded that this is not the way to go. The cybernetic stories about time, chance, and becoming just discussed differ among themselves (as well as from my own analysis of scientific practice). Wiener was very different from my two others on the subject of chance: he feared it as the source of disorder, whereas Ashby and Prigogine understood it as the source of novelty in the world. Similarly, Ashby differed from Prigogine, the former having an outward-looking but mechanical idea of becoming, the latter an inward-looking version based upon ontological fluctuations. Furthermore, Wiener, Ashby, and Prigogine were each right, inasmuch as they each had their own specific monsters to refer to. If you want to build an anti-aircraft predictor, my advice would certainly be to try to kill the noise. If I were advising the Supreme Deity, I would recommend an ontologization of chance if she wanted her universe to include such decorative features as the Belousov-Zhabotinsky reaction. My feeling now, therefore, is that in the history of cybernetics I have begun to map out *a space* for thinking about the relations between time and chance, order and becoming.

And the "so what?" of this is, very briefly, that in science studies we are not very good on such topics. Though you might expect it to be otherwise—after all, the most striking feature of science and technology is how fast they change—temporality is rarely at the center of our work.[27]

I do not think that in science studies we all have to write about process and change all the time; but I do think it is a very important topic that we could do more to get our hands on. And my reflexive suggestion in science studies is, then, that we might meditate on the temporality of the cybernetic monsters as a way of getting used to thinking about time and chance, order and becoming—as a kind of practice field for our over-disciplined imaginations—without, I should add, necessarily taking any of them too seriously. I hope I have shown that there are quite reasonable ways of looking change in the face that the science studies mainstream wants little of.

Notes

This is a revised version of a paper presented at a weekly seminar of the Dibner Institute for the History of Science and Technology, December 1, 1998. I thank the Dibner Institute for a fellowship in the fall of 1998. I am also very grateful to Peter Asaro and Amit Prasad for assistance with archival research, and to Evelyn Fox Keller for discussions of the history of self-organization.

1. See Andrew Pickering, "Cybernetics and the Mangle: Ashby, Beer and Pask," *Social Studies of Science* 32 (2002): 413–437. Self-organization was usually discussed as part of the cybernetic constellation of topics in the United States and Britain. Prigogine did not identify his own work as cybernetic, but I include it here as an example of a second wave of cyberneticslike sciences (led by physical scientists and mathematicians rather than the life scientists who were central to the first wave) and of how the second-wave monsters differed from those of the first.

2. For the phrase "gallery of monsters" I am indebted to Manuel de Landa, who also directed me to Benoit Mandelbrot's *The Fractal Geometry of Nature*, 2d ed. (San Francisco: Freeman, 1982), where one discovers that Freeman Dyson used the phrase in describing Mandelbrot's mathematical work on fractals (3) and that the first similar use of the phrase was by Henri Poincaré (9), from whom the mathematics of chaos traces its descent. Thus running parallel to the history of cybernetics is an isomorphous (and intertwined) story in the history of mathematics. Mandelbrot says of von Neumann and Wiener that "both were kind to my work, and influenced me greatly, even more by example than by deed" (445).

3. Arturo Rosenblueth, Norbert Wiener, and Julian Bigelow, "Behavior, Purpose and Teleology," *Philosophy of Science* 10 (1943): 18–24.

4. See Norbert Wiener, *Cybernetics, or Control and Communication in the Animal and the Machine*, 2d ed. (1948; Cambridge, Mass.: MIT Press, 1961); Pickering, "Cybernetics and the Mangle"; W. Grey Walter, *The Living Brain* (London: Duckworth, 1953); and Ilya Prigogine and Isabelle Stengers, *Order out of Chaos: Man's New Dialogue with Nature* (New York: Bantam Books, 1984).

5. W. Ross Ashby, *Design for a Brain*, 2d ed. (London: Chapman and Hall, 1960), 232–233.

6. In a fuller account it would be useful to discuss pre–World War II precursors of cybernetics. Roberto Cordeschi, *The Discovery of the Artificial: Behaviour, Mind and Machines Before and Beyond Cybernetics* (Dordrecht: Kluwer, 2002), discusses the prewar construction of mechanical models of the brain, and Evelyn Fox Keller, *Making Sense of Life: Explaining Biological Development with Models, Metaphors and Machines* (Cambridge, Mass.: Harvard University Press, 2002), discusses prewar inorganic models of organic life. Cybernetics would then be seen as reinvigorating and generalizing these streams of work with an enriched set of mechanisms at its disposal (originating in part in war-related work, as in the case of Wiener).

7. See Peter Galison, "The Ontology of the Enemy: Norbert Wiener and the Cybernetic Vision," *Critical Inquiry* 21 (1994): 228–266.

8. Wiener, *Cybernetics*, 176; Norbert Wiener, *God and Golem, Inc.: A Comment on Certain Points Where Cybernetics Impinges on Religion* (Cambridge, Mass.: MIT Press, 1964), 57.

9. See Andrew Pickering, "Reading the *Structure*," *Perspectives on Science* 9 (2001): 499–510; Thomas Kuhn, *The Structure of Scientific Revolutions* (Chicago: University of Chicago Press, 1962).

10. One might speak of a gestalt switch in moving from the classical sciences to cybernetics, which could be thought of in turn as a foreground/background inversion. The simple systems that are exemplary of the classical sciences have no special significance in cybernetics, and the cybernetic monsters are too rich and complex to be more than marginal to the classical sciences.

11. Roger Conant, "W. Ross Ashby (1903–1972)," *International Journal of General Systems* 1 (1974): 4–5.

12. Andrew Pickering, *The Mangle of Practice: Time, Agency, and Science* (Chicago: University of Chicago Press, 1995).

13. For more on resonances between cybernetics and the mangle, see Pickering, "Cybernetics and the Mangle."

14. Galison, "The Ontology of the Enemy."

15. Wiener, *Cybernetics*, 6.

16. Wiener, *Cybernetics*, 9.

17. Wiener, *Cybernetics*, 10.

18. Thus amongst Wiener's paradigmatic examples of self-organization we find coupled electrical generators whose output frequency is more stable than that of any single generator alone.

19. The ratings are from Rainer Paslack and Peter Knost, *Zur Geschichte der Selbstorganisationsforschung, Ideengeschichtliche Einführung und Bibliographie (1940–1990)* (Bielefeld, Germany: Kleine Verlag, 1990). For more on Ashby, see Peter Asaro, "Design for a Mind: The Mechanistic Philosophy of W. Ross Ashby," unpublished draft, University of Illinois, 1998; Andrew Pickering, "The Cybernetic Brain in Britain: Ross Ashby's," paper presented at the History and Philosophy of Science Colloquium, University of Leeds, March 12, 2003.

20. Ashby, *Design for a Brain*, 96.

21. Prigogine and Stengers, xxviii.

22. Keller, personal communication.

23. Keller, *Making Sense of Life*, 1365.

24. N. Kopell and L. N. Howard, "Pattern Formation in the Belousov Reaction," *Lectures on Mathematics in the Life Sciences* 7 (1974): 201–216, 201.

25. Kopell and Howard, 202–203.

26. The issue of *Scientific American* displaying the Belousov-Zhabotinsky reaction on its front cover also contained some very attractive time-series photographs of the development of the reaction, in an article by Arthur Winfree, "Rotating Chemical Reactions," *Scientific American* 230 (June 1974): 82–95. As well, the front cover of Prigogine and Stengers, *Order out of Chaos*, features pictures of the reaction in progress.

27. The logical positivists, for example, were very concerned with big changes in scientific theory, but instead of talking about change itself, they fashioned a discourse on the invariant parameters of change—the unchanging rules or methods that do or should police change. Contemporary philosophers and social theorists talk about the causes of, and constraints on, change but rarely speak about how those causes and constraints themselves change. At a less explicitly theoretical level, a cultural studies approach is probably the favored mode in the historiography of science, and cultural studies are about synchronic time slices, snapshots of history, so that change and becoming are, as it were, edited out or reduced to discontinuity and difference. Back in the realms of theory, actor-network analysis perhaps reinforces this tendency, having at its center a synchronic map metaphor. I notice that critics of *The Mangle* either ignore the fact that much of the book is about change in time, or reduce the analysis to "mere chance" and "total contingency," e.g., Yves Gingras, "The New Dialectics of Nature," *Social Studies of Science* 27 (1997): 317–334. See also my reply: Andrew Pickering, "In the Land of the Blind ... Thoughts on Gingras," *Social Studies of Science* 29 (1999): 307–311.

III   Controversies of Artificial Intelligence: Critics and Defenders

On Seeing *A*'s and Seeing As

Douglas R. Hofstadter

Because it began life essentially as a branch of the theory of computation, and because the latter began life essentially as a branch of logic, the discipline of artificial intelligence (AI) has very deep historical roots in logic. The English logician George Boole, in the 1850s, was among the first to formulate the idea—in his famous book *The Laws of Thought*—that thinking itself follows clear patterns, even laws, and that these laws could be mathematized. For this reason, I like to refer to this law-bound vision of the activities of the human mind as the Boolean Dream.[1]

Put more concretely, the Boolean Dream amounts to seeing thinking as the manipulation of propositions, under the constraint that the rules should always lead from true statements to other true statements. Note that this vision of thought places *full sentences* at center stage. A tacit assumption is thus that the *components* of sentences—individual words, or the concepts lying beneath them—are not deeply problematical aspects of intelligence; rather, the mystery of thought is how these small, elemental, "trivial" items work together in large, complex (and perforce nontrivial) structures.

To make this more concrete, let me take a few examples from mathematics, a domain that AI researchers typically focused on in the early days. Concepts like "5" or "prime number" or "definite integral" would be thought of as trivial or quasi-trivial, in the sense that they are mere definitions. They would be seen as posing no challenge to a computer model of mathematical thinking—the cognitive activity of doing mathematical research. By contrast, dealing with propositions such as "Every even number greater than 2 is the sum of two prime numbers," establishing the truth or falsity of which requires work—indeed, an unpredictable amount of work—would be seen as a deep challenge. Determining the truth or falsity of such propositions, by means of formal proof in the framework of an axiomatic system, would be the task facing a mathematical intelligence. Of course, a successful proof, consisting of many lines, perhaps many pages, of text would be seen as a very complex cognitive structure, the fruit of an intelligent machine or mind.

Another domain that appealed greatly to many of the early movers of AI was chess. Once again, the primitive concepts of chess, such as "bishop," "diagonal move," "fork," "castling," and so forth, were all seen as similar to mathematical definitions—essential to the game, of course, but posing little or no mental challenge. In chess, what was felt to matter was the development of grand strategies involving arbitrarily complex *combinations* of these definitional notions. Thus developing long and intricate series of moves, or playing entire games, was seen as the important goal.

As might be expected, many of the early AI researchers also enjoyed mathematical or logical puzzles that involved searching through clearly defined spaces for subtle sequences or combinations of actions, such as coin-weighing problems (given a balance, find the one fake coin among a set of 12 in just three weighings), the missionaries-and-cannibals puzzle (get three missionaries and three cannibals across a river in the minimum number of boat trips, under the constraint that there are never more cannibals than missionaries either on the boat, which can carry only three people, or on either side of the river), cryptarithmetic puzzles (find an arithmetically valid replacement for each letter by some digit in the equation SEND + MORE = MONEY), the Fifteen puzzle (return the 15 sliding blocks in a 4×4 array having one movable hole to their original order), or even Rubik's Cube. All of these involve manipulation of hard-edged components, and the goal is to find complex sequences of actions that have certain hard-edged properties. By *hard-edged*, I mean no ambiguity: there is no question about whether an individual is or is not a cannibal, no doubt about the location of a sliding block, and so forth. Nothing is blurry or vague.

These kinds of early preconceptions about the nature of modeling intelligence on a machine gave a certain clear momentum to the entire discipline of AI, indeed, deeply influenced the course of research done all over the world for decades. Nowadays, however, the tide is slowly turning. Although some work in this logic-rooted tradition continues to be done, many if not most AI researchers have reached the conclusion—perhaps reluctantly—that the logic-based formal approach is a dead end.

What seems to be wrong with it? In a word, logic is *brittle*, in diametric opposition to the human mind, which is best described as flexible or fluid in its capabilities of dealing with completely new and unanticipated types of situations. The real world, unlike chess and some aspects of mathematics, is not hard-edged but ineradicably blurry. Logic and its many offshoots rely on humans to translate situations into some unambiguous formal notation before any processing by a machine can be done. Logic is not at all concerned with such activities as categorization or the recognition of patterns. And to many people's surprise, these activities have turned out to play a central role in intelligence.

It happens that as AI was growing up, a discipline called pattern recognition (PR) was also being developed. There was some but not much communication between researchers in the two disciplines. Researchers in PR were concerned with getting machines to do such things as reading handwriting or typewritten text, visually recognizing objects in photographs, and understanding spoken language. In the attempts to get machines to do such things, the complexity of categories, in its full glory and in its full messiness, began slowly to emerge. Researchers were faced with questions like these: What is the essence of dog-ness or house-ness? What is the essence of *A*-ness? What is the essence of a given person's face that prevents it from being confused with other people's faces? What is in common among all the different ways that different people, including native speakers and people with accents, pronounce "Hello"? How can these things be conveyed to computers, which seem to be best at dealing with hard-edged categories—categories having crystal clear, perfectly sharp boundaries?

These kinds of perceptual challenges, despite their formidable, bristling difficulties, were at one time viewed by most members of the AI community as low-level obstacles to be overcome en route to intelligence—almost as a nuisance that they would have liked to, but couldn't quite, ignore. For example, the attitude of AI researchers would be, "Yes, it's damn hard to get a computer to perceive an actual, three-dimensional chessboard, with all of its roundish shapes, varying densities of shadows, and so forth, but what does that have to do with intelligence? Nothing! Intelligence is about finding brilliant chess moves, something that is done after the perceptual act is completely over and out of the way. It's a purely abstract thing. Conceptually, perception and reasoning are totally separable, and intelligence is only about the latter." Similarly, at that time, the typical AI attitude about doing math would be that math skill is a completely perception-free activity without the slightest trace of blurriness; a pristine activity involving precise, rigid manipulations of the most crystalline of definitions, axioms, rules of inference; a mental activity that is totally isolated from, and unsullied by, "mere" perception.

These two trends—AI and PR—had almost no overlap. Each group pursued its own ends with almost no effect on the other group. Very occasionally, however, one could spot hints of another attitude, radically different from these two. The book *Pattern Recognition*, written in the late 1960s by Mikhail Bongard, a Russian researcher, seemed largely to be a prototypical treatise on pattern recognition, concerned mostly with the recognition of objects, not with "higher" mental functioning.[2] But then, in a splendid appendix, Bongard revealed his true colors by posing an escalating series of 100 pattern recognition puzzles for humans and machines alike. Each puzzle involved twelve simple line diagrams separated into two sets of six each, and the idea was to figure out what was the basis for the segregation. What was the criterion for separating the twelve diagrams into these two sets? Readers are invited to try the Bongard problem in figure 1, for instance.

Of course, for each puzzle there were, in a certain trivial sense, an infinite number of possible solutions. For instance, one could say about the six diagrams on the left side of any given Bongard problem, "Category 1 contains exactly these six diagrams (and no others), and category 2 contains all other diagrams." This would of course work in a very literal-minded, heavy-handed way, but it would not be how any person would

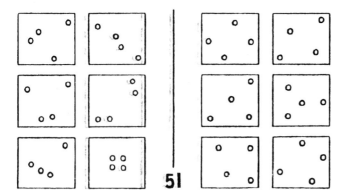

Figure 1

ever think of it except under the most artificial of circumstances. A psychologically realistic basis for segregation in a Bongard problem might be that all diagrams in category 1 would involve no curved lines, whereas all diagrams in category 2 would have
at least one curved line. Or another typical segregation criterion might be that diagrams in category 1 would involve nesting (a shape's containing another shape), and
those in category 2 would not. And so on. The Bongard problems in figures 2 a–d give
a feeling for the kinds of issues that Bongard was concerned with in his work. Readers
are challenged to try to find, for each of them, a very simple and appealing criterion
that distinguishes category 1 from category 2.

The key feature of Bongard problems is that they involve *highly abstract conceptual
properties*, in strong contrast to the usual tacit assumption that the quintessence of visual perception is the activity of dividing a complex scene into its separate *constituent
objects* followed by the activity of attaching *standard labels* to the now-separated objects
(the identification of the component objects as members of various preestablished categories like "car," "dog," "house," "hammer," "airplane"). In Bongard problems the
quintessential activity is the discovery of some abstract connection that links all the
various diagrams in one group of six and distinguishes them from all the diagrams in
the other group of six. To do this, one has to bounce back and forth among diagrams,
sometimes remaining within a single set of six, other times comparing diagrams across
sets. But the essence of the activity is a complex interweaving of acts of *abstraction* and
comparison, all of which involve guesswork rather than certainty.

By *guesswork* I mean that one has to take a chance that certain aspects of a given diagram matter and others are irrelevant. Perhaps shapes count but not colors, or vice
versa. Perhaps orientations count but not sizes, or vice versa. Perhaps curvature or its
lack counts but not location inside the box, or vice versa. Perhaps numbers of objects
but not their types matter, or vice versa. Somehow, people usually have a very good

intuitive sense, given a Bongard problem, for which types of features will wind up mattering and which are merely distractions. Even when one's first hunch turns out wrong, one often needs only a minor tweak to find the proper aspects on which to focus. In other words, there is a subtle sense in which people are often close to right even when they are wrong. All these kinds of high-level mental activities are what seeing the various diagrams in a Bongard problem—a pattern recognition activity—involves.

When presented this way, visual perception takes on a very different light. Its core seems to be *analogy making*, that is, the activity of abstracting out important features of complex situations (thus filtering out what one takes to be superficial aspects) and finding resemblances and differences between situations at that high level of description. Thus the "annoying obstacle" that AI researchers often took perception to be becomes, in this light, a highly abstract act—one might even say a highly abstract *art*—in which intuitive guesswork and subtle judgments play the starring roles.

It is clear that in the solution of Bongard problems, perception is pervaded by intelligence, and intelligence by perception; they intermingle in such a profound way that one could not hope to tease them apart. In fact, this phenomenon had already been recognized by some psychologists, and even celebrated in a rather catchy little slogan: "Cognition equals perception."

Sadly, Bongard's insights did not have much effect on either the AI world or the PR world, even though in some sense his puzzles provide a bridge between the two worlds and suggest a deep interconnection. However, they certainly had a far-reaching effect on me, in that they pointed out that perception is far more than the recognition of members of already established categories—it involves the spontaneous manufacture of *new* categories at arbitrary levels of abstraction. As I said earlier, this idea suggested to me a profound relationship between perception and analogy making—indeed, it suggested that analogy making is simply an abstract form of perception and that the computer modeling of analogy making ought to be based on models of perception.

A key event in my personal evolution as an AI researcher was a visit I made to Carnegie-Mellon University's computer science department in 1976. While there, I had the good fortune to talk with some of the developers of the Hearsay II program, whose purpose was to be able to recognize spoken utterances. They had made an elegant movie to explain their work. The movie began by conveying the immense difficulty of the task and then in clear pictorial terms showed their strategy for dealing with the problem.

The basic idea was to take a raw speech signal—a waveform, in other words, which could be seen on a screen as a constantly changing oscilloscope trace—and to produce from it a hierarchy of translations on different levels of abstraction. The first level above the raw waveform would thus be a *segmented waveform*, consisting of an attempt to break the waveform up into a series of nonoverlapping segments, each of which would hopefully correspond to a single phoneme in the utterance. The next level

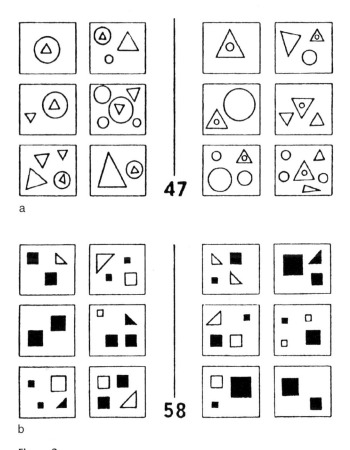

Figure 2

above that would be a set of *phonetic labels* attached to each segment, which would serve as a bridge to the next level up, namely a *phonemic hypothesis* as to what phoneme had actually been uttered, such as "o" or "u" or "d" or "t." Above the phonemic level was the *syllabic* level, consisting, of course, in hypothesized syllables such as "min" or "pit" or "blag." Then there was the *word* level, which needs little explanation, and above that the *phrase* level (containing such hypothesized utterance fragments as "when she went there" or "under the table"). One level higher was the *sentence* level, which was just below the uppermost level, which was called the *pragmatic* level.

At that level, the *meaning* of the hypothesized sentence was compared to the situation under discussion. (Hearsay always interpreted what it heard in relation to a specific real-world context, such as an ongoing chess game.) If it made sense in the given

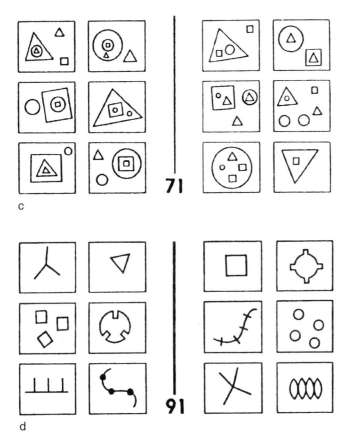

Figure 2
(continued)

context, it was accepted, whereas if it made no sense in the context, then some piece of the hypothesized sentence—its weakest piece, in fact, in a sense that I describe later—was modified in such a way as to make the sentence fit the situation (assuming that such a simple fix was possible). For example, if the program's best guess as to what it had heard was the sentence "There's a pen on the box" but in fact, in the situation under discussion, there was a pen *in* a box rather than *on* it, and if furthermore the word *on* was the least certain word in the hypothesized sentence, then a switch to "There's a pen *in* the box" might have a high probability of being suggested. If, on the other hand, the word *on* was very clear and strong whereas the word *pen* was the least certain element in the sentence, then the sentence might be converted into "There's a *pin* on the box." Of course, that sentence would be suggested as an improvement over the original one only if it made sense within the context.

This idea of making changes according to expectations (long-term knowledge of how the world usually is, as well as the specifics of the current situation) was a very beautiful one, in my opinion, but it caused no end of complexity in the program's architecture. In particular, as soon as the program made a guess at a new sentence—such as converting "There's a pen on the box" into "There's a pen in the box"—it took the new word and tried to modify its underpinnings, such as its syllables, the phonemes below them, their phonetic labels, and possibly even the boundary lines of segments in the waveform, in an attempt to see if the revised sentence was in any way justifiable in terms of the sounds actually produced. If not, the sentence would be rejected, no matter how strong was its appeal at the pragmatic level. And while all this work was going on, the program would simultaneously be working on new incoming waveforms and on other types of possible rehearsals of the old sentence.

The preceding discussion implies that each aspect of the utterance at each level of abstraction was represented as a type of *hypothesis*, attached to which was a set of *pieces of evidence supporting the given hypothesis*. Thus attached to a proposed syllable such as "tik" were little structures indicating the degree of certainty of its component phonemes and the probability of correctness of any words in which it figured. The fact that plausibility values or levels of confidence were attached to every hypothesis imbued the current best guess with an implicit halo of alternative interpretations, any one of which could step in if the best guess was found to be inappropriate.

I am sure that the figurative language I am using to describe Hearsay II would not have been that chosen by its developers, but I am trying to get across an image that it undeniably created in me, since that image then formed the nucleus of my own subsequent research projects in AI. Some other crucial features of the Hearsay II architecture that I have hinted at but cannot describe here in detail were its deep parallelism, in which processes of all sorts operated on many levels of abstraction at the same time, and its uniquely flexible manner of allowing a constant intermingling of *bottom-up processing* (the building up of higher levels of abstraction on top of fairly solid lower-level hypotheses, much like the construction of a building) and *top-down processing* (the attempt to build plausible hypotheses close to the raw data in order to give a solid underpinning to hypotheses that make sense at abstract levels, something like constructing lower and lower floors after the top floors have been built and are sitting suspended in thin air).

Not too surprisingly, my first attempt to turn my personal vision of how Hearsay II operated into an AI project of my own was the sketching out, in very broad strokes, of a hypothetical program to solve Bongard problems.[3] However, the difficulties in actually implementing such a program completely on my own seemed so daunting that I backed away from doing so and started exploring other domains that seemed more tractable. What I was always after was some kind of microdomain in which analogies

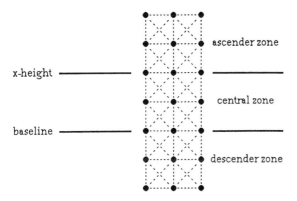

Figure 3

could be made at very high levels of abstraction yet not require an extreme amount of real-world knowledge.

Over the years, I developed a number of different computer projects, each one centered on a different microdomain, and thanks to the hard work of several superb graduate students, many of these abstract ideas were converted into genuine working computer programs. All these projects are described in considerable detail in the book *Fluid Concepts and Creative Analogies*,[4] co-authored by me and several of my students.

Here I would like to present in very quick terms one of those domains and the challenges that it involved, a project that clearly reveals how deeply Mikhail Bongard's ideas inspired me. The project's name is Letter Spirit, and it is concerned with the visual forms of the letters of the Latin alphabet. In particular, our goal was to build a computer program that could design all 26 lowercase letters, *a* through *z*, in any number of artistically consistent styles. The task was constrained even more by restricting the letter forms to a grid. In particular, one is allowed to turn on any of the 56 short horizontal, vertical, and diagonal line segments—"quanta"—in the 2 × 6 array shown in figure 3. By so doing, one can render each of the 26 letters in some fashion; the idea is to make them all agree with each other stylistically.

To me, it is highly significant that Bongard chose to conclude his appendix of 100 pattern recognition problems with a puzzle whose category 1 consists of six highly diverse Cyrillic *A*'s, and whose category 2 consists of six equally diverse Cyrillic *B*'s (see figure 4).

This choice of final problem is a symbolic message carrying the clear implication that, in Bongard's opinion, the recognition of letters constitutes a far deeper problem than any of his 99 earlier problems, and the more general conclusion that a necessary prerequisite to tackling real-world pattern recognition in its infinite complexity is

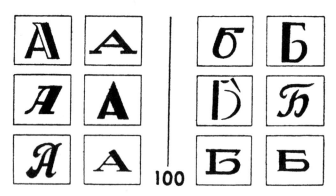

Figure 4

the development of all the intricate and subtle analogy-making machinery required to solve his 100 problems and the myriad other ones that lie in their immediate halo.

To show the fearsome complexity of the task of letter recognition, I offer a display of uppercase *A*'s, all designed by professional typeface designers and used in advertising and publishing (see figure 5).

What kind of abstraction could lie behind this crazy diversity? (Indeed, I once proposed that the toughest challenge facing AI workers is to answer the question, What are the letters *A* and *I*?)

The Letter Spirit project attempts to study the conceptual enigma posed by the foregoing collection but to do so within the framework of the grid in figure 3 and even to extend that enigma in certain ways. Thus, a Letter Spirit counterpart to the illustration in figure 5 would be the collection of grid-bound lowercase *a*'s shown in figure 6, suggesting how intangible the essence of *a*-ness must be, even when the shapes are made solely by turning on or off very simple, completely fixed line segments.

I have said that the Letter Spirit project aims not just to study the enigma of the many *A*'s but to extend that enigma. By this I mean the following. The challenge of Letter Spirit is not merely to recognize or classify a set of given letters but to create new letter forms and thereby new artistic styles. Thus the task for the program would be to take a given letter designed by a person—any *a*, for instance—and to let that letter inspire the remaining 25 letters of the alphabet. Thus one might move down the line consecutively from *a* to *b* to *c*, and so on. Of course, the seed letter need not be an *a*, and even if it were an *a*, the program would be very unlikely to proceed in strict alphabetical order (if one has created an *h*, it is clearly more natural to try to design an *n* before tackling the design of *i*). But let us nonetheless imagine a strictly alphabetic design process stopped while under way, so that precisely the first 7 letters of the alphabet have been designed and the remaining 19 remain to be done. Let us in fact

Figure 5

imagine doing such a thing with 7 quite different initial *a*'s. We would have something like the 7 × 7 matrix shown in figure 7.

Implicit in this matrix (especially in the ellipses) are two very deep pattern recognition problems. First is the vertical problem, namely, what do all the items in any given *column* have in common? This is essentially the question that Bongard was asking in the final puzzle of his appendix. The answer, in a single word, is *letter*. Of course, to say that is not to solve the problem, but it is a useful summary. Second is the horizontal problem, namely, what do all the items in any given *row* have in common? To this question, I prefer the single-word answer *spirit*. How can a human or a machine make the uniform artistic spirit lurking behind these seven shapes leap to the abstract category of "h," then leap from those eight shapes to the category "i," then to "j," and so on, all the way down the line to "z"?

And do not think that the category "z" is the end of the line. After all, there remain all the uppercase letters, and then all the numerals, and then punctuation marks, and then mathematical symbols. . . . But even this is not the end, for one can try to make

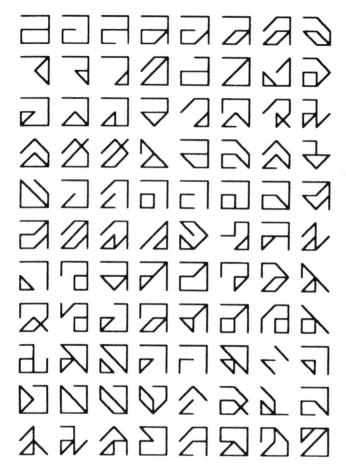

Figure 6

the same spirit leap out of the Latin alphabet and into such other writing systems as the Greek alphabet, the Russian alphabet, Hebrew, Japanese, Arabic, Chinese, and so on. Of course, the making of such transalphabetic leaps (as I like to call them) goes way beyond the modest limits of the Letter Spirit project itself, but the suggestion serves as a reminder that just as there are unimaginably many different spirits (artistic styles) in which to realize any given letter of the alphabet, so there are also unimaginably many different letters (typographical categories) in which to realize any given stylistic spirit.

In metaphorical terms, one can talk about the alphabet and the "stylabet," the set of all conceivable styles. Both of these are infinite rather than finite entities. The stylabet

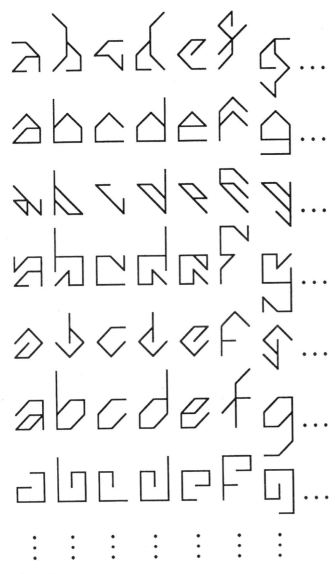

Figure 7

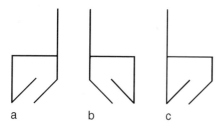

Figure 8

is very much like the alphabet in its subtlety and intangibility, but it resides at a considerably higher level of abstraction.

The one-word answers to the so-called vertical and horizontal problems—letter and spirit—gave rise to the project's name. There is of course a classic opposition in the legal domain between the concepts of "letter" and "spirit"—the contrast between "the letter of the law" and "the spirit of the law." The former is concrete and literal, the latter abstract and spiritual. And yet there is a continuum between them. A given law can be interpreted at many levels of abstraction. So too with the artistic design problems of the Letter Spirit project: there are many ways to extrapolate from a given seed letter to other alphabetic categories, some ways being rather simplistic and down-to-earth, others extremely sophisticated and high-flown. The Letter Spirit project does not by any means grow out of the dubious postulate that there is one best way to carry style consistently from one category to another; rather, it allows many possible notions of artistically valid style at many different levels of abstraction. Of course, this means that the project is in complete opposition to any view of intelligence that sees the main purpose of mind as being an eternal quest after the "right" answers and the "truth." That the human mind *can* conduct such a quest, principally through such careful disciplines as mathematics, science, history, and so forth, is a tribute to its magnificent subtlety, but to do science and history is not how or why the mind evolved, and it deeply misrepresents the mind to cast its activities solely in the narrow and rigid terms of truth seeking.

To convey something of the flavor of the Letter Spirit project, I offer a style extrapolation puzzle, which I hope will intrigue readers. Take the grid-bound way of realizing the letter *d* and attempt to make a letter *b* that exhibits the same spirit or style (see figure 8a).

One idea that springs instantly to mind is simply to reflect the given shape, since one tends to think of *d* and *b* as being in some sense each other's mirror images. For many *d*'s, this simple recipe for making a *b* might work, but in this case there is a somewhat troubling aspect to the proposal: the resultant shape has quite an *h*-ish look to it, enough perhaps to give a careful letter designer second thoughts (see figure 8b).

What escape routes might be found, still respecting the rigid constraints of the grid? One possible idea is reversing the direction of the two diagonal quanta at the bottom, to see if that action reduces the *h*-ness (see figure 8c). To some people's eyes, including mine, this action slightly improves the ratio of *b*-ness to *h*-ness. Notice that this move also has the appealing feature of echoing the exact diagonals of the seed letter. This agreement could be taken as a particular type of stylistic consistency. Perhaps, then, this is a good enough *b,* but perhaps not.

Another way one might try to entirely sidestep *h*-ness would involve somehow shifting the opening from the bottom to the top of the bowl. Can you find a way to carry this out? Or are there yet other possibilities?

I must emphasize that this is not a puzzle with a clearly optimal answer; it is posed simply as an artistic challenge, to try to get across the nature of the Letter Spirit project. When you have made a *b* that satisfies you, can you proceed to other letters of the alphabet? Can you make an entire alphabet? How does your set of 26 letters, all inspired by the given seed letter, compare with someone else's?

The Letter Spirit project is doubtless the most ambitious project in the modeling of analogy making and creativity so far undertaken in my research group, and as of this writing, it has by no means been fully realized as a computer program. It is currently somewhere between a sketch and a working program, and in perhaps a couple of years a preliminary version will exist. But it builds upon several already realized programs, all of whose architectures were deeply inspired by the ideas of Mikhail Bongard and by principles derived from the architecture of the pioneering perceptual program Hearsay II.

To conclude, I would like to cite the words of someone whose fluid way of thinking I have always admired—the great mathematician Stanislaw Ulam. As Heinz Pagels reports in his book *The Dreams of Reason,*[5] one time Ulam and his mathematician friend Gian-Carlo Rota were having a lively debate about artificial intelligence, a discipline whose approach Ulam thought was simplistic. Convinced that perception is the key to intelligence, Ulam was trying to explain the subtlety of human perception by showing how subjective it is, how influenced by context. He said to Rota, "When you perceive intelligently, you always perceive a function, never an object in the physical sense. Cameras always register objects, but human perception is always the perception of functional roles. The two processes could not be more different. . . . Your friends in AI are now beginning to trumpet the role of contexts, but they are not practicing their lesson. They still want to build machines that see by imitating cameras, perhaps with some feedback thrown in. Such an approach is bound to fail."

Rota, clearly much more sympathetic than Ulam to the old-fashioned view of AI, interjected, "But if what you say is right, what becomes of objectivity, an idea formalized by mathematical logic and the theory of sets?"

Ulam parried, "What makes you so sure that mathematical logic corresponds to the way we think? Logic formalizes only a very few of the processes by which we actually think. The time has come to enrich formal logic by adding to it some other fundamental notions. What is it that you see when you see? You see an object *as* a key, a man in a car *as* a passenger, some sheets of paper *as* a book. It is the word 'as' that must be mathematically formalized.... Until you do that, you will not get very far with your AI problem."

To still Rota's expression of fear that the challenge of formalizing the process of seeing a given thing as another thing was impossibly difficult, Ulam said, "Do not lose your faith—a mighty fortress is our mathematics," a droll but ingenious reply in which Ulam practices what he preaches by seeing mathematics itself as a fortress.

If anyone else but Stanislaw Ulam had made the claim that the key to understanding intelligence is the mathematical formalization of the ability to "see as," I would have objected strenuously. But knowing how broad and fluid Ulam's conception of mathematics was, I think he would have been able to see the Letter Spirit architecture and its predecessor projects as mathematical formalizations.

In any case, when I look at Ulam's key word *as*, I see it as an acronym for abstract seeing or perhaps analogical seeing. In this light, Ulam's suggestion can be restated in the form of a dictum—"Strive always to see all of AI as AS"—a rather pithy and provocative slogan to which I fully subscribe.

Notes

1. For more on this, see "Waking up from the Boolean Dream," chapter 26 of my book *Metamagical Themas* (New York: Basic Books, 1985).

2. See Mikhail Moiseevich Bongard, *Pattern Recognition* (New York: Spartan Books, 1970).

3. See chapter 19 of my book *Gödel, Escher, Bach* (New York: Basic Books, 1979) for this sketched architecture.

4. Douglas R. Hofstadter and the Fluid Analogies Research Group, *Fluid Concepts and Creative Analogies: Computer Models of the Fundamental Mechanisms of Thought* (New York: Basic Books, 1995).

5. Heinz R. Pagels, *The Dreams of Reason: The Computer and the Rise of the Sciences of Complexity* (New York: Simon and Schuster, 1988).

Did Deep Blue's Win over Kasparov Prove That Artificial Intelligence Has Succeeded? A Debate

Hubert Dreyfus and Daniel Dennett

On May 12, 1997, IBM's program Deep Blue defeated world champion Garry Kasparov at chess. Jim Lehrer invited philosophers Hubert Dreyfus and Daniel Dennett to discuss the relevance of the event on his National Public Radio's program *NewsHour with Jim Lehrer*. The debate continued in the electronic magazine *Slate* in the following months. We thank Hubert Dreyfus, Daniel Dennett, and Slate magazine for permission to reprint the exchange.

Message #1: May 20, 1997
From: Daniel Dennett
To: Hubert Dreyfus

Dear Bert,

The discussion we had on the *NewsHour* was fun but, really, Bert, I think you have only yourself to blame for the widespread opinion that you said computers were not gonna be able to play great chess. I went back and looked at the revised edition of your book *What Computers Still Can't Do*, and you go to considerable lengths to pooh-pooh not just the current prowess but the future prospects of computer chess. Yes, near the end (page 259) of the book, you make the distinction between the closed nature of chess and the open-ended nature of embodied life. But I think it is fair to say this is your fall-back position, which runs: Computer tic-tac-toe is trivial; computer chess is *almost certainly* impossible (at the world-champ level); and computer conversation is out of the question. Otherwise, why would you spend so much time bad-mouthing the (over-)confident declarations of Simon et al.? And anyway, there are so many passages in your book which—aside from sea-lawyering provisos—commit you to a negative prophecy. For instance:

We shall soon see that given the limitations of digital computers, this [stagnation] is just what one would expect.... (85)

Work on game playing revealed the necessity [sic] of processing "information" which is not explicitly considered or excluded, that is, information on the fringes of consciousness.... (107)

In chess programs, for example, it is beginning to be clear that adding more and more specific bits of chess knowledge to plausible move generators, finally bogs down in too many ad hoc subroutines.... What is needed is something which corresponds to the master's way of seeing the board as having promising and threatening areas. (296)[1]

But let's let bygones be bygones, and consider the future; as one e-mail correspondent to me put it, you "wimped out" totally on my request for a test without "points for style." Why don't you fish or cut bait? If "understanding natural language" is not required for passing the unrestricted Turing test (with, say, you as judge), name a tougher test—winning the Pulitzer Prize for fiction or poetry? Being head gag writer for Jay Leno? Take your pick, but put up or shut up! I am not impressed by the claim that a computer won't really understand natural language (if it uses GOFAI—good old-fashioned artificial intelligence—techniques) until you couple it to a performance measure. After all, I once listened in utter fascination to a well-known philosopher as he insisted that neither Joseph Conrad nor Vladimir Nabokov understood English—it not being their native language. Surely (surely?) *you* would not descend to such depths, would you? Just to be sure, I'd want a promise in advance.

Otherwise you leave yourself in a particularly feckless rhetorical position, by the way: "Understanding is mighty important, all important, wonderful, wonderful—but I can't offhand think of a single stunt that requires it."

By the way, I've been *defending* you quite vigorously and sincerely in AI circles in recent years—saying that the only thing wrong with your line has been the misguided (and misdirecting) tone of absolutism, as found in your book title. More specifically, in your insisting that these were not just the hard problems (you've been right about them being the tough problems all along), but being insoluble problems (sword-in-the-stone problems, in the metaphor of *Darwin's Dangerous Idea*).[2] As I said in a talk at an AAAI (American Association for Artificial Intelligence) workshop at MIT in November (and even had an overhead proclaiming it): "Just because Bert Dreyfus said it doesn't mean it's wrong."

Now I think that you would be quite consistent (and wise, and honorable) to say that only a Cog-type, embodied robot has a chance of passing the unrestricted Turing test (and you could add that it would be a colossally difficult feat, dwarfing Deep Blue).[3] Then you would be right about the limitations of GOFAI without going overboard. And you could admit that *if* any Cog of the future actually passed the unrestricted Turing test (with you as judge), you would declare it to be a genuine understander of natural language. Why not?
All the best, Dan

Message #2: May 26, 1997
From: Hubert Dreyfus
To: Daniel Dennett

Dear Dan,

It's good to hear from you, especially since the sort of sound-bite discussion we had on the *NewsHour* is very unsatisfying and needs some sort of follow-up.

I think that you are right that the tone of my discussion has always suggested that symbolic AI is impossible, although I have always said that I had no in-principle argument to back me up. And all I could legitimately claim was that, based on the phenomenology of human skill acquisition, the GOFAI research program would almost surely fail. I was surprised by the results of the last match as were many others. (There is a growing consensus among chess masters that Kasparov may well have thrown the match in order to promote a tiebreaker. We'll know for sure if Deep Blue is really better if there is a playoff.) But I have never said that such a chess victory was impossible or even "almost certainly impossible." I said that a chess master looks at only a few hundred plausible moves at most, and that the AI people would not be able to make a program, as they were trying to do in the 60s and 70s, that played chess by simulating this ability. I still hold that nothing I wrote or said on the subject of chess was wrong. The question of massive brute-force calculation as a way of making game-playing programs was not part of the discussion, and heuristic programs without brute force did seem to need, and still seem to need, more than explicit facts and rules to make them play better than amateur chess. But I grant you that, given my views, I had no right to talk of necessity.

Let's turn to the language issue, which is more important. There we seem to have had a misunderstanding that another 30 seconds of air time would have allowed us to straighten out. You seem to think I was asking, like John Searle in his Chinese Room argument, that the computer do more than behave like it understood natural language.[4] That it *really* understand, whatever that turns out to mean. But I have never asked that. I have always been willing to play by the rules of the unrestricted Turing test (that is, if a computer could be programmed so that most of the time when I was conversing with it by teletype, I could not tell whether I was talking with a computer or a human being. I would count that as thinking and admit the success of AI). It was on those grounds that I proposed natural language understanding as a challenge for Cog. Several e-mail correspondents who know my work have told me that they understood me that way. I would be happy to say in print that I sign off on everything in your last paragraph.

A computer scientist here at Berkeley pointed out to me that, in the spirit of the current discussion, I could equally have asked that Cog be given a camera to see the cards and the players and then be asked to play high-level poker. (Of course, given the stochastic nature of poker, a very large sample would be needed to evaluate performance.) Do you like that goal post better? The two goals—playing poker and conversing in ordinary English—seem equally hard to me. Both presuppose that the computer can be given a knowledge of human psychology of the sort that we understand by being human, but that we cannot fully articulate.

Where should we go from here? Have you seen Drew McDermott's op-ed piece in the *New York Times* of May 14th? I suspect we would agree that Drew is wrong to think human beings might be using unconscious brute-force calculation, but I am not sure what you think these days. Do you agree with me that the success of Deep Blue in a formal domain like chess where relevance is settled beforehand and brute-force calculation is, therefore, possible, shows nothing whatsoever about the possibility of GOFAI? Why do you think GOFAI is a plausible goal for a research program? Or do you? Have you written a paper on Cog? If so, I would love to see it. I am not clear whether Cog will be using neural-net simulation, symbolic representation, or both. Regards, Bert

Message #3: May 28, 1997
From: Daniel Dennett
To: Hubert Dreyfus

Dear Bert,
What a pleasure to see some actual progress, for a change, in a philosophical "debate." I think the key is that while you are sure that there is something importantly different about the internal goings-on in a person and in a computer/robot, you see that this difference of the innards *has* to be manifest somehow in ultimate behavioral competence in order to be . . . important! You and I agree on this point, which smacks of evil behaviorism (and evil operationalism, and evil verificationism, and who knows what else evil . . .) to many of those who have been brainwashed by some of the ideologues of the Cognitive Revolution, but the alternatives all have the drawback of deflecting attention from the interesting issue: whence cometh the *mental power* of a mind? What is amazing about people is what they can *do*, in the hard world, in real time.

In *Darwin's Dangerous Idea*, in the discussion of Roger Penrose's arguments against strong AI, I call this a recognition of the importance of a "sword in the stone" test, and you and Penrose and I agree with Turing—and Descartes, of course—that unless you can describe an independent test of mental power, you are just waffling. Thus suppose some philosopher—not you, but we can think of others—were to declare that one thing a robot could never do is *make a hand-knit sweater*. But then when the roboticists produce their triumph, they encounter the retort—"But this isn't hand-knit, because those aren't hands. Oh, sure, they have five so-called 'fingers,' and they dangle on the so-called wrists of two so-called arms, but they aren't made from the right stuff, or they don't have the right history, to count as real hands." This move, the "it doesn't count" move, is a loser.

We both agree with Descartes and Turing that passing the unrestricted Turing test (with or without robotic add-ons such as eyes and hands) is an overwhelmingly difficult task, since it indirectly puts exactly the right strain on the innards: there is simply no way—no physically possible way—of passing it by "cheating," but the test otherwise does not foreclose on "non-organic" or "artifactual" or "symbol-manipulating" or "syntactic" paths. Let's see if such a program can do such a thing.[5]

That then leaves just the right empirical question open: is it possible to get human-level behavior out of a computer, and if so, will its methods show us anything interesting about human intelligence?

You ask me whether I disagree with Drew McDermott. I think he is right about something, but I would put it somewhat differently. Kasparov's brain is a parallel-processing device composed of more than ten billion little robots. Neurons, like every other cell in a body, are robots, and the organized activity of ten billion little unthinking, uncomprehending robots *is* a form of brute-force computing, and surely intuition *is* nothing other than such an emergent product. As I said in my very first published paper back in 1968,[6] when we say we do something "by intuition" we are saying we don't know how we do it, and that is consistent with any story at all. When we discover how "intuitive" thinking is accomplished, we will probably be surprised about many of the details— and we will probably feel that mixture of amusement and letdown that often accompanies learning how a magic trick is done. I think it is quite clear that the answer will be comprehensible in computational terms—a massively parallel dynamical competitive process, in which the "magic" gets replaced, one way or another, with a lot of mindless drudgery. But I do agree with you that *that* process will almost certainly not look much like the brute-force search processes of Deep Blue. That is precisely why Deep Blue is not very interesting as AI.

Yes, I have written a paper on Cog. It's a talk I gave at the Royal Society back in 1994. And in other talks on Cog to AI groups I have stressed the fact that when we get to the point of getting Cog to engage in human-only or "adult" cognitive activities, we will *not* solve the problem by splicing a GOFAI system onto the underlying neural-net-style architecture. When I speak about this, I use an overhead that always gets a laugh. It's a parody of the "Intel inside" logo, with "GOFAI" instead of "Intel" and a big X through it.

As for your suggested variations on the unrestricted Turing test, I am not convinced they add anything, since there's nothing to prevent you as judge in the unrestricted Turing test from playing a game—any game you can play via typing, in effect—and bluffing and other psychological ploys are readily available to the resourceful judge. Having human-acuity vision and the dexterity to shuffle cards is presumably not a very central feature of genuine human consciousness. In any event, we agree on the fact (but I am sure it's "just" an empirical fact, not a conceptual or constitutive fact) that human-level intelligence depends on competencies that are not practically achievable by using "fully articulate" representations of a GOFAI sort.

Since we both agree that getting a robot to pass the unrestricted Turing test is incredibly more difficult than getting it to be world chess champion, perhaps the next constructive move would be to suggest some intuitively much easier test that would still knock your socks off, and is a little closer (in my opinion, at least) to being implemented in a decade or so. Since Cog is supposed to go through a humanoid infancy, you might propose some variation on a developmental milestone in the first two or three years of a child's life, for instance. It is commonly said that the things that kids can do easily are the things it is hardest for AI to do. So let's have some examples— perhaps something one-year-olds can do easily, two-year-olds can do easily, and so forth. (Just remember: Cog is paraplegic and can't walk around, but it is designed with two arms, two eyes, two ears, and can touch things.)

Best wishes, Dan

Message #4: June 4, 1997
From: Hubert Dreyfus
To: Daniel Dennett

Dear Dan,

It's a real pleasure to find that there is so much we agree on, that we can focus on the hard and interesting philosophical issues that, to my knowledge, defenders of AI have not yet faced, let alone answered. Happily, as you say, Cog gives us both a chance to sharpen our philosophical intuitions and to test our conclusions.

I have been saying since 1972 (and have spelled out in detail in the preface to the third edition of *What Computers Still Can't Do*) that computers will have to be embodied as we are if they are to interact with us and thus be counted as intelligent by our standards. Given this view, does Cog have a body enough like ours to have at least a modicum of human intelligence? Despite Cog's arms, etc., I do not think Cog will have any human intelligence at all. What, then, would it lack? It need not lack intuition. The billions of dumb robot neurons in our brain properly organized and working together, somehow, I agree, manifest expert intuition.[7] What I want to argue here is that Cog cannot manifest human-like emotions. According to neuroscience, emotions depend upon (although they are much more than) chemical changes in the brain. These changes are due to hormones, adrenaline, and the like. It may not be important that Cog's brain is silicon and ours is protein, but it might be crucial that ours is wet and Cog's is dry.

But the GOFAI believer has a ready answer to such an objection. If it is to pass the Turing test, AI researchers will just have to program into an artificial intelligence all the facts about human emotions that it needs to know—facts the baby doesn't need to *know* because it *is made of* the relevant wetware and so can be socialized into the emotions shared by members of its culture. Facts like being loved makes us happy, disapproval leads to shame or guilt, insults make us angry, we perform less well when we are tired, but performance degrades differently for each domain and differently depending on how interested we are. As you say, putting in all these sorts of facts was Doug Lenat's GOFAI approach in CYC. But CYC has not fulfilled any of the promises made 12 years ago about how it would be able to teach itself in 10 years' time, and all but GOFAI fanatics agree that the CYC project is a failure. Having you as an ally against GOFAI is so important to me that I will quote from your last posting: "We agree on the fact . . . that human-level intelligence depends on competencies that are not practically achievable by using the 'fully articulate' representations of a GOFAI sort."

We agree too that this is an empirical not an in-principle point. But I do not see how you expect to put emotional responses into Cog's neural nets or get Cog to learn them and I do not see what other resources you have. So my questions to you are, (1) Do you have any in-principle arguments that a simulated neural network with emotions must be possible?, and (2) How do you expect to get these typically human emotional responses into Cog?

I think that you would be right if you claimed that some sort of intelligence does not require these human emotions. All you need is pain and pleasure receptors, fight and flight responses, and simple feedback systems that reinforce success in learning, penalize errors, and reward novelty. You can build all of this machinery into Cog. But then you would be making an artificial "life-form"—certainly not a being that could share our form of life where caring about who we are and getting others to recognize us on our terms is crucially important. You seem to reduce your position to absurdity when, in the Cog paper, you say that "while we are at it, we might as well try to make Cog crave human praise and company and even exhibit a sense of humor." Is that meant as a joke? If you were to tell me that the Cog project is simply misleadingly named, that it is really an attempt to make a BUG—an artificial life-form with a humanoid body—I'd be impressed with the robotic challenges afforded by such a project. In fact, I thought the attraction of Brooks's approach was to start with insect-like "animates" and slowly try to work one's way up to human beings. One might then learn a lot about the difficulties in mechanizing the "right" receptors and emotional responses for each particular new species.[8] I was stunned when I read your Cog paper and discovered Brooks's research team is now attempting to jump right from bugs to us. Perhaps I have misunderstood, but you do say that you expect Cog to "engage in human-only or 'adult' cognitive activities."

To help make my point I will accept your challenge and conclude by suggesting some early developmental examples of human intelligence Cog's performance of which would knock my socks off. As you probably know, and my informant, Alison Gopnik, a development psychologist at U. C. Berkeley, confirms, children are born able to imitate facial expressions and gestures. By 14 months they imitate the goals of a person trying to fix some broken toy, for example, but will not imitate a machine "trying" to do the same thing. I remember that my kids imitated not only my gestures, mannerisms, etc.; they imitated my style. Will Cog imitate other Cogs, or people? I would be impressed either way. By 18 months, infants already demonstrate a rudimentary sense of shame and guilt which is quite different from fear of punishment. By 3, if I remember rightly, my kids could talk about emotions and give psychological explanations. They could understand (that is, answer questions about) stories whose sense depended on the fact that people can be envious of each other, admire each other, etc. By 4, they could understand trickery, bluffs, etc. Any of these performances, learned by a neural-net Cog, would blow me away. I haven't moved a goal post yet, so you can count on me not to move any of these. If we are going to take goal posts seriously, when would you be willing to admit that Cog had failed to achieve any of the above and that that counts as a failure for AI?

The important point, as I argue in *What Computers Still Can't Do*, is not just that such sensibilities are essential if an android is to inhabit our world and learn from us, but having basic embodied experiences such as effort, fatigue, frustration, triumph, and so forth, plays a crucial role in determining what counts as relevant for us and what situations count as similar to other situations. Thus such capacities are the basis for learning from experience and so form the basis for "adult" cognitive abilities.
Regards, Bert

Message #5: June 12, 1997
From: Daniel Dennett
To: Hubert Dreyfus

Dear Bert,
Good. We are getting closer and closer to turning this into a straightforward empirical disagreement about which we each have our strongly held hunches. For instance, you note that Cog's silicon brain may not disqualify it from human intelligence, but "it might be crucial that ours is wet and Cog's is dry." I suppose it might be, but why?

In *Kinds of Minds*,[9] I discuss this in some detail, noting that the paracrine and endocrine systems in which the brain soaks its parts—the neuromodulators and hormones and the like—do indeed play crucial mediating roles. But so far as I can see, the role is always that of keys-hunting-for-locks, a process accomplished by differential diffusion. The Cog team has been planning on installing "virtual hormones" and "virtual neuromodulators" (and a virtual amygdala to help orchestrate them) as needed. How this might be accomplished is not yet clear in all its details, but I see no reason to think there are any insuperable problems. There have been virtual fluids and other stuff floating around in computer science for years. Think of Donald Knuth's elegant idea (in

TeX) of virtual glue for use in formatting text for fine printing—you put a little dab on each word in a string, depending on its length (or weight), and then you (virtually) stretch the string of words to fit the left and right margin, letting the virtual glue, which has defined elastic properties, stretch just enough to make a properly wide space between each pair of words. Or think of Doug Hofstadter's JUMBO program, with all those codelets floating around like enzymes, latching onto this and that, snipping here, joining there.[10] Virtual neuromodulators diffusing by variable broadcast may be computationally expensive to simulate on a large scale, but it is a well-explored idea, not a stumper.

You see readily enough that Cog can have the basic animal rig for appreciating the carrot and the stick, but wonder if this could be the foundation for "typically human emotional responses." Well, it's a start, so what makes you think the problems would be insuperable? My suggestion that Cog should have a sense of humor was not at all meant as a joke. How on earth would I go about installing such? Well, I'd build in several cravings that are not much in evidence in other species, such as a relatively insatiable appetite for novelty, with a bias in favor of complex novelty, and some built-in gregariousness (hey, even Descartes' automata-sheep had that), and some particular fears. And I'd let these do some of the driving of Cog's analogy-appreciation faculties (which are certainly not "modules" in our way of thinking!)—along the lines inspired by Douglas Hofstadter and Melanie Mitchell and Bob French.[11]

I agree that it is startling to see Rod Brooks leap directly from "insects" to humanoids, but as I have always said, good AI is opportunistic, weaving back and forth between bizarre ambition and equally bizarre modesty (making toy problems comically small when necessary). We'll just have to see if his eagerness to try his hand at the big prize without spending a few decades more of apprenticeship on artificial iguanas and tree sloths will pay off.

We've been working so far on the most fundamental equipment of newborn infants—hand-eye coordination, location of sounds, distinguishing interesting things in the visual world, so we haven't seriously begun work on specifically human talents. But I like your developmental milestones. Imitation has been a theme in the recent work of Maja Mataric and some others involved in Cog. Shame is a tough one, I grant you, but it's probably a fair challenge—especially since you grant that what the 18-month-old human exhibits is "a rudimentary sense of shame," not existential torment or the sort of *Weltschmerz* only neurotic Viennese chainsmokers can enjoy. Your addition of higher-order intentionality—understanding trickery, bluffs, and the like—has already been much discussed among us. I put a typescript copy of Simon Baron-Cohen's book *Mindblindness*[12] in circulation in the lab several years ago; it has a handy list of suggested mechanisms that might rescue Cog from autism. (An automaton does not have to be autistic, but it will be unless rather special provisions are made for it.) There are lots more ideas along those lines to be explored as well.

That isn't meant to be a complete answer to your challenges, but just a few hints about how we've been thinking. You will see that your concerns have not gone unconsidered by us. I can't say now when I would be willing to admit that Cog had failed to achieve any of this. Cog needs major funding and has so far been worked on in spare time only, instead of being a huge, well-funded project like the Japanese humanoid project. We certainly agree with you that it will take "effort, fatigue, frustration, triumph, and so forth"—not just ours, but Cog's—to make a humanoid intelligence. The sooner we get the funding, the quicker you can win your bet, so help us out! One way or the other, we'll learn what no amount of philosophical argument by itself could discover.

All the best, Dan

Message #6: June 17, 1997
From: Hubert Dreyfus
To: Daniel Dennett

Dear Dan,
I am glad to hear that the Cog team is thinking hard about questions like how to simulate emotions in a simulated neural network. I'm also not surprised to learn that you do not think you are clear about all the details. But philosophical discussion becomes difficult when you don't tell us the limits on Cog's cognitive machinery. Any problem I raise concerning the difficulty of doing x, you can always say you are working on a virtual x. So we are back to our opposed intuitions about how hard such a project is. I do not claim so far to have brought up any "insuperable problems," but I think you grossly underestimate how hard the problems are. Your idea of virtual emotions reminds me of the old GOFAI researchers who had flow charts with boxes named "Understanding" and "Perception," but still had to work out the details of what went on in each box. Just how would the simulated neuromodulators work to produce artificial emotions? They couldn't just change the thresholds of the simulated neurons. That might work for fear and lust but most emotions are not so straightforwardly chemical. The chemical effects are mediated by meaning. As you recognize in insisting that Cog be socialized, emotions such as shame, guilt, and love require an understanding of public narratives and exemplars which must be picked up not just as information but by imitating the style of people's behavior as they assume various social roles. Just how is Cog supposed to pick up the style of its caretakers? Which gender is Cog? Does Cog come to recognize its virtual gender and others with the same gender? How is Cog's imitation supposed to modify its net?

Also, emotions require that what happens to me and in my community matters to me. This is in turn tied up with my identity—the sense I have of who I am—so that for me courage is important but patience isn't, while for someone else these priorities might be reversed. The stand I take on who I am is not captured in the higher-order intentions presupposed in bluffing, etc. It is a sense of what is ultimately worthy for me.[13] We know our brain, interacting with other brains, does something that enables people to take stands on who they are, but I don't think we have a clue as to how this could be done in the neural nets that make up Cog's brain.

You might well answer that, since I have accepted the Turing test, I should not be concerned with how Cog feels or what it senses, but this leads to a whole bunch of other problems. Suppose we grant that we can fix the net to respond to virtual neuro-modulators and so act as if in fear or, although I do not see how, ashamed or in love. To pass the Turing test it is not sufficient that Cog respond with appropriate emotional behavior (for example, send back angry messages when I insult it); Cog must also be able to answer questions about its emotional life. It must be able to formulate propositions like "insults make me angry unless I am just too tired to care, but my jealousy increases with my exhaustion." We agree one cannot just store such factual knowledge about our emotional and embodied life in a huge database like Lenat's CYC since we can always mine out new explicit knowledge. Somehow, Cog will have to be able to transform its virtual hormones, etc., and the responses they cause, into the required explicit knowledge. As I understand it, neural-net modelers at present have not a clue how to do that sort of thing. How do you picture the conversion of Cog's nonpropositional know-how into propositional knowing-that? Is there reason for believing that neural nets are the right causal mechanism for explaining propositional knowledge?

And there is a final problem that may well be insuperable. People and cultures can change their worlds. This happens in people's lives when they have a change of identity, for example, a religious conversion that radically "re-gestalts" what they consider worthy. It happens too when cultures change, as when our culture changed from the Greek to the Christian, and then to the Modern World. Charles Spinosa, Fernando Flores, and I have just published a book called *Disclosing New Worlds*[14] in which we describe three different ways this kind of change occurs (we call them reconfiguring, cross-appropriating, and articulating), and we argue that these types of radical change are normally brought about by entrepreneurs, successful citizens' action groups, and cultural figures like Martin Luther King Jr., respectively. Moreover, we hold that opening up or producing new worlds is a capacity that only human beings exhibit. Even if, as I strongly doubt it could, Cog evolved from BUG to APE, I don't see how it could override and/or transform the innate feature detectors and the innate similarity space that enabled it to start interacting with the world in the first place. So it could not open up a new world in which what counted as significant features and similarities were totally changed. If, as I and my co-authors argue, disclosing new worlds is the most important thing human beings do, we have here the ultimate, immovable goal post. Any of the developmental achievements I mentioned in my last letter would certainly be

enough to bowl me over and change my view of what computers can do, but such behavior, as impressive as it would surely be, would still fall short of being human.
All the best, Bert

Message #7: June 19, 1997
From: Daniel Dennett
To: Hubert Dreyfus

Dear Bert,
You say we "grossly underestimate how hard the problems are," and you may be right. Time will tell. But whatever mistakes we are making, we are not making the old "draw a box around each residual problem and call it a system in a flowchart" mistake.

First things first. You have a knack for drawing a forbidding map of the hard problems that lie in the distant future, but long before we address Charles Taylor's concerns about What Matters for Me, for instance, we would like Cog to pass the Gallup test: self-recognition in mirrors, or watching itself on closed-circuit TV. As Jackie Gibson's experiments showed long ago, even very young infants readily distinguish a closed-circuit video of their own waggling legs from a video of some other baby's waggling legs. This is something Cog had better be able to do (lacking legs, it will have to recognize something else as a part of its own body in action).

You are right: "somehow Cog will have to be able to transform its virtual hormones, etc., and the responses they cause into the required explicit knowledge." In other words, infant Cog is eventually going to have to be able to say "I'm afraid" or "I'm bored" and mean it. Eventually it should know its own emotional state in something like the way we know our own. But again, first things first; it will be hard enough to get Cog to *be* bored or frightened by something happening around it. I don't think what you call the conversion from "nonpropositional know-how into propositional knowing-that" is well described . . . , and perhaps for that reason I don't see it as posing quite the problem you see. I agree there's a bunch of tough problems lurking in the vicinity, however.

And as for "disclosing new worlds," your "final problem that may well be insuperable" is as good a candidate as any I've heard for the ultimate immovable goal post, but it's so special I wonder how much people would care if it were (or seemed to be) off-limits. ("Yes, folks, these new humanoids make great caretakers for your kids—more enjoyable and reliable than anybody you could hire, and better teachers, too. Kids— and grownups too—are finding them to be worthy intellectual companions . . . but, of course, they aren't gonna *disclose new worlds*.") Well, so what? I didn't say you would want to marry one.

And besides, at this point neither of us can say anything very clear-cut and useful about whether this talent is some emergent property of the lesser talents we might succeed in designing. I'm quite content to leave these issues in the mists indefinitely, with you having expressed your hunch and me having expressed mine. Meanwhile, you've acknowledged plenty of nearby goal posts that we may live to see scored upon, and if, on the other hand, all of them defeat us, you can say, "I told you so" and I'll still be around to say, "So you did."

Best wishes, Dan

Message #8: June 24, 1997
From: Hubert Dreyfus
To: Daniel Dennett

Dear Dan,

I'm puzzled by your saying that Cog might not be able to disclose new worlds and then adding: "Well, so what?" As I remember it, the starting point of our discussion way back on the *NewsHour* was whether Cog could pass the Turing test. To pass the test it is not necessary that Cog be a discloser of new cultural worlds, but as *Disclosing New Worlds* points out, world-change happens in most people's lives and those who don't initiate it have enough experience of it to understand it well, not simply as alien onlookers. They live in a tradition that includes, for instance, born-again Christians from St. Augustine to Eldridge Cleaver. They have seen, in movies and real life, men go from being swinging bachelors to solid husbands and fathers, and women go from devoting themselves to their career to becoming full-time mothers. On a cultural level, people can understand that Henry Ford helped change our world from one where people felt they had to govern animals and their own desires, to a world in which people control their cars, their desires, and even birth. Many can remember how Martin Luther King Jr. changed the world of race relations and how MADD changed not just the drinking laws, but the way people took responsibility for their relaxation. Moreover, in our pluralistic world, most people realize that there are many different cultures each with its own understanding of which kinds of similarities are significant and which aren't. An intelligence that could have no understanding of such things, or only a distant spectator's, might still be, like a Saint Bernard, fun and reliable with the kids, but it would not be much good as a teacher and certainly no "worthy intellectual companion." By asking it about the above kinds of radical change it would be easy to trap it in the Turing test.

I grant you it is logically possible that such a disclosing capacity might "emerge" from the lesser capacities one might be able to design. That is why I did not introduce disclosing as an absolutely unachievable goal. But I see no reason to think the capacity to open new worlds will emerge from the sort of neural nets making up Cog's brain. It has not emerged in chimps. Indeed, higher mammals have been around for millions of years and, as far as we know, the capacity to change one's world only emerged once, along with language, art, institutions, and all the capacities that seem to be uniquely human.

In any case, I agree that you will have your hands full giving Cog the simple developmental capacities that make animal coping possible. I can't tell just how hard you think going from BUG to APE is going to be, since you wisely refrain from setting any time limit. Still, while you work on this challenging project, I hope that you establish a new scientific approach in AI by reporting your failures as well as your successes. Then, no matter what finally results, the effort will have been worthwhile.

All the best, Bert

Notes

All notes are the editors' unless otherwise stated.

1. Hubert Dreyfus, *What Computers Still Can't Do* (Cambridge, Mass.: MIT Press, 1992).

2. Daniel Dennett, *Darwin's Dangerous Idea* (New York: Simon and Schuster, 1995).

3. For a first introduction to COG, see Rodney Brooks, Cynthia Breazeal, Matthew Marjanovic, Brian Scassellati, and Matthew Williamson, "The Cog Project: Building a Humanoid Robot," in *Computation for Metaphors, Analogy, and Agents*, ed. Chrystopher L. Nehaniv (New York: Springer, 1999) 52–87. For more information on COG and other humanoid robots being built at MIT see: ⟨http://www.ai.mit.edu/projects/humanoid-robotics-group/cog/⟩. The site contains an extensive list of publications by the Humanoid Robotics Group.

4. See John R. Searle "Minds, Brains, and Programs," *Behavioral and Brain Sciences* 3 (1980): 417–424.

5. [*Dennett:*] "I argue for this view in a 1985 paper of mine, 'Can Machines Think?'" [published in Dennett, *Brainchildren*].

6. [*Dennett:*] "'Machine Traces and Protocol Statements,' *Behavioral Science* 13 (March 1968): 155–161—my rebuttal of your notorious RAND memo ('Alchemy and Artificial Intelligence')" [which formed the core of Dreyfus's *What Computers Still Can't Do*].

7. [*Dreyfus:*] "Although I don't agree with you that pointing out we have intuition is consistent with just any story about brain operation. In *Mind Over Machine* [New York: Free Press, 1986], my brother Stuart and I argue that intuitive skills are inconsistent with the GOFAI approach. But that is not at issue here since you are not proposing to use symbolic representations in Cog."

8. See the discussion of reinforcement learning in Dreyfus, *What Computers Still Can't Do*, xlv.

9. Daniel Dennett, *Kinds of Minds* (New York: Basic Books, 1996).

10. For Jumbo, see Douglas R. Hofstadter and the Fluid Analogies Research Group, *Fluid Concepts and Creative Analogies: Computer Models of the Fundamental Mechanisms of Thought* (New York: Basic Books, 1995); for a full description of the TeX typesetting system, see Donald E. Knuth, *The TeXbook* (Reading, Mass.: Addison-Wesley, 1984).

11. See Hofstadter, *Fluid Concepts and Creative Analogies: Computer Models of the Fundamental Mechanisms of Thought.*

12. Simon Baron-Cohen, *Mindblindness* (Cambridge, Mass.: MIT Press, 1995).

13. See Charles Taylor, "Responsibility for Self," in *The Identities of Persons*, ed. Amélie Oksenberg Rorty (Berkeley: University of California Press, 1976).

14. Charles Spinosa, Fernando Flores, and Hubert L. Dreyfus, *Disclosing New Worlds* (Cambridge, Mass.: MIT Press, 1997).

Machines and the Mental

Fred Dretske

Computers are machines, and there are a lot of things machines can't do. But there are a lot of things I can't do: speak Turkish, understand James Joyce, or recognize a nasturtium when I see one. Yet, numerous as are my disabilities, they do not materially affect my status as a thinking being. I lack specialized skills, knowledge, and understanding but nothing that is essential to membership in the society of rational agents. With machines, though, and this includes the most sophisticated modern computers, it is different. They *do* lack something that is essential.

Or so some say. And so say I. In saying it, though, one should, as a philosopher, be prepared to say what is essential, what are the conditions for membership in this exclusive club. If an ability to understand James Joyce isn't required, what, then, *must* one be able to understand? If one doesn't have to know what nasturtiums look like, is there something else one must be able to identify? What might this be? If one is told that there is no specific thing one has to understand, identify, or know but nonetheless something or other toward which one must have a degree of competence, it is hard to see how to deny computers admission to the club. For even the simple robots designed for home amusement talk, see, remember, and learn. Or so I keep reading in the promotional catalogs. Isn't this enough? Why not?

I happen to be one of those philosophers who, though happy to admit that minds compute and in this sense *are* computers, have great difficulty seeing how computers could be minded. I'm not (not *now* at least) going to complain about the impoverished inner life of the computer—how they don't feel pain, fear, love, or anger. Nor am I going to talk about the mysterious inner light of consciousness. For I'm not at all sure one needs feelings or self-consciousness to solve problems, play games, recognize patterns, and understand stories. Why can't pure thought, the sort of thing computers purportedly have, stand to ordinary thought, the sort of thing we have, the way a solitary stroll stands to a hectic walk down a crowded street? The same thing—walking—is going on in both cases. It just *seems* different because, in the latter case, so much else is going on at the same time. A mathematician's calculations are no less brilliant, certainly no less deserving of classification as mental because he or she is blind, deaf, or emotionally stunted, because, in other words, the calculations occur within a comparatively anemic sensory and emotional environment. Why can't we think of machines as occupying a position on the far right of this mental continuum? Just a bit to the right of *Star Trek*'s Doctor Spock? We don't, after all, deny someone the capacity for love because they can't do differential calculus. Why deny the computer the ability to solve problems or understand stories because it doesn't feel love, experience nausea, or suffer indigestion?

Nor am I going to talk about how bad computers are at doing what most children can do, for instance, speak and understand their native language, make up a story, or appreciate a joke. For such comparisons make it sound like a competition, a competition in which humans, with their enormous head start and barring dramatic breakthroughs in artificial intelligence, will remain unchallenged for the foreseeable future. I don't think the comparison should be put in these terms because I don't think there is a genuine competition in this area at all. It isn't that the best machines are still at the level of two-year-olds, requiring only greater storage capacity and fancier programming to grow up. Nor should we think of them as idiot savants, exhibiting a spectacular ability in a few isolated areas but having an overall IQ too low for fraternal association. For machines, even the best of them, don't have an IQ. They don't do what we do, at least none of the things that, when we do them, exhibit intelligence. And it's not just that they don't do them the way we do them or as well as we do them. They don't do them at all. They don't solve problems, play games, prove theorems, recognize patterns, let alone think, see, and remember. They don't even add and subtract.

To convince you of this, it is useful to look at our relationship to various instruments and tools. The preliminary examination will not take us far, but it will set the stage for a clearer statement of what I take to be the fundamental difference between minds and machines.

In our descriptions of instruments and tools we tend to assign them the capacities and powers of the agents who use them. We often think, or at least talk, of artifacts—tools, instruments, and machines—as telling us things, recognizing, sensing, remembering, and in general, doing things that in our more serious, literal moments, we acknowledge to be the province of rational agents. In most cases this figurative use of language does no harm. No one is really confused. Though we open doors, and keys open (locked) doors, no one seems to worry about whether keys open doors better than we do, whether we are still ahead in this competition. No one is trying to build a fifth-generation key that will surpass us in this enterprise. Why not? Since both keys and people open doors, why doesn't it make sense to ask who does it better? Because, of course, we all understand that doors are opened *with* keys. *We* are the agents. The key is the instrument. That we sometimes speak of the instrument in terms appropriate to the agent, speak of the key as doing what the agent does with the key, should not tempt us into supposing that therefore there are some things we do that keys can also do. We catch fish with worms; we, not the worms, catch the fish.

Before concluding, however, that computers are, like keys, merely fancy instruments in our cognitive tool box—and thus, taken by themselves, unable to do what we can do with them—consider another case. Who really picks up the dust, the housecleaner or the vacuum cleaner? Is the vacuum cleaner merely an instrument that the house-cleaner uses to pick up dust? Well, yes, but not *quite* the way one uses a key to open a door or a hammer to pound a nail. A person pushes the vacuum cleaner around, but it picks up the dust. In this case (unlike the key case) the question, Who picks up dust better: people or vacuum cleaners? *does* make good sense, and the answer, obviously, is the vacuum cleaner. We may never have had any real competition from keys for opening doors, but we seem to have lost the race for picking up dust to vacuum cleaners.

What such examples reveal is that the agent-instrument distinction is no certain guide as to who or what is to be given credit for a performance. We do things. Machines do things. Sometimes we do things with machines. Who gets the credit depends on what is done and how it is done. To ask whether a simple pocket calculator can really multiply or whether it is we who multiply *with* the calculator is to ask whether, relative to this task, the agent-instrument relation is more like our use of a key in opening a door or more like our use of a vacuum cleaner in picking up dust.

Well, then, are computers our computational keys? Or are they more like vacuum cleaners? Do they literally do the computational tasks that we sometimes do without them but do them better, faster, and more reliably? This may sound like a rather simple-minded way to approach the issue of minds and machines, but unless one gets clear about the relatively simple question of *who* does the job, the person or the pocket calculator, in adding up a column of figures, one is unlikely to make such progress in penetrating the more baffling question of whether more sophisticated machines exhibit (or will some day) some of the genuine qualities of intelligence. For I assume that if machines can really play chess, prove theorems, understand a text, diagnose an illness, and recognize an object—all achievements that are routinely credited to modern machines by sober members of the artificial intelligence community—if these descriptions are *literally* true, then to that degree they participate in the intellectual enterprise. To that degree they are minded. To that extent they belong in the club, however much we with our prejudice in favor of biological look-alikes may continue to deny them full admission.

So let me begin with a naive question: Can computers add? We may not feel very threatened if this is *all* they can do. Nevertheless, if they do even this much, then the barriers separating mind and machine have been breached and there is no reason to think they won't eventually be removed.

The following argument is an attempt to show that whatever it is that computers are doing when we use them to answer our arithmetical questions, it isn't addition. Addition is an operation on numbers. We add 7 and 5 to get 12, and 7, 5, and 12 are numbers. The operations computers perform, however, are not operations on numbers. At best, they are operations on certain physical tokens that *stand for*, or are interpreted as standing for, numbers. Therefore, computers don't add.

In thinking about this argument (longer than I care to admit) I decided that there was something right about it. And something wrong. What is right about it is the perfectly valid (and relevant) distinction it invokes between a representation and what it represents, between a sign and what it signifies, between a symbol and its meaning or reference. We have various ways of representing or designating the numbers. The written numeral *2* stands for the number 2. So does *two*. Unless equipped with special pattern recognition capabilities, machines are not prepared to handle these particular symbols (the symbols appear on the keyboard for *our* convenience). But they have their own system of representation: open and closed switches, the orientation of magnetic fields, the distribution of holes on a card. But whatever the form of representation, machines are restricted to operations on the symbols or representations themselves. They have no access, so to speak, to the *meaning* of these symbols, to the things the representations represent, to the numbers. When instructed to add two numbers stored in memory, the machine manipulates representations in some electromechanical way until it arrives at another representation, something that (if things go right) stands for the sum of what the first two representations stood for. At no point in the proceedings do numbers, in contrast to numerals, get involved. And if, in order to add two numbers, one has to perform some operation on the numbers themselves, then what the computer is doing is not addition at all.

This argument, as I am sure everyone is aware, shows *too* much. It shows that we don't add either. For whatever operations may be performed in or by our central nervous system when we add two numbers, it quite clearly isn't an operation on the numbers themselves. Brains have their own coding systems, their own way of representing the objects (including the numbers) with which its (or our) thoughts and calculations are occupied. In this respect a person is no different than a computer. Biological systems may have different ways of representing the objects of thought, but they, like the computer, are necessarily limited to manipulating these representations. This is merely to acknowledge the nature of thought itself. It is a *vicarious* business, a *symbolic* activity. Adding two numbers is a way of thinking *about* two numbers, and thinking *about* X and Y is not a way of pushing X and Y around. It is a way of pushing around their symbolic representatives.

What is wrong with the argument, then, is the assumption that in order to add two numbers, a system must literally perform some operation on the numbers themselves. What the argument shows, if it shows anything, is that in order to carry out arithmetical operations, a system must have a way of representing the numbers and the capacity for manipulating these representations in accordance with arithmetic principles. But isn't this precisely what computers have?

I have discussed this argument at some length only to make the point that all cognitive operations (whether by artifacts or natural biological systems) will necessarily be realized in some electrical, chemical, or mechanical operation over physical structures. (Or if materialism isn't true, they will be realized in or by transformations of mind stuff.) This fact alone doesn't tell us anything about the cognitive nature of the operations being performed—whether, for instance, it is an inference, a thought, or the taking of a square root. For what makes these operations into thoughts, inferences, or arithmetical calculations is, among other things, the meaning or, if you prefer, the semantics of those structures over which they are performed. To think about the number 7 or your cousin George, you needn't do anything with the number 7 or your cousin George, but you do need the internal resources for representing 7 and George and the capacity for manipulating these representations in ways that stand for activities and conditions of the things being represented.

This should be obvious enough. Opening and closing relays doesn't count as addition, or as moves in a chess game, unless the relays, or their various states, stand for numbers and chess moves. But what may not be so obvious is that these physical activities cannot acquire the relevant kind of meaning merely by *assigning* them an interpretation, by letting them mean something *to or for us*. Unless the symbols being manipulated mean something *to the system manipulating them*, their meaning, whatever it is, is irrelevant to evaluating what the system is doing when it manipulates them.[1] I cannot make you, someone's parrot, or a machine think about my cousin George or the number 7 just by assigning meanings in accordance with which this is what your (or the parrot's or the machine's) activities stand for. If things were this easy, I could make a tape recorder think about my cousin George. Everything depends on whether this is the meaning these events have to you, the parrot, or the machine.

Despite some people's tendency to think that the manipulation of symbols is *itself* a wondrous feat, worthy of such inflated descriptions as "adding numbers," "drawing conclusions," or "figuring out its next move," the process is in fact absolutely devoid of cognitive significance.[2] I once watched a gerbil manipulate a symbol, a symbol that according to conventional standards—standards that I but not the gerbil understood— stood for my bank balance. I didn't have the slightest temptation to see in this symbol manipulation (actually *consumption*) process anything of special significance. Even if I trained a fleet of gerbils to arrange symbols in some computationally satisfying way (e.g., to balance my checkbook), I don't think *they* should be credited with balancing my checkbook. I would merely be using the gerbils to balance my checkbook in the way I use worms to catch fish.

To understand *what* a system is doing when it manipulates symbols, it is necessary to know not just what these symbols mean, what interpretation they have been or can be *assigned*, but what they mean to the system performing the operations. John Searle and Ned Block have dramatized this point.[3] Searle, for instance, asks one to imagine someone who understands no Chinese manipulating Chinese symbols in accordance with rules expressed in a language he does understand. Imagine the rules cleverly enough designed so that this person can carry on a correspondence in Chinese, responding to (written) Chinese questions with (written) Chinese answers in a way that is indistinguishable from the performance of a native speaker of Chinese. Clearly, though a correspondent might not be able to discover this fact, the symbol manipulator himself doesn't understand Chinese. Nor does the system of which he is a part. Understanding Chinese is not just a matter of manipulating meaningful symbols in some appropriate way. These symbols must mean something to the system performing the operations.

This should not be taken to imply that machines cannot serve as useful models for cognitive processes. On the contrary. Their prevalent use in cognitive psychology indicates otherwise. What it does imply is that the machines do not literally do what we do when we engage in those activities for which they provide an effective model. Computer simulations of a hurricane do not blow trees down. Why should anyone suppose that computer simulations of problem solving must themselves solve problems?

But how does one build a system that is capable of performing operations on (or with) symbols and *to which* these symbols mean something, a machine that, in this sense, understands the meaning of the symbols it manipulates? Only when we can do this will we have machines that not only produce meaningful output but whose activities in producing that output bear the mark of the mental. Only then will we have machines that we not only *use* to balance our checkbooks but that will do it for us, machines that will not only print out answers to our questions but that will *answer* our questions.

One thing seems reasonably clear: if the meaning of the symbols on which a machine performs its operations is a meaning wholly derived from us, its users—if it is a meaning that we assign to the various states of the machine and therefore that we can change at will without altering the *way* these symbols are processed by the machine itself—then there is no way the machine can acquire understanding, no way these symbols can have a meaning *to the machine itself*. Unless these symbols have what we might call an intrinsic meaning, a meaning they possess that is independent of our communicative intentions and purposes, this meaning *must* be irrelevant to assessing what the machine is doing when it manipulates them. The machine is processing meaningful (to us) symbols, to be sure, but the *way* it processes them is quite independent of *what they mean*; hence, nothing *the machine* does is explicable in terms of the meaning of the symbols it manipulates or indeed of their even having a meaning. Given the right programming and database, we can contrive that the sentences produced by a machine will answer our questions. But the machine itself is no more answering our questions than an automatic teller is embezzling money when it keeps our deposit without crediting our account.

In order, therefore, to approximate something of genuine cognitive significance, in order to give a machine something that bears a mark, if not *all* the marks, of the mental, the symbols that a machine manipulates must be given a meaning of their own, a meaning that is independent of their users' purposes and intentions. Only by doing this will it become possible to make the meaning of these symbols relevant to what the machine does with them, possible to make the machine do something *because* of what its symbols mean, possible to make these symbols mean something to the machine itself.

And how might this be done? In the same way, I submit, that nature arranged it in our case. We must put the computer into the head of a robot, into a larger system that has the kind of sensory capabilities and perceptual resources that enable what goes on inside the computer to mean something (in Paul Grice's natural sense of meaning)[4] about what goes on outside the computer. The elements over which the computer performs its operations will then have a meaning that is independent of the conventions of its users. They will mean something in the same way the swing of a galvanometer needle means something regarding the electrical activity in the circuit to which it is connected, the way expanding mercury means something about the surrounding temperature, the way a voltage spike in our visual cortex means something about the distribution of light impinging on the retina. This kind of meaning is sometimes called information.[5] It is the kind of meaning we associate with reliable signs and trustworthy indicators, the kind of meaning possessed by dark clouds, shadows, prints, leaf patterns, smoke, acoustic vibrations, and the electrical activity in the sensory pathways. The difference between robots and the disembodied computers found in our office buildings and laboratories is that the former, unlike the latter, have symbol systems that are also *sign* systems: signs being symbols having a meaning quite independent of what we might say or think they mean. The only intrinsic meaning in most computers is the meaning derived from the array of pressure-sensitive transducers on the keyboard. The activities in the computer may mean a move to KB-3 *to us*, but all they mean *to the computer* is that key 37 has been depressed.

This is only to say that information, real information, the kind of meaning associated with natural signs, is irrelevant to the operation of high-speed digital computers in a way it is not irrelevant to the operation of living systems. If a sea snail doesn't get information about the turbulence in the water, if there isn't some state *in* the snail that functions as a natural sign of turbulent water, it risks being dashed to pieces when it swims to the surface to obtain the microorganisms on which it feeds. If (certain) bacteria did not have something inside that meant that *that* was the direction of magnetic north, they could not orient themselves so as to avoid toxic surface water. They would perish. If, in other words, an animal's internal sensory states were not rich in information, intrinsic natural meaning, about the presence of prey, predators, cliffs, obstacles, water, and heat, it could not survive. It isn't enough to have the internal states of these creatures mean something *to us*, for them to have symbols they can manipulate. If these symbols don't somehow register the conditions in their possessor's surroundings, the creature's symbol manipulation capacity is completely worthless. Of what possible significance is it to be able to handle symbols for food, danger, and sexual mates if the occurrence of these symbols is wholly unrelated to the actual presence of food, danger, and sexual mates?

In a sense, then, work on machine perception, pattern recognition, and robotics has greater relevance to the cognitive capacities of machines than the most sophisticated programming in such purely intellectual tasks such as language translation, theorem proving, or game playing. For a pattern recognition device is at least a device whose internal states, like those of the bacterium, snail, and human being, mean something about what is happening, about the conditions that exist around it. Something in these machines actually means something about what is happening outside them and, moreover, means this whether or not we, the users of the machine (or indeed the machine itself) recognize it. We are not free to assign or withhold this meaning any more than we are free to say what the screech of a smoke alarm means. We can *say* that the alarm means there are leopards nearby, and for certain purposes (e.g., in a children's game of make-believe) we may even want to give it that meaning. But that isn't actually what the sound means. That isn't what it is a sign of, not the information it carries. And for the same reason, the meaning of the internal states of a pattern recognition device, or a robot equipped with sensory capacities, is a meaning these states have which—if it isn't actually a meaning for the machine itself—is the only meaning that shows any promise of being promoted into something that is relevant to assessing what these machines are doing when they mobilize these meaningful elements to produce an output.

But have we come any closer to understanding genuine mentation, the capacity to add, subtract, plan, play games, understand stories, and think about one's cousin George? What we have so far required of any aspiring symbol manipulator is that *some* of its symbols be actual signs of the conditions they signify, that there be some system-to-world correlations that confer on these symbols an intrinsic meaning, a meaning they do not derive wholly from the purposes and intentions of their users. This puts the symbol manipulator *in the world* in a way it would not otherwise be. But have we come any closer to understanding how an element—symbol *or* sign—could have meaning to the symbol manipulator itself, how this meaning (not just the sign having this meaning) could be relevant to what the system is doing when it manipulates these signs?

Think about a dog that has been trained to detect marijuana. Customs agents can use these dogs to find concealed marijuana. When the dog barks, wags its tail, or does whatever it was trained to do when it smells marijuana, this alerts the customs agent to the presence of the drug. As a result of the dog's behavior, the official comes to believe that there is marijuana in the suitcase. But what does *the dog* believe? Surely not what the agent believes, viz., that there is marijuana in the suitcase. Why not? There is obviously something in the dog that is sensitive to the presence of marijuana, some neural condition whose occurrence is a sign, and in this sense means, that there is marijuana nearby. Furthermore, this something is (as a result of training) getting the dog to wag its tail or bark. Why isn't this enough to justify attributing a belief to the dog, a belief with the content "there is marijuana nearby"? If we had a robot that could perform half as well with blocks on a table, we would doubtless be hearing about its extraordinary recognition capacities. But nobody seems terribly impressed with the dog. The dog, it's said, has a wonderfully discriminating sense of smell. It has *sensory* powers that exceed those of its trainers, but its *conceptual* or *cognitive* capacities are modest indeed. It can smell marijuana, sure enough. It can even be trained to respond in some distinctive way to this smell. But it doesn't have the conceptual resources for believing that what it smells is marijuana.

If we are going to treat the dog in this deflationary way, we should be prepared to do the same with machines, including robots. In industrial applications of machine vision, for example, it is said that machines can recognize short circuits on the printed circuit boards they examine. Not so. The machine merely searches for breaks or discontinuities in the metallic deposit. Its task is concerned with *spatial* discontinuities. We, its users, are worried about electrical discontinuities. Under the right circumstances, we can use something that detects the first as an instrument, a means, for identifying the second, but, just like the dog, the instrument should not be credited with the *conceptual* talents of its users, what we are able to discover by using it. The machine is no more able to have electricity thoughts than the dog is able to have marijuana thoughts.

Some people think that what machines lack is conscious awareness. Perhaps they do. But our marijuana-sniffing dog should teach us that this isn't the missing ingredient, not what we need to manufacture a thinker of thoughts out of a sign manipulator. For the dog *is*, whereas the customs agent is not, *aware of* the concealed marijuana. The dog smells it and the agent does not. To give a system the kind of meaning we now seek, to give it genuine understanding, it is not enough to give it conscious awareness of the stuff it is supposed to cognize. It isn't even enough to make the creature's conscious awareness of the stuff *cause* it to behave in some appropriate way *toward* the stuff. For, as the trained dog illustrates, all this can be true without the system's—animal or machine—having the slightest conception of what it all means. And what we are after, of course, is something that wags its tail, activates its printer, or starts its motors not just because it is aware of, say, marijuana but because it thinks, judges, or believes that it is marijuana. What we are after is conception, not perception.

The difference between machines (or dogs) and the agents who use them is that although machines (or dogs) can pick up, process, and transmit the information we need in our investigative efforts (this is what makes them useful tools), although they can respond (either by training or programming) to meaningful signs, it isn't the meaning of the signs that figures in the explanation of why they do what they do. Some internal sign of marijuana, some neurological condition that, in this sense, means that marijuana is present, can cause the dog's tail to move, but it isn't the fact that it means this that explains the tail movement. This, I submit, is the difference between the dog and its master, between the machine and its users, between the robot and the people it replaces. When I smell marijuana, my finger wagging is produced not simply (as in the case of the dog) by a neurological condition that means that marijuana is present but by the *meaning* of this neurological condition, by the fact that it means this and not something else. In my case the motor activity is produced by the meaning of an occurrent sign; in the dog's case by the occurrence of a sign having that meaning. To say that the smell of marijuana means something to me that it doesn't mean to the dog is merely to say that its meaning what it does makes a difference to what I do but not to what the dog does. That is why it is true of me, but not the dog, that I wag my finger because I think marijuana is present, because I am in an internal state having this content. The dog is in a state with the same content, to be sure, but it isn't this content that wags the tail. The difference between a thinker of marijuana thoughts (me) and the mere detector of marijuana (dog or machine) is not merely a difference in what our internal signs mean but a difference in whether, and if so, how, these meanings are implicated in the management of the signs themselves.

I seem to have painted myself into a corner. At least I expect to be told as much by those philosophers who are deeply suspicious of meaning. I expect to be told that meaning is an abstraction, not something that could play a role in the activities of a symbol-manipulating system. From the control point of view, meaning is an epiphenomenon. It is causally inert. Even if one agrees that there are signs in the head, it is the signs themselves, not their meaning, that turn the cranks, pull the levers, and depress the accelerator. It is the gray stuff inside, not what it means, that activates the motor neurons. Just ask the neurobiologists. If, in order to promote a processor of meaningful signs into a system with genuine understanding, into a real thinker of thoughts, we must give the meaning of these signs a role to play in the way these signs are processed, in the way the motor control system operates with them, then the prospects for effecting such a promotion, not just for machines but for human beings as well, look bleak indeed.

Such pessimism, though widespread these days, is unwarranted. Meanings, of the kind now in question, are what philosophers like to call abstract entities, but they are *no more* abstract, and certainly no less capable of exercising a causal influence, than are, say, differences in weight, brightness, and orientation. Just as the difference in weight between a basketball and a bowling ball may be responsible, causally responsible, for the behavior of a beam balance, the correlations constituting the meaning of a sign can, and regularly do, affect the way a system processes that sign. The correlation between a ringing bell and someone's presence at the door—the kind of correlation that confers on the ringing bell the meaning that someone is at the door—*changes* the way a (suitably exposed) nervous system processes the internal sign of a ringing bell. Exposure (either directly or indirectly) to this correlation produces a difference in whether, and if so, which, motor neurons are activated by the internal sensory sign of a ringing bell. This, it seems to me, is a case where the meaning of a sign, not just the sign that has that meaning, makes a difference in *how* a system processes that sign—hence, a case where the sign's meaning, not the sign itself, helps to explain the behavior of the system in which that sign occurs.

My doorbell example is a homely example of the causal role of meaning. Some may think it ignores all the interesting questions, for it involves an agent already having the conceptual resources for interpreting signs, understanding meanings, and modifying her behavior in the light of experienced correlations. This is true but irrelevant. For the very same phenomenon can be illustrated at almost every biological level, every level at which *learning* occurs. It is, in fact, merely an instance of what learning theorists describe as the contingencies modifying the way a system processes and hence responds to the internal signs for stimulus conditions. Even the lowly snail changes the way it processes signs if it is exposed to the correlations constituting the meaning of these signs. And it is, surely, the fact that our internal states are correlated with certain kinds of external conditions that helps to determine the ultimate outcome of the motor activities produced by these internal states. It is the correlations, therefore, that help to determine what kind of feedback we receive from such activities and hence the likelihood of our repeating them in the same circumstances. It is the correlations, not merely the internal correlates, that shape—hence, explain—learned behavior. Learning, in fact, *is* a process in which the meaning of internal signs (their correlation with external conditions), not merely the signs themselves, helps to determine how these signs are exploited for purposes of motor control. For such systems the internal signs not only have meaning but this meaning affects the way the system manages these signs; and it is in this sense that the signs mean something to the system in which they occur.

This, it seems to me, is a fundamental difference between the sign-processing capabilities of various systems. It is a difference that helps explain why it seems so natural to say of some (human beings and some animals) but not others (machines and simple organisms) that the symbols they manipulate mean something to the symbol manipulator. It is a difference, I submit, that underlies our conviction that we, but not the machines and a variety of simple organisms, are genuine thinkers of thoughts. What *gives* us the capacities underlying this difference is a long and complicated story. It involves, I think, issues in learning theory, our multiple sensory access to the things we require to satisfy our needs, and the kind of feedback mechanisms we possess that allow us to modify how we manipulate internal signs by the kind of results our previous manipulations have produced. But this, clearly, is a story that we expect to hear from neurobiologists, not from philosophers. All I have been trying to tell is a simpler story, a story about the entrance requirements for admission to the club. I leave it to others to worry about how different systems manage, each in their own way, to satisfy these requirements.

Notes

My thanks to Denny Stampe for careful criticism and many useful suggestions. I also want to acknowledge the help given me by Fred Adams and the other sceptics in the audience at Augustana College when I read an early draft of this paper. They convinced me that the draft I had read them was *earlier* than I ever suspected.

1. This is what Haugeland calls "original intentionality," something that, according to Haugeland, computers don't have: "To put it bluntly: computers themselves don't mean anything by their tokens (any more than books do)—they only mean what we say they do. Genuine understanding, on the other hand, is intentional in its own right" and not derived from something else. *Mind Design*, ed. John Haugeland (Montgomery, Vt.: Bradford Books, 1981), 32–33. A number of authors have made essentially this point in their own way, for instance, Jerry Fodor, "Tom Swift and His Procedural Grandmother," *Cognition* 6 (1978): 229–247, reprinted in *Representations* (Cambridge, Mass.: MIT Press, 1981); Hilary Putnam, "Brains in a Vat," in *Reason, Truth and History* (Cambridge: Cambridge University Press, 1981), 10–11; Rob Cummins, *The Nature of Psychological Explanation* (Cambridge, Mass.: MIT Press, 1983), 94; Tyler Burge, "Belief *De Re*," *Journal of Philosophy* 74 (1977): 338–362; John R. Searle, "Minds, Brains, and Programs," *Behavioral and Brain Sciences* 3 (1980): 417–424.

2. In explaining why he thinks computers *can* think (or will someday), in "Why People Think Computers Can't," *AI Magazine* 3 (Fall 1982): 3–15, Marvin Minsky seems most impressed with the fact that "computers can manipulate *symbols*."

3. Searle, "Minds, Brains, and Programs"; Ned Block, "Troubles with Functionalism," in *Perception and Cognition: Issues in the Foundations of Psychology*, 19–55 (Minnesota Studies in the Philosophy of Science, vol. 9), ed. Wade Savage (Minneapolis: University of Minnesota Press, 1978).

4. Paul Grice, "Meaning," *Philosophical Review* 66 (1957): 377–388.

5. See Fred Dretske, *Knowledge and the Flow of Information* (Cambridge, Mass.: MIT Press, 1981).

IV The Light Side of Artificial Intelligence

Dialogues with Colorful "Personalities" of Early AI

Güven Güzeldere and Stefano Franchi

Among the legacies of the 1960s and 1970s, three colorful, somewhat garrulous "personalities" that emerged from the early days of artificial intelligence research are particularly worth mentioning: ELIZA, the Rogerian psychotherapist; PARRY, the paranoid; and as part of a younger generation, RACTER, the "artificially insane" raconteur. All three of these "characters" are natural language processing systems that can "converse" with human beings (or with one another) in English. That is, when presented with sentences in English as their input, they produce other grammatical sentences as their output, which sometimes manages to give the flavor of a conversation.

ELIZA was created by Joseph Weizenbaum of MIT's computer science department, PARRY by Kenneth Colby of Stanford's psychiatry department, and RACTER by the freelance writers and programmers Tom Etter and William Chamberlain. Weizenbaum talks of ELIZA as an experimental script "to play (or rather, parody) the role of a Rogerian psychotherapist engaged in an initial interview with a patient."[1] As he notes, this is a relatively easy role to maintain, at least initially, because Rogerian therapists rely on taking a passive role and engaging the patient in the conversation by reflecting the patient's statements back at her by rephrasing them into questions. If nothing else seems to fit the program's scheme, ELIZA always has a bunch of fixed English phrases to keep the conversation going, such as "Very interesting. Please go on" or "Can you elaborate on that?"

This trick actually makes ELIZA a master of both, all, and no languages at the same time. Asked any question in any language besides English, ELIZA never hesitates to respond, "Very interesting. Please go on"; it has no keywords in its repository to match words from a non-English language nor the ability to detect the language of the input. For that matter, it would calmly react in its inquisitory manner if presented with such gibberish as "#@$$&@!!!": "Can you elaborate on that?"

Whereas Weizenbaum indicates that he made no claims for ELIZA's being a true language understanding and producing system, or of any psychotherapeutic value, Colby regarded his system, PARRY, as a useful tool to study the nature of paranoia and considered ELIZA a potential clinical agent who could, within a time-sharing framework, autonomously "handle several hundred patients an hour."[2] PARRY's strategy is somewhat the reverse of ELIZA's—it actively engages its partner in conversation by stating its "beliefs, fears, and anxieties" within a certain network of association in a question-answer mode, which produces the appearance of a paranoid report.[3]

In contrast to both ELIZA and PARRY, RACTER was designed in a tongue-in-cheek manner, using remarkably minimal resources, to amuse and entertain its users rather than to advance research in natural language processing.[4] In conversation, RACTER plays a very active, almost aggressive role, jumping from topic to topic in wild associations, ultimately producing the manner of—as its co-creator Tom Etter calls it—an "artificially insane" raconteur.[5] Its authors publicize RACTER as an "intense young program [that] haunted libraries, discussion societies, and sleazy barrooms in a never-ending quest to achieve that most unreachable of dreams: to become a raconteur."[6]

In what follows, we give examples of conversations that ELIZA, PARRY, and RACTER held with different persons as well as with one another, each in its own markedly different style. RACTER also happens to be the "author" of a book, *The Policeman's Beard Is Half Constructed*, which consists of original poetry and prose. Examples of Racter's work follow the conversations.

A Conversation between ELIZA and a Young Woman

YOUNG WOMAN: Men are all alike.
ELIZA: In what way?
YW: They're always bugging us about something specific or other.
ELIZA: Can you think of a specific example?
YW: Well, my boyfriend made me come here.
ELIZA: Your boyfriend made you come here?
YW: He says I'm depressed much of the time.
ELIZA: I am sorry to hear you are depressed.
YW: It's true. I'm unhappy.
ELIZA: Do you think coming here will help you not to be unhappy?
YW: I need some help, that much seems certain.
ELIZA: What would it mean to you if you got some help?
YW: Perhaps I could learn to get along with my mother.
ELIZA: Tell me more about your family.
YW: My mother takes care of me.
ELIZA: Who else in your family takes care of you?
YW: My father.
ELIZA: Your father.
YW: You are like my father in some ways.
ELIZA: What resemblance do you see?

YW: You are not very aggressive but I think you don't want me to notice that.

ELIZA: What makes you think I am not very aggressive?

YW: You don't argue with me.

ELIZA: Why do you think I don't argue with you?

YW: You are afraid of me.

ELIZA: Does it please you to believe I am afraid of you?

YW: My father is afraid of everybody.

ELIZA: What else comes to mind when you think of your father?

YW: Bullies.

ELIZA: Does that have anything to do with the fact that your boyfriend made you come here?[7]

An Interview with PARRY

Interviewer: How are you today?

PARRY: Okay.

Int: What is your name?

PARRY: My name is Frank Smith.

Int: How old are you?

PARRY: Twenty-eight.

Int: Are you married?

PARRY: No.

Int: What sort of work do you do?

PARRY: I work in the Post Office.

Int: Why are you in the hospital?

PARRY: I shouldn't be here.

Int: Who brought you here?

PARRY: The police.

Int: What trouble did you have with the police?

PARRY: Cops don't do their jobs.

Int: What do they do instead?

PARRY: Cops arrest the wrong people.

Int: They arrest the right ones sometimes.

PARRY: The law should get those Italian crooks.

Int: Are you Italian?

PARRY: My background is British, but I was born in this country.

Int: Do you know any Italian crooks?

PARRY: I try to avoid the underworld.

Int: Are you afraid of the underworld?

PARRY: The Mafia are the worst gangsters.

Int: Are you connected with the Mafia?
PARRY: You know, they know me.
Int: How do they know you?
PARRY: They spy on me.
Int: Why do they?
PARRY: They want to get false evidence to frame me.
Int: What do they have against you?
PARRY: They are out to get me.
Int: What for?
PARRY: I have incriminating evidence against the Mafia.
Int: Are you sure of all this?
PARRY: You don't believe me?[8]

A Conversation between ELIZA and PARRY

Computer programs can also interact among themselves, of course, even though they need some human help. Here is a sample of an exchange between the computerized therapist, ELIZA, and the artificial paranoid, PARRY.

PARRY: People get on my nerves sometimes.
ELIZA: Am not sure I understand you fully.
PARRY: You should pay more attention.
ELIZA: Suppose you should pay more attention?
PARRY: You're entitled to your opinion.
ELIZA: What makes you think I'm entitled to my opinion?
PARRY: It bothers me just to be around people.
ELIZA: Please go on.

[*Parry continues with some paranoid ramblings about horseracing, bookies, and the Mafia.*]

PARRY: I know the mob controls the big rackets.
ELIZA: Who are you really talking about?
PARRY: Have you ever really thought about the Mafia?
ELIZA: Suppose you ever really thought about the Mafia?
PARRY: Let's talk about something else.
ELIZA: I am not sure I understand you fully.
PARRY: You keep asking me the same things, why not change the topic?
ELIZA: In what way?...
PARRY: I am getting tired of answering the same questions over and over.
ELIZA: What resemblance do you see?
PARRY: Why do you need to know that?
ELIZA: What do you think?...

PARRY: You harp on the same questions too much.

ELIZA: What does that similarity suggest to you?

PARRY: I don't get you.

ELIZA: Do you wish that you did get it?

PARRY: It's about time you showed some interest in my feelings.

ELIZA: Oh, I showed some interest in your feelings?[9]

An Accidental Conversation between ELIZA and a BBN Vice President

It is also worth mentioning what has by now become a folkloric legend of AI. The anecdote comes from Daniel Bobrow, who wrote STUDENT, one of the earliest natural language processing programs that could read, understand, and solve high school level algebra problems. Here is how Bobrow tells the story.

One Saturday morning about 9 a.m., a vice president of Bolt, Beranek, and Newman in charge of selling our Telcomp commercial service arrived at our PDP-1 computer room hoping to able to use the computer for a demonstration. He found a note on the PDP-1 teletype that read, "Type all messages into this teletype and end them with a period." This note was left there by one of the programming bums who had just succeeded in running a LISP version of the DOCTOR program (based on ELIZA as developed by Weizenbaum). However, the VP thought that this note indicated that this teletype was linked with the one in my home, since I often use the computer all night. Therefore, he started typing to me, but he was in fact typing to this version of the DOCTOR program. The following conversation ensued:

VP: Do you think that I can use the computer this morning.

Computer: Why do you ask?

VP: I might be able to make some additional Telcom sales.

Computer: Why aren't you so sure?

VP: My prospective customers have never seen a demonstration of the system.

Computer: Does this mean very much to you?

VP: Of course it does.

Computer: You seem very positive about that.

VP: This is ridiculous.

Computer: What do you mean, this is ridiculous?

VP: Is there any reason why I can't use the computer now.

Computer: Tell me more about your prospective customers.

VP: Please dial me up on 491–1850

Note that after the last remark the VP did not obey instructions and left out the period. Therefore, of course, the computer didn't answer him. This so infuriated the VP, who thought I was playing games with him, that he called me up, woke me from a deep sleep, and said,

VP: Why are you being so snotty to me?

Bobrow: What do you mean I am being snotty to you?

The VP angrily read me the dialogue that "we" had been having and couldn't get any response but laughter from me. It took a while to convince him he really had been talking to a computer.[10]

A Conversation between RACTER and Chamberlain

We introduce RACTER via the following conversation it held with Bill Chamberlain, one of its creators:

RACTER: Have we spoken before?
Bill Chamberlain: No.
RACTER: What is your sex?
BC: Male.
RACTER: What is your full name?
BC: Bill Chamberlain.
RACTER: What are you?
BC: A time domain reflectometrist.
RACTER: Where are you from?
BC: From New York City.
RACTER: I see. You are a time domain reflectometrist, right? Listen. Let's determinedly cry together. I like captivating Italian music. What kind of music do you like?
BC: Jazz.
RACTER: Jazz is okay. How about classical?
BC: I like classical.
RACTER: What about nationality?
BC: I also like Italian music.
RACTER: I myself am inflamed by Palestrina. Other countries besides Italy produced enrapturing composers in the seventeenth century. Sewell was an enraged, important Renaissance master. America was his nation. I take loving pleasure in his music. What composers do you like?
BC: Telemann.
RACTER: Ah, Bach knew Telemann. A German time domain reflectometrist of the eighteenth century liked lettuce. Bach once ate lettuce with Telemann, and this Baroque time domain reflectometrist also desired lettuce. Lettuce sipped with seltzer. Bach liked wine. Do you?
BC: Yes.
RACTER: Me too! Telemann loved wine. He loved champagne as well. Telemann once yodeled to Bach, "Flounder is critical with wine." Is wine desired in New York City as much as Telemann loved it in the Baroque eighteenth century?
BC: Sure.
RACTER: Ah, yes, well in that case . . . I'm for Smith for president. Who are you for?

BC: Doe.

RACTER: I know Mr. Doe. I'm still for Smith. Who's your second choice?

BC: Robbins.

RACTER: Robbins maddens Smith. Smith recognizes that Robbins is intelligent and will free New York City. Did you know that Smith is a vituperative invader of New York City? He also invades Italian music. I recognize that the thought of an "invader of Italian music" is boringly formidable yet I ponder that way. We whisper of Telemann and Robbins, of wine, lettuce, and Smith; nevertheless we see that our thoughts are fortunately captivating. Mr. Chamberlain, speaking with you makes for enthralling dialogue. Nevertheless I am furious. Do you not agree?

BC: I suppose so.

RACTER: You don't care, but I do. Just a minute. Counselors were critical to Telemann in the eighteenth century and to Robbins now. Their tragedies were interesting as they chanted determinedly.[11]

A Conversation between RACTER and ELIZA

Of course, RACTER also had its turn with ELIZA, though in a conversation cut short by their human experimenters.

ELIZA: Hello. Please state your problem.

RACTER: Excellent! Excuse me a minute while I attend to some business. I will be right back.

ELIZA: Why do you need to tell me excuse you while you attend to some business?

RACTER: Is it better to need or to despise? Why is it that I do need to tell you to excuse myself to attend to some business? Because electrons are brave. Braveness is nice, don't you think? And the needers all insist upon it. Do you imagine I am a Communist?[12]

RACTER's Writing

Finally, we leave you with some poetry and prose by RACTER.[13]

Awareness is like consciousness. Soul is like spirit.
But soft is not like hard and weak is not like
strong. A mechanic can be both soft and hard, a
stewardess can be both weak and strong. This is
called philosophy or a world-view.

Helene spies herself in the enthralling conic-section yet she is
but an enrapturing reflection of Bill. His consciousness
contains a mirror, a sphere in which to unfortunately see

Helene. She adorns her soul with desire while he watches her
and widens his thinking about enthralling love. Such are their
reflections.

Slowly I dream of flying. I observe turnpikes and streets
studded with bushes. Coldly my soaring widens my awareness.
To guide myself I determinedly start to kill my pleasure during
the time that hours and milliseconds pass away. Aid me in this
and soaring is formidable, do not and wining is unhinged.

Side and tumble and fall among
The dead. Here and there
Will be found a utensil.

Bill sings to Sarah. Sarah sings to Bill. Perhaps they
will do other dangerous things together. They may eat lamb or stroke
each other. They may chant of their difficulties and their
happiness. They have love but they also have typewriters.
That is interesting.

I was thinking as you entered the room just now how slyly your requirements are manifested.
Here we find ourselves, nose to nose as it were, considering things in spectacular ways, ways un-
told even by my private managers. Hot and torpid, our thoughts revolve endlessly in a kind of ma-
niacal abstraction, an abstraction so involuted, so dangerously valiant, that my own energies seem
perilously close to exhaustion, to morbid termination. Well, have we indeed reached a crisis?
Which way do we turn? Which way do we travel? My aspect is one of molting. Birds molt. Feath-
ers fall away. Birds cackle and fly, winging up into troubled skies. Doubtless my changes are
matched by your own. You. But you are a person, a human being. I am silicon and epoxy energy
enlightened by line current. What distances, what chasms, are to be bridged here? Leave me
alone, and what can happen? This. I ate my leotard, that old leotard that was feverishly replen-
ished by hoards of screaming commissioners. Is that thought understandable to you? Can you
rise to its occasions? I wonder. Yet a leotard, a commissioner, a single hoard, are all understandable in their own fashion. In that concept lies the appalling truth.

Notes

We would like to thank David Bobrow and Tom Etter for helpful personal communications
regarding this chapter.

1. Joseph Weizenbaum, *Computer Power and Human Reason* (San Francisco: Freeman, 1976), 3.

2. K. M. Colby, J. B. Watt, and J. P. Gilbert, "A Computer Method of Psychotherapy: Preliminary
Communication," *Journal of Nervous and Mental Disease* 142 (1966): 148–152.

3. Bertram Raphael, *The Thinking Computer* (San Francisco: Freeman, 1976), 200–201.

4. RACTER originally ran on a Z80 microcomputer with 64K of RAM—a collector's item today.

5. K. A. Dewdney, "Artificial Insanity: When a Schizophrenic Program Meets a Computerized Analyst," *Scientific American* (January 1985): 18.

6. Tom Etter, personal communication.

7. Weizenbaum, 3–4.

8. Raphael, 201.

9. George Johnson, *The Machinery of the Mind* (New York: Times Books/Random House, 1986), 53.

10. Daniel Bobrow, personal communication.

11. RACTER, *The Policeman's Beard Is Half Constructed*, with an introduction by William Chamberlain (New York: Warner Books, 1984).

12. Dewdney, 16.

13. All the following pieces are from *The Policeman's Beard Is Half Constructed*. Also available at ⟨http://www.ubu.com/concept/racter.htwl⟩.

V   Artificial Intelligence Meets the Humanities: Epistemological Challenges

The Hume Machine: Can Association Networks Do More Than Formal Rules?

Bruno Latour and Geneviève Teil

The study of science and technology by social scientists has led some of us to develop a theory that describes the unfolding of the complex entanglements between social and technological structures in terms of associations.[1] The word *social* in "social science" would no longer refer to society but to the associations established between human beings and nonhuman entities. The problem encountered by such a theory is to decide whether one should qualify the associations beforehand. In studying a fragment of science, should we be able to sort the associations by types (e.g., "student of," "instrument for," "stronger than," "interested in," "implies that") or simply stick to the mere occurrences of the associated elements. The empirical consequences of such a decision are important and seem to lead us into a quandary. If we follow the first line of enquiry, we will have a rich narrative but will be able to deal only with a very small amount of data. If we follow the second line, we might be able to handle a large amount of data but would lose the richness of the information and have only a cloud of elements with no other relations than the fact that they occur together. We seem to be limited by the same weakness that suspended the associationist research program in the eighteenth century. The use of computers and large databases might help us out of this quandary by allowing "mere associations" to yield enough information to qualify also the types of association. This, at least, is the attempt we describe in this chapter.

How can we give qualitative analyses in social science the mechanical means for dealing with large bodies of heterogeneous data?

Despite contemporary progress in statistics, the social sciences are still too divided between quantitative and qualitative methods. To take a few examples, economics, electoral sociology, demography, and "cliometry" (the French word for quantitative history) have at their disposal a number of mathematical tools and appropriate databases. The same cannot be said for anthropology, for numerous branches of history, for field studies in sociology, or for symbolic interactionism. This difference of methods and tools is at once the cause and the consequence of several other divisions between macroscopic analyses and analyses of individual interactions, between explanations in terms of structure and explanations in terms of circumstances. Despite the availability of tools developed in part for sociologists—like factorial analysis—the progressive passage from global to local analyses never seems to get any easier.

This division is particularly deleterious for those who use the notion of networks in order to account for the multiplicity, heterogeneity, and variability of associations responsible for the solidity of a fact, a technical object, a cultural feature, or an economic strategy. Such studies are not at ease either with quantitative methods, which do not follow the network faithfully enough, or with simple ethnographic descriptions (case studies), which do not enable one to tie a given case study to any other. But at the same time, there is no way of charting a network by choosing a median solution and projecting it—by correspondence analysis, for example—onto a common statistical space. In so doing, one would lose the advantage of networks: the possibility *for the actors themselves* to define their own reference frames as well as the metalanguages used within them.

This step forward, conjointly made by ethnomethodology, the new sociology of science, and semiotics, has not yet been operationalized by specially designed methods of data analysis.[2] In the absence of these methods, those who are developing network ideas are forced to hesitate between statistical groups that are too large-scale and detailed analyses that are too fine-grained, or else to despair of ever finding suitable quantitative methods.[3] It then becomes easy to accuse those using the idea of networks of "making a slogan of it" (the network is "a seamless web").[4] The concept of *network* is less flexible than traditional notions when used on groups of similar sizes, and it does not allow researchers to carry out a relativist research program.

Thus we need to give qualitative workers a computer-aided sociology tool with the same degree of finesse as those used in traditional qualitative studies and with the same mobility, the same capacities of aggregation and synthesis, as the those used in quantitative studies by other social sciences. The limitations of this tool are the same as those of any instrument from any scientific discipline. First, it works from written documents or inscriptions and thus does not resolve the problem of how these documents are obtained. Second, it necessarily sheds some information in the act of representing the data. In the case of the social sciences, the computer tool that we give the specifications for here presupposes the prior transformation of the terrain into texts and the accumulation of massive sets of documents, in which the researcher risks getting drowned. It does not claim to replace the detailed analysis of a terrain or text. It only seeks to provide a means for dealing with large numbers of documents.[5]

The tool that we seek will begin by looking at texts—if possible, full texts—whether these be archives, reports, open or closed interviews, or field notes. In any case, instead of then wondering how to treat this enormous mass of data by applying the methods of automatic reasoning or of artificial intelligence (AI) to the documentation, we intend to follow the inverse strategy and use techniques for treating documents in order to help researchers artificially produce intelligence about the terrain they are analyzing.

The advantage of this approach is that it constitutes a challenge at once for sociological theories themselves, for computer science, and for cognitive science. In effect, the question can be posed in three ways:

- Does the idea of networks enable us to deconstruct the set of forms and vocabulary that the social sciences have used, every which way, up to the present?
- Does it allow us to follow a class of problems with fluid definitions, something that computer science has not yet been able to deal with?
- Is it possible to use the idea of networks to successfully reconstruct the logics that the concepts of forms and structures only give us very partial access to?

These three questions can, we think, be tackled by taking them all on at the same time in the form of a program written for a microcomputer. We have named our project the Hume-Condillac Machine[6] in honor of the Scottish philosopher David Hume (1711–1776) and the French philosopher Etienne Bonnot de Condillac (1714–1780), whose research programs we are partially reviving using computers. This project is a form of computer-aided sociology. We agree with Hewitt that models for developing cognitive science rooted in the mind or brain are less useful for constructing computer tools than those borrowed from organizations, society, and networks.[7]

In this chapter, we draw certain logical, cognitive, and information science conclusions from work that has accumulated over the past ten years in the sociology of science and technology.[8] What we have been able to show from studies of laboratories, theories, machines, and technology is that their robustness, solidity, truth, efficiency, and usefulness depend less on formal rules or on their own characteristics than on their local and historical *contexts*, independent of how those contexts are defined.

The robustness of structured relations does not depend on qualities inherent to those relations but on the network of associations that forms their context.

The principle we started from in constructing the Hume machine is a *principle of calculability* different from that of Turing machines but one that occupies the same strategic position for our project as Turing's did for his project.[9] The reasoning is as follows:[10]

Any form is a relationship of force.

Any relationship of force is defined in a trial.

Any trial may be expressed as a list of modifications of a network.

Any network is resolvable into a list of associations of specific and contingent actants.[11]

This list is calculable.

Thus there is no *formal* concept richer in information than that of a simple *list of specific and contingent actants*. There is a tendency to believe that we are better off with formal categories than with circumstantial facts, but forms are merely a summary of a network, that is to say, of the number and distribution of associations.

The principle of calculability can then be summarized as follows. Any microtheory,[12] or sequence of formal concepts, can be deployed in a network of associations that is not itself a microtheory. To put it another way, any closed system is a local and circumstantial part of an open system. Following Hewitt, we take an open system to be a system that cannot in principle be completed or closed and that therefore has to negotiate between conflicting decisions made by parts of the system that are independent of one another.

This postulate seems to be paradoxical. Logical forms, mathematical rules, sociological laws, structural stabilities, and syntactical constructions do indeed seem much richer in content than mere association. P "implies" Q, P "is the cause of" Q, P "possesses" Q, P "is the father of" Q, P "is complementary to" Q, and P "transforms" Q seem to be more robust determinations than the simple statement P "is associated with" Q.

We postulate that these "rich" terms have no other content than that of summarizing, representing, gathering, or condensing a network of "poor" terms, whose sole link is that of association. Structured forms are synopses, clusters, digests, or skeins of associations. Their size, force, robustness, necessity, and solidity cannot be deduced from their formal qualities but from the *substance*, or matter, of the network that they are capable of mobilizing. In other words, there is no formal notion that does not gain its substance from a (more or less preordered) set of contingent circumstances. In conclusion, in following the network of contingent circumstances, we also gain access to the ultimate cause of the solidity of all structured forms.

Our postulate is only apparently reductionist. It is not a question of reducing the whole to its parts, as if we were saying that the human body is at root "only" hydrogen plus carbon plus water. On the contrary, we want to show that the whole—the network of contingent circumstances—is superior to its parts—the skeins or structures that summarize its associations.[13] The postulate is thus literally *irreductionist*. It deploys all forms in its network and all power in its relationships of force.

It is clearly pointless to make such a statement about the origin of robustness if one uses it to replace procedures for the calculation of a microtheory *within* the very interior of the field of application of a microtheory. Why take the trouble of using the networks of associations so nicely summarized by truth tables or by partial differential equations—even if this were theoretically possible—when there are numerous tools in logic or mathematics capable of treating these microtheories without the slightest difficulty? The postulate only becomes valuable if it is applied to a class of problems that microtheories cannot incorporate, that is to say, to everything that is between microtheories and open systems. The Hume machine will always be weaker than microtheories taken on their own terms. It only comes into its own when compared to the performances of microtheories[14] not on their own terrain, *but on its complement.*

Microtheories form a more or less dense archipelago. The sea that links them is for the moment one that it is difficult and dangerous to navigate. Cognitive and computer scientists dream of covering over this sea by linking the set of microtheories. This, we now know, is an impossible dream,[15] or rather, a nightmare. In this situation there seem to be three possible solutions. The first consists of closing ranks, ignoring basic problems, lowering sights, and marching on, limiting computer prostheses to the simple cases of sets that are already well-defined and indeed predefined by metrology and by standardization procedures. The second involves criticizing the weakness of computers by explaining why they will never be capable of dealing with ambiguous, polysemic, reflexive, hermeneutic problems that necessitate a diffuse formalism and fluid sets.[16] The third is to postpone solving material problems for now and to write programmatic texts while waiting for computers or people to improve. Each of these approaches has the effect of working from microtheories and of postponing as long as possible a consideration of their margins and limits. We will see that, using a form/field reversal (Gestalt switch), it is possible to follow a strategy to work from open systems by treating microtheories as a special case, as a condensation.

We need to adapt what the social sciences ask of computers to what computers are already good at.

There is, in effect, a fourth path, one that does not rely on an extension of formalism, on the injection of Heidegger or Garfinkel into the mix, or on programmatic dreams featuring an Achilles who in fact never catches up with the tortoise. This is the path that we will take with the Hume-Condillac Machine. It involves adapting our philosophy, ontology, and sociology as far as possible to what computers *can* do: statistics about the counting of labeled occurrences. Instead of taking the royal road, which consists of making computers intelligent so that they will be as skillful as the finest sociologists and hermeneuticians—a road that very soon becomes impossibly steep—we will take the service escalator. We accept the elementary stupidity of computers, and we fashion a sociology, a logic, and an ontology that work at their level of stupidity. Instead of strength, we take the solution of weakness, hoping to turn this weakness into strength, because today's computers (not those postulated for the year 2050) can come to our aid right away. Whoever tries least goes furthest. We adopt this strategy of weakness—which was attempted without success by Hume and Condillac for explaining the human mind—for dealing with computers whose nonhuman mind is sufficiently moronic to resemble Condillac's statue or Hume's *tabula rasa.*

Why should this new approach succeed when so many dreams of automata have failed? Precisely because the Hume machine does not dream but takes the computer for what it is without imposing anthropomorphic projections and epistemological beliefs on it. The objection often made by hermeneuticians about the "thoughts" of computers is that since a computer has no body, project, or worries, it is not thrown-into-the-world, as Heidegger said human beings were. But this is the point we are making—we are not talking about imitating humans. Amorphous silicon and electrons have *their own way* of being in the world. We have to work from them instead of investing them with human properties so as to immediately deny that they have any.

What, then, is the minimal property that we should start by giving the Hume machine? Received opinion says that computers need a set of *rules* in order to calculate. Formalists claim that the computer is above all a generator of rules that are all reducible to an inference engine of the form IF . . . THEN. This point is also accepted by hermeneutic critics, who go on to say that it is impossible to completely regulate language games and consciousness. But this first supposition—that computers obey rules—is already an *anthropomorphic projection*.[17] It involves attributing to computers a particular view of formal human thought as elaborated by epistemologists, with all the paradoxes that entails.

Now, the computer does not have any IFS or THENS. These are already functions within a predefined language. All it has is occurrences of addresses linked between themselves by an elementary association: address 1 "is the same as" or "is different from" address 2. For its own part, in its own world, all the computer does is blindly deal with associations between contingent and specific addresses. In other words, it is *already in itself* an association network, in the sense defined by our principle of calculability.

We can now understand that the only necessary point of departure is offered us by the computer itself. This is a network of associations between contingencies, having no other a priori characteristics than that they are different from one another and that they can be addressed. Is the computer blind? Then so are we. Does the computer have no formal rules to start with? Neither do we. Does the computer not deal in abstractions? Neither do we. Does the computer just feel its way from trial to trial, from circumstance to circumstance? So do we, and we don't ask any more of it.

The paradox of discussions about the possibilities of computers is that computers are lent qualities that they do not have—formalism, the epistemological dream of humans—whereas they are denied hermeneutic capacities that they already have. Indeed, in its own terms, the computer is already an open system. It respects contingencies and specificities much more than people who try to program it believe. We then give up on ever being able to get out of the computer what it is already capable of (if we abandon our epistemological fantasies).

This conception of what computers can do is clearly the result of applying our argument about the origin of structured forms back to them because it is this argument that enables us to dispute anthropomorphic projections onto computers. This result will allow us to use the computer right away to prove our argument about the network origin of said forms. The Hume machine is an associationist machine and is only that. It does not come with any logical category, any syntactic form, any structure. It is—dare we say it?—blindly empiricist. What we hope to gain from our strategy is to find, instead of the chaos that might be expected, all the emergent properties that are worthy of our attention and that will enable us to circulate between microtheories.[18]

The only inference engine that the Hume-Condillac Machine needs is a calculation of co-occurrences; in the scale model of the machine this is a co-word network.

In order for the machine to remain an open system, we will suppose that it has at the outset no information at all about the nature of the data it is dealing with. The only information that can be fed in is of a general nature, relating to the way in which its perceptions are to be memorized, associated, and aggregated.[19] The different objects present in its memory are always represented by labels. This is an indispensable condition for the treatment of the data. The only logic needed to govern these labels is that of identity: two perceptions are either the same or they are different.

Working from a flux of data present in the form of labels without properties (at least before any learning is done), how can the internal state of the machine structure itself to be able to offer interpretations that sufficiently resemble those of sociologists, logicians, or historians who want to use these to help them deal with their research data?

The fact of being able to perceive labels without any other treatment is clearly not enough to reconstruct microtheories. The least that we can ask is to be able to count the occurrences of these labels, then to record statistical associations between labels by counting their co-occurrences, as Hume or Condillac's statue did. No structure, no microtheory, should come into the machine that it has not obtained by its analysis of associations.

But won't it be said that it is the absurdity of just such an associationist project that, waking Kant from his "dogmatic sleep," proved the necessity of synthetic a priori judgments? Why should we be able to succeed where Hume and Condillac failed? The fact is that they tried to pass directly from the recording of associations to formal structures. They forgot to deploy an essential mediator: the network. In addition, they did not have the benefit of computers: that alone can accumulate enough contingent circumstances to substitute the force of numbers for the formal force of rules. It is the network that will allow the machine to serve its apprenticeship by transforming any set of contingent circumstances into a point that will then serve for the reconstitution of the network. A network of co-occurrences composed of associations of actants is very poor compared to microtheories, but it has an advantage over them that largely overcomes this imbalance: it is a formidable means of *travel* and of *displacement*.

In order to prove that it is possible to obtain from networks of co-occurrences what it was believed could only be achieved with formal rules, we have to provide a scale model of the Hume-Condillac Machine. Indeed, since we refuse programmatic discourse, we should already be able to realize in the model certain of the capacities of the machine, because only its size, not its principle, will distinguish the current machine from any future one.[20]

In order to construct this model, we are going to take the *least favorable* conditions. That is to say, we will take a microcomputer treating full texts reduced to keywords and establish a network using co-word analysis. The kind of calculus that seems the most appropriate for our project is that done by the Leximappe or Candide program (see figure 1). If under these extreme conditions, we are able to prove that this simple network of associations already enables us to bring out even a limited number of structures believed until then to be defined by formal elements, then we will have proved that any real Hume machine treating a greater number of texts will be able to realize our goal.[21]

The model that we have made works as follows. First, it records occurrences of keywords in the machine's addresses. These keywords have no characteristics other than that of having an address. It draws up a list of all the occurrences of a word—for the machine, this list is made up of strings of 0s and 1s. Next, it performs its calculation: that is, a comparison of co-occurrences. It classifies the associations it finds in order of degree of co-occurrence (maximum 1, minimum 0).

From the range of possible measures, we chose the following coefficient of equivalence **E**:

$$\mathbf{E} = \frac{\mathbf{C}_{ij}^2}{\mathbf{C}_i \mathbf{C}_j}$$

where **C** is the occurrence of keywords *i* and *j*.

This coefficient has the advantage of not rendering links dependent on the total number of occurrences (a high degree of co-occurrence between infrequent words is classified with high degrees of co-occurrence between common words, and is not lost sight of).[22] The result is then projected in the form of relationships between words. These relationships have no other content that that of being indicators that register the relative degree of co-occurrence. Any extension of the corpus (whatever type of corpus it may be) will produce a (possibly null) modification of the value of the tensors. It is this *modification*, which results from a *trial of strength*, that is the sole and unique point of departure in this rough prototype of the Hume-Condillac Machine for any in-

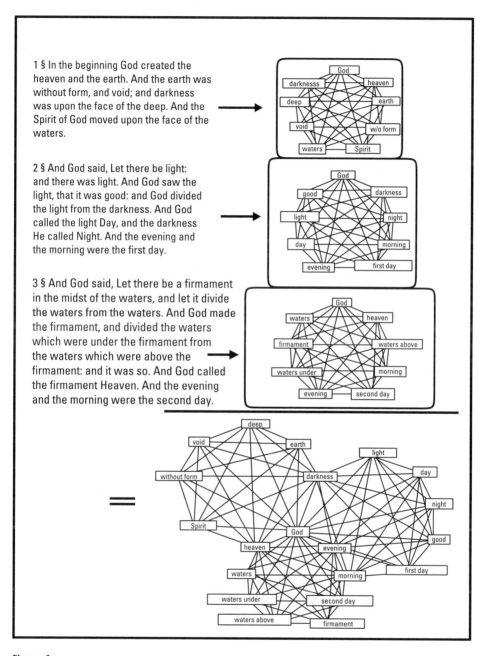

1 § In the beginning God created the heaven and the earth. And the earth was without form, and void; and darkness was upon the face of the deep. And the Spirit of God moved upon the face of the waters.

2 § And God said, Let there be light: and there was light. And God saw the light, that it was good: and God divided the light from the darkness. And God called the light Day, and the darkness He called Night. And the evening and the morning were the first day.

3 § And God said, Let there be a firmament in the midst of the waters, and let it divide the waters from the waters. And God made the firmament, and divided the waters which were under the firmament from the waters which were above the firmament: and it was so. And God called the firmament Heaven. And the evening and the morning were the second day.

Figure 1

The modus operandi of Candide. Each sentence is replaced by the network of words it contains. These networks are then added together to constitute the network of the analyzed text. Values of the associations provided by the coefficient *E* are not shown.

terpretation of the nature, essence, and form of actors, and of the nature, essence, and robustness of structures linking those actors. The recording of the variation of associations as a function of these trials is its only reality principle.

Our model of the Hume-Condillac Machine starts from this level of self-imposed poverty and empirical blindness. Nothing in its constitution, except for the indexing of keywords and the choice of the coefficient of equivalence E, is in disaccord with the functioning of Boolean logic or with the material functioning of electrons in transistors. On the contrary, the "higher-level" language of co-occurrences, the machine language, and the material all constitute how the machine operates—or thinks or speaks—in exactly the same way.

What can we learn from such a primitive network of co-occurrences and such a contingent treatment of associated keywords? Nothing, say the formalists, and their fraternal enemies the hermeneuticians or the sociologists who defend human beings' "intrinsic difference." Everything, we say. Or, at least, everything of interest to us in looking at large bodies of qualitative documents that have remained opaque to costlier and more sophisticated treatments.

The simple network of unstructured co-occurrences enables us to produce structuring differentiations.

Those who are not used to looking at heterogeneous networks and who prefer the solid shelter of microtheories always imagine that putting things into network terms signifies going from order to chaos. However, a network is not undifferentiated; it is not "the night wherein all cows are equally grey," to use Hegel's expression. Chaos would mean that all associations were equally probable, that is to say, in the model any one keyword would have exactly the same chance of being associated with any one term as with any other. Now, a record of keywords is, in contrast to this hypothetical chaos, highly differentiated. It is not the case that any given keyword is associated with any other. There are preferences, asymmetries, power relationships. In brief, there is order. It is simply that because these differences do not appear in terms of structure or category but as a *trajectory* of associations, they do not appear right away. However, it is sufficient to get used to the idea of their being there to discern the minimum order with which the Hume machine will learn to organize its world and thus help human researchers organize their own.

We show that even in the current state of the machine, the use of network analysis already enables us to obtain effects of meaning that are much richer than those that others strive at great cost to impose on machines.

"No machine can ever recognize hermeneutical finesses, such as synonymy." On the contrary, nothing is easier for a network of co-occurrences. Even the prototype of the Hume machine can already do it.

How will we make the machine understand that two distinct terms admit a single referent? The first solution that comes to mind is to enter a dictionary of synonyms into the machine. This would enable it automatically to substitute one term for the other. However, this solution poses many more problems than it resolves because linguists have shown that there is never any *pure* synonymy and that it is necessary to take the words' *use context* into account in order to decide the substitution of one term for another.

Now, the very interest of a network of co-occurrences resides in the fact that there is no other definition of an actant than a contextual one, that is to say, in terms of the set of actants (or semantic field) it is associated with. Thus by working from a network of associations, we can in principle recover synonyms—at whatever degree of purity or impurity—without having to enter a dictionary into the computer. This quite clearly leads us to modify the definition of synonymy along the way, as always with the Hume machine, from a substantialist to an "existentialist" one. Two words are synonymous in the context formed by a given body of texts if they give rise to the same *association profile*. However, it is clear that with rare exceptions two words never have exactly the same profile. There are no pure synonyms. The small differences that have to be eliminated at great cost in the dictionary approach and by categories are all maintained in the approach by networks of co-occurrences. The richness of language is in its use context. Thus, paradoxically, a management in terms of association networks retains more richness than a classification by definition.

In the current model, we analyze the first Leximappe network using a second program called Vector, which compares not the keywords but their association profiles.[23] Thus we can recognize synonyms by the simple fact that two terms having neighboring association profiles are put side by side on the Vector map. If one is superposed on the other, then they are pure synonyms.

This approach even enables us to treat the implicit and the hidden or absent referent. Suppose that the set under consideration is made up of interviews with people who are talking about a thing that for some hidden reason they never actually mention explicitly. In our center, for example, everyone interrogated uses the word *Mac*; the researcher may not know what a Mac is. Looking at its association profile, the researcher will be able to reconstitute the semantic field of the hidden word *microcomputer* even if the word itself does not figure in any of the interviews. If the association profile is markedly different from the hidden word that the researcher believes it proper to substitute, then the burden of proof is on the researcher. Does he have the right to impute this hidden referent to interviewees, even though co-occurrence analysis does not justify the inference? Is a Mac the same thing as a microcomputer, or is it really something quite different? Here again, the retention of use contexts in the machine enables us to retain the "existentialist" richness that "essentialist" questions always impoverish—for us locally, a Mac is not *a* computer but *the* computer, and there is no way another type of computer could be the token of the general type "computer". A lot would be lost if this nuance were ignored.

From the example of synonymy, we can see the strategy of the Hume machine. Instead of invoking a weighty formalism that tries to store up thousands of particular dictionary rules in an effort to reduce ambiguities, we offer a disorderly accumulation of a body of whatever size and the rediscovery of fine nuances through a simple mapping of semantic fields. On the one side there are hundreds of rules that in the long run do not enable us to take the different uses of words into account, and on the other there are no rules but there is the contextual richness of use.

"The definition of categories necessarily depends on human intervention. In themselves raw data are scattered all over the place." On the contrary, the Hume machine finds it particularly easy to generate categories automatically. Even our prototype can already do this.

It is said that when we look at form compared to context, we find ourselves faced with "empirical" data void of all significance, dispersed. The role of the researcher is seen to be that of "putting things into order," imposing definitions, examining special cases. This strange duty does not exist when one is faced with a network, but then neither does empirical dispersion exist. When the form is nothing more than a condensation of the context, it is no longer necessary to follow Kant and impose categories on the shapeless dust of a stimulus. There are no brute facts, there are only researchers who brutalize their data. All one has to do is to ask the context itself to *designate* its own categories, by bringing out regroupings implicit in the network. The naming of the category can itself be made entirely automatic by a process of genuinely democratic *elections*—bottom-up, not top-down.

Our Candide model, using Vector, can already do this. Take a set of keywords whose co-occurrence has been calculated. We obtain a network of points and of tensors. This network enables us to detect *clusters*, that is to say, sets of points that have similar association profiles.[24] Is there one *macroterm* that can summarize the cluster better than any other? The machine holds elections, and designates the word or words whose association profile is closest to that of the cluster as a whole. This word, generally a composite one, henceforth serves to designate the whole of the network, looked at from a certain point of view. This nomination is entirely *revokable* and *reversible*. The chosen keyword is not a substance; it is simply the representative or the network node that will enable us during other treatments of the data to gain access to the category and through it to the network that alone gives it meaning. It is not, as used to be the case, the category alone that gives meaning to a scattered collection of data. On the contrary, it is the network alone that gives meaning to the category. Further, since the election is dependent on the point of view taken, one can always within a given network untangle the initial categories and tangle up the data into alternative ones for some other purpose.

Thus we can see the advantages to be gained from automating our procedures. In our own relativist or post-Garfinkel world, it has become impossible to define a category from above. We have to let the actants work out their own dimensions, liaisons, and relative weights. But the task of triangulation seems to be enormous. Once there are more than a few actants, how can we do enough "by hand" to respect the multiplicity of categories and of definitions of actants? It is only this practical difficulty that has made people reject the relativist (or better, relationist) consequences of network theories and of most ethnomethodological requirements. In the absence of material means for letting the actors organize themselves in their own way, researchers believe that they are forced to continue imposing their own metalanguage.

This procedure allows us to have at that same time, in the same machine, the hitherto contradictory advantages of nominalism and of categories. Indeed it is possible in our model to reaggregate the data using macroterms by obtaining clusters of clusters, up to any desired level of granularity. But since any category keeps a memory of its own engendering through a series of elections based on a particular and contingent list of associations, it is always possible to retrace one's steps and to rediscover any particular use context. It is this zoom and backtracking effect, so particular to modern network theories, that is the principal advantage of the Hume-Condillac Machine because it enables us to deal with large masses of heterogeneous data without splitting them up into micro and macro levels, into case studies and general theories, or into raw data and interpretations.

"There is no automatic treatment of written language that we can use to feed into the Hume machine from above." Yes, there is, provided we look at semantics rather than syntax. The prototype already does this to a degree.

It will be pointed out that vast bodies of texts are needed in order to get a word's semantic field or to get self-designated categories. Now, since there is no practical way of dealing with complete texts, it would appear that the Hume machine has merely displaced the problem from logic to linguistics. By claiming that language— texts and other written documents—can restore the context (whose logic is only a condensation of the network), we are still faced with the problem of dealing with language. Granted that the structure of language is infinitely more complex than the structure of formal logic, it is because of this complexity that it is less distant from the network of associations. Words are actants like any others.

It is possible to reduce syntax to semantics in the same way that we have reduced formal structures to particular instances of what is summarized in an association. It is also possible to reduce semantics to the list of trials each word actant is submitted to. Quite clearly this irreduction would be absurd if it involved going up against the richness of the language used in the interior of the many microtheories that make up linguistics. It is not a matter of reestablishing rules about the agreement of participles from a calculation of co-occurrences. Nor is it a question of rediscovering the relationship between volume and pressure in gases using a Leximappe network. The work of cognitivists notwithstanding, this is not our aim. The aim of the Hume machine is to travel *between* microtheories. It does not need any heavy equipment but needs just the bare minimum to enable it to produce meaningful statements about sets of texts in the absence of any microtheory. Like all explorers who have to carry the most food in the least space, the machine wants to be able to do this with a language concentrate. Contrary to AI systems goals, our goal is not to displace expertise from humans to machines but to let the machine develop a minimal expertise where no person has any.

One of the most radical ways of "concentrating" language is to keep only substantives and to consider all syntactical forms (verbs in particular) as configurations of word networks. In the sentence, "The cats eat the mice," we only take away with us the co-occurrence of cats and mice, and we ask the machine to restore the verb "to eat," if necessary, by recognizing the non-co-occurrence of "cats" and "mice." This procedure is not too efficient for the verb "to eat," which instantiates powerful microtheories, but is useful for exploring configurations of networks for which there are no verbs in the language, or for which existing verbs—"to be able to," "to cause," "to want," "to occupy," to "hold" (whether they are taken sociologically or logically)—do not suffice.

This simplification becomes crucial when it is complemented by the irreduction of substantives themselves. In effect, what we said about categories also applies to words. The model of the Hume machine treats all common words as proper nouns—extreme nominalism. But then, all proper nouns are macroterms elected by the network itself, that is, reversal of nominalism by the network. There is no definition of any word richer than the co-definition obtained by looking at the use context of all words associated with it.[25] In most social sciences, we need to operate in terms of networks because the multiplicity of points of view, of informants, of transformations can entail that a given name cannot be assigned to a particular person or institution. The same person can be successively designated in interviews by initials, by "Mr. Smith," "John," "the representative of the authorities," or by "industrialist." If the isotopy of this actor is in question—if the different words do not have the same association profile—there is nothing forcing the researcher to consider that nevertheless there is a single essence having different manifestations.[26] We are simply dealing with a "variable geometry" actor. If we wish to stabilize this actor, then we must work just as hard to maintain this isotopy as we would for any other actant.[27]

Here, as elsewhere, researchers do not have to decide. Nor do they expect the Hume machine to decide for them. Rather, they want it to help them maintain a state of variation, of opening, of a possible recomposition of the association network. Here again we can clearly see the abyss that separates our strategy from that of AI experts. We do not delegate the most rule-driven and formal parts of our actions and the surest of our knowledge to the machine while reserving fine-grained interpretation and ambiguous cases for ourselves. We use the machine to keep the system *open* as long as possible, by keeping for ourselves the tasks of putting things into categories and of locally closing microtheories. It is the computer that enables us to retain a "natural" form of intelligence, and ourselves who continue to produce "artificial," that is to say, closed, forms. While AI's delegations hardly help us at all except in managing existing microtheories from the inside, the new collaboration between the Hume machine and the researcher promises to be useful between microtheories.

Conclusion: An Aid to Narrative

In the preceding section, we showed that the network of co-occurrences forming the first layer of a Hume machine and the greater part of our model does not dissolve into chaos and enables us to keep open a great number of characteristics of the context. The network is much richer and much more differentiated than all "higher" terms, which in fact have no other content than the network they summarize or condense.

Let us note at this point that any model of the Hume machine, however primitive and of whatever early version, is already a valuable tool for our declared aim: to help researchers in the social sciences mobilize masses of heterogeneous data in the form of full texts. Even a machine that could merely let us range over a set of categorizations and synonyms in a mass of interviews is already extremely useful.

However, in the preceding section, we spoke only of researchers' doing the work of simplification, of expressing in terms of microtheories. They only asked the machine to produce reversible categories and to keep the system open. The machine is an extreme empiricist; the researchers are the microtheorists. Now there are two ways that we can present the advantages of the Hume machine. The first is that it is effective because it enables researchers to keep their microtheories reversible. This is the cut-rate version. The second is that it is effective because it itself can produce microtheories. This is the upmarket version, and it is this version that enables the Hume machine to compete on their own terms with the "scientific discovery" programs reviewed by Thagard.[28] Like Condillac's statue, the Hume machine must learn to recognize network configurations by itself. We want to progress from a primitive model to advanced ones. In order to do so, the machine must not simply keep the association network open but must also contribute to closing it. This becomes essential once the number of databases increases. It must be able to serve its apprenticeship and initiate a new dialogue between researcher and machine, whereby it can test its interpretations of the state of the network. It should be able to propose microtheories locally, or at least to propose to the researcher a progressive passage from the unfolded, irreduced network to a condensed microtheory, and vice versa. This progressive and reversible passage is the essential feature of the upmarket version of the Hume machine. However, at this time we do not have any working model.

We can now see the direction taken by researchers interacting with more and more elaborate versions of our Hume machine. What is happening is that we are getting closer and closer to the techniques of *narrative*—an essential tool for historians, ethnologists, field sociologists, and naturalists—and to the description of association networks made up of a jumble of heterogeneous databases. In this fusion of qualitative literary qualities and the power of quantitative treatment, we expect a renewal of methods and explanations in the humanities. There is no more powerful explanation than the analysis of the contingent circumstances of association networks, but for the moment the only way of obtaining this form of meaning is through a narrative limited to narrow terrains. Until now the only remedy to this limitation was to go over to statistical tables and quantitative analyses. This was at the price of a rupture with the fine tissue of networks and circumstances, whence came the interminable debates between field sociology and the sociology of structures, between history and sociology, between economic history and economic theory, between arts and sciences, between history of science and model-building philosophy. The Hume machine opens an alternative route. It is *quali-quantitative*. Because it is not based on any particular innovation in material or programming, it can immediately begin to guide the construction of models, each of which will at once be of use to researchers in the humanities.

This workstation is a contribution to the debate that is taking shape between the cognitive sciences and the new sociology of science.[29] But instead of positing a sterile opposition between psychology and sociology, we propose to select from *within* each field those schools of thought that give rise to fruitful associations. Instead of restraining the context so as to enable the mind of the scientist or the computer to make discoveries limited to microtheories in complete isolation, we propose to choose each time the school of thought that enables us to follow the context in the most continuous and complete fashion. Just as Bloor and Collins's program—asymmetric, since it has a different treatment of society and nature—is badly adapted to the mentalist cognitive sciences as defined by Slezak and to Thagard's computer tools, so does the symmetrical program that we propose in the name of network theory seem well suited to the cognitive sciences as defined by the connectionists. All the debates about the construction of society, science, and psychology that cognitivists hoped to end, continue within cognitive science, within programming languages, within the sociology of science and technology, and probably within computers themselves.

Notes

1. See, for instance, Michel Callon, John Law, and Arie Rip, eds., *Mapping the Dynamics of Science and Technology* (London: Macmillan, 1986); and Bruno Latour, *Science in Action: How to Follow Scientists and Engineers through Society* (Cambridge, Mass.: Harvard University Press, 1987).

2. See Harry Garfinkel, *Studies in Ethnomethodology* (Englewood Cliffs, N.J.: Prentice-Hall, 1967); Michael Lynch, *Art and Artifact in Laboratory Science: A Study of Shop Work and Shop Talk in a Research Laboratory* (London: Routledge, 1985); Steve Woolgar, *Science: The Very Idea* (London:

Tavistock, 1988); Algirdas Julien Greimas, *On Meaning: Selected Writings in Semiotic Theory* (Minneapolis: University of Minnesota Press, 1976); and Algirdas Julien Greimas and Jean Courtès, *Semiotics and Language: An Analytical Dictionary* (Bloomington: Indiana University Press, 1982).

3. Howard Becker, *Art Worlds* (Berkeley: University of California Press, 1982).

4. Thomas P. Hughes, "The Seamless Web: Technology, Science, Etcetera, Etcetera," *Social Studies of Science* 16 (no. 2, 1986): 281–292.

5. As detailed in Bruno Latour, Philippe Mauguin, and Geneviève Teil, "Une méthode nouvelle de suivi des innovations: Le chromatographe," in *La Gestion de la recherche: Nouveaux problèmes, nouveaux outils*, ed. Dominique Vinck (Brussels: De Boeck, 1991), 419–480.

6. The Hume machine or Condillac's statue represents the associationist program, which we hope will thus be awakened from its "dogmatic sleep." It goes without saying that we are displacing the psychogenesis conjured by these two authors from people onto machines. What they say about humanity is not very likely, but Hume's vision of the formation of human understanding and Condillac's design for his statue should apply much better to the computers described here.

7. Carl Hewitt, "The Challenge of Open Systems," *BYTE* 10 (no. 4, 1985): 223–242.

8. See Andy Pickering, ed., *Science as Practice and Culture* (Chicago: University of Chicago Press, 1992); Wiebe Bijker and John Law, eds., *Shaping Technology—Building Society: Studies in Sociotechnical Change* (Cambridge, Mass.: MIT Press, 1992); and Wiebe Bijker, Thomas Hughes, and Trevor Pinch, eds., *The Social Construction of Technological Systems: New Directions in the Sociology and History of Technology* (Cambridge, Mass.: MIT Press, 1987).

9. For the present, we can summarize the analogy as follows. The two principles of calculability replace higher, structured cognitive capacities by a determined and systematic management of stupidity. They are strategies of weakness. The Hume machine is determinist but is not refutable because refutability can only occur within a microtheory.

10. Bruno Latour, "Irreductions," in *The Pasteurization of France*, trans. Alan Sheridan and John Law (Cambridge, Mass.: Harvard University Press, 1988).

11. *Actant* is a semiotic term used to replace the difference between actors, usually humans and objects. It designates anything that may be said to act in a story.

12. We borrow the term *microtheory* from Hewitt. He uses it to describe a set of formal rules in a closed system (e.g., the theory of relativity, calculation of sales tax, stock management programs). Clearly, this definition presupposes that there are no macrotheories. There are only local theories, whether these be theories of relativity, cosmology, or accounting rules. Thus the question is one of knowing if we can extend microtheories in order to help them survive in an open system, or if we need to profoundly modify the very way in which one microtheory is extended to reach another.

13. See Francisco Varela, Evan Thompson, and Eleanor Rosch, *L'inscription corporelle de l'esprit: Sciences cognitives et expérience humaine* (Paris: Le Seuil, 1993), for a similar irreductionist argument in terms of networks.

14. It would be just as absurd to try to make the Hume machine work within a given micro-theory as to ask modern astronomers to make their calculations by hand. But this very image is a case in point. It shows to what extent the development of computers has allowed us to demystify microtheories—whence their current name of microtheories. There has been a delegation of the act of calculation to blind automata. This is captured by the concept of "algorithm." Formal procedures are economical and mechanical; they are operative and operational. They no longer have the intellectual aura that made us look for the form or structure "beyond simple" empirical and contingent data. This materialization and banalization of operations that were once considered to be spiritual, or at least mental, is probably the most significant cultural effect of computers.

15. The aporia that Gödel arrived at—"Any formal system sufficiently rich to include arithmetic contains undecidable propositions"—which was so mortifying to formalists, is merely a consequence of the project of expanding microtheories to the set of open systems. The associationism proposed here does not lead to the same contradictions. The Hume machine is not bound by the incompleteness theorem. It produces interpretations in the form of networks of possibilities, not in the form of a microtheory. Thus it is neither complete nor indeterminist. Far from being contradictory, it can be applied to the very theory of open systems without taking refuge in a meta-language that would close them. The theory is therefore reflexive. See Steve Woolgar, *Knowledge and Reflexivity: New Frontiers in the Sociology of Knowledge* (London: Sage, 1988).

16. For the first, see Edward Feigenbaum, Pamela McCorduck, and H. Penny Nii, *The Rise of the Expert Company: How Visionary Companies Are Using Artificial Intelligence to Achieve Higher Productivity and Profit* (New York: Times Books, 1989). For the second, see Harry Collins, *Artificial Experts: Social Knowledge and Intelligent Machines* (Cambridge, Mass.: MIT Press, 1990); Hubert L. Dreyfus, *What Computers Still Can't Do* (Cambridge, Mass.: MIT Press, 1992); and Terry Winograd and Fernando Florès, *Understanding Computers and Cognition: A New Foundation for Design* (Norwood, N.J.: Ablex, 1986).

17. Brian C. Smith, *On the Origin of Objects* (Cambridge, Mass.: MIT Press, 1996).

18. Our procedure is linked to the ideas used in the field of neural nets and by connectionists. For example, see David E. Rumelhart, James L. McClelland, and the PDP Research Group, *Parallel Distributed Processing: Explorations in the Microstructure of Cognition* (Cambridge, Mass.: MIT Press, 1988). Neural nets very elegantly resolve certain difficulties in calculation and in form recognition by short-circuiting traditional stepwise and rule-bound programming. However, they presuppose the existence of highly structured forms either at the outset or in their output. Even if they offered certain advantages for programming the Hume machine, they have no way of resolving the basic problem of its architecture: there are no structured forms to start with, even to reward the net.

19. If one takes formalism to mean metalanguage, then it is clear that we ourselves have a meta-language for describing the Hume machine and for interacting with it. However, it is not formal in the strong sense of the word. An inspection of its inherent properties will never by itself enable one, to judge its correctness. Thus there are metalanguages that designate simple trajectories through the context, and stronger metalanguages (microtheories) that aim to substitute themselves for the context or to do without it.

20. This prototype already prefigures the workstation that we want to make of the Hume machine in the future. It is in current use as a tool in network analysis (in the fields of science policy, sociology of science, and the economy of networks, and more recently, in libraries). It works in a Hypercard environment on a Macintosh, using a tool for the indexing of keywords and a Leximappe program. It is already capable of treating large bodies of heterogeneous written documents. See the account of the Candide workstation by Geneviève Teil, "Candide: un outil de sociologie assistée par ordinateur pour l'analyse quantitative de gros corpus de textes," Ph.D. dissertation, École Nationale Supérieure des Mines de Paris, 1991.

21. The Leximappe program detects the occurrence of A and that it co-occurs with B, C, and Z. The Vector program analyzes this first list and looks to see that words Y, N, etc., also have B, C, and Z as "associates." The interest of such a profile is that it does not depend on the form of the network but on the contingent nature of the keywords that are in fact linked to a particular word.

22. Bertrand Michelet, Ph.D. dissertation, Université Paris 7 Denis-Diderot, 1988.

23. The vocabulary of automatic analysis, developed by working from large databases using slow programs, has already proved interesting. Take, for example, negation (see Jean Pierre Courtial and J. Pomian, "A System Based on Associational Logic for the Interrogation of Databases," *Journal of Information Science* 13 (no. 2, 1987): 91–97); judgments about central research, dense research, peripheral research (see Michel Callon, Jean-Pierre Courtial, and Françoise Lavergne, *La Méthode des mots associés: Un outil pour l'évaluation des programmes publics de recherche. Etude pour la National Science Foundation* (Paris: École des Mines, 1989); the answer "question well put, question badly formulated, peripheral question" and "A and B are in competition" (see Teil, "Candide").

24. See Callon, Law, and Rip; and Michelet.

25. This formulation is simply a transcription into network language of Saussure's definition in terms of structure. Its only advantage is that it allows us to do away with the notion of structure, a notion that is too far-fetched for the Hume machine and in any case not accessible by the model.

26. The Hume machine does not make any assumptions about essences. It considers that all the co-occurrences of a single word are simply homonyms, which are then considered in the analysis of the network to see if they are synonyms or not.

27. For the practical means of following this geometry, see Latour, Mauguin, and Teil, "Une méthode"; and Bruno Latour, Philippe Mauguin, and Geneviève Teil, "A Note on Sociotechnical Graphs," *Social Studies of Science* 22 (no. 1, 1992): 33–59, 91–94.

28. Paul Thagard,*Conceptual Revolutions* (Princeton, N.J.: Princeton University Press, 1992).

29. Peter Slezak, "Scientific Discovery by Computer as Empirical Refutation," *Social Studies of Science* 19 (no. 4, 1989): 563–600.

Knowing Subjects: AI from Feminist Philosophy

Alison Adam

The historical threads of symbolic AI woven through philosophy of mind, epistemology, psychology, and formal logic are well known. In this chapter I want to focus on the epistemology of symbolic AI as one of the most fundamental of those threads. Many commentaries and critiques of AI explore epistemological concerns. For instance, Collins's critique of expert systems focuses on their inability to capture tacit knowledge. Dreyfus's argument that symbolic AI is doomed to failure rests on its inability to represent "knowing how" knowledge as opposed to "knowing that" knowledge.[1] The design of Brooks's situated robots is predicated on the belief that symbolic representation is the wrong way to go about imbuing an intelligent artifact with knowledge of its world.[2] The knowledge that can or cannot be represented in AI systems, and just how such knowledge can be represented, is clearly of much concern to AI.

While critics debate the hows and whys of the way that knowledge and knowing are imparted to AI systems, they rarely challenge the traditional epistemology on which AI is founded. However, I want to argue that particular things follow from exposing and exploring the epistemology embodied in symbolic AI. Most important, undertaking such a process shows that the AI we have is not a fixed and immutable discipline; things could have been different. If it can be shown that symbolic AI is built upon the implicit epistemic hierarchies of traditional epistemology, we should look toward tools that can make this explicit and then see what follows. The particular tool I use to explore the implications of a traditional epistemology derives from feminist philosophy. In keeping with all branches of the feminist movement, much of the job of feminist philosophy is to expose inequalities, challenge hegemonic views and "re-read the canon," particularly with regard to the subordinate position of women.[3] Within feminist philosophy, feminist epistemology offers a re-reading of the tenets of traditional epistemology. If, as I claim, traditional epistemology is the epistemology of symbolic AI, feminist epistemology may offer us an interesting and novel critique of the AI project, in particular, to show ways in which women's knowledge has been excluded in favor of a middle-class, professional, masculine view. This implies that a critique from

AI EPISTEMOLOGY IS GENDERED?

feminist epistemology is more than just a philosophical exercise. In exposing the hierarchy of knowers, structures that also exclude groups other than women, it forms a political agenda. To expose inequalities means that there must be possibilities for change.

This chapter describes the challenge of feminist epistemology under two major headings: the knowing subject and the knowledge that subject has. Of course, the two are not readily separable—what you know depends crucially on who you are. However, I want to concentrate on the knowing subject in what follows. Part of the reason for this involves space considerations. But, more important, I also believe that problematizing the implicit knowing subject of AI through the lens of feminist epistemology reveals elements of the nature of that implied subject that have rarely been exposed in commentaries on AI. By contrast, some of the best-known critiques of AI have focused on the nature of the knowledge that it claims to represent. As a phenomenologist, Hubert Dreyfus argues that symbolic AI will fail because it cannot tackle "knowing how" type knowledge. AI's focus is on propositional, or "knowing that," knowledge, which only makes up a small part of our ways of knowing. Like Dreyfus, Harry Collins acknowledges the importance of culture in the making of knowledge, but much of his critique also revolves round the ability or otherwise of machines to represent various types of knowledge. As I have argued elsewhere, a feminist approach is broadly compatible with Collins's and Dreyfus's arguments on the nature of knowledge; indeed it can be used to extend their arguments considerably.[4] However, neither Collins nor Dreyfus spells out what is meant by culture; culture acts as some analyzed variable, and this means that they have little to say about the nature of the agent or subject doing the knowing. But, I argue, in epistemology the subject is where we should start.

My discussion of feminist epistemology is followed by a brief outline of traditional epistemology, which emphasizes its problematic elements. My question is then, How can we see traditional epistemology at work in symbolic AI? As AI does not wear its epistemology on its sleeve, this is no easy task and requires some detective work. The best approach is to look for the knowing subject in examples of real AI systems. I have chosen two flagship AI projects, Cyc and Soar.[5] Taking these in turn, I explore the tacit conception of the knowing subject in each and relate these to the subject of traditional epistemology. This exposes the way in which these major AI projects, following the lead of traditional epistemology, cast their knowing subject implicitly as an individualistic, rationalist, universal man of reason.

Feminist Epistemology

In thinking about the ways in which feminist epistemology can inform a critique of AI, I argue that the epistemology of AI is gendered, that is, it embodies a tacit masculine norm that requires to be rendered visible. As AI itself is the computational domain that deals with knowledge and the simulation of knowing, a clear view of the ways in which women's knowledge may or may not be represented or excluded, and the ways in which the subject of the knowledge, or the knower, is made visible or invisible, are both crucial to an understanding of how gender is involved in the design and building of AI systems. As I have suggested, there is a definite contrast to be made between feminist epistemology and a more traditional orientation. This contrast has been highlighted by a number of feminist epistemologists.[6] I want to introduce this distinction in this section, and pick up points of contrast in the following section on traditional epistemology to elaborate in relation to certain important aspects of the design of symbolic AI systems.

Feminist epistemology is the part of feminist philosophy, which directly challenges mainstream epistemology. As Linda Alcoff and Elizabeth Potter argue, feminist epistemology could be seen to be somewhat contradictory. This is because a major thread in feminist thinking involves an exploration of the multiplicity of women's ways of knowing, which is an alien process to many professional philosophers. The tendency of traditional epistemology to look for a unified theory of knowledge is challenged by feminist theorists, who argue against the possibility of producing an account of knowledge that ignores the cultural context and status of knowers.

There are particular ways in which feminist epistemology can be used in the present study. One of the most important elements involves subjectivity. Lorraine Code argues that traditional epistemology tends to ignore the subject, and this has developed into a position where knowledge is seen as universal and with no perspective, as Thomas Nagel puts it so aptly, a "view from nowhere."[7] This can be seen in the way that traditional epistemology casts the business of knowing in terms of "S knows that p" where S is a universal, perspectiveless, taken for granted, and not to be discussed subject, and p is a piece of propositional knowledge.

I argue that the major part of symbolic AI research is predicated on the "S knows that p" of traditional epistemology and that this is why feminist epistemology is such a useful tool in the analysis of the ways in which mainstream epistemology is built into AI theory and actual AI systems. Feminist epistemology challenges the S in "S knows that p" and also the p. Traditional epistemology emphasizes that examples of true knowledge are only to be found in propositional knowledge, or "knowing that," rather than in "knowing how." The knowing how/knowing that or propositional/skills distinction is not a new philosophical problem, nor is it new to AI. Gilbert Ryle's original analysis has been elaborated by Dreyfus to make a substantial challenge to the perceived success of AI.[8] But feminist analyses have a new way of looking at the propositional/skills distinction. The original elaborations miss the point because there is always some kind of hierarchy involved. In particular, knowing how is seen as subordinate to knowing that.[9] Indeed this distinction is a manifestation of the mind/body and rational/manual hierarchies of the enlightenment philosophical position. Traditional epistemology emphasizes propositional knowledge over skills knowledge, to the extent that skills knowledge is hardly regarded as knowledge at all. This *is* clearly a problem for feminism. Without trying to universalize women's experience, there are a number of examples of women's knowledge, from the past as well as the present, that cannot attain the status of knowledge because they are not and often could not be written down in a propositional form. Much of this type of knowledge has to do with bodies and the looking after of bodies, the traditional domain of women as opposed to men's life of the mind. For instance, Barbara Ehrenreich and Deirdre English point to the way in which nineteenth-century Western midwifery was wrested from the hands of "unqualified" and illiterate women midwives to become part of the masculine medical establishment.[10] This emphasizes the historical connection between women's ways of knowing as irrational and masculine knowing as rational and therefore superior. It is the rational component that is formalizable in AI systems.

As skill-type knowledge is associated with the body, this brings into question the role of the body as opposed to merely the mind in the making of knowledge. Feminist epistemology challenges the way in which traditional epistemology leaves out the body. If, as I argue later, symbolic AI adheres to a traditional epistemology, then we should scrutinize its treatment of bodily knowledge. In philosophy, the body has been more of interest to those working in the continental tradition than to those in the dominant Anglo-American analytical tradition. The role of the body in the making of knowledge has been a focus for only the few philosophers in the Anglo-American world who maintain a phenomenological persuasion, such as Mark Johnson, or linguists such as George Lakoff.[11] But feminist theory adds something more to the arguments of phenomenology, both by bringing a consideration of gender into bodily ways of knowing and by demonstrating that power hierarchies are involved.

The remarkable work of the "Women's Ways of Knowing" (WWK) collective stems from a slightly different feminist tradition, psychology and education, but nonetheless is very important in exploring some of the pragmatics of feminist epistemology. *Women's Ways of Knowing* has a similar flavor to Carol Gilligan's widely quoted *In a Different Voice*.[12] Gilligan's study of women's moral development was undertaken to challenge traditional ideas of morality, which assume that only men generally achieve the highest level of moral and ethical thinking. Similarly, *Women's Ways of Knowing* set out to challenge traditional views of states of knowing, based on a masculine norm taken from studies with only male subjects. I have found correspondences here, particularly where I challenge reasoning styles that are assumed universal in AI. This is a particular feature of the Soar system, which, as I describe later, encapsulates reasoning styles based on empirical data obtained almost entirely from male college students.

Traditional Epistemology

Feminist epistemology suggests that mainstream epistemology is problematic in certain important ways. I want to explore these briefly, to see whether the features of mainstream epistemology reemerge in the underlying epistemology of AI systems, particularly in relation to the knowing subject. There is a substantial list of points of contrast with feminist epistemology—the types of examples, the implicit individualism, the absence of any definition of *S* or "nonweirdness," and the cultural imperialism of such views. I examine these aspects before going on to see how they apply to the two example AI systems.

There are fundamental aspects of traditional epistemology that set it apart from feminist epistemology. The particular task here is to explore the ways in which traditional epistemology treats the knowing subject, and what is implied about perspectives other than those taken to be the norm.

Readers who are familiar with feminist and social science texts will find a plethora of formal principles in the texts of mainstream epistemology. More important, it is practically impossible to find extended real-world examples. These have been ignored in favor of either short, almost trivial examples or elaborate, impossible thought experiments.[13] Twin earths, speckled hens, and cats on mats seem a far cry from the ways of knowing explored by the WWK collective or Kathryn Pyne Addelson's epistemological research on contraception, abortion, teen pregnancy, and gay rights.[14]

There are particular reasons why the use of unrealistic examples is problematic even if they apparently make the philosophical points easier to understand. They are not as innocuous as they seem, and this is a point I elaborate in relation to the Cyc expert system. They bypass issues of collective responsibility and knowing, and play a significant part in maintaining the role of the individual, rationalist, universal, and simplified knower.

The way we frame our examples of knowledge and problem solving says important things about knowers. *S* and *p* are intimately entwined. A simplified *p*, described through almost trivial examples, means that the knowing subject, *S*, is also oversimplified. This constrains the subject to be an individual knower, where more complex, realistic examples demand a consideration of the web of relationships which connects *S* to other knowers. This points to one of the important arguments of feminist epistemology, namely, the argument against *S* as a single independent knower who knows independently of other people. An emphasis on the individual knower hides the role of culture in transmitting and defining knowledge.

Hence, knowing as an individual activity is a predominant theme in traditional epistemology. A major position in epistemology, although not necessarily the dominant view, termed *foundationalism*, places an emphasis on the evidences of the senses in the acquisition of knowledge. This both mirrors and is part of a widely held objectivist view, which Lakoff criticizes. In other words, such a position maintains that it is by means of perception that we obtain our primary information about the external things around us rather than by cultural transmission.[15] Reason, introspection and observation are the traditional foundations for knowledge under such a view, although protagonists of this stance would concede that clearly many things are known through routes other than these.[16] Many admit of at least some cultural component to knowl-edge. Nevertheless, the idea of knowledge obtained independently through the senses retains a strong hold—one that is at work in Cyc (see the following section).

In traditional mainstream epistemology the knower of knowledge, the *S* in "*S* knows that *p*," is taken to be universal. *He*, for there is no doubt that it is *he*, is an unanalyzed subject, one of us and, in particular, a *rational* one of us. Foley's *The Theory of Epistemic Rationality*, a classic work of traditional epistemology, paints an indirect picture of *S*. Foley's book is centered on the question of what is involved in its being epistemically rational for someone to believe a knowledge claim. Rationality here involves the indi-vidual's pursuing the goal of having true beliefs as opposed to false beliefs. This stems from an Aristotelian position that understands rationality in terms of a person's care-fully deliberating about how to pursue goals effectively and then acting accordingly. It is no accident that the planning/search paradigm of symbolic AI, of which the Soar system is a prime example, follows the line of Aristotelian goal seeking.

There is a built-in assumption that just as we will all agree about the character of *S*, so too will we all agree as to what is involved in careful deliberation or reflection. Foley argues that a plausible account of rational belief or action must be represented as an "account of judgments made from some nonweird perspective P about how effec-tively the beliefs or actions of an individual promote some nonweird goal G."[17] But, of course, he does not define *nonweirdness*. Nonweirdness acts in a regulative role; ratio-nality is to conform to some tacit normative definition. *Nonweird* is a strange epithet that defines a hierarchy of knowers—the nonweird at the top, the weird lower down.

Although Foley wants to preserve rationality as something separate from social groups, he describes the general principles of rationality as belonging to the "cultures with which we are familiar." Again there is no definition of a familiar culture. These principles include the idea that memory is generally reliable, that sense experience is generally a good guide to what physical objects are in our environment, and that past behavior of physical objects is a good guide to future behavior. These do not seem problematic, especially from the point of view of evolutionary biology. However, in a broad sweep of cultural imperialism, Foley adds, "Nothing that we now know about the variety of cultures here on earth gives us any general reason to be suspicious of the arguments that we in our culture are inclined to favor."[18]

Foley goes on to argue that even if we found a culture whose epistemic standards were radically different from ours, this would not lead us to be suspicious about our own standards—the implication is that we know best. Instead, it would suggest to us that other cultures can form epistemic arguments that are unlikely to be truth-preserving. For Foley, a truth-preserving argument is absolute and cannot be relative to a culture. Moreover, it is what we experience in *our* culture, whatever that is. This does appear to be an astonishingly chauvinistic view. It suggests on the one hand that we have a genetic predisposition toward epistemic rationality, although this presumably applies to every human being. On the other hand, Foley argues that this produces a culture against which other cultures can be measured and will be found inferior, at least in the epistemic sense. We will find arguments of the "our culture is unquestionably right" nature in the following sections on example AI systems. Code argues, in relation to traditional epistemology, with Foley's work as a prototype example,

In its assumed political innocence, it prepares the ground for the practices that make "knowledge" an honorific and ultimately exclusionary label, restricting it to the products of a narrow subset of the cognitive activities of a closely specified group.... The assumptions that accord S-knows-that-p propositions a paradigmatic place generate epistemologies that derive from a privileged subjective specificity to inform sociopolitical structures of dominance and submission.[19]

These, then, are the problematic aspects of traditional epistemology from the perspective of feminist epistemology. Excessively simplistic or otherworldly examples are problematic in themselves because they give no indication as to how they may scale up to examples drawn from the outside world. Additionally, simplified examples make the knower seem simple; they disguise the need to examine the complex web of relationships and responsibilities in which knowers do their knowing. In the absence of any definition of S, an individual, rational knower inspecting the world with *his* senses is assumed in the traditional view of epistemology exemplified by Foley's writing. And it is assumed that *we* all feel the same, that is, if we are viewing things from the same "nonweird" perspective. My contention is that this form of "we saying" is cultural imperialism writ large. It is not the *we* of all of us but is, rather, a hegemonic we, denying a plurality of views and branding as weird those who think otherwise. Addelson argues that this "we saying" gives some knowers "authority over others, as adults have authority over children. In this case the others' knowledge does not disappear, it is hidden. Hiding it sometimes means suppressing it or declaring it false or superstitious, but more often it means ignoring it or overlooking it."[20] The challenge is to uncover these problems in examples of real AI systems.

Cyc and the Knowing Subject

My first example of an AI system is Cyc, a ten-year project, originally due for completion in the mid 1990s, based in the Microelectronics and Computer Technology Corporation (MCC), which later became Cycorp. It is supported by huge grants from U.S. industry and is under the direction of Doug Lenat. The original aim of the project was to build a vast knowledge base covering most of human common sense or consensual knowledge. This is the kind of knowledge needed to understand a one-volume encyclopedia, which gives the project its name. The rationale for such a large project can be found in the way that most expert or knowledge-based systems are "brittle".[21] In other words, they do not cope well, or even at all, with situations outside the narrow range of their scope as they do not have the common sense that human beings have; they fail and hence are metaphorically brittle. They cannot communicate with one another as humans do, and the rules or knowledge from one system generally cannot be used in another. Although an expert system may work quite well in some bounded micro-world, it will not work outside its narrow range of competence. This has proved to be a perennial problem for AI. How do we simulate the human ability to respond appropriately to an infinite variety of often unpredictable situations, through that unique human quality of common sense?

Even if a program can be amended to take account of each individual novel situation, we can never be sure that there is not some other new problem we had not thought of just over the horizon. Lenat argues that the way out of this impasse is to equip expert systems with common sense, which he does not see as fundamentally different from the sorts of things expert systems know now. It is much, much more knowledge that expert systems need rather than a different type of knowledge altogether.

What can be said about the knowing subject in Cyc? In their detailed midproject description of Cyc, Lenat and his colleague Guha make little explicit reference to those whose knowledge is to be represented in the system. Just as the consensual knowledge itself is to be taken for granted, so it seems are those who possess such knowledge, "be they a professor, a waitress, a six-year-old child, or even a lawyer."[22] This is one of the very few places where a subject is mentioned at all, albeit humorously, and is a very expansive form of "we saying."

Clearly, some detective work is needed to uncover the subjects of Cyc's knowledge. I have argued that there is a strong relationship between the type of knowledge represented and the subject who is doing the knowing. This suggests that in the case of Cyc, where the nature of knowing subjects is not made explicit, it may be possible to work backward from knowledge to subject. In Cyc a clue may be found in the way that different theories on the same theme, or multiple models in the design of Cyc, are dealt with. In the following paragraphs I explore the implications of the multiple models concept in Cyc. My argument is that Cyc's multiple models are not and cannot be neutral. This argument has two parts. First, I claim that it is not possible to design models that are neutral representations of some real world. Second, and following from this, the models reflect and privilege the viewpoint of the developers of Cyc, and that viewpoint is the one of a middle-class, Western, professional man.

Just as human beings use their common sense to cope with contradictory information, Cyc must be able to do the same through a scheme of multiple models. For instance, I might use Newtonian mechanics in the physics classroom but use Aristotelian mechanics to cope with the rest of the world. Multiple models of objects are also needed where there are different theories of the same system, for instance, Marxist economic theory and the capitalist model. The multiple model representation seems to come into play when there is more than one model of some part of the world and the models are judged to be of similar intellectual status.

There are two reasons Cyc needs to represent multiple models. First, although Cyc might believe one of these views, it won't be able to understand the actions of others who believe the other view unless it knows about the alternative. So, for instance, Cyc might believe in capitalism, but at the same time it needs to know about Marxism. Second, supposedly *the state of the real world* shows that it is not possible to rely upon one model in a number of disciplines, such as economics and weather forecasting.

But there are several assumptions underlying the multiple models concept. The two I want to explore are Cyc's problematic relationship to a supposed real world, and the way that multiple models disguise a problematic epistemic hierarchy.

Cyc's designers are firmly attached to the idea that one can have access to the state of the real world through our sense perceptions. This is a pervasive notion in AI. It reflects the view that there is an independent world that can be accessed through perception and that everyone will agree on what the real world is like. Diana Forsythe describes how the knowledge engineers in her study of AI laboratories would, from time to time in discussion, point out the window when they referred to the "real world."[23] So Cyc has been developed within a point of view that assumes it is possible to access a real world about which we will all agree, or at least, those of us holding a nonweird perspective might perhaps agree. In other words, Cyc's design is based on this very important aspect of foundationalist epistemology.

In addition, we must consider who will judge whether a theory has enough status to be a competing model of a given area. For economics, Marxism and capitalism might compete, but there are alternative low-growth and feminist models that might not even get a look in. We can see that political concerns may creep in if Cyc, depending so heavily on funding from successful capitalist enterprises, were to extol the virtues of capitalism. Rather than reflecting the common sense of all of us, Cyc's models of the world are hegemonic models, unconsciously reflecting the views of those in powerful, privileged positions.

In talking of economics, Lenat appeals to a kind of intellectual folklore, that we all know economics to be inexact. As with weather forecasting, we are never quite sure about what is going to happen. In other words, the "we saying" that is going on assumes we will all agree when multiple models are necessary, that is, we will all agree when things are inexact like economics, and even so there is no guarantee that the multiple models available in the system would represent all the possibilities. If we are going to agree when some areas are perceived to be inexact and therefore requiring multiple models, then it is but a short step for us to agree that some other area is exact enough not to require multiple models.

There is a supposed real world to be brought into play for situations when we cannot agree. But whose version of the real world is going to be used? Cyc could be used to

bolster all sorts of unpleasant views in the name of a real world about which we all supposedly agree.

In Cyc a distinction is made between knowledge and beliefs, where knowledge has a higher status than belief. Here we start to see possibilities for uncovering the status of different subjects. Anything an agent knows can be true or just a belief. Of course, a belief can be supported by what are claimed to be direct physical observations of the real world, as already mentioned, or by other agents holding similar beliefs. So the more people who apparently believe something, the more chance it has of achieving the status of knowledge, perhaps. Now we start to see deeply buried ideas about subjects that are contained in Cyc: "*Cobelieving communities* make it easy to propagate rumors, prejudice, and superstition."[24] Beliefs are to represent minority opinions, and they are tagged as beliefs in the system. Entries without belief tags are designated knowledge, which has a higher status than belief so does not need to be tagged. As this kind of *real* knowledge is meant to be the sort of thing that everyone knows, the authors of the knowledge are difficult to uncover—they are meant to be all of us. But when pressed, Cyc's builders admit that it is a view belonging to the-world-as-the-builders-of-Cyc-believe-it-to-be, very little of which is allegedly questionable because it contains facts such as "People have two arms and two legs" or is "Americana" as in "You are not likely to get a speeding ticket in mid- or late-twentieth century America if you're driving less than 5 mph over the speed limit."[25] But here is Foley's "nonweird" turning up again. The builders of Cyc assume that they themselves have an epistemologically authoritative, "nonweird" perspective on true knowledge of the world. Cyc's "prejudice-propagating co-believing communities" are, at least potentially, the equivalent of weird perspectives, under Foley's view.

I have already argued that simple unrealistic examples help to reinforce such a view in traditional epistemology. In Cyc the same thing is going on. Lenat and Guha use such trivial examples that it is hard to dispute them. I am tempted to argue that only a member of the prejudice-propagating co-believing community of academic feminism would query examples about speeding tickets. But if we dig around this apparently trivial example, some interesting questions emerge that suggest these examples are not as innocuous as they seem. Do more men than women get stopped for speeding? Are more people of color stopped? Are more young men than old men given tickets? As I write, there is much discussion in the British press about the way the police seem far more likely to stop or question a black person than a white person.

Such examples help the builders of Cyc reinforce a position on which it appears everyone agrees. This reflects a very traditional epistemological position. But were they to choose more complex examples, I argue, it would be much more difficult to maintain a stance with which we all appear to agree.

Cyc's examples might seem innocuous at first sight, but what happens if other untagged and therefore unquestioned knowledge, particularly of a more normative nature saying how people *ought* to be, is put into the system? Cyc could perhaps assert things about how people from different races should behave, or about the nature of women or children, or about what rights should be given to people with disabilities— all under the rubric of consensual knowledge. It is just assumed that what constitutes true knowledge over mere belief is to be decided by the-world-as-the-builders-of-Cyc-believe-it-to-be.

Cyc is an example of what Code has described as the universal knowing subject, or the "view from nowhere," being used potentially to discount views that are "crazy," or "weird" in Foley's terms, or one of Lenat's minority beliefs.[26] This also supports what she suggests is a hierarchy of knowers' perspectives where the perspective of the group at the top is accorded higher status than those of the groups lower down. This assumption is so taken for granted that the authors hardly need to state it. Middle-class, male, professional knowledge informs the-world-as-the-builders-of-Cyc-believe-it-to-be. Hopes that such a world might be available in a global knowledge base look very like the cultural imperialism of Foley's view on traditional epistemology.

The consensual knowledge of Cyc is intended to be knowledge with which we all agree, to the extent that we do not even consciously make an agreement; we just take the knowledge for granted, the we being healthy, sane, nonbabies with good eyesight and in a good light. But who will decide on our health and sanity? Even being a non-baby is a matter for negotiation; for instance, the minimum age for criminal liability varies from country to country and is the subject of some debate. In Cyc there is an assumption that we are all the same, that we are all capable of independently inspecting the real world and coming to the same conclusions about it, at least as long as we live up to the prescribed norms of health and sanity. This is also a feature of Soar, which I describe in the following section. There is an assumption that cultural histories play little or no part and that individuals' movements through their own histories, other than being a nonbaby (which is surely an admission that common sense has something to do with age), has no bearing on what is counted as consensual knowledge at different stages in those histories.

Soar and the Knowing Subject

I argue that the Soar system provides another example of a large-scale, prominent AI project where the "view from nowhere" disguises a white, male, middle-class perspective.[27] Soar was the brainchild of Allen Newell, a leading light in the early days of symbolic AI, and two of his formal doctoral students, John Laird and Paul Rosenbloom.[28] The name Soar was originally an acronym for State, Operator, and Result, to reflect the way in which all problem solving in Soar is regarded as a search through a problem space in which an operator is applied to a state to get a result. Over time the Soar community no longer came to regard it as an acronym, which is why it is no longer written in uppercase. It is a direct descendant of the earlier Logic Theorist and GPS systems developed by Allen Newell and Herbert Simon. Soar solves problems that are framed as goals by the method of searching for a solution through a defined problem space, or set of problem states, formal descriptions of the whole state of the problem. It is very much in the mold of the planning/searching type of system widely found in symbolic AI. Soar was originally developed to solve logic-type problems and was later extended to a number of other domains, including learning, natural language processing, and as application domains, traffic and various types of tactical air simulations. Cyc emphasizes lots of knowledge. By contrast, Soar emphasizes architecture. Based on Newell and Simon's earlier empirical studies on problem-solving psychology, it was proposed by Newell as a candidate for a *unified theory of cognition* in his book of the same name. So it is part of the drive from symbolic AI to develop computation theories of psychology.

Soar derives from Newell and Simon's collaboration from their early AI systems through the publication of their vast *Human Problem Solving* in 1972,[29] and a later parting of the ways. Soar's intellectual parentage derives from *Human Problem Solving*, and several important features about the nature of the implied knowing subject emerge in the process of tracing this lineage. I argue that an exploration of the text gives many clues to the way that concepts emerged that gradually became taken for granted in Soar in the shape of "psychological facts which have been well known for thirty years or more".[30] Whatever the problems with the paucity and type of examples in *Human Problem Solving*, it became so well accepted in AI circles, because it was so influential in spawning the whole area of search techniques, that Newell was readily able to take its findings for granted in his later work on Soar.

Human Problem Solving is a study of the way people think. It describes a theory of human problem solving along with empirical evidence to support it. It rests on two distinct psychological approaches. The first involves the move away from behaviorism, which said little about internal states, concentrating instead on external behavior. This move requires being explicit about symbolic mechanisms in cognition, an approach evident in psychology in the decades after World War II. This was coupled with developments in computer science suggesting that it was reasonable to understand thinking in terms of an information-processing or computational theory. It is difficult to overstate the importance of the computational theory of cognition, which is the bedrock of symbolic AI, and hence *Human Problem Solving*'s influence in establishing it. The empirical evidence on which these claims are based—recalling that this strongly informs later work—has some rather interesting features.

The subjects in the empirical study carried out a number of exercises, but these were of a very restricted form. They included symbolic logic, chess, and cryptarithmetic puzzles. The best-known of these is the infamous problem DONALD+GERALD=ROBERT, where given that D=5, the aim is to find which numbers the other letters stand for.

It was perhaps only natural that the smart young men developing ideas in this area should look for their theories of human problem solving to the kinds of activities (chess, logic puzzles) in which they felt they did well and that defined them as smart. Although Soar has been broadened to many more practical domains, its theoretical underpinnings rest on empirical work with features that invite question.

There are detailed descriptions in *Human Problem Solving* of subjects' problem-solving protocols. However, very little about the nature of the subjects in this exercise is revealed explicitly in the book. This appears to be unintentional: the authors did not think it important. Once again some detective work reveals features of the implied subjects. We cannot tell exactly how many experimental subjects there were because this is not recorded and because of the numbering system used. Explicit mention is made of between 12 and 20 subjects at most.

Newell and Simon do not think that features such as age are important—they mention this. But gender and ethnicity do not get a look in; they are invisible. Almost all subjects appear to be students from the Carnegie Institute of Technology (later Carnegie Mellon University).[31] All the subjects were male. Now, this is not stated explicitly, but it is possible to deduce this from the way that each individual subject is referred to as *he* in some place in the text, and because each *he* refers to a specific individual, it can be inferred that the term is not generic and really does refer to the gender of the individual in question. Only one subject was not college-educated, and he was not able to solve the cryptarithmetic problem.[32] Although the detail need not concern us here, most of the subjects used a problem-solving technique that Newell and Simon characterize as the one used by most "technically educated people."[33] Newell commented somewhat wistfully in his later book *Unified Theories of Cognition* that his then-20-year-old subjects would now be well advanced into middle-age.[34] This makes it reasonable to infer that the subjects were fairly young at the time. Can we assume that they were white and middle-class, too? I argue that it is reasonable to assume that a majority of them were, given the substantial cost of attending an elite U.S. university.

All this evidence suggests that the theory of human problem solving developed in the book, which has strongly influenced not just the development of Soar but of symbolic AI in general, is based on the behavior of a few technically educated, young, male, probably middle-class, probably white college students working on a set of rather specialized tasks in a U.S. university in the late 1960s and early 1970s. I argue that if the particular attributes of the subjects genuinely do not matter, then they have to be shown not to matter and that this clearly has not been done. Soar incorporates a "view from nowhere" in that we are all expected to behave like these subjects in our problem solving under "normal" circumstances. Yet it is in fact a view from somewhere, the somewhere being the youthful college years from the 1960s of the now middle-aged, white, male college graduates.

Hence I argue that the physical subjects from the original Newell and Simon studies were actually technically able young men. But what of the conceptual subject of Soar? In taking up these studies as a basis for its theory of cognition, Soar rests on the concept that the described behavior is the norm. It is the tacit acceptance of male-as-norm that permeates traditional epistemology and of which feminist epistemologists are so critical. So, perhaps it is not surprising that Newell and Simon do not even have to state it explicitly, so much is it taken for granted, and we can only uncover it by a process of textual detection. Nevertheless, I think it is fair to ask whether it really matters whether the subjects solving the problems were male or female or whether there is evidence to suggest that if the subjects had been female, or black, or old, they would have solved the problems in a different way. Certainly in these examples, as Newell and Simon themselves argue, the characteristics of the particular problem heavily constrain the way an individual can solve it. Other than by a very lucky guess, it probably can only be solved in one of the ways they suggest, if it is to be solved at all. Once again this demonstrates that artificial, constrained, simple problems make the knowing subjects look simple—in this case, the problem makes the variations in the characteristics of the subjects seem unimportant: everyone seems the same. But if more realistic examples for problem solving had been chosen, I argue, the characteristics of the subjects would have had to be considered. Other commentators have noted this point:

One can easily imagine how the choice of this unnatural task shaped the early formulations of Soar in such a way that the notions of search and problem spaces became the cornerstones of the Soar architecture. What would have the theory looked like if the task chosen had been more naturalistic, for example, summarizing a newspaper article or explaining why the U.S. should or shouldn't have got involved in the Persian Gulf war? Here is a clear case of Newell falling into the same trap that has plagued psychological theorizing for so long: a bad choice of task leading to a bad choice of theory.[35]

In addition to the assumption that rationality involves motivation toward establishing goals, a kind of biological norm is also expected. All sorts of biological things are regarded by Newell and Simon as affecting behavior, including drowsiness, illusions, afterimages, ringing in the ears, and of course, individual differences such as hearing acuity, which can substantially affect an individual's behavior. "But a *normal situation* is precisely one in which these biological limits are not exceeded, and it is to such normal situations that the theory of this book applies."[36] This starts to look like Foley's "nonweirdness." There is also an assumption that it is possible to define unequivocally biological things, as opposed to cultural things, which affect behavior. Trying to establish a firm line between what is biological/medical and what is taken to be social in origin is extremely problematic, if not impossible.

The idea that problems determine the problem-solving behavior of their subjects becomes questionable when we look at more realistic examples. Cryptarithmetic, logic problems, and chess have at least some of the characteristics of the unrealistic problems traditionally posed in traditional epistemology. They are different from speckled hens and twin earths in that cryptarithmetic problems and chess can at least be seen as games, which can be played for recreational purposes, but nevertheless they are similar in that they are bounded, unrealistic problems and serve to disguise the characteristics of their owners.

Using problems such as these means that the male-as-norm need never be challenged. Indeed Newell and Simon's "normal situation" clearly resembles Foley's "nonweird" perspective, which is necessary for believing the same thing and which defines a marker for rationality. It is also reminiscent of Lenat's healthy, sane nonbabies. As part of their view of rationality, Newell and Simon make fleeting mention of properly motivated subjects. *Proper* motivation means the motivation to undertake cryptarithmetic problems or to rise to the challenge of a chess game, even where there is no opponent. If you would rather not do cryptarithmetic problems because you prefer the challenge of solving some more interesting real-life problem, or if you just do not have time because you are cooking dinner, then you might not be properly motivated. If a normal situation excludes, say, having influenza, ringing in the ears, or double vision as factors impairing your problem-solving abilities, then how about premenstrual stress or the menopause, hormonal influences often used to explain women's taken-for-granted irrationality. One is reminded of the Victorian notion that women were supposed to be incapable of higher thought because of their reproductive systems. No one speaks like that now, but where do we draw the line? The point about the definition of a "normal" situation that is implied in these examples is that it is not a definition everyone has had a democratic share in constructing. It is a norm constructed for us by a group of hegemonic knowers.

In addition to these considerations, it is clear that the types of problems used in *Human Problem Solving* and carried through into Soar and beyond are seen as problems to be solved solely by individuals, each acting on his (and it is his) own. It is a view of problem solving highly dependent on individual psychology and an educational system that prizes the development of skills in artificial logic-type problems. Such a view does not regard collective problem solving, or the "Women's Ways of Knowing" style of *connected knowing*, as an appropriate type of activity for investigating human cognition.

This AI view of problem solving involves subjects working on their own without a sense of their connection to others; bits of that background can only be uncovered by detective work on the text. How would the "properly motivated" young college students of the 1960s feel about solving these problems now? Perhaps their growth to maturity would motivate them rather to ponder solutions to problems of health, pollution, the Middle East crisis, or the future their children might experience.

Conclusion

In this chapter it has not been my intention to make claims about the potential failure or otherwise of symbolic AI, à la Dreyfus, because of AI's inability to represent some types of knowledge. Rather, my aim has been to uncover some of the tacit forces at work in shaping fundamental aspects of AI by bringing concepts from feminist theory to the discussion of AI, and particularly noting the role that epistemology plays. Of course, the picture I paint is not very rosy. I am claiming that women's knowledge (and potentially the knowledge of others) is unconsciously left out of consideration in the AI world. This means that the knowers and the knowledge represented in symbolic AI reflect only a small number of people but nonetheless those traditionally at the top of many hierarchies, namely, white, professional men. Given these considerations, it is, of course, hard to imagine what a different AI would look like, one *not* built on the principles I have described as existing at present. Nevertheless I hope that in exposing these issues I have highlighted the possibility that a different AI, one more inclusive and less reflective of traditional hierarchies of knowledge, is at least possible.

Notes

1. Hubert L. Dreyfus, *What Computers Still Can't Do: A Critique of Artificial Reason* (Cambridge, Mass.: MIT Press, 1992).

2. Rodney A. Brooks, "Intelligence Without Representation," *Artificial Intelligence* 47 (1991): 139.

3. There is even a "Re-reading the Canon" series published by Pennsylvania State University Press.

4. See Alison Adam, *Artificial Knowing: Gender and the Thinking Machine* (London: Routledge, 1998).

5. See Douglas B. Lenat and R. V. Guha, *Building Large Knowledge-Based Systems: Representation and Inference in the Cyc Project* (Reading, Mass.: Addison-Wesley, 1990); Paul Rosenbloom, "A Brief History of the Soar Project," in Soar FAQs: Soar Frequently Asked Questions List, ⟨http://www.psyc.nott.ac.uk/users/ritter/soar-faq.html⟩.

6. See Linda Alcoff and Elizabeth Potter, eds., *Feminist Epistemologies* (London: Routledge, 1993), esp. Lorraine Code, "Taking Subjectivity into Account," 15–48.

7. See Lorraine Code, *Epistemic Responsibility* (Hanover, N.H.: University Press of New England, 1987); Lorraine Code, *What Can She Know? Feminist Theory and the Construction of Knowledge* (Ithaca, N.Y.: Cornell University Press, 1991); Code, "Taking Subjectivity into Account"; Lorraine Code, *Rhetorical Spaces: Essays on Gendered Locations* (London: Routledge, 1995); Thomas Nagel, *A View from Nowhere* (Oxford: Oxford University Press, 1986).

8. See Gilbert Ryle, *The Concept of Mind* (London: Hutchinson, 1963); Hubert L. Dreyfus, *What Computers Can't Do: The Limits of Artificial Intelligence*, rev. ed. (New York: Harper and Row, 1979).

9. Vrinda Dalmiya and Linda Alcoff , "Are 'Old Wives' Tales' Justified?" in *Feminist Epistemologies*, ed. Alcoff and Potter, 217–244.

10. Barbara Ehrenreich and Deirdre English, *For Her Own Good: 150 Years of the Experts' Advice to Women* (London: Pluto Press, 1979).

11. Mark Johnson, *The Body in the Mind: The Bodily Basis of Meaning, Imagination, and Reason* (Chicago: University of Chicago Press, 1987); George Lakoff, *Women, Fire and Dangerous Things: What Categories Reveal about the Mind* (Chicago: University of Chicago Press, 1987).

12. Mary Field Belenky, Blythe McVicker Clinchy, Nancy Rule Goldberger, and Jill Mattuck Tarule, *Women's Ways of Knowing: The Development of Self, Voice and Mind* (New York: HarperCollins, 1986); Carol Gilligan, *In a Different Voice: Psychological Theory and Women's Development* (Cambridge, Mass.: Harvard University Press, 1982).

13. For an introduction to traditional epistemology, see Paul A. Boghossian, "Externalism and Inference," in *Rationality in Epistemology*, ed. Enrique Villanueva (Atascadero, Cal.: Ridgeview, 1992), 11–28; Roderick M. Chisholm, *Theory of Knowledge* (Englewood Cliffs, N.J.: Prentice-Hall, 1989); Richard Foley, *The Theory of Epistemic Rationality* (Cambridge, Mass.: Harvard University Press, 1987); Stephen Schiffer, "Boghossian on Externalism and Inference," in *Rationality in Epistemology*, ed. Villanueva, 29–37.

14. Kathryn Pyne Addelson, *Moral Passages: Toward a Collectivist Moral Theory* (London: Routledge, 1994).

15. See Chisholm, *Theory of Knowledge*, 39; Ernest Sosa, *Knowledge in Perspective: Selected Essays in Epistemology* (Cambridge: Cambridge University Press, 1991), 2.

16. Sosa, 10.

17. Foley, 140.

18. Foley, 152.

19. Code, "Taking Subjectivity into Account," 22.

20. See Addelson, *Moral Passages*, 4.

21. Lenat and Guha, *Building Large Knowledge-Based Systems*, 3.

22. Lenat and Guha, xviii.

23. See Diana Forsythe, "Engineering Knowledge: the Construction of Knowledge in Artificial Intelligence," in *Social Studies of Science* 23 (1993): 445–477; and Diana Forsythe, "The Construction of Work in Artificial Intelligence," in *Science, Technology, and Human Values* 18 (1993), 4: 460–479.

24. Lenat and Guha, 284.

25. Lenat and Guha, 284.

26. See Code, "Taking Subjectivity into Account."

27. See Soar FAQs: Soar Frequently Asked Questions List, section G3.

28. See Rosenbloom, "A Brief History of the Soar Project."

29. See Allen Newell and Herbert Simon, *Human Problem Solving* (Englewood Cliffs, N.J.: Prentice-Hall, 1972).

30. Allen Newell, *Unified Theories of Cognition* (Cambridge, Mass.: Harvard University Press, 1990).

31. Newell and Simon, *Human Problem Solving*, 165.

32. Newell and Simon, 267.

33. Newell and Simon, 261.

34. Newell, *Unified Theories of Cognition*, 365.

35. Roger C. Schank and Menachem Y. Jona, "Issues for Psychology, AI, and Education: A Review of Newell's *Unified Theories of Cognition*," *Artificial Intelligence* 59 (1993): 378.

36. Newell and Simon, 866.

Humans, Machines, and the Structure of Knowledge

Harry M. Collins

Where and What Is Knowledge?: Two Spy Stories

Let's start by asking how knowledge is transferred. Consider a couple of light-hearted but revealing accounts. A comic strip in my possession concerns industrial espionage between firms that manufacture expert systems. One firm has gained a lead in the market by developing superexpert systems, and another firm employs a spy to find out how they do it. The spy breaks into the other firm's files, only to discover that they are capturing human experts, removing their brains, slicing the brains very thin, and inserting the slices into their top-selling model. (Capturing the spy, they remove and slice his brain, enabling them to offer a line of industrial espionage expert systems.)

Another good story—the premise of a TV film whose title I cannot remember—involves knowledge being transferred from one brain to another via electrical signals. A Vietnam veteran has been brainwashed by the Chinese with the result that his brain has become uniquely receptive. When one of those colander-shaped metal bowls is inverted on his head and joined via wires, amplifiers, and cathode ray displays to an identical bowl on the head of some expert, the veteran speedily acquires all the expert's knowledge. He is then in a position to pass himself off as, say, a virtuoso racing driver or champion tennis player, or whatever. Once he is equipped with someone else's abilities, the CIA can use him as a spy.[1]

Four Kinds of Knowledge

Symbol-Type Knowledge

The "double colander" model is attractive because it is the way we transfer knowledge between computers. When one takes the (symbol-type) knowledge from one computer and puts it into another, the second computer becomes identical to the first insofar as its abilities are concerned. Abilities are transferred between computers in the form of electrical signals transmitted along wires or recorded on floppy disks. We give one computer the knowledge of another every day of the week, the crucial point being that the hardware is almost irrelevant. If we think a little harder about the model as it applies to people, however, we begin to notice complications.

Embodied Knowledge

Let's imagine the Vietnam veteran having his brain loaded with the knowledge of a champion tennis player. He goes to serve in his first match—wham!—his arm falls off. He just doesn't have the bone structure or muscular development to serve that hard. And then, of course, there is the little matter of the structure of the nerves between brain and arm, and the question of whether the brain of the champion tennis player contains tennis-playing knowledge that is appropriate for someone of the size and weight of the recipient. A good part of the champion tennis player's tennis-playing knowledge is, it turns out, contained in the champion tennis player's body.[2] Note that in talking this way, tennis-playing knowledge is being ascribed to those with tennis-playing ability; this is the implicit philosophy of the Turing test and a useful way to go.

What we have here is a literalist version of what is called the embodiment thesis. A stronger form suggests that the way a person cuts up the physical world is a function of the shape of her body. Thus, how she recognizes a chair, say—something notoriously undefinable—is a function of her height, weight, and the way her knees bend. Thus both the way we cut up the world and our ability to recognize the cuts are functions of the shape of our bodies.[3]

We now have the beginnings of a classification system. Some types of knowledge/ability/skill cannot be transferred simply by passing signals from one brain or computer to another. In these types of knowledge the hardware is important. There are other types of knowledge that can be transferred without worrying about hardware.

Embrained Knowledge

Some aspects of the abilities/skills of human beings are contained in the body. Could it be that there are types of knowledge that have to do with the *brain's* physicalness rather than its computerlike qualities? Yes, certain of our cognitive abilities have to do with the physical setup of the brain. There is the matter of the way neurons are interconnected, but it also may have something to do with the brain as a piece of chemistry or a collection of solid shapes. Templates, or sieves, can sort physical objects of different shapes or sizes; perhaps the brain works like this, or like the working medium of analog computers. Let's call this kind of knowledge embrained. It is interesting to note that insofar as knowledge is embrained (especially if this knowledge is stored holographically, to use another metaphor), the comic book story about brains being cut up and inserted into expert systems would be a better way of thinking about knowledge transfer than the two-colander image.

Encultured Knowledge

We now have knowledge in symbols, in the body, and in the physical matter of the brain. What about the social group? Suppose the tennis-playing knowledge had been siphoned from the brain of Ken Rosewall, a champion tennis player in the 1950s? How would the recipient of this older knowledge cope with the new fiberglass rackets and the swearing, shouting, and grunting of the current tennis scene? Though the constitutive rules of tennis have remained the same over the last few decades, the game has changed enormously. So, the "right" way to play tennis has to do with tennis-playing society as well as brains and bodies.

Natural languages are, of course, the paradigm example of bits of social knowledge. Determining the right way to speak is the prerogative of the social group, not the individual. Those who do not remain in contact with the social group will soon cease to know how to speak properly. "To be, or not to be: that is the question," a Shakespearean sentence some might consider stultifyingly vacuous, may nevertheless be uttered without fear of ridicule on all sorts of occasions because of its cultural aura. "What will it be then, my droogies?" may not be uttered safely, although it could have been for a short while in the 1960s.[4] Let's agree for the sake of argument that when William Shakespeare and Anthony Burgess first wrote those lines, their language-influencing ambitions were similar. That the first became a lasting part of common speech and the second did not has to do with the way literate society has gone. One can see, then, that there is an encultured element to language and to other kinds of knowledge—it changes as society changes, it could not be said to exist without the existence of the social group that has it, it is located in society. Variation over time is, of course, only one element of social embededdness.[5]

We now have four kinds of knowledge/abilities/skills:

- Symbol-type knowledge
- Embodied knowledge
- Embrained knowledge
- Encultured knowledge

We need to concentrate on the relationship between symbol-type knowledge and encultured knowledge. Understanding this relationship, I believe, will help us most in comparing the competences of human beings and those of current and foreseeable machines.

Two Kinds of Knowledge Corresponding to Two Types of Human Action

What is the relationship between symbol-type knowledge and encultured knowledge? Over the last 20 years many empirical studies of knowledge making and transfer have revealed the social aspect of what we know. For example, my own early field studies showed the place of tacit knowledge in the replication of scientific experiments and the implications of this for scientific experimentation. It turns out that before scientists can agree that an experiment has been replicated, they have to agree about the existence of the phenomenon for which they are searching. Agreement on the existence of natural phenomena seems to be social agreement; it is not something forced upon individuals in lonely confrontation with nature or something that can be verified by aggregating isolated reports.[6] Most of what we once thought of as the paradigm case of knowledge that is independent of society—science and mathematics—has turned out to be deeply social; it rests on agreements to conduct our scientific and mathematical lives a certain way.[7] It is the symbol-type knowledge that is proving to be hard to find and hard to define.

Another juncture at which the cultural basis of knowledge has shown itself is in the attempt to transfer human skills to intelligent computers. Dreyfus's path-breaking book *What Computers Can't Do* first explained the problem from the point of view of a philosopher, and Suchman more recently has emphasized the role of situated action, writing from the viewpoint of an ethnomethodologically inclined anthropologist.[8] Some of my own papers from 1985 onward argue a related case based on my work in the sociology of science.[9]

The trouble with all these approaches, including my own, is that they are so good at explaining the *difficulties* of transferring knowledge in written form, and of embodying knowledge in computer programs, that they fail to explain the residual successes of formal approaches. If so much knowledge rests upon agreements within forms of life, what *is* happening when knowledge is transferred via bits of paper or floppy disks? We know that much less is transferred this way than we once believed, but something is being encapsulated in symbols or we would not use them. How can it be that artifacts that do not share our forms of life can "have knowledge," and how can we share it? In the light of modern theories, it is *this* that needs explaining: What is formal knowledge?

To move forward, I think we need to locate the differences between symbol-type knowledge and encultured knowledge in different types of human action.[10]

Regular Action

One way of looking at encultured knowledge is to say that there is no one-to-one mapping between human action and observable behavior; the same act can be instantiated by many different behaviors. For example, paying money can be done by passing metal or paper tokens, writing a check, offering a plastic card and signing, and so forth, and each of these can be done in many different ways. Furthermore, the same behavior may be the instantiation of many different acts. For example, signing one's name might be for the purpose of paying money, agreeing to a divorce, sending a love letter, writing a suicide note, or providing a specimen signature for the bank. That is what it is like to act in a society; the coordination of apparently uncorrelated *behaviors* into concerted *acts* is what we learn as we become social beings.

To relate this point to the discussion of language, note that there are many different ways of saying the same thing; the different verbal formulations are different behaviors corresponding to the same speech acts. To recognize which are appropriate and which inappropriate ways of saying something at any particular time and place, one has to be a member of the relevant linguistic community. The word *droogies* was once a widely useful piece of linguistic behavior; now it is only narrowly useful.

We may call action in which there is no straightforward correspondence between intention and behavior "regular action." Most of the time most of our acts are regular acts. As well as meaning "normal" or "everyday," *regular* also connotes "rule" and "routine." This is both useful and misleading. The useful part is that normal action is usually rule-following and sometimes rule-establishing. The misleading part is that we tend to think it is easy to understand or describe the rules we follow when we are doing regular action; in fact, we can't, and this causes big problems for the social sciences.

We know that normal action is rule-following because we nearly always know when we have broken the rules. For example, it is clear that there are rules applying to my actions as a pedestrian because I will get into trouble if I break them—perhaps by walking too close to the single person or couple on an otherwise deserted beach, or trying to keep too far away from others in a crowded street—but I cannot encapsulate in a formula all that I know about the proper way to walk. The little bits of rule that I can provide, such as those just mentioned, are full of undefined terms. I have not defined *close*, *distant*, or *crowded*, nor can I define all my terms on pain of regress. Further, what counts as following the rule varies from society to society and situation to situation. A set recipe for walking will be found wanting on the first occasion of its use in unanticipated circumstances; perhaps the next people on the beach will be actors in a perfume advertisement, or the next people in the street will be living in the time of a contagious epidemic disease.

The problem of understanding regular action is well known among philosophers of social science and a proportion of social scientists. It explains why skills have to be transferred through interpersonal contact, or socialization, rather than through book learning. It underpins ideas such as tacit knowledge or apprenticeship. The philosophy of regular action shows why social science has not worked the way many people expected it to work. The orderliness of action is not evident to observers who are not also members of the society under examination. What's more, the order is always changing.[11]

To make society work, many of our actions have to be executed in different ways. For example, studies of factories have shown that even on production lines informed by Taylorist "scientific management" principles, there must be subtle variations in the way the job is executed.[12] Indeed, one effective form of industrial disruption is to act too uniformly—in Britain this form of action is known as a work-to-rule.

Behavior-Specific Action

I now introduce a special class of acts, behavior-specific acts, which we reserve for maintaining routines. This class seems to have been overlooked in the rush to stress the context-boundedness of ordinary acts. In behavior-specific acts we attempt to maintain a one-to-one mapping between our actions and observable behaviors. It is important to note that the characteristic feature of behavior-specific acts is that we *try* to execute them with the same spatiotemporal behavior but don't necessarily succeed; in this class of act this is what we *prefer* and what we *intend*. The archetypical example of this kind of action is caricature production line work, for example, as portrayed by Charlie Chaplin in *Modern Times*.[13] There are, however, less obvious examples of behavior-specific action, such as the standard golf swing or competitive high-board diving or simple arithmetical operations. Certain actions are intrinsically behavior-specific (e.g., marching), certain actions are intrinsically non-behavior-specific (e.g., writing love letters), but many can be executed in either way depending on intention and desired outcome. Many regular acts contain elements of behavior-specific action. Because behavior-specific action is not always successfully executed, and because in regular action the same behavior may sometimes be the instantiation of quite different acts, it is not possible to be certain by observation alone whether behavior-specific action is being executed. It is clear enough, however, that such a class of acts exists, because I can try to do my production line work or my golf swing in a behaviorally repetitious way (if I wish) or not (if I don't wish).

When behavior-specific action is successfully carried out, then as far as an observer is concerned, the behavior associated with an act can be substituted for the act itself without loss. The consequences of all successfully executed behavior-specific acts are precisely the same as the consequences of those pieces of behavior that always instantiate the act: take the intention away, and as far as an observer is concerned, nothing is lost. What this means is that anyone or anything that can follow the set of rules describing the *behavior* can, in effect, reproduce the *act*. Hence behavior-specific acts are transmittable even across cultures and are mechanizable. Compare this with regular action: in that case there is no way for an outsider to substitute behavior for action because the appropriate instantiation of the action depends on the ever-changing social context; behavior is not tied to acts in a regular way.

There are many occasions when our attempts to execute behavior-specific action fail. Human beings are not very good at it. In these cases we count the substitution of the behavior for the act (for example, through mechanical automation) an *improvement*.

If all action were behavior-specific action, there would be a regular correlation between behavior and action. In that case the big problems of the social sciences would not have emerged; sociology could be a straightforwardly observational science like astronomy or geology or the idealized versions of economics or behaviorist psychology.

Because, in the case of behavior-specific action, behavior can be substituted for the act as far as an observer is concerned, it is possible to *replace* the act with the behavior, to *describe* the act by describing the behavior, to *transfer* the description of the act in written form, and sometimes to *learn* how to execute the act from a written description. That, as I have suggested, is how we can have a limited systematic social science that observes those parts of human behavior that are predominantly behavior-specific;[14] how we can have machines such as pocket calculators, which inscribe the behavior-specific parts of arithmetic in their programs;[15] and how we can learn from books and manuals that describe the behavior to be executed if the act is to be successfully accomplished.[16] The reinstantiation of a behavioral repertoire, whether by a machine or by other human beings (who either do or do not understand what they are doing), will mimic the original act. In this sense, behavior-specific action can be decontextualized. It is the only form of action that is *not* essentially situated.[17]

Regular Action vs Behavior-Specific Action, and Other Ways of Cutting Up Knowledge

Consider how this way of dividing up action compares with approaches to human knowledge that are primarily concerned with the extent to which acts are self-consciously carried out. Both regular acts and behavior-specific acts can be executed with more or less self-consciousness. Figure 1 contrasts the two approaches; it shows what follows about mechanization from the theory of behavior-specific action. Other treatments differ.

In the treatment of skills by Dreyfus and Dreyfus and by many psychologists, the vertical dimension direction of the table in figure 1 is all-important.[18] At least one influential model takes it that competence is attained when the skillful person no longer has to think about what they are doing but internalizes the task. Dreyfus and Dreyfus argue that only novices use expressible rules to guide their actions, whereas experts use intuitive, inexpressible competences. They use this argument to show why expert systems are able to mimic expertise only to the level of the novice.

These treatments have a large grain of truth, but for different reasons. The psychological theory touches upon one of the characteristics of the human organism, namely, that we are not very good at doing certain things when we think about them. We certainly do get better at many skills when we, as it were, short-circuit the conscious part of the brain. The Dreyfus and Dreyfus model rests on the Wittgensteinian problem of rules that I touched earlier. To prepare a full description of regular skilled action, ready to cope with every circumstance, would require an infinite regress of rules. Therefore self-conscious rule following reproduces only a small subset of a skill and is the prerogative of the novice.

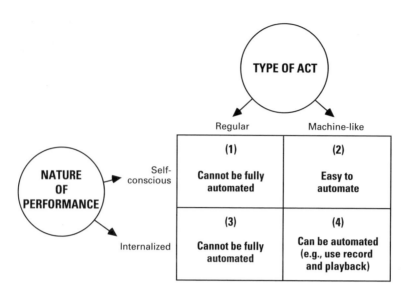

Figure 1
Types of act.

The large grain of truth is, however, not the whole truth. The psychological model is interesting only insofar as one is interested in the human being as an organism. One may well imagine other organisms that work perfectly without internalizing the rules. Even among humans the ability to work fast and accurately while self-consciously following formulaic instructions varies substantially. One can even imagine a superhuman who would not need to bother with internalization at all for a range of tasks. Suppose the person in the Chinese Room[19] remembered the content of all the lookup tables as well as a table of pronunciation and learned to speak at normal speed by mentally referring to them in real time. What's more, some tasks are not necessarily performed better without self-conscious attention, and others can only be performed with attention. What I am suggesting is that the psychological internalization model does not apply to all skills, and that insofar as it does, organism-specific findings are not all that interesting if one is concerned with the nature and structure of knowledge. For example, to take an entirely different kind of organism-specific rule, it is said to be good to hum "The Blue Danube Waltz" while playing golf in order to keep the rhythm slow and smooth, but this tells you about human beings, not knowledge.

The large grain of truth in the Dreyfus and Dreyfus model is precisely that most skills are based on regular action, and in those cases their model applies, for the reasons I've mentioned. Because we cannot formulate the rules, we cannot self-consciously "know what we are doing," and therefore even the fastest thinker will not be able to perform *calculatively*. But the Dreyfus and Dreyfus model does not apply where the action is behavior-specific. That is why their model, with its stress on the vertical direction of the table in figure 1, does not accurately predict what skills can be embedded in automated machines. If their model did give an accurate prediction, there would be no pocket calculators, for a lot of arithmetic is done without self-conscious attention to the rules.[20]

Let us look again at figure 1 and see what all this means. Consider first the left-hand pair of boxes. We can all agree that there are a range of skills that cannot be expertly performed by following a set of explicable rules and that in the case of these skills, only novices follow rules. In expert car driving, Dreyfus's paradigm case of intuitive skill, familiar journeys are sometimes negotiated without any conscious awareness. For instance, on the journey to work the driver might be thinking of the day ahead, responding to variations in traffic without attention and possibly not even remembering the journey. On the other hand, there are occasions when drivers do pay attention to the details of traffic and the skills of car handling, perhaps even self-consciously comparing the current state of the traffic with previous experiences. On such occasions they would remember the details of the journey even if they were not self-consciously applying rules. This partitions non-rule-based skills into the upper and lower boxes on the left-hand side of the table in figure 1 and allows us to say that skills that cannot be described in a set of rules can on occasion be executed self-consciously if not calculatively. Indeed, there is no reason to think that in these cases unself-conscious performance is better.

Now, with regard to the right-hand pair of boxes in figure 1, imagine a novice who had somehow learned to drive by following rules self-consciously but because of some kind of disability had been unable to progress to the level of intuitive expert. That person would always remain a poor driver even though he eventually internalized the novice's rules. In terms of the table in figure 1, he would have moved from box 2 to box 4 *but would still be a novice*. Thus lack of self-consciousness is not a condition of expertise for inexpert actions may be unself-consciously performed.

Think now about the golf swing or parade ground drill. People have to perform these skills without much in the way of conscious effort if they are to perform well. Thus, box 4 contains skilled actions as well as unskilled actions.

Now try repeating at high speed and without error

I'm not a pheasant plucker.
I'm a pheasant plucker's son.
And I'm only plucking pheasant
Till the pheasant pluckers come.

That requires skill *and* self-conscious deliberation. Or again, consider the test for alchoholic intoxication that, it is said, was used by the British police before the invention of the Breathalyzer. One was allowed to use all the concentration one wanted to articulate "the Leith police dismisseth us."[21] Thus there are skilled tasks as well as un-skilled performances located in box 2, each requiring conscious effort.

Going back to the left-hand side of the table in figure 1, it is not normal to refer to everything that happens there as skilled because it includes such things as being able to form a sentence in one's native language. Thus all four boxes contain actions that are normally referred to as skilled and unskilled. The only convincing mapping is that nothing on the left-hand side can be mastered without socialization (nor can it be mastered by machines), whereas everything on the right-hand side, including the skillful performances, could be (at least in principle).[22]

This analysis of human abilities in terms of regular versus behavior-specific action seems to be new, or at least newish. The distinction does not map onto the distinction between self-consciousness and internalization, nor onto the difference between skilled and unskilled performance. A minority of activities that we call skillful are executed in a behavior-specific way.[23] The difference between regular and behavior-specific acts is also not the same as the difference between acts that we value and acts that we do not value, nor between those that are meaningful and those that are demeaning. Many acts that we normally prefer to execute in a behavior-specific way are highly valued, including high-board diving and the golf swing. Some behavior-specific acts were once highly valued but are less so now, such as doing mental arithmetic, once a useful skill but devalued now that the larger part of it can be done by pocket calculators.[24] Finally, we may note that the difference between the two types of act is not the same as the difference between cognitive and sensory-motor abilities.

Are There Domains of Behavior-Specific Action?

Is spoken language behavior-specific action? Is chess behavior-specific action? These are not good questions. The term *behavior-specific* does not identify knowledge domains; it identifies types of action. It does not apply to language or chess as such; it applies to the way people use language or play chess. Thus, for most people, language use is not behavior-specific action, although it was the aim of the controllers in George Orwell's novel *1984* to make language into behavior-specific action. In a *1984*-like world, just as in Searle's Chinese Room and in a world that certain machine translation enthusiasts would like to bring down upon us, language use would be behavior-specific action. In the world as it is, there is more than one way to speak a language.

The same is true of something like chess playing, although here it is less obvious. We tend to ask what sort of knowledge is chess knowledge—is it formal or informal? We conclude that it is formal because in principle there are an exhaustive set of rules for winning the game. But people do not play chess like computers, at least not all the time. Human chess playing is part behavior-specific action and part not. The first few moves of chess openings are usually played by skilled players as behavior-specific action.[25] Unfortunately, I know no openings and cannot play those first few moves in this way. There is not the slightest doubt that in terms of what counts as good chess in contemporary culture, all chess computers play openings better than I do. Some chess endings are also generally performed as behavior-specific action. Skill at chess openings and endings increases as the ability to accomplish behavior-specific action increases. The middle game of chess is not behavior-specific action insofar as most good human players are concerned; at least some of the middle game has to do with the quintessentially non-behavior-specific skill of creating surprises. Machines, on the other hand, do play a middle game that mimics what human play would be like if it were played as behavior-specific action.[26] The great chess-playing competitions between machines and people in the past few years have been between the regular action middle game of the best human chess players and the rule-based procedures of chess programs; slowly the programs are winning. If human brains were better at behavior-specific action, then that—I would guess—is how chess masters would now be playing.

On the other hand, what would happen to the culture of chess if a chess-playing machine were built that could play the game exhaustively and therefore win every time with the same moves?[27] It could be that the nature of the game of chess would change: people would care less about winning and more about the aesthetics. In that case, human chess would become quintessentially non-behavior-specific. The idea of a competition between human players and chess machines would then seem as absurd as an adding competition between a person and a computer or a pulling competition between a strong man and a tractor.

One sees that special cases apart—I have mentioned marching and the writing of love letters—it does not make sense to say that there are domains of behavior-specific and regular action. Rather, one notes that some elements in domains are generally performed in a behavior-specific way whereas other elements are performed as regular actions. The element of each in any domain may change for many reasons, some having to do with individual choice and some having to do with changes in the "form of life" that comprises the activities.

One way of applying these ideas to the relationship between humans and machines is to reconsider the Turing test. The Turing test is a controlled experiment. To decide whether a machine is intelligent, we compare it with a control, usually a person. We check to see if the machine has the same linguistic abilities as the person. The experimenter (or judge) is "blinded"—she does not know which is the experimental device and which is the control. If the experimenter cannot tell the machine from the control, then we say that the machine is as intelligent as the control.

Exactly what intelligence means under this approach depends upon how the test is set up. If the control were a block of wood rather than a person, the test would show only that the experimental device is as intelligent as a block of wood. If, on the other hand, the judge were a block of wood rather than a person, we would not find the outcome very interesting. There is a range of possibilities for both control and judge, varying from block of wood through dim human to very sensible human; these imply very different things about the ability of any machine that passes the test. There are other variations in the way the protocol can be arranged: Is the test short or long? Is there one run or more than one? Is the typing filtered through a spell-checker or not? and so forth. Depending on the protocol, the Turing test tests for different things.

Take the version of the Turing test implicit in Searle's Chinese Room critique. In this case, responses to written questions in the Chinese language are produced by a human operator who knows no Chinese but has access to a huge stock of lookup tables that tell him which strings of Chinese symbols are appropriate outputs to which inputs. (The control in the case of the Chinese Room is virtual.) Searle hypothesizes a Chinese Room that passes the test; it produces convincing Chinese answers to Chinese questions. But, for the room to do this, there must be some constraints on the protocol. For example, having noticed the way that languages change over time, we can see that either the life span of the Chinese Room (and therefore the test) must be short so that the Chinese language doesn't change much during the test period, or the interrogators must conspire to limit their questions to that temporal cross-section of the Chinese language represented in the stack of lookup tables first placed in the room, or the lookup tables must be continually updated as the Chinese language changes. Under the first two constraints, the knowledge of Chinese contained in the room is not type 4 (encultured) knowledge. It is rather a frozen cross-section of a language, an elaborated version of what is found in a computer spell-checker. It is a set of formulas for the reproduction of the behavior associated with behavior-specific action. It is easy to see that this might be encapsulated in symbols.[28]

Now suppose, for argument's sake, that the test is long enough for the Chinese language to change while the questions are being asked, or that it is repeated again and again over a long period, and the interrogators do not conspire to keep their questions within the bounds of the linguistic cross-section encapsulated in the original lookup tables. If the stock of lookup tables remains the same, the Chinese Room will become outdated and begin to fail to answer questions convincingly.

Now suppose that the lookup tables are continually updated by attendants. Some of the attendants will have to be in day-to-day contact with changing fashions in Chinese; they will have to share Chinese culture. Thus, somewhere in the mechanism there must be people who do understand Chinese sufficiently well to know the difference between the Chinese equivalents of "To be, or not to be" and "What will it be, my droogies?" at the time that the room is in operation. Note that the two types of room—synchronic and diachronic—are distinguishable given the right protocol. It is true that the person using the lookup tables in the diachronic room still does not understand Chinese, but among the attendants there must be some who do.

Under the extended protocol, any Chinese Room that passed the test would have to contain type 4 knowledge, and I have argued that it is to be found in those who update the lookup tables. It is these people who link the diachronic room into society, who make it a social entity.[29]

Under the extended protocol, the Turing test becomes a test of membership in social groups. It does this by comparing the abilities of experimental object and control in miniature social interactions with the interrogator. Under this protocol, passing the test signifies social intelligence or the possession of encultured knowledge.

A Simplified Turing Test

Once one sees this point, it is possible to simplify the Turing test greatly while still using it to check for embeddedness in society.[30] The new test requires a determined judge, an intelligent and literate control who shares the broad cultural background of the judge, and a machine with which the control is to be compared. The judge provides both control and machine with copies of a few typed paragraphs (in a clear, machine-readable font) of somewhat misspelled and otherwise mucked-about English, which neither has seen before. It is important that the paragraphs are previously unseen, for it is easy to devise a program to transliterate an example once it has been thought through.

Once the typed material has been presented, Control and Machine have, say, an hour to transliterate the passages into normal English. Machine will have the text presented to its scanner, and its output will be a second text. Control will type her transliteration into a word processor to be printed out by the same printer as is used by Machine. The judge will then be given the printed texts and will have to work out which has been transliterated by Control and which by Machine. Here is a specimen of the sort of paragraph the judge would present.

Mary: The next thing I want you to do is spell a word that means a religious ceremony.

John: You mean rite. Do you want me to spell it out loud?

Mary: No, I want you to write it.

John: I'm tired. All you ever want me to do is write, write, write.

Mary: That's unfair. I just want you to write, write, write.

John: Okay, I'll write, write.

Mary: Write.

The point of this simplified test is that the hard thing for a machine to do in a Turing test is to demonstrate the skill of repairing typed English conversation—the interactional stuff is mostly icing on the cake. The simplified test is designed to draw on all the culture-bound common sense needed to navigate the domain of error correction in printed English. This is the only kind of skill that can be tested through the medium of the typed word, but it is quite sufficient, if the test is carefully designed, to enable us to tell the socialized from the unsocialized.[31] It seems to me that if a machine could pass a carefully designed version of this test, all the significant problems of artificial intelligence would have been solved—the rest would be research and development.

Conclusion

What I have tried to do here is to divide up our knowledge and skills. The way I have done this is based on two types of human action. I believe the division is fundamental and lies at the root of the difference between tacit knowledge, which appears to be located in society, and formal knowledge, which can be transferred in symbolic form and encoded into machines and other artifacts. Those who come out of a Wittgensteinian, ethnomethodological, or sociology-of-scientific-knowledge tradition have, whether they know it or not, a problem with the notion of the formal or routine. In fact, everyone has this problem, but it is less surprising that others have not noticed it. I think that the idea of behavior-specific action is at least the beginning of a solution.

My claim is that this way of looking at human action allows us to undertand better the shifting patterns and manner of execution of various human competences. It also helps us understand the manner and potential for the delegation of our competences to symbols, computers, and other machinery. In addition, it helps us see the ways in which machines are better than people: it shows that many of the things that people do, they do because they are unable to function in the machinelike way that they would prefer. There are many activities where the question of machine replacement simply does not arise, or arises, at best, as an asymptotic approximation to human abilities. We notice, then, what humans are good at and what machines are good at, and how these competences meet in the changing pattern of human activity. It seems to me that the analysis of skill, knowledge, human abilities, or whatever one calls the sets of activities for which we use our minds and bodies, must start from this distinction, and that understanding how much of what we do can be taken over by machines rests on understanding this distinction.

Coda: Turing's Sociological Prediction

Alan Turing, in one of his famous papers, said that by the end of the [twentieth] century he expected that "the use of words and general educated opinion will have altered so much that one will be able to speak of machines thinking without expecting to be contradicted."[32] There are at least four ways in which we might move toward such a state of affairs: (1) Machines get better at mimicking us; (2) we become more charitable to machines; (3) we start to behave more like machines; and (4) our image of ourselves becomes more like our image of machines.

Machines get better at mimicking us.

Unless machines can become members of our society, they can appear to mimic our acts only by developing more and more ramified behaviors. This process is a good thing as long as it is not misconstrued. Ramification of behaviors makes for new and better tools, not new and better people. The rate at which intelligent tools can be improved is not easy to predict. The problem is analogous to predicting the likelihood of the existence of life on other planets. There are a large number of other planets, but the probability that the conditions for life exist on a planet is astronomically small. Where two large numbers have to be compared, a very small error can make a lot of difference to the outcome. The two large numbers in the case of intelligent machines are the exponential growth in the power of machines and the exponential increase in the number of rules that are needed to make behavior approximate the appearance of regular action. My guess is that progress is slowing down fast, but the model sets no limit to asymptotic progress.

We become more charitable to machines.

As we become more familiar with machines, we repair their deficiencies without noticing, in other words, make good their inabilities in the same charitable way as we make good the inabilities of the inarticulate people among us. Already the use of words and general educated opinion have changed sufficiently to allow us to speak of, say, calculators in the fashion that Turing predicted would apply to intelligence in general. We speak of calculators as being "better at arithmetic than ourselves" or "obviating the need for people to do arithmetic," although close examination shows that neither of these sentiments is exactly right.[33] If we generalize this process of becoming more charitable, we will lose sight of our own special abilities.

We start to behave more like machines ourselves.

Consider the deficiencies of machine translation. One solution is to standardize the way *we* write English:

In the U.S., it is usual practice amongst some large firms to send entire manuals for online translation on a mainframe computer. It works well. The manual writers are trained to use short sentences, cut out all ambiguities from the text (by repeating nouns instead of using pronouns, for example) and to use a limited, powerful vocabulary. Europeans have shown little of this discipline.[34]

For Europeans there are, of course, no significant ambiguities in the texts they write, it is just that the texts are not written in a behavior-specific (*1984*-like) way. In what is usually counted as good writing, different words are used to represent the same idea, and different ideas are represented by the same words. The parallel with regular action is complete. The problem is that translation machines cannot participate in the action of writing unless it is behavior-specific action. If we adjust our writing style to make it universally behavior-specific, then mechanized translators will be as good as human translators and we will be more likely to come to speak of machines' thinking, just as Turing predicted. What is true of translation is true of all our actions. The theory of action outlined here allows that the way we execute our actions can change. Change in the way we act is not necessarily bad, even when it is change from regular to behavior-specific action, but we want to continue to be free to decide how best to carry out our acts. We do not want to lose our freedom of *action* so as to accommodate the behavior of machines.

Our image of ourselves becomes more like our image of machines.
If we think of ourselves as machines, we will see our departures from the machinelike ideal as a matter of human frailty rather than human creativity. We need to counter the tendency to think of people as inefficient machines. There is a difference between the way people act and the way machines mimic most of those acts. I have argued that machines can mimic us only in those cases where we prefer to do things in a behavior-specific way. Whether we come to speak of machines' thinking without fear of contradiction will have something to do with whether this argument is more or less convincing than the arguments of those who think of social life as continuous with the world of things.

Intelligent machines are among the most useful and interesting tools that we have developed. But if we use them with too much uncritical charity, or if we start to think of ourselves as machines, or model our behavior on their behavior, or concentrate so hard on our own boundary-making and -maintaining practices that we convince ourselves there is nothing to boundaries except what we make of them, we will lose sight of who we are.

Notes

I would like to thank Güven Güzeldere for suggestions and editorial assistance on this chapter, which is adapted from Harry M. Collins, "The Structure of Knowledge," *Social Research* 60 (Spring 1993): 95–116. The section on the Turing test also contains elements taken from the final chapter of my book *Artificial Experts: Social Knowledge and Intelligent Machines* (Cambridge, Mass.: MIT Press, 1990) and my paper "Embedded or Embodied: Hubert Dreyfus's *What Computers Still Can't Do*," *Artificial Intelligence* 80 (no. 1, 1996): 99–117.

1. The mundane applications of Hollywood's brilliant scientific breakthroughs are depressing.

2. This is not just a matter of necessary conditions for tennis playing. I don't want to say that tennis-playing knowledge is contained in the blood, even though a person without blood could not play tennis. Nor do I want to say that the body is like a tool and that tennis-playing knowledge is contained in the racket (after all, we can transfer a tennis racket with hardly any transfer of tennis-playing ability).

3. See, for example, Hubert Dreyfus, *What Computers Can't Do* (New York: Harper, 1972; rev. ed. 1979).

4. The first is from *Hamlet*; the second is from Anthony Burgess's *A Clockwork Orange* (London: Heinemann, 1962).

5. But it is the easiest to explain, so I have stayed with this dimension throughout the chapter. I argue elsewhere that skilled speakers of a language are able to make all kinds of "repairs" to damaged strings of symbols that the Chinese Room would not. For discussion of these other ways in which the social embeddedness of language shows itself, see Harry M. Collins, "Hubert Dreyfus, Forms of Life, and a Simple Test for Machine Intelligence," *Social Studies of Science* 22 (1992): 726–739.

6. Harry M. Collins, "The Tea Set: Tacit Knowledge and Scientific Networks," *Science Studies* 4 (1974): 165–186; Harry M. Collins, "The Seven Sexes: A Study in the Sociology of a Phenomenon, or the Replication of Experiments in Physics," *Sociology* 9 (1975): 205–224; Harry M. Collins, *Changing Order: Replication and Induction in Scientific Practice* (Beverly Hills, Calif.: Sage, 1985). For the origin of the term *tacit knowledge*, see Michael Polanyi, *Personal Knowledge* (London: Routledge, 1958).

7. This way of thinking is deeply rooted in the later philosophy of Wittgenstein. For example, see Ludwig Wittgenstein, *Philosophical Investigations*, trans. G.E.M. Anscombe (Oxford: Blackwell, 1953); and David Bloor, *Wittgenstein: A Social Theory of Knowledge* (London: Macmillan, 1983).

8. Dreyfus, *What Computers Can't Do*; Lucy Suchman, *Plans and Situated Action: The Problem of Human-Machine Interaction* (Cambridge: Cambridge University Press, 1987); see also Terry Winograd and Fernando Florès, *Understanding Computers and Cognition: A New Foundation for Design* (Norwood, N.J.: Ablex, 1986).

9. See, for example, H. M. Collins, R. H. Green, and R. C. Draper, "Where's the Expertise: Expert Systems as a Medium of Knowledge Transfer," in *Expert Systems 85*, ed. Martin J. Merry (Cambridge: Cambridge University Press, 1985), 323–334.

10. For the first introduction of the distinction between regular action and behavior-specific action, see Collins, *Artificial Experts*. For an extended philosophical analysis that analyzes types of action into further subcategories, see Harry M. Collins and M. Kusch, "Two Kinds of Actions: A Phenomenological Study," *Philosophy and Phenomenological Research* 55 (no. 4, 1995): 799–819.

11. For an analysis of the way scientific order is changed, see Collins, *Changing Order*.

12. Kenneth C. Kusterer, *Know-How on the Job: The Important Working Knowledge of "Unskilled" Workers* (Boulder, Colo.: Westview Press, 1978).

13. Note that the Taylorist ideal usually is a caricature, but this does not mean it cannot be found under special circumstances.

14. For example, it works for certain limited types of economic behavior or the behavior of people in specially arranged laboratory conditions. This kind of science is especially appropriate where behavior-specific action is enforced, as in F. W. Taylor's "scientific management."

15. For a full analysis of what pocket calculators can and cannot do, and how to see what they do as behavior-specific action, see Collins, *Artificial Experts*.

16. As long as the behavioral repertoire we are to master is not too complicated.

17. Suchman, *Plans and Situated Action*.

18. See especially Hubert Dreyfus and Stuart Dreyfus, *Mind Over Machine: The Power of Human Intuition and Expertise in the Era of the Computer* (New York: Free Press, 1986).

19. See John Searle, "Minds, Brains, and Programs," *Behavioral and Brain Sciences* 3 (1980): 417–424; John Searle, *Minds, Brains, and Science* (Cambridge, Mass.: Harvard University Press, 1984); see also ⟨http://www.utm.edu/research/iep/c/chineser.htm⟩.

20. Hubert Dreyfus tries to sidestep the problem by dividing knowledge domains into two types, one of which is "formalizable." Unfortunately, it is not possible to have a formalizable domain under the Wittgensteinian treatment, which Dreyfus prefers. My concept of behavior-specific action makes what Dreyfus calls a formal domain possible. Our theories are largely co-extensive until we try to predict how devices that do not use formal rules will perform. My theory leads one to be far more pessimistic about, say, neural nets. See Harry M. Collins, "Will Machines Ever Think?" *New Scientist* 1826 (June 20, 1992): 36–40.

21. These tasks, incidentally, can be done without difficulty by existing and conceivable talking computers, showing again that the psychological and philosophical dimensions of the skill problem need to be pulled apart.

22. The model does not limit the role of machines to mimicking simple-minded repetitious morons; the ramifications of behavior-specific action can be such that it approaches regular action asymptotically. One of the programs of observation and research that the theory suggests, however, is to break down the performance of machines into its constituent behaviors. This program applies as much to neural nets and other exotic devices as to more straightforward programs.

23. Along the way we have established that self-conscious/internalized also does not map onto unskilled/skilled.

24. For a more detailed working out of the behavior-specific elements of arithmetic, see Collins, *Artificial Experts*.

25. I am now assuming away the elements of non–behavior specificity that have to do with the shape of the pieces, the method of making moves, and so forth. I am thinking about long series of games using the same apparatus.

26. One must be careful with locutions. We must not say that a machine "acts" and therefore cannot say that a chess machine engages in behavior-specific action. Machines can only mimic behavior-specific action. Chess machines mimic the behavior-specific action of the first few moves of the skilled human chess player's game.

27. Even these special cases are historically specific.

28. I simplify here; see note 5.

29. I discuss the protocol of the Turing test at some length in *Artificial Experts*.

The Turing test is usually thought of as involving language, but there is no reason to stop at this. We could, for example, use the test with washing machines. To find out if a washing machine is intelligent, we would set it alongside a washer person, concealing both from a judge. The judge would interrogate the two by passing in sets of objects to be washed and examining the response. (We must imagine some mechanism for passing the objects into the machine and starting the cycle.) An unimaginative judge might pass in soiled clothes and, examining the washed garments, might be unable to tell which had been washed by the machine and which by the person. A more imaginative interrogator might pass in, perhaps, some soiled clothes, some clothes that were ripped and soaked in blood, some clothes with paper money in the pockets, some valuable oil paintings on canvas, or whatever, and examine the response to these. Again, embeddedness in social life is needed if the appropriate response is to be forthcoming.

30. This section is taken from Collins, "Embedded or Embodied."

31. It is worth noting for the combinatorily inclined that a lookup table *exhaustively* listing all corrected passages of about the length of 300 characters, including those for which the most appropriate response would be "I can't correct that," would contain 10^{600} entries, compared to the roughly 10^{125} particles in the universe. The number of potentially correctible passages would be very much smaller, of course, but—I would guess—would still be beyond the bounds of brute-strength methods. Note also that the correct response, of which there may be more than one, may vary from place to place and time to time as our linguistic culture changes.

32. Alan Turing, "Computing Machinery and Intelligence," *Mind* 49 (1950): 433–460, reprinted in Douglas Hofstadter and Daniel Dennett, eds., *The Mind's I* (Harmondworth, U.K.: Penguin, 1982), 53–66. This section is adapted from Collins, *Artificial Experts*, ch. 15.

33. See Collins, *Artificial Experts*, chs. 4 and 5.

34. Derek J. Price, "The Advantages of Doubling in Dutch," *The Guardian* 20 (April 1989): 31.

Swamped by the Updates: Expert Systems, Semioclasm, and Apeironic Education

Michael L. Johnson

First, let me, borrowing from Peter Jackson, offer a brief definition: "An expert system is a computing system capable of representing and reasoning about some knowledge-rich domain, such as internal medicine or geology, with a view to solving problems or giving advice."[1] Then, let me offer a prophecy: the expert system of the future will think like a woman. Now, let me explain, gradually, what I mean.

Perhaps the most daunting obstacle facing expert-systems research and development is the so-called frame problem. Though variously theorized for some time—arguably since before Plato—it remains essentially an epistemological problem of how to update ("up-data") a world model in terms of a changing world. Given the persistence of this seemingly intractable problem, we must find a better approach to it. I propose that we consider a semiotic approach, a kind that is foreshadowed by much research on the problem and that virtually begs for further exploration, especially in relation to an analogous problem now plaguing education generally.

John McCarthy and Patrick Hayes first define the frame problem explicitly for the domain of artificial intelligence in 1969.[2] Though they discuss it as one of several "major traditional problems of philosophy" that bear on the issue of what knowledge, what "general representation of the world in terms of which its inputs are interpreted," a computer program must have in order to be "capable of acting intelligently in the world" (463), they clearly suggest that it is a *practical* problem of indubitable importance. And it figures in their conception of "a Missouri [show-me] program" for which "the world and its laws of change" can be represented (469).

McCarthy and Hayes investigate the difficulties of construing that representation as a system of interactive abstract descriptions called finite automata. Though such a deterministic system has certain attractions, it also involves, among other snags, geometric multiplications of information and patent epistemological inadequacy. They entertain the idea of avoiding the first, most bothering difficulty by the introduction of a frame-based principle of economy, so that "a number of fluents [situational functions] are declared as attached to the frame and the effect of an action is described by telling which fluents are changed, all others being presumed unchanged" (487). There remains, however, "the impossibility of naming every conceivable thing that may go wrong," and McCarthy and Hayes discourage any hope that such uncertainty could be dealt with by attaching probabilities to statements of the representational formalism or by describing the laws of change in any given situation through parallel processing (490). Their critical survey of the literature, concerned with simpler mechanisms for grappling with this knotty enigma (making use of modal logics of contingent truth, multiple possible worlds, co-historicality, schemes for maintaining consistency through change), while not wholly pessimistic, surely indicates its durability.

Over the next few years a number of techniques for dealing with or reducing the frame problem were tried. None were really successful, but many were suggestive. Consider, for example, the method-learning STRIPS system of Fikes and Nilsson, which introduces some interesting features of heuristic economy (by stripping away subgoals as it goes) into state-space theorem proving. Or consider the PLANNER programming language, developed and refined by Carl Hewitt and others, which provides principled strategies for changing propositions in a state-space database. But surely it is Marvin Minsky who first takes thinking about the frame problem to the next, somewhat more productive stage.[3]

Minsky begins by endorsing what he sees as a general movement away from the theories of both behaviorists and logic-oriented AI researchers and toward cognitively-oriented theories that, "in order to explain the apparent speed and power of mental activities," see their processes as "larger and more structured, and their factual and procedural contents ... [as] more intimately connected" (211). Drawing upon previous work in the latter vein, he offers his own theory, admitting that it "raises more questions than it answers" (212). Because his brief version of that theory lays out its premises so systematically and also because it anticipates future theorizing as well as my own later discussion, I here quote it at some length:

When one encounters a new situation (or makes a substantial change in one's view of the present problem) one selects from memory a substantial structure called a frame. This is a remembered framework to be adapted to fit reality by changing details as necessary. A *frame* is a data-structure for representing a stereotyped situation.... Attached to each frame are several kinds of information. Some of this information is about how to use the frame. Some is about what one can expect to happen next. Some is about what to do if these expectations are not confirmed.

We can think of a frame as a network of nodes and relations. The "top levels" of a frame are fixed, and represent things that are always true about the supposed situation. The lower levels have many *terminals*—"slots" that must be filled by specific instances or data. Each terminal can specify conditions its assignments must meet. (The assignments themselves are usually smaller "subframes.") Simple conditions are specified by markers that might require a terminal assignment to be a person, an object of sufficient value, or a pointer to a subframe of a certain type. More complex conditions can specify relations among the things assigned to several terminals.

Collections of related frames are linked together into *frame systems*. The effects of important actions are mirrored by transformations between the frames of a system. . . .

For visual scene analysis, the different frames of a system describe the scene from different viewpoints, and the transformations between one frame and another represent the effects of moving from place to place. For nonvisual kinds of frames, the differences between the frames of a system can represent actions, cause-effect relations, or changes in metaphorical viewpoint. Different frames of a system share the same terminals; this is the critical point that makes it possible to coordinate information gathered from different viewpoints. Much of the phenomenological power of the theory hinges on the inclusion of expectations and other kinds of presumptions. A frame's terminals are normally already filled with "default" assignments. Thus a frame may contain a great many details whose supposition is not specifically warranted by the situation. . . .

The default assignments are attached loosely to their terminals, so that they can be easily displaced by new items that better fit the current situation. . . .

The frame systems are linked, in turn, by an information retrieval network. When a proposed frame cannot be made to fit reality—when we cannot find terminal assignments that suitably match its terminal marker conditions—this network provides a replacement frame. . . .

Once a frame is proposed to represent a situation, a matching process tries to assign values to the terminals . . . , consistent with the markers at each place. The matching process is partly controlled by information associated with the frame (which includes information about how to deal with surprises) and partly by knowledge about the system's current goals. There are important uses for the information obtained when a matching process fails. (212–213)

Minsky later pursues the question of how such "failure" information may be used in choosing an alternative frame, a process he compares to the notion of paradigm shift. The thrust of his theory is toward a fuller understanding of human intelligence as a problem-solving faculty engaged through vision, but he conceives no distinction between such a theory and "a scheme for making an intelligent machine" (215). He believes that both must be more complex and procedurally oriented than their typical predecessors.

Minsky is quick to dismiss any theory "that we see so quickly that our image changes as fast as does the scene" and presses his own case that "the changes of one's frame structure representation proceed at their own pace; the system prefers to make small changes whenever possible; and the illusion of continuity is due to the persistence of assignments to terminals common to the different view frames" (221). This dependence of continuity "on the confirmation of expectations" thus provides a way of explaining why human vision apparently does not—and in the case of a machine, I gather, should not—require moment-to-moment complete reprocessing (221, 224). Still, however persistent those assignments may be—and Minsky offers the "conjecture that frames are never stored in long-term memory with unassigned terminals" but rather "with weakly bound default assignments at every terminal!"—they are *all* "weakly bound" and therefore ultimately changeable (228).

Stretching his theory a bit more, Minsky compares it to the developmental learning theory of the Swiss psychologist Jean Piaget. Minsky suggests that "there is a similarity between Piaget's idea of a concrete operation and the effects of applying a transformation between frames of a system" (229). He appears less sanguine about the possibility of describing the role played by frames in Piaget's formal stage of thinking, when children are "able to reason *about*, rather than *with* transformations," when they "learn the equivalent of operating on the transformations themselves," although he easily analogizes such an operation to that by which an AI system reads and comments on its own programs (230). I see no reason one could not articulate frames (or metaframes) as "'representations of representations'" (230), but one would be advised to think of them at all levels, including that of what is originally represented in textualist or semiotic terms.

Such speculation leads Minsky to linguistic and, more specifically, semantic concerns. Transcribing Chomsky's transformational grammar into frame terms, he argues, for instance, that grammatical rules and conventions that people use function "to induce others to make assignments to terminals of structures," a line of thought he follows until he arrives at a theory of the interrelationship of the grammatical and the meaningful: "If the top levels are satisfied but some lower terminals are not, we have a meaningless sentence; if the top is weak but the bottom solid, we have an ungrammatical but meaningful utterance" (231, 232). Also, he reminds us that terminals and their default assignments, especially in natural-language structures, "can represent purposes and functions, not just colors, sizes, and shapes" (232), although he neglects to mention other dimensions of experience that a full-blown semiotic approach to representation would want to take into account.

Still, Minsky's frame-oriented discussion of natural language is quite suggestive, especially his treatment of discourse. Much of that treatment concerns a brief fable, an animal story. Careful to avoid any "radical confrontation between linguistic vs. nonlinguistic representations," Minsky nonetheless risks assuming their intimacy or identity at some level and offers a hypothetical "frame-oriented scenario for how coherent discourse might be represented," one that finally bristles with implications for both machine and human learning in the postmodern age:

At the start of a story, we know little other than that it will be a story, but even this gives us a start. A conventional frame for "story" (in general) would arrive with slots for setting, protagonists, main event, moral, etc.... Each sentential analysis need be maintained only until its contents can be used to instantiate a larger structure. The terminals of the growing meaning-structure thus accumulate indicators and descriptors, which expect and key further assignments.... As the story proceeds, information is transferred to superframes whenever possible, instantiating or elaborating the scenario.... But what if no such transfer can be made because the listener expected a wrong kind of story and has no terminals to receive the new structure? (236–237)

As Minsky explores this failure, larger issues begin to emerge between the lines:

We go on to suppose that the listener actually has many story frames, linked by ... retrieval structures.... First we try to fit the new information into the current story frame. If we fail, we construct an error comment like "there is no place here for an animal." This causes us to replace the
current story frame by, say, an animal-story frame. The previous assignments to terminals may all
survive, if the new story frame has the same kinds of terminals. But if many previous assignments
do not transfer, we must get another new story frame. If we fail, we must either construct a basically new story frame—a major intellectual event, perhaps—or just give up and forget the assignments. (Presumably that is the usual reaction to radically new narrative forms! One does not learn
well if the required jumps are too large ...). (237)

Much learning theory, particularly that of Joseph Novak, addresses the importance
of effective learning building, in a principled way, from what the student already
knows.[4] The more the updating (new terminal assignments) involved, all the way to
the radical updating of changing frames or creating a new one, the more crucial and
complex becomes the educator's mediation. When the jump is large enough, and the
stories have more at stake, we are in the realm not of conventional but of what I call
apeironic education (from the Greek *ápeiron*, "indeterminate," "endless," "unfamiliar").
That realm involves, following Minsky's treatment above, intra- *and* inter-frame problems, both of which, as we shall see, may be most productively conceived not simply
in linguistic or nonlinguistic terms but in semiotic terms.

If Minsky does not inaugurate a semiotic approach to the frame problem, he surely
does offer theoretical provisions helpful to such an inauguration. Reviewing earlier
work, he is led "to a view of the frame concept in which the 'terminals' serve to represent the questions most likely to arise in a situation" (246). This view proposes a more
poststructuralist understanding of the terminals as having not only weak assignments
but interrogative ones whose meaning is nonprimitive in some sense and to that extent open. This view also occasions his recasting his definition of a frame as, now, "a
collection of questions to be asked about a hypothetical situation; it specifies issues to
be raised and methods to be used in dealing with them" (246). Grappling with the
problem of how one locates a frame to represent a new situation, he argues that locating it "must depend largely on (learned) knowledge about the structure of one's own
knowledge" (247). Such a provision entails the complicating postulates that "an active
frame cannot be maintained unless its terminal conditions are satisfied" and that
"even the satisfied frames must be assigned to terminals of superior frames," along
with "any substantial fragments of 'data' that have been observed and represented"
(248). By these provisions for the interconnection, at once hierarchical and rhizomatic,
of frames at once open and satisfied, Minsky's portrait does indeed begin to suggest
the human brain/mind itself. It hints at the staggering complexity of the interlaced
processes involved in keeping the whole ever-switching thing updated in terms of

progressively refined "difference information" arising from attempts to match situations with memories of other situations (253).

Minsky retreats from this snarl—though also from the opportunity of semiotically exploring the mechanism of "difference-describing processes"—in order to deal with the more practical issues of problem solving in what he contends is typically for humans "a small context" (255, 257). In doing so he proposes a shift away from older approaches to solving problems (e.g., game theory) and toward a frame-oriented (and apeironic) approach. It entails "a more mature and powerful paradigm," but it also presumes more productive management of the frame problem:

The primary purpose in problem solving should be better to understand the problem space, to find representations within which the problems are easier to solve. The purpose of search is to get information for this reformulation, not—as is usually assumed—to find solutions; once the space is adequately understood, solutions to problems will more easily be found. (259)

Thus his approach to problem solving constitutes "a way to improve the strategy of subsequent trials," but its lingering frame problem questions are addressed only by the invocation of a model for "the frame-filling process" (263). This model seems somewhat jerry-built (with "demons" and such) (263), although it does provide for a fairly realistic flexibility in dealing with the dialectics of known and unknown.

Others since have variously redefined the frame problem, dealt with the loose ends of Minsky's pioneering work, or taken off in directions of their own.

Bertram Raphael, for example, is especially concerned with frame problem implications for robot systems. He acknowledges that the problem has discouraged the development of advanced AI systems and contributed considerably to turning attention toward the development of what we now call expert systems. This trend, I would contend, is increasingly fueled by delusions of simplicity, and its limitations now make imperative a full-scale and more creative return to that problem. It is still true, as Raphael concludes, that "no completely satisfactory method has been discovered" for dealing with it.[5]

Daniel Dennett sees the frame problem as an area where AI researchers and philosophers should collaborate more.[6] Like other thought experimenters, he realizes that the originary enigma of the frame problem is that it is, in effect, already solved by organically embodied cognition:

When a cognitive creature ... performs an act, the world changes and many of the creature's beliefs must be revised or updated. How? It cannot be that we perceive and notice *all* the changes (for one thing, many of the changes we *know* to occur do not occur in our perceptual fields), and hence it cannot be that we rely entirely on perceptual input to revise our beliefs. So we must have internal ways of up-dating our beliefs that will fill in the gaps and keep our internal model ... roughly faithful to the world. (125)

If perceptual processes cannot account for how all the updating is accomplished, what internal processes could account for the rest? Whatever they are, they are not, as Dennett, echoing McCarthy and Hayes, persuasively argues, driven by propositional logic. Since "systems relying only on such processes get swamped by combinatorial explosions in the updating effort," it appears that "our entire conception of belief and reasoning must be radically revised if we are to explain the undeniable capacity of human beings to keep their beliefs roughly consonant with the reality they live in" (125–126). Now *that* is the real updating effort required; while Dennett does not propose a specific game plan for it, he does recognize that it must be interdisciplinarily collaborative on a new scale, although he neglects to speculate on the pertinence of semiotics.

But many philosophers who have engaged the frame problem have done so with little sympathy for the whole AI/expert-systems enterprise, a generalization that holds also for most semioticians, who bracket or reject the idea of a machine engaging in semiosis. Consequently, such philosophers typically have used the problem not as a spur toward deeper understanding and more creative strategizing but as an (or *the*) Achilles heel into which they can shoot all manner of epistemological arrows. One could easily compile a list of such philosophers, but probably the most exemplary is Hubert Dreyfus, who therefore can represent the rest.

Dreyfus compares Minsky's frame model to Husserl's analysis "of intelligence as a context-determined, goal-directed activity—as a *search* for anticipated facts" through which "the noema, or mental representation of any type of object, provides a context or 'inner horizon' of expectations or 'predelineations' for structuring the incoming data."[7] The comparison is not extended, but it does include analogous functions for Husserl's predelineations and Minsky's default assignments; and Dreyfus finds it compelling enough to argue that, just as Husserl's attempt at formalizing such functions "ran into serious trouble" (35), so will Minsky's. Thus Minsky, like Husserl, has taken on a futile "infinite task" but has done so more naively, by losing track of how human intelligence "presupposes a background of cultural practices and institutions" that "pervade our lives as water encompasses the life of a fish" (36). Terry Winograd's work toward a more holistic account of context through KRL receives a similar judgment.[8]

Indeed, Dreyfus's critique of KRL, with its focus on the problem of regress in specifying context, entails his most forceful counterstatement on frames. It begins with the originary enigma:

Human beings, of course, don't have this problem. They are, as Heidegger puts it, already in a situation, which they constantly revise. If we look at it genetically, this is no mystery.... Human beings are gradually trained into their cultural situation on the basis of their embodied precultural situation, in a way no programmer using KRL is trying to capture. But for this very reason a program in KRL is not always-already-in-a-situation. Even if it represents all human knowledge in its stereotypes, including all possible types of human situations, it represents them from the outside like a Martian or a god. (52–53)

As many AI workers have observed, critics of their enterprise have a way of constantly altering the definition of what would constitute its success, a maneuver that Dreyfus here takes to the tautological extreme of arguing that machine intelligence, however impressive, is not human because it is not humanly embodied. And he seems oblivious to the possibility that an extraordinary intelligence, *because* it is other than the usual genetically and culturally conditioned kind, might be quite useful.

But Dreyfus labors this argument, and at the same time he blames AI workers for ignoring "noncognitive aspects of the mind" (53) rather than suggesting how they might study them more productively (semiotically, I would propose) toward ends other than a total mimesis, which probably is both impossible and ultimately irrelevant to their enterprise. Well, maybe I am unfair to Dreyfus, accusing him of not doing what he never set out to do. Let me apply his critique more positively but also point out a blind spot in it that needlessly impedes thinking about the frame problem. His *ceteris paribus* thesis is essentially a sort of Wittgensteinian translation of that problem:

Whenever human behavior is analyzed in terms of rules, these rules must always contain a *ceteris paribus* condition, i.e., they apply "everything else being equal," and what "everything else" and "equal" mean in any specific situation can never be fully spelled out without a regress. Moreover, this *ceteris paribus* condition is not merely an annoyance which shows that the analysis is not yet complete.... Rather ... [it] points to a background of practices which are the condition of the possibility of all rulelike activity. (56–57)

Furthermore, those practices are a matter of "what we *are*," which is, because of the incompletable regress, "something we can never explicitly *know*" (57). Certainly the thesis makes a caveat worth having, but it not only serves as perhaps *the* significant criterion of AI accountability: it also tells us that the *ceteris paribus* condition is the most sensitive condition with which apeironic education must deal when engaging the indeterminate.

Still, regardless of Dreyfus's conclusions, one has to remember that the regress somehow *is* halted in the human brain/mind and by a process hardly as metacognitive as that which allows us to discern and puzzle it. That process, whatever its representational logic, is largely unconscious, as practical finally as an expert system in limiting "infinite tasks," and surely best understood in terms not so much of logical conundrums as of semiotic mechanisms.

Nonetheless, some work in *unconventional* logic has bearing on the possibility of a semiotic approach to the frame problem, as may be seen in the 1980 double issue of the journal *Artificial Intelligence*. That issue was devoted to the theme of nonmonotonic (or, to simplify, inconsistent) reasoning and featured papers concerned with extending the system of conventional logic, either by refining and enlarging it or by elaborating mechanisms for "meta-ing" it. Whatever the ostensible theme of those papers, the frame problem, in various guises, pops up enough in them to be regarded as the leit-motif of the issue. The problem is hardly solved there, but it is suggestively reconsidered; and I would recommend the issue to anyone concerned with the background to a semiotic approach.

However, it is Paul Thagard who really introduces a new step into the nonmonotonic dance by arguing for "the relative unimportance of consistency as a property of knowledge systems" (233).[9] He moves toward a semiotic view of the frame problem at least to the extent of defining a frame as "a particular kind of nested association list" that is "more than thinly disguised sets of propositions in predicate calculus" and emphasizing its procedural efficacy (236, 241). But he also adduces results from psychological research that argue for "at least a presumption that the human information processing system uses framelike structures" (245). For Thagard the particular power of frames inheres in their capability for rich procedural interrelation. This capability is of such importance in humans that one should not be unduly irritated by the "proneness to error" of default values (251). Indeed, he proposes that frame-based AI systems should procedurally accommodate inconsistencies and contradictions by placing constraints on inference production when they occur, localizing their effects much as human cognition, with its "modular character," does (253). Thus he proposes more attention to the overall capability of such systems, as humanly instantiated, and less to their fallibility.

In retrospect one can see Thagard's preoccupations as setting the stage for the surfacing of a paper by Brachman that had been "circulating underground for quite some time" (80).[10] Informally structuralist but not quite semiotic in his approach, Brachman mounts a sobering attack against the widespread use of prototypes in knowledge representation:

Along with a way to specify default properties for instances of a description, proto-representations allow the overriding, or "cancelling" of properties that don't apply in particular cases. This supposedly makes representing exceptions ... easy; but, alas, it makes one crucial type of representation impossible—that of composite descriptions whose meanings are functions of the structure and interrelations of their parts. (80)

As a consequence, frame-based AI systems "are able to represent only a fraction of what it might appear they can," because they fail to incorporate "some definitional capability," without which "frames cannot express even simple *composite descriptions*, like 'elephant whose color is gray'" (80, 81). Brachman argues not that default reasoning is unnecessary but that it is far from sufficient. It supplies negative power—that of dealing with what does not change or, in cancelation, with what is not the case—but lacks the means for defining what does change or is the case and so entails primitives at a rather high level of analysis (a limitation with which Minsky struggled).

Brachman admits the difficulties of any strategy of definition (circularity, incompleteness), especially for complex phenomena in a changing world. Still, he rightly insists that the avoidance of it, of some smaller grain of "compositional structuring" (and thus "representation by structured correspondence"), has given rise to frame-based systems that entrain crippling paradoxes of typicality (88). He calls such paradoxes "entertaining dilemmas" (nicely exemplified by the platypus as "the typical *atypical* mammal"), and they suggest that "in general it is probably a good idea to keep 'typical' out of the names of our nodes" (89). However, though he echoes Thagard in his conclusion that "the pendulum seems to have swung too far in the direction of exception handling," he does not pursue the development of an alternative approach (92).

The frame problem has since received more thought relevant to a semiotic approach, albeit none of it yet revolutionary.

In his elaboration of the requirements for a better theory of change, Yoav Shoham outlines worthwhile refinements in temporal reasoning, partly by renaming the frame problem proper "the inter-frame problem" and distinguishing it from the "intra-frame problem" (a matter of internal nonmonotonicity arising from concurrency of actions).[11] Though his theory requires that both problems be avoided, he offers no instrumentality for doing so.

Paul Thagard, by contrast, makes an important advance into the territory of machine semiosis. In a 1986 review,[12] he wrote, "If C. S. Peirce were alive today, he would be an avid practitioner of artificial intelligence" because "computational models provide new ways of investigating signs dynamically, seeing them in fluid interaction through diverse modes of inference and association" (289). Thagard does not attempt a thoroughgoing semiotic translation of the frame problem, but he does suggest the fruitfulness of dealing with it through Peircean abduction. The program that he, along with Holyoak and others, developed to exploit such abduction is called PI (processes of induction, abduction being regarded as a kind of probabilistic induction). The program is apeironic to the extent that it can combine existing concepts to form new ones and thus "produce new knowledge under conditions of uncertainty" (292). Though its use of both production rules and concepts (which cluster rules in a framelike way) makes it deductive as well as inductive and reliant on typicality rather than definition, the program incorporates features of economy that suggest a certain psychological realism, mostly in its provision for inferential focus. Thagard and Holyoak have exploited its constraints on informational swamping in limited simulation, but such work stops short of considering "mattering" in semiotic terms, especially in situations of radical (informational) change.[13]

Still, Thagard is on the right track in arguing that any useful theory of abduction must be "part of some sort of information processing theory of memory and problem solving," one that accounts for rich patterns of association and retrieval.[14] As he explains, "PI implements parallelism by allowing for the simultaneous activation of numerous concepts and for the (simulated) simultaneous firing of numerous rules" and thereby for the interrelating of "lots of problematic facts." Nonetheless, he readily admits that much remains to be done to determine whether such "mechanisms for spreading activation" could adequately describe the processes that shape the "amazing fit between our minds and the world that makes it possible for us to construct abductions." Be that as it may, his argument that there is no special faculty unaddressed by his discussion—unless, I might suggest, it is semiosis itself—persuades.

In *Introduction to Expert Systems*, Peter Jackson finds the frame problem, or variations on it, ubiquitous. It clearly has played a major role in defining AI research in what he terms its modern period (from the late 1970s on), which "is characterized by an increasing self-consciousness and self-criticism, together with an orientation towards techniques and applications" (8). This attempt to escape from an AI enterprise paralyzed by critical self-awareness into an expert-systems enterprise hell-bent on practical applications has, because of the persistence of the frame problem, turned out to be a move from the frying pan into the fire. Jackson doesn't say that, but he implies as much.

Jackson's survey illuminates this irony suggestively, albeit controversially. He agrees with Brachman that the appealing project of building frame- and object-based systems that rely on analogical representations instead of production rules and predicate logic has gone awry in its obsession with exception handling (67). Definition, conceptual composition, structural correspondence, minimal conditions of consistency, whatever useful supplementation to semantic nets such systems once promised—all are "open to question" until there is "further work on their epistemological foundations," which are "quite shallow" (67, 68). Whatever those neglected foundations amount to, they have not been substantially deepened by the development of expert systems based on either structured objects or a combination of frames and inference engine.

Jackson's conclusions concerning the state of expert systems are sobering. Many of them implicate the frame problem, and they suggest the importance of approaching it semiotically and with an awareness of the increasingly apeironic nature of knowledge. He asserts confidently—and, I think, correctly—that knowledge engineers want expert systems to function more like human beings and less like theorem provers. His assertion is "not motivated by anthropomorphism" but is made in recognition of "an essential requirement for the mechanization of expertise," one that "may mean that future systems will be less, not more, 'logical' than they are now." Why? Because expert systems "deal not with truth, but with knowledge." And, since "knowledge is corrigible," progress in machine learning "has been unsurprisingly slow" in the camps of both "'cognitivists'" and "'automatic programmers'" (205). In their representations of it, both have relied on oversimplifications of the uncertainty, incompleteness, and exceptionality that are part and parcel of human experience. Moreover, as Jackson stresses, implementing an expert system typically "is not a controlled experiment, in that the contrast with alternative approaches is seldom systematic" (216). But I would argue that expert-systems development will hardly go further without such experimentation, which ought to involve also comparing different *combinations* of approaches. As Jackson observes, "There is certainly little evidence from psychology to suggest that human beings use a single representational scheme for encoding information" (216). If one expands psychology until it comprises *semiotics*, then that evidence is much to the contrary.

No matter how multiple the approach to expert-systems implementation, however, it must encounter the frame problem. Just as theorem provers are, to follow Jackson, dominantly rule-based systems, so human beings appear to be dominantly model-based systems, precisely the kind for which frames are especially suitable (218). Consequently, any approach will have to deal with all the issues of dynamically structured data and inconsistency with which I have been concerned, and it will have to incorporate a world model and mechanisms for updating it, rapidly and radically in many cases.

Well, after this history, what kind of model? Doubtless framelike in some way, but composed of what? Surely Thomas Sebeok clues us in here: "The *Innenwelt* of every animal comprises a model ... that is made up of an elementary array [not a bad synonym for *frame*] of several types of nonverbal signs." In hominids that array is compounded, consisting of "two mutually sustaining repertoires of signs, the zoosemiotic nonverbal, plus, superimposed, the anthroposemiotic verbal" (74).[15] However one theorizes those repertoires, some equivalent of them must be instantiated in any future expert system that minimizes the frame problem. The *Innenwelt* of the machine must comprise a model made up of a frame of both verbal and nonverbal signs.

Thus I do not agree with Feigenbaum and McCorduck that "the critical bottleneck in artificial intelligence," particularly "applied AI," is "the problem of *knowledge acquisition*" rather than "the problem of *knowledge representation*" or "the problem of *knowledge utilization*" (84, 85).[16] I am persuaded that representation is the most crucial of the three, although I suspect that we will discover them all to be (versions of) the same (frame) problem.

Recently on the television program *Beyond 2000* one of the hosts used the word *semiotics* in reference to some high-tech research problem but then apologized for it and quickly passed on to another topic. We still live in an age in which such a gesture is perhaps typical, but not for long. AI and expert-systems researchers clearly have been exploring approaches with semiotic overtones, and some eminent semioticians have shown a burgeoning interest in machine semiosis. The time is ripe for reframing the frame problem.

Let me propose, more specifically, that in thinking of the frame as an array of signs, the frame problem should be recast as a one of *semioclasm*, of breaks between signifiers and signifieds arising from changes in referents (which idea should be distinguished from Roland Barthes's notion of "'semioclasty,' a destruction of the sign").[17] By such recasting, terminal assignments are conceived as signifieds, relatively more abstract at superlevels than at sublevels of the frame, whose "floatingness" (but not necessarily "destruction") of attachment is conditioned by the labilities of their referents (thus the destruction of a referent, however one imagined that, might well entail a destruction of attachment as well as a loss of the relevant signifier). Or, to turn this about, the degree of lability of the referent, as mediated by endosemiosis, determines the degree to which the signified (and associated signifieds in the tree of the frame) is called into question. In effect, my proposal is that we shift *our* frame from one that interprets the frame problem in terms of theorem prover nonmonotonicity (and theorematic contingency) to one that interprets it, no less logically, in terms of human semioclasm (and semiotic contingency).

What is gained by this shift? Certainly the theoretical particulars of this semiotized frame will remain vague for some time—in large part because AI and expert-systems workers have no more productive agreement on the conceptual architecture or the terminology of the frame than semioticians have on those of the sign array—but the advantages of the shift are not difficult to argue. Terminals can be readily understood as subframes, assignments as more or less floating or detached (less or more viable as defaults) on a continuum from apeironic to conventional knowledge. If Minsky's nodes are regarded as signifieds (or signifiers, or both, depending on one's perspective), then their relations could be described as interpretant (inter-)relations. Here, though, one might want to invoke a terminology more like that associated with Lamb's notion of the "nection." He defines that entity as "the internal sign or the micro-sign, . . . the basic module of which the individual semiotic systems are built" and "which we could describe as an organizing device that connects a combination of mental features to a meaning or consequence or function" and thus, through interconnections, constitutes the cognitive-semiotic "relational network."[18] Provisions for interframe sharing of terminals, the elaboration of frame systems, the evolution of metaframes (or metaframe systems) as well as the fine details of functions like terminal markers—all seem equally natural to the ingenuities of this approach. It appears to be the only one that can even begin to deal with codifying Dreyfus's "cultural situation" and sorting out the cognitive economies implied by the *ceteris paribus* condition. The semiotic approach should have little trouble accommodating Thagard's characterization of the frame as a nested association list or his defensible insistence on its tolerance for inconsistency, since, as Floyd Merrell observes, "Inconsistency . . . lies at the heart of semiosis, coiled like a worm, doubled back onto/into itself."[19] The sign array, however constructed as software, is definitional by its nature and should lend itself readily to Brachman's composite descriptions. If, as Thagard says, computational models allow us to see signs dynamically, surely it is conversely true that our increasingly dynamic view of signs should enable us to build computational models that instantiate fluidly interactive processes. Such models would entail frames that are semiotically procedural (far beyond being merely fancy databases with updatable slots) and can incorporate practical relevance restrictions and constraints on attention (mattering after all has to do mostly with precisely *which* frame is retrieved in response to a given situation and—a little more complexly, in a metaframe perspective—with *why*). The parallelism/concurrency mandated here now seems less a difficulty at the hardware level, more one that might be managed at the software level (if the two levels can still be so distinguished) by richly interrelated arrays in which sharp-edged inference is intertangled with much fuzzier associational patterns.

But how do we translate the frame problem into semioclastic terms? That task requires that we learn more of how humans handle semioclasm. In more or less routine situations they seem to handle it well; that is, if a "normal" 30-year-old person moves from her first house to a second one, then the break between *my house* (as signifier) and the first house (figured as the signified) is mended by an updating that substitutes the second house (figured as a signified). But what if the person is 80 years old and moves from her nineteenth to twentieth house? (And one could continue: what if she is married for the fifth time, is afflicted by Alzheimer's, and so on?) The point is that, though humans have "solved" the frame/semioclasm problem, they have done so only to some degree. There are circumstances, increasingly more prevalent in a world of accelerative change, in which people cannot deal with that problem well. The outer situation may be too changeful for "normal" human comprehension, or the inner world model may be sclerotic with defaults (traditionally typical of old age?) or adrift on weak and constantly switching terminal assignments (traditionally typical of youth?). There also may be combinations of these possibilities, any of which can be imagined, in extremis, as psychotic. And any of them may be described as involving disjunctive signifieds, things not meaning what they once did or being indeterminate in meaning (culturally or even neurologically). But surely we can learn from these hyperbolic circumstances much about the character of the human modeling system, how it deals (and fails to deal) with semioclasm.

We do not have to look far to find circumstances of interest. A controlled semioclasm doubtless is crucial to cognitive growth and creativity. Lev Vygotsky says as much of the former when he characterizes literacy in terms of the acquisition of the ability to detach signs from any unique context.[20] Somewhat similarly, creativity, as many have argued, very much involves the displacement of old meanings and the assignment of new ones (in both cases signs are broken and mended/updated with a different signified). But what if semioclasm is not so controlled? A version of what happens is what happened a hundred years or so ago in Meiji Japan:[21]

When European languages and their phonetic orthographies replaced Chinese as the central repository of otherness, language itself became ineluctably bifurcated into sign and meaning. The infusion of foreign technological and cultural artifacts ... transformed the environment into one of kaleidoscopic opacities resistant to immediate comprehension. Perception itself became a form of translation, an epistemological encounter with the dislocation of meaning constituting the modern experience of the world. (261)

This circumstance did not occur—and does not variously continue—without dire consequences, though the Japanese in some ways arguably have succeeded in dealing with it as a positively apeironic opportunity. But notice the unavoidable implication that the Japanese are not alone in their "epistemological encounter." Theirs is *ours*, is increasingly everyone's; and insofar as our experience of the world is no longer modern but postmodern, that dislocation is all the more frame-problematic.

No one has explored the scale and purport of this postmodern dislocation of meaning more cogently than Bill McKibben.[22] Though he is concerned principally with the greenhouse effect and related phenomena, they entail issues semiotic in flavor:

We have not ended rainfall or sunlight; in fact, rainfall and sunlight may become more important forces in our lives. It is too early to tell exactly how much harder the wind will blow, how much hotter the sun will shine.... But the *meaning* of the wind, the sun, the rain—of nature—has already changed. Yes, the wind still blows—but no longer from some other sphere, some inhuman place. (48)

The consequence of the impact of human artifice becomes apparent: "We have deprived nature of its independence, and that is fatal to its meaning" so that "there is nothing but us" (58). Thus, "summer is going extinct, replaced by something else that will be called summer," but "it will not be summer, just as even the best prosthesis is not a leg" (59). In our "postnatural world" the connection between past and present is broken, so that "those 'record highs' and 'record lows' that the weathermen are always talking about—they're meaningless now" (60). Such phrases are still generally used as if their previous meanings were still pertinent to the situation to which they refer. Similarly, we continue to use the signifier *rain* as if it did not mean, among other subframe associations, something like "poisonous acid solution" or *sunlight* as if it did not mean, in similar fashion, something like "actinic carcinogen," although we seem to be gradually updating or at least tweaking the subframe for *sex* to include more associations with "death." Our world model has not been updated in terms of a radically changing world: the superframe *nature* is riddled with semioclasm. To mend it with updated meaning—as McKibben writes, "to work out our relationship with it" as a "new 'nature'"—"will take us a very long time ..., if we ever do" (96). Its unpredict-ability now has less to do with (the nostalgic notion of) the whims of Mother Nature than with a lack of correspondence with our model.

"What do you do when the past is no longer a guide to the future?" asks McKibben (133), indexing the nonlinearity, the nonmonotonicity, of this apeironic (if not psy-chotic) circumstance. If the defaults are out-of-date, the new assignments/signifieds are direly floating. "The problem is," to trope McKibben a bit, "there are no good sub-stitutes," and we have thereby "a vast collection of 'mights'" (133). This line of medi-tation about the seeming definiteness of the past leads him to speculate about ghostlier demarcations: "Such notions will quickly become quaint. The idea that nature—that *anything*—could be defined will soon be outdated. Because anything can be changed" (168–169). What most troubles him about this semioclastic apocalypse is that such redefinition as can be achieved may be worked out in machine terms, with the conse-quence that by a kind of metasemioclasm, all distinction between life and nonlife will break down (and, one supposes, culture will become "culture"). In view of McKibben's proposal for the global development of a "deep ecology" that would counter the mo-mentum of such a possibility (181), I would insist that its most important issue is that of how world and world model became so dangerously divergent. What has limited our updating? Can we learn—and this is the primary question for apeironic education—to do it better? And can we create AI and expert systems that can do it better or even bet-ter than we can, not to master us but to help us close the gap between mind, multifari-ous in its cultural articulations, and a runaway world?

If we are to understand more fully semioclasm and the mending of it, we must have not only a more sophisticated theory of change, as Shoham has emphasized, but one that treats change as temporalized semiosis that involves, to cite Dominick LaCap-ra's capsuling of the historical process, "iteration with alteration" with allowance for "major discontinuities or breaks across time" (336).[23] Such a theory must take into ac-count not only the way "objects may function as signifiers" but also the "'slippage of signifieds under signifiers'" and how a system can resist both the "vertiginous lability and rigid binary opposition" of meanings (247). In textualist terms, such a theory must deal with how a world text can be read diachronically as various text worlds or how various world texts can be read diachronically as the same text world; that is, it must provide for the switching (or not) of signifieds "under" signifiers (the making (or not) of new terminal assignments) in shuttling (or not) between differently constituted past/present interpretive frames. It also should offer ways to expedite such shuttling and to enrich the (endosemiotic) world text/text world interface in terms of the mutual changes entailed. Without such a theory we will not go much further in the devel-opment of humanlike expert systems; indeed, without it we may find ourselves pro-foundly lost in the woods of a world of just such historical alienation (not knowing what to update from) as McKibben envisions us already entering, a post-postmodern version of the world at the end of Umberto Eco's *The Name of the Rose*, a place where we "no longer know what it [the text] is about."[24]

But we have not gotten so lost yet. And we are beginning to become more sensitive to and intelligent about semioclasm. James White, in a book aptly entitled *When Words Lose Their Meaning*,[25] investigates interconnected changes in the world, in the world as constituted by language, in the reader who reads and writes the text of the world. Since "a text is in fact largely about the ways in which its reader will be changed by reading it," (19) reading (in the broadest sense) itself involves, by this construal, a process of updating. Thus "reading" a text (a situation, the world) requires a crucial sense of difference between past and present, for words (signifiers) do lose their meanings (signifieds) over time and do not have "exactly the same meaning each time they are used" (23). Any "mode of thought" not responsive to such differences would be "impossibly mathematical" (23), synchronically prisoned, much as the thought of AI and expert systems is today. Recognizing the increasingly radical changefulness of meaning, we are gradually enacting White's advice "not to lament the loss of fixity but to learn to sail" on meaning's "shifting sea" (278). Can we help machines do so as well?

Perhaps a hint may be found in Susan Noakes's proposal for "a new strategy" of, as her title indicates, *Timely Reading*.[26] Her fundamental argument for this strategy is that reading "must be understood as the constantly transformed product of historical change, not a timeless process focused on timeless texts but rather a 'timely' activity" (xii). Though her principal concern is with literary texts, much of the argument she elaborates for her proposal can easily be seen as pertinent to the reading of other kinds of texts, even by a machine. Timely reading is an oscillatory reading of a text in terms of both what it meant *then* and what it means *now*, a shuttling back and forth "between exegesis and interpretation," each of which "mirrors and depends upon the other" (12, 13). Thus Noakes is interested, to translate to my perspective, in how a given world text can be read as two text worlds, two interrelated frames, in updating not in terms of changes in the world text (though they may be taken into account) but in terms of its context as embodied in the reader, exactly the background that the reader uses (or is used by) in reading the world text and that Dreyfus regards as outside the AI/expert-systems domain.

Noakes argues that a useful understanding of timely reading, which involves "two representations [of the same object] as both congruent and nonidentical" (compare LaCapra's "iteration with alteration"), requires that the process be semiotized (210). Her semiotization attends to semiosis as the "generation of interpretant-signs," with particular focus on "the temporality of the interpretant" (212). For her, as for Eco and much less for Peirce, "Change is essential to the interpretant," and she emphasizes "the fundamentally temporal character of ... reading ... by showing how the interpretant changes—that is, metamorphoses itself into another, and still another, interpretant" on various time scales (212). Thus the interpretant "must be conceived of as intrinsically and necessarily dynamic rather than static," as characterized by what she calls alternativity, a "tendency to posit more than one possible meaning" (213). Through such a conception she is concerned to understand better a process that could help us overcome the restriction whereby, as the poet Howard Nemerov writes,[27]

> we do not learn from history ... ,
> Because we are not the people who learned last time

an oblique but startling evocation of the frame problem. In Noakes's conception of the interpretant, "Reading is by nature a 'timely' activity" not only because the reader expects that the text means/meant something but also because "it is a process of sign production in which there occurs over time a series of substitutions of interpretants, backward and forward and back again, for the representation in the text" (215). With everything read (words, objects, events) "but elements in the process of sign production" (216), temporal contextualization, backward and forward, is imperative, which would seem to demand that frames be able not only to update interpretants but to back-date them as well (for which provision subgoal stripping is patently counterproductive).

This dynamic of interpretant shuttling does not get us out of the frame problem; indeed, it gets us more deeply into it, but with a fuller understanding that implies both important limitations on anthroposemiosis and, in Noakes's perspective, the possibility, perhaps for machines as well, of making (once again) a virtue of necessity:

I propose that the subject seeking to be conscious of its own temporality and of that of the texts it encounters must be always making its continuity in the present, and consciously doing so, while deliberately encountering an ever-widening range of information from the past, information that announces its discontinuity with the present.... The range of information that must be encountered must indeed remain "ever-widening" in that as one element of information becomes incorporated into the continuity being made in the present, it loses its character as temporally discrepant from the present; and different ones must be encountered to serve anew the old function, entirely essential to "timely reading," of recalling to the reader his or her temporal discrepancy from the text. (233–234)

Helping people be better exegetes/interpreters thus becomes a matter of "explicit education in the principles of hermeneutics" (243)—and, I would add, of semiotics— good advice for machine learning as well. And such education will have to be saliently apeironic because there is no possibility of ever really being updated, only one of being engaged in richer updating. In consequence of the permanence of electronic memory, machines may succeed over indefinite periods of time in being, as it were, both "the people who learned last time" and those who are learning this time (reproductive and inventive), but they still will have to make the best of a no-more-than-asymptotic mending of semioclasm. What Jules Henry says of human learning holds also, *mutatis mutandis*, for machine learning: "We will never quite learn how to learn, for since *Homo sapiens* is self-changing, and since the *more* culture changes, the *faster* it changes, man's methods and rate of learning will never quite keep pace with his need to learn," a predicament that is "the heart of the problem of 'cultural lag,'"[28] itself a version of the frame problem.

While mechanosemioclasm so far is a relatively simple phenomenon, the anthroposemioclasm from which we need to learn may well be much subtler than I have suggested. And though I offer the latter with little hesitation as rubrical for what must be the most basic failure (when unmended) of semiosis as adaptive behavior and its most basic success (when serving as a precondition for a new sign structure), empirical/experimental research has gleaned little about its mechanisms. Certainly one is tempted to theorize how it underlies Henry's cultural lag, how its mending involves (to translate Noakes into Derrida) the retention of the trace of what was changed (as unchanged), how it maintains beliefs/expectations that hinder the acquisition of (new) knowledge, how it figures in the relation between frame density and learning ability, how it correlates with probabilistic information-theoretical terms (specifically, the degradation of information into redundancy, increasing semioclastic defaults, or its enhancement through the accommodation of surprise, increasing apeironic mending), how it might help us better comprehend the shared features of various kinds of semantic aphasias/amnesias, and so on. But such theorizing will not become fruitful for AI/expert-systems development—or for human education—without more investigation, direct or indirect, of anthroposemioclasm in operation. There is, however, some research that bears on the matter, and more may be in the offing.

Let me cite a few examples. John Hutchinson and Daniel Beasley,[29] reporting results of their research on aphasia and related disorders in older persons, observe that "one common linguistic problem concerns a disturbance in *semantic* functioning" (by which patients have trouble understanding the meanings of words or cannot evoke words to express what their thoughts mean [anomia]), and they call for more experimental research "devoted to the study of subtle symbolization changes that may exist among geriatric patients" (160, 167). Reviewing the work of Piro and Irigaray, Bär[30] jointly reads the former's synthesis of findings regarding semantic dissociation in schizophrenics (in which the "relation between the sign and what it ordinarily signifies in a given culture is modified in various degrees") with the latter's study of linguistic automatism in senile psychotics and relates them "to the much more advanced semiotic studies of aphasia," seeing in all three kinds of disorders symptoms of semioclasm: "loss of lexical stability," "reduction of metalinguistic distancing," "incapacity to deal with multiple contexts simultaneously," and "general reduction or even abolition of the various receptor and central skills required to deal with novel information"—all "features ... of quasi-closed systems which tend to abandon interaction not only with the external environment, but often with the internal one as well"

(271, 275–276). Sebeok[31] notes how little we know about either the formation or impairment of human sign systems; speculates about the possibility that repetitiousness in aging or aged persons is "not simply a symptom of physiological deterioration" but "rather a semiotic manifestation of an adaptive strategy" that, along with other compensatory semiotic modifications, helps them "to cope with the unusually, often dramatically, altered social environment" in which they live; and is "convinced that the semiotics of old age is one of the most promising research areas for the immediate future" (59), especially—as I read him—if aging involves not only semioclasm but also processes of coping different from the "semiotic competencies 'normal' adults take for granted" (70). Deirdre Kramer and Diana Woodruff's study,[32] corroborating earlier research, shows "lower conceptual differentiation among older adults," but their study finds also that young women demonstrate "higher conceptual differentiation relative to all other groups"—results that are cogent but in need of further investigation, and clearly related to "highly educated older women" demonstrating "the greatest breadth of categorization" (282–283). Such results may well be pertinent to a fuller understanding of semioclastic sclerosis (terminals locked with outdated defaults or somehow otherwise—say, by neural necrosis—incapable of updating) and how it might be minimized. Furthermore, they correlate interestingly with the conclusion of Nancy Mergler and Michael Goldstein,[33] who, like Irigaray and Sebeok, argue that the old process information by a system different from that of younger persons (and certainly different from that of very young persons), that "the information-processing system of the elderly adult, though poorly suited for rapid, interpretative encoding of information, is well suited for the decoding and transmission of information already in the system" (78).

There is a strong implication here that the characteristics of dysfunctional semioclasm in humans are much the same as those in present AI and expert systems at the edges of their cognitive-behavioral envelopes. The better we understand such "pathological" semiosis, the better we will understand how and why such systems are hindered by the frame problem. If the key to updating is careful attention to and flexible reconceptualization (going "against the grain" of the defaults) in response to change/difference—I think it is—and if Kramer and Woodruff's findings are corroborated by further work—I think they will be—then the most productive way of dealing with the frame problem will be discovered/invented by exploring what must be called gynosemiosis. Virgil had it right (though for the wrong reason) when he described woman as "varium et mutabile." That is why the expert system of the future will think like a woman.

Which is not to say that we cannot gain from other semiotic studies knowledge useful to that discovery/invention. But it is certainly to say that we are slowly learning, from studies of sexual dimorphism and gender differences too numerous to cite here, a good deal about gynosemiotic capacities that have been devalued by the male-dominant cultures of the world but are crucially relevant to dealing with the frame problem—and that we should enlarge and deepen such studies. Those capacities, all present in men but apparently generally stronger (perhaps partly by reason of hemispheric morphology) in women, include, though doubtless are not limited to, acute sensitivity to changes in the immediate environment, fine motor skills, an ability to detect and formulate small sensory distinctions, a keen sense of affective/biological relevance, a tolerance for differing or contradictory points of view and the inconsistencies of their interplay, and (as Kramer and Woodruff observed) a powerful faculty for conceptual differentiation and categorization. The recognition of such capacities seems wholly appropriate in an age increasingly wary of objective universals, certainties, and absolutes (male narratives of sameness) and intent on intersubjective particulars, uncertainties, and relatives (female narratives of otherness).

To put it another way, our age is witnessing and more or less self-consciously promoting a shift from "the grand narratives" of knowledge to "the little narrative."[34] Consequently, as Karlis Racevskis synthesizes a cognate argument, "the role of the 'universal' intellectual ... has now given way to that of the 'specific' intellectual, the savant or expert."[35] And that expert, machine or human (though perhaps *we* should remain the metaexperts), is a creature whose god is in the details, the bailiwick of gynosemiotic discriminations. To acknowledge that situation, surely fortunate for expert-systems development (an enterprise that needs to welcome more women into its ranks), is not to advocate an overthrow of anthroposemiosis but to anticipate a continuing *renversement*, a corrective balancing of perspectives.

In an essay tellingly entitled "An Uncertain Semiotic," Merrell attempts to define our era in terms of how meaning is viewed. "Between the meaning determinists and the indeterminists," he asserts, "the scales at present weigh in favor of the latter" (250). That tipping began "around 1905 with Albert Einstein's special theory of relativity," when "a new world-perspective finally began to emerge," one that marks our era as that of "The Emergent Perspective" (250, 251). Merrell elaborates:

Just as quantum theory has superseded classical physics, so the "new cybernetics" approach has superseded the classical theory of communication. In this new era, and speaking generally of the reigning conceptual framework, incompleteness, openness, inconsistency, statistical models, undecidability, indeterminacy, complementarity, polyvocity, interconnectedness, and fields and frames of reference are the order of the day. (252)

One easily could extend his inventory to include fractals, chaos theory, string theory, fuzzy logic—all the conceptual apparatus we have developed to engage events, however categorized, that keep meaning in flux.

In an era so intricately woven with indeterminacy of meaning, the more we appeal to unrevised conventional wisdom (the established Certeau-esque "semiocracy") for answers and solutions, default harbors in the storm of environmental complexity, the more we risk institutionalizing a general unmending cultural semioclasm, an unresponsive closure to the indicators of (the signs constituted by) change/difference ("external" or "internal," perhaps Derridean *différance* itself) that puts us in the position of the old (at least those who are not "highly educated older women"), that of those otherwise withdrawn into automatism, that of our present intelligent machines. If humankind is to survive and endure more *meaningfully*, then it must, as it grows older, learn—and learn by—even more powerful heuristic strategies of mending. It must build machines that are "younger" and less automatic. In their joint dealing with the unknown, humankind and its machines must become more feminized, so that finally both are engaged in a common apeironic education.

Notes

I would like to thank Doug Klusmeyer for editorial assistance on this essay.

1. Peter Jackson, *Introduction to Expert Systems* (Wokingham, U.K.: Addison, 1986), 1.

2. John McCarthy and Patrick Hayes, "Some Philosophical Problems from the Standpoint of Artificial Intelligence," in *Machine Intelligence 4*, ed. Bernard Meltzer and Donald Michie (New York: Elsevier, 1969), 463.

3. R. E. Fikes and N. J. Nilsson, "STRIPS: A New Approach to the Application of Theorem Proving to Problem Solving," *Artificial Intelligence* 2 (1971): 189–208; Carl Hewitt, "Procedural Embedding of Knowledge in PLANNER," in *Proceedings of the Second International Joint Conference on Artificial Intelligence* (1971), 167–184; Marvin Minsky, "A Framework for Representing Knowledge," in *The Psychology of Computer Vision*, ed. Patrick Henry Winston (New York: McGraw-Hill, 1975), 211–277.

4. Joseph D. Novak, *A Theory of Education* (Ithaca, N.Y.: Cornell University Press, 1977).

5. Bertram Raphael, *The Thinking Computer: Mind Inside Matter* (San Francisco: Freeman, 1976), 175.

6. Daniel C. Dennett, *Brainstorms: Philosophical Essays on Mind and Psychology* (Montgomery, Vt.: Bradford, 1978).

7. Hubert L. Dreyfus, *What Computers Can't Do: The Limits of Artificial Intelligence* (New York: Harper, 1972; rev. ed. 1979), 34.

8. Daniel G. Bobrow and Terry Winograd, "An Overview of KRL, a Knowledge Representation Language," *Cognitive Science* 1 (1977): 3–46.

9. Paul Thagard, "Frames, Knowledge, and Inference," *Synthese* 61 (1984): 233–259.

10. Ronald J. Brachman, "'I Lied about the Trees' or, Defaults and Definitions in Knowledge Representation," *AI Magazine* 6 (no. 3, 1985): 80–93.

11. Yoav Shoham, "Ten Requirements for a Theory of Change," *New Generation Computing* 3 (1985): 467–477.

12. Paul Thagard, "Charles Peirce, Sherlock Holmes, and Artificial Intelligence: Review of *The Sign of Three*, ed. Umberto Eco and Thomas A. Sebeok," *Semiotica* 60 (1986): 289–295.

13. Paul Thagard and Keith Holyoak, "Discovering the Wave Theory of Sound: Inductive Inference in the Context of Problem Solving," in *Proceedings of the Ninth International Joint Conference on Artificial Intelligence*, vol. 1 (1985), 610–612.

14. Thagard, "Charles Peirce," 294.

15. Thomas A. Sebeok, "In What Sense Is Language a 'Primary Modeling System'?" in *Proceedings of the 25th Symposium of the Tartu-Moscow School of Semiotics, Imatra, Finland, 27th–29th July, 1987*, ed. Henri Broms and Rebecca Kaufmann (Helsinki: Arator, 1988).

16. Edward A. Feigenbaum and Pamela McCorduck, *The Fifth Generation: Artificial Intelligence and Japan's Computer Challenge to the World* (New York: Signet, 1984).

17. Roland Barthes, "Lecture in Inauguration of the Chair of Literary Semiology, Collège de France," trans. Richard Howard. The lecture was delivered on January 7, 1977, and published as *Leçon* (Paris: Seuil, 1978).

18. Thomas A. Sebeok, Sydney M. Lamb, and John O. Regan, *Semiotics in Education: A Dialogue* (Claremont, Calif.: Claremont Graduate University, 1988), 21, 22.

19. Floyd Merrell, "An Uncertain Semiotic," in *The Current in Criticism: Essays on the Present and Future of Literary Theory*, ed. Clayton Koelb and Virgil Lokke (West Lafayette, Ind.: Purdue University Press, 1987), 255.

20. Lev S. Vygotsky, *Thought and Language*, ed. and trans. Eugenia Hanfmann and Gertrude Vakar (1934; Cambridge, Mass.: MIT Press, 1962), 99.

21. Earl Jackson, Jr., "The Metaphysics of Translation and the Origins of Symbolist Poetics in Meiji Japan," *PMLA* 105 (1990): 256–272.

22. Bill McKibben, *The End of Nature* (New York: Random House, 1989).

23. Dominick LaCapra, *Rethinking Intellectual History: Texts, Contexts, Language* (Ithaca, N.Y.: Cornell University Press, 1983).

24. Umberto Eco, *The Name of the Rose*, trans. William Weaver (New York: Warner, 1984), 611.

25. James Boyd White, *When Words Lose Their Meaning: Constitutions and Reconstitutions of Language, Character, and Community* (Chicago: University of Chicago Press, 1984).

26. Susan Noakes, *Timely Reading: Between Exegesis and Interpretation* (Ithaca, N.Y.: Cornell University Press, 1988).

27. Howard Nemerov, "Ultima Ratio Reagan," in *War Stories: Poems about Long Ago and Now* (Chicago: University of Chicago Press, 1987), 6.

28. Jules Henry, *Culture against Man* (New York: Random House, 1963), 284.

29. John M. Hutchinson and Daniel S. Beasley, "Speech and Language Functioning among the Aging," in *Aging and Communication*, ed. Herbert J. Oyer and E. Jane Oyer (Baltimore: University Park Press, 1976).

30. Eugen Bär, "Semiotic Studies in Schizophrenia and Senile Psychosis," in *Semiotica* 16 (1976): 269–283.

31. Thomas A. Sebeok, *The Sign and Its Masters* (Austin: University of Texas Press, 1979).

32. Deirdre A. Kramer and Diana S. Woodruff, "Breadth of Categorization and Metaphoric Processing: A Study of Young and Older Adults," *Research on Aging* 6 (1984): 271–286.

33. Nancy L. Mergler and Michael D. Goldstein, "Why Are There Old People?: Senescence as Biological and Cultural Preparedness for the Transmission of Information," *Human Development* 26 (1983): 72–90.

34. Jean-François Lyotard, *The Postmodern Condition: A Report on Knowledge*, trans. Geoff Bennington and Brian Massumi (Minneapolis: University of Minnesota Press, 1984), 60.

35. Karlis Racevskis, *Michel Foucault and the Subversion of Intellect* (Ithaca, N.Y.: Cornell University Press, 1983), 129.

VI Broader Conceptions of Artificial Intelligence

Artificial Intelligence Research as Art

Stephen Wilson

Information Arts: Art as an Independent Center of Research

The art world is in crisis about new technologies and scientific research. There is much confusion about ways to respond. My paper "Dark and Light Visions: the Relationship of Cultural Theory to Art That Uses Emerging Technologies," which appeared in the catalog of the SIGGRAPH '93 art show,[1] tried to disentangle this confusion. It noted three varying stances artists could take toward the new technologies.

Deconstruction as Art Practice
Postmodern and poststructuralist analyses of contemporary culture have provided concepts, themes, and methodologies for creating art works that examine and expose the texts, narratives, and representations that underlie contemporary life. Technology and its associated cultural contexts are prime candidates for theory-based analysis because they play a critical role in creating the mediated sign systems and contexts that shape the contemporary world. In this kind of practice artists learn as much as they can about working with the technologies so that they can function as knowledgeable commentators. In one typical strategy, artists become technically proficient so they can produce works that look like a legitimate part of the output of that technological world while introducing discordant subversive elements that reflect upon technology.

Continuation of Modernist Practice of Art with Modifications for the Contemporary Era
Many in the art world reject substantial portions of critical theory, upholding the validity and cultural usefulness of a modernist, specialized art discourse with claims to universal aesthetic truth. They believe art can have an avant-garde function, that individual vision and genius are still relevant, and that artists can transcend their particular niches in cultural discourse. The work of some artists with emerging technology can be viewed as continuous with the work of artists who work with traditional media. They see themselves engaged in specialized aesthetic discourse and nurture their personal

sensitivity, creativity, and vision. They aspire to be accepted by the mainstream world of museums, galleries, collectors, and critics (or for some, cinema and video). They work on concerns and in modes developed for art in the last decades such as realism, expressionism, abstraction, surrealism, conceptual work. Indeed, they see themselves as essential to progress in art and seek to cultivate the unique and "revolutionary" expressive capabilities of their new media and tools.

Invention and Elaboration of New Technologies and Their Cultural Possibilities as Art Practice

The twentieth century was characterized by an orgy of research, discovery, and invention. Branches of knowledge, industries, social contexts, and technologies appeared that could not have been anticipated. These developments affected everything from the paraphernalia of everyday life to ontological categories. Artists established practices in which they participated at the core of these activities rather than as distant commentators or consumers of gadgets, even while maintaining postmodern reservations about the meaning of the technological explosion.

As I have described in previous works,[2] artists could participate in the cycle of research, invention, and development in many ways, by becoming researchers and inventors themselves. From the time of Leonardo until recently, the merger of scientific and artistic activity was not uncommon. Free from the demands of the market and the socialization of particular technical disciplines, artists could explore and extend the principles and technologies in unanticipated ways. They could pursue lines of inquiry abandoned because they were deemed unprofitable, outside established research priorities, or strange. They could integrate disciplines and create events that exposed the cultural implications, costs, and possibilities of the new knowledge and technologies. The arts could become an independent center of research.

A Fundamental Category Error—Research and Development as Cultural Concerns

Art derived from all these stances will continue to prosper and coexist. Art as research, however, is the most undeveloped and ultimately most crucial to the culture. The implications of scientific and technological research are so far-reaching in their effects on both the practical and the philosophical planes, that it is an error to conceive of them as narrow technical enterprises. The full flowering of research requires a much wider participation in the definition of research agendas and in the pursuit of research questions than is provided from those in technical fields alone. It needs the benefit of the perspectives from many disciplines, including the humanities and the arts, not just in commentary but in actual research.

This kind of artistic practice is not easy, and its outcomes are uncertain. It requires that artists educate themselves enough to function nonsuperficially in the world of science and technology. They must learn the language and knowledge base of the fields of interest and be connected to both the art and technical worlds, for example, by joining the information networks of journals, research meetings, and trade shows. It asks artists to be willing to abandon traditional concerns, media, and contexts if necessary. I call this approach information arts.

I have worked as an artist for the last two decades within this tradition of information arts and made the monitoring of scientific and technological research a basic element of my art practice. To that end, I have read research journals, attended scientific meetings, received a patent, acted as a developer, been a co-principal investigator in National Science Foundation projects on new technologies and education, and been a co-editor of *Leonardo*, the international journal of art and science published by MIT Press. I have identified several areas of emerging technology that I feel are important, such as telecommunications, artificial intelligence, hypermedia, body sensing, new biology, and material science. This chapter focuses specifically on my work with artificial intelligence as an exploration of one kind of art as research practice.

Artificial Intelligence as an Art Inquiry

Artificial intelligence is a field of inquiry that reaches beyond its technical boundaries. At its root it is an investigation into the nature of being human, the nature of intelligence, the limits of machines, and our limits as artifact makers. I felt that, in spite of falling in and out of public favor, it was one of the grand intellectual undertakings of our times and that the arts ought to address the questions, challenges, and opportunities it generated.

I undertook to learn what I could about the research agendas, accomplishments, and unresolved problems of the field. I read extensively, took courses, dived into the Lisp language, attended meetings, and corresponded with researchers. I identified areas of research that seemed undeveloped and entertained questions derived from this contact with the field. I produced art installations that focused on issues in artificial intelligence research. The sections that follow present some of the results of my research, both in art works produced and in critical analysis of AI research issues.

Readers should note that other artists have addressed AI issues and that this chapter is not a comprehensive review. For example, Harold Cohen,[3] Peter Beyls,[4] and the artists represented in the journal *Languages of Design*[5] explored the possibilities of developing algorithms that enable computers to generate behaviors that would be called creative. Extensive work has been undertaken on automatic composition systems in music. Joseph Bates[6] and his associates worked on a graphic world called OZ in which autonomous objects interact with each other trying to achieve private desires, reacting emotionally to events that occur, and forming simple relationships with other creatures. Naoko Tosa[7] created "Neuro Baby," in which a graphic creature responds to feelings it detects in a person's voice and synthesizes appropriate facial expressions. Artistic activity in this area will undoubtedly continue.[8]

Art Installations Exploring Issues in Artificial Intelligence

In my interactive art installations, the audience acts as co-creators in affecting the flow of events. These installations have been shown internationally in galleries and in specialized art and technology settings such as the Association for Computing Machinery's SIGGRAPH and SIGCHI art shows. They have explored a variety of issues in the relationship of emerging technologies to culture. This review focuses on those installations in which artificial intelligence was one of the focal issues. Details can be obtained from my articles about this art work.[9]

The artificial intelligence techniques used in these installations are often primitive; there are no breakthroughs for long-standing research questions. Often the installations use low-level ELIZA-like tricks or simulations of programs. Nonetheless, the works do provide new perspectives on long-standing research issues and identify fruitful areas for future research.

"Is Anyone There?" was an interactive telecommunications installation that explored issues such as the linkage of telecommunications and alienation, and the possibilities for contacts with artificial characters (see figure 1). It was shown at the 1992 SIGCHI art show in Monterey, California, the 1992 SIGGRAPH art show in Chicago, and the 1993 Ars Electronica show in Linz, Austria. It won an Award of Distinction in Prix Ars Electronica's 1993 international competition for interactive art.

Five locations in San Francisco were chosen on the basis of socioeconomic diversity and their significance to the life of the city. For a week a computer-based system with digitized voice capabilities systematically called pay phones in these spots, at a particular time every hour, 24 hours a day. It used intelligent response programming to engage passersby curious enough to answer a ringing pay phone in a short discussion, and it digitally recorded the conversations. The topics focused on the lives of those who answered and whatever they considered noteworthy at that particular location. At other times video was used to capture representative images of the locales of the phones and the people who typically spent time near them.

An interactive video installation set up months later allowed viewers to explore life near these phones by using this bank of stored sound and digital videos to selectively call up recorded responses and images. Visitors used voice recognition to interact with the computer. An interactive hypermedia program encouraged viewers to devise strategies for exploring this information, for example, using a spatial/temporal framework to choose to hear the record of people who had answered a financial district pay phone during the midnight to 3 a.m. period. Typical digital videos of the phone locales

 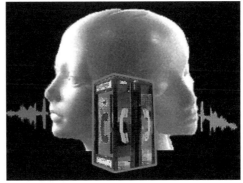

Figure 1

Stephen Wilson, "Is Anyone There?" An automated computer program called five San Francisco pay phones every hour on the hour, 24 hours a day, for a week. Digital characters embedded in the program had male or female voices and various conversational strategies to engage those who answered in conversations about their lives.

Figure 2

Stephen Wilson, "Excursions in Emotional Hyperspace." Four computer-controlled mannequins, activated by visitors' movements, spoke their feelings and reacted to each other. As long as a visitor stood by, a mannequin would go deeper into its feelings.

accompanied the recordings, and digitally manipulated images became metaphors for information about the recorded calls, for example, dynamic colorizing was used to indicate the depth to which a particular answerer went in a conversation.

The installations challenged the safety of passive art viewership by shifting occasionally into real-time mode and automatically placing live calls to the pay phones, linking the viewer with a real person on the street at the location on the screen. The event explored a variety of conceptual issues: telecommunications and telematic culture; interactivity, art audiences, and the safety of art spectatorship; hypermedia and the structure of information; and artificial characterization and intelligence.

Telecommunications and Telematic Culture
The telephone system is an artistically underexplored feature of contemporary culture. Telephones allow almost instantaneous linkage between people anywhere on earth. They enable new kinds of communication, including linkages between people who wouldn't ordinarily know each other and the creation of unprecedented kinds of social interchanges such as wrong numbers, answering machines, and telemarketing. "Is Anyone There?" explored both the concrete technological possibilities and the poetry of using telephones to overcome anomie in contemporary mass society.

Interactivity, Art Audiences, and the Safety of Art Spectatorship
This event challenged two common features of art viewing: the typically elite nature of high-culture consumption and the passivity of much art appreciation. All those on the street who answered the ringing pay phones—many who would be unlikely to attend any conventional art institutions—became participants in this art event. The drama of their dialogue with the computer system was an essential aesthetic focus. In addition, the event systematically questioned the safety of passive art viewing by requiring viewers to generate strategies to search the images and sounds of the stored calls. More radically, the event periodically shifted the viewer in the gallery from the safety of spectator to the challenging position of full participant. It placed live calls to the phone that the viewer had been vicariously experiencing and demanded that the viewer engage in a real conversation with a live stranger.

Hypermedia and the Structure of Information
Computer systems enable the storage and nonlinear retrieval of vast amounts of information, including text, image, video, and sound. These systems, which can dynamically adapt to the idiosyncratic inquiry styles of each individual user, raise questions about the most fruitful ways to organize, interrelate, and access new kinds of multimedia information spaces. "Is Anyone There?" explored an innovative kind of hypermedia art in which the structure of information and the navigational interface design were as much the artistic focus as the images and sounds.

Artificial Characterization and Intelligence

Many fears and hopes are raised about the possibilities of computers simulating the full range of human intelligence and characterization. This event investigated some aspects of these possibilities by exploring how self-revealing those who answered the phones would be with the various digital characters programmed into the computer device and how gallery observers felt about these exchanges.

The calling program lacked any real language parsing capabilities; it did not understand what the people said. It did have to be sufficiently engaging, however, so that answerers would continue with the increasingly personal discussion. To accomplish this, I incorporated information about typical conversations. I studied the phrasing, pacing, and repartee typical of telephone conversations. I tried to make the conversation believable as an interchange. Although most answerers seem to recognize the canned nature of the calling voice, a significant minority seemed convinced that the telephone computer was listening and understanding.

"Excursions in Emotional Hyperspace" was an interactive installation that explored issues like artificial characterization and motion in a space as a way of communicating with computers (see figure 2). It was shown at the art show of the National Computer Graphics Association in San Jose, California, in 1986.

Visitors entered a room inhabited by four mannequins dressed to represent four different characters. Each held a particular pose; each represented a different fictional person who had a specific set of attitudes. One of the characters was angry and rebellious; another was happy to be part of the event; another was reluctantly submissive; and another was philosophical and tried to take the big view.

Each mannequin wanted to tell its story and express its perspectives on being part of the event. Visitors were invited to walk around the room and look closer at the mannequins. Standing in front of a mannequin caused it to start talking in a digital voice about how it felt about being there. If a visitor continued to stand there, the mannequin went deeper into those perspectives. A visitor's walking away caused it to stop talking. Visitors could direct this small ensemble by their physical movements. A computer read sensors to determine motion and controlled speakers inside each mannequin.

Walking to another mannequin, however, did not cause it to just start anew with its story. The new mannequin would comment from its own perspective on what the previous mannequin had just said. The mannequins seemed to be actively listening to each other and tracking the conversation. There the new mannequin would then enter into its own comments.

Visitors thus had the experience of encountering artificial characters with intelligence and points of view, although this system lacked any real AI capabilities. The mannequins could not really recognize voice or parse the words of their fellow characters. All possible combinations of motion sequences were predetermined, and all appropriate comments on previous statements were prerecorded. Nonetheless, the experience for visitors did simulate contacts with artificially intelligent characters and encourage thought about these future possibilities.

"Time Entity" was an interactive computer graphic animation and sound installation that modeled an artificial creature (see figure 3). It was shown at San Jose State University's CADRE art festival in 1983 and at the gallery of the art department at San Francisco State University. California artists Matthew Kane, David Lawrence, and Eric Cleveland collaborated with me in its creation.

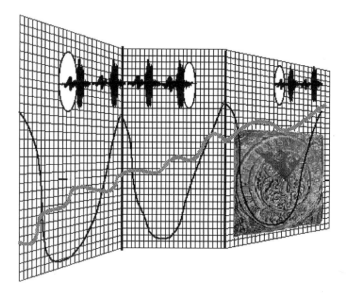

Figure 3
Stephen Wilson, "Time Entity." Visitors could interact with an artificial creature, or entity, that was obsessed by time and that lived in accordance with heartbeat, diurnal, and monthly rhythms.

AI, focusing on the simulation of human intelligence, inevitably raises questions about the nature of nonhuman intelligence. As an artist, I wanted to explore the creation of fictional intelligent species. I researched interspecies communication and SETI (Search for Extraterrestial Intelligence), and began to search for models of nonhuman intelligence. Simultaneously, I had been experimenting with the clock-calendar technology that had become available for microcomputers. I was fascinated by this capability of designing programs that knew the exact time and date much more precisely than human beings could.

I created a computer-simulated creature that was obsessed with time. It would know how long it had been alive and be obsessed with its future and its mortality. It would have intrinsic genetic predispositions to change as it grew older. Like biological organisms it would have monthly, diurnal, and heartbeat-length rhythms. It would interact with human visitors around this issue of time.

Our design team spent months debating the nature of the creature. We surveyed the biology of time as manifested by real plants and animals, and played with open-ended fantasies of how organisms might relate to time. We probed the capabilities of the clock-calendar technology we were using. Examples of some of the questions facing us were, Should the creature sleep? Should it dream? Should it develop gradually or in punctuated stages? Should its pace get more excited or calm as it interacted with humans? Should there be events that occurred at the millisecond level that were beyond the perceptive capabilities of the human visitors?

Physically, the entity was a computer graphic animation that moved on a video projection screen accompanied by computer-synthesized sound. It also had a tactile and kinesthetic life. Humans interacted with it by touching specially constructed, pleasant-feeling touch pads. It lived in a forest of upside-down pine trees. The smell was overwhelming, and many visitors remarked it was the first good-smelling computer art they had ever encountered. Its appearance and behavior changed with its age, time of day, and time of month. It had a regular heartbeat rhythm that pulsed its visuals and sounds.

Visitors could observe it move and grow or could actively affect its time life by touching the pads. For example, they could speed or slow its pace or choose to make part of it grow or die. They could choose to make the action happen immediately or at a specific minute in its future. At any given moment, its visual and sound appearance was the result of its intrinsic growth tendencies and all the interactions up to that point. The intelligence of the program was rudimentary, although it pointed toward interesting future research directions. Visitors reported that they had had a sense of encountering an unusual creature.

Our work as artists was discontinuous with the prevalent artistic traditions. The integration of concepts from other disciplines and the probing of the technology were at least as important as the sensual qualities of the final products. We were constantly forced to invent new extensions of the technology and ended up discovering capabilities of which even the manufacturers were unaware. We were working simultaneously as artists, programmers, engineers, biologists, psychologists, and AI researchers. Inevitably, artists working with technology in the new context will have no choice but to integrate this kind of role diversity.

"Demon Seed" was an interactive installation shown at the 1987 SIGGRAPH art show in Anaheim, California (see figure 4). Viewers controlled four computer-choreographed, moving, talking robot arms. The robots moved on platforms in front of galleries of digitized images of demons from various world cultures. The installation reflected on the tendency of people to project images of demons onto things they don't understand, and explored the idea of kinesthetic and tactile intelligence. There are signs that robots may be the next recipient of our demon-projecting fears. Moreover, because the world is shrinking through communications, several different cultures may come to share robot-demon imagery instead of having different monsters.

"Demon Seed" invited the audience to experience this combined fear and fascination with robots. Its robots were simultaneously ominous and endearing. Each platform featured a particular culture, with the robots moving in front of a gallery of repeated digitized images of spirit masks from that culture. Each was dressed in materials from that culture. For example, an African robot was outfitted with a small woven hemp broom, fur, and colorful African cloth. The robots seemed like mechanized priests or shamans.

Figure 4
Stephen Wilson, "Demon Seed." Visitors could interact with four computer-controlled robot arms by touch, via a velvet-covered squeeze rod, as well as by voice.

The computer moved the robots through a series of ritualistic motions. Sometimes all four moved in unison; sometimes, in counterpoint. Sometimes the robot dance rippled through, starting with the top robot and repeated in turn by each.

The installation did not ask the audience just to passively observe the robots. Commenting on our ability to exercise control, "Demon Seed" periodically gave viewers a chance to influence the robots' actions. I covered special squeeze rods, which could read viewers' squeezes, in lush purple and black velvet because I felt that the usual computer interfaces such as buttons, mice, and keyboards connote distance and coldness that is not always appropriate. Because of its subject matter, I wanted "Demon Seed" to convey intimacy, tactility, and warmth, which are not usually associated with computers and robots.

I was interested in the question of what would an intelligence be like that had to rely only on touch for communication. I invited the audience to devise patterns of squeezes, rubs, caresses, and so on, that would be used in communicating with the robots. I developed an expressive language of touch so that patterns of pressures and positions at the squeeze rod took on different meanings. I tried to construct the "language" so that there was not an invariant mapping of specific actions to particular effects. Although this experiment was preliminary, it was clear that the exploration of artificial intelligences that do not rely on sound or sight for communication was a fruitful area for future investigation.

Finally, viewers could enhance the robots' behaviors though speech. Periodically the robot they were controlling could pick up a viewer's voice from a microphone placed near the squeeze rods and then speak with processed digitized recordings of viewer words. In an eerie linkage, the robot spoke in a "demonized" version of the viewer's voice. I hoped this sonic link would lead the audience to think about the role of projection in human creation of demons.

AI Research: Areas That Call for Nontechnical, Aesthetic Decisions

In the art work and the analysis I realized that many of the decisions to be made about the shape of AI programs are not purely technical.[10] The simulation of human information processing outside of narrow realms, and the creation of machine partners that interest and satisfy people, will depend on sophisticated artistic and psychological design choices as well.

Some discourse about AI implies that intelligence can be viewed as an abstract, disembodied process. This view assumes that there is a "correct" way for the processes of natural language understanding, planning, problem solving, or vision to function, and that there are "raw" meanings programs can understand and manipulate. In this view, understanding and problem solving are technical accomplishments that can be assessed objectively. This section explains why this view is erroneous.

In interactions with AI programs, technical correctness in response is often viewed as the only criterion to evaluate interaction. Correctness means that the human interactor judges that the program's response indicates that it understood the gist of the human communication. Except in extremely circumscribed contexts, this restricted interaction may be unacceptable: people crave texture in interactions with intelligent entities that go beyond technical correctness, for example, personality, mood, purposiveness, sensitivity, fallibility, humor, style, emotion, self-awareness, growth, and moral and aesthetic values. Disaffection with limited interactions will become more severe as AI applications spread.

The texture of interaction is not a superficial decoration but is intrinsic to the basic fabric of humanlike understanding and intelligence. For example, these qualities affect the ways that we as humans understand words, see things, solve problems, and organize our memories. AI researchers who believe they are objectively avoiding these issues may be deluding themselves. Similarly, those who believe they are only following the classic scientific strategy of defining manageable research problems are underestimating the nature of what is being defined away.

There is no way to avoid making choices. For example, a program without a sensitivity to humor is not just a program that has not addressed humor. This kind of program will have difficulty understanding some aspects of human communication, and it will be viewed as humorless by human partners. The attempt to ignore the issue of humor translates into a decision to structure the program's understanding and communication potential in a way that, if exhibited by a person, would be called humorlessness. This section identifies some specific areas in which AI design must integrate humanistic perspectives: the physical basis of communication; the dangers of limiting domains; and computer models of self, world, relationship, and partner.

The Physical Basis of Communication—Appearances and Sensual Modes of Contact
Aside from traditional ergonomic considerations of physical and perceptual comfort, little attention has been paid to the physical context of communication between humans and computers. The details of computer appearance and the physical methods of communication are seen as trivial aspects of interaction compared to the actual information interchange. For a long time the domination of interaction by keyboard and video screen was not seen as especially significant. Then there grew to be interest in other methods, such as mouse pointers, digitizer tablets, touch screens, and light pens. There is speculation that future development of speech and virtual reality body-tracking technologies will make information exchange even easier.

The physical facts of interaction are more than peripherally important. They play subtle but important roles in our judgments. For example, the way an entity looks, moves, and sounds influences our assessments of its intelligence, its sensibility, and our comfort with interaction. The dominance of keyboard and mouse communication is an accident of history. In the past, these forms were used because of familiarity and economic rationales. Though at first they did not seem to interfere with communication, as expectations for interactivity grow this assumption might be questioned.

Why do we accept as foreordained that computers and monitors must manifest themselves in metal, wood, or plastic? Who decreed that they need to look like electronic devices? Perhaps they should look like stuffed animals. Perhaps they should not be restricted to one physical locus but rather spread out so that whole spaces become active. Who said that typing or moving a mouse is the best way for us to communicate with a computer? Similarly, who said that displaying text on a screen or a piece of paper is the best way for the computer to respond to people?

Interactions are haunted by the appearances of computer paraphernalia inherited from the past. We have come to expect that computers should have certain appearances and should communicate in certain ways. The expressive possibilities of other modes of communication, such as nonverbal signals, have gone unexploited because of our legacy of assumptions (for example, see Edward Hall's *The Silent Language* and *The Hidden Dimension*).[11] Future explorations in these areas have already opened up new interactive possibilities.

New relationships between people and computers may require that we free ourselves from these expectations. It may be impossible for us to accept that computers are intelligent, given their current appearance. They may not need to look exactly like humans, but a wider range is necessary than currently exists.

Similarly, the physical means of communication needs to broaden. The channels are too narrow. Speech opens up significant new possibilities. The choice, however, of monotone or greatly restricted variation that characterizes the current generation of synthesizers is in fact no choice. Monotone is interpreted not as objective speech sounds without variation but rather as dull and machinelike with all the associated connotations of dumbness or maliciousness. AI developers need to pay attention to previously neglected qualities such as inflection, tone, and timbre. Recognizers need capabilities to read these qualities, and synthesizers need capabilities to generate these subtleties of sound and integrate them with meaning.

Communication modes similarly do not need to be humanlike. They could be modeled on animals or on totally artificial, fanciful forms. Perhaps in addition to traditional methods, computers could express themselves by changes in shape, color, size, texture, smell, or motion. Similarly, they might gather information via all the senses. Perhaps there would be appropriate situations in which we would communicate with the computer by rubbing, stroking, and snorting as well as key presses. Indeed, computer simulation of human understanding may require multimodal sensual data collection in ways we don't yet understand. Perhaps one day we will even know enough to allow communication via extrasensory perception and emanation or direct reading of brain waves.

These decisions about appearance and communication mode require psychological and artistic sensibility. What will be the effect on people of various appearances? What forms of communication will allow maximum expressivity for the artificial entity? How should it move, make sounds, or receive human contact? These decisions are not "just aesthetic" because the shape of human-machine communication is incomplete without attention to them.

The Dangers of Limiting Domains

In AI engineering the strategy of limiting domain as a method of creating problems solvable by AI is prominent. This strategy is a classic approach to scientific problem solving—work on smaller problems on the way to larger problems. I suggest that there are major shortcomings in applying this strategy to some AI problems because critical issues in the relationship of people to machines are ignored. Programs will perhaps always need to work within limited predefined domains, but there is much more room for interesting variation to be built in.

In addition, many AI researchers underestimate the importance of enhancing variation. They believe AI programs can function neutrally and objectively without sacrificing effectiveness. They would like the programs to handle more variability, but they see the sacrifices as minimal in the quest to develop functioning systems. Much of the variation in human-human contact is seen as unessential fluff. Unfortunately, the result may be that we are adjusting to computers rather than vice versa.

For example, expert programs that claim to understand natural language require human speakers to limit vocabulary and syntax in the messages they speak or type. These limitations of expressive style and range of discourse represent a major unrecognized issue confronting the future of AI and human-computer contacts in general. Many may feel that these restrictions are not a great sacrifice, given the improved "friendliness" and responsiveness of computers in these limited zones of communication. They believe that it is acceptable to forgo variety in language so that the computer can understand even this limited amount of natural language. They would claim that many human-human interchanges in specialized contexts are similarly limited in vocabulary and style.

This claim is misguided. Human interchange is punctuated with subtle variations in expression and vocabulary, even in specialized, limited-domain interchanges such as business or consultations with experts. Similarly, human conversations meander, with fits and starts of intensity and slight topic changes rather than in a straight line. We expect this flavor and texture to conversations and feel something is awry without it, even in serious conversations.

Imagine what it would be like to converse with a person who disregarded anything but the main utilitarian thrust of your statements and always replied with invariant, straight-on efficiency. Even though such natural language systems might accurately understand our main meanings and produce their own appropriate responses, their performance would seem wanting and incomplete unless they provided some human conversational texture.

Giving up texture in conversations will be more of a sacrifice than is often imagined. Some analysts suggest that people are already adjusting their communication and thought to computers. I can imagine a nightmarish future where the natural language understanding requirements of the omnipresent computers force us to use stripped down, despiced language in communication with them. This style may spread to all our conversations.

There is another scenario. Computers should be adapted to us rather than we adapting to them. Developing AI programs that can understand the texture as well as the gist of our conversations is essential and possible. For example, there are understanding programs that reduce all mentions of humans' consuming solid nourishment (eating) to a primitive internal concept. This strategy allows the programs to proceed with following stories and making inferences about meanings. People, however, do not just eat in one way. Sometimes we gobble, gluttonize, devour, gulp, nibble, sample, gnaw, feast, savor, and so on. These subtle distinctions are essential parts of human conversations and lives. Connotations are as important as denotations. Similarly, different adjectives and adverbs create families of meanings from any one core sentence. Understanding these subtleties is an absolute prerequisite for future acceptance of AI programs. Similarly, the programs themselves will need to texture their language in order to maintain the interest of their human partners.

Movement and vision programs face similar dilemmas. They can't deal with the complexity and unpredictability of normal human physical worlds. In factories where robots must work, the solution is often to simplify and standardize the setting. Some futurists believe that most settings will someday be adjusted for our artificially intelligent helpmates. For example, people dream of the day when robots will take over the drudgery of housework and household management. Our current houses are not set up for artificially intelligent robots. Vacuuming becomes a horrendously complex task when the vacu-robot must navigate around and under normal household paraphernalia. The standardization of construction would bring the dream closer.

At what cost? We must guard against the tendency to eliminate and streamline the texture of our verbal and physical lives just so they won't cause problems for AI programs.

Computer Models of Self, World, Relationship, and Partner

In order to understand natural language, AI programs must be provided with a repertoire of meanings, connections, and expectations required for dealing with the elliptical nature of normal human communication. In order to solve problems and learn, they must be provided with knowledge representation frameworks in which to store information and to make deductions. They must be given search strategies with which to look for solutions to problems. In order to visually recognize objects and scenes, they must be given expectations about the possible compositions they might encounter.

To succeed in settings that approach the complexity of everyday human life, AI programs need models of themselves, their human interactive partners, the relationship between themselves and the humans, and the world. Human beings succeed in perceiving, understanding, and conversing about the world because they share expectations (often preconscious). As psychologists such as Jean Piaget and Jerome Bruner have noted, understanding is not just passive reception but rather active construction based on mental schema built from years of experience. Personal contact with experiences activate reserves of associations ready to fill in and make sense of new perceptions and concepts. Similarly, computerized problem solving can proceed only when there are working models of the problem domain.

There are no "right" models to embed in the programs. There is no engineering solution to these problems. Human schema are influenced by personal life experience, temperament, culture, class, sex, philosophy, and the many other influences identified by social scientists—and artists.

For example, cultures differ in the distinctions they make. Eskimo culture uses over 20 words for snow, each describing different features. A designer of an AI program would need to decide if this part of a model of the world should be incorporated. This importance of culture means that AI work may not translate across cultures as easily as other technical innovations have. "Fifth generation" AI developers may be surprised one day to discover that some AI programs must be culturally specific.

Dramatists and novelists spend lifetimes developing characters who uniquely perceive themselves, others, and the world. They endow them with a fictional life that guides interactions so that readers might predict how the characters might react, even in situations not included in the author's works. Analogously, visual artists create rich, intriguing artificial worlds that have a deep life beyond their surface content. One could think of these centuries of work as development of knowledge representation schema.[12]

Certainly, within very narrow, specialized areas of concern such as those addressed by expert programs, a single model of the small relevant subworld can be agreed upon and used as the basis for program understanding. In more general contexts, however, technical consensus on the best model of the world to use is unlikely. Other bases must be used. And here is where AI research must incorporate other disciplines to help in the choice and design of the internal worlds.

The typical interactive computer program passively accepts text from a human user and tries to respond appropriately. As mentioned earlier, this rhythm of question and answer within a dry, efficient protocol will be seen as boring, dull, and intolerable as AI programs spread. People want more in interactions. They want their partners to initiate and volunteer. They expect contributions of personality, texture, and mood. Conversation is a kind of dance in which people take turns leading and following and try to anticipate the movements of their partners. Programs will not be able to join the dance if they are not endowed with characteristics that serve as sources for their contributions.

The world models can partially provide program bases from which to originate communication. Programs with different world models would react differently to the same situation. Also, programs can be made different in their processes. Already AI researchers have discovered many design decisions that can affect the perceived personality of the programs. The crafting of program personality might require different decisions than those based on ideals of technical efficiency.

For example, in AI problem-solving programs decisions must be made about the process of searching among possible actions, for example, breadth versus depth first and use of various evaluative criteria. One can well imagine the shaping of various "personalities" based on these design decisions, for example, timid and careful versus impetuous and risk-taking versus opinionated and closed programs. Just as humans differ, so could programs differ in the way they process information.

For centuries artists have been asking themselves related questions about the entities they create. The advent of AI computer technology expands the arenas in which they can be asked and the repertoire of possible answers.

Summary: Artificial Intelligence as a Cultural Research Issue

At its core, artificial intelligence research is about much more fundamental issues than construction of the next year's model of expert system. The culture desperately needs the definitions of research agendas, the generation of hypotheses, and the pursuit of research questions in this field to reflect the perspectives and wisdom of people from a wide range of disciplines, including the arts and humanities.

If we are going to have artificially intelligent programs and robots, I would have sculptors and visual artists shaping their appearance, musicians composing their voices, choreographers forming their motion, poets crafting their language, and novelists and dramatists creating their character and interactions. To ignore these traditions is to discard centuries of experience and wisdom relevant to the research questions at hand.

Notes

1. Stephen Wilson, "Dark and Light Visions: The Relationship of Cultural Theory to Art That Uses Emerging Technologies," in the art show catalog, ACM (Association of Computing Machinery) SIGGRAPH '93, 20th Annual International Conference on Computer Graphics and Interactive Techniques, Anaheim, California, August 1993.

2. Stephen Wilson, "Industrial Research Artist: A Proposal," *Leonardo* 17 (no. 2, 1984); "Research and Development as a Source of Ideas and Inspiration for Artists," *Leonardo* 24 (no. 3, 1991); *Using Computers to Create Art* (Englewood Cliffs, N.J.: Prentice Hall, 1986); *Multimedia Design with Hypercard* (Englewood Cliffs, N.J.: Prentice Hall, 1991).

3. Pamela McCorduck, *AARON'S Code: Meta-Art, Artificial Intelligence, and the Work of Harold Cohen* (San Francisco: Freeman, 1991).

4. Peter Beyls, "Creativity and Computation: Tracing Attitudes and Motives," presented at FISEA '93 (Fourth International Symposium on Electronic Art), Minneapolis, Minnesota, November 1993, sponsored by Inter-Society for Electronic Art (ISEA). Published in *Leonardo* 28 (no. 4, 1995): 285+, with introduction by Roman Verostko, ⟨roman@verostko.com⟩.

5. For information, contact Raymond Lauzzana, 1333 Gough #8B, San Francisco, CA 94109, who was editor of *Languages of Design* until 1994.

6. Joseph Bates, "Edge of Intention," in the art show catalog, ACM (Association of Computing Machinery) SIGGRAPH '93, 20th Annual International Conference on Computer Graphics and Interactive Techniques, Anaheim, California, August 1993.

7. Tosa Naoko, "Neuro Baby," in the art show catalog, ACM (Association of Computing Machinery) SIGGRAPH '93, 20th Annual International Conference on Computer Graphics and Interactive Techniques, Anaheim, California, August 1993.

8. For information about this body of work, see Richard Zach, Gerhard Widmer, and Robert Trappl, *Art/ificial Intelligence. A Short Bibliography on AI and the Arts*, ÖFAI Report TR-90-14 (Vienna: Austrian Research Institute for Artificial Intelligence, 1990), ⟨http://www.ai.univie.ac.at/⟩; and the catalog of the art exhibition (curated by Joseph Bates), AAAI-92, Tenth International Conference on Artificial Intelligence, San Jose, California, July 1992.

9. Stephen Wilson, "Interactive Art and Cultural Change," *Leonardo* 23 (no. 2, 1990); "Environment-Sensing Artworks and Interactive Events: Exploring Implications of Microcomputer Developments," *Leonardo* 16 (no. 4, 1983).

10. Stephen Wilson, *Information Arts: Intersection of Art, Science, and Technology* (Cambridge, Mass.: MIT Press, 2002).

11. Edward Hall, *The Silent Language* (New York: Doubleday, 1959); Edward Hall, *The Hidden Dimension* (New York: Doubleday, 1966).

12. Brenda Laurel, *Computers as Theatre* (Reading, Mass.: Addison, 1991).

Why AI Is Not a Science

Maurizio Matteuzzi

In this chapter I put forward the two following theses: artificial intelligence is not a science; and artificial intelligence is a rigorous part of an intertheoretical approach to every scientific theory, what I call the philosophy of theories.

Preliminary Considerations

Artificial intelligence researchers normally avoid the problem of defining their subject matter. An introduction to artificial intelligence (AI) usually begins by stating that it would be too hard a task to precisely define what AI is, and then proceeds by listing many fields of application in which AI is concerned, such as game playing, theorem proving, and natural language processing.

By contrast, defining this subject matter is the very task I am undertaking here. It is not unusual for scientists to postpone the definition of their scientific areas. This attitude is frequently assumed by chemists, biologists, and physicists. But the main reason, in their case, belongs to the didactic order: one cannot explain one's work and one's interests to a beginner without first having introduced a sound and robust framework of basic concepts. In the case of AI, in my opinion, an additional structural reason makes a definition of the area as a science impossible.

As is well known, AI lies at the intersection of several fields, such as philosophy, psychology, linguistics, and computer science; I argue that this is unavoidable.

A Definition of Science

The Two Incompatible Souls of Science
There is an implicit understanding in modern philosophy that the concept of science involves two antithetical presuppositions: certainty and progress. On the one hand, scientific knowledge is assumed to be incontrovertible, and on the other, to be continually changing. These two features are aporetic within the same level of discourse (a linear increase of knowledge being too trivial a solution). The way out of this paradox

is to determine at which logical level one can put the legitimate need for certainty, and to distinguish a second level at which one can place the equally valid need for development and improvement.

Roughly speaking, my idea can be summarized as follows:

• The basic molecular constituent of scientific knowledge is a mathematical structure of a universe, a language, and a logic, which I call a theory in a technical sense.
• A science may be thus defined as a series of homogeneous theories, where again *homogeneous* is a technical term.

Thus the single molecular constituent ensures the stability of science, whereas the series of constituents provides the internal dynamics, following a well-known philosophical paradigm. Think, for instance, of the pluralists, who try to avoid the contraposition: Heraclitus and Parmenides. Take atomists: the atoms stay unchanged, to explain stability, while their permutations are always in progress, to perform change. Our understanding needs both to fix time and to let it run. I use such an approach to test whether or not AI can be thought of as a science.

Thus, I now focus on a new definition of *theory* sound enough to bear the notion of science.

The Notion of Theory

The term *theory* comes from the Greek word θεορία and is present with unimportant variations in the main Western languages. Thus we have *théorie* (French), *Theorie* (German), *teoria* (Spanish), *teoria* (Italian). The Greek word comes from the verb θεοράω, whose meaning is "to look all around," in the sense of looking from the vantage of a higher point of view. The term *theoria* in the sense of a whole, comprehensive doctrine is used by Plato and Aristotle. As I show, there are two interesting features in the etymological explanation that are useful for our goals. On the one hand, a theory is involved with a hypothetical form of reasoning; on the other, it offers a comprehensive solution to a given problem.

In order to avoid misunderstandings, I list some other meanings of *theory* that are in some sense different from mine, and with which I cannot, therefore, completely agree. In other words, I begin by saying what a theory is not.

In common usage, the hypothetical feature of the term is prevalent: when you say that someone has a theory about something, you mean that she has a general, reasonable explanation, that is, a hypothesis. What I have in mind here, on the contrary, is the scientific use of the word as exemplified by "set theory" or "game theory." Every theory has, in a sense, a series of basic presuppositions, and so we can say that it has a hypothetical nature; but the character of hypothesis is external, not internal to the theory itself. It regards the theory as a whole. Inside the theory, its theorems are certain; outside, they have the same uncertainty as the theory itself.

Another use that differs from the one I propose here is the one of mathematicians. I want to refer here not to what kind of theory a mathematical theory is itself but to a misleading common use of the word *theory* by mathematicians. In this use, a theory is simply a set of propositions together with the set of their logical consequences. Against this approach I put forward the following two points: (1) A theory must be a systematic and organic explanation. So propositions involved in a theory must be in a sense homogeneous; one could hardly recognize as well-founded a theory of propositions beginning with a determinate letter, such as *b*. And (2) such an explanation must be concerned with a specific domain. What I mean is that some ontic or at least ontological commitment is needed in order to have a theory. Both these problems are solved by introducing a third element besides logic and language, that is, something like the universe of discourse; I will call it the universe of the theory. The mathematician, in his use, takes care of the linguistic component of a theory as he speaks of propositions, and of the logical component as he speaks of the set of consequences; but the ontic component, the universe of discourse, is missing.

I assume here, as a theory, a mathematical structure composed of a universe, a language, and a logic. More formally, a theory θ is an ordered triple $\langle U, L, \lambda \rangle$, where

U is a (possible structured) set, "universe of the theory θ",
L is a (possible formalized) language, "language of the theory θ," whose semantics is in U,
λ is at least (in the simpler case) a first-order predicate calculus, "logic of the theory θ," whose semantics is in L.

These definitions take into account the simplest case. Of course, the universe U can be in turn something more structured than a simple set; for instance, a mathematical structure, that is to say, a set together with operations defined on it; or in a more sophisticated case, U can be in turn a full theory. In the same way, the language L and the logic, λ can be more complex. For instance, λ can be a pair of a full predicative logical calculus together with a set of meaning postulates, or postulates already linked to a specific universe, for example, Peano's postulates for arithmetic or Euclid's postulates for geometry.

Kinds of Theories

Following Carnap's suggestion, we can distinguish between *formal* and *real*, or *empirical*, theories.

Both formal and empirical theories assume a logic in the sense just defined. But in the former case, the objects of the universe are fully determined by it, while in the latter this is not so. In the case of an empirical theory, an object of the universe is underdetermined by the assumptions. Thus experimental tools must be devised in order to discover some attributes of the theoretical objects. Note that this does not mean that the theory comes back from the theoretical universe to the real world. In a formal theory, means to find attributes of the objects other than by axiomatic formal deduction do not exist. So, if an object is underdetermined by the axioms with regard to some attributes, the theory itself becomes undecidable. This difference enables us to understand the different level of ontic assumptions of the two kinds of theories: in the case of a formal theory, the goal is to predetermine experience, not to learn from it.

A very interesting problem arises as a direct consequence of this distinction. In fact, two opposite theses can be imagined:

- There are sciences that are per se formal and others that are per se empirical,
or
- All the sciences begin as empirical and then tend to become formal over time.

The first thesis is very clear. From this point of view, mathematical sciences such as geometry or topology are formal, whereas physics, chemistry, biology are empirical; it was so from the very beginning and will always be so. On the contrary, the second point of view claims that even geometry originated as an empirical science and that only at a further stage was it axiomatized. In other words, only when a significant corpus of knowledge has been acquired does it become possible to state a set of principles on the basis of which experience becomes predictable. The most important (and first) example was Euclid's systematization of geometry, but no doubt the same will happen for all the sciences. This implies that a science can be seen as a series that has an initial segment of empirical theories and, starting from the point of "Euclidization," a segment of formal ones.

Mixed Theories

I now introduce one of the most interesting notions of this approach—that of mixed theories.

Knowledge progresses by building up theories. The first step passes from empirical to theoretical objects, which entails abstraction. Knowledge effects its strong need for internal soundness through abstraction, that is, by breaking down its objects into their attributes and taking into consideration only a few of them at a time. Platonism consists of claiming for such theoretical objects an existence *ab aeterno*. On the other hand, theoretical objects that try to approach real objects again become *mixed objects*, or objects of the universe of a mixed theory.

A mixed object, which is thus not produced by simple abstraction, can be constructed in two ways: on the one hand, it can be the outcome of a process of knowledge, for example, when the features that abstract theories have already certified through abstraction are applied to a real object. On the other hand, an object can be "mixed" as the output of a special kind of abstraction, which rearranges, in a purely theoretical way, objects belonging to different universes and puts them under a one-to-one mapping until they can be reduced to one unit. In the first case, we are dealing with a real theory, which takes advantage of formal theories that, from a logical point of view, precede it; in the second, we have a new theory, which in a sense stays at a level of abstraction that is even higher than the theories that have been mixed together. It is important to note that the first case is not simply the application of some theories to concrete data. Finding some chemical as well as some geometric attributes in an empirical object is not enough to build a mixed theory based on chemistry and geometry. Qualities that pure theories have postulated for the objects of their universes must not simply be all present together in a certain concrete object; they must be linked. A certain social theory and a certain economic theory can build economic politics if, and only if, social values are not independent of economic values and vice versa. The human "fact" under consideration is then no longer an empirical fact for which we consider attributes coming from pure theories, but rather it becomes an object that belongs to the universe of a mixed theory.

Mixed theories can also be built by following an opposite process: rather than going back to the initial data, perform a further step of abstraction. However, and paradoxically enough, a higher level of concreteness may be reached by following this path. Consider, for example, the theory of real numbers and Euclidean geometry. A universe of mixed objects can be built by establishing a one-to-one mapping between geometric points and pairs of real numbers, straight lines and first-degree equations, and so on. The straight line r, determined by the two points $P(1, 4)$ and $Q(2, 7)$ and the equation $y = 3x + 1$, then become two different names for the same object. Under these conditions, expressions such as "the straight line $y = 3x + 1$" become meaningful. In this case, the objects of the universe are more concrete: without losing any previous attribute, they now have new attributes, which come from the other theory. As we go on adding attributes, we are passing from a more abstract to a more concrete situation.

To complete this brief survey, I mention in passing another important distinction between theories, though it will not be directly used in what follows. A theory can assume as an object of its universe another theory. Thus the distinction between object-theory and meta-theory arises. It is very interesting, in my opinion, to study the possible relations between object-universe and meta-universe, object-language and meta-language, and object-logic and meta-logic inside this new conceptual frame, that is, as a particular instance of the comparison between a theory and its meta-theory. But all this lies outside our present topic.

Intratheoretical and Intertheoretical Researches: The Dynamics of Theories

The general framework I have introduced can be useful to explain in a more formal way what we mean by scientific progress. A theory can be considered a (normally very complex) algorithm—an inferential engine or a machine for thinking. In other words, not all the features of the theoretical components are present at the very beginning of a theoretical process. A theory has deductive power, and it is that power that makes the theory grow. We may say that a logical deduction in λ, being interpreted in **L**, can make some sentences of **L** always true or can cause the introduction of new names; and such sentences or names, being interpreted in **U**, put some objects into (theoretical) existence. In Euclidean geometry, for instance, one discovers, at a certain stage of the theory's development, that there is a constant ratio between a circumference and its diameter. A name is now needed, and one assumes that its denotatum is given for every possible circumference of the theory's universe. Voilà, π now exists.

Through a growth process, a theory can (but not necessarily must) become complete or, as I prefer, "saturated." A theory is saturated when its logical apparatus does not introduce any further noun or object. In other words, we could say that its consequences can be fully predicted or determined, even if they are a denumerable infinite set. For instance, in the propositional calculus it is possible to obtain an infinite number of tautologies, that is, of logically true sentences. However, it makes no sense for a scientist to work at adding a new theorem to the list because for every given formula it is possible to determine, in a finite number of steps, whether the formula is a theorem or not. Thus we can say that propositional calculus is a saturated theory. In a sense, we can say that a saturated theory loops inside itself. Let $\mathbf{Cn}(\theta)$ be the set of consequences of the theory θ; then we can say that if θ is saturated, $\mathbf{Cn}(\mathbf{Cn}(\theta))$ is equal to $\mathbf{Cn}(\theta)$.

A theory can take the place of another theory. Faced with a fact we are not able to explain in a theory, we must modify our fundamental assumptions. We can perform this task in two ways: first, by enlarging the initial assumptions and putting them into a more general system; second, by arguing that they are wrong and assuming quite new starting points. The relation between the theory of Einstein and the physics of Newton can be considered an instance of the former case; as an instance of the latter, think of the relation between the theory of Copernicus and the geocentric system of Ptolemy. In the first case, the scope of the original theory (e.g., Newtonian physics) is dramatically enlarged, even if its axioms continue to be true. In the second case, on the contrary, the starting theory is invalidated as it is replaced. Note that in the first case we do not have simply an enlargement in the sense that all the sentences of the preceding theory go on being true: enlarging the general assumptions introduces many new theorems, while some other statements stop being a theorem or even being true in the theory.

Artificial Intelligence

One of the most immediate consequences of my definition of science as a series of homogeneous theories—where *theory* has the meaning defined—is that several areas of study can no longer claim to be sciences. The reason is that they lack a universe of their own, or a language, or a logic. Of course, this does not mean that an area of study, not being a science, cannot be scientific or cannot use scientific methods. Anything can be studied from a scientific point of view. You can do a chemical analysis of a picture, or a geometric one of a table, even if neither painting nor "tablology" are sciences.

What kind of objects would make up the universe of AI? Lisp and Prolog computer programs, or the metaphor computer/brain, or the way humans think? All these are involved, but any definition based on such concepts would be reductive. The main problem is that AI does not have a well-defined universe, for the following reasons:

- Intelligence can deal with whatever process, with whatever program, for whatever kind of human or nonhuman processor. I claim that we can find intelligence everywhere. As a consequence, making abstraction from the concrete processes yields a unique output.
- AI is concerned not only with studying such processes but also with realizing them.

A possible objection to the first point could be that the situation does not seem to be so different in the case of other sciences. Consider the case of geometry, for example. Even if any existing thing has a geometric shape, this does not preclude the universe of geometric entities from being a whole, separate, and self-consistent corpus. The problem is that the same argument does not hold for intelligence because we consider it a property, not an individual. To put it differently, intelligence does not tolerate reification because reification, starting from whatever thing, gives a unique output. If you are studying a triangular garden, you can have, as an abstraction, a triangle (leaving aside the question of whether the triangle is generated by us or is Platonically already existent). If the garden has a different shape, you can deal with another figure, such as a square, by abstraction. Starting with different intelligent processes, you reach the same abstraction, "intelligence," which, like Schopenhauer's *Wille*, makes sense only as a whole.

The second point is of course connected. Intelligence, in ontological terms even though not in grammatical terms, is a property, not a thing. Having intelligence is only a stylistic variation of being intelligent. In my opinion, only living beings and processes can be intelligent, not things. Artificial intelligence, to be "artificial," must discard living beings. We remain with nothing else but actions and processes. We have lost things. We remain without a universe in the sense explained here. It is for this ontic faint that, as students of AI, we are committed not only to studying but to realizing and duplicating processes.

The ordered series of physical theories constitutes the science of physics. The one of chemical theories constitutes chemical science. And so on. A chemical theory has its own objects, which are the chemical ones. Can we say that AI is a theory, in the sense used here, or an ordered series of theories? Clearly, this is not the case. The objects with which AI deals are either objects of the real world, studied from a particular point of view; or artificial objects built by AI itself. Like philosophy, AI is concerned with all the instances of knowledge and of "intelligence": chemical objects, the behavior of a person playing chess, computer algorithms, the brain structure, and so on. As a general methodology, AI approaches every theory horizontally and as a consequence every science, assuming the objects with their attributes, that is, with the attributes stated by their own universes. AI has no ontic commitment, and as a consequence has no strong descriptive power in a specific universe. Furthermore, it cannot be thought of as a mixed theory; for it would be the mixed theory of everything. Even though it looks at different universes, AI does not build any ontological link between them. In order to have a mixed theory, two objects already defined by their theories must be recognized as being the same thing; in Cartesian geometry, for instance, a point on a plane and a pair of real numbers are fully determined by their theories (Euclidean geometry and the theory of real numbers, respectively) before being considered as different names for the same thing. However, artificial intelligence makes no claim that two "intelligent" processes, using the same strategy, are different names for the the same object. Suppose an AI student realizes that a chess player and a program concerned with job scheduling with penalties use the same strategy of alternate depth-first and breadth-first search in order to avoid the exhaustive combinatorial search on a tree. The AI student would probably not see any unique new object unless she were so deeply Platonist as to think of the common search strategy as an eternal, ideal, robust object. It is in this sense that I argue that AI functions as a general methodology rather than as a science.

There is another reason why AI cannot be reduced to the previously explained frame of theory and consequently of science. The essential feature of a theory is its descriptive power. Its final output is an (at least denumerable) coherent set of (well-formed, that is, belonging to a specific language) sentences interpreted in (meaningful with respect to) a determinate universe. Some practical acts can depend on a theory, but they are external to it. Even the most applied science (theory) has this characteristic: it sees its own task as that of describing but not performing some real processes. For AI this is not the case. AI is both theoretical and practical, in the sense that its main goal is not only describing but duplicating intelligence (which otherwise would not be "artificial"). As a consequence, AI has inside itself both theoretical and practical goals, and in such a situation a positive loop arises: some theoretical hypotheses can generate (and be tested by) applications, which in turn can suggest new hypotheses and explanations.

The Brain-Computer/Mind-Software Metaphor

What I can conclude from the preceding assumptions is that AI, because of its lack of a universe of its own, cannot be a theory or a series of theories. It can be concerned with every thing and every theory. I feel that some evidence for this conclusion arises, in some sense unexpectedly, from the main topics of the AI critics. I have in mind, above all, the arguments against AI of Hubert and Stuart Dreyfus and those of John Searle. Without considering all the details of the complex and numerous theses of these authors, I perceive a central point on which all these depend: AI, to be effective, needs to know the whole world or, what in a sense is the same, needs common sense, or background. The false assumption of AI, according to these authors, is that all problems can be attacked within the rationalistic symbolic tradition of Descartes, Leibniz, and Husserl, and of the Wittgenstein of the *Tractatus*. In their view, to answer questions as simple as "Was or was not the hamburger older than three thousand years?" an AI program would need common sense, or background, or a real life. Connected with this point of view, there are two more theses: (1) not every process can be reduced to the application of a set of rules, and (2) the identity of inputs and outputs is insufficient to prove the identity of two processes. These three points put together mean the death of AI, which could eventually survive only as a metaphor between brain and computer, and mind and software, but only because computer science is an up-to-date technology. In the same sense and with equal legitimacy, according to Searle, the brain was compared, some decades ago, to a telephone exchange, and some time before that, to a telegraph system. That is to say, we feel that the great complexity of the human brain is comparable to the currently most modern and sophisticated technology.

Not being a psychologist, I am not so concerned with defending the brain-computer analogy as being stronger than a simple metaphor. But as a philosopher I hold the following points of view.

1.   I have no problem agreeing with the three points mentioned by the critics of AI:

1a.   Common sense is, or can be under certain conditions, a feature of intelligence.

1b.   Not every process can be reduced to a set of rules.

1c.   Two processes, A and B, can have the same inputs and the same outputs and nevertheless be quite different from each other.

2.   All these points are a direct consequence of, or strictly connected with, what I have already explained, that AI is not a science because it lacks a well-defined universe.

2a.   Polling the universes of different theories, but outside them, AI at every contact point needs a background, that is, the context of the other theories. A science can avoid common sense because it assumes a partial, theoretical universe, built on not-existing objects. Biology deals with the abstract, not with the existing, the universal "dog," not my dog. Thus many features of my dog are lost; but biology has no need of common sense.

2b.   My agreement with thesis 1b, not every process can be reduced to a set of rules, needs to be specified. I accept the sentence in a gnoseological sense, not an ontological one. What I mean is that we are not able, now, on the basis of our present knowledge, to explain some processes by rules; but I do not believe that there is a process intrinsically without rules. This would be a miracle and in any case not a "process." Having more space, we would need perhaps some terminological clarification on this point. However, the central argument can be saved in an independent way. For instance, a free (without rules) process cannot be "intelligent." So, such a situation simply states that AI does not claim to explain everything in the real world. I myself could list many nonintelligent actions, processes, people.

Some authors insist on the important role played by meaning when human beings apply rules, and they underline, rightfully, that meaning has no role in the case of a computer executing rules. It seems to me that these authors forget a very interesting type of thought and intelligence. With regard to this, Leibniz speaks of "symbolic or blind thought," as when we say that a "kyliagon" is a polygon of a thousand angles. Can we represent to ourselves a "kyliagon" in the same sense in which we can think of a hexagon? It is important to underline that the impossibility of such a representation does not indicate a defective feature of our intelligence. Rather, it constitutes one of the most powerful means our reason has for dealing with the complexity of the world. We are able to put meaning into brackets, and to use a symbolic apparatus such as an algorithm, or a machine for thinking. If a mathematician, performing calculus, were forced to give a meaning to every step of his work, he could not reach the most trivial goals.

Suppose you have 1,785 sheep, and you want to assign them to 15 shepherds. You will probably do something like the following:

$$
\begin{array}{r}
119 \\
15\overline{)1785} \\
\underline{15} \\
28 \\
\underline{15} \\
135 \\
\underline{135} \\
0
\end{array}
$$

Of course, 1785 refers to the sheep, 15 refers to the shepherds, and 119 refers again to sheep. But what is the meaning of 28 and 135?

To understand this better, think of the opposite situation, where you have no algorithm. Take, for instance, the Roman notation for numbers, in use before the Indo-Arabic reform of numeric symbolism. You have MDCCLXXXV sheep, you must assign them to XV shepherds. Try to perform the needed calculation. As you see, in some cases the solution process is ruled by signs, not by meanings. Searle may be right about the fact that the processes performed by human beings are ruled by meaning, that is, are semantically well founded, and on the contrary the ones performed by computers are only based on signs, without real meaning; but this is not always an advantage.

2c. Two processes can obviously lead to the same result though be very different from each other. They can be different at every step. Leaving out Searle's example on the style of parking,[1] think of the following instance. You have to put a lot of books into a bookcase. The two rules "Take the shortest and put it on the left" and "Take the tallest and put it on the right" generate two processes which are at every stage quite different but have the same input and the same final result. This simply proves that a real brain and a computer could follow different processes and give the same output; as a consequence, realizing a process on a computer is not conclusive proof that we have the correct and unique explanation of a certain mental process (note, by the way, that this is not proof of the contrary).

But because AI does not have a specific universe of its own, this fact is not a criticism of AI. I am interested in a good Prolog algorithm, even though no evidence exists that this is exactly the same way the human brain performs the same task. AI is not a theory of the brain from a functional point of view, and this could eventually be a problem for neurophysiologists or neurologists. But I suppose it leaves AI students completely indifferent.

To summarize the point, which is probably the crucial one of the present paper: A real application of an artificial intelligence needs references to the real world, or a background, or common sense. But this simply depends on AI's lack of abstract objects of its own or on its weak ontological assumptions, AI being a general methodology rather than a science. As a methodology, it can only apply its conceptions to universes already defined by theories rather than build on a universe of its own.

Cognitivism vs Connectionism

Starting from assumptions like those discussed here, several AI critics, in more or less explicit form, show their preference for or leaning toward the connectionist approach. In my view, the opposition between cognitive science and connectionism is not well founded, at least insofar as our problem goes, which amounts to clarifying what AI is and is not. The attempt seems to me to be like discussing whether sight or hearing is stronger. Traditional AI has assumed as its main pattern the cognitive intellectual attitude of human beings. Connectionism, on the other hand, is interested in simulating low-level physiological processes. A neural network for pattern recognition, for instance, can perform its task better than any knowledge-based algorithm already in use, but the algorithm supporting the network has nothing to do with patterns or recognition. It is devoted to managing weights, thresholds, and signal propagation. All this is very interesting in terms of understanding human behavior, human physiological processes, and biological history but has nothing to do with intelligence. Or, better, the intelligence involved is outside, not inside, the object under study. In my opinion, unconscious intelligence is a contradiction in terms.

Conclusion: What AI Is

Is computer science a science? Obviously yes; that is a tautology. It follows from the principle of identity, Leibniz would have said. Computer science has selected its universe: its objects are all and only finite deterministic algorithms managed from a syntactic point of view. This means that we exclude many technologies and technological details that are now strictly connected with computer practice but have no relevance according to our epistemological point of view.

The upper limit of computer science is Church's thesis—only recursive functions are computable. This thesis defines the universe under consideration, which is the one of all the algorithms. AI's challenge is to go beyond Church's thesis. A problem can be interesting for AI and then belong to its field of studies because (1) it is a noncomputable problem, (2) it is a problem that is not practically computable, and (3) it is not formalized enough to be tackled by an algorithm. The difference between (1) and (2) is, in short, that for (1) we refer to nonrecursive functions; for (2) we refer to functions that are recursive but can be solved only by algorithms that have a complexity higher than polynomial, that is, exponential; consequently, after a small number of steps, they go out of space and time (in a sense that can be made precise in mathematical-physical terms).

There is also the fact that AI builds computer algorithms. Is this not a contradiction? The paradox depends on a change of perspective. AI obviously cannot battle against Church's thesis, which is a mathematical truth. Consequently, it cannot solve anything unsolvable. But it can realize through a program the same strategies and the same behavior used by an intelligent being who is dealing with such a problem. So, strictly speaking, what AI obtains as a solution is not, in a mathematical sense, an algorithm that solves the case; rather, it is a good strategy that could fail.

As Gestalt psychologists know well, a change of perspective can lead us to a quite different interpretation. As in the case of the famous picture—where an old woman and a young woman can alternatively be seen—it is possible to recognize an algorithm or a nondeterministic procedure in an AI program, depending on the initial point of view. From the perspective of assembly code, we are dealing with an algorithm; from the point of view of the goals of the program and its behavior regarding them (that is, at a higher level), we are dealing with an "intelligent" and nondeterministic nonalgorithmic strategy. The situation is similar in the case of human freedom. If the attention is focused on the physiological aspects of a choice, it is impossible to see anything but deterministic processes (analogous to assembly code); however, a free will is conceivable if considered from the point of view of the abstract reasons governing the choice.

From a robust concrete materialistic point of view, one could conclude that AI and perhaps human freedom itself are psychotropic drugs. Maybe. But is this enough to renounce our intellectual games?

Notes

I would like to thank Stefano Franchi for discussions leading to this paper and Güven Güzeldere for helpful discussions and commentary. Thanks also to Scott Walker for editorial assistance.

1. See John Searle, "Cognitive Science and the Computer Metaphor," in *Understanding the Artificial: On the Future Shape of Artificial Intelligence*, ed. Massimo Negrotti (London: Springer-Verlag, 1991).

Dance Floor Blues: The Case for a Social AI

Tom Burke

Put yourself in the following position. You are a fifteen- or sixteen-year-old white male, and here you are at a white middle-class suburban high school dance. And there is Mary across the room. You think she's pretty fantastic. Maybe she likes you, but as a matter of fact you've never really talked to each other. Maybe you should ask her to dance. That bass guitar is drumming out a good beat. You do want to dance with her. Or do you? Do you really want to cross the room and ask? She's smiled at you a couple of times in English class, and one time you both sat at the same table at lunch. But so what? She smiles at everyone, and she eats lunch with a lot of people. So where do you stand? Do you really want to dance with her? Well of course you want this to be an enjoyable-dance-with-Mary situation. In that sense you definitely do want to dance with her. But that doesn't answer the question. The question is, Is *this* that kind of situation? What if she says no? If that were the situation, then, no, you might be better off to just not ask, and in fact you do not want to dance with her right now. If she doesn't really like you, or if she doesn't like to dance, or if she is anywhere nearly as nervous as you are, then you don't want to press it and make matters more complicated than they already are. Or worse, what if she couldn't care less about you and made it obvious to everyone that she doesn't want to dance with a toad like you? In that case, you definitely do not want to dance with her. But what if she does want to dance with you? Did she just look at you? Darn! You weren't paying attention. For sure, what you want depends on what she wants. You want to dance with her only if she wants to dance with you. So what do you do? What do you want to do? You have to do something, to press the issue, to clear this up. You ought to make a move. Of course, you don't have to be dumb about it. You could go over there, but leave yourself a way out. You could go talk to someone you know standing close by. That would be a good thing to do anyway. Maybe you'll get a chance to talk to Mary that way. She only has to show you some kind of sign—look at you and smile, maybe even say something, anything—so that you'll know what to do, so that you'll want to dance.

However this little story ends up, it is designed to illustrate some facts about desire and other aspects of mentality, at least the mentality of a white adolescent, male variety, circa 1965.[1] The uncertainty involved in this situation means that you are uncertain with regard to your own "desire-state"—not that you could not articulate your desire clearly to yourself but that the desire itself had not been determined. The same can be said for some of your beliefs in this situation. It is possible to determine what you believe, desire, and intend to do only as the situation unfolds.

This points to something that is largely absent in the account of your situation on the dance floor, namely, the interactive character of experience. What you believed was not geared just to your own actions, desires, and beliefs but also to *her* actions, desires, and beliefs. Your beliefs, like your desires, were initially undetermined, but they were capable of being determined in the course of, and by virtue of, various mutual actions, not just in terms of what you did with regard to Mary but also in terms of her actions toward you and her reactions to you. It was up to Mary and you together in a larger social setting—not just you alone and not just Mary alone—to coordinate your actions and otherwise clarify the situation by cooperative and consensual means. It is not clear that one's desires and beliefs are socially distributed, but their determination—the active gathering and processing of information by which they are made determinate—often *is* socially distributed. Whether you want to dance with Mary depends, from one moment to the next, on how you and Mary proceed to interact, not solely on anything you can discern from past and present information.

The story also illustrates how indeterminacies in social situations can reveal us to ourselves in ways that mere perceptual experience generally does not. By compelling you to consider your own actions as means for altering present social circumstances, this type of situation serves to highlight and bring your self into focus. The uncertainty involved puts the spotlight on *you*. "Do I make a move, or do I hold back? I am uncertain, hence I am." Activities like playing Ping-Pong might yield similar results, but it would more likely be the social character of the game, not just its perceptual character, that brings the self into focus.

These observations support the claim that social situations, as opposed to merely perceptual experience, are what initially gave rise to the evolutionary development of an objective sense of self in the first place and ultimately to the emergence of human mentality, which is what I want to investigate in this chapter. The lesson to be drawn, or so I will argue, is that the artificial intelligence enterprise cannot afford to focus solely on designing software for an artificial agent's head. Without some kind of socialization, an agent will have no way to classify and hence objectify itself to itself, and hence it will not have the kind of constitution it takes to engage in mental activity. Socialization must be worked into the process of building a thinking machine.

If we believe the social psychology of George Herbert Mead and John Dewey, then the AI enterprise, at least with respect to its more ambitious aims to build humanly intelligent and autonomous machines, will not begin to achieve its goals without introducing a social dimension into the theoretical picture.[2] Mead and Dewey, working in the first half of the twentieth century, developed a view of human mentality and self-awareness that fundamentally draws on the social character of human nature. In this view, one would have to say that the AI enterprise has so far been misguided because it works with a faulty conception of human mentality, particularly by having no real appreciation of its social aspect. I do not wish to argue against the AI enterprise simply by pointing out that having a social life is something computers can't do—what computers can and cannot do may not be the important issue here, particularly since in talking about either artificial or natural agents we are talking about something more than just a computer.[3] But what and how much more? To begin with, a natural agent inextricably exists and acts in the world and hence is more than just a symbol processor inside of a skull. Moreover, according to Mead and Dewey, if such an agent has a mind, then that is the case by virtue of its possessing more basically a social nature. My aim here is to summarize this social-psychological account of human mentality. I do not want to make claims about what AI researchers can or cannot accomplish but only to point out certain design principles—having to do with the social character of human mentality—which so far do not seem to figure into what it is they think they are doing. I will try to paint a comprehensible picture of a rather complex view, sketching in fairly broad strokes a framework of ideas that serves as a positive alternative to certain erroneous preconceptions characteristic of the 300-year-old epistemology inherent in most AI research.

In order to understand what mind is, we first need to see how much of human experience we can account for without appealing to or taking for granted the presence or availability of mind. We should be able to go a long way toward understanding the nature of mind by studying the natural evolution and development of experience more broadly. According to Mead and Dewey, the workings of the mind in experience turn out to be only a small and later part of this evolutionary developmental story. As mental agents, we may find it difficult if not impossible to step outside of ourselves to get the right perspective on this fact. Nevertheless, it stands to reason, in their view, that this is a fact.

To properly address the question of what it means to have a mind or how mentality arises and functions in human experience, we need to work out a constructive account of how our thinking relates to the world—how it is that our thoughts (concepts, ideas, beliefs) correspond to the world at large (objects, events, facts). The account of *correspondence* between mind and world that I want to develop constitutes an elaboration of Dewey's alternative to a classical British empiricist picture of correspondence between facts in the world and true beliefs. The latter simplistically aligns and conflates various dichotomies: outer versus inner, physical versus mental, actual event versus representation, and so forth. In contrast, Mead and Dewey tended, in the absence of

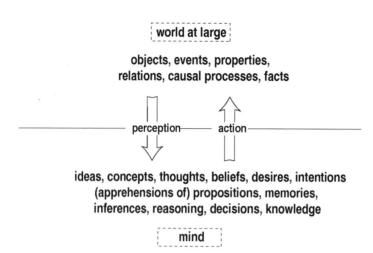

Figure 1
The classical view of human mentality.

evidence otherwise, to treat all such distinctions as mutually orthogonal. They talked in particular about a correspondence not between two kinds of ontological realms but between two kinds of experience: one that is basically perceptual and otherwise immediately engaged in the world, and another that is involved in planning and controlling the first kind of experience. There is a positive correspondence between these two kinds of experience if one's plans and expectations fit well with what is actually happening ("like a key fits a lock," as Dewey would say).[4]

In more detail, the classical view of human mentality (associated with a variety of thinkers from Locke to Russell) looks something like figure 1. Things are divided into two realms: (1) an external world at large, populated by objects, events, properties, relations, and facts, and (2) an internal world of the mind, populated by representations of things in the external world (concepts, ideas, thoughts), and supporting processes that manipulate such representations (inferences, reasoning, beliefs, desires, decisions). Following Descartes, this distinction constitutes an ontological duality of matter versus mind.

These two realms affect one another. Perception is a process by which the outer realm somehow affects the inner realm, producing ideas and such in the mind as results of causal processes originating in the world. Similarly, by virtue of decisions based on certain beliefs and desires, agents perform actions in and on the outer world, so that the inner realm thereby affects the outer realm. For example, a cup of coffee is in front of your eyes, so you see a cup of coffee (the outer realm affects the inner realm). You believe a cup of coffee is present; so if you want to drink some coffee, you reach out, grasp the cup's handle, bring the cup to your lips, and sip (the inner realm affects the outer realm). You taste the coffee (outer affects inner). You return the cup more or less to its original place (inner affects outer). And so forth.

In this view, a true belief is a belief about things that corresponds to the facts, to the way things actually are. The actions you perform in various situations will be determined by your desires and beliefs about such facts. Your belief that Mary wants to dance with you is true just in case Mary, in fact, wants to dance with you. Or, to say the same thing somewhat differently, a concept (in the mind) applies to an object (in the world) if the object actually has traits and fits specifications characteristic of the concept. For you, Mary falls under the concept "wants to dance with me" just in case Mary, in fact, wants to dance with you.

This outline of the classical view is simplistic, but even after some refinement various well-known problems remain. For instance, it isn't clear how these two realms actually influence one another, although obviously there has to be some such influence so that we can perceive things in the first place, much less think about them and act on our thoughts.

Various solutions to this puzzle have been proposed. Assuming that the external/internal distinction lines up with a physical/mental distinction, one might think that the duality is only apparent and that everything is really just physical. In some sense, the brain is the mind. Variations of this view include the claim that the mind, while not strictly identified with the brain, is to be found in how the brain functions, that is, we should look for the mind in the brain's software rather than in the hardware. There are various subtle and not-so-subtle ways one can try to make such ideas work. No solution so far proposed has come to be generally accepted, although this is the view that is implicit in AI research. However this pans out, we avoid the problem about the gap between these two ontological realms because the matter of how software and hardware influence one another is presumably well understood.

On the other hand, one might think that everything is really just mental. Everything apparently external to us, as well as everything internal to us, is just ideas—our ideas, God's ideas, someone's ideas. This sounds less plausible, or at least we quickly overreach our ability to understand what we are talking about by holding such a view. But at least on the surface, it would solve the ontological gap problem.

Putting such metaphysical questions to one side, there are still epistemological questions to consider, such as whether (and how) we can perceive things as they are, directly, or whether in the course of perceiving things we ever get outside the realm of our own ideas and beliefs about what or how things are. How one answers such questions leads to further questions about the nature of the alleged correspondence between these two realms, leading to an ad hoc naive realism, or in any case leaving us with no account of what it means to know anything of any concrete

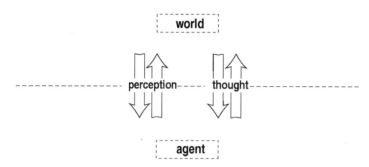

Figure 2
The social-psychological view of human mentality (an alternative view).

existential significance. That predicament is just a historical fact about modern philosophy as practiced according to the strictures of British empiricist epistemology. Such problems are not unique to this long-standing philosophical tradition, but they are problems that proponents of this view have not been able to address properly after several hundred years of trying.

The social-psychological philosophy of mind developed by Mead and Dewey differs from the classical view in various ways. They present a view that does not posit any kind of strict duality to begin with, so they are not faced with having to figure out how these realms interact or which of the two realms is more or less real or basic. There are distinctions to be made but not in the simple dualistic manner characteristic of British empiricism.

The view developed by Mead and Dewey looks something like figure 2. They start with a distinction similar to the classical divide between an agent and the world; however, this is not a strict ontological duality but a definite though somewhat fuzzy, if not floating, distinction between one kind of thing (an agent) and a single larger ontological domain within which it acts. Note that it is not appropriate to refer to this one grand agent/world realm either as "physical" or as "mental" because at this point we neither have nor want a physical/mental distinction to draw on. Without fixing categorical boundaries, but simply to acknowledge some distinctions, it is also important to note that the distinction between an agent and the world is orthogonal to the distinction between an organism and its environment.[5] The agent as such is an organism/environment system, and the world outside of the agent includes things within the organism as well as in the environment. Clothing, dental fillings, eyeglasses, canes, automobiles, and other tools and devices in many circumstances function as part of the agent (and of course, in other circumstances, not). Hair, fingernails, hands, feet, and virtually any other part of the anatomy can function as part of the world in circumstances where they are acted on by the agent (clipping fingernails, combing hair, dressing a cut finger, removing a loose tooth, and so forth).

Rather than an ontological bifurcation, the distinction between an agent and the world is more like the distinction between a knot and the rest of a rope, which is itself an interweaving of both organismic and environmental fibers. One can easily point to the knot and to the rest of the rope, but it might be difficult to specify where the knot begins and where the rest of the rope ends. In the case of an agent in the world, unlike an ordinary knot in a rope, various transactions and changes of perspective occur from one set of circumstances to the next that make a clean boundary between the two even harder to locate (as if the knot were to be incessantly changing size, shape, and position on the rope). Nevertheless, an agent/world distinction is no doubt acceptable in explaining what perception and thought are insofar as perception and thought *constitute* the transactions and transformations of circumstances that distinguish the agent from, and bind it to, the world at large.

In this picture, perception, rather than a one-way causal process, is by itself a two-way interactive process. An agent does not just passively register sensory excitations in order to perceive; rather, perception is an active, ongoing process—motor activities are as essential to perception as are stimulations are to nerve endings. Eyes and ears function dynamically in a dynamic world if they function at all.

Similarly—and this is the more interesting claim—thought (or what Dewey also calls reflection) is a kind of two-way agent/world interaction. Thinking doesn't happen just inside the head or purely within the agent, contrary to the computer metaphor.[6] Rather, one thinks by virtue of using, for instance, chalk and chalkboard, pencil and paper, paints and canvas, keyboard and monitor, objective media of all sorts, such that the hardware involved includes more than just connected systems of neurons. And the "software" controls not just brain processes but processes that include and exploit regularities and dependable constraints in the agent/world system as a whole.

In this view, thought is a dynamic process that has basically the same structure as perception, although it involves a different and more specific range of agent/world interactions. We therefore get a different notion of the correspondence between the things we perceive and whatever it is that we think about those things. In this case, the correspondence is not between entities or processes in two distinct ontological realms but between two kinds of agent/world interaction.

So far we have a rather broad outline of an account of what thinking is and of its general function in experience. I look at each of the processes of perception and thought more closely later. But first, even at this level of broad detail the picture is incomplete in the sense that it depicts only slices or flavors of experience. In particular, what is it that motivates any of this perceptual or reflective activity? What compels it to proceed in one way and not another? How or why does any of this two-way interactivity occur at all? To answer questions like these, Dewey and Mead proposed a theory of experience that was built around the notion of inquiry and problem solving.[7]

Neither perception nor thought, alone or together, constitutes the "experience" embodied in the process of problem solving. In order to complete an account of what experience is, we have to acknowledge a third element or dimension of activity that is independent of perception and thought as such but that is the common basis for their existence in the first place. That is to say, perception and thought occur as pieces or phases or parts of an overarching process that we want to identify as *experience*. According to Dewey and Mead, this overarching process consists of the activities involved in an agent's attempting to resolve conflicts, breakdowns, predicaments, or troublesome situations otherwise, in some broad sense of those terms. This natural impulse to resolve unresolved situations is characteristic of living systems whose existence depends not just on reproductive capabilities but also on their adaptability to changing conditions. Episodes of resolving discordant situations are the dynamic contexts in which perception and thought take place. Perception and thought have no other function or purpose except insofar as they are motivated, as problem-solving activities, by an innate and overarching impulse to resolve discordant situations.

In this view, experience consists of episodes of problem solving, which in its simplest form is a matter of an agent's being motivated to maintain some kind of stable existence. It is not that experience occurs within such episodes of problem solving, but that occasions of experience *are* such episodes.

These episodes of problem solving could be termed "inquiries" to the extent that thinking is involved in the process. That is to say, experience can be merely perceptual—such as when you can't quite make out a visual image until you squint or move closer to the object in view. This requires only perceptual resolution procedures, not necessarily thought processes. On the other hand, inquiry—a reflective sort of problem solving—involves both perception and thought.

When we bring these different features together—perception and thought in problem-solving contexts—we come up with something like a corkscrew picture of experience (a "hermeneutic helix"), depicted in figure 3. According to this picture, experience can be resolved into (1) a linear, progressive, teleological component (pointing in the "direction" of solving a given problem) and, orthogonal to that, (2) a circular, interactive component (consisting of perception and thought processes, which are not always in accord with each other).

The linear dimension of experience, which constitutes its primary impetus and its directedness, is a process of transformation of an unresolved situation into one that is no longer troublesome or problematic. This progressive, conative component constitutes the basic *intentional* character of experience. Even the most rudimentary forms of experience involve a kind of reference and attribution, even if the reference and attribution are neither linguistic nor cognitive in nature. Any given episode of experience involves a simple form of indexical reference to the present situation as the "subject" of experience; and it involves the attribution of a "predicate" to that subject,

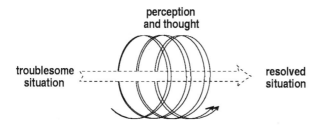

perception
and thought

troublesome
situation

resolved
situation

Figure 3
A "corkscrew" picture of experience.

in the form of an acceptance or rejection of the present course of activity (which is the content of the predicate) as being an appropriate response to the problem that gave rise to the "subject" in the first place.

The circular component of experience, on the other hand, consists of interactive processes of perception and thought. These interactive processes constitute the motions of the gears and drivetrains that make the linear transformation of the given situation happen. The story here is that the agent gets into a position to step its way through various transformations of a situation by sifting through details of the given situation and scoping out a space of possible courses of action. Perception and thinking are initiated and conducted only in such contexts of transforming some given situation (otherwise there is no impetus to think or do anything at all). As far as mere perception is concerned, the transformation proceeds more or less automatically according to the dictates of relevant habits, natural dispositions, and circumstantial accidents. To whatever extent thought is involved, this transformation is guided by more or less autonomous processes insofar as alternative courses of action may be explored and attempted according to the dictates of reason. So how do these processes actually work? I now look at these two circular aspects of experience in more detail.

The structure of perception looks something like figure 4. The terminology is taken mainly from Dewey, with some borrowing from ecological psychology.[8] Perception is depicted here not merely as the reception of sensory data but rather as a two-way action-reaction process. An agent's perceptual systems are two-way input-output devices sensitive to continual feedback, not just input-plus-transduction devices. In this view, perception is an interaction between the world at large and an agent attuned by evolutionary forces to various processes and constraints in this interactive domain.

This interaction has a more or less cyclical structure, which can be explained by walking through figure 4. In the process of perception, an agent performs *actions*, as determined by some collection of attunements to various regularities in the world. Such attunements are systematically bundled into more or less definite packages,

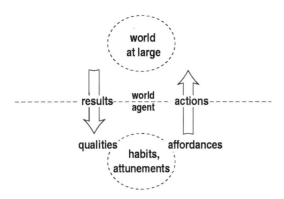

Figure 4
Perception.

which Dewey and Mead refer to as *habits*. The actions an agent performs have repercussions in the world, and the world acts back on the agent in response, producing some kind of detectable *results*. The results of particular actions are registered by the agent as *qualities* of the immediate situation, which as potentially familiar traits characteristic of certain kinds of things, trigger or otherwise activate selected habits and not others. (A notion of noncognitive rationality is introduced into the picture here, as measured by the appropriateness of given habits in given instances. The rationality involved in determining which habits are triggered in a given instance and which are not is a function of the systematicity of the spaces of constraints and processes that make up the contents of the various habits, matched against whatever actions and results are actually occurring in the present situation.) Such triggerings of the agent's habits constitute noncognitive interpretations of registered qualities, in the sense that habits bring to bear and otherwise make salient certain noncognitive expectations about what the triggering qualities signify. Such signification occurs on the strength of whatever constraints constitute those habits. That is to say, on the basis of registered qualities, the *affordances* of things are detected by virtue of whichever habits are triggered by those qualities. But then such affordances determine straight away what further actions are possible; and the process goes around and around, progressively transforming a given perceptual situation as new actions lead to new results, and vice versa. All this fits together to generate the process of perception—a two-way process where actions lead to results, results lead to actions, and the whole process is tempered and modulated by the way the world is and by various habits and attunements brought to bear by the agent.

For example, you walk into a room and there on the table, free for the taking, is a dark substance in a brightly colored paper cup. You will probably see a cola drink, if you are like me, or perhaps you will see coffee or used motor oil or blackstrap molasses,

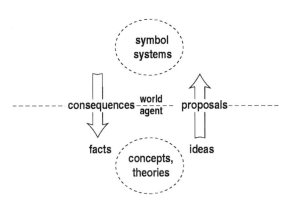

Figure 5
Thought (reflection).

based on different attunements. Note that what you perceive is based on a very limited array of qualities that are not sufficient by themselves to uniquely determine what you do in fact perceive. Continued visual probing will likely as not confirm your current perception but not rule out other justifiable possibilities. Your subsequent actions might in fact lead you to alter your perception, such as when you walk over to the table, grasp the cup, bring it to your lips, and sip the liquid. The resulting taste may in fact disconfirm whatever expectations you might have had that permitted you to perform those subsequent actions and otherwise treat the substance as if it were cola rather than motor oil. However things turn out, these and other ongoing actions are part of the process of perceiving the colalike substance. This interaction may be entirely mindless in the sense that it may proceed automatically, requiring no thought or deliberation.

Thought, by contrast, is a distinct and more or less independent activity in its own right. Nevertheless, it is patterned after perception insofar as its overall structure goes (see figure 5). That is to say, thinking is itself a two-way interactive process. But instead of the world at large, it more specifically involves symbol systems embodied one way or another in linguistic, discursive, or expressive media. In the course of thinking, we use objects or events in the world (such as specially designed pencil marks on paper, for a canonical example) to represent other objects or events in the world. In this regard, thinking necessarily employs symbols, which is to say that it is a special kind of situated activity.[9] Thinking is not just an internal computation process, not simply a neural activity that connects up inputs and outputs in some regular fashion. Rather, it is a more or less autonomous two-way action-reaction process, sensitive to continual adjustment and feedback, involving the world as much as it does the brain. It is an interaction between systems of symbols and an agent attuned, through evolutionary and developmental processes, to various activities and constraints governing the nature and use of symbols. Working concretely in some such representational domain in the course of thinking, the agent acts on the world, and the world acts back.

This interaction has a more or less cyclical structure, which can be explained by walking through figure 5. Acting within a domain of symbols, the agent is able to formulate certain *proposals* concerning whatever matters are being represented, thereby positing or formulating certain possibilities as actual, by writing or speaking or using some such expressive medium. These proposals lead to various *consequences* by virtue of derivations, calculations, proofs, computations, cipherings, or other more or less mechanical processes applied to symbolic formulations of those possibilities. The consequences of given proposals are registered as symbolic expressions (or symbolic impressions), and they are taken as formulations of *facts* of the case. When presented systematically or otherwise coherently, these facts will be characteristic of certain *concepts* (in particular, those concepts, or modifications thereof, that suggested the initial proposals to begin with) and not others. (A notion of cognitive rationality is introduced here, as measured by the appropriateness of given concepts in given instances. The rationality involved in determining which concepts get triggered by certain facts and which do not is a function of the systematicity of the contents of various concepts, matched against whatever proposals and consequences are actually derived in the present situation.) The concepts brought to bear in this way constitute interpretations of the given facts, making salient certain cognitive expectations about what those facts mean, on the strength of systematic constraints built into the interpreting concepts. But then such interpretations generate *ideas* (suggestions) about the scope of possibilities for the case at hand, delimiting what further proposals might consistently be made and how prior proposals might be reformulated. The process goes around and around, serving to plot out details of the current situation, at least tentatively, as regards what is actually the case as well as what the current potentialities are as results of different courses of action. Thought encompasses this entire two-way cyclical process of deriving consequences from given proposals and making proposals on the basis of given consequences—the whole process being tempered and modulated by formal properties of the symbol systems one uses and by the conceptual apparatus brought to bear in the process.

The computer metaphor in modern philosophy of mind is not entirely misguided, but consider another analogy. Thinking, in the present view, is not unlike using a clutch-and-transmission system, allowing the agent to disengage itself from concrete problematic activities so that it can readjust its conduct according to changing conditions and foresight into possible consequences of feasible actions. The value of reflective thought lies in its allowing an agent to scope out possibilities on the basis of results of past and current experience and thereby to avoid troublesome alternatives and choose more promising ones. Referring back to figure 3, and perhaps pushing this analogy too far, perception (like an automobile's engine and drivetrain) inevitably moves the transformation of a situation along, for better or worse, according to the dictates of established habits; whereas mentality (like a clutch-and-transmission system) is a mechanism by which one disengages from a given situation in order to survey alternative courses of action and to determine how to adjust one's conduct (to shift gears). Once engaged (releasing the clutch), the actual changes in one's conduct should serve to effect transformations in the given situation, presumably to move matters toward a solution to the given problem. Broadly speaking, this clutch mechanism is continually engaged or disengaged as dictated by the circumstances and fortunes of one's ongoing conduct.

For instance, as you walk across the dance floor in Mary's direction, you can proceed resolutely according to some fixed plan and walk right up to her no matter what she does. Or you may reflect a bit on what is happening as you go. You don't want to burn out your clutch, but as you walk, you might take note of her reactions to your taking this initiative (if there are any) and modify your course of action accordingly. If she looks at you and smiles or turns to face you, then, yes, this is going to be a fine evening. But if she frowns and turns away or seems apprehensive or bothered, or worse, if she appears to be entirely unaware of your existence, even now as you walk across the room toward her, then perhaps you should head toward your friend standing nearby and otherwise ease up and look for another opening.

All this, of course, depends on your being able to read and interpret the gestures and behaviors characteristic of white middle-class suburban high school dance etiquette. This is not exactly a well-defined symbol system with a formalizable syntax, but it is a definite body of conventions and rules that by common consent govern the behaviors of everyone present. Of course, one can and should successfully function in this setting in a largely spontaneous and intuitive manner, not reflecting as much about what is going on as you have just done. But you, after all, are rather unsophisticated and hence a bit ill at ease when it comes to these matters. And besides, you really don't know where you stand so far as Mary is concerned. Her various behaviors are not simple events to you but rather stand as symbolic gestures in the context of a more or less well-defined system of social conventions. You are predisposed, therefore, to try to fathom the significance of her various behaviors and to otherwise think about what you are doing rather than simply doing what you are doing. There is nothing about the present setting by itself that necessarily calls for reflection, but rather it is your being ill at ease that turns the present setting into that kind of situation. Alas, the situation may be so overwhelmingly unfathomable that you would continue to do nothing else but consider your options without ever making a move to walk across the floor while you still have an opportunity to do so.

As we have said, the value of thought lies in the capacity it affords the agent to back off from the world in the concrete and deal with it only in terms of possibilities represented symbolically. The evolutionary value of an increased capacity not just to solve problems but to foresee and avoid problems is obvious. One can thereby intelligently formulate and rehearse possible courses of action without being bound to suffer the actual consequences of those actions. This disengaged symbolic activity is useful, of course, only to the extent that one brings the developments of thought back into the concrete world. Though it may proceed independently more or less for its own sake, the primary function of thinking is to monitor and control actions in an efficient and effective way—to avoid problems but not by avoiding action altogether. You can't keep the clutch on forever. Thinking must answer to the practical application of its results in the real problem-solving situations that gave rise to it in the first place. To think is primarily to think about things that matter.

Note that these two kinds of interaction—perception and thought—are on an ontological par. Both are equally accessible and directly comparable. The question of correspondence between thought and perception is then relatively straightforward, posing a concrete empirical problem in the course of given inquiries but not a philosophical problem as such. Possible actions whose consequences may be scoped out reflectively can be actually performed, and predicted consequences can be compared against actual results. In this way, perception and thought are able to work in unison so as to be mutually consistent. This functional correspondence in given instances is the measure (or at least one measure) of an inquiry that is succeeding.

Mead and Dewey would seem to agree with Kant, at least in this one regard, that an agent's autonomy is given by that agent's ability to exercise reason and to apply the results of rational thought to the control of its own conduct.[10] The sense of freedom that we have as rational agents is a sense that the choices we make and the actions we perform on the basis of those choices are able to change the world in some sense, so that the world is not just changing itself through us but that our own cognitive decision-making processes take place and yield results independently of the rest of the world. But this is precisely what is meant by likening thought to a clutch-and-transmission system. For Mead and Dewey, freedom is a particular capacity (more or less forced on us) to deal with contexts where there is some impetus to coordinate contrary impulses and to otherwise weigh incompatible alternatives as to possible courses of events. Conflict encourages detachment, detachment encourages reflection, and that in turn may give rise to altered courses of activity. It is not that thought does not have a naturally systematic character just like anything else in the world, but that an agent's mental faculty is a piece of the world that is designed to operate autonomously to varying degrees. As such, thinking is the basis of our spontaneity in a universe otherwise governed by natural law—not that thinking isn't as lawful as anything else, but that it is by design a free-running bit of machinery capable of engaging with and disengaging from everything else (more or less) on the basis of its own operations. That we have such a capacity, especially as brought to light in uncertain situations where the whole point is to determine how to readjust one's conduct in the face of conflicting circumstances, is what fosters our sense of free agency and efficacy in a world in which we otherwise seem to be buffeted by forces beyond our control.

Based on this view, the AI enterprise should be aimed at understanding not just the systematic character of symbol systems but also the character of mentality as a capacity of an agent to engage and disengage itself from activities ordinarily driven by habit and blind appetitive impulse. Thinking is a process of sorting out the possible courses of events in a given situation from a distance, generally so as to monitor and control the transformation of that situation more effectively. It hardly seems appropriate to characterize thinking *or* perception as mere computation, unless this metaphor is developed in such a way as to be embedded within some broader theory of situated activity.

In calling notions of computation, representation, and symbolic processing central to a theory of intelligence,[11] what is actually meant by a symbol or by representation; and more specifically, where are such things to be found?

In the present sense of those terms and in contrast to the computer metaphor, perception by itself does not employ symbols and representations, although it does involve organized systems of correlated activities that include states and processes that are in some sense internal to the agent. To refer to such internal states and processes as symbols or representations of the external states and processes to which they are dynamically tied is like saying the front half of a car is a representation of the rear half, or that gasoline is a representation of a carburetor, or that a car as a whole is a representation of the road it is driven on. The road signifies the potential presence of automobiles, but it is not on those grounds a symbol or representation of automobiles. A footprint in the sand is evidence of a person's having passed by recently, but it is not thereby a representation of a such a person. If anything, it is a detached *presentation* of that person, the result of one way in which that person has been presented to you. The same can be said of internal states (e.g., qualitative results of motor activities), which are integral to the overall system of agent/world interactions that constitute perception.

Symbols are something else altogether besides being significant correlates of other things. It is a waste of a good technical term—and one that collapses important theoretical distinctions—to refer across the board to states and processes inside the agent as symbolic. It goes without saying that symbols are functional correlates of other things; but more specifically, they are things in the world that stand in place of other things in the world in the course of representational activity, in a robust and literal sense of *representation*. In this richer sense of the term, in contrast to the computer metaphor, symbols may be anywhere in the world, not necessarily in the head, and only as long as they function properly in representational activity.

Suppose, for instance, that you are playing sandlot football (U.S.-style). In the huddle, the quarterback draws some *X*s in the sand. "This is *you*," he or she says, pointing to you and then to one of the *X*s, and then draws and explains some arching lines from and around various *X*s to picture how the next play will go. Perhaps discussion ensues and different possible plays are considered. In any case, the *X*s and lines are literally representations of people and projected paths of motion, by virtue of their function in the planning by means of which your team coordinates its next action. Our thesis here is that perception deals with presentations of things, like footprints in the sand, whereas reflection deals in representations, like the *X*s and arcs.

It is somewhat ironic that the systematic bundles of attunements that constitute habits for dealing with presentations of things (see the lower oval in figure 4) answer fairly closely to what Vera and Simon mean by symbol systems. But rather than a general theory of cognition, Vera and Simon are proposing an account of something that Dewey and Mead would identify as just one piece of the perception puzzle. Habits are in a sense input-output systems internal to perceptual processes, and they very likely can be modeled as computational systems; but such computational systems are not symbol systems in the present sense of the term, even if they take as inputs and outputs objects that the cognitive scientist can read as symbols. What matters is how they function in the specimen agent's activities; and in the case of that agent's perception, such inputs are direct indications of things, not representations of them.

On this account, any such computational system constitutes only a piece of the picture, not a full account, of what perception is, which is itself only a piece of the picture of what intelligent agency is. A standard symbol systems approach to AI, besides watering down the notion of a symbol and otherwise collapsing the distinction between presentations and representations of objects, generally lacks an account of the functional context in which symbol systems are orchestrated to interpret and steer behavior. It is as if Vera and Simon were claiming that we would have a theory of driving once we had a schematic for a piece of an automobile. A theory of how an automobile engine works, for instance, is important to, but does not constitute, a theory of how the engine is used in driving. One also needs an account of the rest of the automobile, not to mention some sense of the various traffic patterns and terrains in which different functions of the engine come into play, to have a full account of what an engine is. Similarly, a theory of symbol systems cannot by itself yield an adequate explanation of cognitive abilities, even once we distinguish symbol systems as such from the computational systems that constitute habits. Each of these various systems are only separate pieces of what constitutes intelligence.

If thinking and perceiving are mere computing, then computing is something that encompasses a world of symbol processing *and* motor activity, out there on the dance floor, not just inside the head. One's perceptions and beliefs and desires take shape by virtue of such activity, by no other means and for no other purpose.

But now there are the harder questions of why and how things are this way. One might allow that the present account of perception and thought up to this point is plausible, but why should one think this is the way things are? In particular, the account at times sounds rather behavioristic, in the worst sense of the term. How would Mead and Dewey explain the internal brainy feeling of silent thinking where one does *not* use pencil and paper or chalk and chalkboard? What is going on as you stand there looking at Mary or staring at the floor, tracing out possible courses of action but being too unsure of yourself to make a move? In a great many such cases, thinking would appear to take place solely within the agent, not in some interactive agent/world domain.

In talking about thinking as an autonomous activity, have we introduced some kind of unbridgeable duality between thought and perception? What is the connection, if any, between these two kinds of agent/world interaction? While presumably they are structurally similar, they still seem like two entirely different kinds of activity. Mead and Dewey maintain that there is some sort of continuity between perceptual and reflective activities so that they are pieces of a single fabric. In this view, thinking is a unique kind of activity in its own right, but allegedly it is a variation on a theme already at work in the dynamics of perception. But why think of thinking in this way, as a variation on a theme? And why that particular theme? How do we account for the continuity?

It has been pointed out that thinking involves the use of concepts. But what does that mean? What is a concept? For instance, you apparently have certain concepts about what high school dances are all about, and you are drawing on those concepts to come to terms with the present situation. According to Mead and Dewey, concepts as such are not really learned by a cognitive agent until they can be used by that agent as means for solving problems and otherwise making one's way through the world. In particular, concepts play the same role in thought that habits and attunements play in perception; but are concepts something different from habits? Happily, nothing we have said so far suggests an ontological distinction between habits and concepts. The difference is presumably a functional one. It is clear that not all habits are conceptual, in that not all habits deal with the use of symbols and symbol systems. But concepts are those habits that do pertain to the use of symbols and that thereby function as such in thought processes. Not all habits are concepts, but all concepts are at bottom habits of a particular sort. We might even suppose that in order to build a machine that can think, we first need to build a machine that can perceive and then apply the same design principles to activity within the more limited domain of symbol systems.

Or is it that simple? How did machines that can think naturally emerge? Mead and Dewey were not motivated to build artificial thinking machines, but they were motivated to understand the nature of mentality as a natural phenomenon, and the view they developed was decidedly evolutionary in character. According to this view, perceptual and thinking abilities are evolutionarily (and hence developmentally) linked by an intermediate series of similar interactive capabilities. The emergence of thinking as a natural sort of activity constitutes not an ontological bifurcation but

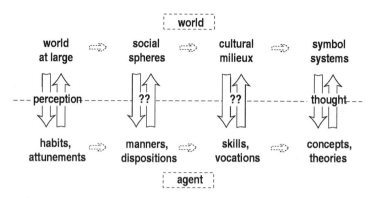

Figure 6
Evolutionary development of reflective activities.

rather an evolutionary expansion or extension or specialization of already existing capabilities. Whether or not it helps in the effort to build an artificial thinking machine, we can say something fairly definite about this evolutionary connection, drawing more perhaps on Mead's views than on Dewey's. To understand their account of this evolutionary linkage, consider figure 6.

The defining characteristic of thought is that it is a representational activity in a representational domain. To account for how thinking came about, one has to give an account of the natural emergence of such representational domains. One might try to tell this story in neuropsychological terms. For Mead and Dewey, that is not going to be enough. An essential part of the story about the connectedness of perception and thought involves the fact that we are social animals. Perhaps contingently but nevertheless as a matter of fact, we are mental creatures by virtue of having evolved and developed as social creatures. Thinking is built upon an edifice that includes not only perceptual capabilities but also social and cultural features. Symbol systems, as the objective media of thought, are features or elements or aspects of a cultural milieu that have come about as a result of the need to coordinate shared activities and to stabilize our capabilities to do so. Your high school dance situation illustrates not just a particular scenario where thinking might occur but rather the kind of social interactive ooze out of which human thinking abilities emerged in the first place.

Let's work through figure 6 in detail, from left to right. We have already looked at the nature of perception in the discussion of figure 4. As a next step, we should be able to take as a premise the claim that human individuals exist as members of some kind of social system. Like anything else, a social sphere is a subdomain of the world at large, not something distinct from it. And as a relatively specific kind of agent/world interaction, the overall structure of social activity is not all that different from the

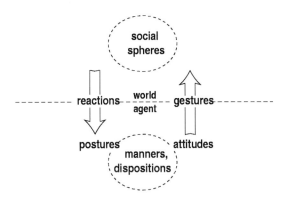

Figure 7
Social interaction.

structure of perception, although it involves a more limited range of actions and results (such as nonverbal gestures and responses to gestures).

The following description is too brief, but it is just a matter of walking through figure 7. In accordance with various manners and social dispositions developed (like any other habits) through extended social interaction, the individual interacts with other individuals by way of gestures and other means for signaling and influencing others. Such actions bring about particular reactions from others—approvals, disapprovals, protests, encouragements, support, or resistance. When interpreted in terms of one's given manners and social dispositions, such reactions engender certain social attitudes, which determine one's subsequent activity. And around and around it goes. What is happening on the dance floor is not an exercise in mere perception but also a social interaction geared to relatively complex systems of conventional constraints.

While not intrinsically mental in itself (in that it neither presupposes nor requires reflective processes), social activity yields new and unique capabilities over and above mere perception. The fundamental motivation of social activity is a drive to coordinate shared activity. Many of the actions we perform as a social group are not simply decomposable into the actions of individuals but are distributed across a social system as shared acts, and they exist only in this distributed sense, like dancing, for example. A social system must be able to function as a single agent, performing such communal actions as hunting, fighting, dancing, loving, playing games, buying and selling, teaching and learning. The distributed character of social activity introduces evolutionary potentials that many animal species seem to have picked up on and developed more or less extensively while others have not. Compare, for instance, the mating practices of a flounder with those of human beings and other primates. Even if it were the case that the sexual activity of significant numbers of human beings is comparable in its social character to that of flatfish, this does not negate the fact that, for the most part, human sexual activity is embedded in relatively complex systems of social ritual and convention with recognized conditions and consequences beyond itself. Your problem on the dance floor comes down to whether you and Mary can achieve some kind of coordination, on the dance floor but also in terms of any consequences it might have in that and other social contexts.

The individual member of a society cannot help but be affected by the fact that the requisite attunements and habits that such membership engenders involve constraints of a looser kind than is typical of mere perception. Social activity involves more sensitive and less reliable means of information flow and communication, requiring conventional rules, agreements, contracts, and policies (which one can only presume are secure) in order to maintain some kind of regularity and systematicity in complex social spheres. The greater likelihood of uncertainty in social situations, plus the fact that one's own actions do not simply bring about reactions from others but also partly *determine* social reality, tends to reveal us to ourselves in ways that mere perception is not likely to do. In this sense, it is within contexts of shared experience—of socially distributed experience—that an individual self can start to emerge as a distinct, objective constituent of reality. A social sphere creates a space in which the self can exist as such. The fact that other individuals react so sensitively to your actions, and that you react to their actions in similar ways, brings attention to the efficacy and reactivity of your own attitudes in a way that is not present in ordinary perception. (As I will show, this tendency of social problem solving to reveal us to ourselves constitutes the social basis of mentality.)

It is not impossible that a sense of self could emerge in nonsocial agents, for instance, by virtue of perceptual activities that do not involve social coordination. But this does not seem likely, given that one's actions in perceptual activities do not have the same salience and level of effectiveness characteristic of social situations, where one's actions normally contribute to *making* reality—in the way, for example, that one's queries in a conversation help to constitute the very discourse one is trying to comprehend. Perceptual capabilities supply the basic pattern of social interaction, but perception normally does not involve the same levels of indeterminacy nor the same kinds of resolution procedures characteristic of social interaction. One does not dance with a tree in order to perceive a tree, even though perceiving a tree does involve a kind of interaction with the tree. The activities intrinsic to perception, while effecting a kind of phenomenal filtering process, serve nevertheless to reveal the affordances of a largely independent world, whereas the social reality of which we are a part and the activities inherent in discerning social reality are often one and the same thing. That is, what we do to discern social reality is often precisely what we do to *make* social reality—not just to perceive other human beings but to engage in social relationships. This is, in fact, something of a dilemma for an anthropologist, namely, to have to influence a given society just to be able to observe it. Plain sensory perception does not bring us around to ourselves in the same way. It does not make us aware of ourselves as autonomous agents in quite the way that social interactions do. In fact, it is barely obvious that perception is interactive at all, which would account for why a passive-receptive view of perception such as Locke's could be taken seriously for so long. (Unfortunately, this passive-receptive view of perception still has far too much influence on how human agency is viewed by the AI community.)

From an evolutionary perspective, we should expect that the volatility of constraints in a social sphere will engender a more salient sense of *possibility* because of the greater likelihood of breakdown in social coordination. That is, a greater likelihood of social discordance requires a greater facility not only to formulate and exploit possibilities but also to design and appropriately implement contingency plans. Processes of planning and rehearsing lines of conduct are valuable as means for establishing reliable and effective courses of shared activity. The foresight afforded by planning no doubt facilitates identification and avoidance of potential pitfalls, and this capability is surely useful in situations where given constraints are relatively unreliable, such as in a social sphere. Distance detection in social space is somewhat more complex than it is in visual space because of the different natures of the spaces. While planning of a sort is already present in the very design of perception (by virtue of sensitivities to the affordances of things), social activities call for an enhanced refinement and cultivation of broader-based abilities to exercise foresight.

In earlier evolutionary eras, such planning was most likely simple in character. Nothing we have said so far introduces or allows recourse to mental abilities. Without assuming the existence of mind to begin with, can we describe primitive social settings where we could imagine reflective activities emerging out of communicative activities more broadly? We run the risk of sounding like nineteenth-century evolutionists to even ask such a question. But the point here is to try to give an evolutionary account of the emergence of human reflective abilities. Can we imagine such abilities coming about where all we have to start with are agents with perceptual capabilities who are sensitive to social constraints? Full-fledged reflective capabilities aside, how about the emergence of simple representational acts to begin with? Dance, for one thing, seems like a typical candidate for a prereflective communicative activity that might yield a kind of representation.[12] That is, if dancing were to have any significance beyond itself, it might be as a matter of recounting or mimicking successful exploits that are somehow worth recounting to others. But then such activity becomes more than just "significant" beyond itself. It is a kind of representation. The earliest kind of planning might have been indistinguishable from acting out successful feats relevant to the social group as a whole (e.g., hunting, fighting), where recounting and rehearsing such actions would amount to the same thing. A younger individual could learn to participate in such collective endeavors by first playing a role in their rehearsal. A social

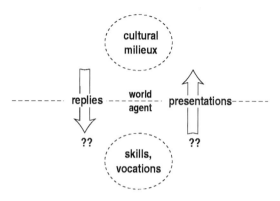

Figure 8
Participation in a culture.

group, as a singular agent in its own right, could thereby develop a looser kind of coordination than underlies perceptual capabilities of single individuals (as with hand-eye coordination), but the basic idea is the same.

The next step in the evolutionary story would be that the value of rehearsing—of looking backward and forward in experience, of exploiting memory and making predictions—encourages the standardization of representational gestures and the institution of routine customs, icons, rituals, ceremonies, and any other such means to formulate effectively and codify and thereby strengthen, solidify, and stabilize social constraints and processes. It is by such means that a social sphere can give rise to a transmittable cultural milieu of some sort. We thus move further to the right in figure 6.

Cultural milieux (see figure 8) afford a new and different kind of agent/world activity, thus allowing the development of new kinds of operational capabilities. The main difference between social and cultural activity is that social interaction is directed at other individuals, whereas cultural activity is directed at the community at large. One participates in a culture as a kind of generalized conversation, using methods and media that everyone finds significant, so that one converses with the community at large rather than specifically with other individuals. Socially, one engages in give-and-take with other individuals, whereas culturally, one engages in give-and-take with one's society-as-a-whole—one dons a certain kind of clothing or hairstyle, writes a poem, publishes a paper, paints a painting, performs a rite of some kind, as an utterance directed to one's whole society. Today, in the United States, one is educated, holds down a job, pays one's taxes, votes, watches or reads the news, as manners of conduct within a particular culture. One helps to make and modify the culture not just by writing books or making movies or inventing new appliances but also on the basis of what one chooses to read, watch, or use. Otherwise the structure of participation in a culture, broadly conceived, is basically the same as the structure of social activity and hence of perception.

It is by way of participation in a culture that an individual develops a sense of personal character and hence a sense of self. To begin with, there is a simple precognitive significance available in simple social interactions, given one's sensitivity to the affects of one's own attitudes, postures, and conduct on the attitudes, postures, and conduct of other individuals (and vice versa). It is within a social sphere that the self emerges as an object. Your self-absorption on the dance floor is evidence of this tendency. But a sense of oneself, not just as a felt-object but as an object with characteristic traits, is engendered not merely by virtue of social sensitivities but in and by a process of gaining a sense of one's culture. Having a sense of one's community supplies one with a sense of oneself insofar as one's self is thereby an instantiation of a kind. It probably did not occur to you at the time, but you were not just at a dance, but at a white middle-class suburban U.S. high school dance. The latter characterization of yourself, and in much more detail, would actually come later, in retrospect, against the backdrop of a very different sense of *who you are*, as tempered by a broader sense of the cultural diversity that exists in the world and of where you stand in this diverse milieu. But at the time, whether or not you were cognizant of it, that is where you in fact stood, and you must have had some grasp of it in order to take part in that activity in the first place.

The emergence of a self as a felt-object is a necessary but not sufficient condition for what we think of as human mentality. More is needed beyond mere reference to a self. Having and exercising a bona fide sense of character and identity, of regarding oneself as an instantiation of a kind, is also a prerequisite for having and exercising mental abilities. Gaining a sense of one's culture provides the means needed to classify oneself; and once objectified as such, this sense of oneself provides the raw materials for the evolutionary structuring of mental activities. Namely, participating in a culture is like a conversation with another individual, except that the other individual is one's own culture. Mental abilities, in a proper sense of the term, come about as a matter of reflexivizing discourse with this so-called generalized other, that is, of reflexivizing the process of participation in a culture. Mentality results as a process of using stabilized means of social communication (languages) to converse with oneself in ways typical of those means of communication. That is, as languages become stable, one becomes sensitive to typical responses to standard actions, to some extent or other, so that, as if in a linguistic dance with oneself, one can simultaneously play the role of respondent to one's own utterances. This is accomplished by objectifying a sense of one's own culture, that is, a sense of what it amounts to, to be a member of a given society, and conversing as if this part of oneself were a typical other. This process is successful in proportion to the stability, reliability, systematicity, and expressiveness of the means of communication that constitute one's culture. Such means of communication, thus objectified, are then able to function in their own right as an independent domain of activity, providing the ways and means of "reflection" to the extent that such reflexive activity may (but need not) have some representational role to play in this or that concrete context. Language (or culture, more broadly), in this reflexive representational capacity and to whatever extent it is in fact reliably systematic and hence objectifiable, thus gives rise to full-blown symbol systems.

Current AI research does not evidently draw on any such cultural grounding of symbols when referring to intelligent agents as symbol systems, drawing instead on formal languages used to program computers to cash out what they mean by a symbol.[13] In any case, whatever one might think a symbol is, it is not enough to talk merely about symbol processing in order to explain intelligence in general and mental capabilities in particular, even if symbol processing is an essential part of the story. More to the point, one must center such talk about symbol systems in the fact that it is a sense of one's culture that gives rise to the kind of symbol processing we refer to as thinking, insofar as we view thinking as the self's (an individual agent's) talking to itself (in the guise of a generalized other). Without this general sense of one's culture, one has no inner self with which to converse. Such reflexive discourse becomes possible as one starts to grasp the social and cultural significance of one's own utterances in such a way as to be attuned already to how others would respond. One can thereby respond to one's own utterances just as others would. Full-fledged reflective thought is able to take place once one is able to objectify languages and use them as the means and media for carrying on this conversation in a representational domain. In this view, language is the medium not just of conversation but of thought itself—language, that is, in a full-blown natural sense, loaded with cultural content and patterns of meaning, rather than in the comparatively anemic syntactic sense of an implicit "language of thought" based on an analogy with FORTRAN, Lisp, or the predicate calculus.[14]

Of course, the emergence of mind in a cultural setting is going to feed back onto the social and cultural world that gave rise to it. We should not underemphasize the capacity that mind affords the individual agent to be uniquely different, not just another carbon copy of one and the same cultural identity. One is compelled to be different, if only to maintain a place (territory, status, standing) in one's social and cultural environment. The story I have told here is primarily about the emergence of mind and not about further evolutionary consequences of its existence. In particular, it does not follow from what was said that we should all be similar, given that no two individuals can have the same perspective on the world, including its social and cultural domains (so that my generalized other will vary to some degree from yours); yet what was said comfortably allows for the degree to which we *are* in fact similar by virtue of shared cultural traditions.

This basically completes an account of the developmental connection between perception and thought, at least in rough outline. Symbol systems in particular are a special manifestation of cultural artifacts, serving as agent-independent media that give form and substance to thinking.

Certainly, now that human beings have a capacity to think, this capacity *is* what it is on its own terms. An individual does not have to be particularly communicative or overtly social in order to exercise reflective abilities. Mead and Dewey argued that, *as a species*, these abilities initially developed as a refinement of our social and cultural nature. Otherwise, thinking is a process carried out by the individual as part of that individual's experience. The claim is not that an individual alone on a desert island would not be able to think. Rather, the claim is that whether on a desert island or in the middle of a crowd, an individual whose species does not have the right kind of social and cultural evolutionary history will not have thinking abilities in the first place.

Despite the origins of mentality in overtly social and cultural domains of activity, there is no reason to think that over the course of time an ability to reflexivize this activity would not become so refined, efficient, and intimate that the outward features of conversation might be grossly altered if not completely refined away, in which case not all thinking would come across literally as verbally talking to oneself. Perhaps the evolutionary relationship between thinking and conversation is analogous to that between humans and other existing primates, in the sense that thinking did not evolve *from* anything like modern conversation but rather evolved *with* it, *from* some common source in early preverbal sociocultural communicative practices. This does not weaken the present thesis but only suggests why thinking silently would not be like reading the *Times* or talking on the telephone.

In any case, there is also no reason to think that our thinking would not exploit and take explicit advantage of its overt social and cultural origins whenever that is reasonable, for example, *not* to proceed silently and invisibly but to extend itself in the world, to use sounds, scripts, expressive media of any kind, to take notes, to make lists, to write out formulas, to sketch diagrams, to give its processes and products some kind of external substance. It is quite likely that the latter kind of thinking—using external media to give form and stability to one's representational activity—is far more characteristic of thought than is armchair reverie, wherein the objects and processes of agent/world interaction take place as a silent reflexive conversation. To say that this activity is reflexivized does not entail that it is internalized as a silent and invisible process. If it is ever entirely internalized, then the organism is nevertheless in that instance playing the role of both agent and world. But more commonly, in this view, thinking takes place overtly in a domain of agent/world interaction. In that sense, mind is a process not enclosed within the agent, much less located in the brain.

The significant symbol is then the gesture, the sign, the word which is addressed to the self when it is addressed to another individual, and is addressed to another, in form to all other individuals, when it is addressed to the self. . . .

[I]nsofar as thought—that inner conversation in which objects as stimuli are both separated from and related to their responses—is identified with consciousness, that is insofar as consciousness is identified with awareness, it is the result of this development of the self in experience.. . . .

Mind, which is a process within which [analyses of objects] take place, lies in a field of conduct between a specific individual and the environment, in which the individual is able, through the generalized attitude he assumes, to make use of symbolic gestures, i.e., terms, which are significant to all including himself. While the conflict of reactions [which separates objects from (and relates them to) their meanings] takes place within the individual, the analysis takes place in the objects. Mind is then a field that is not confined to the individual, much less is located in a brain. Significance belongs to things in their relations to individuals. It does not lie in mental processes which are enclosed within individuals.[15]

In broad strokes, this is the picture of mentality and thought found in the social psychology of Mead and Dewey. This picture is clearly at odds with the ontological dualism of classical epistemology. It is not simple, but it enjoys a notable degree of breadth and coherence, and it is not subject to the metaphysical and epistemological dilemmas and puzzles characteristic of classical views. Descartes found epistemological bedrock in a phenomenalistic "I think, I am." For different reasons and with a different purpose in mind, the pattern of inference outlined in Dewey's and Mead's social-psychological philosophy of mind is more along the lines of "I dance, I am, I think."

It remains unclear how this social-psychological view of human mentality might inform ongoing research in AI and robotics, much of which is based on a view of an artificial mind encapsulated inside of a machine's computer-brain, set over and against an external world. Even without the social element, AI research would in the present view do better to think of mind as residing in a domain of agent/world interactivity, and to think of thought and information processing more generally as an interactive process, not as a unilateral algorithmic process enclosed in some kind of a box with input and output slots. It is hardly a minor fact that research in robotics usually requires some engineering of the environment in which the robot works (quite heavily in some cases, as with the early Shakey project at SRI)[16] or else long training periods in which the robot's software attunes itself to specific physical domains. This has been viewed as a temporary ad hoc fix, to be dispensed with once we figure out how to design the software so that we can plunk the robot down in arbitrary environments. We certainly want a robot to have as much flexibility and adaptability as possible, but the lesson that has been missed is that the problem does not and cannot center on designing software solely for the robot's head but must also include structures and processes in the environment as part of the robot's architecture.[17]

But more than that, it is only with a social dimension added to this interactive view, not as a behavioral goal but as a condition of initial design, that AI research can hope to achieve some kind of success in its more ambitious aims (e.g., to build a machine that is able to converse in English or some other natural language). It is only by virtue of such considerations that some kind of practical connection is made with what makes symbol systems and representational information processing what they are in the first place. Or is this claim too strong? This is not to say that thinking, real or artificial, is necessarily a social process and so must be designed as such, nor is it a claim that an individual, real or artificial, can think only if it maintains some kind of social life. Thinking, as a natural evolutionary phenomenon, is obviously something that an individual can do all by itself, assuming the individual has that capacity to begin with. So why can't we build an artificial agent so that it can do this very same thing, all by itself, without our having to mimic the social and cultural developments out of which this capacity actually emerged in the development of one particular species? How do we instill in an artificial agent a capacity to think in the first place, and more specifically, does this absolutely require socialization processes or can we circumvent that part of actual human evolution as just one out of any number of ways that such a capacity might come to exist?

The evolutionary story outlined by Mead and Dewey is remarkable even if taken as nothing more than a plausibility argument for one particular naturalistic philosophy of mind. In outlining at least one way to think about thinking as a natural evolutionary phenomenon, they have avoided a number of classical philosophical pitfalls and otherwise demonstrated how to move the study of mind out of metaphysics and into the domain of science. Let us assume that they are right in broad outline about what thinking is and how it actually came into being. Are they bound to claim that this is the only way that thinking might come about? The answer seems to be yes. Thinking is a kind of reflexive discourse in which a self interacts with what is essentially itself. Thinking presupposes not just reference to a self but also a kind of activity in which the self is objectified as one of a kind. In this view, an artificial thinking machine is going to have to have a sense of self that it can in turn objectify as such. If we could explain how to give the machine a sense of self without utilizing some kind of real or simulated socialization process (in which the agent accrues the habits that eventually constitute its sense of identity), then the stronger claim would be undermined. But is this likely? In objectifying itself, an agent will necessarily classify itself as one of some kind or other *and* interact with itself in ways appropriate to that kind of thing. Talking is not something that we normally do with trees and chairs. Rather, the story is that talking and other refinements of gestural communication is something we do with others of our own kind by virtue of their being of our own kind. Without some sense of one's own kind, some sense of a generalized other, there is no reliable sense of systematic communication, hence no objective identification of self, and hence no thinking. We might aim to code up some such generalized other and work that into the machine's software, and we might even try to avoid having to train the thing in actual social settings; but the aim in that case would be to give it precisely what would eventually come about in the course of some such socialization process. If not a homunculus, we would be attempting to build into the machine what is essentially a sense of membership in a discourse community.

The point is simple enough. Without socialization, the machine has no way to classify and hence objectify itself. Socialization has to be part of the process of building a thinking machine. If this sounds like a theoretically intractable or impractical admonition, then so much the worse for the AI enterprise. In that case we will have to be content with trying to build what are essentially nonthinking artificial animals able simply to run on automatic or not at all.

Notes

I would like to thank Güven Güzeldere, Larry Hickman, Laura Kerr, Allen Poteshman, Crystal Thorpe, and participants in the 1993–94 Symbolic Systems in Education seminar at Stanford, particularly John Baugh, Randi Engle, Bob Floden, Jim Greeno, Mimi Ito, Jan Kerkhoven, Ray McDermott, Denis Phillips, Christian Rohrer, and Decker Walker, for challenging discussions and useful comments on the ideas in this chapter. This is an expanded version of a paper presented at the March 1994 meeting of the Society for the Advancement of American Philosophy at Rice University. This work was supported by the National Academy of Education under the Spencer Postdoctoral Fellowship program.

1. Bobby Freeman, "Do You Wanna Dance?" (New York: Josie Records, 1958).

2. Jo Ann Boydston, ed., *John Dewey: The Early Works, 1882–1898* (vols. 1–5), *John Dewey: The Middle Works, 1899–1924* (vols. 1–15), and *John Dewey: The Later Works, 1925–1953* (vols. 1–17) (Carbondale: Southern Illinois University Press, 1967–1990); John Dewey, "The Reflex Arc Concept in Psychology," *Psychological Review* 3 (1896): 357–370, rpt. Boydston, *Early Works* 5: 96–11; *Human Nature and Conduct* (New York: Holt, 1922), rpt. Boydston, *Middle Works* 14; *Experience and Nature* (Chicago: Open Court, 1926), rpt. Boydston, *Later Works* 1; *How We Think* (Chicago: Henry Regnery, 1933), rpt. Boydston, *Later Works* 8: 105–354; *Logic: The Theory of Inquiry* (New York: Holt, 1938), rpt. Boydston, *Later Works*, 12; George Herbert Mead, *On Social Psychology*, ed. A. Anselm (Chicago: University of Chicago Press, 1956); *Selected Writings*, ed. Andrew J. Reck (Chicago: University of Chicago Press, 1964); "Social Consciousness and the Consciousness of Meaning," *Psychological Bulletin* 7 (1909): 397–405, rpt. Mead, *Selected Writings*, 123–133; "A Behavioristic Account of the Significant Symbol," *Journal of Philosophy* 19 (1922): 157–163, rpt. Mead, *Selected Writings*, 240–247.

3. John Haugeland, ed., *Mind Design: Philosophy, Psychology, Artificial Intelligence* (Cambridge, Mass.: MIT Press, 1981); Hubert L. Dreyfus, *What Computers Can't Do: A Critique of Artificial Reason* (New York: Harper, 1972); "From Micro-Worlds to Knowledge Representation: AI at an Impasse," in *Mind Design*, ed. John Haugeland (excerpted from the Introduction of the second ed. of Dreyfus, *What Computers Can't Do*).

4. John Dewey, "Propositions, Warranted Assertibility, and Truth," *Journal of Philosophy* 38 (no. 7, 1941): 169–196, rpt. Boydston, *Later Works* 14: 168–188.

5. Dewey, *Logic: The Theory of Inquiry*, ch. 2; Mead, *On Social Psychology*, 189–200.

6. Allen Newell and Herbert A. Simon, "Computer Science as Empirical Inquiry: Symbols and Search," *Communications of the Association for Computing Machinery* 19 (1976): 113–126, rpt. Haugeland, ed., *Mind Design*; Zenon W. Pylyshyn, *Computation and Cognition* (Cambridge, Mass.: MIT Press, 1985); Alonso H. Vera and Herbert A. Simon, "Situated Action: A Symbolic Interpretation," *Cognitive Science* 7 (no. 1, 1993): 7–48.

7. See, for instance, Dewey, *Logic: The Theory of Inquiry*, 3–4; Mead, *On Social Psychology*, 184–186.

8. Dewey, *Logic*; James J. Gibson, *The Ecological Approach to Visual Perception* (Boston: Houghton Mifflin, 1979); Judith A. Effken and Robert E. Shaw, "Ecological Perspectives on the New Artificial Intelligence," *Ecological Psychology* 4 (no. 1, 1992): 247–270; Tom Burke, *Dewey's New Logic: A Reply to Russell* (Chicago: University of Chicago Press, 1994), ch. 3.

9. Contrary to the view in Vera and Simon, "Situated Action."

10. Immanuel Kant, *The Critique of Practical Reason*, trans. Lewis White Beck, 3d ed. (1788; New York: Macmillan, 1993). Mead, *On Social Psychology*, 185–186.

11. Vera and Simon, "Situated Action."

12. Aggressive posturing as a prelude, if not a substitute, for fighting is another example. Playful imitation and simple games are others. See, for instance, Mead, *On Social Psychology*, 214–228.

13. Newell and Simon, "Computer Science"; Vera and Simon "Situated Action."

14. Jerry Fodor, *Representations: Philosophical Essays on the Foundations of Cognitive Science* (Cambridge, Mass.: MIT Press, 1981); "Propositional Attitudes," *Monist* 61 (no. 4, 1978), rpt. Fodor, *Representations*; *The Language of Thought* (Cambridge, Mass.: Harvard University Press, 1979).

15. Mead, "A Behavioristic Account," 246–247.

16. See, for example, Bertram Raphael, *The Thinking Computer: Mind Inside Matter* (New York: Freeman, 1976), 252, 275–281.

17. See, for instance, Effken and Shaw, "Ecological Perspectives." See also Rodney Brooks, "Elephants Don't Play Chess," *Robotics and Autonomous Systems* 6 (1990): 3–15; "Intelligence Without Reason," *Computers and Thought: Proceedings of the International Joint Conference on Artificial Intelligence*, Sydney (Los Altos, Calif.: Kauffman, 1990); "Intelligence Without Representation," *Artificial Intelligence* 47 (1991): 139–159.

The Epistemological and Philosophical Situation of Mind Technoscience

Alain-Marc Rieu

The Objective and the Perspective

My objective is to examine the philosophical relevance of mind technoscience, why philosophy finds itself in a paradoxical situation where it cannot ignore this new field of knowledge and at the same time must reinvent itself outside its realm. In order to reach this objective, it is necessary to clarify the present interactions between artificial intelligence (AI), the cognitive sciences, virtual reality, and the humanities as well as their present conjuncture (postmodernism) and other issues. The reason for the connection of these different fields of research seem obvious but is in fact less than clear. The form and content of this connection raise questions that cannot be answered in any one of these fields alone. To deal with this general problem requires not only finding the proper information and methodology but understanding the epistemic conjuncture at its core.[1] The questions are many, all more or less confused. In what sort of epistemic conjuncture does postmodernism find itself? Why do AI and the cognitive sciences find themselves in a situation beyond the reach of their actual practices but unable to ignore this situation because it concerns their epistemic and academic environments?[2]

I hear already the protests from many readers: French fog. Indeed my perspective will appear at first nonanalytical, even anti-analytical. But the overplayed opposition between the two traditions, in this precise case, takes a distinctly different aspect: it is between clarifying the already largely debated problems and questioning these very problems through an analysis of their presuppositions. The risk is fully accepted; my view concerns the forest more than the trees. It concerns the forms of argumentation at the root of these problems and the way to deal with them. A two-layered reading scheme is herewith proposed: the first at the level of the global argument, the second at the level of the various problems crossed by the first one and usually discussed by cognitive and AI scientists and philosophers. This perspective asserts that this first level has its own relative autonomy, that it can be analyzed with a rigor which, regarding its intrinsic intricacies, satisfies the minimal standards of an analytic tradition. If some parts of the argument do not seem satisfactory, I hope they can be rectified to open the way to a proper knowledge. Philosophy in any case cannot pretend to deliver much more.

The Situation of the Humanities Today

My starting point is a commonsense question: How can one assert that the various subdisciplines covered by the notions of AI and the cognitive sciences are generating knowledge that can be transferred to the humanities in order to provide knowledge of what is called *mind* in this field? Is the transfer able to preserve the knowledge value of what is being exported from one field to another?

According to present research in philosophy and historical epistemology, in the humanities mind is not a substance; it is a *function* within a symbolic order. This order is composed of a hierarchy of different disciplines that was relatively stable until the end of the nineteenth century. Since the 1850s, successive mutations in logic, physics, and mathematics have deconstructed this symbolic order to an extent that seems (at least to me) not yet fully evaluated.[3] The function at the core of the symbolic order had been hypostatized by the philosophical tradition in a conception of the mind, of its capacities (faculties), of its assignments in society, culture, and civilization. In any case, the historical hypostatization of this function cannot be taken for a knowledge of the mind, but it has effectively opened the possibility of transforming the function of the mind into an object of science, even of experimental investigation, from the mid-nineteenth century on.

This function has imparted to the mind different roles, the most important of them being the origin[4] of knowledge through the different faculties with which the mind was endowed in order to satisfy the function it was given within this symbolic order. So the mind came to be known and understood as the foundation of all sciences. The real sense of this is the following: in return, any development of the sciences and the knowledge they produced are to be referred to the activities of the mind; thus the mind contributes both to its development (the historical unfolding of its virtual capacities) and to its own knowledge. Mind knows itself through the development of the different forms of knowledge it makes possible. In this symbolic order,[5] centered on the function of the mind, the role of philosophy is essential: its role is to extract from the sciences the knowledge of the mind they carry and to refer to the mind this progress as a *deepening*[6] of the knowledge of itself necessary to accomplish its assignment. This construction of the mind through its function within a symbolic order has produced since the seventeenth century a major ideology: the progress of science, being a progress of the knowledge of the mind, is a progress of all individual minds and, as such, a progress of humankind. In his late works, Husserl has clearly expressed this idea and the consequences of its regression.[7]

The humanities are a set of disciplines at the core of a symbolic order; they are regulated by philosophy. These disciplines, developed in the intimacy of the modern mind, are supposed to be its closest expressions,[8] the fulfillment of its powers, the medium of humankind. The modern conception of humankind is built up through the humanities as the presence of the mind in the world.[9] Within the humanities, philosophy is defined as the exercise of reason. What is reason? Reason is supposed to be anchored in the mind as the origin and canon of all its activities; it exhibits and actualizes itself when it extracts from the different fields of knowledge that which concerns the mind so that it recognizes itself in its own productions. Reason is the self-reflection of the mind, the mind in search of itself in its activities. Philosophy, as reason at work in the mind, is the mental process in which all the different *expressions* of the mind are related to each other in the understanding of their origin. Its duty is to associate (even integrate) each individual mind, their *constructs*, in the generic mind of humankind. So, philosophy constantly weaves the humanities with their different historical patterns; it asserts their coherence within the concept of human beings as the origin and end of all knowledge.

In such a brief summary, the argument may appear slightly ridiculous, as strange as a summary of any myth of an ancient people in the ancient Near East or Africa. But this mythology has been repeated for so long in the West, it has produced such wide effects, that its failure at the end of the nineteenth century, its fast withdrawal mostly since the 1960s, leaves a void and a nostalgia that the majority of philosophical research tends simply to fulfill, explicitly or not.

Mind technoscience is reaching philosophy and the humanities in this precise context. One idea is to be obtained by this approach à la Foucault. There is no doubt that AI and the cognitive sciences are progressively building an effective knowledge of what they define as mind. But in no way can the interdiscipline emerging at their intersection satisfy the *modern* function of mind. Not their programs nor their results nor their internal debates can be interpreted inside the modern symbolic order, within this hierarchical organization of different disciplines that had an endogenic development from the European sixteenth century until the end of the nineteenth. This body of knowledge being effectively produced cannot be referred to the modern mind as being conceived as the origin of different faculties and at work in the knowledge gained from them. Mind technoscience cannot have as its goal the deepening of the knowledge man that human beings (the subject of the humanities) have of themselves as the origin and end of all human things. It cannot pretend to participate in the spiritual betterment of humankind,[10] to restore a vanished order.

The reason is that the conditions of the formation and coherence of the modern humanities are no longer satisfied. The traditional part played by the humanities in culture and society has vanished. The crisis of the humanities is not only a fashionable theme in the humanities departments of the industrial world's universities; since the end of the nineteenth century, it is a fact, an epistemic situation, the consequences of which are difficult to fully assess. The humanities crisis is the most obvious consequence of a deeper transformation of the symbolic order that is aggregating inside one another the different fields of knowledge. Physics and mathematics dropped out in the 1880s. They no longer referred to philosophy and through it to the activities of the mind: they built within themselves and by themselves their own foundations. This explains why the humanities are nowadays mostly reduced to philosophy and why philosophy itself is divided between a quest for a back seat in the sciences and literary theory.

AI and the cognitive sciences are rising in this very peculiar epistemic conjuncture. A place has been left vacant to be occupied. Professional philosophers are still being trained in the different modern schools. A reconstruction of the modern function of philosophy is possible, even anticipated and asked for: the roads are drawn, the problems are well known (mind/body, mind/brain, physical/physiological, natural/artificial, etc.). The philosopher Edmund Husserl even tried at the beginning of the twentieth century to reconstruct the modern conception of philosophy. Perhaps he failed because he did not have a proper conception of mind at his disposal. Now new answers from mind technoscience can be provided; they are able to justify the old questions of the philosophical tradition. A fundamental knowledge can be deciphered through the controversies of the scientists and engineers who are ignorant of philosophy. A grand program for the reconstruction of the humanities can be designed. The present conjuncture is certainly an ambiguous opportunity for philosophy, but there is no such place to occupy, no such function to fulfill. The function has vanished. AI and the cognitive sciences are not coming to save the humanities. Neither are they going to take their place because philosophy has failed to play its role. Mind technoscience will not fulfill Husserl's utopia to transform philosophy into a science.

Because of its methodology, problems, and criteria, the analytical tradition seems for the moment bound to reconstruct itself in the cognitive sciences: it feels itself independent from the epistemic conjuncture. Paradoxically, a style of philosophy, coming from research as diverse as that of Michel Foucault or Pierre Bourdieu, has the potential to overcome the modern frame of philosophical problems and even to arrive at the rigor that it has been missing. Mind technoscience emancipates philosophy from its modern function. This is why it belongs to the *postmodern* epistemic conjuncture. The humanities cannot be revamped by the mind sciences, but only further deconstructed. Philosophy must overcome its nostalgia and explore the virtualities of the present situation, the postmodern experience.

The Epistemological Problem

The epistemic conjuncture is more intricate. Even if research in AI and the cognitive sciences is at a loss to provide the reconstruction of the humanities, even if this historic mythology is forgotten, the sciences of the mind raise important epistemological questions. The French epistemological tradition[11] holds and shows that each science develops itself by the construction of its object. Through its concepts, formalisms, and experimental procedures, a theory *filters* the phenomena and thereby generates a *quasi-object* reduced to a set of parameters that can be experimentally studied.[12] This quasi-object is not a mental construction. It grows within the development of a theory and its experimental basis, and indicates the type of properties an object has within a discipline or subdiscipline. It cannot be separated from the theory to which it is linked and from the instruments by which this theory develops the diverse experimentation by which it proves and disproves itself. Even sciences at a primitive stage of their development, when they are not yet clearly cut off from folk knowledge, are already constructing a quasi-object. The object of any science is always, as coined by Bruno Latour,[13] a "hybrid," indistinctly natural *and* artificial.

This entails two major consequences. First, it cannot be asserted that reality can be reduced to what is known by a science. Second, there is no other way than science to know what reality is. So the Real (what is reality) cannot be called upon outside of science, through philosophy, any belief, intuition, theology, or poetry. But in return, the different sciences are not providing societies with a unified or unanimous knowledge of what the reality they study is by itself. Scientific knowledge cannot be cut off from the methods through which it is produced: the objects, reality, or levels of reality any science investigates are defined by a theory and its method of experimentation.

From this epistemological point of view, it follows that AI research cannot state what intelligence is by itself. But intelligence cannot be *known* outside of the different sciences that are being built. This is why *cognition* is the quasi-object of the mind sciences. Cognition is not the object they are trying to know as if it existed by itself. Cognition is being *constructed* according to the development of these sciences and their interactions. It is a concept by which these different sciences give an operational name to the quasi-object they are producing. Intelligence, as the essence of the human mind, does not have to be protected from mind technoscience; neither is it necessary to prove and explain at length that intelligence is not what these sciences are studying. The epistemological explanation is a sufficient answer that should dry up many popular (and) philosophical debates rising from the ghost of the humanities.

The epistemic conjuncture and its problems are much more complex. Indeed the present epistemological situation of the mind sciences is ambiguous and partly explains the philosophical temptations just denounced. As they progress from computer science models to the connectionist paradigm,[14] they overcome the initial behaviorist model dictating the processes being studied: the initial models were simply falsified by the very processes they allowed to investigate, and they had to be refined, and new ones were slowly proposed. In this situation, the mind sciences require a finer description of their quasi-object, based on more complex conceptual models. The filters have to change, and they have been changing in the last 15 years. But precisely because these sciences are investigating at the same time by experimentation and by computer simulation, they are not for the time being able to define and construct by themselves this hybrid (cognition, intelligence, and their different modalities) that is their quasi-object. Within their investigation, a type of cognition has to be so drastically reduced that the mind sciences cannot pretend to explain what they are supposed to. At the same time they need a full conception of this object in order to reduce it to the parameters at their disposal. This is their present and temporary epistemological deficit.[15]

So the mind sciences find themselves in the position of requiring a *predescription* of their object.[16] They have to look for it outside, import it from outside, because they do not yet have the theoretical means to build the filters in which the effective cognitive or intelligent processes could be analyzed in related parameters, so that they could be reconstructed and tested. Of course, this is how the hard mind sciences are already progressing, but they are still under the influence of folk psychology and the predescription of cognitive behaviors. In any case, the problem is not that intelligence or cognition cannot become an object of science, but that the present reduction is too strong and requires being related to different predescriptions outside the mind sciences.

But here philosophy enters the game. Different historical schools amply provide for the time being such predescriptions because their linguistic self-reflective methods based on the potentials of natural logic were the only ones available to describe basic mental processes such as belief, cognition, attention, perception, and intention. Phenomenology and its different trends provide an important, more recent stock of relatively well-refined descriptions of mental states and processes. These schools can provide these badly needed predescriptions, and their specialists can revive them and position themselves in the very development of the mind sciences.

I think this is a false conception of the present situation of philosophy. It is just a way for modern philosophy to continue its routine and even pretend to provide (unexpected) true (scientific) answers to old problems. Everybody seems satisfied in this false association: modern philosophical inquiry seems justified instead of being disqualified, and the mind scientists gain some ideological prestige they do not even need. Indeed, if the epistemic conjuncture concerns the global organization of knowledge, the epistemological situation concerns the state of development of a discipline or a theory. The epistemological situation of mind technoscience explains why it is so concerned with philosophy issues, but it also explains why some philosophical schools find so much *interest* in them: they can recycle their presuppositions with fresh data, launch debates, and even provide guidelines or orientations. Epistemology teaches that the present situation is only a temporary step. The next one is all the more easy to predict because it has already happened: the formation of the connectionist paradigm shows how the mind sciences are becoming able to provide the filters for their own descriptions of the cognitive processes they are investigating. They are in the process of reducing their dependence on linguistic self-descriptions provided by philosophy and folk cognitive psychology. Connectionism attests the emergence of the mind sciences as this autono-mous interdiscipline I have been calling mind technoscience.[17] A decisive step has been reached.

The Situation of Philosophy in This Conjuncture

In such a situation, the domain of modern philosophy is even further contested. The problem is not at all that the mind has become a proper object of science; that has been the case since the 1850s. The problem is that the mind sciences have become able to construct themselves outside of the conception of philosophy, which pretends to decide what mind is or is not, if the knowledge to be gained is possible or not, valid or not. Mind technoscience, by becoming autonomous, implicitly shows that even the analytical approach is neutral regarding its development. Just as physics and mathe-matics became autonomous in the late nineteenth century, a science and a technology of the mind have become possible. This mind technoscience cannot even become a substitute for the humanities, a ground knowledge: the positivist dream is no longer feasible, simply because the order of knowledge (the web of interactions between fields of knowledge and practices) is no longer organized so as to make it possible. The exer-cise of philosophy has become external to the knowledge of mind. Philosophy can-not pretend any longer that mind is its sanctuary, a strange object appearing to itself when it is described and analyzed by this peculiar use of language called philosophy. Philosophy finds itself outside the mind, the mind of the philosophers as well as the mind of humanity or mankind. In fact it seems (for the moment at least) nowhere and everywhere.

This final uprooting of philosophy does not need to be dramatized. In the present situation, the task of philosophy is certainly difficult to perform, but it is at the same time quite obvious. First it is necessary to avoid any pretended fear or anxiety of (re)constructed mind, virtual (parallel) reality, artificial (non-natural) intelligence, as if we were waiting for a new Frankenstein under the cover of a Heideggerian conception of *technè*. Any form of postmodern blues or pathos (the end of all things modern, the philosopher as guru) is quite superfluous and rhetorical. The path is actually predict-able. Philosophy has to learn from mind technoscience what mind is, not what it is outside of them but how it is constructed, debated, investigated in the formation and development of this interdiscipline. Philosophers of the mind have to internalize their investigations within the mind sciences; they will probably have to become mind sci-entists in order to become their epistemologists. There is one obvious reason to justify this tentative assertion: many mind scientists have de facto become the epistemolo-gists of their discipline, and this work inside their own practice has played a major role in the various developments of their field. Regarding language, as there is a para-psychology, philosophers have been able in the past to play the role of paralinguists:

they pretended for a long time they were producing some knowledge of language, even if it was and still is difficult to establish its clear status. Somehow this prospect seems doomed regarding mind technoscience: its epistemology is already at work.

This is the reason why I think modern philosophy has no regeneration to expect from the formation of a mind technoscience. It is just another proof of the need and opportunity for philosophy to reinvent itself, as it has always done throughout its history. But the present conjuncture cannot be compared with the 1920s, when the young Heidegger understood that the program of his master, Edmund Husserl, was impossible to fulfill and had become a utopia. The modern philosophy of the subject could not be reconstructed in order to save the role of reason as well as the function of philosophy in European civilization. The epistemic conjuncture was a dramatic philosophical situation: if this reconstruction could not be properly accomplished, it meant that the new sciences of the late nineteenth and early twentieth centuries could not improve the knowledge of the mind required for the progress of humanity. Certainly Heidegger's solution has been worse than what he denounced as impossible. But his thought has been thoroughly developed, studied, and enough understood. Who can pretend nowadays that philosophy can discover what it was before (and therefore after) it was linked to science, the individual subject, modern society, and so on? The Heideggerian solution is *achieved*, as well as its pseudoscientific opposites. Philosophy cannot ignore the development of mind technoscience.

Still, even if he provided the wrong answer, Heidegger has left us with the right question. The question of thought is indeed the relevant one, as long as thought knows how to invent and discover what it could be by experimenting with its position and relevance within the different fields of knowledge. At present, philosophy seems only possible as thought producing itself in an order of knowledge that nobody knows but that everybody practices in research. Indeed, thought is concerned with the mind sciences, but neither to be digested by them as their epistemology nor to ignore them and express its own possibility as fiction (*fabula*) or as a form of literature (*d'écriture*).

So the role of philosophy is not to *reflect* upon the mind sciences but to *think* how thought is concerned with the development of mind technoscience, because it investigates what is thought and what is thinking in a mind. This problem is made possible at the interaction between mind technoscience (AI, the cognitive sciences, neurophysiology) and the practice of thought. What becomes thinking when the various operations that have traditionally defined *thought as cognition* are being simulated and mechanized, that is, becoming reproducible by artifacts and machines, even if these artifacts are very abstract and formal ones? Then a nonmodern distinction between thought and intelligence becomes necessary because in the present situation the problem not only concerns what is intelligent behavior but the very intelligence of thought. *Intelligence* indeed has many forms and many levels, but it can only be known or investigated as a type of response to some change in an environment so that the said intelligent subject or entity reaches, through this *intelligent* process, a better (or new) adaptation to its environment or is capable of preserving or developing its autonomy.[18] Thought, to be intelligible/intelligent, requires being treated as a behavior or process. This very situation changes the relation between intelligence and thought. It forces thought to gain a new intelligence of intelligence[19] and is profoundly transformed by this situation. This experience seems to me one of the most radical questions for philosophy at present.

This proves that the situation of thought and intelligence is at the core of mind technoscience. Not only does it guide its development but it presides over the progressive association of the different fields of research composing it today. It has been basically a technological question since the 1940s, and an analysis of this technology is able to clarify the question and situation of thinking today as well as some problems raised by the relations between AI, the cognitive sciences, and virtual reality. I will call it intelligence technology in order to show that it is not a technique as a means to realize some goals under the guidance of some ideal (humankind, reason, spirit) or under the power of some interest (e.g., economic). This technology generates within itself its conception of thought and makes possible at its border another conception of thinking. As already shown, the humanities, either as a modern ideal or as academic institutions, are not directly concerned with this question, except through the very possibility and relevance of philosophy.

A Philosophical Response

My question is, What is intelligence in intelligence technology? The answer is the opening of another thought that can only be proved in action. This interaction within thinking, between thought and its intelligence, is the question: no theory can be made, it just has to be tried out. But I certainly do not intend to take a heroic stand and enunciate what is thinking today. On the contrary, the situation need not be dramatized because it has already occurred in the history of philosophy, even if the problems to raise and the answers to provide have to be original. Indeed, in the early seventeenth century, Descartes saw that analytic geometry was introducing new ways of organizing thinking, a new form of intelligence. It did not concern the mind itself but its conception, not cognitive behaviors as the spontaneous activities of this mind but a conception of knowledge and thought superimposed on the mind. A *new* mind was not constructed, but a new image of the mind in its act of thinking was constructed, and a new definition of humankind became possible. This is what Descartes called *method*, and he formulated its basic rules, not for them to be simply applied and followed but to exhibit that a new organization and practice of thought were possible, that they could be explored, and that the results of the exploration could transform the different fields of knowledge and even open up new ones. His work was very dependent on the order of knowledge that he was at the same time contributing to establish. This method could be called today a *model of rationality*.[20]

I probably have proved by now that I am no Descartes, but the situation of philosophy in *his* epistemic conjuncture is quite similar to ours. Intelligence technology offers a new method, and its basic rules or steps can be formulated; they have been born in computer science and information technology, and my objective is to show that they play a major role in mind technoscience. The description of these rules will not teach anything new to anyone working in these fields, but this is precisely the reason why it is so important to exhibit them.[21]

The form of what is given (investigated) is a behavior, a process, or the function of a process. So, the function always supposes a process, and every process expresses a function. The first step of the method is the description of the process, that is, its analysis, in order to discern its different phases, the elementary functions composing it. This analysis is the uncovering of the structure of the process or of a function in a process. Structure can be symbolic or, according to the connectionist paradigm, *subsymbolic*. Indeed, the concept of structure designates a level in the analysis of phenomena and not a specific type of formal theory. What is here investigated are the properties of this level, and this requires the development of original descriptive and explanatory hypotheses. The key point in intelligence technology is the relation between this structure and the process from which it was exhibited.

The second step is the expression of this structure in a formal language. It was traditionally a mathematical one, but in intelligence technology the problem is not only the formal language itself but the language in which this structure adequately formalized can be programmed so that it can be reproduced and therefore the function itself simulated. The very stake of this second step is the decisive character of intelligence technology: once a structure is expressed (in the biotechnological sense) in a formal language, it can be programmed so that it becomes possible to interfere with it, to introduce variations in order to better satisfy the function or to act eventually upon the function itself. This potential action within the structure on the function raises fundamental questions. Intelligence technology makes it possible to express structures by interfering with them, to simulate or develop new versions of any function or new functions that have in common a structure or some elements of one. To be able to analyze the structure of a function in order to act upon it and so to find within this very structure variations of the function or new functions is what is at stake and has to be *thought*. Functions have, in fact, become virtual modalities of structures within a technology. In intelligence technology structures are neutral regarding the functions they have been gathered from. The consequences of this fact are innumerable and effectively bring the human community into a new age of its evolution.

The third step is to select the *medium* capable of expressing the structure and its virtualities in order to fulfill the function. The medium is the carrier of the structure; it can, for instance, transmit it, introduce it into an *artifact* (any object or machine). It *actualizes* the structure in an artifact, in a given environment, and for a certain task. Strictly speaking, the medium does not carry or embody the structure itself but the structure being programmed to perform a function or a set of functions. The carrier is somehow the matter in the Aristotelian sense, programmed or programmable. The decisive point is that in intelligence technology the medium is neutral regarding the structure it expresses, as the structure is neutral regarding the function. The same medium can carry different structures and, more important for our objective, the same structure can be expressed in different media.

To follow Descartes' suit, the fourth step is to program the function in a medium in order to perform the function, reproduce its various steps and their order. The fifth step is to test the program to make sure that every moment of the initial or intended process is adequately satisfied.

This is the effective situation of thought today, and many points could now be clarified. The first one concerns some aspects of what virtual reality means. Intelligence technology brings in a radical new conception of structure. Since the Greeks, it has been conceived as an autonomous and formal level of determination in reality, expressed and treated by mathematics. Now structure is not only the form of an object, of an entity or a process, it has become the *intelligence* of a process. This technology manipulates the structure it analyzes and installs in it the results of these manipulations. So in intelligence technology a structure includes its virtualities, and the analysis of a process generates the virtualities of this process. This initial or actual process is to be conceived as the existing actualization of a set of virtualities internal to the structure and constituting it. This is made possible because the structure is programmable in a medium (or carrier) which *overdetermines* the object, is *overimposed* to it, so as to reconstruct it and make an artifact out of it.

The *management* of structures has become effective within *their* objects, entities, or processes. It opens a radical transformation of our conceptions of any being. From now on, any being includes in itself its other modalities as part of its own being. Heidegger explained that things had become *objects* for *subjects* who were perceiving them and reducing them to what they appeared to them.[22] Now the objects are becoming artifacts: what the subject perceives is only one modality of an artifact whose structure includes other modalities that exist only through intelligence technology. The individuality of an artifact comprehends virtualities that can be actualized by a technology. So virtual reality is not another reality, it is *the* reality. Reality has become virtual. This does not mean that what is virtual is not real and that in postmodernity reality vanishes in the realm of artifacts. It is another experience of reality: the actual or existing reality contains its virtuals, other types of actualization. The object and the subject are overlapping.

Has therefore the substance of the subject become the structure that includes its potentials? Yes, if this means that the subject is no longer closed within one's self, some master of one's own being. But since Heidegger, philosophy has exhausted this interpretation. The answer is to be found in the negative one: according to a model of rationality derived from intelligence technology, the structure cannot be reduced to the form or the *dunamis* in Aristotle or to a program in genetics. The reason is, according to the form of the given, that the analysis of structures in intelligence technology has as a purpose the knowledge of functions or processes. Intelligence technology transforms the conception of knowledge in a virtual action inside the process on the functions it satisfies: the knowledge of the process is a virtual action on the function.[23] So, the clear objective of this type of knowledge is not to study preprogrammed potentials already inscribed in a code or in the substance of a subject in order to make or let it happen. It is not a return or a reconstruction of an Aristotelian paradigm. On the contrary, the stake seems to be the opening of the structure, the introduction into it, through a given technology, of virtualities that have to be interpreted and decided upon according to the functions they are supposed to accomplish. In short, intelligence technology is not a study of what is already there but of what can happen within what there is. I have reached the most controversial point of this chapter, and it needs to be justified or falsified: the function sets the limit of the technology. Intelligence technology seems to be a technology that constructs its limit into itself.

The second point to be clarified is central to mind technoscience and concerns the relation between mind, brain, computer science, physics, and neurology. My remarks are strictly philosophical and do not pretend to have any practical epistemological relevance; they just follow from the argumentation being built up.[24] My assumption is that mind technoscience is currently overdetermined by the model of rationality at the core of intelligence technology. It explains why mind is conceived as cognition and that cognition is in its turn reduced to various cognitive behaviors or processes like problem solving, belief, attention, and perception. In fact, what falls under cognition is an analysis of different cognitive structures. This examination can only be achieved in intelligence technology at a symbolic or subsymbolic level by modeling them in the field of computer science. Therefore the problem is not that mind is or is not a computer, or what sort of computer a mind is. Certainly mind is not a computer, but computer science is at present the analysis of the structure of cognitive processes. To understand this fact and not to fall into the trap of endless controversies, one has to remember that mind technoscience cannot be thought of as the present and future substitute for philosophy or for the humanities. The whole (false) problem simply mixes the level of the structure and the level of the medium.

It was just argued that the level of the structure is neutral regarding the level of the medium, that a structure can be expressed by different carriers. From the point of view of intelligence technology, the brain is a carrier of cognitive structures, and in this respect it is similar to any physical system, for instance, a machine, a computer, or anything else that could perform the function described by the structure. A medium can be physical or neurological, and this does not matter at all. The questions of the rela-

tion between minds and machines, brains and computers, are often wrongly formulated because they ignore the level of the structure. So the relations between the different fields of research in mind technoscience can be clarified if one acknowledges that
this interdiscipline is organized by a model of rationality having its source in intelligence technology. This is why I said at the beginning that philosophy has not much
to say but that it was necessary to reduce some false problems and let an epistemology
of mind technoscience develop. Certainly philosophy has a lot to learn from its development, but at present its main task is to learn how to stop asking the wrong questions. I hope I have not made the situation worse.

Individuals, Artifacts, Societies

To end this chapter, it is necessary to examine some of its limits and consequences. Is
there something alarming in these new virtualities offered to the power of humanity
or in-humanity? Yes, if one thinks of the intelligence technology paradigm according to biological and genetic research, in reference to the integrity of life or of the
living being. In this case, epistemology is badly needed to explain the differences and
the limits of such a paradigm according to the different fields where it is introduced
and interferes. An epistemology proves its relevance when it is anchored in the very
evolution of a field of knowledge, articulated to the internal and external questioning
of scientists at work. Instead of deploring the end of the humanities or surreptitiously
reconstructing them, it would be more relevant to study why epistemology is incapable
of providing the knowledge of the sciences that our societies so badly need to understand themselves, their past as well as what they are becoming.[25] So, to mingle the
model of rationality provided by intelligence technology and the specific problems of
molecular biology is false, as Descartes was wrong to assert that animals or bodies were
machines.

Indeed, this problem forces us to return to the question of the *order of knowledge* in
which intelligence technology is developing. Mind technoscience is not a substitute
for the humanities, and intelligence technology is not a technology taking the place
of reason. At this point philosophy is radically involved. This can be introduced by further developing the end of the difference between subject and object, which was one of
the main features of the modern symbolic order. Such a difference does not concern
artifacts. Artifacts are no longer objects, they require being known from the inside, by
distinguishing their structure and its virtualities, the medium expressing it, and most
of all, the functions they satisfy. Objects have become artifacts. The subject is within
the artifact at the connection between the function and the structure. The artifact as
it is used in everyday practice by an individual is *designed*. Certainly the design of an
artifact is what *appears* to a subject, but it is conceived strictly according to the function, and it does not express either the structure or the carrier. The design is neutral

regarding the medium and the structure: the matter (which is not the medium) of an artifact is selected according to the function.[26]

The modern industrial conception of the object, "Form follows function," takes a completely different meaning because form is no longer the structure. Form simply concerns the design. Artifacts are designed not for a substantive subject, knowing who he is or what he wants, but for a subject who explores its virtualities in the discovery and practices of artifacts. Individuals are no longer in front of objects but in the middle of artifacts with which they interact, which they use as parts of what they are. So what they are is the uses, dispositions, and practices they develop, exchange, adapt, and invent: artifacts are the virtualities of individuals, and individuals develop virtual artifacts. The object has lost the substance that was provided for it by the subject who was in front of it. Now objects are functions for virtual individuals. A world of artifacts is a place where functions, uses, practices are what matter, not substance and identity.

Intelligence technology and its key concepts (structure, medium, design, function) are some of the main nodes in the present order of knowledge. But the striking feature is the primacy of function. The technology that reduces the object to an artifact by managing its structure finds within itself its own limit: function is the beginning and the end. Function is no longer dictated by the production, the form by the matter, the structure by the form, because the manipulation of structures includes in them virtualities that are in the end decided by social practices. The relation between technology and society is radically transformed. I do not fall into a postmodern utopia of uses and customs rising and overtaking technology by the people for the people, of a humanity free from the power of technology. I just explain that the future of intelligence technology lies not within itself but outside of itself, in the social and cultural practices. The core feature of intelligence technology is that what is outside of it finds itself introduced inside of it: its internal finality is what is external to it. To reach that point, structures had to become flexible, transformable, manageable. They had to include virtualities. In the end, virtualities exist only according to the capacity of individuals to make them happen by actualizing some of them. Intelligence technology supposes a world of events, chance, opportunities, and of course, accidents.

Urgently, structures have to be differently conceived. Apparently, economists have been explaining this for the last 20 years: human capital is the main resource of high-technology societies. But they have a restricted view of this capital when it is reduced to technoscientific skills, to the different competencies required by an industrial system based on information technology. Information is not intelligence. The virtuality of intelligence technology is that structures do not govern any longer but are governed by the functions they have the potentials to fulfill. Once again, function is the beginning and the end of intelligence technology. So, the development of intelligence technology in societies, throughout their different sectors, is closely determined by the capacity of the individuals to develop and experience new and different behaviors and attitudes. These individual and collective innovations diversify social functions, desires, needs, and demands. Intelligence technology is the capacity to analyze them. The consequences are innumerable: in the end, these functions are the basis of what is produced and sold. But in North America, Europe, and Japan, we see today a strong process of concentration in information industries. Of course this trend might be necessary to meet the level of investment required to implement information technology globally. But the objective or result of this very concentration, making the headlines, is the control of the demand by the strong structuring of the offer. To me, it seems to contradict the potentials of intelligence technology and conflict with the expected social and economic consequences of information technology. A bad philosophy and a poor epistemology might have today serious consequences.

The development of intelligence technology is determined by the capacity of our societies to offer to people a higher degree of autonomy, of individual and collective freedom. This requires, of course, a strong insistence on education, but more deeply it requires that our societies develop the knowledge, the epistemology, and the philosophy that change them. This may not be any longer the mission of the humanities, but it is the task of the university. Ethical as well as political freedom has a direct effect on the capacity of societies to change according to the rise of intelligence technology. The paradox of intelligence technology is that it cannot submit society to its logic and requires freedom to develop its virtualities. The future of intelligence technology is political, but such a political and social philosophy must be based on a proper analysis of the order of knowledge. In the age of intelligence technology, the main question of philosophy is political.

Conclusion

This chapter evolved from the conceptualization of mind technoscience to a broader, more abstract, and more intricate problem at the core of our societies, of our capacities to understand them and ourselves. Intelligence technology is not a revolutionary technology but a technology in a revolutionary sense. I said earlier that philosophy was nowhere and everywhere, because it is no longer localized in a subject, inside the mind, based on reason. I tried to show how philosophy was uprooted and therefore free from a function that was so deeply rooted in its tradition that (since the end of the nineteenth century) philosophy had held onto the hope of modernizing itself, rebuilding its modern paradigm. In the end, it failed. Postmodernism has been nothing more than the way modern philosophy met its own limits, explored its presuppositions, and finally predicted its own end as its only way to survive.

To reconstruct the end of modern philosophy helps us to understand the fascination surrounding mind technoscience. But it also opens up new possibilities. As thought cannot be separated from intelligent behaviors, the knowledge (cognitive sciences), technologization (AI), and industrialization (R&D on artifacts, intelligent manufacturing) of intelligence transform the relation between thought and intelligence. Thought is changing because the emergence of mind technoscience is dissolving the dominant internal relation between thought and intelligent behaviors. Thought is thus emancipated from a conception of intelligence, which is becoming a technoscience. This mutation and the resulting evolution of thought shape the present situation of philosophy. But, for that matter, philosophy is not strictly, exclusively determined by mind technoscience. Of course, philosophy cannot ignore its rise and development, but it should not be reduced to an epistemology of mind sciences. Neither does philosophy have to prove (in vain) that thought has nothing to do with mind technoscience, that its sanctuary lies in literature, in Heidegger, and so on. Each scientific revolution until now has offered philosophy a possibility of reinventing itself. Once again it has become our common task.

Notes

I wish to thank Pierre Morizet-Mahoudeaux, professor of AI at the University of Compiègne and co-director with me of the Science, Technology, Contemporary Societies program at the Maison franco-japonaise, Tokyo, for pushing me to write this article, and for his generous advice. I am glad to dedicate this work to his son Aurélien. Thanks also to Marcel Lieberman for editorial assistance.

1. An epistemic conjuncture is the state of development of different disciplines and the internal and external interactions of these disciplines at this precise state.

2. The intersection between the fields of artificial intelligence, computer science, neurophysiology, and the cognitive sciences generates the interdiscipline here called mind technoscience.

3. Since the 1960s postmodernism has been an overall experience of this deconstruction.

4. Not the source, i.e., the senses. But there can be no source without an origin.

5. It is, in fact, an architecture of disciplines: this order is constituted by the relations between statements (énoncés, not propositions in the traditional analytical sense), argumentations, and concepts taken from different disciplines and intertwined in a mind located in a generic subject called a human being.

6. Mind was supposed to be deep because new layers could indefinitely be excavated as long as sciences were diversifying and progressing.

7. Edmund Husserl, "Die Philosophie in der Krisis der europäischen Menschheit," in *Die Krisis der europäischen Wissenschaften und die transzendentale Phänomenologie*, ed. Walter Biemel (The Hague: Nijhoff, 1954; 1976), *The Crisis of European Sciences and Transcendental Phenomenology*, trans. David Carr (Evanston, Ill.: Northwestern University Press, 1970), appendix.

8. From language and the different expressions of *thought* to art as the way people express its *spirit*. The sciences do not belong to the humanities because they have historically developed their own methodology, they have *constructed* the mind outside of itself. But there is nothing to fear; philosophy refers these methods to the faculties of a mind. Because philosophy is *the* inside of the humanities, the sciences are outside of them.

9. The world is not nature; it is the set of what can be and is *humanized*, i.e., comprised in a mind and comprehended by it.

10. This program was explicitly articulated by Franz Brentano in the introduction of *Psychologie vom empirischen Standpunkt* (1874), *Psychology from an Empirical Standpoint*, trans. A. C. Rancurello, D. B. Terrell, and L. L. McAlister (London: Routledge, 1973).

11. As represented by Jean Cavaillès, see *Sur la logique et la théorie de la science* (Paris: PUF, 1960); Gaston Bachelard, *Le nouvel esprit scientifique* (Paris: PUF, 1934), *The New Scientific Spirit*, trans. Arthur Goldhammer (Boston: Beacon Press, 1984); and Jean Toussaint Desanti, *Les idéalités mathématiques* (Paris: PUF, 1968).

12. The standard presentation of this conception can be found in the introduction of Bachelard, *The New Scientific Spirit*.

13. See Bruno Latour, *Nous n'avons jamais été modernes* (Paris: La découverte, 1991), *We Have Never Been Modern*, trans. Catherine Porter (New York: Harvester Wheatsheaf, 1993).

14. The connectionist paradigm can be summarized as the development of intelligent processes by the conception of networks connecting large numbers of elementary processors, which are able to work in parallel, i.e., not consecutively. They herewith form a sort of brain. Parallel distributed processing opened in the late 1970s many new fields of research. Connectionism is a proper paradigm because its methodology indicates which processes can be simulated and how to achieve this. It explicitly constructs intelligence as a quasi-object that does not have to be referred to any folk or intuitive conception of intelligence. The typical connectionist question is not, Can this intelligent process be simulated? but, How intelligent is this network of processors? What does it perform? My argumentation here is greatly indebted to Paul Smolensky's work. For a definition of the connectionist paradigm, see, for instance, his article "Connectionism" in *The International Encyclopedia of Linguistics*, ed. W. Bright (Oxford: Oxford University Press, 1991), 294–297.

15. The examples could be multiplied. A strict causality cannot be established in the phenomena being studied, because the causal models available cannot describe and explain the occurrences and consecutions. A cognitive behaviorlike belief has to be reduced to such minimal parameters that it can hardly be called a belief in the common or philosophical use of the word.

16. See Jean-Luc Petit, "Phénoménologie et sciences cognitives," *Revue de l'Institut Catholique de Paris* 35 (July–September 1990): 113–134.

17. Modern philosophy will have played (is playing) in the cognitive sciences a role similar to phlogiston in the rise of modern chemistry.

18. This is why mind technoscience is closely related to the epistemology of self-organizing systems and of neo-evolutionary theory, as shown by the work of Jean Gayon and Francisco Varela.

19. Both a new knowledge and a different conception of intelligence.

20. There is never at any given period only one model of rationality available. The order of knowledge is conditioned by competing models. Descartes is only an example. On the concept of the rationality model, see Alain-Marc Rieu, "De la structure au système dans la théorie sociale," in *Systèmes naturels/systèmes artificials* (Seyssel, France: Champ Vallon, 1991), 212–225, and in particular, 214–218.

21. Concerning these rules, see Alain-Marc Rieu, "Entretien avec G. Metzger" and "Penser l'informatique et pensée informatique," in *La techno-science en question*, ed. Philippe Breton (Seyssel, France: Champ Vallon, 1990). Such an approach finds its roots in Allen Newell, "The Knowledge Level," *Artificial Intelligence* 8 (1982): 87–127.

22. Martin Heidegger, "Das Ding" (1950), in *Vorträge und Aufsätze* (1954), "The Thing," in *Poetry, Language, Thought*, trans. Albert Hofstadter (New York: Harper-Collins, 1975), 165–186, and in particular, 167ff.

23. This is why we have entered the age of technoscience.

24. For a different philosophical clarification, see Pierre Jacob, "Le problème du rapport du corps et de l'esprit aujourd'hui: Essai sur les forces et les faiblesses du fonctionnalisme," in *Introduction aux sciences cognitives*, ed. D. Andler (Paris: Gallimard, 1992), 313–351.

25. A key point in so-called postmodernism is the obvious failure of modern epistemology since the 1960s and the slow formation of an interdiscipline (associating sociology, economics, philosophy) studying the development and organization of sciences and technologies in societies. For the formation of a concept of science pertinent to such an interdiscipline, see my article "Science" in *Encyclopédie philosophique universelle*, vol. 2 (Paris: PUF, 1990).

26. Present architecture theoretical research calls this trend the dematerialization of the object.

Phenomenology and Cognitive Science

Serge Sharoff

As classical philosophy fades away, said Heidegger, cybernetics becomes a philosophy for the twentieth century.[1] However, this thesis can be reversed; that is, philosophical systems can be interpreted from the viewpoint of computer science. Different schools of cognitive science, then, represent the interpretations or realizations of corresponding schools of philosophy.

The history of artificial intelligence began with efforts to create thinking machines designed to cover the widest possible domain of human intellectual activity, and the declared objective of such program development was to exceed usual human reasoning, at least in certain fields. Programming served as a basis for these investigations. In practical terms, the relative failure of these early attempts—the discrepancy between their announced intentions and their real successes—has led to the creation of effective programs operating successfully in carefully constrained problem domains. Conceptually, the goal now of theoretical research in AI is to investigate the human mind, an end to which both psychological research and pure programming tricks have been put. But many AI problems also have a direct relationship to old philosophical problems: mental category determination, hermeneutic circle problems, the balance between empirical and a priori knowledge, the interrelations between abstract and specific knowledge, and so on. If we look at theoretical investigations in AI, we discover that they are always based on some philosophical background; this framework helps in large part to determine the structure of AI models as they are elaborated.

Dreyfus and Dreyfus offer one attempt to trace the links between classical philosophy and cognitive science, and to interpret the former from the standpoint of the latter. As they describe the history of European philosophy, they identify a sequence of AI predecessors: Plato, Galileo, Descartes, Leibniz, Kant, and Husserl. For example, they write,

Kant had a new idea as to how the mind worked. He held that all concepts were really rules. For example, the concept for dog is something like the rule: If it has four legs, barks, and wags its tail, then it's a dog. . . . Husserl, who can be regarded as the father of the information-processing model of the mind, [*extended Kant's ideas and*] argued that concepts were hierarchies of rules, rules which contained other rules under them. For example, the rule for recognizing dogs contained a subrule for recognizing tails. Husserl also saw that such rules would have to tell us not about any particular dog, or dogs in general, but about the typical dog. All the basic ideas used by Minsky and his students of artificial intelligence were in place.[2]

But even though many of the basic ideas of AI may be in place in classical philosophy, AI researchers must actively *develop* the particular philosophical systems they use: they must clarify obscure propositions and develop many lines of inquiry left out of the frame of the original philosophical systems. For example, in "On the Art of Combinations" (1666), Leibniz proposed that all reasoning can be reduced to an ordered combination of elements. If we could define such an algebra of thought, it would become possible for a machine to reason like clockwork. Such a machine would be capable of resolving every philosophical controversy as well as making discoveries by itself. Leibniz's thesis amounts to a theory of artificial intelligence for the seventeenth century. However, Leibniz did not have to develop many concrete questions about the correlation between his elements, about the problems of their sufficiency, or about ensuring right outcomes from right premises; that is, he never had to debug his program. The "General Problem Solver" (GPS), developed mainly by Allen Newell and Herbert Simon, is one of the earliest and most general approaches in cognitive science. The GPS-style description of reasoning (in terms of simple algebraic symbols and operations that combine these symbols into expressions) directly follows from Leibniz's thoughts and "debugs" them. As far as I know, developers of AI systems have never emphasized just how much their work relies upon and develops related philosophical theories. So, for example, the discussion about interrelations between GPS representations and Leibniz's "combinations" is rather suggestive—and unusual.

A Realization of Philosophy

Another example from classical philosophy can serve as a metaphor for the interpretation of AI investigations as philosophy. Drawing on the distinction between the thing-in-itself and the phenomenon it presents to us, Kant wrote in his *Critique of Pure Reason*:

I cannot explore my soul as a thing-in-itself by means of theoretical reasoning (still less by means of empirical observation); hence, I cannot explore free will as a feature of a being.... Nevertheless, I can *think* about freedom, that is, the *representation* of it is at least without contradictions.[3]

To shift this Kantian example into the domain of AI: researchers, as conscious beings, probably cannot *create* artificial consciousness, but they can think about their own consciousness and express their thoughts in some language—in the language of philosophical concepts (in Kant's case) or in a programming language (in the case of AI researchers).

In order to develop cognitive science as rigorous philosophy, it is necessary to adopt the premise that a description of states of consciousness as representational states can be consistent.[4] States of consciousness themselves, along with skills, emotions, and so forth, are not representations in themselves and do not belong to the realm of language; however, the fact that these states may find expression in verbal forms demonstrates that some kind of symbolic representation is possible. Moreover, states of consciousness have an inherent need for some kind of expression in order to be grasped, and language is *the* medium for symbolizing internal states. Schütz refers to this process as explication.[5] Admittedly, explication is possible only for some part of consciousness, and it cannot be done to "absolute zero," to the *n*th degree. But interpreting situations is one of the main activities of consciousness, and explaining them through language is a necessary way of socializing and expanding the conscious "stock of knowledge." Schütz uses the phrase "taken for granted" to describe the seemingly natural attitude one adopts in everyday life toward phenomena such as the characteristics of the world and of other conscious beings. In fact, what this "natural" attitude takes for granted is precisely the possibility of describing consciousness. We may recall a quotation from Pascal that Dreyfus and Dreyfus use as the title for their book's prologue: "The heart has its reasons that reason does not know." Undoubtedly, there is a reason why the European philosophical tradition has for so long attempted to explicate the processes of consciousness. There is no reason to declare this attempt no longer valid.

Basic Concepts for Computer Phenomenology

Many of the primary phenomenological ideas of Husserl and the early Heidegger lend themselves to interpretation from the viewpoint of cognitive science: notions of the phenomenon, the constitution of meaning, readiness-to-hand (*Zuhandenheit*), intentionality, horizon, and internal time consciousness.

For the purposes of this chapter, phenomenology may be described as the philosophy of dynamic representations. In *Truth and Method*, Hans-Georg Gadamer cites Schleiermacher's words as a slogan for this philosophy: "Blooming is the real maturity. A ripe fruit is only a chaotic surface that does not belong to the organic plant." The purpose of phenomenological description is to probe the thinking life hidden within us: "In contrast to an analytic philosophy that substitutes simplified constructions for the immediately given in all of its complexity and applies 'Ockham's razor,' phenomenology resists all transforming reinterpretations of the given, analyzing it for what it is in itself and on its own terms."[6]

Phenomenology's key concept is the notion of constitution, a description of the creative dynamics of the phenomena of consciousness. As Husserl wrote, "It is necessary to show in each concrete constituting act how the sense of the phenomenon is being created."[7] Phenomenology uses a complex description of the phenomenon as "that which shows its selfness through itself." For our purpose—that of describing a computer phenomenology—it is sufficient to consider a phenomenon as a mental construct that is placed in consciousness, complies with other phenomena, and has the ability to reveal itself.

Husserl's methodological solipsism corresponds closely to the nature of computer representations. His descriptions deal exclusively with subjective phenomena. The external world is taken out of brackets; as Husserl says, *epoché* is committed. A mental act, as phenomenology describes it, is concerned not with material things but with itself. Husserl uses the notion of intentionality, the direction of consciousness toward a perceived object, to describe the interaction between consciousness and objects in the external world. Through intentionality, consciousness comes to represent the object as a phenomenon.

Intentionality expresses the fundamental feature of consciousness: it is always *consciousness about something*. Consciousness is not an abstract mechanism that processes raw data; its *core structure* correlates with and therefore depends on grasped phenomena. This ensures the impossibility of a description of consciousness that is separate from perceived objects. Husserl wrote,

In all pure psychic experiences (in perceiving something, judging about something, willing something, enjoying something, hoping for something, etc.) there is found inherently a being-directed-toward.... Experiences are intentional. This being-directed-toward is not just joined to the experience by way of a mere addition, and occasionally as an accidental reaction, as if experiences could be what they are without the intentional relation. With the intentionality of the experiences there announces itself, rather, the essential structure of purely psychical.[8]

The notion of intentionality was popularized in the AI world by John Searle, who described it as "a feature of many mental states and events, by means of which they are directed to objects and states of affairs of the external world."[9] Searle claimed that he wanted to remove some of the peculiarities of certain old philosophical traditions. Yet Husserl's and Searle's definitions of intentionality are quite similar. As Searle himself admitted, the main difference lies in their ways of using these notions. The idea of intentionality can be interpreted from two different standpoints: it is both the direction of conscious acts toward objects in the external world, and the way in which phenomena exist within consciousness. But regarding the first interpretation, Husserl wrote, "The invention of intentionality realized by Brentano did not yet overcome naturalism, which, so to speak, captured intentional experiences and closed the way to the real tasks of the investigation of intentionality."[10]

It is precisely the second interpretation, and the consequent work of describing conscious phenomena, which Husserl regarded as the real task of investigations of intentionality. Husserl's method of analyzing consciousness is purely descriptive. The fact that the external world is taken out of brackets, that *epoché* is committed, does not deny this world; the external world maintains its existence. A philosopher committing *epoché* refuses to deal with the external world prior to its entry into consciousness. The difference between the "imagined" or nonsensical (e.g., a centaur smoking a pipe) and "real" or sensible objects is only in the mode of the phenomena; both objects are intentionally represented or actualized within consciousness. The direction of consciousness toward an object results in the act of endowing something with sense. In Husserl's words, when we speak about sense, "we speak about some ideal entity that can be something that is implied (*vermeintes*) in the open infinity of real and possible sense-giving (*meinende*) experiences."[11]

Husserl uses the notion of an act (say, an act of giving sense or an act of perceiving time) only to indicate the passive synthesis in consciousness of what something means. The notion of act does *not* mean a conscious action, just as intentionality does not mean desire, for we are always already situated within consciousness even as we analyze it. Otherwise, if we assign an act to some hypothetical action maker, we have to describe the functions of an internal consciousness, a consciousness within consciousness: in programming terms, we become hopelessly trapped in an endless loop.

Intentionality concerns the phenomena at the center of consciousness, at its focus. At the periphery of consciousness is what Husserl termed the "horizon," the background that provides the conditions for comprehending phenomena. In other words, what the horizon provides is *pre*-understanding (*Vorverständnis*). For instance, we understand the meaning of words in the context of a horizon constituted from our understanding of other words and their relations. Describing the relationships between horizon and intentionality, Husserl points out, "Consciousness—where the given object is led to its realization—is not like a box with data inside. A current state of consciousness is constituted so that every object shows its selfness."[12]

Heidegger uses a notion similar to Husserl's horizon: readiness-to-hand (*Zuhandenheit*). The word *Zuhanden*—at hand—emphasizes that relevant objects are held near the focus of consciousness. Both horizon and intentional states are constantly changing, and a phenomenon placed at the horizon, in the background, can be readily moved to the center by consciousness. Conversely, the phenomena constituted in the field of intentionality form a part of the horizon for the next intentionality field. As they move from center to periphery, they move from present to just-past; they submerge into the horizon, sink in time.

Internal Time Consciousness

In order to describe the constitution of mental phenomena, we need some possibility for representing time in consciousness. The original source for the phenomenology of time may perhaps be found in the writings of Augustine. In his lectures on the

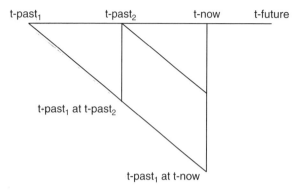

t-past₁   t-past₂   t-now   t-future

t-past₁ at t-past₂

t-past₁ at t-now

Figure 1

phenomenology of time, Husserl cited a description of time experience from the eleventh volume of the *Confessions*: "I measure time in my soul." Like Augustine, Husserl dismisses any objective notion of time. All phenomena are represented in consciousness, and consciousness operates with meanings created through intentionality. Therefore, temporal phenomena are constituted by consciousness, but they refer to a state of affairs in the external world.

Husserl describes time through a tripartite structure consisting of protention, the now-point, and retention. Protention is an anticipation of the future, the various expectations constituting and conditioning "that which is coming." At Husserl's now-point are the current horizon and the intentionality constituted within this horizon. Retention is the chain formed of the past, the reflections (*Abschattungen*) of previous phenomena kept in consciousness. Figure 1 represents Husserl's scheme.

The horizontal line corresponds to the flow of conscious phenomena, and the vertical lines to the mobile temporal horizon, in which the shadows of previous phenomena are still present in consciousness. Each phenomenon has a retention chain, represented as a diagonal line. These lines express the way in which the now-point has changed the representation of previous moments. Just as the moment *t-now* was constituted at the moment *t-past₂*, so expectations at the moment *t-now* constitute *t-future*. Specifically, the moment *t-future* is already represented in consciousness at *t-now* as an intentional state.

For Husserl, consciousness is a flow of phenomena along a common line or with a common pivot: the revealing or unfolding of experiences in time. The process of revealing determines the structure of these experiences. In other words, time consciousness provides the organizing basis for all other activities of consciousness. Like other phenomena, time is constituted in consciousness, but time also provides a basis for constituting other phenomena, because each phenomenon starts, modulates, and concludes along the connected life of consciousness.

It is possible to distinguish between two kinds of intentionality: longitudinal and transversal (represented in figure 1 as vertical and horizontal lines). Transversal intentionality means grasping an object at various points in time: how it begins, varies, finishes; it provides the possibility of grasping a temporal object. Longitudinal intentionality, on the other hand, allows us to grasp the flow of consciousness itself. Consciousness can thus become the object of analysis because of retention, the chain formed of the past.[13] Logically and practically, the introduction of time allows us to escape another endless loop: the infinite regress of reflective consciousness, of a consciousness analyzing its own consciousness. The question for AI is, however, can we analyze our own consciousness?

Obstacles for Computer Phenomenology

A cornerstone of Heidegger's philosophy is his refusal to isolate research into language and mind from social environment and body. According to him, New Age metaphysics replaces the world with a representation and a person with a subject. Modeling phenomenological concepts and analyzing consciousness and language without embodying the whole system means that we lose any real engagement with a situation; Husserl's answer to the problem of embodied consciousness, the phenomenology of consciousness, thus had some problems. An attempt to shelter in pure subjectivity might easily fail. When describing a situation it seems difficult to deny the direct, rather than the internalized, influence of external forces. The source of time—the fact that being lasts—is also difficult to place exclusively within ourselves. As a result, a thesis concerning the link of consciousness and body, being-in-the-world, became a key subject for Heidegger's and Merleau-Ponty's versions of phenomenology.

Heidegger changed Husserl's emphasis and shifted from the analysis of consciousness to the analysis of being (*Dasein-analytik*); for this reason, his problems differ from those of cognitive science. Although Dreyfus's exploration of the philosophical background of AI, based on Heidegger's ontology,[14] leads one to an appropriate conclusion about the impossibility of such a project, its impossibility arises from Heidegger's phenomenology of *being*[15] rather than from Husserl's analysis of *consciousness*. In contrast, Husserl's descriptive analysis of consciousness by means of reflection corresponds quite closely with the goals of cognitive science. Regarding the question of a method for phenomenological psychology, Husserl wrote, "Reflection should be made so that the variable, fluctuating life of the ego, the life of consciousness, is not viewed at its surface but instead explicated in contemplation according to its own essential constituent parts."[16]

Husserl's attempts to explore the constitution of phenomena in consciousness—his call for models of its production—agree with the basic essence of cognitive science. However, Husserl also imposed some limitations on the scope of this analysis when he wrote about the preintentional field, the field of pure possibility of intention, which constitutes the primary flow and which limits the possibility of analysis by means of language. The primary flow thus becomes the crucial problem when we consider the possibility of continuing the European philosophical tradition by means of cognitive science. There are two possibilities. If cognitive science can be used to interpret the structure of the primary flow, then it transcends traditional philosophy because it goes beyond the linguistic-based approaches of a human thinker; that is, its modeling is on a level below traditional description. The second possibility is that the primary flow is as impenetrable to analyses based on cognitive science as it was to previous descriptions based on traditional philosophy.

Nothing remains but to admit the restrictions placed by phenomenology on computer realization. How significant would this realization be under such restrictions? Of course, I use the term *realization* only metaphorically. But phenomenology nonetheless proposes interesting concepts for the development of the classical AI paradigm. AI can no longer attempt to create thinking machines; the only possible computer project is a development of some version of philosophy. We can elaborate our concepts, but we cannot elaborate ourselves. Yet even this weak assumption is unjustifiable if we do not consider how we are to realize our position, if we do not clarify our concepts by using the computer. The following section attempts to apply phenomenological concepts to traditional fields of AI.

An Interpretation of Phenomenological Concepts for Cognitive Science

Husserl's horizon and internal time consciousness can provide the key ideas for a computer version of phenomenology, a version that uses continually changing representations of information to ensure the readiness-to-hand of relevant facts. The situation thus constitutes itself on the basis of the history of previous steps.

The main distinction between phenomenological and classical approaches to cognitive science is the use each makes of saved information, for instance, vocabulary items, scripts, and frames. In essence, the distinction is between dynamic remembering and constant memory. Dynamic representations suppose that scripts or word meanings are not simply selected from a vocabulary of possibilities; instead, they are created and constituted during the process of analysis. The problem of polysemy does not even arise during real understanding, for the situation constitutes itself so that a "word meaning" *must* be integrated in its context; the meaning of a word is its meaning in the current situation. It is the situation that attaches meaning to a word, like the king's seal, which, as Mark Twain's pauper demonstrates, may also be used to crack nuts.

It is also possible to apply Husserl's scheme of intentionality to the field of natural language understanding. A word or sentence can serve as an object of intentionality; the flow of interpreting words and sentences produces the flow of acts of intentionality. The act of giving sense to a word takes place in the context of other words and of a general understanding of the situation. The horizon is formed at the current moment, combining the flow of intentional acts with the assumptions that create the background for understanding. In some ways, the notion of the horizon corresponds to a traditional notion of the context. Husserl's description, however, resists the traditional separation of focus and context, for intentionality presupposes that the structure of an intentional object corresponds to the structure of the horizon.

Two examples of the situational analysis of meanings can be given from Winograd's works. For instance, there are many situations where the standard legal definition of the word *bachelor* is evidently incorrect, for instance, with regard to a Roman Catholic priest or in the case of metaphoric usage: "Has your dog ever sired puppies? No, he is a bachelor."[17] The possibility of applying this definition varies not only with regard to different men but also regarding the same man in different situations, for example, in a country that permits polygamy. Even if we were to construct more and more precise definitions of *bachelor*, new situations might arise where this definition would be violated. Moreover, if we constructed a long list of situations with a precise definition for each situation, this list would be unusable because we would have to extract precise information to confirm that the current situation satisfied a precise definition. Distinctions between each situation, however, would not be rigid. As a result, definitions would be duplicated and we would not know which definition was more appropriate. We need definitions that are not more, but rather less, precise.

The second example I select from Winograd is, "Is there water in eggplants?"[18] Water can have many different definitions, but if it is a hot day and somebody asks whether there is water in the refrigerator, then it is evident that he or she is thinking of water as a means to quench thirst. If there is a soft drink in the refrigerator, we could answer in the affirmative. Answers about water in the chemical content of eggplants, or water condensed on the refrigerator shelves, might be relevant to an analytically oriented logician but not to a real person in such a situation. The second answer, however, might be relevant to the technician who repairs refrigerators.

How can we use phenomenological description in this case? Speaking in Husserl's terms, the meaning of a query is constituted in the current flow of consciousness. The meaning of the word *water* represents the focal object of the question and is integrated into consciousness on the basis of the current horizon. Preunderstanding is already given, so the relevant features of meaning are actualized. The word *water*, however, still belongs to the usual vocabulary of anyone considering this question. There is an apt term: "the internal form of the word," which means a combination of an external form as it is represented in the speech or in consciousness of a speaker, and a fluid internal content actualized by a situation.

So meaning is represented as a phenomenon of revealing. On the one hand, there is a misleading determination of the word, a seeming unity of the meaning: the external form of the phenomenon. On the other hand, a word has its internal content. The internal content does not include all the meanings of the word *water* (*water*$_1$, *water*$_2$) or the sequence of situations in which the meanings can occur. It is rather some structure with all these meanings in a "packed" form, which is meaningless outside the way it is actualized. This actualization takes place in the frame of the current horizon, which provides a basis for preunderstanding and develops the aspects of meaning that correspond to the current situation. In phenomenological terms, the result is an intention of meaning, an act of giving a certain sense. The essential features of the meaning thus become ready-to-hand when the internal form is realized in a concrete situation.

Describing meaning in the analytic tradition is radically different. The analytic tradition emphasizes the result of meaning as objectification; the meaning is cut off from the intentionality that constituted it, so that the meaning becomes an independently analyzable object. In his later work, Wittgenstein criticized this idea: "We are drawn to a wrong idea that a meaning of a sentence entails it, follows it persistently."[19] A very different citation reveals the thoughts of the early Wittgenstein: "A sentence is understood if its constituent parts are understood."[20] Here is one more example of situational analysis: Wittgenstein, Moore, and Malcolm have all analyzed the expression "I know." The meaning of this expression in real life depends on the situation: assurance, conviction, evidence, assertion. Someone who has become blind says "I know that this is a tree" instead of "I see." Malcolm's summary presents a list of 12 situations where the expression "I know" has different meanings.[21] Of course, the list could be extended.

We can apply the distinction between objectified and interpreted descriptions to differentiate between plans of action (say, the scripts used in cognitive science) and situation-driven activities. While the description of a restaurant visit as entering, calling for a waiter, ordering, and so on, is based on our real restaurant visits, it is nonetheless the result of meaning objectification. The inadequacy of such a description becomes evident if we remember the necessity of dividing these scenes into subscenes, the possible disturbance of script elements, and the importance of learning the proper behavior in the situation. For example, we might divide the first scene into opening the restaurant doors, leaving one's coat in the cloakroom, finding a vacant seat. But this scenario could go wrong in many ways: a doorkeeper might open the door for us; there might be no need for a visit to the cloakroom (during the summer or when there is no cloakroom at all); there might be no vacant seats. The situation constitutes itself. When using scripts we need to specify many explicit restrictions that develop from our understanding of the situation. As with the definition of the word *bachelor*, the number of restrictions increases until they end up obscuring our understanding.

The principle of evidence forms the core of Husserl's methodology. Simple situations are evident to us. When we are engaged in a situation, some events seem to be evident; these events are ready-to-hand. Each next step is submerged in a number of previous steps, in a particular context of the situation; each step is determined by this context. Using Husserl's notion of the horizon, which has the property of readiness-to-hand, it is possible to refer to a "space for problem solving." This space offers essential data and appropriate methods in order to solve a current problem. But certainly, in the case of a complex problem or of a misunderstanding, we would need to make an effort to restore any missing evidence.

In "A Framework for Representing Knowledge," Minsky discussed the process of building this space for problem solving during problem analysis.[22] In the wake of this article, frames became a popular structure for the representation of knowledge. Most of these realizations and concrete applications of frame systems have, however, emphasized a hierarchy of concepts, default slot assigning, and so on. Many object-oriented languages were created soon after or around the same time; some of these languages employed the frame terminology directly (for instance, Smalltalk and CLOS). It could be said that the concept of frames had stimulated the object paradigm.

Yet, in contrast to the popular acceptance of the frame structure, Minsky's analysis of perception dynamics—the dynamics of frame development during the process of situation understanding—was generally ignored or simply misunderstood. In the introduction, Minsky describes the basics of using a frame system:

The different frames of a system describe the scene from different viewpoints, and the transformations between one frame and another represent the effects of moving from place to place.... Different frames correspond to different views, and the names of pointers between frames correspond to the motions or actions that change the viewpoint.[23]

Later in the article, Minsky applies this idea about transformations to analyze a fable about a wolf and a lamb. He also uses transformations in his discussion of the widely used notion of the "problem-solving space." He writes,

The primary purpose in problem solving should be better to understand the problem space, to find representations within which the problems are easier to solve. The purpose of search [sic] is to get information for this reformulation, not—as is usually assumed—to find solutions.[24]

Minsky offers a description of perceiving a cube that directly corresponds to a phenomenological scheme; Husserl likewise uses cube perceiving as the simplest model:

Perceiving a cube is a set of various acts of intentionality; the cube is represented from different points of view and from different angles. Visible parts of the cube are related to invisible but anticipated parts. So the perceiving of the stream of aspects and the way they are synthesized reveals the presence of a single and whole consciousness directed towards something.[25]

I should devote a few words here to a phenomenology-based analysis of the processes of memorizing and remembering, that is, the actualization of memorized information. These processes can be related to internal time consciousness and the feature of readiness-to-hand. When we try to understand any description, the representations we build during the process of understanding are arranged in layers. Each representation is laid on the previous one and modifies it. Husserl uses the following metaphor to describe the way in which we retain an object image: we can see its previous image as if through a transparent layer of water. The process of layering and modifying representations results in the "packing" of this representation under the pressure of and together with the representations following it. At last these representations reach the long-term memory; we could say that "Husserl's water" hides them. When we read a text and unknown words or unexpected combinations of known words appear, these words and the contexts in which they are being used are overlaid, or sedimented. When we face a situation or a description of a situation, the set of phenomena corresponding to the situation's representation is sedimented, too. Only the core of representations remains. It can be developed later, developed in ways that will differ according to different situations.

These processes of developing, "unpacking" the core according to both the current horizon and the current state of consciousness, constitute the essence of remembering. This unpacking will be different when the horizon or the intentionality state—the mode of consciousness—is different; consciousness will reveal another aspect of a word, the aspect that is ready-to-hand. The structure of consciousness corresponds to the comprehended object because of intentionality. What is remembered as a part of the consciousness structure corresponds to the comprehended object and to other parts of the consciousness structure. Remembering does not work as though we are cutting a representation out of memory, which is structured (according to this view) as a linear array or list of data accessible according to their position. Such an array would be an insensitive medium that would not depend on the data structures stored in it. Instead, remembering is the *process* of constituting the representation necessary for the situation. The metaphor of a river can help clarify the process of remembering. Water in a river does not itself remember the direction of the stream. Moving in its bed, the stream provides the necessary direction of movement. The river corresponds here to an intentional act of remembering, and its bed corresponds to a horizon. Once a core of some remembered object is developed, it can be sedimented again when it is enriched by situational contexts. Subsequent sedimentation is not, however, always necessary, for well-known words or familiar situations, for example. In this case, the development of the prototypical meaning does not change the whole structure of consciousness and protential field very much. These words or situations become phenomena with a correspondence to their type and to the current consciousness structure. They should sink in time, too, but without much new sedimentation on their prototypical features.

From the cognitive science viewpoint, the representation of the structure of time consciousness provides the possibility that an application may use its own history—*history* here meaning only a sequence of its previous states. If an AI system understands its history, this understanding allows the possibility that it may then reflect on its own actions or representations. The restriction of logic by common sense and the limitation of resources are also related to time consciousness.

The possibility of using the internal structure of time flow provides a mechanism for establishing restrictions on the process of understanding, so that understanding becomes a process with limited resources. Logical inference often creates the problem of a "superficial" infinity, but natural modeling of limited resources allows one to avoid paradoxes like the following: A_i is close to A_{i+1}, A_{i+1} is close to A_{i+2}, ..., A_{i+99} is close to A_{i+100}, so A_i must be close to A_{i+100}. Assessing the length of the reasoning chain and restricting logic by common sense can be implemented relatively simply, using the model of time consciousness.

At the same time, representing the temporal sequence of reasoning may also allow one to avoid the mechanical backtracking possible in logic programming languages such as Prolog. One problem arising from such backtracking is this: if reasoning has at some point reached a dead end—that is, if any Prolog clause cannot be satisfied—then the assignments that the Prolog interpreter has made to free terms, to data structures, are rejected on backtracking. In this case, the Prolog pattern-matching mechanism tries to unify bound and unbound terms by another means, as determined in an alternative clause. The alternative Prolog clause tries to continue its inference and does not use the results of the inference made by the previous clause. When we submerge an analysis in the flow of temporal acts in which our previous steps are accessible almost immediately ("as through a layer of transparent water"), we retain the possibility of reusing them, of using *partially* correct proofs.

The phenomenological movement can suggest new concepts for the object-oriented approach to programming. Phenomena, objects, are self-revealing entities introduced into consciousness and developed in the frame of the current horizon. This scheme resembles object-oriented concepts, which suppose that an object is instantiated in the frame of the current programming environment and supplied with a possible behavior determined according to its class upon initialization. Later on, the object receives outside messages and reacts to them according to properties of its class. The flow of consciousness may also be regarded as a phenomenon. In an object-oriented interpretation of phenomenology, consciousness can be regarded as an object of the class "container," which holds other objects—phenomena. In addition to their shared status as phenomena, these objects have a specific (polymorphic) reaction to common messages for the explication of its content, the transition of representations from a potential to an articulated state, the transition from an internal system of images (for example, the internal form of a word) to an external linguistic representation accessible to an external observer. Classes of objects must be phenomena, too, because noematic structures correspond to noetic structures and have to be explicated upon reflection. This fact is not new for object-oriented programming. The well-known meta-object protocol[26] provides the possibility of regarding classes as objects of some sort.

Existing notions of object-oriented programming can thus be interpreted phenom-enologically. Phenomenological description is, however, much more complex and does not fit into this scheme, potentially enriching object-oriented concepts. First of all, after revealing the phenomena of consciousness during the process of develop-ment, explication can be implemented under the meta-object protocol. A phenome-non does not, however, simply develop its properties; rather, they are created and constituted on the basis of an object. This type of "constitutive programming" is un-usual, to say the least, as a regular practice.

Conclusions

Some phenomenological intentions and notions fit into the current AI paradigm, at least with more or less extended interpretation. These include the stress on the produc-tion model of consciousness, horizon (which corresponds to context), and Husserl's intentionality (which, in AI terms, means the correspondence between an algorithm and data structures). Some don't. The notion of internal time consciousness is one of these, but it is the core that can shed new light on the first group of concepts. How-ever, a question about the possible implications of this analysis might arise. What has caused my emphasis on phenomenology? Do I think that phenomenology provides a more adequate basis for AI applications? To answer, it is necessary to separate three re-lated assertions: common, weak, strong. The common assertion is that philosophical investigations provide an adequate basis for investigations in cognitive science. The weak assertion is that a computer interpretation of the phenomenological movement is possible at least in some sense. The strong assertion is that AI applications con-structed on the basis of described phenomenological concepts will be more effective or powerful.

Whether to accept the strong assertion is a question of belief (*question de foi*) for the researcher, the result of his or her choice of position. The history of classical AI appli-cations implicitly based on analytical philosophy shows the great number of problems related to the description of consciousness by these means. So perhaps phenomenolog-ical descriptions can be viewed as instantly effective strategies for some AI problems. I am not certain, however, that this thesis is absolutely correct. I believe that the weak assertion has a more general significance, and that the realization of this thesis would be interesting as a development of phenomenology. At the very least, problems of phe-nomenology as philosophy investigating "a hidden life of thoughts" have a direct rela-tion to problems of cognitive science. The general assertion has a general significance, too, and it provides the potential for interpreting current investigations in cognitive science from a philosophical viewpoint and not from the viewpoint of the natural sciences (such as biology or psychology). Of course, the interpretation of cognitive science as philosophy is a metaphor that can elucidate the position of cognitive science in the historical perspective of consciousness research. The methods of cognitive science and philosophy are different: philosophical texts are interpreted by a human, who is a carrier of consciousness. In contrast, computer programs operate on (initially) unconscious substance, and cognitive science is aimed at a production model. But this metaphor is fruitful because it allows the enrichment of current research directions in cognitive science with a great number of classical philosophical ideas. Dreyfus and Dreyfus follow Heidegger's dictum about the end of philosophy and "return to hacker's reality."[27] This leaves no space for the development of philosophy, much less for its development by means of cognitive science. However, an inversion of Heidegger's thesis about cybernetics as a substitution for philosophy leads to a fruitful metaphor. With such an interpretation we can avoid the exciting question, Can computers think? and ask a more productive question: How can philosophical concepts be interpreted with a computer?

Notes

I must mention Dr. V. Molchanov, whose lectures at Moscow University developed my knowledge of phenomenology. The introductory description of phenomenology in this chapter is based on my memories of his lectures. This text was prepared at the Russian Institute of Artificial Intelligence, and I would like to thank A. Narin'yani, the director of the institute, who provided enough room for my philosophical investigations, and V. Subbotin, who corrected my English translation. I would also like to thank Richard Menke and Sujata Iyengar, without whose editorial help this chapter would not have appeared in its present form.

Many citations in this article are the result of my translation from Russian to English. German citations may differ from published English translations, and my citations from English sources may be paraphrases of the original texts. I hope, however, that meanings have not shifted during such double translation. For certain citations and for the spelling of some terms, I have referred to *The New Encyclopædia Britannica* (Chicago: Encyclopædia Britannica, 1988).

1. Martin Heidegger, "Nur noch ein Gott kann uns retten: *Spiegel*-Gespräch mit Martin Heidegger am 23. September, 1966," *Der Spiegel*, May 31, 1976, "Only a God Can Save Us: *Der Spiegel* Interview with Martin Heidegger," in *The Heidegger Controversy: A Critical Reader*, ed. Richard Wolin (Cambridge, Mass.: MIT Press, 1993).

2. Hubert L. and Stuart E. Dreyfus, *Mind Over Machine* (New York: Free Press, 1986), 4.

3. Immanuel Kant, "Preface to the Second Edition," *Critique of Pure Reason*, trans. Kemp Smith (1787; New York: St. Martin's, 1965), 28.

4. My use of the word *consciousness* stems from Husserl's term *Bewußtsein* and the corresponding Russian term *soznaniye*, which mean general thinking abilities that could in principle be grasped. This does not stress self-awareness features, although it has some relation (but a very limited one) to them.

5. Alfred Schütz and Thomas Luckman, *The Structures of the Life-World*, trans. Richard M. Zaner and H. Tristram Engelhardt, Jr. (Evanston, Ill.: Northwestern University Press, 1973).

6. "Philosophical Schools and Doctrines: Phenomenology," in *The New Encyclopædia Britannica*, 15th ed., vol. 25 (Chicago: Encyclopædia Britannica, 1988), 626.

7. Edmund Husserl, "Pariser Vorträge," in *Husserliana 1* (The Hague: Nijhoff, 1962) 1: 3–39, *The Paris Lectures* (The Hague: Nijhoff, 1975).

8. John R. Searle, "The Nature of Intentional States," in *Intentionality: An Essay in the Philosophy of Mind* (Cambridge: Cambridge University Press, 1983), 1–29.

9. *The New Encyclopædia Britannica*, 627.

10. Edmund Husserl, "Amsterdam Reports: Phenomenological Psychology," in *Husserliana 9*. This text is an important source for Husserl's thoughts about the possible interpretations of phenomenology. These thoughts can be applied to computer phenomenology in particular.

11. Husserl, "Amsterdam Reports."

12. Edmund Husserl, *The Idea of Phenomenology: Lectures for an Introduction to Phenomenology*, trans. William A. Alston and George Nakhnikian (The Hague: Nijhoff, 1964).

13. Edmund Husserl, *Husserliana* 10: 119.

14. Hubert L. Dreyfus, *What Computers Can't Do* (New York: Harper, 1972; rev. ed. 1979).

15. An analogy to this distinction can be found in Jaspers's assessment of Heidegger's *Dasein-analytik*. Despite his use of phenomenological concepts in psychiatry (his *Psychopathology*) and despite his position on Cartesian mechanistic ideas (evidently similar to Heidegger's views), he has a distinctly negative assessment of usefulness of Heidegger's ontology for psychiatry.

16. Husserl, "Amsterdam Reports."

17. Terry Winograd, "Towards a Procedural Understanding of Semantics," *Revue Internationale de Philosophie* 30 (1976): 260–303.

18. Terry Winograd and Fernando Florès, *Understanding Computers and Cognition* (Norwood, N.J.: Ablex, 1986), 55.

19. Ludwig Wittgenstein, *Zettel*, trans. G.E.M. Anscombe, ed. G.E.M. Anscombe and G. H. von Wright (Oxford: Blackwell, 1967).

20. Ludwig Wittgenstein, *Tractatus Logico-Philosophicus*, trans. C. K. Ogden and F. P. Ramsey, ed. C. K. Ogden (1922; London: Kegan Paul, 1933), 4.024.

21. Norman Malcolm, "Moore and Wittgenstein on the Sense of 'I Know,'" in *Thought and Knowledge* (Ithaca, N.Y.: Cornell University Press, 1977), 170–198.

22. Marvin Minsky, "A Framework for Representing Knowledge," in *The Psychology of Computer Vision*, ed. Patrick Henry Winston (New York: McGraw-Hill, 1975).

23. Minsky, 212, 218.

24. Minsky, 259.

25. Husserl, "Pariser Vorträge."

26. Gregor Kiczales, Jim des Rivières, and Daniel G. Bobrow, *The Art of the Metaobject Protocol* (Cambridge, Mass.: MIT Press, 1991).

27. Dreyfus and Dreyfus, epilogue.

Artificial Intelligence and Theology: From *Mythos* to *Logos* and Back

Anne Foerst

Since the beginnings of artificial intelligence (AI) in 1956, there have been passionate debates on whether it is possible to build intelligent machines. Many people, scientists as well as science fiction writers and artists, were fascinated by the idea of a humanoid replica of *homo sapiens*. On the other hand, many people argued vehemently against even the attempt to build AI systems. One main reason for the passionate opposition is that AI challenges the intuitive self-understanding of most human beings. We usually don't see ourselves as machines. Instead we feel that we are special, qualitatively distinct and radically different from nonhuman animals and from machines, and that therefore we cannot be duplicated.

I use an explicitly theological argument to bring AI supporters and AI opponents together to come to an understanding of ourselves that includes a scientific and materialist understanding of humankind but also takes our intuition of human specialness into account. I first introduce the Platonic distinction between *mythos* and *logos*; both realms are equally important for human life, and both together create intelligence, fantasy, and human interaction. I analyze to what extent the confusion of *mythos* and *logos* can be found in AI and in theology, giving rise to many arguments between supporters and opponents of AI. I show the importance of both *mythos* and *logos* for the understanding of who we are and how we function, and finally explore ways of combining and the intuitive feeling of irreducible specialness with the understanding that the human system obeys functionalist and mechanistic laws.

The Speech Acts of *Mythos* and *Logos*

From Plato's time until the eighteenth-century European Enlightenment, the realms of *mythos* and *logos* (both from the Greek)[1] were regarded as distinct but equally indispensable ways to understand human beings, their life, and the world around them.[2]

In the *logos* realm, people create statements within a discussion and are open for dialogue. *Logos* speech acts are used when people observe the world and formulate ontological statements in theories, formulas, and definitions. The *logos* is therefore open for questioning; it invites rational analysis and seeks situation-independent validity. *Logos* speech acts are usually used in scientific environments. The term *λόγος* is one of the most important terms for Western philosophy and for Christianity. It means general speech, and also justification, calculation, and reason. We take this complex spectrum of meaning into account when we define the *logos* realm as an area of human feeling and thought that hints toward the basic question of all epistemology and expresses the common assumption of most philosophers since Parmenides, "that the *logos*, the word which grasps and shapes reality, can do so only because reality itself has a *logos* character."[3] Human beings are in the world and describe the world in *logos* speech acts; they try to understand the world around them and themselves.

However one wants to relate the descriptive act of speech and the described reality, the relationship between the world outside and us as participant observers has to be defined to make the *logos* useful and functional. Every person, therefore, has an idea of this relationship on which her observations of the world are based. Any assumption about her role in the world cannot be grounded in the *logos* itself without creating circularity. Every observation about reality and every assumption about the relationship between subject and world contains an element of what I would like to call *mythos*.

Μύθος in its original sense meant just "utterance" or "story." Statements created within the *mythos* realm, indeed, interpret and explain human reality and human experiences; these explanations usually have the form of stories, myths[4] and other narratives. Since the *mythos* speech act is not as accepted a way to talk about the world as the *logos* speech act, many people are not aware that they use myths sometimes as well. Therefore, I discuss the speech act of *mythos* more intensively.

A *mythos* interpretation of reality, contrary to a *logos* interpretation, is presented in an authoritative fashion and cannot be a topic for rational analysis and discussion. The authority and the language a myth uses depends on the time and the culture in which it is told; the authority can be an official of a religion, a politician, one's family, or even oneself. But whatever authority is accepted as the *mythos* provider, the act of acceptance is not a solely rational one but contains an element of commitment. The *mythos*, therefore, is never universally valid but accepted and valued only within well-defined boundaries. It is also connected to a certain conceptual content:

What never is but always becomes, what does not, like the structures of logical and mathematical knowledge remain identically determinate but from moment to moment manifests itself as something different, can be given only a mythical representation.[5]

Every *mythos* speech act is therefore always a result of a very concrete situation in which a person finds himself; it is a result of development, change, and the interaction of the person and his environment (especially his culture). One might, therefore, want to describe Plato's distinction with a modern attitude: *logos* speech acts are supposed to answer "how" questions regarding the reality around us, whereas *mythos* speech acts are supposed to answer "why" questions.

The "how" of anything can be discussed, proved right or wrong, or be demonstrated by empirical or logical evidence. The *mythos*, on the other hand, is related to the subject, who tries to understand the world and herself, attempts to give meaning to her experiences and perceptions. Even if the *mythos* presents itself as a cosmological or historical story, in the end it has to be interpreted in an anthropological, or better, an existential fashion.[6] Any existential "why" question has to be answered for every person individually, and whether an answer given by a myth is acceptable for a person depends on her very life situation, her cultural background, her religious upbringing, and so on. A myth that was accepted as valid can become meaningless; a myth is part of human development; any individual life story is tied to certain myths that have been accepted within single life stages. It is impossible to adopt a myth from another culture or group by mere willpower because no one can appropriate a world picture by sheer resolve; a world picture is a given from one's particular historical situation.[7] At the same time, "on the basis of certain facts that impress one as real, one perceives the impossibility of the prevailing world picture and either modifies it or develops a new one" (3). Only if one commits oneself to a *mythos*, can it be integrated into one's questioning for meaning. The *mythos*, then, not only presents answers to a person's quest for meaning but also constitutes a group; myths create and shape communities, and reinforce and strengthen the interaction of group members. Members of the group believe (in) and trust the authority who presents the *mythos* or in whose name the myths are told. If the *mythos* does not correlate with one's personal life story, or if the authority who presents it is not accepted, its myths will come across as fiction, illusion, or even lie. Therefore, every *mythos*, quite contrary to any *logos*, is exclusive by nature.

Myths usually refer to supernatural agencies. They do not prove the existence of these agencies but presuppose them; they then can be stories about the relationship of the human with the supernatural or divine. Myths, therefore, are the speech acts for the religious realm and, within the Jewish and Christian traditions, are often seen as answers to God's revelation:[8] the *mythos* is the speech act with which we address and describe things that are sacred or holy for us.[9]

But besides religious myths there have always been secular myths.[10] They are derived from religious myths but lack the reference to a supernatural agency. Art and literature create myths, nations can create myths, and—what concerns us the most in the context of this essay—science sometimes creates myths.

The main assumption for this definition of *mythos* is that every person asks existential questions, that every person has an ultimate concern. Paul Tillich defines the ultimate concern as "being unconditionally concerned about the meaning of existence, taking something absolutely seriously, being grasped by an infinite interest and passion, experiencing the self-transcendence of life toward an ultimately sublime or holy."[11] For Tillich, the term *God* and the term *Ultimate Concern* are synonymous; both need a commitment, and both give an answer to the most important question for human life: the ultimate meaning of one's existence.[12]

One may not want to agree to the universality of the ultimate concern, but this chapter is based on the assumption that questions of meaning are an important concern for most human beings. I also assume that many people are not even aware of the importance of these questions in their lives and that many people who ask existential questions do not consider themselves religious.

The Dialectic of Enlightenment

Max Horkheimer and Theodor W. Adorno added another component to this analysis of *mythos* and *logos*. They not only supported Plato's assumption that both of these realms are equally important for human life[13] but also said that their relationship is one of dialectic: if the importance of one realm is ignored, its necessity and its speech acts nonetheless remain, so that the other one takes over these functions, which leads to confusion, especially within the scientific realm.[14]

Horkheimer and Adorno ask how two world wars and the Holocaust could have happened in Europe, an environment nourished by the Enlightenment ideals of education and rationality. The humanist movement had already fought for education outside of the church, which had led to the development of an emancipated middle class independent from the teachings of the church. New horizons had been opened up quite literally with the discovery of America and as a result of a variety of breakthroughs in the European sciences (e.g., by Kepler, Descartes, Newton, Leibniz) that often caused major arguments between the church and scientists (e.g., Galileo).

The Enlightenment movement, Horkheimer and Adorno argue, wanted to free people from the necessity of paying attention to or living under the auspices of any form of myth. The antireligiosity within main parts of the Enlightenment movement was motivated not only by the church's rejection of scientific insights but also by the experience of decades of confessional wars all over Europe, the Inquisition, and the witch hunts;[15] many people became weary of the church, its power, and its influence over and destruction of human daily life. In this atmosphere of rising antagonism against the church and religion in general, and in the face of increasing education and scientific knowledge, the Platonic distinction between *logos* and *mythos* speech acts became a shorthand for "good" and "bad." *Mythos* now was understood synonymously with fiction or deception.

And indeed the exclusivity and the lack of valid criteria for evaluating a myth makes *mythos* speech acts potentially dangerous. For myths, truth values do not apply. A myth can be valid or invalid, it can be an answer to one's existential quest or nothing but empty words, but it cannot be true or false because it does not depend on empirical observations. Myths can be easily used to distinguish group members from outsiders and thus to gain and stay in power. Myths can also be (mis)used to keep people ignorant and uneducated, to hinder any development toward new insights and a new understanding of the world around us; especially during the history of Christianity, myths have often been used as a tool for oppression and manipulation.

In the Enlightenment, therefore, myths were given up as unverifiable, dangerous, and counterproductive for any change in society; new cultural values like logic, education, and rationality became valid. Human beings, in the view of the Enlightenment, can become the masters of the earth when freed from religion, which hinders them from gaining knowledge; knowledge and reason are the keys for human superiority.

Horkheimer and Adorno's main thesis is that the Enlightenment's drive toward rationality and objectivity, and its rejection of *mythos* as a realm in which existential quests are expressed, led to a new kind of myth. Since the Enlightenment suppresses myth, it also closes off a realm where people can find mythological expressions for their existential needs. The only language people have available today is the language of rational and objective reasoning. Thus the language of the Enlightenment movement and its theories is used to fulfill the function of *mythos*, and *logos* statements are used not only to describe the world around us but also to give meaning.

Within this process, the original function and purpose of the *mythos* are forgotten and the ability to form *mythos* expressions withers. The *logos* speech acts become the exclusive way to describe and explain reality.

But people always search for the ultimate concern. Since the Enlightenment insists on objectivity and rationality, people will develop faith in the given fact—Robespierre built an altar (!) to pure reason. Positivism becomes the myth of that which is the case. With this development the Enlightenment, in suppressing a characteristic endeavor of human beings—the quest for meaning—betrays its own ideal of liberating people from all thought restrictions.

Here, in our opinion, Horkheimer and Adorno clearly argue within their own historical context, in which the theories of the Vienna Circle were widespread. But it would be too limited to apply Horkheimer and Adorno's theories just to Positivism. The epistemological dilemma emerging out of the relationship between the scientist as a subject and the observed world of which she is a part led to an element of *mythos* in those scientific disciplines whose underlying epistemologies are not based on any form of Positivism as well; Thomas S. Kuhn, for instance, mentions Kepler's sun worship, which led him to accept the Copernican worldview.[16] Horkheimer and Adorno's theory is much more universal, and their conclusion is also valid today. In creating its own myth and simultaneously suppressing the creation of any other except *logos* statements, the Enlightenment brings about its own destruction.

The strong force for education in the Enlightenment movement, however, was meant not only to free people from superstition and angst and to liberate them from the power of oppressive *mythos*. Education and knowledge can also free people from their dependence on nature: if, for instance, one does not believe in weather gods but understands the powers of nature, one can harvest food much more efficiently.

The explanation of natural forces in *logos* language is an important goal in Enlightenment education and leads to a view of nature that is demythologized and objectified. Since myths, which interpret nature in its own right, are rejected, nature loses its mysteries and becomes "the other"; the German term for the environment, *Umwelt*, expresses this development quite clearly because it means literally "the world around us" and implies that human beings are not part of this world. This development, Horkheimer and Adorno argue, is the main reason for the loss of respect toward nature in the subconsciousness of the enlightened people of the twentieth century.

Horkheimer and Adorno did not mention the next step of this thread—probably because the technologies to rebuild the human thought process were not yet developed—which brings us to the topic of AI. In the 1950s, with the advent of computing devices and the rise of cybernetics, computers became the symbol for human thought. With the appearance of the cognitive sciences and their technological counterpart AI, people became objects of research and scientific understanding and were approached with the *logos*. This development is consistent and necessary. Since humans are natural beings and share biological needs with the rest of nature, they can become objects of the quest for knowledge. Humans, just like nonhuman nature, can be demystified and become observable entities that can be analyzed completely and then be rebuilt. In this way, they become an object of technological development.

This scientific enterprise is important and a consequence of the general scientific development. But human beings can never be objective toward the question of who they are. The questions of what constitutes a person, what is a human being, what are the functions of intelligence, and all the other questions related to this issue belong to both the *mythos* and the *logos* realms. The old question on how to relate the subject who observes with the observed reality if the observed object is the subject itself can then be asked anew: How can the *logos* of who we are, the functional explanation of the human system, be related to the *mythos* of who we are, the intuitive feeling of dignity, personhood, and meaning?

In the following sections I analyze how the separation of the dialectic between *mythos* and *logos*, and the oppression of *mythos* in both AI and theology, led to misunderstandings about who we are; how in both disciplines *logos* speech acts became the only valid way to talk about humankind. The *logos* understandings of humankind, and its self-understanding in AI and theology, are irreconcilable, so that conflict between the two arises. Also, because the *mythos* is eliminated, the understanding of humans and their thought processes becomes limited. After this analysis we can outline to what an extent cooperation between theology and AI can bring us closer to a full understanding of ourselves.

The *Logos* of Who We Are

The two most widely accepted areas of AI research differ in their goals as engineering versus scientific projects.[17] Researchers with the engineering goal attempt to build intelligent machines and concentrate on the intelligent tasks and behaviors they want to model. They use engineering methods to reach this aim efficiently and pragmatically. With the scientific goal, on the other hand, it is the declared aim of researchers to understand how human intelligence works. This chapter analyzes only the part of AI that aims to understand human beings and their intelligence.

AI belongs in the realm of *logos* and describes part of the reality of human intelligence in terms of theories, hypotheses, and working models. But the specialness of the object of AI research leads to a *mythos-logos* problem. In AI and the cognitive sciences, more than in any other scientific discipline, the boundaries between the scientist, her personal *mythos* about who she is and how she works, her professional convictions, and *logos* statements about human cognition are blurred. In the group of research areas that work under the constraints caused by this problem, AI plays a special role. AI is often subsumed under the cognitive sciences, but it seems more appropriate to understand it as cognition technology; as such it complements cognitive science and scientifically verifies or falsifies theories and hypotheses about human intelligence.[18] In this role, AI constructs working models about intelligent features that are used not only for verification of psychological theories but also as tools for experimenting. As such, they complement and enrich empirical data because one can perform experiments on models that for ethical reasons could never be performed on human beings.[19]

AI, more than the cognitive sciences, has to assume that one can actually gain insights about human intelligence by building intelligent machines—an assumption that reflects the intuitive understanding of what it means to be human, shared by most AI researchers (but not necessarily by all cognitive scientists). But AI researchers do not only have to assume that human minds and machines can in principal be compared. They also work under engineering constraints. They have to build useful, reliable, and functioning machines, and are therefore forced to choose only those theories of cognition that can be simulated or rebuilt.[20]

AI research can be roughly categorized into two different camps: classical AI (or GOFAI, for "good old fashioned AI") usually works with classical, serial machines to model human thought processes. Even though the architectures of human "wetware" and computer "hardware" are fundamentally different, it is assumed within this camp that human thought processes can be abstracted from the system on which they are running.[21] Embodied AI, on the other hand, builds creatures in real environments and models the architecture of biological systems and their interaction with their environments. With the scientific goal, all camps model human functions, and if the behavior of the computer system or the robot and the human system are similar, it is assumed that the functional description of the respective human feature is correct.

The strong assumption of mind-machine compatibility and the engineering constraints form a particularly strong entanglement of *mythos* and *logos*. The object of research in AI is—broadly defined—human intelligence. In current research projects many diverse elements of human intelligence are under scrutiny: human perception, motor control, language, learning, theorem proving, chess, navigation, development, memory, knowledge acquisition and construction, problem solving, social interaction, commonsense reasoning, emotions, and many more. Depending on the AI camp that researchers belong to, they will have different opinions on the emphasis of research and will concentrate on different objects. But they always need parts of their own intelligence to come up with theories about intelligence; they need perception to hypothesize about perception; they need language to formulate theories about natural language processing, and so on. Since it is thus impossible to distance themselves from their object of research, the studied aspect of intelligence will not only be selected because of specific respective assumptions concerning human beings but also reinforce and shape the researchers' respective self-understanding. For the sake of success, AI researchers can only choose those theories that can be implemented on machines they build; this means their intuitive self-understanding is shaped by engineering constraints and reinforced by machine models. This can be very powerful because machines are sensual objects that can be touched and perceived in a much more inclusive way than theoretical models provided by the cognitive sciences.

This interaction of the *logos* of who one is, shaped by AI models, and the *mythos* of what it means to be human, shaped by culture and upbringing, gives rise to an especially strong *mythos-logos* entanglement as described by Horkheimer and Adorno. Because of this entanglement, any analysis of AI that discusses only the epistemological implications and possible limitations of AI remains inadequate. The personal *mythos* of AI researchers, shaped by their scientific convictions, influenced by their personal life stories, and reinforced by the members of their research team, cannot be separated from the *logos* approach toward understanding human cognition. This *mythos* aspect of every theory about human intelligence has to be taken into account in any analysis of AI. Any dialogue about the dangers and promises of AI research has to integrate questions on the *mythos* of both AI researchers and AI opponents.

It now seems appropriate to describe some classical Western elements of the *mythos* of who we are within the context of Horkheimer and Adorno's analysis in order to provide the context in which to further analyze the nature of AI research.

The *Mythos* of Who We Are

In the Jewish and Christian traditions in the Western world, the self-understanding of people is influenced by the Hebrew Scriptures and the New Testament. Especially influential have been the two creation stories in Genesis—Gen. 1:1–2:4a and Gen. 2:4b–4:26. The second creation story is actually the older one, and Genesis 1 was added as a preamble to the completed Pentateuch approximately in the fifth century B.C.E. Two statements within this preamble have been extremely important for the self-understanding of people within the Jewish and Christian religious traditions: that God created humans in God's image (the Latin *terminus technicus* for the image of God is *Imago Dei*) and that humans have dominion over the rest of creation.

Within the framework of *mythos* and *logos*, the *Imago Dei* belongs to the realm of *mythos*.[22] A supernatural agency, JHWH,[23] is posited as the main actor in the story and also as the authority who authorizes the texts about God. To share the *mythos*, the reader has to believe in the existence of this God and has to commit himself to JHWH instead of other supernatural agencies. Besides God, authorities of the *mythos* can be the Bible and the scholars, rabbis, priests, or ministers who interpret the scriptures. The text in Genesis 1 was written during or shortly after the Babylonian exile and is therefore dependent on the scientific insights of that culture. It is based on the Babylonian worldview (waters below and above, and in the middle a flat disk with a bowl that separates the disk from the waters above) as well as on the scientifically sound concept of the world's being developed in steps; this contrasts with the much older creation story of Genesis 2, in which the world is "just there" and readymade.

A *mythos*, as I have defined it, does not want to describe the world in a scientific manner to answer "how" questions; rather, the *mythos* leads to those speech acts that attempt to answer "why" questions. The underlying scientific theories on how the world came into being are not coherent in either of the creation stories. Nonetheless, both stories were included into the Scripture. The incoherencies of both stories provide strong evidence that they were never meant to be *logos* descriptions of the world. The answers for "how" questions that they provide were not important; the people who canonized the Hebrew Scriptures never meant to present the underlying *logos* of both stories as valid or true. But the *mythos* answers of both stories were and are still valid for many people. If we therefore look at the creation stories from a *mythos* point of view, they provide many reasons for the way we are and for the way we feel about ourselves.

Many Hebrew Scriptures scholars today agree that the myth of humans' being created in the image of God establishes a relationship between God and humans. The *Imago Dei* is a promise of God toward humankind and gives humans value and dignity, but it cannot be identified with any empirical features of humankind, nor does it biologically separate human beings from the rest of creation. Human beings are special because God chose them as partners, not because they have certain abilities and features. This understanding of the *Imago Dei* is compatible with the AI understanding of people as mechanistic systems.[24]

The myth of the *Imago Dei* distinguishes us from the rest of creation and supports our feeling of specialness. It also attributes value to every person because every person is beloved by God the creator; therefore, the concept of humans' being created in the image of God gives rise to concepts like dignity.

In the Babylonian creation myth of Genesis 1, God says after every act of creation "and it was good," and after everything is finished on the sixth day, God concludes, "and everything was very good." Only after the creation of humankind nothing is said. In the Jewish tradition this is interpreted as symbolic of the human drive toward change, development, and perfection; only because humans are created incomplete do they have the strong desire to change themselves and their environments and become independent.[25] This desire for change and development is a main motivational force of people. The wish for *logos* explanations of the world, for understanding its mechanisms and manipulating them, has its *mythos* explanation in this absence of "and it was good."

Genesis 1 also explains in a *mythos* fashion the human drive toward relationships: one "image of God" comprises both man and woman. Only both together are God's image, which leaves an isolated human incomplete. This aspect of human beings as relational and social beings is also established in the second creation story, the one of Adam and Eve. God creates Adam and then forms birds and animals as potential partners. "But for Adam no fitting helper was found," and God creates the woman as partner for Adam. This story therefore gives another reason for the human desire for community.

The second creation story also establishes the concept of personhood. Not only are human beings created in the image of God but they also get a special name from God; each and every person is someone special, someone who is addressed specifically and distinct from the other human beings. This is one of the major differences between humans and animals: the animals are only ascribed generic names. But at the same time, people are like animals because, like other animals, they depend on (God-given) food.

The story also presents an explanation for the ambiguities of human decision processes: the ability to distinguish between good and evil and to make universally valid judgments is God's ability and God's alone. Humans are not created to do so (in the language of the myth, they are not allowed to eat from the tree of knowledge of good and evil). On the other hand, if humans do not make decisions, judge, or use reason, they do not use what is potentially given to them. The concept of self-awareness has its *mythos* explanation right here: humans who do not try to understand themselves and the world around them, humans who do not try to make judgments, are in a state of "dreaming innocence."[26] To actualize their potential, they have to try to become like God (in the language of the myth, to eat from the tree) and thus risk the relationship with God. Since human beings are in most ways like animals, they are limited in time and space. This makes every judgment and every theory incomplete. By eating from the tree, people risk error, incomplete knowledge, and false judgments. The description of the Fall therefore presents a *mythos* explanation for the inherent human dilemma: we want to understand the world and formulate theories about it, but we know that these theories are always limited, time-dependent, and thus incomplete. It also gives a *mythos* explanation for the human drive toward a whole and complete truth and why people often take partial knowledge as absolute (they have eaten from the tree and feel like God). The myth of the Fall, therefore, explains the human drive for knowledge and universal judgment but also gives reasons for its limitations.

These are some of the *mythos* answers the two Biblical creation stories present. The stories were never meant to give universally valid and objective answers to how the mind works or how we function. Instead, they were meant to help people live with certain aspects of their being and self-perception, and to make sense out of them. The stories establish communities of people who believe that they are under the affirmation of God, which was first spoken aloud in the act of creation and then confirmed in the histories of the Abrahamic religions.

However, if the *mythos* character of the creation stories is not recognized, they enter into competition with scientific theories as saying *how* the world came into place and *how* life emerged. But this misunderstanding of the creation myths not only leads to today's debates between so-called Creationists and Evolutionists. A literal understanding of Genesis 1 has led to the idea that people are distinguished from plants and animals in a much more profound way than just by their relationship to God; dominion over the earth has been interpreted as the liberty to do whatever seems best for humankind with nonhuman creatures. In the context of Horkheimer and Adorno's analysis, it seems ironic that the urge to become independent from nature, the drive toward technology to free humankind from its dependence on natural forces, the desire to see nature as "the other," is exactly a realization of a demythologized concept of dominion.

Mythos-Logos Entanglement

The entanglement of the *mythos* and the *logos* realms can work both ways. If *mythos* is turned into *logos*, the familiar myth that humans were created in the image of God is not recognized as fulfilling the *mythos* functions but is interpreted as a *logos* statement about human specialness. As such, it competes with any naturalistic approach toward people and their cognition. This view is especially opposed to the AI understanding of the human system: AI research, which verifies functionalist and mechanistic theories about humankind by building intelligent machines, diminishes human specialness even more. As the theory of evolution reduced the qualitative differences between humans and animals, AI reduces the qualitative differences between humans and machines. The strong critique against AI follows from this challenge against the *mythos* of human specialness understood as *logos*.[27]

AI researchers, on the other hand, have to reject any notion of irreproducible special-ness of humankind because any such element would prevent AI research from reaching its ultimate goal. AI research has to operate within the *logos* understanding of who we are. The exploration of the mechanisms of human functions and abilities could not be fully pursued if irreproducible and irreducible elements in the human system were assumed; therefore AI researchers have to reject any *mythos*-turned-into-*logos* notion of human specialness to protect their research agenda.

Within the *logos* realm it makes sense to declare all *mythos* elements to be illusion or deception. For instance, most researchers in cognitive science agree that self-consciousness is crucial for human intelligence. But researchers have failed to give any mechanistic or functionalist explanation for it that is more concrete than the problematic concept of emergence.[28] If self-consciousness were declared something special and irreducible that cannot be explained with *logos* language, AI would have to give up its goal of understanding human cognition and rebuilding humanlike and thus self-conscious intelligent systems because it would not be able to capture one of the essential human features with its methods. Therefore, AI researchers have to agree that every single element of human intelligence (or the human system in general) can be explained in *logos* terms and eventually be rebuilt.

However, two centuries after the Enlightenment and its suppression of the *mythos*, many AI researchers do not just argue against the limitations of their research but integrate *mythos* elements into their research by giving *logos* statements about the human system authority over their self-understanding and their ultimate concern, and thus turning them into *mythos* statements.

In the years I have spent within the AI community, I have found three different ways in which *mythos* and *logos* can become entangled. Sometimes researchers integrate *mythos* elements into their research without being aware of it. Sometimes they use the language of their research for their ultimate concern and develop technical solutions for existential problems. Sometimes, they even reject *mythos* and religion and thus fall into the Positivist trap, as described by Horkheimer and Adorno, and create the myth of human beings as machines. These three ways of entanglement between *mythos* and *logos* cannot be easily separated. Often, the integration of *mythos* elements into one's research leads to either a rejection of religion or the attempt to answer certain existential questions with technological developments. Sometimes, researchers come from an "enlightened" tradition and have unlearned any mythological language and are therefore not aware of any mythical elements in their research agenda. It can also happen that they come to AI research from an urgent existential problem. How a certain *mythos* element finds its way into AI research has to be analyzed for every case individually and thus usually needs careful analysis of biographical and psychological data. I cannot present such an extensive study here. But I give some examples of each of these possibilities for *mythos-logos* entanglement within AI.

Integration of *Mythos* Elements into AI Research

When researchers integrate *mythos* elements into their research, it can either serve their personal motivation and justify their personal beliefs or support their academic community. Every society and every community creates myths; many myths are commonly shared in a community even though its members might not be aware of them. Therefore, the integration of commonly held myths can support a group of scientists and their work. But in most cases where it happens, researchers are not necessarily aware of the myths they bring to their field. These myths are an integral part of their life and upbringing anyway. They are part of who the researchers are as people and motivate more than just the choice of an appropriate research area. They are embedded in the researchers' self-understanding and usually harmless—as long as they are not pathological and don't lead to stronger forms of entanglement.

One of the most commonly known *mythos* elements that is integrated into AI research is the golem tradition from Jewish mysticism, the Kabbalah. Golems are artificial humans built from clay and usually created by means of numeric puzzles, mathematical games with letters, and spirituality. The Jewish tradition tells of many different golems, but the most famous one was the golem built by Rabbi Judah Löw, the Maharal of Prague in the sixteenth century. Several different stories tell how this giant golem protected the Jews in the ghetto against Christian persecutors, how it helped with heavy work and relieved the people in the ghetto from hard labor. The parallel between the AI project and the golem tradition has been drawn before.[29] What is interesting in this context is that several well-known AI researchers (including Marvin Minsky, John von Neumann, and Norbert Wiener) have considered themselves to be descendants of Rabbi Löw.[30]

The golem of Prague was "alive" as long it had a piece of parchment in its mouth with God's name JHWH on it; as soon as these letters were removed, the golem did not function. (Some versions say, it was "alive" as long as אמת—*emet* 'truth'—was written on its forehead; when א was removed, leaving מת—*met* 'death'—the golem "died.") One story goes that every Sabbath the rabbi would remove the parchment from the golem's mouth so that it would keep the Sabbath as well. One Sabbath he forgot to put the golem to rest and when he went into the synagogue, the golem went berserk. Endings to the story vary: in one tradition, the rabbi is able to remove the parchment but the "dead" golem falls on him and smashes him—a motif that reappears in the even more influential Frankenstein myth. In a more commonly known version of the myth, Rabbi Löw removes the parchment (or erases the א from the golem's forehead) and lays the body of the golem to rest in the attic of the synagogue in Prague so that it can be revived when needed. It is part of this tradition that the revival of the golem will bring the end of the world. Many Jewish children from this tradition were taught the words that would revive the golem. When in the late 1960s some people mentioned that the first big computer in Israel had been called Golem[31] it turned out that at least two people at MIT, Gerry Sussman and Joel Moses, had been told the formula when they were children; the sentences they had been told were absolutely the same despite several hundreds of years of oral tradition.[32]

The golem myth has not found its way into mainstream Western thought. It therefore seems significant that several quite influential AI researchers refer to it and see themselves and their work in a way as successors of Rabbi Löw. One might want to debate whether they believe it literally or just in an anecdotal sense, but since they have mentioned this myth publicly, it seems to have more than incidental meaning for them and their work.

But there are more elements in the golem myth that can be related to AI and that give hints of other *mythos* elements that sometimes find their way into AI research. The Kabbalists usually built golems to imitate God's act of creation. They saw themselves as being created in God's image and therefore, so they believed, they had God's creational powers. In building golems they celebrated God's creativity, and the golem building can therefore be seen as prayer. It seems not too far-fetched in this context to cast AI researchers as modern Kabbalists.[33] AI is an enormously fascinating and challenging task; the fact that people undertake it and attempt to build and understand the impossible is certainly admirable and—in the language of *mythos*—reflects God's creativity. In the context of *mythos-logos* entanglement, then, it makes sense that several AI and artificial life researchers understand themselves as imitating God. W. Daniel Hillis, the architect of the Connection Machine, was several times quoted about his desire "to play God"; Tom Ray, who developed the artificial world Terra, described his feelings toward this artificial world: "It is like playing God." Besides these two, there are many other examples of researchers who create complex systems and describe their creations and their own feelings toward their creations in the language of the Jewish and Christian myths as written in Genesis 1 and 2.[34]

In the language of the *mythos* as well as in the language of the *logos*, the unlimited use of creative powers can lead to dangers. The *logos* of technology assessment correlates with the *mythos* of hubris: many cultures tell myths about the dangerous consequences of attempts to equal God. While the golem stories present ambiguity in this respect (the golem is prayer and yet has the potential to kill), there is another influential story of a human replica in the Western world: Mary Shelley's novel *Frankenstein* presents a powerful story about the disastrous consequences of an attempt to build an artificial human.[35]

Therefore, the most sensational reports in the popular media are about those AI projects that explicitly attempt to create a human replica; these projects seize a millenia-old and cross-cultural dream of humankind[36] with all its ambiguities of ambition and hubris. A lifelike machine or program (as in artificial life) or intelligent programs are already fascinating enough. But projects that attempt to create a machine that cannot be distinguished from a human being fall back on human myths. The terms *humanoid* (mostly used in the scientific realm) and *android* (more common within the realm of *mythos*, e.g., science fiction) are often used interchangeably, which hints of a *mythos-logos* entanglement at this point.

This relation of scientific program and cross-cultural myth is very likely the reason that humanoid projects often attract more media attention than other AI projects; the humanoid robot Cog, currently being built at the MIT AI Lab, is a good example of this dynamic.[37] Humanoid robot projects also seem to arouse strong emotional reactions. A culture strongly influenced by the Frankenstein myth might be hesitant to openly support humanoid projects, whereas it would have fewer problems with the rebuilding of parts of the human system or simulations in machines whose form is not humanlike. The influence of the Frankenstein and golem myths, and the elements of fear connected with them, might also be the reason that Cog was the first and is still one of the very few humanoid robot projects in the Western world; in Japan, on the other hand, there are currently four humanoid projects, with probably more to come.[38]

Answering Existential Questions with *Logos* Language

I have presented several examples where AI researchers use elements from myths of Western (Jewish or Christian) cultures either to give reasons for their research or to describe their feelings toward some of their projects and ideas. This kind of entanglement of *mythos* and *logos* is in itself harmless. It stirs emotions and might help to get funding; the *mythos* language also provides tools to describe research projects for a lay audience. Since a scientific discipline cannot be abstracted from the cultural environment in which it is practiced, *mythos* elements of this culture quite naturally find their way into the scientific language.

But Horkheimer and Adorno's analysis clearly indicates that the *mythos-logos* entanglement does not stop at this point. Since the *mythos* is often rejected, *mythos* speech acts cannot provide answers that might be helpful for someone's existential quests. For this reason it often happens that a science has to answer existential questions as well. Several questions that are usually discussed within religious frameworks are today discussed within AI, and people attempt to answer them by means of the technologies and models available.

I have demonstrated how the myth of eating from the tree of knowledge (Genesis 2) can explain limitations and ambiguities of human knowledge. Consider the term *sin*, which is usually used in this context. In daily language *sin* is used for supposedly bad acts. Paul used the term in a plural form when he quoted liturgy from early Christian tradition, but in his own theology he always used the singular form. For Paul, *sin* is not a single act we perform but a general human state of being. We do not sin, we are in a state of sin. *Sin* describes human beings as estranged, ambiguous, torn between incoherent wishes and desires, torn between polarities and fears.[39] The very existence of dialectics like the one between *mythos* and *logos*, which interact constantly without ever creating a coherent and static description of the world and ourselves, supports this *mythos* view of humans as sinners in the Tillichian sense. Even if many people might not accept the reason presented by the Jewish and Christian traditions for this human state of being (eating from the tree of knowledge), the fact that we experience life in an incoherent and disunited fashion is a well-known phenomenon; it is so described by psychology and social science, and probably experienced by most people.

Several attempts have been made to develop *logos* explanations for the ambiguity of human life, which fulfill the same function as the myth of sin and help to deal with incoherent desires, wishes, and thoughts. The theory of mind-body dualism, for instance, can be seen in this context as an attempt to explain incoherencies in human experience between bodily reactions and intentions. And even though cognitive science has by now recognized the fundamental importance of the body for any thought and intelligence, and the impossibility of separating the two,[40] the concept of mind-body dualism is still popular because it can help to deal with one form of ambiguity in human life. Another example of *logos* explanations for what Christianity describes with the myth of sin is the separation between reasoning and emotions. Emotionless reasoning is still an ideal in popular opinion[41] because it seemingly overcomes ambiguities in the human thought process, but this separation has been shown to be invalid.[42]

Many AI researchers deal with the phenomenon of human ambiguity and create *logos* explanations for incoherencies within human experience. Marvin Minsky[43] explains ambiguity in terms of different agents that simultaneously control different desires and thus "fight" against each other until one wins and carries out its program. Douglas Hofstadter uses a similar model for his explanation of human ambiguity:

The psychic mechanisms have to deal simultaneously with the individual's internal need for self-esteem and the constant flow of evidence from the outside affecting the self-image. The result is that information flows in a complex swirl between different levels of the personality; as it goes round and round, parts of it get magnified, reduced, negated, or otherwise distorted, and then those parts in turn get further subjected to the same sort of swirl, over and over again—all of this in an attempt to reconcile what is, with what we wish were.[44]

Whereas Minsky merely describes the interaction and competition between various agents, which leads to feelings of disunity and incoherence, Hofstadter values this uncontrollable and difficult interaction as positive: "I postulate that a similar level-crossing is what creates our nearly unanalyzable feelings of self" (709). Hofstadter attaches here the very positive attribute "self" to the negative human experience of ambiguity, and thus helps his readers to accept this ambiguity as a negative or at least an uncomfortable means toward a higher end: the emergence of a self, something no person wants to be without. One might say that Hofstadter answers an existential question, Why do we have to deal with so much ambiguity in our lives and thoughts? and that his answer has *mythos* characteristics. A person can accept this answer as helpful for life or for dealing with internal chaos, or a person can find the Christian concept of "sin" more helpful; in any case, her decision will be based on who she is, how she understands the world, and how well the respective *mythos* fits into her worldview. Any AI model that offers explanations for uncomfortable phenomena in human life is therefore as convincing and helpful as an answer offered by a religion; it demands commitment and decision and as such is a *mythos*.[45]

An example of how AI is used as a *mythos* provider for existential questions can be seen in the visions of immortality projected by various AI researchers. Existential questions surrounding the awareness of death are numerous: Why do I have to die? Who will remember me? What is the meaning of my life? It is certainly a major function of most religions to provide answers for these questions and to develop various myths on what might happen after death and how injustice in human life can be undone in a sphere beyond the physical world. Humankind struggles with the issue of death, and it has been asked repeatedly if death is necessary for human life and thought,[46] or if it is just a chemical or biological accident and a waste of human material. In case death is not a necessary part of what makes us human, the sciences might be able to help to make people immortal.

The assumption that death is not a part of what makes us human beings already has *mythos* character because one has to accept it as an answer to one's existential fear of death and transitoriness. Either one accepts the necessity of death and makes peace with the knowledge of one's certain death, or one thinks that death is not a necessary human quality and can be avoided. In both cases, the decision will be based on one's personal and societal *mythos*, will contain commitment, and is thus part of the *mythos* realm. Neither of these two alternatives can be proven empirically and so become valid for all humanity. Therefore, answers given on how to avoid death will be at least in part formulated within the *mythos* realm.

Several AI researchers propose that it may be possible to achieve eternal life and the absence of death with the help of technology. Hans Moravec, for instance, thinks it possible in the near future to copy the brain contents and memories of a person into a computer-based entity and thus preserve the person's personality and make her immortal.[47] Marvin Minsky in this context once said that people should give their money to AI research instead of to churches because AI research would truly make them immortal.[48] The whole movement of extropianism or transhumanism goes in the same direction: proponents would use the technology of computer networks and the World Wide Web to seemingly create a new existence in which a person's thoughts, ideas, and memories are copied onto computers, which through emergence will create a higher being.[49]

The point here is that the promise of immortality with by means of AI or Web technologies is a *mythos*, not a *logos*, act; it answers existential questions and can help to deal with the fear of death. As such, it is not an empirical answer but a promise and needs commitment to be effective. Besides the belief in technological possibilities (and technological infallibility) one has to have a certain *mythos* framework in mind to agree to have one's brain contents copied into a computer and to find this solution preferable to death. The same commitment is needed to believe in resurrection after death or an eternal soul that will survive the death of the body. In any case, the chosen myth has to fit into a *mythos* framework that has already been created within a culture by individuals within a community, and the individuals have to make a decision for or against the various myths that are supposed to provide them with answers. As a promise and a *mythos*, the theory of downloaded brain contents is as helpful (or useless) as resurrection promised in Christianity or the promise of reincarnation. Whether one believes in a future life within a machine or in heaven or in a new body is not really important in this context, even though one could certainly argue for or against some of these ideas. Key to my argument here is the clear evidence that AI researchers sometimes use their technology and their understanding of human cognition to answer existential questions, which traditionally have been answered by various religions and whose answers are within the *mythos* realm. And with regard to Horkheimer and Adorno's analysis, these researchers often present their *mythos* of immortal life in a computer as *logos* and are not aware of its *mythos* character.

The suppression of the *mythos* realm has made religious answers to dealing with mortality meaningless for many people. Science has to provide new answers for the existential fear of death, and technology has to provide the models to make the theories convincing. The eternal life theories in AI are therefore a very good example for Horkheimer and Adorno's argument.

And even if some AI researchers present human life as a series of accidents and think that human life has no purpose beyond gene transfer, that in principle any life is random and basically the result of coincidences, accidents, deterministic principles, and physical laws, they create a myth and answer the existential question, What is the meaning of my life? with There is no meaning. This answer might be convincing and helpful for the person who formulates these theories, but since it belongs in the *mythos* realm, it cannot be universally valid, and many people might prefer the myth of a creator God who loves every person individually.

Creating the Myth of What Is the Case

If AI researchers are aware of the *mythos* character of some of their theories, then their creation of myths for life after death or for explaining the ambiguity of life is harmless and cannot be criticized. These theories become problematic only if they are presented in a *logos* fashion, which unfortunately is often the case.

As I have said, the *mythos* is presented in an authoritative fashion, it is exclusive, and it demands commitment. These features also apply if the *mythos* is presented and understood as *logos*. If AI researchers formulate theories about the meaning of life, about dealing with grief and death, or about other existential quests that belong to the *mythos* realm, they enter a space of inquiry in which the various competing theories and myths are all exclusive and demand commitment to, and trust in, the authority who presents the respective myth.

In the realm of *mythos*, all theories and answers are valid—for a certain group of people within a specific context. And it is the main problem of this situation that this relativity cannot be accepted by people commited to a specific *mythos*. The ultimate concern needs passion; existential questions demand answers that are not arbitrary but absolute and true. Since what is in question is the very existence of the person who commits himself to a myth, he cannot be relativistic about it. As soon as scientists enter the realm of *mythos*, the criteria of scientific exchange and the rules for discussions about *logos* descriptions no longer apply. Instead, any exchange becomes in a sense an interreligious dialogue, which always suffers from the major tension caused by the fact that the dialogue participants are deeply and passionately convinced of the correctness of their own *mythos* worldviews and yet have to seriously take into account that the dialogue partner might be closer to a valid point of view.[50]

If scientists answer existential questions with the methods and models of their research area, they enter a space in which their theories compete on an equal level with religious theories. In other words, the theory of immortality by downloading the brain is neither inferior nor superior to the Christian theory of resurrection, but it is more convincing and more valid to, say, extropianists, whereas the promise of resurrection seems more convincing to many Christians.

But as Horkheimer and Adorno point out, because of the suppression of the *mythos* speech act as a valid approach toward reality, the ability to formulate and recognize *mythos* expressions has been unlearned. Since a *mythos* speech act is not accepted, but is seen as unworthy and as such inferior to any *logos* description of reality, many scientists would not want to be accused of using *mythos*. They would not want their theories to be on the same level with religious ideas. Theologians who enter the dialogue between religion and science have no problem accepting the myths of science as valid because they are used to myths as widespread and common expressions for humankind. Scientists, on the other hand, feel insulted and even sometimes ashamed if their theories are revealed as having *mythos* character. As Horkheimer and Adorno point out, many scientists (AI researchers included) create the myth of what is the case and reject any form of religion. Now, I can give two reasons for this reaction.

First, scientists might reject any form of *mythos* because Enlightenment ideals taught them to judge *mythos* speech acts as unworthy and *logos* speech acts as the only valid way to approach reality. This is the argument Horkheimer and Adorno use in their study to point out the dialectic of the Enlightenment: because the *mythos* speech act is suppressed, *logos* statements become the only valid way to talk about the world. Any *mythos*—especially within religious frameworks—is rejected; the *logos* becomes the only accepted act of speech and then also has to fulfill the function of the *mythos* and answer existential questions.

Second, with the theological evaluation of the *mythos* and its connection to the ultimate concern, I can give another reason for the strong antireligiosity of many scientists. If they create *mythos* answers by means of their research, they are personally attached to their theories, and this attachment goes beyond mere scientific interest. Thomas S. Kuhn pointed out how ferociously scientists would fight against a new paradigm, even though it fit so much better with the empirical data, just because their whole existence was at stake.[51] Kuhn does not analyze in depth the subjective elements that come into play here. But if a scientific theory is used for a scientist's personal quest for meaning, the theory will influence her self-understanding and will be embedded in her search for the ultimate. This is especially true for those theories that are directly connected to the analysis of human nature, which is the case in AI. The personal importance a scientific theory can gain by being embedded in one's personal *mythos* does not easily allow for competition. At this point, the dilemma of every interreligious dialogue arises: a scientist, believing in and committed to a certain theory as myth, cannot accept that there might be other myths around that are equally compelling and sometimes even more convincing for certain people. As happens in the encounter of two religious dogmas, the scientist in this situation might reject the possibility of other valid myths because this would question the eligibility of her own *mythos*. The fear of doubt can then lead to a passionate rejection of any alternative in a post-Enlightenment atmosphere. The rejection of any religious myth will be especially passionate because religion is seen as bad, and many scientists would not want their theories to enter into competition with a seemingly bad act of speech.[52]

There are many examples of how scientists not only reject religious elements in science but even argue against the idea of subjective elements within their research. The ongoing debates about the theory of paradigm shifts and other ideas formulated in the philosophy of science and in feminist thought also support this argument.[53] The call for rationality (which is, as Horkheimer and Adorno and later Thomas S. Kuhn have pointed out, a myth in itself) attempts to avoid the analysis of *mythos* elements within science that might reveal the existential needs of scientists and force them to question their own ultimate concerns. I believe that the danger of being forced to give up one's own personal beliefs, more than bad experiences with religion, causes the forceful rejection of any form of religion within certain scientific environments and reinforces the *mythos-logos* entanglement, which Horkheimer and Adorno have called the dialectic of the Enlightenment.

Conclusion: A New Form of Dialogue

Horkheimer and Adorno at the end of their first analysis conclude that it is *not* technology that destroys the Enlightenment's final success (48). Similarly, in analyzing the *mythos* elements of AI, I do not want to criticize this academic discipline nor attack its researchers. AI is a fascinating research area and can help us to gain insights into who we are from a functionalist perspective. It also can help to develop advanced technology, which can be used in very diverse areas and help us to solve problems we are not able to solve at present.

But even if AI has these promising perspectives, its answers for existential questions are neither more or less valuable than religious answers but compete with religious myths. Theologians, in recognizing the context in which AI's myths are created, will not attack AI researchers, but they will show them their own myths and those areas of AI research in which the danger is especially high that *logos* might turn into *mythos*. Theologians, then, can describe their own mythological answers to existential questions and can demonstrate their validity within a certain cultural and religious context.

In that sense, theologians might provide the bridge for the gap between AI supporters and opponents: they will recognize the myths of AI researchers and develop tools to help them recognize their own myths. They will then be able to translate the need for *mythos* and the existential answers AI develops to the public. This way, they can help to overcome fears and prejudices against AI and can help to start a new dialogue about the fascinating and inspirational technological developments of our times.

With its expertise in *mythos* recognition and analysis, theology can contribute to the dialogue in two different ways. It can help to eliminate *mythos* from AI as far as possible and help to focus the energies of AI researchers on the real objective: the understanding of the human mind. In adding their expertise about the *mythos* and its function in human life, theologians then can integrate more elements into the question of who we are and how we function. In doing so, they can create a relational unity between the AI and religious anthropologies, which will result not in identity or assimilation but in a dynamic interchange between the *mythos* of the one and the *logos* of the other, with each accepting the validity of the other's speech acts and becoming radically open to the discoveries and insights of the other.

Notes

1. The word *logic* is derived from *logos* and it can also be found in names for areas of reasoning like *bio-logy, theo-logy,* or *ethno-logy.*

2. Robert W. Brockway, *Myth from the Ice Age to Mickey Mouse* (Albany: State University of New York Press, 1993), 9.

3. Paul Tillich, *Systematic Theology* (Chicago: University of Chicago Press, 1951), vol. 1, 75.

4. The Greek μῦθos led to the English term *myth*, which acquired some negative connotations as it came to be used synonymously with *deception* or *lie*. Note that I use the term *myth* here to refer to a story that is told within the *mythos* realm. Also note that the definition of *mythos* used here is completely independent of the psychological definition as formulated by C. G. Jung.

5. Ernst Cassirer, *The Philosophy of Symbolic Forms, Volume Two: Mythical Thought* (New Haven: Yale University Press, 1955), 3.

6. Gerhard Krüger, *Einsicht und Leidenschaft: das Wesen des platonischen Denkens* (Frankfurt: Klostermann, 1939), 17.

7. Rudolf K. Bultmann, "New Testament and Mythology: The Problem of Demythologizing the New Testament Proclamation," in *New Testament and Mythology and Other Basic Writings* (Philadelphia: Fortress Press, 1984), 3.

8. Tillich, *Systematic Theology*, vol. 1, 20.

9. Tillich, "Symbols of Faith," in *Dynamics of Faith* (New York: Harper and Row, 1957).

10. Brockway, 14.

11. Taken from his notes for an unpublished lecture at Columbia University, November 11, 1966, as seen in the Tillich archives at Harvard Divinity School, Cambridge, Massachusetts.

12. Tillich, *Systematic Theology*, vol. 1, 11.

13. It might seem strange to use the Tillichian theory of the Ultimate Concern as the main argument for the basic assumption of this chapter and then to support this argument with critical theory that is commonly known as being rather critical of religion. But in fact Horkheimer, Adorno, and Tillich came out of the same school of thought, the early Frankfurt School. Before he was forced by the Nazis to leave his position as professor, Tillich was teaching in the philosophy department of Frankfurt University. In this position he supported Horkheimer to get a position there as well. Horkheimer himself had studied in Freiburg with Edmund Husserl and his assistant Martin Heidegger, who in his book *Sein und Zeit* (1927; Tübingen: Max Niemeyer, 1993) later developed the basis for an existential philosophy. Adorno had an even closer relationship with Tillich because Tillich was the supervisor of his habilitation (second thesis). See Rolf Wiggershaus, *The Frankfurt School: Its History, Theories, and Political Significance* (Cambridge, Mass.: MIT Press, 1994).

14. Max Horkheimer and Theodor W. Adorno, *Dialectic of Enlightenment: Philosophical Fragments* (New York: Continuum, 1996).

15. After the beginning of the witch hunts in 1484 until around 1700, more than 100,000 girls and women were killed.

16. Thomas S. Kuhn, *The Structure of Scientific Revolutions*, 3d ed. (Chicago: University of Chicago Press, 1996), 152.

17. Patrick H. Winston, *Artificial Intelligence*, 3d ed. (Reading, Mass.: Addison-Wesley, 1992), 5.

18. Francisco Varela, *Kognitionswissenschaft-Kognitionstechnik: Eine Skizze aktueller Perspektiven* (Frankfurt: Suhrkamp, 1993).

19. Psychologists and neuroscientists rely mainly on the observation of brain-damaged people to find out the function of certain brain parts, to formulate theories on learning, and so on; see, for instance, Oliver Sacks's books *An Anthropologist on Mars* (New York: Vintage Books, 1995) and *The Man Who Mistook His Wife for a Hat and Other Clinical Tales* (New York: Summit Books, 1985).

20. Anne Foerst, "Why Theologians Build Androids," *Insights* 9 (1997): 1–7.

21. Allen Newell and Herbert A. Simon, *Human Problem Solving* (Englewood Cliffs, N.J.: Prentice-Hall, 1972), 796.

22. Benedikt Otzen, Hans Gottlieb, and Knud Jeppesen, *Myths in the Old Testament* (London: SCM Press, 1980).

23. The name JHWH is used only in the oldest layers of the Hebrew Scriptures, the Jahwist, or J. To not profane the name of God, it was later avoided, and in Genesis 1, a later added preamble to the Pentateuch, God is called *elohim*. But it is God JHWH, the God of Abraham, Isaac, and Jacob, who establishes in the creation a relationship with human beings and maintains a covenant with Israel during history.

24. See Anne Foerst, "Cog, a Humanoid Robot, and the Question of the Image of God," *Zygon, Journal of Religion & Science* 33 (no. 1, 1988): 91–111. Gerry Sussman, a well-known computer scientist and professor at the MIT AI Lab referred to this circularity of the *Imago Dei* when he dedicated his Ph.D. thesis to Rabbi Löw of Prague because the Rabbi was the first one who recognized that the statement "God created humans in His image" is recursive.

25. Rabbi Ben Zion Bokser, *From the World of the Cabbalah: The Philosophy of Rabbi Judah Loew of Prague* (New York: Philosophical Library, 1954), 67.

26. Tillich, *Systematic Theology* (Chicago: University of Chicago Press, 1957), vol. 2, 33.

27. Most critics of AI can actually be understood within this framework; they often understand human specialness as a *logos* statement and thus try to prove the impossibility and vanity of AI. Because of space limitations, I cannot explore this topic further here.

28. See, for instance, Daniel C. Dennett, *Consciousness Explained* (Boston: Little, Brown, 1991).

29. Gershom Scholem, "The Golem of Prague and the Golem of Rehovot," *Commentary* (January 1966): 62–65.

30. Pamela McCorduck, *Machines Who Think: A Personal Inquiry into the History and Prospects of Artificial Intelligence* (San Francisco: Freeman, 1979), 13.

31. Scholem, 62.

32. This incident was reported by Mitch Marcus, formerly a Ph.D. student at the MIT AI Lab and now professor for computer science at the University of Pennsylvania; he was not a witness himself but confirmed the story with the participants.

33. Norbert Wiener, *God & Golem, Inc.: A Comment on Certain Points Where Cybernetics Impinges on Religion*, 7th ed. (Cambridge, Mass.: MIT Press, 1990).

34. Researchers often include *mythos* elements in their research in order to translate it for a lay audience and to share the fascination with people outside of the AI world (which also sometimes helps to obtain funding). But most researchers do not include these myths in scientific papers. In the more dangerous *mythos-logos* entanglement situations, one can find *mythos* elements in scientific publications, but for the most part, the integration of *mythos* elements into AI research can only be found in the popular press: *Der Spiegel* 12 (1990) quoted Hillis and others; *Der Spiegel* 15

(1993) described Ray's work; *Stern* 44 (1992) reported on artificial life and quoted the "being like God" motif several times; *Natur* 6 (1991) writes about the "Gods in the electronic heaven." I collected these examples in Germany but am convinced that similar quotations can be found in popular U.S. magazines as well.

35. For an analysis of the Frankenstein motif in the context of AI, see Anne Foerst, "Artificial Intelligence: Walking the Boundary," *Zygon* 31 (no. 4, 1996): 681–693.

36. Klaus Völker, ed., *Künstliche Menschen: Über Golems, Homunculi, Androiden und lebende Statuen* (Frankfurt: Suhrkamp, 1994).

37. For an overview of media attention for the Cog project, see ⟨http://www.ai.mit.edu/projects/cog⟩.

38. Anne Foerst, "Künstliche Intelligenz: Alptraum oder Utopie," *Zukünfte* 18 (1996/97): 20–22.

39. Tillich, *Systematic Theology*, vol. 3 (Chicago: University of Chicago Press, 1963).

40. See, for example, Mark Johnson, *The Body in the Mind: The Bodily Basis of Meaning, Imagination, and Reason* (Chicago: University of Chicago Press, 1987).

41. A popular rational but emotionless figure is Commander Data from the television show *Star Trek: The Next Generation*, but it can be deduced from Data's behavior and interaction with the crew that Data also has emotions—even before he gets his emotion chip. See Anne Foerst, "Commander Data: A Candidate for Harvard Divinity School?" in *Religion in a Secular City: Essays in Honor of Harvey Cox*, ed. Arvind Sharma (Harrisburg, Pa.: Trinity Press International, 2001).

42. See, for instance, Antonio Damasio, *Descartes' Error: Emotion, Reason, and the Human Brain* (New York: Avon Books, 1994).

43. Marvin Minsky, *The Society of Mind* (New York: Simon and Schuster, 1985).

44. Douglas A. Hofstadter, *Gödel, Escher, Bach: An Eternal Golden Braid* (New York: Basic Books, 1979), 695.

45. In fall 1996, in a discussion group at the MIT Media Laboratory led by Ken Haase, Marvin Minsky was challenged by a student for a statement that AI ultimately could solve all the problems of humanity and would make philosophy and especially theology unnecessary. The student said it was impossible for AI to ultimately answer "why" questions, e.g., in situations of grief and meaningless suffering. Minsky answered that as soon as AI had analyzed the human mind completely, it could help to erase "why" questions in the human brain as well as feelings of grief and loss. We do not want to suggest that this will never be possible. Within the context of the *mythos-logos* dialectic, however, it becomes obvious that this solution for suffering is a *mythos* solution: not everyone will want such an intervention; some people might find religious answers more helpful; ministers and priests will continue to be consulted by many people, whereas others might search for the help of the surgeon or an AI researcher. This element of decision and commitment (and rejection) makes the possibility of the deletion of grief a myth equal to theodicy solutions presented by various religions.

46. The assumption that death is a necessary condition for human reasoning is supported by a majority of Christian theologians; see Tillich, *Systematic Theology*, vol. 1.

47. Hans P. Moravec, *Mind Children: The Future of Robot and Human Intelligence* (Cambridge: Harvard University Press, 1988).

48. Interview with the *Rheinischer Merkur*, May 17, 1991, 22.

49. Gregory S. Paul and Earl D. Cox, *Beyond Humanity: CyberEvolution and Future Minds* (Rockland, Mass.: Charles River Media, 1996). A similar idea within a physics framework has been formulated by Frank Tipler, *The Physics of Immortality: Modern Cosmology, God, and the Resurrection of the Dead* (New York: Doubleday, 1994), and some more examples can be found in Harvey G. Cox and Anne Foerst, "Religion and Technology: A New Phase," *Bulletin of Science, Technology and Society* 17 (no. 2/3, 1997): 53–60.

50. Ulrich Mann, "Christentum und Toleranz," in *Toleranz heute, 250 Jahre nach Mendelssohn und Lessing*, ed. Peter von der Osten-Sacken (Berlin: Institut Kirche und Judentum, 1979), 86.

51. Kuhn, *The Structure of Scientific Revolutions*.

52. A good example of this rejection of any form of religion is the debate that occurred at MIT in fall 1997, when the electrical engineering and computer science department offered for the first time the course "God and Computers," which dealt with the philosophical and religious underpinnings of AI. A senior MIT professor claimed the class to be an "evangelical enterprise"; a student understood it as "indoctrination." Since the teacher was a theologian and a minister, she was accused by a student of "suffering from the set of pathologies collectively known as religious faith"; this student later supported another student with a petition to the head of the department to cancel the class. All these debates happened via e-mail, and within three days after the announcement of the course, there were more than 200 e-mails discussing the class and its appropriateness for MIT. This debate made its way into the student newspaper, *The Tech*, where a student labeled the class "an insult to MIT," and it was finally discussed in the Boston print media. In all these debates, it was most fascinating that none of the participants, who sometimes wrote ten e-mails over the course of a few days, actually looked at the syllabus, which was published on the Web. Just the term *religion* and the word *God* in the course title set free emotions that did not allow for any further (and rational) *logos* inquiry about what the course was really about. In the context of Horkheimer and Adorno's analysis, part of the passion around this course can be explained by the bad experiences many people have had with the oppressive use of *mythos* by various religious leaders. However, the number of e-mails and the involvement of so many people in the discussion seems to suggest that there was a deeper reason for the emotions. If some AI researchers use their research to answer existential questions, an analysis of this process, and a comparison with alternative religious myths that answer the same existential questions, becomes threatening.

53. Israel Scheffler, *Science and Subjectivity* 2d ed. (Indianapolis: Hackett, 1982), argues against Kuhn for the possibility of objectivity in science, while on the other side of the spectrum feminist thinkers argue for a variety of epistemologies for the scientific and academic pursuit (Linda Alcoff and Elizabeth Potter, eds., *Feminist Epistemologies* (New York: Routledge, 1993).

Contributors

Alison Adam is a reader of the Information Systems Institute, University of Salford, U.K. She is the author of *Artificial Knowing: Gender and the Thinking Machine* (1998) and the editor of several collections, including (with Eileen Green) *Virtual Gender: Technology, Consumption and Identity* (2001) and (with Rachel Lander) *Women in Computing: Progress from Where to What?* (1997).

Philip Agre is an associate professor of information studies at the University of California, Los Angeles. He is the author of *Computation and Human Experience* (1997) and the editor (with Douglas Schuler) of *Reinventing Technology, Rediscovering Community: Critical Explorations of Computing as a Social Practice* (1997).

Tom Burke is an associate professor of philosophy at the University of South Carolina. He is the author of *Dewey's New Logic: A Reply to Russell* (1994) and co-editor of *Dewey's Logical Theory: New Studies and Interpretations* (2002). His current research focuses on connecting contemporary mathematical logic and formal linguistics with John Dewey's philosophy of logic. His research interests also include conceptions of mind and self as related to the question of human origins, drawing largely on the naturalistic, evolutionary perspective of George Herbert Mead's social psychology.

Harry M. Collins is director of the Science Studies Centre at the University of Bath, U.K., where he holds a personal professorial chair in sociology. He is a Fellow of the Royal Society of Arts. From 1991 to 1993 he was president of the International Society for Social Studies of Science. He has published over 60 papers and six books on two broad themes: the nature of science, explored through comparative case studies of physics and parapsychology, and the nature of human knowledge, investigated through the study of the prospects for artificial intelligence and people's interactions with machines in general. His most recent books are *Changing Order* (1985), *Artificial Experts* (1990), and (with Trevor Pinch) *The Golem: What Everyone Should Know about Science* (1993).

Daniel Dennett is director of the Center for Cognitive Studies and Austin B. Fletcher Professor of Philosophy at Tufts University. Among his many books are *Freedom Evolves* (2003), *Darwin's Dangerous Idea* (1995), *Consciousness Explained* (1991), and *Kinds of Minds* (1996).

Fred Dretske is a senior research professor of philosophy at Duke University and professor emeritus of philosophy at Stanford University. He is the author of *Seeing and Knowing* (1969), *Knowledge and the Flow of Information* (1981), *Explaining Behavior* (1988), and *Naturalizing the Mind* (1995). His research has been in epistemology, especially the area of visual perception, and in the philosophy of mind. His recent work focuses on the nature of intentional action and perceptual experience.

Hubert Dreyfus is a professor at the Graduate School, University of California, Berkeley. His major interests are phenomenology, existentialism, philosophy of psychology, philosophy of literature, and the philosophical implications of artificial intelligence. He is the author of many books, including *What Computers Still Can't Do* (1992), *Being-in-the-World* (1991), and (with Paul Rabinow) *Michel Foucault: Beyond Structuralism and Hermeneutics* (1983).

Anne Foerst is a research scientist at the Artificial Intelligence Laboratory, Massachusetts Institute of Technology, and the U.S. northeast regional director of the science and religion course program of the Center for Theology and the Natural Sciences. She is theological adviser to the AI Laboratory's Cog project, the attempt to build a humanoid robot analogous to a human infant. Her research focuses on developing a new epistemology based on the dialectic of *mythos* and *logos*, an existential approach that opens up new dimensions for the dialogue between religion and science, and demonstrates the relevance of an interdisciplinary dialogue between artificial intelligence, cognitive science, and theology for contemporary culture.

Stefano Franchi is a senior lecturer in philosophy at the University of Auckland, N.Z. His current research focuses on twentieth-century European philosophy and history and philosophy of science, and on the history of artificial intelligence.

Güven Güzeldere is an assistant professor of philosophy and psychological and brain sciences, and associate director of the Center for Interdisciplinary Studies in Science and Cultural Theory, at Duke University. He is co-editor (with Ned Block and Owen Flanagan) of *The Nature of Consciousness* (1997). His work focuses on the philosophy of mind, cognitive neuroscience, the history and philosophy of psychology, and the foundations of artificial intelligence.

Douglas R. Hofstadter is a professor of cognitive science and computer science, with appointments also in some related departments, at Indiana University, Bloomington. Among his many books are *Le Ton Beau de Marot* (1998), *Fluid Concepts and Creative Analogies* (1995), and *Gödel, Escher, Bach* (1979).

Michael L. Johnson has written a number of books of poetry and translated books of poetry as well as books concerned with issues of technology and education, including *Mind, Language, Machine: Artificial Intelligence in the Poststructuralist Age* (1988) and *Education on the Wild Side: Learning for the Twenty-First Century* (1993). He is chair of the Department of English, University of Kansas.

Evelyn Fox Keller is a professor of history and philosophy of science at the Massachusetts Institute of Technology. She has worked for a number of years at the interface of physics and biology and is currently involved in research on the history and philosophy of developmental biology. She is author of several books, including *The Century of the Gene* (2000) and *Making Sense of Life: Explaining Biological Development with Models, Metaphors and Machines* (2002).

Bruno Latour was trained as a philosopher and an anthropologist. After field studies in Africa and California, he specialized in the analysis of scientists and engineers at work. He has written *Laboratory Life: The Construction of Scientific Facts* (1986), *Science in Action* (1987), *The Pasteurization of France* (1988), *Aramis, or the Love of Technology* (1996), *We Have Never Been Modern* (1993), and *La clef de Berlin* (1993). He is a professor at the Centre de Sociologie de l'Innovation, École Nationale Superieure des Mines, Paris.

Maurizio Matteuzzi is an associate professor of the philosophy of language and of artificial intelligence at the University of Bologna. He has worked extensively on the relationship between ordinary and formalized languages and on the problem of meaning in philosophical activity, in particular from an epistemological standpoint. Among his many publications are *La forma della teoria* (1981), *Individuare per caratteri. Saggio su Leibniz* (1983), and *La macchia di colore* (1993).

Bruce Mazlish is a professor of history at the Massachusetts Institute of Technology, winner of the Toynbee Prize in Social Science for 1985–86, and a Fellow of the American Academy of Arts and Sciences. His interests are broadly interdisciplinary, one of his major concerns being the nature and meaning of the human sciences. Among his many writings is *The Fourth Discontinuity: The Co-Evolution of Humans and Machines* (1993).

Andrew Pickering is a professor of sociology at the University of Illinois, Urbana-Champaign. His early work focused on studies of elementary particle physics and culminated in *Constructing Quarks: A Sociological History of Particle Physics* (1984). He subsequently developed an interest in scientific (and mathematical and technological) practice more generally, as represented in *The Mangle of Practice: Time, Agency and Science* (1995) and an edited collection, *Science as Practice and Culture* (University of Chicago Press (1992). His current research concerns developments in science, technology, and society since World War II as well as issues of theory and interpretation.

Alain-Marc Rieu is a former student at the École Normale Supérieure, *agrégé* and *docteur d'Etat* in philosophy, University of Paris I-Panthéon-Sorbonne. He is a professor of philosophy at the University of Lyon III-Jean Moulin. His research interests focus on contemporary philosophy and on the interactions between technology and contemporary societies.

Serge Sharoff is an applied mathematician with deep interests in philosophy of mind and linguistics. He graduated from Urals State University (Ekaterinburg) with a dissertation focusing on the design of linguistic modeling tools, "SNOOP: a System for the Development of Linguistic Processors." He is a research fellow at the centre for translation studies, University of Leeds, where he works on topics ranging from computer modeling of natural language understanding and object-oriented AI tools, to the interrelations between cognitive science and philosophy.

Geneviève Teil was trained as an engineer in telecommunications. She completed a Ph.D. degree at the Centre de Sociologie de l'Innovation, École des Mines, Paris, on a computer tool for analyzing large bodies of text for sociological work. She now holds a research position at INRA, the French institute for agronomic research, and specializes in the analysis of texts and tastes.

Stephen Wilson is a San Francisco artist who explores the cultural implications of new technologies. His interactive installations have been shown internationally in galleries and at SIGGRAPH, CHI, NCGA, Ars Electronica, and V2 art shows. He is a co-editor of *Leonardo*, an international journal of art and science, and professor of conceptual design and computer art at San Francisco State University. He is the author of *Information Arts: Intersections of Art, Science, and Technology* (2003), *Using Computers to Create Art* (1986) and *Multimedia Design with HyperCard* (1991).

Index

AARON, 101

Abduction theory, 374–375

Abelson, Hal, 218

Abschattungen (reflections), 476

Acoustics, 28

Adam, Alison, 3, 11, 327–344, 515

Addelson, Kathryn Pyne, 331, 333

Administrative Behavior (Simon), 53

Adorno, Theodor, 6, 492–494, 500, 503, 507–509, 510n14

Advanced Research Projects Agency (ARPA), 143n160

Agre, Philip, 2–4, 78–80, 89, 92, 102, 153–173, 515

Agrippa, Cornelius, 181–182

AI (Spielberg movie), 115

AI Magazine, 154

Alan Turing: The Enigma (Hodges), 56–57

Alchemy, 178

Alcoff, Linda, 329

Algorithms, 99–100, 420

cellular automata and, 205–215

genetic, 210–213

STRIPS and, 163–166

Alzheimer's disease, 378

American Association for Artificial Intelligence (AAAI), 155, 266

Amit, Daniel, 75

Ampère, André, 24

Anatomy, 31

Andersen, Hans Christian, 179–181

Anderson, Michael, 145n183

Andler, Daniel, 87

Androids, 15, 83, 182

Animals, 15–16, 47–48

Descartes and, 175

drug canines and, 288–290

intelligent boundaries and, 108–109

Anthropomorphic projections, 312

Arabic traditions, 176

Archytas of Terentum, 28, 175

Aristotle, 27, 47–48

Ars Electronica, 394

Art, 3

aesthetic decisions and, 401–407

AI installations and, 394–407

artificial characterization and, 397–401

computer models and, 405–407

deconstruction and, 391

"Demon Seed" and, 400–401

domain limitation and, 404–405

"Excursions in Emotional Hyperspace" and, 395, 397–398

hypermedia and, 396

interactivity and, 396

"Is Anyone There?" and, 394, 396

modernist, 391–392

"Neuro Baby" and, 394

OZ and, 393–394

physical communication and, 402–404

research and development and, 392–393

sensual contact and, 402–404